Uneven Encounters

AMERICAN ENCOUNTERS / GLOBAL INTERACTIONS

A series edited by Gilbert M. Joseph and Emily S. Rosenberg

This series aims to stimulate critical perspectives and fresh interpretive frameworks for scholarship on the history of the imposing global presence of the United States. Its primary concerns include the deployment and contestation of power, the construction and deconstruction of cultural and political borders, the fluid meanings of intercultural encounters, and the complex interplay between the global and the local. American Encounters seeks to strengthen dialogue and collaboration between historians of U.S. international relations and area studies specialists.

The series encourages scholarship based on multi-archival historical research. At the same time, it supports a recognition of the representational character of all stories about the past and promotes critical inquiry into issues of subjectivity and narrative. In the process, American Encounters strives to understand the context in which meanings related to nations, cultures, and political economy are continually produced, challenged, and reshaped.

Uneven Encounters

*Making Race and Nation in Brazil
and the United States*

Micol Seigel

Duke University Press
Durham and London 2009

Library of Congress Cataloging-in-Publication Data
Seigel, Micol, 1968–
Uneven encounters : making race and nation in Brazil and the
United States / Micol Seigel.
p. cm. — (American encounters/global interactions)
Includes bibliographical references and index.
ISBN 978-0-8223-4426-1 (cloth : alk. paper)
ISBN 978-0-8223-4440-7 (pbk. : alk. paper)
1. Racism—Brazil—History—20th century.
2. Nationalism—Brazil—History—20th century.
3. Brazil—Race relations—History—20th century.
4. Racism—United States—History—20th century.
5. Nationalism—United States—History—20th century.
6. United States—Race relations—History—20th century.
I. Title. II. Series.
F2659.A1S44 2009
305.800981—dc22
2008041804

For my father:
thank you.

Contents

Illustrations   ix

Preface   xi

Note on Language   xvii

Acknowledgments   xix

Introduction   1

1. Producing Consumption:
   Coffee and Consumer Citizenship   13

2. Maxixe's Travels:
   Cultural Exchange and Erasure   67

3. Playing Politics:
   Making the Meanings of Jazz in Rio de Janeiro   95

4. Nation Drag:
   Uses of the Exotic   136

5. Another "Global Vision":
   (Trans)Nationalism in the São Paulo Black Press   179

6. Black Mothers, Citizen Sons   206

   Conclusion   235

   Abbreviations   241

   Notes   243

   Discography   321

   Bibliography   323

   Index   367

Illustrations

Figure 1. "You can take my word for it—this is <u>REAL</u> Coffee!" Butter-Nut ad, 1922. Hills Bros. Collection, National Museum of American History. Archives Center, Behring Center, Smithsonian Institution. 14

Figure 2. "My reputation depends on COFFEE." JC ad in series "Coffee—the universal drink," 1920. N. W. Ayer Advertising Agency records, National Museum of American History. Archives Center, Behring Center, Smithsonian Institution. 28

Figure 3. "Mrs. Thomas Was Housecleaning." JC ad, 1923. N. W. Ayer Advertising Agency records, National Museum of American History. Archives Center, Behring Center, Smithsonian Institution. 32

Figure 4. "Places to talk business." Terry Gilkiron [?], "Kernel Koffee" (cartoon). Hills Bros. Collection, National Museum of American History. Archives Center, Behring Center, Smithsonian Institution. 36

Figure 5. Carter, Macy advertisement, 1918. Science, Industry, and Business Library, NYPL, Astor, Lenox and Tilden Foundations. 38

Figure 6. All America Cables advertisement, 1921. Science, Industry, and Business Library, NYPL, Astor, Lenox and Tilden Foundations. 39

Figure 7. W. R. Grace advertisement, 1920. Science, Industry, and Business Library, NYPL, Astor, Lenox and Tilden Foundations. 40

Figure 8. W. R. Grace advertisement, 1918. Science, Industry, and Business Library, NYPL, Astor, Lenox and Tilden Foundations.   41

Figure 9. "Thoroughbreds." Hills Bros. ad, 1931. Hills Bros. Collection, National Museum of American History. Archives Center, Behring Center, Smithsonian Institution.   54

Figure 10. "COFFEE .. is .. America's Favorite Drink." BACPC ad, 1929. N. W. Ayer Advertising Agency records, National Museum of American History. Archives Center, Behring Center, Smithsonian Institution.   60

Figure 11. Caribou Coffee flier. Collection of the author.   64

Figure 12. Duque at Luna Park. Jerome Robbins Dance Division, The NYPL for Performing Arts, Astor, Lenox and Tilden Foundations.   78

Figure 13. Le Corbusier drawing of Josephine Baker and Le Corbusier, 1929. Artists Rights Society (ARS), New York/ADAGP; Paris/ FLC.   124

Figure 14. José Fortunato, "Os 'Batutas' em Paris." Reproduced in Cabral, *Pixinguinha*.   134

Figure 15. Stella F. Simon, Olga Burgoyne as Mother Kanda in a scene from *Run, Little Chillun!*, 1933. Photographs and Prints Division, Schomburg Center for Research in Black Culture, NYPL, Astor, Lenox and Tilden Foundations.   165

Figure 16. Carl Van Vechten, Portrait of Elsie Houston. Library of Congress, Prints and Photographs Division, Carl Van Vechten Collection.   177

Figure 17. *Evolução*, 1933, front cover. Jornais Negros Brasileiros— Arquivo do Instituto de Estudos Brasileiros [Brazilian Black Newspapers—Archive of the Institute of Brazilian Studies], University of São Paulo.   186

Figure 18. Mãe Preta statue, São Paulo. Photo by Denise Botelho.   207

Figure 19. Front page of *Chicago Defender*, May 22, 1926. Courtesy of *Chicago Defender*.   223

Preface

Over the years I have been working on this book, some of the circumstances that prompted its writing have shifted. There is now not quite such a dearth of transnational history or work on U.S. empire, for example. Yet other pieces of its prompting conditions remain intractably in place. One of the most recalcitrant is the comparative mindset people bring to the contemplation of race in the United States and Brazil. Even when I feel I have cleanly explained my objections to comparing race in national contexts, some of my interlocutors, academic and non-academic alike, will have failed to hear them. It is as if comparison were so essential to long-distance contemplation that no other lens were possible. Isn't it true, people offer, that U.S. and Brazilian racial systems are really different? Isn't Brazil a much more racially mixed society than the United States? In terms of racism, isn't Brazil/the United States better/worse? I wish my work would shift the frame of analysis so that such questions become not just unanswerable, but also unaskable.

My objections to these questions can be briefly and simply put.[1] Comparisons require generalizations about U.S. and Brazilian national racial identities that cannot be right because they cannot be *national*, for truly, nothing is. No single social trait characterizes a whole nation and nothing but the nation, and no single ideological framework pertains evenly across an entire national space. Most of these comparisons also biologize race by implying that mixture occurred in one of the two nations earlier or later than the other, measuring against an ostensible purity or positing a moment of purity at some previous point.[2] Notions of national racial ideologies of the United States and Brazil get nation wrong and race wrong, and they get the specifics wrong too. That is, the perfectly opposed guiding myths of racial purity in the United States and racial harmony in Brazil reference social systems that have an awful lot in common. North Americans lived amid constant racial mixing, interracial social intimacy, a huge range of racial identities neither black nor white, and evidence everywhere of how hollow were the claims of white supremacy.[3] Brazil's virulent, socially structuring racism included explicitly racialized processes of criminalization and discipline, the circumscription of social opportunities for darker citizens even to the point of lynching, and constant attempts by whiter citizens to deny African ancestry and prevent further Afro-descended members from branching into their family trees.[4] Both Brazil and the United States leaned heavily on "race" to structure social hierarchy, and within both vast territories, the experience of that reliance varied greatly.

This opposition, while wrong, is useful. It is useful in the unfortunate sense that it does ideological work. It helps people articulate and recirculate notions of purity and mixture and reassert the primacy of black and white at the exclusion of categories such as "Asian" or "Latino" that might disrupt the national narratives these fictions underlie. But it is also useful in the more productive sense of being "good for thinking," for such striking, impossible parity highlights the artifice of its own formation. It points us to the fact that comparison is a construction site, where U.S. and Brazilian racializations are built up together.

To get at that process of transnational racial construction, I have tried to develop a method that can serve as a counterpoint to comparison. Despite the full country names in the book's title (a concession to publisher and bookstore needs), this book does not compare the United States and Brazil or any subset thereof. It seeks instead a sample of the myriad connections linking people who resided (most of the time) in cities within the geographic borders of those two territories. Sometimes people gazed out at each other to understand themselves as national beings, using their viewfinders to locate useful touchpoints. More often in this book, they did so not as representatives of their national units but as members of other social formations, imagining themselves in relation to and in solidarity with each other. The communities they imagined in that process (to paraphrase Benedict Anderson) were odd-shaped beasts, neither fully within nor simply larger than their nation-states. They wove global filaments into local social worlds, operating at "scales that are both smaller and larger than the nation-state."[5]

This is my working definition of "transnational" and of transnational method. Where international history explores the relations of nation-states (or just states) as well-bounded subjects, transnational history explores the global in the local, via interactions of groups or entities that do not fit national borders, whether because they are greater or lesser or both. Examples of such border-disrespecting units include geographic features such as rivers, political spaces such as borderlands, and far-flung people who imagine themselves in community. These could include individuals who identified within and across national borders as "men" or "law-abiding citizens" or "Christians" or even "coffee drinkers" and, of course, as members of the African diaspora. Diasporas and the African diaspora principally are the quintessential transnational units, unevenly distributed and defined, shaped in opposition to nation-states and in contested collaborations across national lines. "Diasporan subjects *are* transnational subjects," as Robin Kelley points out, and in that sense African diaspora studies and its predecessors have always been transnational and are critical guides for transnational method now.[6] As these examples suggest, transnational subjects are not the exception but the rule, at least in globalized eras such as the past half-millennium of European expansion, capitalism, and African slavery. Everything has a transnational aspect or two, for every local has global threads woven through.

What I have delineated above is far from the only definition of transnational method in circulation today. Other scholars prefer other definitions, and the term "transnational" is in such vogue that many use it without any particular definition in mind at all. Some assume "transnational history" is a synonym for "world history," as if "trans" meant merely "bigger." Some posit any border crosser a "transnational" subject, with similarly dulling effect. I remain unconvinced that there is any difference between a migrant who crosses national borders and a "transmigrant."[7] Many observers think transnational method assumes the obsolescence of nations. On the contrary; in my view, the value of transnational method is its ability to examine and critique the nationalism that remains a powerful political and intellectual force. Transnational subjects overflow and challenge national borders not in blithe disregard for those borders but because nation-states so profoundly, even violently, constrain them. Nationalism has ceded to globalized formations neither in world politics nor in the academy, where national frameworks continue to define both fields of study broadly and individual research projects.

In addition to its debt to African diaspora studies, this version of transnational method owes much to radical geographers extending the legacy of theorists of world systems, themselves in turn extending the legacy of that obscure nineteenth-century transnationalist, Karl Marx. I phrase in this way to emphasize again that transnational method is not new, despite its neologism, and to underline my debt to and continuity with such theorists, despite a critical difference. Where theorists of global economic exploitation tend to emphasize the power of the core over the periphery, I trace vectors of influence in opposite directions, from colony to metropole, marginal subject to enfranchised elite, black to white, and cultural to political (among others). That is not to minimize the power of the center to wreak enormous violence on regions under its control. The exchanges explored in this book do not right the imbalances of race, nation, gender, class, or region, for none escaped their hierarchical matrices cleanly. Still, the stories they animate both reflect and complicate our understandings of such imbalance and perhaps uncover ways in which people today might intercede.

Transnational method is well set to pay such attention to bottom-up flow thanks to another set of debts, these owed to scholars and thinkers struggling against colonialism, including internal colonialism. Elsewhere I have tried to elaborate this relationship and its implications for academic method.[8] *Uneven Encounters* reflects this debt to those post- and anti-colonial scholars within and outside the United States who have explored the ways identity and experience are shaped in relation—through such factors as proximity, distance, similarity, difference, affinity, and conflict. Scholars in queer studies have incorporated these insights as well, so that their arguments and mine regarding passing and drag or the key roles of gender and sexuality in the elaboration of national identity all contain a doubling back to Third World and U.S. women of color scholars writing since the 1930s.[9] That foundation is too often overlooked, just as coffee drinkers rarely remember the travels of the sweat-soaked bean. Their cumulative insights point to the transnational contours of the nation, which, like the self, emerges in relation to others.

Straddling diaspora studies, Brazilian history, and U.S. history, and drawing sustenance from postcolonial and queer theory, this book is engaged in disciplinary Twister™. If it stands squarely anywhere, it is among American studies' work on empire, which in the last decade and a half has grown into a vibrant field.[10] Amy Kaplan, whose essay in a 1993 anthology sounded a resonant call to address the absence of empire in the study of U.S. culture, pointed her 2002 book toward the "confounding of the borders between the foreign and the domestic."[11] Christina Klein more straightforwardly calls a critical perspective transnational if it "enables us to see how the local and the global are inextricably bound up with one another."[12] Seth Fein calls transnational those "forces produced by the presence of one nation *within* another."[13] While Kaplan and Klein focus on the world's presence within the United States and Fein considers U.S. presence in Mexico, their applications of transnational method all pursue versions of the global in the local, as do mine.

The field of American studies has embraced transnational method in order to critique U.S. nationalism in the era of U.S. imperialism. Such work leans on the increased attention to nationalism in the wake of postwar, postcolonial, and post-Soviet "national explosions" (as Benedict Anderson called them) and the growing willingness to see the United States as an empire after the demise of the USSR and the invasions of Afghanistan and Iraq.[14] By paying attention to the cultural aspects of international politics, non-elite agency, resistance, and hybridity(for example), and by historicizing the nation, revealing it changing over time rather than transcendent or essential, transnational scholarship can powerfully critique the nation form at a moment when we need such a critique badly.

In American studies, many scholars are pursuing the study of empire in imaginative and productive ways, yet few works extend themselves fully into the history and historiography of the places whose traces they track. Focusing only on the country in which one lives keeps a scholar from certain fertile encounters. Language acquisition, the assimilation of scholarly literatures, and the personal contacts of collegiality are investments that create both stakes and debt. If the only North Americans who enter into such commerce, reaping its benefits in insight, are scholars *of* those other places, then the entire fields of North American history, culture, and social life remain untouched by that insight, while all the theoretical wealth of American studies, such as queer and postcolonial substreams, explorations of intersectionality, and analyses of racial construction, can elude North American scholars of other places.

North America–focused work on U.S. imperial history or culture can posit but not pinpoint the agency of foreign subjects. Nor, in tracing the global in the local, can it see what foreign subjects do with those traces as they watch their ideological and cultural production resonate and distort in North American contexts. Nor can it see the reworked phenomena as they alter local conditions and then travel yet again. The point is simply this: global circuits of culture and ideas never come to rest. To follow a single journey is to miss the previous trips woven into the slope and speed of the next. *Uneven Encounters* follows some of the multiple travels woven into ideas of race and nation by looking at a particular set of historical subjects who grabbed and manipulated them, infusing them with another dose of energy and sending them once again into motion.

The language of motion here is slightly misleading, for often the only traveling is done by ideas or cultural forms, which are subsets of each other (ideas are cultural forms, and cultural forms are also ideas; race and nation are both). In some ways a metaphor of conversation better conveys the dynamic this book explores, in which most people are standing more or less still, exchanging information about certain consequential social categories.[15] A conversation, though, is awfully calm. It fails to capture the violence that keeps some people in some places and sends others into motion and the resulting ways people engage, singing to and yelling at each other across achingly distant, distorting caverns of geography, language, station, time, and so on. Across these multiple distances and distortions, their suggestions and contentions reach intended and unintended targets who then—not willfully yet very carefully—misinterpret, rework, and recirculate them in their intimate environs, propelling their collective, conflictive work once again to the echoing canyon.

Looking in this way can reveal some things that otherwise often remain obscure, particularly in comparative frameworks: the power of non-elite subjects to see very far afield; to understand the world as well as anybody can; and to influence people, institutions, and ideas that seem unyieldingly more powerful than they. It shows disfranchised people actively making careful decisions, sharply constrained by complex economic and political factors as well as outright repression, and it shows how their decisions matter. Eroding assumptions of the passivity, ignorance, and impotence of marginalized people, this optic would encourage imperial subjects who desire global justice to try to follow rather than assume they must lead.

Note on Language

The descendants of Africans in Brazil in the 1920s called themselves and each other a broad array of terms. They used *negro, de côr, de classe, preto, pardo, mulato*, other color terms, and all the terms for white shades as well, of course—and many refused racial or color identifications at all, sometimes successfully. Historical actors are as inconsistent as contemporary subjects; all of us encounter and use the instability of racial categories. So how should a historian write of such subjects when discussing the impact of race?

For historians to use a single term carries elements of coercion, forcing people into categories they resist or exceed, and ironing over bountiful heterogeneity. Yet the use of multiple, inequivalent terms makes it difficult or impossible to recognize the organizing power of racism. Worse, accepting the classification system on the ground in the period studied can strengthen those elements in contemporary ideology that are the legacies of that period. I negotiate between these twin dilemmas with a split decision. In my own writing, I embrace the artifice of anachronistic umbrella terms that highlight rather than conceal that process of coercion and allow, albeit imperfectly, for a discussion of racism. For Brazilian subjects I choose "Afro-Brazilian" and "Afro-descended," the terms emerging from anti-racist activism in Brazil since the late 1970s, avowals of solidarity with Portugal's ex-colonies in Africa and with Afro-diasporic communities worldwide. I use "African American" for Afro-descended North Americans not from Canada (gritting my teeth about the equation of "America" with the United States as the alternative is simply too unwieldy). More happily, I use "Afro-American" for people of African descent from anywhere in the Americas, including the United States and Brazil. I even indulge in "black," most often in the pursuit of readability. I tend to prefer "whiter" to "white" to recognize the equally fluid, relative quality of this adjective and often use "elites" rather than "whites" in a nod to the imperfect convergence of race and power.

These are my choices for my own prose. When it comes to reprinting and translating primary sources, I take an opposite tack toward the same goals. The texts cited in this work adhere strictly to the original. I have not smoothed over errors nor modernized the Portuguese. Attentive readers will find occasional "errors" such as "paes" rather than "pais"; "cor" as well as "côr" (once even in the same sentence); and variations in the orthography of names (writers in the Afro-Brazilian press sometimes spelled their own names differently in different bylines; I do not presume to decide which one was their true name). For the most part these are offered unencumbered by the textual clutter of [*sic*]. Preserving these variations sustains the beacon of anachronism—that disjuncture that reminds the reader she is encountering a foreign country, the past. It respects the material and also the reader, who can more confidently form her own opinion in relation to sources free of yet another layer of mediation.

Yet my goal is not to provide a clear view based on unaltered primary sources—on the contrary. So many strata of mediation interfere in contemplating the history of race in the United States and Brazil from this book's twenty-first century U.S. perspective: translating Portuguese to English, locating Brazilian racial systems in North American terms, and bridging past and present. Any rendering of Brazilian racial terms into U.S. English is necessarily multiply inadequate. I address the question of translation substantively in chapter six, but throughout the book I engage it implicitly by leaving many words for race in the body of the text alongside their translations, or untranslated words within translated sections when the meanings will be evident from context. I hope the awkwardness of anachronism and untranslated terms will help to highlight inequivalence, the changing of racial terms over time, the struggles behind those changes, and the ultimate irretrievability of precise meanings for extinct racial categories. This strategy contains a plea to recognize and accept a certain measure of ignorance about terms for race. Only such ignorance genuinely respects the status of race as a social construction—if we knew what race "really" was, what would we know it to be?

Acknowledgments

There is great joy in owing so much to the many people who have guided and supported me through this work. I thank them here in roughly chronological chunks but with no particular internal order. In the dissertation stage, I was blessed with a brilliant set of mentors: my adviser, Robin D. G. Kelley; exam and dissertation readers Lisa Duggan and George Yúdice; and dissertation readers Diana Taylor and Olívia Gomes da Cunha. I benefited immeasurably from my other professors and mentors at NYU, including Nikhil Pal Singh, Robert Stam, Martha Hodes, Ada Ferrer, and Judith Halberstam.

From my first dissertation research to my last moments of revision, I have leaned heavily on Rio de Janeiro friends and mentors, including Olívia Gomes da Cunha, Flávio dos Santos Gomes, Tiago de Melo Gomes, Rose Sant'anna, Edmeire Exaltação, Jurema Verneck, and Luciene Fortuna and Brazilianist colleagues and friends Judith Williams, Amy Chazkel, Darien Davis, Sonia Roncador, Kim Butler (who gave wonderful, generous comments on an early version of the manuscript and again at a later date), Michael Mitchell (who read and encouraged me via e-mail for months during the first revisions), Denise Ferreira da Silva, James Green, Jerry Dávila, Bryan McCann, Edward Telles, David Hellwig (without whose edited volume I could not have conceived of my dissertation), Jeffrey Lesser (who before we ever met sent me documents from his own research in an archive that had since closed and later supported me generously at Emory), Barbara Weinstein (admired friend and my model of academic integrity), Daryle Williams (inspiring co-director of the Driskell Center), and Steven Topik (tireless correspondent on any coffee-related query).

At Bowdoin College I appreciated the supportive enthusiasm of Randolph Stakeman, Allen Wells, Patrick Rael, Krista Van Vleet, and Marilyn Reizbaum, and at the University of Maryland, I basked in the sweet wisdom of Driskell Center director Eileen Julien and extended my research base in inspiring conversation with her, Daryle Williams, Barbara Weinstein, Mary Kay Vaughan, Elsa Barkeley Brown, Clyde Woods, and the incredibly generous and insightful Julia Foulkes. My research that term at the Smithsonian Institution was deftly guided by Fath Ruffins and radical poet-archivist Reuben Jackson.

In Los Angeles I was buoyed up by my wonderful colleagues at the California State University, Los Angeles (CSULA): Mark Wild, Peter Sigal, Alejandra Marchevsky, Victor Viesca, Christopher Endy, Beth Baker-Cristales, colleagues in the Center for the Study of Genders and Sexualities and the Rockefeller Program and by astonishing students, including Gustavo Lopez, Jasmine Guerrero, and Kyelynn Chiong; by members of the Los Angeles Latin American History reading group: Robin Derby and Maria Elena Martinez; and especially by my trusted friend David Sartorius, who consulted with endless goodwill and great judgment. Three other beloved scholarly friends in Los Angeles cheered and advised this project: Teo Ruiz, Vanessa Schwartz, and Ruthie Gilmore—thank you. Also absolutely sustaining was the collaboration and inspiration of Critical Resistance rudders Melissa Burch, Ruthie Gilmore, Craig Gilmore, Roy San Filippo, and Rose Braz. Thank you, Robs. Thank you, Maxa. Thank you, WH_2O. Thanks to the participants in the Tepoztlán Institute on Transnational History, who have supported and guided my thinking on transnational method, especially Jocelyn Olcott and the institute's huge-hearted directors, Pamela Voekel and Elliott Young.

In an outstanding year at Cornell's Society for the Humanities (SOH), I benefited from the rich companionship of my brilliant fellow fellows, in particular those who read large portions of this manuscript or talked thorny points all the way through with me: Lucinda Ramberg, Sarah Evans, Suman Seth, and Jeff Cowie; thanks to Andy Hobarek for my title, to Matthew Hart for productive provocations on the question of modernity, and to director Brett de Bary for sweet guidance; thanks to Cornell faculty participants in the Comparative History Colloquium: Ray Craib, Mary Roldan, and especially my old new friend Duane Corpis; thanks to these and all the fellows for Gimme! daytime and sudsy evening debates over the global post . . . whatever: Gabriela Vargas-Cetina, Igor Ayora-

Diaz, Belinda Edmondson, Stanka Radovic, Noa Vaisman, Natalie Melas, Erin Hyman, Jenny Mann, Phil Stern, Petrus Liu, and, up the road at Syracuse, the fearless Jenna Loyd. I could not have finished this project without the incredible structure the soh provided and am profoundly grateful to its organizers.

Thanks for helpful e-mailing and discussion to Frederick Cooper, Doris Witt, Timothy Brennan, Deborah Cohen, and Steven Selka; thanks to M. Elizabeth Ginway for extensive correspondence regarding Elsie Houston and for sharing her unpublished interview notes with me. Thanks to David Kazanjian for reading a long excerpt and for subsequent helpful comments; to Jordana Rosenberg for readings and thinkings-through; thanks for help in musical analysis to pianist and music historian Clifford Korman; Cornell musicologist Steven Pond; and flutist Jayn Rosenfeld, my mother, who in addition read and helped hone most if not all of the chapters while listening to all the, how shall I say, background noise. Thanks to Peter Winn and to my treasured friend Karen Krahulik, both of whom read the entire manuscript and gave wonderful comments, a labor of loving collegiality for which I am deeply grateful. Thanks to the excellent Duke University Press (DUP) readers, especially the three of whom identified themselves to me and extended their already enormously helpful comments in subsequent conversations, Kim Butler, Sueann Caulfield, and Maria Josefina Saldaña-Portillo. Thanks to my brilliant and dear friend Seth Fein, eminent theorist-practitioner of transnational history, who among many other acts of selfless and sweet support helped shepherd this book into this series; thanks to series editors Gil Joseph and Emily Rosenberg for receiving it there; thanks to Valerie Milholland, Neal McTighe, and Miriam Angress of DUP for constant encouragement and expertise.

For financial and institutional support for this work, I gratefully thank the Rockefeller Foundation, first at UNICAMP and later at CSULA; the Foreign Language and Area Studies Program of the Department of Education, also twice, first for language study and then for archival research in Brazil; the New York University (NYU) Center for Latin American and Caribbean Studies; the NYU Dean's Dissertation Fellowship program; the Centro de Estudos Afro-Asiáticos; the Universidade Federal do Rio de Janeiro (UFRJ)'s Programa Avançado de Cultura Contemporânea; Bowdoin College; Emory University; the Driskell Center for the Study of the African Diaspora and the Arts at the University of Maryland, College Park; CSULA; the Cornell University SOH; and Indiana University, Bloomington. Perhaps this will strike some readers as odd, but I am also grateful to this book itself. Its provocations and demands in themselves at times sustained me.

Finally, one person is responsible for this work in more ways than is usually possible: my father. As a child, I would hang around his study, reading titles off the spines of his library and asking what each book was about. He answered with such joyous interest that it did not occur to me that I was interrupting him until I became a reader of similar books. All my life my father has engaged, disagreed, and debated with me with this same interested, fierce respect. At the same time, he has met my every joy with joy and every sadness with unmatched empathy. I am the scholar and the person that I am because of him.

Introduction

All his life, anti-racist activist José Correia Leite, co-founder of the longest-lived newspaper in the São Paulo black press, retained a global perspective he had acquired just after the First World War. In his memoirs, Leite recalled in particular the window the war opened onto transatlantic racial politics:

> The American Negroes in France, when they marched separately from the whites, began to notice that the United States was heavily criticized for its racial discrimination. And also when they saw how the Senegalese army marched in Paris—those Frenchwomen draped around the necks of those big Negroes [negrões]—they saw that they were wrong to think that American whites' racial discrimination was a generalized thing.... That came to our attention here. We also began to use those facts as example.... All that was published in the papers, and we saw it as based in the influence of the First World War.[1]

While Leite's local social sphere in São Paulo included few African American or African subjects, his understanding of the world incorporated them and more. Gazing over equator and ocean with the help of the newspaper press, Leite was entranced by the range of Afro-diasporic subjects and racial attitudes he observed, and he was transformed by his revelations, as was a generation of his peers in all the places he noted.

Perhaps it is surprising that such a modest figure paid so much attention to such far-away places and people in this moment prior to electronic telecommunication. From a twenty-first century vantage point, it is hard to grasp "how effectively illiterate people with such particularist loyalties could communicate on a global scale, bridging continents," as another observer of non-elite world travelers has noted.[2] It is easier to succumb to the evolutionist feeling that only now could such communication occur—as if, as one U.S. scholar of Brazil suggested, until "the 1970s, black Brazilians had little information about U.S. blacks due to the barrier of language."[3] A related misconception imagines that marginalized people are too oppressed to act on their own behalf. As another North American academic wrote, explaining Afro-Brazilians' "failure" to fight racism, "day-to-day survival [is] so difficult and time consuming that it is virtually impossible to concentrate on politics."[4] As Leite confirms, these statements are simply not true.

The notion that non-elites in global peripheries were isolated rests upon the idea that the technology required for global communication has only recently emerged—that only in the last forty years or so has the world entered the age of "globalization."[5] It underestimates the efficacy of all previous communications technologies from print media and music all the way back to the canoe, discounting as well the abilities of people in earlier moments to use them. The view that poverty prohibits politics forgets those for whom day-to-day survival *is* political. It erases the agency of non-elite historical subjects and confines politics to the tiniest formal arena, denying the utility of cultural politics.[6] While those to whom luxury travel and formal education are denied certainly have avenues of global encounter and action closed to them, no one stops thinking or negotiating the world around them just because they are working.

Communication among the enslaved is the quintessential refutation of such misconceptions. It bridged divides of distance, language, time, and culture since the first forced migrations of the Atlantic slave trade.[7] Slave resistance mocks the idea that the overworked cannot engage in political acts, and it often grew or grew bolder due to long-distance communication.[8] Slave communication routes across the Americas and the Atlantic, evolved and reworked by commerce and technological change, undergird the twentieth-century channels of transnational exchange that are the subject of this book.

Transnational exchange reflects the global imagination and reach of people enmeshed in global systems, whether they toiled and traveled the reaches of the Roman or Mongolian empires, the trade routes of the thirteenth-century Mediterranean world, or the networks of capitalism,

European expansion, and African slavery that have traversed the planet in the last five hundred years. This framing reminds us that global links are forged in violence and resistance, a fact neglected by those who celebrate blithe, frictionless digital-age globalization. It also moves toward the recognition of the global formation of the largest units of social relation in our global era, the categories of race and nation. Situating Leite in his rightful place as an agent of transnational exchange adds a third point, distinctly hopeful: not only did non-elites develop large-scale social imaginations, but they used them to resist and reshape their local worlds. *Uneven Encounters* presents a cast of characters situated along the full range of international and domestic social hierarchies, who used their global vision to rework lived ideas of race and nation.[9]

Leite and his fellow journalists and their community of supporters and readers saw, understood, and acted. As Leite pointed out, they "began to use those facts as example." The transnational exchange of views Leite described provided material for political struggle: Afro-Paulista (from São Paulo) newspaper readers and writers used the supposed lack of racism on the part of the French as well as the mileage U.S. African Americans made from a similar vision to inspire pride, fear, a sense of duty, honor, and hope among their various audiences, from fellow recreational and mutual aid society members to local and national elites. They drew on and enhanced a mental map that charted people and events in Africa, Europe, and the Americas and even included an understanding of how people in those places saw each other. Their global vision doubled up and back over the Atlantic and across the equator, revealing the complex self-awareness of subjects on multiple margins. From such a standpoint, people often develop achingly sharp insights on the structures that keep them in such precarious positions. Not despite but because of their marginal geographic and social positions, Leite and his peers knew about the world and put their awareness to use. While they did not make history exactly as they pleased, their tactics pulled a host of interlocutors into consequential interactions.

Uneven Encounters explores the ways people used the transnational mental maps they developed out of cultural exchange. In particular it focuses on the ways Brazilians and North Americans gleaned from transnational exchange to reshape two of the most consequential social categories structuring their lives: race and nation. The book selects a transnational lens in order to highlight the broad contexts in which these constructs form. Race and nation must be understood together, I argue, for in our age these two categories are so profoundly intertwined that their relationship is constitutive of the meanings they both make.[10] Racialized national categories draw their shape and meaning not only from other social categories such as gender or region, but also from each other—that is, from other racialized national categories. Their process of construction therefore involves international and transnational relations. This insight carries implications for historical practice and social action: both must refuse the corrosive of nation(alism), still terribly powerful in what some would call a postnational age. To historicize race, one must consider multiple scales, including those both smaller and greater than the nation-state. To dismantle racial hierarchies, one must also target nationalism. So historians of race must surpass national frameworks, just as anti-racism must forego the seductions of nationalism.[11] The reverse is also true—to confront nationalism, one must ferret out racisms of all textures—but few readers these days will need to be reminded of that.

Race and nation are made together, this book contends, in cultural as well as political or economic realms, by non-elites as well as elites and out of pieces gathered very far away, as well as local, regional, and national elements. To support this claim, the chapters follow a motley set of 1920s characters crossing barriers of many sorts, reinforcing or undermining prevailing conceptions of race and nation in the realm of public, commercial, and popular culture. The cultural forms through which the characters work include ads (chapter 1), dance (chapters 2 and 3), music (chapters 3 and 4), vaudeville and other genres of popular stage performance (chapter 4), newspapers (chapters 5 and 6), and public monuments (chapter 6). All the forms detailed transcend the national: the advertisements are made by U.S. and Brazilian merchants together, and they market an import (coffee); the dance is Brazilian, enjoying a vogue in the United States; the music is jazz in Rio de Janeiro, and its players embrace its supposed foreign qualities explicitly; the vaudevillians are North Americans literally performing foreignness, either by dancing foreign dances and speaking foreign languages or pretending to be foreign; the newspapers are organs of the black Brazilian press that report intensely on external, particularly North American news and eventually enter into direct conversation with the U.S. black press; the monument is a figure of Brazilian history commemorated precisely because of what her champions hoped she would demonstrate about Brazil abroad.

Chapter 1 begins with a topic that permits a sketch of political and economic background: the coffee trade. This most concrete channel of U.S.–Brazil exchange in the post–First World War period brought together such elite actors as planters, businessmen, and politicians as they moved in ideological fields increasingly organized by the possibilities of mass culture. The chapter focuses on the quintessence of the culture industry, advertising — art in the service of capital — tracking the political unconscious it organized and that organized it. It tracks this unconscious, paradoxically, through the highly conscious ideological production circulated by relatively privileged people to middle-class North American audiences. They did not see the conditions of possibility for their work, set by their negotiations with less visible and less apparently powerful cultural producers, who are the subjects of the rest of the chapters.

Chapters 2–4 deal with popular performance. Their quick stops on a tour of the wartime and post–First World War entertainment world engage different aspects of leisure culture during a period of fervid celebration of racially marked cultural production. Chapter 2 follows the breakneck travels of the Brazilian dance *maxixe* into the limelight and then very far out. Remaining with the previous chapter's focus on elites, it traces some of the ways culture industry avatars in imperial centers incited and appealed to exoticist tastes. Following this process helps explain how the profound hybridity of "American" culture could continue to escape observers, for the mechanisms through which maxixe was introduced to the United States and with which it won such acclaim were also those that ensured its quick erasure from collective memory.

Moving beyond elite subjects, chapters 3 and 4 consider the ways popular cultural producers used the exoticisms of the moment as fuel for artistic creation, professional advancement, and even collective and political possibilities. Chapter 3 listens to the ways performers of jazz in Rio de Janeiro played racial and social justice into their musical reality. In concert with fellow travelers such as religious officials, black press journalists, and popular audiences, mostly Afro-Brazilian performers used the transnational context of the "Negro vogue" to emphasize the virtue and value of blackness. Their overtures reconfigured notions of citizenship, modernity, and Brazilian national identity that have been attributed primarily to intellectuals and elites. Chapter 4 appreciates similar work by North American artists. Their exoticist performances cracked open space for black success onstage or stepped outside the category "black," whether by passing as foreign or via a national masquerade whose unworried admission of artifice places it closer to drag — nation drag.

From the elite (white, mostly North American) subjects of chapters 1 and 2 to the popular performers of chapters 3 and 4 (a mix of racial and national subjects), the book moves in chapters 5 and 6 to people who actively identified as black and engaged explicitly in political struggle. These two chapters take place largely in Brazil, following the anti-racist activists of the São Paulo black press as they wrestled to reimagine their several overlapping communities. Here we rejoin José Correia Leite as he and his peers moved in conversation with other Afro-Paulistas, Brazilians regardless of color, and Afro-diasporic subjects in and beyond Brazil, including black press readers and writers in Chicago. Chapter 5 highlights some of the uneven qualities and quantities in black North American and Brazilian subject positions that frustrated comprehension when people actually met and that frustrate any hope of comparing blackness across the two national contexts. Chapter 6 juxtaposes these fluid, inequivalent conceptions of race by examining a controversial plan to build a monument to the Black Mother of slavery times. As African American and Afro-Brazilian journalists read and translated reports of distant sets of events, they generated mismatch after mismatch in conceptualizations of social categories. Working to construct usable solidarities, journalists papered over yawning gaps in definitions of race with ostensibly coherent, constant categories of gender. Their strategic misunderstandings sprang from the same set of hopes mobilizing the Rio jazz musicians of chapter 3: that the tools to realize Brazil's much-touted "racial democracy" lay in international realms.

Routes of Contact/Grounds of Relation

The backstory here involves the conditions that made these rounds of cultural exchange possible, and they are many and complex. Trails were blazed by previous travelers, trade routes and cowpaths, traditions of mutual interest or antagonism, and so on, all the way back to the slave communication networks that laid the groundwork for so many later webs of exchange.

Related to slave networks and more visible to historians, abolitionist complexes leaned on and expanded those networks in the nineteenth century. Abolitionists throughout the Atlantic world gestured to and invoked

Brazil, for its ostensibly peaceful racial relations seemed to prove the unnecessary cruelty of slavery in the United States. In their newspapers, lectures, plays, and presentations and through capacious oral networks of story and rumor, abolitionists gave wings to news of Brazil.[12] Abolitionists' opponents also found the apparent existence of a place of racial harmony useful. Proponents of slavery cited Brazil as proof that slavery could be benign or, in later years, as evidence for the terrible degradations of racial mixture.[13] That both sides in the debate over slavery found Brazilian conditions particularly relevant augmented its symbolic importance for considerations of Afro-descendants in the Americas. This is part of the historical basis that set Brazil in its prominent position in the transnational construction of race in the United States.

The images of Brazil conveyed to North American observers by travelers prompted several waves of migration in the nineteenth century, and these in turn strengthened and expanded webs of exchange. Disaffected white confederates set up relatively ill-fated settlements in the Brazilian interior just after the U.S. Civil War.[14] Brazil's peaceful abolition of slavery in 1888 and its transition from a monarchy to a republic the following year also commanded much U.S. attention.[15] After the end of Reconstruction, Brazil was one of the places to which African Americans dreamt of moving to find a haven from racism. By the mid-1920s, growing North American investment in South America and patterns of labor migration from the United States and the Caribbean had established a noticeable group of black foreigners in São Paulo and probably other cities as well.[16] These emigrants and events brought U.S. racial arrangements to Brazilian attention and vice versa.

Brazilians traveling to the United States have also contributed to the widening of avenues of exchange, though significant numbers of Brazilian immigrants did not appear in the United States until the 1980s.[17] In the nineteenth and early twentieth centuries, many Brazilian travelers were sons of the elite sent to the metropole for finishing educations. They followed commercial and military sailors, those quintessential Atlantic voyagers. Seafarers bring back news of the places they have been, weaving a subtle transnational filament into the worldview and expectations of their circles of friends and acquaintances. Such voyagers have been key to Afro-American intercommunication, given the high proportion of Afro-descendants in navies, in port work (for example, stevedores), and as crew on commercial craft.[18] One cohort of Brazilian navy sailors disembarking in Brooklyn provoked in Brazilian anthropologist Gilberto Freyre, then a student at Columbia University, the tormented musings on the degradations of Brazilian miscegenation that would spark his inordinately influential comparative history of Brazil. Other sailors on shore leaves left impressions equally striking, if less resonantly recorded.[19]

Long-distance communication and awareness, of course, are geopolitically uneven — "lumpy," in Frederick Cooper's wonderful characterization of globalization (too bad "Lumpy Encounters" doesn't work so well as a book title).[20] People in peripheral places are often more aware of conditions and events in the powerful metropoles than people in the centers of power are about their counterparts in the periphery. Certainly Brazilians were more aware of the comings and goings of their northern neighbors than North Americans were of them. Brazilian popular culture was suffused with the output of Hollywood, Madison Avenue, and Tin Pan Alley, as well as with locally produced items that made reference to them (though often more parodic than reverential). Formal political spaces lined themselves with citations of Brazil's most powerful hemispheric neighbor, and more informal public spheres, such as the press, made constant allusion to the social relations prevailing there. In the United States, the view of Brazil was more blurry. Occasionally Brazilian cultural forms enjoyed brief vogues with U.S. audiences, and thanks to the mass marketing of its coffee, Brazil could take its place as one of a number of tropical countries whose laborers bent their dark backs to the pleasure of the U.S. consuming public. The privileges of power include ignorance, and some of this book is about the construction of ignorance through the careful erasure of the lessons of transnational exchange. North Americans worked hard to assimilate images of Brazil into the iconography of empire, which in the opening decades of the twentieth century contributed profoundly to the always ongoing construction of racial and national identity. Still, multiple, overlapping fields of power and privilege mean that sometimes subsets of metropolitan populations have reasons to know about peripheral places and often choose not to erase — and even to expand — the information they encounter into usable fields of knowledge.

The example of this dynamic that is most important to this book is the interest in Brazil sustained by North Americans who identified as black. Brazil's reputation as a place of peace among the races was intriguing to African Americans, who amassed a serviceable storehouse of information about this supposedly non-racist New World state and set about drawing attention to its example. Unconcerned to be projecting a utopian desire onto a deeply racist place, African Americans and allies used Brazil's image as a "racial paradise" to attack fear of miscegenation, to argue that racism was neither natural nor inevitable, and to invoke international disapproval of racial animosity in the United States.[21] African American and other travelers to Brazil updated and extended the transnational conversations forged by abolitionists, slave and free.

The First World War accelerated Pan-American exchange dramatically. Wartime innovations sparked interconnected booms in communications technologies, mass culture, and urbanization; these developments then in turn widened the paths for the travel of goods, services, ideas, and cultural products. The war realigned trade routes—for example, forcing Americans to seek markets within their hemisphere for the goods they had previously shipped to Europe.[22] As the largest two nations in the region, Brazil and the United States sought each other's markets for their exports with particular hope and zeal. Advances in communications technologies spurred the growth of mass culture, a swift and fluid traveler, and commercial realignments in those communications technologies further expanded inter-American exchange, as in the case of a German news service that telegraphed from Brazil and left in 1918, ceding its place to the Associated Press.[23] Another powerful spark to both commerce and cultural exchange was the advertising industry, which expanded in the early twentieth century in tandem with the rise of mass culture, postwar economic growth, the popularization of Freudian psychology, and innovations in media from print to wax to radio waves.

The war launched another set of developments that accelerated the pace of Brazil-U.S. exchange and Afro-American communication more broadly. It spotlit global racial relations and questions of racial justice as the Allies' rhetoric of democracy and equality caught on the snag of their own racially stratified societies. As José Correia Leite made explicit in another forum, "the war, distributing ideas of liberty and equality, presenting itself as the great struggle for democracy, awoke in the laboring masses of color aspirations for a better fate."[24] Demobilization precipitated activism. Black soldiers had been highly visible in the conflict, whether in segregated U.S. troops, African and Caribbean colonial units, or European armies, and they remained visible in pacifying operations after the Armistice. During the peace African culture caught more than the passing fancy of metropolitan citizens, who reveled in jazz, primitivism, futurism, and surrealism. Yet racist hierarchies failed to budge. Soldiers' determination to enjoy the rights earned by their patriotism spurred anti-racist activism, both in the United States and, as Leite reminds us, far beyond.[25]

Activism fed reaction. The U.S. anti-racist movement that followed the return of African American troops met a wave of anti-black race riots and lynchings, most notoriously during the nationwide "Red Summer" of 1919. Intensified racial terror constricted the segregationist codes of Jim Crow.[26] In this book, chapters 2 and 4 recount some of the ways popular cultural figures were a part of these reconfigurations. Brazilian elite response took a seemingly opposite path to the rhetorical embrace of racial harmony while staunchly reinforcing racial hierarchy in less audible ways. Chapters 3, 5, and 6 detail the roles of Afro-Cariocas (from Rio de Janeiro) and -Paulistas in delimiting the parameters of this elite response.

This process added yet another segment to the long tale of U.S.–Brazil exchange as postwar activism and reaction refreshed North Americans' and Brazilians' mutual focus. Brazilians of various sorts circulated news of U.S. racial violence because of its useful contrast to their supposedly harmonious nation's moral superiority. Racial terror sparked another wave of African American emigrationism, bringing Brazil back to center in an African American public sphere and making the renewed possibility of black migration once more an issue in Brazil.

These developments were far from limited to Brazil and the United States. The interwar period nurtured a range of global imaginaries, all irretrievably racialized. Leite's view from the south joined the Marxist vision of W. E. B. Du Bois's "dark and vast sea of human labor in China and India, the South Seas and all Africa; in the West Indies and Central America and in the United States—that great majority of mankind," and both found a paranoid counterpart in Lathrop Stoddard's "rising tide of color." From imperial imaginaries to anti-imperialisms to black internationalisms in Pan-American, Pan-African, Black Atlantic, and countless other variations, these global racial imaginaries encompassed solidarities of many kinds, helping both to build momentum for social change and to hold the line against it, transforming ideas about race and racial configurations around the world.[27] These imaginaries would bear fruit in Depression-era radicalism, but their matrix was cultural exchange in the decade and a half before.

This context makes U.S.-Brazil exchange in the 1920s compelling to narrate as a consequential piece of the construction of race and nation in both places. The United States and Brazil were not necessarily more important to each other in this process or moment than other places were to either one. In fact the United States and Brazil are good candidates for the conjoined historicization of their racialized nationalisms because their connections are not obvious. They share no border, speak different languages, exchanged relatively few migrants before the late twentieth century, are incommensurate in political and economic power, and were never in a formal colonial relationship to each other. Yet as I shall show, they are bound up in each other in discursive and material arenas in uneven, awkward, sometimes brutal ways, earlier and with greater consequence than most observers have been willing to admit.

Uneven Encounters helps backdate the histories of interwar radicalism and globalized interconnection, contextualizing the classic cases of the 1930s and the 1970s, respectively. It does the same for the history of cultural exchange. At the point that these stories mostly end in the early 1930s, cultural exchange in the Americas began to shift in character. The consolidation of the Depression in 1932 preceded by two short years the repeal of the Platt Amendment (which had secured effective U.S. control in Cuba), the withdrawal of U.S. Marines from Haiti, and bilateral trade agreements between the United States and five southern neighbors: Cuba, Haiti, Brazil, Colombia, and Honduras. These events signaled the coming of age of the southern-facing diplomatic stance of the Good Neighbor Policy elaborated by Franklin D. Roosevelt in the 1930s.[28] The United States was increasingly invested in cultivating Pan-American friendship in the thirties and increasingly convinced of the fertility of culture in particular as grounds for political approximation. In the wake of the world war, Brazilians had also come to value the United States as trade partner, political ally, and hemispheric neighbor, and Brazilian president Getúlio Vargas, who came to power in the Revolution of 1930, gave unprecedented attention to cultural matters.[29]

By the end of the period discussed in this book, the state had taken cultural exchange into its jurisdiction.[30] Not exclusively, of course; informal exchange of the kind I explore here continued, often in tension with state-sponsored counterparts. The transnational back-and-forth that had convinced authorities of the potency of culture as a vehicle for politics, however, was neither a state product nor the fruit of elite cultural or intellectual production. Over routes paved by performance, entertainment, pleasure, commerce, activism, journalism, tourism and more, people, ideas and cultural forms flowed abundantly, unevenly, and often at painful cost. Their travel constitutes a complex, consequential conversation. This book listens to it.

CHAPTER ONE

Producing Consumption
Coffee and Consumer Citizenship

Readers of North American popular magazines in 1922 may have paused to admire an intriguing advertisement for Butter-Nut coffee. It featured a coffee grower—a dashing patrician with black mustache and beard, bow tie, cummerbund, large sombrero, pointy boots, and flowing pants with mariachi silver buttons. This cinematic figure stood in front of a field of leafy shrubs (presumably coffee plants), with a group of low buildings behind them (perhaps his plantation) and mountains (probably volcanic) rising in the far background. As befit such a mishmash of geography and culture, the specific place went unnamed. The gentleman grower simply called it "my country," though he made clear reference to the United States: "Coffee is as important an item to my country as wheat is in your United States," he explained. Lest this lack of specificity mar his authenticity, the ad's copywriter had him declare, "You can take my word for it—this is <u>REAL</u> Coffee!"[1]

The ad drew its readers further into the transnational realm of the coffee trade by imagining not only the tropical producer but also his North American consumer. The planter handed a steaming cup across the page to a carefully groomed white man in a conservative suit, at table in a gracious dining room. Behind him, a chandelier, a finely worked wooden dining table, and a mantle with adornments; under his feet, an Oriental rug, and across from him, gazing adoringly at the offer, a lovely blonde, surely his wife. Coffee passed from Latin to Saxon; from raw, authentic nature to refined civilization; and from a place of suggestively virile barbarity into a well-contained domestic space of bourgeois heterosexuality. Its vision of

FIGURE 1. "You can take my word for it—this is <u>REAL</u> Coffee!" Butter-Nut ad, 1922. Hills Bros. Collection, NMAH.

mutual attraction set a textbook Hollywood Latin leading man feminized by his smoldering sensuality (volcanos, barbarous virility, dazzling sartorial display) alongside an Anglo-Saxon lightly emasculated by the taint of citified over-civilization, a favorite fear of metropolitan urban dwellers at the time. Less homoerotic than homologic, the two lean in toward each other as if in the thrall of a "natural" magnetism.

This arrestingly evocative schematization of connection between coffee producers and U.S. consumers is a perfect entrée into an exploration of the local and global interrelationships shaping key facets of twentieth-century U.S. nationalism. Its picture conveys more than a thousand words regarding the process of imagining national community. Its two panels, side by side, encouraged the viewer to contemplate self and Other. If the substance of their link was a cup of coffee, the ad suggested, the substance of their difference was not only race and place but their participation in the acts of production and consumption, respectively. Uninterested in reciprocity, the ad furnished its dining room with multiple items clearly coded as imports, implying that along with their whiteness and adherence to gender conventions, it was the couple's consumption of the world's products, rather than consumption in general, that made them appropriate objects for desire and identification. This was a vision in which undifferentiated Latin Americans produced and proffered, while "Americans" (in "their" United States) consumed.[2]

Such representations of global relations dovetailed with discursive productions of U.S. imperialism but were not reducible to a simple framework of political domination.[3] More directly and consequentially, this ad indexed and promoted the political-economic changes attendant to the rise of consumer capitalism. The Butter-Nut spot and its field of related advertisements helped to midwife the critical idea, emergent in this period, of consumer citizenship.

In this chapter I read 1920s coffee advertisements to argue that consumer citizenship is a racialized nationalism constructed in transnational context. I explore a tiny slice of economic history to introduce the book's overall contention that ideas of race and nation in the United States, as in Brazil, have been constructed in interrelation. To arrive at this contention requires several complicated steps, so let us pause a moment to consider what consumer citizenship is, why it is important, how it relates to U.S. nationalism, and why it ought to be apprehended within a transnational framework.

Notions of "consumer citizenship" emerged from the wedding of consumerism, "the belief that goods give meaning to individuals and their roles in society," to notions of *national* belonging.[4] That wedding was a historical process—that is, it happened slowly, over time. In the nineteenth century, U.S. notions of national identity were more likely to hinge on production, in a loose reflection of its agricultural and industrial output. The economic transition of the United States from a producer to a consumer society was a long process; it began in the eighteenth century and remained less than fully realized until after the Second World War. But representation need not cleave faithfully to economic conditions, and what concerns us in this chapter are the webs of signification spun around ideas of consumption. People in the 1920s experienced consumerism with a palpable feeling of alarm. Critics expressed great discomfort at the thought of allowing self-indulgent (they charged) consumption practices to replace the producerist ethos that had long been a point of national pride. "Consumption" seemed to be spreading like its contagious homonym, and city dwellers worried about "neurasthenia" and "overcivilization," romanticizing the sweat of the farmer or the muscular labor of the manufacturer.[5] Advertisers for all sorts of products, not just coffee, worked diligently to soothe this anxiety and coax audiences to think of themselves as "consumers" to promote the practices needed to drive commodity capitalism.

The short version of this story is that advertisers were successful. Over the course of the twentieth century, consumption has taken an increasingly important place in U.S. definitions of self and society, to the point of defining the parameters of citizenship. As its many critics have pointed out, consumerism has come to organize notions of who is a deserving member of society (those who consume wisely and responsibly), what freedom means (choice at the supermarket), and what constitutes political participation (buying green; the boycott).[6] Consumerism functions accordingly as a form of U.S. nationalism, worth going to war to protect. Further, as race and class remain deeply correlated in the United States (and the world), consumerism is a racially discriminatory nationalism. Its assumptions regarding "good" choices in the market divert attention from the structural factors that keep poor people poor, including racism, and so reinforce those structures.[7]

Many observers have discussed the development of consumer citizenship and criticized its effects, but few have placed it in the transnational context in which it belongs.[8] As illustrative pieces of a broader cultural field, the Butter-Nut ad and its fellow coffee advertisements can help us see the transnational aspects of consumer citizenship, for the ideological work they did hinged on the ways they were transnational themselves.

As I explained in the preface, by "transnational" I mean phenomena unconfined to—both greater and lesser than—the nation-state. The term directs attention to cases in which national borders are not the pertinent containers for the phenomena at hand. It is not intended simply to replace either "international," which refers to the interactions of nation-states or representatives thereof, or "global," a gesture to the earth's largest scale. We might observe, to illustrate, that the global coffee trade was both inter-

and transnational. It was global in its production and consumption on seven continents and its shipping across seven seas; it was international in that it brought together state representatives and market sectors acting in the interests of their states. It was transnational in the shifting loyalties of market and state representatives, sometimes at one with each other, sometimes at odds; the regionalisms that foil a single national interest; and the links laborers (for example, farmhands or stevedores) maintained to their sending communities, for they were often migrants or immigrants. Its transnationalism was also simply a function of the fluctuating formations of cooperation and conflict among the trade's multiple sectors: growers, shippers, importers, greenmen, roasters, advertisers, retailers, bankers and other financiers, politicians (both federal and regional), laborers, and the families and environs of all of these people.

Coffee meant enormously different things to different people. In terms of its social meaning, the coffee that left the Brazilian port at Santos was not the coffee unloaded in New Orleans. Yet there is continuity in some senses. Economic historians speak of "commodity chains"—all the labor and production processes entailed in a commodity's formation—and there is a social level to such linkages as well.[9] As every piece contains traces of the whole, so the social relations entailed in coffee production are a part of its ads, just as they are present in every draft of the brew we sip. The transnational travels of the coffee trade were woven into its 1920s U.S. ads, sometimes via references to far-away places, sometimes in the form of non-state, non-nation concoctions such as "civilization," "the West," or "the Tropics." At times advertisers tried *not* to gesture to the broad geography of the commodity they pushed, and ads certainly often function to obscure, rewrite, and sanitize points along the chain of the commodity they hawk. Yet the effort required to suppress important details of coffee's provenance, as we shall see, often left its mark. Coffee ads inserted their foreign and transnational traces into circulation in the United States, planting them in the cultural fields in which the ads were at play. Those traces may have seemed buried, their impact attenuated and near impossible to specify, but their residue was critical. This chapter will show the ways in which their transnational aspects helped coffee advertisements effect a critical obfuscation: the portrayal of consumption as a national quality rather than the class-specific practice it is.

Such obfuscation is one clear reason to seek to understand the transnational dimensions of ideas of race and nation. Understanding consumer citizenship first as a nationalism, then as a racialized nationalism, and ultimately as a racialized nationalism reliant on transnational context sharpens the tools critics can devise to intervene in the toxic social relations ordered by consumer citizenship, internationally and within the United States. So while a transnational approach forces the critic to work broadly—learning other languages, absorbing multiple historiographies, traveling to distant archives—its advantage is not necessarily that it illuminates a "global picture," as many people construe its purpose. Rather, thinking transnationally reveals the specific mechanisms by which class, race, nation, and other social categories are constructed and the process of their construction occluded.

Few North Americans assume that Brazilian or transnational phenomena shaped U.S. life in any important way. Yet it is logical; everything from the foreign trade that generated profits for U.S. merchants to the nations or peoples against whose images North Americans defined themselves have been critical contributors to U.S. economic and ideological conditions. What historical cultural study can do is show *how* transnational phenomena matter. Where did they enter, and how did they work? Just as important, how was recognition of such contributions erased so that collective popular and scholarly memory meet them as exceptions rather than as rule?

This chapter, then, takes up one concrete instance of the transnational construction of ideas of race and nation: the development of the notion of consumer citizenship in coffee advertisements. After a scene-setting sketch of political-economic background, it narrates the unprecedented transnational collaboration of the Joint Coffee Trade Publicity Committee. It then explains the mid-decade breakdown of cooperative advertising in the wake of controversial attempts to price-protect coffee and finally ends by considering the reprise of the campaign in the late 1920s. Overall, since Brazilian coffee sectors successfully resisted political and market pressure not to "valorize" their country's chief export, this is much more than a story of the United States imposing its will upon a subject of economic colonialism. Yet ultimately, the chapter points out that although Brazil refused to knuckle under in that moment, North American capital may have gained something more valuable in the long run, for the brouhaha in U.S. newspapers and political arenas over valorization helped rally relevant publics to the discourse of consumerism.

This tale unfolds within a complex confluence of circumstances. What were the technological developments that allowed coffee to be consumed so far from its growing fields? Within what economic trends did widespread coffee consumption emerge, and how did it help to shape them? How did political relations in the Americas facilitate connections between growers and markets? Through what sorts of changes in social relations did all these developments occur? Addressing these questions, the following section sets the stage for this and subsequent chapters, whose actions also developed within these contexts.

Politics, Commerce, and the Coffee Campaign

It is no coincidence that coffee was the substance of the first Brazil-U.S. connection examined here, for it had long been a transnational traveler. Coffee was one of the "drug foods" that made up a significant portion of transcontinental trade even before the Industrial Revolution. For its first three hundred years as a commodity, as trade historians Kenneth Pomeranz and Steven Topik put it, the bean was "an Arabian monopoly," grown in Yemen and consumed in the Middle East and Southwest Asia. Over the seventeenth century, European elites acquired the taste. Transatlantic transport and slavery installed the crop in New World plantations during the eighteenth century, lowering the price while standards of living rose, allowing the drink to become the object of mass consumption we know today.[10] Though Brazil was a relative latecomer to the shrub (introduced there only in the eighteenth century), by 1830 coffee dominated the country's export agenda and drove its economic growth. By 1880 Brazil harvested about half the world's coffee, and by the century's close regularly grew three-quarters of the global harvest.

Coffee's growth in Brazil was part of a set of interacting global trends. In the last third of the nineteenth century, scientific knowledge and technological innovation accelerated so much that some historians call the period the "Second Industrial Revolution." Advances in chemical use, electricity, transportation, and agricultural and food processing (among other things) profoundly altered possibilities for commerce and industry.[11] Post-emancipation labor migration patterns within Latin America and transatlantically provided the workforce for these advances; coffee cultivation spread throughout the tropical highlands of Latin America, displacing Caribbean growers, and tropical products enjoyed a global boom, most pronounced in the thirty years before the First World War. Like many Latin American countries with economies based on the export of primary products, Brazil experienced unprecedented growth in the fifty years after 1880. Earlier export cycles, which had focused on sugar and minerals (mostly gold) and lesser quantities of cotton, cacao, and tobacco, gave way to coffee, Brazil's "principal point of linkage to an expanding world economy."[12]

An export economy needs markets, and the largest and fastest-growing in the region belonged to the United States. In part to cater to that potential, Brazil at the turn to the twentieth century consciously shifted its axis of political alliance away from its traditional anchor of England and toward the United States—a shift that was part of a larger trend, as one by one in the new century, other Latin American countries did the same. Directing this turn in Brazil was the brilliant minister of foreign relations, José Maria da Silva Paranhos, Júnior, the Baron of Rio-Branco, who helped close a centuries-long era of territorial disputes and boundary fixing. At peace and buoyed by coffee's prosperity, Brazil under Rio-Branco adopted an extroverted foreign policy, taking a leadership position in the Pan-American movement and currying a close friendship with the United States. The two countries exchanged ambassadors in 1905, with Washington sending Rio the only U.S. ambassador accredited to South America. The largest Southern Cone nation was also the only one to declare war on the Central Powers and contribute militarily to the Allied cause during the First World War. All in all in the early decades of the twentieth century, Brazil was among the warmest political allies of the United States. Brazilian efforts to capture U.S. markets paid off: in the mid-nineteenth century Brazil was supplying two-thirds of the coffee consumed in the United States. By 1876, that figure had risen to three-quarters, where it would remain well into the 1900s.[13]

North Americans imbibed so much of this leisure drink because they could. Over the last two decades of the nineteenth century and through the First World War, U.S. wealth in relation to the rest of the world grew again. Migrants and immigrants swelled U.S. urban industrial centers, stoking manufacturing on an unprecedented scale. U.S. imperialism in Cuba, Puerto Rico, the Philippines, and Hawaii; its control of Panama and jurisdiction over the canal; and its other colonial engagements enriched U.S. coffers through resource extraction, cheap labor, and tariff-free markets for U.S. products.[14] The First World War further augmented

U.S. power by boosting industrial production while sapping the forces of the next closest powers, Britain and Germany, so that the interwar years saw the United States become the most powerful economy in the world.

Its political and economic might allowed the United States to levy subtle forms of diplomatic and financial control, which, like formal imperial domination, expanded opportunities for U.S. trade abroad.[15] Business and state representatives in the United States were hungry for access to all of South America's large and growing markets, Brazil's first among them. To exploit them they used a range of tactics, many of which critics have denounced as imperialist or neocolonial in some form (economic or cultural). The U.S. state contributed to the Brazilian military and educational systems, for example; U.S. missionaries worked to pave the way for Protestantism, and U.S. corporations, for capitalism, going even so far as to purchase land in Brazil for their operations. These efforts were successful in many ways, as North American products saturated Brazilian cinemas, airwaves, newspapers, and roadways.[16] The war made Brazil and the United States even more important trading partners, their commercial rapprochement necessitated by the constriction of transatlantic commerce, strengthened by military alliance, and boosted by Pan-American solidarity over the sickening fratricide in Europe.[17]

In this conscious search for foreign markets on the part of both the United States and Brazil, the advertising industry played an increasingly important role. In the late nineteenth century, U.S. corporations had consolidated into large-scale trusts, creating the sorts of big businesses that would want, need, and be able to advertise nationally. Wartime propaganda and Liberty and Victory Bond campaigns had primed the U.S. public, and the wartime profits tax encouraged businesses to advertise by defining advertising as a fully deductible expense. After the war advertising took off, riding the spread of mass production methods, increasing affluence including that among the working class, fears of overproduction (such as those around the 1920–21 recession), technological innovations in print and other venues of mass culture, urbanization, and the popularization of Freudian psychology. The benefits of advertising became, for businessmen north and south, an article of unquestioned faith.[18]

In this climate of economic growth, adoration for advertising, and U.S.-Brazilian political alliance and commercial approximation, the North American roasters and Brazilian planters who had been working unsuccessfully toward coordinated publicity efforts for years finally cut a workable deal. The U.S.-based National Coffee Roasters Association (NCRA) stepped up its efforts to mount a coordinated publicity campaign funded by its members and other sectors of the U.S. coffee trade, a drive it had supported since at least 1912.[19] In São Paulo in 1917, planters created the Sociedade Promotora da Defesa do Café (Society for the Promotion of Coffee Defense). Drawing enough planter and state support to levy a light tax on each bag of coffee shipped to the ports, the society raised funds for advertising campaigns throughout the world, sending the largest chunk of cash north to create and support the Joint Coffee Trade Publicity Committee (JC).[20]

The JC was made up of North American roasters, other sectors of the U.S. coffee trade, Brazilian planters, and representatives of the government of the state of São Paulo and the Brazilian federal government. Its historic (unprecedented, its members proclaimed) combination of U.S. and foreign businessmen would exist for six years, foundering in 1926 on the shoals of the 1924 coffee crisis. A successor, the Brazilian-American Coffee Promotion Committee (BACPC), would reemerge for another short spate in 1928, folding for good in 1932. For the full life of both committees, 1919 to 1932, minus the hiatus of 1926–28, the admen and women of N. W. Ayer and Son would present the committees' case.[21] Through Ayer, the JC (and later the BACPC) would saturate North American commercial venues with ingenious plugs for coffee.

The JC flooded the pages of trade journals, newspapers, and magazines; the windows and aisles of grocery stores; billboards; and even the airwaves. Always with advance copies sent to "all our subscribers and coffee roasters," the ads found venues in the *Saturday Evening Post, Ladies' Home Journal, Good Housekeeping, Woman's World, The Farmer's Wife, McCall's, Woman's Home Companion, Literary Digest, Country Gentleman, Modern Priscilla*, and the *Christian Herald*, among others. By its own count, the JC estimated that its ads in magazines and newspapers would reach over thirteen million people each month, while the trade magazine *Spice Mill* expected an audience of sixty-five million people.[22] The JC's monthly publication for roasters, salesmen, and retailers boasted a circulation of twenty-five thousand in 1923, and its "educational coffee school exhibit" was sent to fifteen thousand "teachers and scholars." A comparable number of its medical "informational" pamphlets aimed at doctors, factory owners, and restaurateurs.[23] JC supporters claimed that U.S. coffee merchants of all sorts had responded to the committee's urgings and to the opportunities represented by its work, increasing the advertising of their brands "over 300%," or some ten times beyond the JC campaign itself.[24] These non-JC ads, such as the Butter-Nut piece with which this chapter began, were as much a part of the cultural field the campaign seeded as the ones the committee paid Ayer to produce.

The ads clearly reached a wide audience, if not exactly the "America" the industry claimed. More precisely, they hailed North American urban populations, unevenly and incompletely, and people in rural places, probably largely middle class, who encountered the relevant magazines and circulars, grocery store displays, and product packaging. At the end of the 1920s, that audience would expand as the campaign moved into radio. Now that we have understood the campaign's quantitative and geographic scope, we may wrestle with its more abstract effects. What can one conclude from studying these ads?

Scholars of advertising take a range of positions on their source material, from the view of advertising as a conspiratorial imposition of elite consciousness on the working class articulated by such cultural critics as Stuart and Elizabeth Ewen to Gary Cross's celebration of consumerism as a philosophy that saved the world from Cold War destruction; from the meticulously empirical take of a cultural historian such as Roland Marchand, who sees advertising as an inexact but still useful reflection of the social reality it transmutes into image, to the brilliant flights of interpretive fancy taken by Cultural Studies analysts such as Judith Williamson, to the constructionist recognition of Foucauldian exegetes such as Jennifer Scanlon or Simone Davis that marketers helped to produce what they claimed merely to observe.[25] My approach draws from the last three camps. Certainly advertising is more than a simple mirror of society and less than the direct cause of consumer behavior along the lines most audaciously hoped for by its crafters. It weaves between the two, encoding shared sets of cultural resources, revealing the elements people at a given time use to negotiate ideological reproduction. In this way it is like other discursive fields (which is not to say all discursive fields offer equivalent objects of cultural critique). The uniqueness of ads consists in their taut connection to capitalism and consumer culture and their intended expression of popular fantasies. The hopes and dreams ads offer are tense readings of public hopes and preferences by capital, corporate, and state elites. That their readings are neither always right nor passively accepted does not diminish their utility as source material; advertisement remains a field of ideological production even when we recognize that in reception it is frequently reworked or rejected. Indeed, the process of ideological reproduction entails contestation and refusal, incorporated into the next rounds of negotiation. With that in mind, ads can productively offer the critic a complex discursive terrain, one of so many interrelated cultural or textual fields waiting to be read.

The JC campaign provides fodder for analysis on three related fronts then: as a contribution to that weighty socioeconomic institution that is the advertising industry; as an index of its ideological moment as filtered through the judgements of businesspeople and copywriters; and as a discursive field people engaged by reading and rejecting, embracing, or modifying its suggestions. That engagement, not some motor internal to the ads themselves, is the way this field was productive rather than simply reflective of its social context. Ultimately it is impossible to read the process of that production, buried in unrecorded audience reactions. What the critic can do is place the ads in the contexts that generated them and followed, read them closely, and project trajectories of connection. On that basis I argue that this ad campaign was a brick—one of many, no single one necessary but all together sufficient—in the edifice of the racialized nationalism that is consumer citizenship.

This is the stuff of humanities scholarship, of course. The JC didn't consider the social effects of its work. It was simply proud that the ads seemed to have succeeded in boosting coffee drinking.[26] Advertising executives also attributed the rise to the campaign and congratulated the JC for its innovative model of intra-industrial, international collaboration—as well they might, since the campaign hawked the value of advertising as much as it celebrated coffee.[27] Later in the decade, as we will see below, the partnership that had created these ads would dissolve when Brazil refused to accede to North American demands regarding price protection. But in the flush, immediate postwar period, everyone seemed to be rubbing everyone else's back.

"From Brazil Alone . . ."

To kick off its shiny new advertising campaign, the JC fêted its foreign friends. Ads in the first series made constant and explicit references to Brazilians' roles in this innovative advertising blitz. In an all-text ad from

1919 with the bold heading "Brazil is doing its part in the COFFEE campaign," the JC admonished coffee wholesalers, roasters, and presumably retailers: "The coffee interests of Brazil have proven most liberal and progressive in the support rendered to the Coffee Campaign. They have come forward in right royal fashion. Shall it be said that we of this country are less appreciative of enterprise,—less responsive to opportunity?"[28] Another 1919 spot attributed to Brazilians great pride in their national product: "Ask a Brazilian to name his country's greatest service to mankind, and he will proudly answer,—'Brazil furnishes three-fourths of the world's coffee.'"[29]

In subsequent series, text on Brazil shifted to sidebars accompanying illustrated narrative replacing the first series' text-focused declaratives. Sidebars in the 1920 series quantified Brazilian coffee production: "São Paulo, Brazil, has become the acknowledged coffee-garden of the world"; "From Brazil alone we import between 800,000,000 and 900,000,000 pounds a year"; and "From Brazil alone we import nearly three-quarters of a billion pounds a year" (clearly unfazed by discrepancies in accounting).[30] Combining quantifications and praise for Brazilian politicians and planters, 1921 ad sidebars explained: "This advertisement is part of an educational campaign conducted by the leading COFFEE merchants of the United States in co-operation with the planters of the State of Sao Paulo, Brazil, which produces more than half of all the COFFEE used in the United States of America," and "The planters of Sao Paulo, Brazil, who produce more than half of all the Coffee used in the United States, are conducting this educational advertising campaign in co-operation with the leading merchants of the United States."[31] If the reading and coffee-buying public did not associate coffee with Brazil at the end of the war, it would have been difficult to avoid the link as the twenties proceeded.

These early ads did not simply note Brazil in neutral tones. They praised Brazilians as "most liberal and progressive" and called coffee-growing "one of the world's greatest *industries*." They portrayed Brazilian coffee men as full partners, "conducting this educational advertising campaign *in co-operation* with the leading Coffee merchants of the United States."[32] Against prevailing representations of Brazil as a barbaric backwater and coffee as an enervating intoxicant, JC ads aligned both with the dense discursive nodes of "modernity," "progress," and "civilization," the era's highest available words of praise.[33] "Coffee is a civilizer—a stabilizer," and coffee-drinking, "a habit of refined civilization," they claimed.[34] Linking coffee and the progress of knowledge, they countered attacks on the drink's healthiness: "Time dispels our old illusions"; "Wild and weird were our old delusions"; "We outgrow our old foolish fears."[35] The link between coffee and progress was so tirelessly reiterated as to constitute grounds for ridicule. As the JC's radio personality would later quip while promoting iced coffee: "There was plenty of ice in the Ice-age, too, but no coffee — and no whipped cream — and no sugar. Besides, they had no time to relax. They were too busy beating each other over the head with clubs and rocks and other blunt implements. Yet some people say there's no progress!"[36]

Cloaking a labor-intensive commerce in the mantle of mutual cooperation, these ads set coffee, along with its principal producing country, in the "modern" realm of frictionless speed and misery-free production. Such positionings reflected the demands of the JC's Brazilian collaborators at a moment when elite Brazilians bristled with frustrated desire to be treated as modern equals to North Atlantic elites.[37] In addition, these savvy admen well understood the value of turning a nation into a brand name. While the JC was not contractually required to name Brazil in these early ads, Brazilians clearly had ample input. No wonder: Brazil paid the piper to the tune of $250,000 in the campaign's first year, when U.S. contributions totaled only $59,000.[38]

As if in compensation for its reiterated affirmations of coffee's ties to Brazil, the JC also dubbed coffee "the American drink."[39] Less in a spirit of contradiction or confrontation than in a sort of logical symmetry, coffee's "Americanness" met its "Brazilianness" with the appropriate equivalent. "Unquestionably," wrote JC manager Felix Coste, "the temperament of the American people is responsive to the flavor and stimulation of Coffee."[40] A 1921 JC ad explained to the public: "This country drinks nearly one-half of all the Coffee grown in the world. And the American appetite for Coffee is constantly growing. . . . This liking for coffee by Americans is easily understood. America is an active, virile nation. As a nation we require food that sustains body and brain at high efficiency. . . . It helps men and women to endure exposure and withstand hard work."[41]

Such copy underlined its message with the most compelling discursive links available, including the patriotism particularly strong in the wake of war, gendered and even sexualized language, and a nod (in the reference to hard work) to the producerist ethos the JC's own work was helping to replace. The reformulation of consumption *as* production, present in this and many other JC ads (as we will see below in the links they made between coffee and work), was *the* critical move in the development of consumerist ideology.

"Brazil" and "America," then, were both highly prominent characters in the narrative web of the JC campaign. Personified, they appeared in compelling vignettes introducing themselves and performing their interrelations. The protagonist of a 1920 series was fairly representative. This South American coffee man was an attentive, affluent planter, a Latin lover with a Don Juan mustache. "My reputation depends on COFFEE," declared this tall, dark, and handsome business-suited man.[42] Savoring a steaming cup, the patrician figure beamed as a white-uniformed worker in the background drew the brew from a coffeemaker of institutional proportions. This, the ad implied, was a person accustomed to being served and one who would share that quality with U.S. consumers rather than provide it. A text sidebar placing him in São Paulo confirmed that he was indeed Brazilian, and in visual corroboration, the artist tapered the bottom of the image into a wavery triangle reminiscent of the southern borders of Brazil.

Though certainly responsive in part to planters' desires to counter images of Brazilians as naked savages, such representations did not exactly set Brazilians as North Americans' equals. The point was the relation to North American consumers, even as the ads celebrated mutual enrichment among civilized modern sophisticates, and the relationship of consumer and producer lent itself to the representation not of equity but of hierarchy. The planter in "My reputation depends on COFFEE" reads easily as a restaurant manager, not an owner, a clearly subordinate, though respected, position. Further, to a viewer unfamiliar with Brazil's land mass and coastline, the shape of his body suggested less a territorial map than a genie wafting out of an invisible bottle. A mysterious, "exotic" aura, with its mantle of service, draped his shoulders after all. Further, in conflating coffee–Brazil–Brazilians, even in seemingly positive terms, the JC figured them all as available, another favorite Orientalist conceit. Finally, early pieces prodding North American businessmen to contribute to the campaign lest South Americans, those most notorious laggards, surpassed them in "progress" and "enterprise," relied on the touchstone of Latin laziness to make sense, reinforcing as much as undermining notions of Northern or Anglo-Saxon industry and Southern or Latin indolence. The Ayer copywriter exalting Butter-Nut echoed this dynamic even more explicitly in "You can take my word for it." Distributors such as Butter-Nut found themselves in a fortunate position, for not only were they presented

FIGURE 2. "My reputation depends on COFFEE." JC ad in series "Coffee— the universal drink," 1920. N. W. Ayer Advertising Agency records, National Museum of American History. Archives Center, Behring Center, Smithsonian Institution.

with the opportunity to "tie in" to the campaign (a phrase Ayer may have coined in this context) and build on the visibility of their product at the time, but as they were unbeholden to Brazilian interests, they could also give copywriters greater rein to tap into consumer fantasies. The JC campaign in various ways posited Brazilian "civilization" with one word or sketch and compromised it with another.

"Martha Must Have Had a Cup, Too"

As the JC campaign evolved, representations of Brazilians or of planters receded, replaced by vignettes of "Americans" preparing or drinking coffee. As we approach these vignettes, keep in mind that no tale about coffee in the United States could be completely domestic, for on some level all observers knew coffee was an import. Any readers of these tales who had not gathered as much from the generally available repository of information about the world would in this period have gleaned it from newspapers, previous JC ads, or the small text sidebars that continued to invoke and praise the JC's Brazilian partners. This sense of the world abroad framed the narratives the ads related, subtly but inescapably. It pulled back to offer a long-range perspective: the forest, not the trees, a view from which internal differences blurred. Instead a vision of identity—national identity, in the full sense of the unattainable identicality posited in an imagined community—could emerge.[43] Even when an ad's point clearly relied on a staging of social difference, transnational frames worked to minimize and mitigate hierarchy within the nation. That coffee could be *served* provided a perfect platform for the representation of harmonious inequity, whether in the global terms of "My reputation depends on COFFEE" and "You can take my word for it!" or in portraits of domestic space. Ads sketching such portraits embraced the opportunity to represent difference as pleasant and incidental, transferring the supposed benignity of global hierarchies to an equivalently lovely domestic front, where the distinctions portrayed were most often those of race and gender.

Ads for the JC and private distributors virtually reveled in household labor, both the near-effortless fun of dainty white housewives ("Mrs. Stevens was a friendly, companionable little woman and she liked to entertain") and the labor of African American women in white families' homes.[44] In one Hills Bros. ad, an African American woman prepared "corn-cake"; in another, a smiling figure with spatula in hand and spotted kerchief on her head cooked pancakes while a delighted little blonde girl clapped her hands in anticipation.[45]

The image of "Mammy" cooking pancakes for white appetites was fast gaining national name recognition in the twenties, thanks to James Webb Young, the J. Walter Thompson (JWT) advertising executive who created the "Aunt Jemima" advertising campaign for Quaker Oats in 1919.[46] Young deftly yoked white supremacy to the higher cause of increased sales. He applied that strategy to JWT campaigns less well remembered today than that of Quaker Oats, including that for Maxwell House coffee, which courted consumers with a series of images of the aristocratic Old South. "Over this coffee the North and South pledged the new brotherhood years ago," reads Young's Maxwell House copy, yearning for the white nobility made possible by the presence of black servants. Young's copy was in conversation with the work of filmmaker D. W. Griffith, whose 1916 *Birth of a Nation* had recently seized the public imagination. Offering Southern codes of "honor" as national bond, Griffith stitched reconciliation among Northern and Southern rich and poor whites on the grounds of the violent marginalization of African Americans.[47] As racial violence raged nationwide during the "Red Summer" of 1919, JC coffee ads narrated a similar reconciliation, using references to producing countries to bracket a national space as its site.

The JC fawned over the Maxwell House campaign, calling it "the finest coffee advertising we have ever seen."[48] It proved its sincerity with the finest form of flattery. Along with other advertisers, the JC embraced "Mammy's" potential to sell breakfast foods.[49] It updated her for modern urban conditions and made her the fulcrum of a parable entitled "Mrs. Thomas Was Housecleaning":

> For two days she had been packing away the winter clothing, cleaning windows, changing curtains, sweeping floors, dusting furniture and moving things around generally.
>
> It was hard work, even with Martha, a colored woman, helping her.
>
> Along toward mid-afternoon of the second day, Mrs. Thomas felt that she couldn't go a step farther. "I've simply got to rest a while," she told herself, "or I'll have another of those splitting headaches."

Martha was sympathetic. "What you done need, mam, is a good hot cup o' Coffee. It will set you right in a jiffy."

And it did! That night Mrs. Thomas told her husband about it. "Martha must have had a cup, too," she added, "for she seemed to feel better and work better the rest of the afternoon."

Mr. Thomas nodded approvingly. "I'm glad you're so bright and chipper. First housecleaning time it's ever happened. I know how you feel. I've been drinking a cup of Coffee myself every afternoon for a month. Best thing I ever did. I should have told you about it."[50]

This cliff-hanger of an ad was evoked in order to resolve a host of contemporary anxieties. Its heroine was a woman precariously on the edge of a blue-collar home life, a confusing mixture of class signifiers. Engaged in hard domestic labor, "Mrs. Thomas" was salvaged as middle-class only by the introduction of "Martha" in the second paragraph. To illustrate the transfer of the burdens of labor, in the second sketch it is Martha who wears the headkerchief and bow-tied apron that adorn Mrs. Thomas's pert frame in the first. In a textbook example of identity in relation, the white woman's race and class positions emerged via her relationship to the black woman's presence and work.[51] If "Mammy" could save Colonel Higbee of Quaker Oats fame from social misstep by solving the dilemma of what to feed houseguests, she could save Mrs. Thomas from the perils of middle-class homemaking with another suggestion of what to consume.

"Mrs. Thomas Was Housecleaning" drew on white desire to see "Mammy" as a benevolent repository of folk wisdom, enhanced by perceptions of African Americans' particular aptness for manual labor. The copy portrayed folk wisdom and modern science corroborating each other's conclusions: the husband, symbol of professional expertise, confirms the value of coffee. The "primitive" and the "modern" wrapped far enough around "overcivilized" bourgeois urban life to meet on the other side. Not only should modern housewives apply the principles that organized public life in the running of their homes, "Mrs. Thomas" implied, but doing so would allow them to consume the wisdom of the ages, setting them at the apex of the social food chain.[52] Coffee provided nourishment, indeed.

In "Mrs. Thomas," coffee helped order a social hierarchy and division of labor determined by race and gender. It bestowed its caffeinated happy ending upon a white woman safely married and dedicated to regular do-

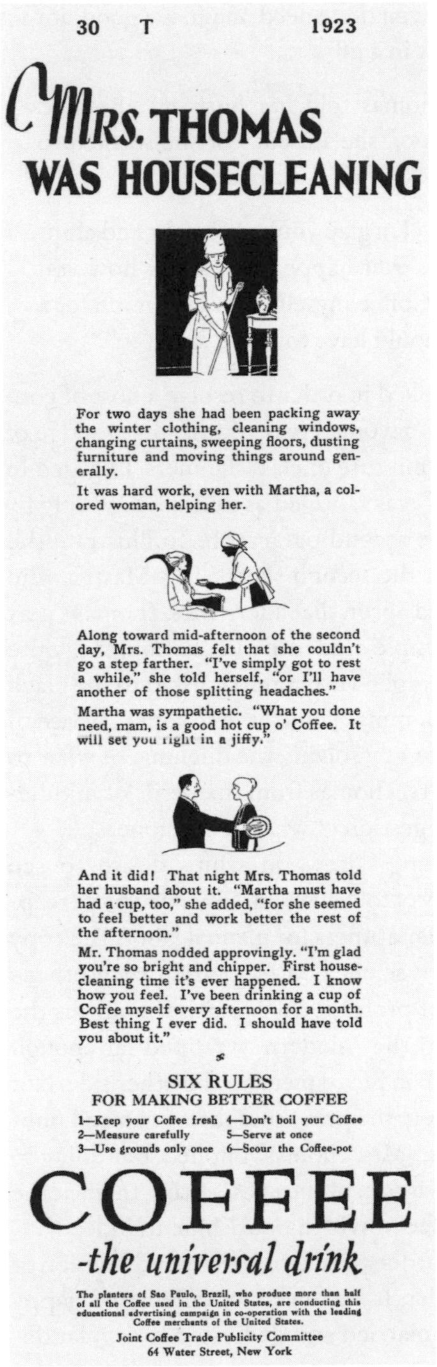

FIGURE 3. "Mrs. Thomas Was Housecleaning." JC ad, 1923. N. W. Ayer Advertising Agency records, National Museum of American History. Archives Center, Behring Center, Smithsonian Institution.

mestic chores, a matching white middle-class husband, and a black laborer "sympathetic" and appropriately respectful ("mam"). It apportioned coffee to the deserving in the spaces appropriate to them: Mr. Thomas at work, Mrs. Thomas at home in an easy chair, and "Martha" presumably in the kitchen or anywhere safely out of sight.

These seductive rationalizations of racialized class difference in the United States were woven subtly to the exposition of global hierarchies. Seemingly a domestic story, "Mrs. Thomas" crystallized as a broader tale thanks to its transnational framing: at the bottom of this fanciful page, a plug for "The planters of Sao Paulo, Brazil" placed the missus, her husband, and her employee in wider relation. The international context helped the reader back up to see in this drama not difference but sameness: all three were "American," members of the "domestic" sphere in its double sense of household and nation, here overlaid in convergent congruity. Thanks to transnational frames, "Mrs. Thomas" is a tale of the American family, black and white, lovingly and willingly maintained even by its subordinate members, who know their places and remain contentedly within them. Two sets of social hierarchies—those within the United States and those that ordered its relation to other nations—buttressed each other with their overlap, trading alibis for inequality across reciprocal, interdependent imagined communities.

In discursive fields seeded by transnational interactions, representations of social differentiation and hierarchy between the United States and other nations fed and fed off representations of hierarchy within the nation, spinning dense cyclical webs of cross-referencing and reinforcement. This is the dynamic that scholars who look only within national borders might miss: the *productive* relationship between transnational and domestic reproductions of inequality. The home was only one site in which coffee ads staged this relationship.

"The Boss Serves It Right Here in the Plant"

"Mrs. Thomas" folded coffee's incidental pleasures—the steaming cup, domestic bliss, white supremacy—into the promise of increased productivity for all: no matter what labor was a person's lot in life, coffee would speed the plow. Coffee's ostensibly privileged relationship to work was another handle advertisers seized to sell their product, again plunging coffee ads into the work of shaping ideas of race and nation in the United States.

Coffee's boon to speedy efficiency—today common sense—was far from a foregone conclusion when the JC was born. Just as close at hand was coffee's fame in the leisurely intellectual worlds of coffee-house Vienna, which the JC evoked to affirm the bean's prestigious European heritage. Occasionally present in the ads were nods to coffee's aristocratic flavor or its supposed impetus to democratic revolution, contradictory qualities still celebrated by some coffee paladins.[53] Neither of these suggests productive labor. Nor could the link to work hinge upon caffeine's stimulant quality, which at the time made coffee medically suspect and still did not necessarily translate into productive work—people could as easily have interpreted stimulation as feeding an inefficient freneticism. Like any other commodity, coffee's meaning is socially produced, varying according to historical context. In the post–First World War United States, its meaning shifted with broader paradigms of value and surely also in response to the JC campaign. The JC worked assiduously to portray coffee not as grease to a genteel world of ideas but as a spark to "productivity" and therefore deeply "American." As other advertisers successfully tied apples to health ("an apple a day . . .") or the nation ("as American as . . .") and diamonds to love, the JC forged a link between coffee and work that today feels utterly natural.[54]

The JC's North American parent organization, the National Coffee Roasters' Association (NCRA), had argued as early as 1912 that "coffee increases the capacity for both muscular and mental work." It funded research into coffee's effect on labor productivity and then made sure employers learned of the results by distributing them directly, along with information on how to set up coffee stations in factories and other workplaces. The JC took up the baton readily. In 1920 it presented its pamphlet *Coffee as an Aid to Factory Efficiency* to factory and white-collar office managers and reported on the thirst for coffee among automobile manufacturers and steelworkers, the epitome of manly "producers."[55]

In arguing that increased consumption (of coffee) would increase production (of anything), the JC soothed North Americans' anxiety about the demise of their productive power. The argument resonated with the logical undertow Henry Ford would tap into with his contention that a system in which producers consumed the products they produced would propel itself to august heights of growth and affluence. Coffee, consumed inside the United States and produced outside it, did not fit a Fordist paradigm, but then again, nothing really did since the United States was neither a cohesive social community nor a closed economic system. Such claims were attractive, however, for they helped paper over the violence of capitalist divisions of labor, obscuring both the local and global conditions of U.S. affluence and helping to manufacture consent on the part of labor.[56]

In 1923, the JC produced a series of plates that could virtually have sprung from the mind of "efficiency expert" Frederick Winslow Taylor, famous proponent of the argument that the interests of labor and management coincided.[57] Highlighting coffee's boon to productivity of all types, the plates reported what "the executive says," "the grocer says," "the mechanic says" (among others) about coffee. The executive reported that his four o'clock cup helped him do "more work now from four to five than I used to do all afternoon." The grocer promised to boost his own sales, pledging to "tie up" with the national campaign via window displays and customer direction. The mechanic urged management to catch up with the folk wisdom of the workers. "We used to bring Coffee to work in a thermos bottle. That's a great idea. Now the boss serves it right here in the plant. That's better yet."[58] The mechanic didn't say he worked harder with coffee, but he didn't have to. That his boss understood the serving of coffee at the plant to be in his best interests spoke worlds.

This vision of cross-class masculinity as basis for national unity (the "American drink," after all) constituted the obverse side of domestic dramas such as "Mrs. Thomas Was Housecleaning." The JC's projects beyond the walls of home-sweet-home envisioned a profoundly homosocial public sphere, bestowing upon coffee the glory of a hypervalorized masculinity. "Coffee is '*man's drink*,'" the campaign promised; "A sturdy, hearty, flavory, savory drink. A real chummy, clubby drink"; "a social, convivial, 'good-fellow' drink. Wherever men meet to dine or deliberate—there is *coffee*."[59] Coffee ads placed their brew in the most macho locations available, such as the (U.S.) West and war.[60] In the heady wake of victory, the JC congratulated "the fighting man's drink," which "did its bit in the war right manfully."[61] "Your Uncle Sam provided his boys with COFFEE," read another JC ad. "Brave, clean, lithe, sturdy fellows they were. . . . Coffee lovers, they were—almost to a man."[62] This strikingly feminine, sensual portrayal—"boys," "clean, lithe," and "lovers" (of coffee)—reflects two related tensions in the JC's task. Not only was it working to construct mas-

KERNEL KOFFEE—

HE TALKS BUSINESS ONLY
IN A COFFEE HOUSE

FIGURE 4. "Places to talk business." Terry Gilkiron [?], "Kernel Koffee"
(cartoon). Hills Bros. Collection, National Museum of American History.
Archives Center, Behring Center, Smithsonian Institution.

culinity via the feminizing anthropophagy (cannibalism) of consumption
but it was also committed to erasing class divisions while buttressing a
system premised upon them.

A similar tension emerges from the JC's attempt to capitalize on Prohibition. Fully expecting a windfall, the JC tried to slip coffee seamlessly
into the niche left empty by spirits.[63] Coffee could be "the modern 'cup
that cheers but not *inebriates*'"; "The cocktail hour has become the coffee
hour."[64] Uninterested in temperance, advertisers wanted simply to make
the most of unquenched thirst.[65] Alcohol's manly prestige made it an irresistible icon, for alcohol had long been discursively located in a masculine
social and cultural sphere.[66] To boost its prestige further, the JC painted
the sphere left bereft by the prohibition of alcohol as a respectable, affluent, patrician space "where men may meet, and mingle in honest, manly,
friendly spirit."[67] No vulgar dive, this was a place that welcomed elites,
especially businessmen: "Over cups of steaming brew men meet of an evening and talk with one another of things that concern them at the moment"; "in the conferences of men of affairs . . . there you will find *coffee*."[68]
One cartoon narrative extended this suggestion to the coffee house's supposed precursor, revising the history of the saloon as a place "to talk business."[69] Quite a stretch for an institution long associated with poor and
working-class men of all colors.

Both the saloon's head-spinning social mobility and its resolutely homosocial space echo the tensions and contradictions in the JC's portrayals of
soldiers. In these two cases and many others, coffee advertisements be-

littled inequalities of class, drawing on and reinforcing the appealing idea of solidarity and similarity among white "American" men. The commitment to the erasure of class conflict stands in sharp contrast to the representational tradition the JC followed and that it was working to displace, a tradition that had eagerly contemplated, perhaps even celebrated, backbreaking labor and obvious social difference. Let us turn for a moment to that tradition.

When Ayer began its work for the JC, advertising in coffee trade journals overwhelmingly featured barebacked manual laborers. Typical was the image proffered by tea importer Carter, Macy, & Co.: a gigantic, powerful ship being loaded by dark-skinned men with muscular, bare torsos. Architectural and sartorial accents provided Asian atmosphere and authenticity, while a tiny Stars and Stripes on the ship's rear deck promised U.S. consumers that the ship's cargo was destined for them.[70] The basic elements of this advertisement were repeated in many others: a ship, usually full of detail, dwarfing the scene; some gesture to the ship's destination; dark-skinned laborers, generally muscular men in some state of undress; work, usually carrying; and details about the distant places producing the goods in question. All-America Cables (telegraph operators) featured a similar ship-loading scene, as did the coffee-buying firm W. R. Grace & Co., in several permutations.[71]

One W. R. Grace iteration of this image illustrates its draw to advertisers before the war and some of the reasons it lost some of that attractiveness to retailers in the twenties. This ad (figure 8) centered a ship's imposing bulwark, graced with great detail.[72] From rowboats on either side, tiny figures oversaw great roped nets raising bundles to the hold. In front, framing the port scene, a silhouette of two laborers rose out of the black foreground. One, larger, was drawn with a round, bare head, bare chest, exaggerated muscles, and loads in both hands; the other was fully clothed, including a soft-brimmed sombrero. The two appear to represent the two main nonwhite figures populating the North Atlantic imagination of Latin America: the African and the Indian, here shown working side by side.

These are typical of the laboring figures in trade journal ads: powerful, dark, and physical. None had faces or names, nor even nationalities, unlike the ships themselves. Such schematizations of the dusky, virile masses sweating for the pleasure of the individual(ized) consumer, confirmed the subservience of the barbaric periphery to the civilized center. In addition to the psychic "wages" of imperialism—the pleasures of sit-

FIGURE 5. Carter, Macy advertisement, 1918. SIBL, NYPL.

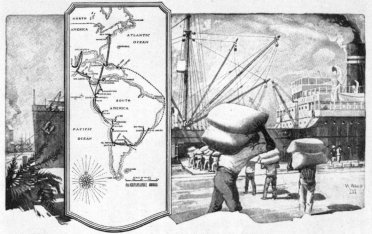

SANTOS, BRAZIL

Where Your Coffee Comes From

"Like the threads of a giant web ALL AMERICA CABLES radiate out from New York commercially enmeshing Central and South America."

Your morning cup of coffee—do you realize that the bracing fragrant starter of your day comes to you eighteen days over seas from a city as modern and as hustling as any in the United States?

Santos with its railroads to all Brazil, and its system of concrete wharfs where steamers load Plimsoll deep with coffee, rice, and hides, keeps in constant touch with the worlds markets, and the cities of the Americas through the All America Cables.

To a great degree, All America Cables has made possible the development of business and friendships of the peoples of our Western Hemisphere. Messages that otherwise would take weeks and months to deliver are flashed back and forth.

And just as they are the only direct means of communication, they are the only American owned cables.

JOHN L. MERRILL, Pres.
*Main Cable Office
89 Broad Street, New York*

To insure rapid, direct and accurate handling of your cables to Central and South America, mark them "Via All America". These words are transmitted free of charge by all telegraph and cable companies.

ALL AMERICA CABLES

CONSULT CLASSIFIED BUYER'S GUIDE IN THE BACK OF THIS ISSUE FOR FURTHER INFORMATION

FIGURE 6. All America Cables advertisement, 1921. SIBL, NYPL.

FIGURE 7. W. R. Grace advertisement, 1920. SIBL, NYPL.

FIGURE 8. W. R. Grace advertisement, 1918. SIBL, NYPL.

ing oneself at that civilized center—was the anthropophagic appeal of consuming these symbols of nature and virility. Indeed, the workers were often drawn bent so low by their bulging sacks that they took on a sack-like shape themselves, and certainly the tea and coffee colors of their skin helped conflate them with the product consumers would eventually imbibe. Coffee drinkers could absorb, these ads implied, workers' considerable "barbarian virtues"—including their labor.[73] What balm for the pangs of a felt loss of the valiant laboring life! Consumption promised access to the people, their labor, and their exotic locales, linked but also comfortingly separated by the great expanse of ocean, premised in the form of the mammoth ship.

The ship suggests both the consumer's hoped-for social and economic mobility and a sense of entitlement to the world delivered to one's doorstep. Yet ship iconography was a resonant tradition in the watery Atlantic world, with an unavoidable ambiguity, despite these drawings' fealty to a transnational capitalist elite.[74] Even in these commercial images, the potential for the transatlantic vessel to become a site of mutiny is an audible overtone, especially in the portrayals of the motley crew laboring to fill its hull. The inordinate strength and hyper-masculinity of the laborer, key to the pleasure of his subordination, entailed an inescapable, titillating suggestion of danger. The ad for W. R. Grace makes this clear. The laboring figures are dead center, in flat, black outline minimizing detail, competing with the ship for control of the image. Though they seem to be focused on the ship, inviting the viewer to look over their shoulders at it, they appear essentially in silhouette as if they might actually be facing the viewer, gazing unflinchingly back.

The representation of raw labor may have offered viewers some pleasurable identifications, but it also entailed risk. The fact of oppression ever threatens to irrupt onto scenes of its depiction, overwriting the narrative of peaceful, profitable interaction. The far less palatable story of coercion, exploitation, and resistance is incompatible with a world sure of the pleasures of consumption. While turn-of-the-century U.S. observers, confident of their imperialist destiny, may have found the idea of laborers bent double under painful burdens delicious, as the world turned in the 'teens, such images became tougher to swallow. In the wake of a war in which those paragons of "civilization," the European powers, had behaved with great savagery, it was more difficult to portray imperialism as benevolence.[75] As the Bolshevik Revolution distributed its messages of labor radicalism, proponents of capitalism worked ever more frantically to obscure the violent coercion entailed in deriving profit from other people's manual labor. Soon "imperialist" would take on its Cold War cast as North Americans refused to apply it to any political unit other than the Soviet Union.

It should come as no surprise, then, that 1920s coffee advertisers worked to distance the image of their trade from the context of open imperialism in which it had most recently expanded. To insinuate harmony and mutual enrichment between producer and consumer, they dispensed with both ship and attendant images of dark figures from unnamed countries laboring for the pleasure of the civilized consumer. Recall the Butter-Nut ad, in which coffee traveled with no help from any vehicle save the planter's outstretched arm. Avoiding any suggestion of coerced labor, risk, or distance, that vision moved coffee north magically, via the waves of goodwill emanating from producer to consumer. No wonder the JC campaign featured enlightened Brazilian businessmen in modern cities, familiar with the latest industrial technology. Shrinking the trade journal trope of ship and laborers to a more intimate, human scale, it had replaced the imagery of colonialism with the terms of contracts and progress, changed the sign of the consumer from ship to individual, and "promoted" the producer from laborer to aristocrat.

IN SUM, THE WORLD is present in consumerist tales of U.S. national identity in all these ways: as condition of possibility of U.S. wealth, as suppressed background, as counterpoint against which to define consumerism as a national identity, and as alibi for the violence wrought by that thoroughly material imagining. Indeed, I have suggested that it is the world's very presence that makes these arguments and their erasures so compelling: the JC's transnationalism underlay the ways this crystallization of the Brazil–U.S. exchange contributed to North American notions of race and nation.

Unfortunately for ambitious North American capitalists, the rest of the world also exists in real life, populated by real people, with ideas of their own. People in other places weren't always willing to play the roles metropolitan capital assigned them. At times they had the audacity to try to sell their goods at a profit, for instance. When the agency of foreign subjects irrupted into advertising's otherwise seamless narratives, marketers and allies found it quite a bit more difficult to ignore global power differentials. At such moments, the position of the United States as coercive world consumer hove into view, sending those invested in the logic of consumption as productive or the universal benefits of international trade scrambling to regain control of the storyline.

An Unfavorable Reaction: Valorization and Backlash

In the late nineteenth and early twentieth centuries, after over a century and a half of fairly gentle growth, coffee production in Brazil rose astronomically. Overproduction brought economic conundra, for the most part unaddressed by Brazilian authorities, whose Darwinian views dictated a hands-off approach to the market.[76] In 1906, finally, after nearly ten years of enormous harvests and accumulating oversupply, the government of the State of São Paulo stepped in. It bought and warehoused the surpluses until they could be sold off at reasonable prices. In 1917 and again in 1920, private merchants and federal and state authorities intervened in the market on behalf of their country's most valuable export, much to the dismay of other sectors of the coffee trade in Brazil and abroad. Amid controversy, support rose for the institutionalization of "valorization," as coffee protectionism was called, as state policy.[77]

The rest of this chapter is concerned with valorization and its aftermath. It sketches the formulation of valorization policy, explores the reaction in the United States, and analyzes the fallout as reflected in late-1920s coffee advertisements. In denouncing valorization, North American commentators apparently felt called upon to defend the consumerist role the United States increasingly adopted in the world, showing the importance of foreigners' agency in provoking and shaping this U.S. nationalism. Even more revealing is what happened when the JC's foundering left the field of coffee ads to private distributors: they removed all references to Brazil. The oxymoron of this overt effacement offers a rare view of the mechanisms of erasure that obscure formative transnational aspects of U.S. ideological and economic structures. For that story, let us look at the precipitating events of the mid-decade crisis.

By 1923, the coffee reserved from the market during the 1920 valorization had been sold and the loans repaid. Proponents of valorization saw their opportunity. In December 1924, they successfully passed legislation creating the Instituto Paulista de Defesa Permanente do Café (São Paulo

Institute for the Permanent Defense of Coffee). This body would rename itself the Instituto do Café do Estado de São Paulo (São Paulo State Coffee Institute) in 1925, removing the words "permanent defense" in a curtsy to valorization's foes. That semantic shift did not change the institute's work to regulate prices, which it would continue to do under the control of the state of São Paulo until it was taken over by the federal government after the coffee exchange "crack" of October 1929, the stock market crash later that same month, and the Revolution of 1930, which brought to power an administration less beholden to the Paulista planter aristocracy. While later observers would be divided about the effect of valorization on industrialization and economic development in Brazil, for the rest of the 1920s the efficacy of this sort of state protection for coffee prices appeared self-evident.[78]

In its valorization policies, Brazil was no lone innovator. Many governments experimented with trade-control policies in the 1920s, including the United States. Having known full well the terrors of overproduction since at least the turn of the century, the United States insulated various industries, especially farming, with protectionist legislation—most notoriously in the 1930 Smoot-Hawley Act, whose ultimate effect on the U.S. economy remains an object of controversy today.[79] Herbert Hoover, secretary of commerce during the 1920s, had embraced protectionism by the time he ran for president in 1927; Smoot-Hawley was in part the fulfillment of promises he had made during that campaign.[80]

Despite their state's equal commitment to protectionism, North American coffeemen and their governmental allies were furious over valorization, as were U.S. businessmen in general over the many foreign government price control policies that cut into their profits.[81] Overcoming long-standing antagonisms of race, region, and market sector, the various segments of the U.S. coffee trade, together with capitalists in related divisions (such as banking and shipping) and U.S. state representatives all united in opposition to valorization.[82]

Within the U.S. coffee trade's precarious unity, roasters were the most active in their opposition to valorization. The NCRA sent at least two "missions," as its members called them, to convert the growers to their market monotheism. The mission of 1922 flopped; Brazilians remained committed to defending the price of coffee.[83] The second mission, in 1925, negotiated with São Paulo's newly created State Coffee Institute, which the NCRA clearly considered a formidable adversary, state power differentials notwithstanding. NCRA delegates cajoled and bullied, sold their services in deterring boycotts and securing loans, and most of all, threatened decreased consumption, holding aloft a familiar banner: "the consumer, without whose goodwill these purposes cannot reach full fruition." The growers were not convinced.[84]

The U.S. state, in the person of Commerce Secretary Hoover, opposed valorization even more vehemently than the roasters. Hoover sent his commercial attaché to Brazil in 1925, and in 1926 held congressional hearings into price control schemes by foreign governments, including Brazil.[85] He leaned on Brazil's need for foreign financing, threatening loans withheld if coffee price controls continued, and he followed his threats up fully. Hoover was able to prevent both the U.S. Treasury and private banks from loaning São Paulo funds. Brazilians found financial support elsewhere.[86]

Hoover's Commerce Department attempted to goad the U.S. banking and coffee industries into more punitive opposition to valorization. A Commerce Department official encouraged the NCRA to use "a little sentiment created through the press," hinting, "the most effective thing would be to scare off some of the European bankers from continuing to finance Brazil's coffee control."[87] Sometimes state and market representatives worked together in genuine collaboration, as when "Hoover personally joined with representatives of the coffee trade in a session intended to convince Brazil Coffee Defense 'that when prices are too high . . . an unfavorable reaction sometimes sets in.'"[88] Yet at other times roasters tried to run interference with their state, promising planters they would support a U.S. loan to Brazil in exchange for guarantees about the number of bags stored at the port city of Santos, a minimum of direct state participation in the market, and monies for propaganda. While shared opposition to valorization helped galvanize U.S. coffee interest blocs to some extent, the U.S. state and its market sector were not simply of one mind.[89]

Despite great resources and frontal assaults, North American forces failed. Brazil repeatedly refused to budge.[90] Thus valorization sounded the JC's death knell. Its contract was set to expire on April 1, 1925, and although a new contract was negotiated, it would not be honored. After a last-gasp attempt to convince the consumer that "coffee is still cheap," the committee ceased its activities, suspending joint advertising for several years.[91] Meanwhile, conflict over valorization raged at fever pitch.

"A Nation Who Had None"

Valorization threatened U.S. business and state interests far beyond the immediate losses involved in higher bean prices, for the controversy interrupted the representation of global trade as an equitable, mutually profitable exchange. Particularly given the great fuss U.S. coffee merchants made over it, valorization revealed the violence of the market, uncovering brutal competition even among different factions of a single commodity sector. This controversy belied the notion of universal benefits from (global) commerce, the fiction that sweetened the bitter loss of a sense of self based on production in exchange for one involving principally consumption. Such a disruption also threatened the related Taylorite fictions of the convergence of management and labor interests. No wonder North American market and state representatives worked as hard rhetorically as they did in formal economic and diplomatic arenas to levy pressure against Brazilian price protection. And work they did, filling public spaces such as the floor of the U.S. Congress and the pages of daily newspapers with vehement responses to valorization, affirming U.S. virtue and Brazilian greed, blaming Brazil for disrupting the supposedly mutual flow of benefits to both consumer and producer.

In June 1924, in the national forum of the Sunday *New York Times*, New York City businessman Emmet Beeson proclaimed the "American Coffee Drinker at the Mercy of Brazil." Beeson used the rhetoric of consumer citizenship to couch his frustration (perhaps involving the trimming of his own profit margins?) in political terms. He denounced "the coffee dictatorship now enjoyed by Brazil," claiming that "the [Brazilian] Government is waxing fat on its monopoly." In this formulation, Brazil's economic control (monopoly) sidled easily into the political (dictatorship), conflating the two as only a deep believer in the inevitable democracy of the "free" market could. Making his nationalist plug explicit, Beeson complained that the poor little rich United States was "practically at the mercy of other nations in the matter of this beverage, as we are in other products."[92]

Another *Times* editorialist pitied the U.S. coffee industry, "rather in a bad way, owing to the mauling it has been getting from South America." "But," he soothed, "it will bear up, in all probability; it will bear up!" Referring to Hoover's commercial attaché, William Schurz, then in Brazil for talks on valorization, he assured readers: "There's Mr. Hoover, and down yonder is Mr. Schurz. You will get your morning cup of coffee as usual."[93] Painting the coffee industry as a poor invalid keeping a stiff upper lip despite wounds inflicted by a savage beast ("mauling"), and the U.S. state as standing up for "you," the individual consumer, this writer rhetorically angled to position the United States as picking on someone its own size. A like-minded *Industrial Digest* reporter smugly championed the small (female) consumer against the Brazilian Goliath. Brazilians might very well flout U.S. "anti-trust laws . . . American law or American sentiment." But, he cheered, "the American housewife . . . has taken a hand in the game and has reduced her purchases to such an extent that Brazilian coffee . . . dropped off . . . 9.5 per cent."[94]

If the "American housewife" stood metonymically for U.S. consumers in anti-valorization rhetoric, there was no question who would play the man of the house. Commerce Secretary Hoover, another *Times* article assured, was "fathering" a congressional investigation into foreign government price control attempts.[95] Hoover also used the language of consumer citizenship to render a commercial dispute in the political terms of freedom and democracy, making the extraordinary stretch required to position U.S. consumers as "victims of monopolistic cupidity." Explaining the congressional investigation into foreign government price controls, he laid out his outrage for the nation's constructive contemplation in the forum of the *New York Times*. "Are consumer nations to sit still and take their punishment?" he demanded. "Would a world made of ten or twelve nations controlling the world's raw material against each other and fifty other nations who have none, be a world of wholesome international relations and good will toward men? Does not our experience in the past twelve months demonstrate that we should take measures to provide independent sources of raw material supplies to our people and the other forty or fifty consuming nations?"[96]

Hoover's portrayal of the United States as a "nation who had none," with himself as Robin Hood come to its defense, is striking in its audacity. His recasting of the U.S. dilemma, away from a recognition of its ill-begotten wealth, hid not only the exploitative relationship the United States sustained with countries whose products it bought dirt cheap, but also the gross disproportion of U.S. wealth in relation to other consuming countries. The United States was not one among "forty or fifty" similarly endowed nations; this assertion was pure politics, a play for gravitas and the semblance of fairness. Such fortuitous rhetorical positioning fed the wave of public approval for Hoover that would carry him through to the presidency two years later.

In his editorial, Hoover called the United States a "consumer nation" several times. What made Hoover stray from conventional characterizations of the United States as the quintessential producer and Latin American nations as far less "enterprising or venturesome," never truly "manufacturing or creative in their desires?"[97] Hoover's biographer and his autobiography suggest that he otherwise embraced these views. The answer, I suspect, lies in the ways focusing on U.S. consumption allowed Hoover to avoid considering his nation a moneylender, despite its having become Latin America's chief capital creditor after the war.[98] The moneylender figure's anti-Semitic overtones of parasitism made the representation entirely uninteresting as national metaphor, nor were free market boosters anxious to acknowledge the leverage this position conferred upon U.S. manufactures. Yet more important, Hoover's hand was forced by the ways Brazilian coffee valorization threw voracious North American consumption into sharp relief. Brazilian decisions created a controversy dominated by evidence of U.S. consumer behavior.

Even as he was forced to acknowledge U.S. consumption, however, Hoover struggled to retain his insistence on his nation's exceptional production. Refusing the targets of his invective the compliment "productive," he portrayed the "foreign Governments" he saw "controlling the world's raw material" as withholding that portion of the world's inheritance that happened to fall within their borders. His words called up no sense of those nations as active, modern subjects whose products reflected industry, technological innovation, or the sweat of their laborers' brows — citizens working just as hard, and "producing" just as much, as workers in the United States. Modern subjects in Hoover's terms were those whose active labor consisted of consumption. Competing with images of Brazil as industrial, productive, and cooperative in ads from the JC's early years, Hoover engaged ongoing debates over the allocation of that hypervalorized concept, "modernity."

With such arguments, anti-valorization journalists, businessmen, and politicians put the language of consumerism to work to portray the United States, then enjoying the heights of its postwar wealth and power, as the underdog, an individual consumer beset by a bloated monopoly. Lobbing discursive grenades up against Brazil's unflappable façade, they portrayed this dependent, monocrop export economy as an inordinately powerful tyrant. Such a behemoth could confirm both the "American" consumer's vulnerability (so small and female) and her omnipotence (the incontestable will of the people). Such a portrayal could pretend that the blood foreign price controls revealed flowed from North American wounds, reiterating soothing promises of harmony if producer and consumer, worker and manager, would simply all act right.

The effectiveness of this rhetoric should not obscure the fact that in this case it was a defensive strategy—a tense, contradictory, tactical position. This suggests that controversies over foreign government price controls in the 1920s were part of the sea change in the ways North Americans thought about economic structure, labor rights, and such consequential concepts as modernity. Earlier obsessions with finding markets for U.S. products slipped beneath equally extreme fears of not being able to afford other nations' goods. In other words, struggles for economic survival on the part of people in places such as Brazil pushed North Americans to rearticulate, strengthen, and embrace the discourse of consumerism as national identity.

"This Time Try Coffees from Central America"

Faced with the failure of their efforts to inspire in Brazil a deferential attitude, North American opponents of valorization availed themselves unabashedly of the power of their imperial state. Most simply, they looked around for more obedient subjects. *New York Times* editorialist Beeson urged his government to learn from the "British, who are past masters in developing industries for their colonies" and encourage coffee growth in some of the "vast areas of coffee lands that are now going to waste in different parts of the world." Echoing Theodore Roosevelt, who had called unindustrialized regions "waste spaces," enthusiasts of the exercise of imperial power didn't worry that the cultivators or inhabitants of these lands might disagree that they were "going to waste."[99] The Chicago *Evening Post*, agreeing, urged the United States to look to "Cuba, Porto Rico, Hawaii and other countries"—places under the formal colonial dominion of the United States—to get "an ultimate relief from the Brazilian monopoly concerns."[100]

Such suggestions struck a chord. As coffee historian Antônio Delfim Netto has written, "during the Hoover Campaign in 1925, it became commonplace to affirm that the United States should interest other countries in coffee production and encourage them by acquiring their products."[101] State support for this aspect of trust-busting was forthcoming, the *New York Times* reported: "A survey will be made by the Department of Commerce to find out what other lands can grow coffee successfully—just such a survey as was made when the rubber situation grew acute. The Philippines have grown fine coffee, but the industry has been allowed to retrograde. Coffee can be grown, in fact, and is grown to some extent throughout the civilized and semi-civilized tropical regions of the world." With an overtone of menace, the reporter pointed to "a possibility that Brazil is strangling the goose which lays her golden eggs."[102]

North Americans tried to hasten the demise of that particular goose, encouraging and investing in other coffee-growing territories increasingly as the decade wore on.[103] The shrubs planted in Central and other South American nations would soon yield multiple import opportunities for North American roasters, though Brazilian coffee would prove its staying power.

Long before the fruits of those shrubs could have hoped to displace Brazil from its central position in global coffee production, North American coffeemen moved to eliminate Brazilian production from U.S. consumers' sight. After 1924, many roasters wrote Brazil out of their advertising parables. They made advertising, the site of previous cooperative arrangements, into pointed jabs at their former friend. In retaliation for the mid-decade valorization, U.S. advertising campaigns pictured a discriminating consumer enjoying products derived from a deliciously indistinguishable panoply of producing countries. No longer interested in portraying a duet of equal partners in trade, they tried their darnedest to paint Brazil out of the world coffee picture.

In a pointed snub of Brazil, a 1925 Maxwell House booklet located coffee's origins primarily in the "dark continent" and the "East." *The Story of Coffee and How to Make It* listed the places coffee grew: "in Abyssinia and Ethiopia—Java, Sumatra and other Islands of the Dutch East Indies; in India, Arabia, equatorial Africa, the Islands of the Pacific—in Mexico, Central and South America and the West Indies."[104] In this period, Brazil provided the majority of the coffee consumed in the world and "practically three-fourths of all coffee consumed in the United States," as the BACPC (the JC's successor) would soon remind the trade.[105] Even taking Brazil out of the lead position required dedicated effort; excising it from the list entirely entailed some resolutely heavy lifting. Subsumed in a broader region (South America) that didn't even garner pride of last-but-not-least, Brazil was blatantly absent from Maxwell House's promotions.

More explicit yet in their repudiation of Brazil were ads for another roaster, Folger's. "This Time Try Coffees from Central America," Folger's suggested. The copy would have left no coffee man, and few coffee devotees, in doubt of the referent: "Ordinarily you note little real difference when you change from one brand of coffee to another. And that is really to be expected. For over 70 per cent of all the coffee entering the United States regardless of brand names comes from one common region—giving it the same common taste. *Nature herself makes Folger's coffee different.* For it is grown in another region altogether—in the high volcanic districts shown in the map of Central America below."[106] Brazilian coffee, the Folger's copy whispered, was the "common" choice of the ignorant masses. This contempt for common folk fits well with consumerism's assurance of the market's meritocracy, which congratulates the rich and blames the poor. So much for "the drink of democracy."

Even as this Folger's ad gestured to a world of freely chosen contracts, it pushed Brazil away from the negotiating table by working willfully to forget Brazil and make its role in U.S. consumers' lives invisible. Coffee ads had begun the 1920s by erasing Brazilian laborers from their scenes; in the mid-'20s, they proceeded to erase Brazil entirely.

Hills Bros. erased not only Brazil but all producing countries from its own ads. In 1922, it had listed Brazil "first in order of importance" among "coffee producing countries."[107] In 1924–25, it published a series tracing coffee's roots to a revisionist West—the U.S. West, that is. "Really, it's a joy to be a Westerner and to have Hills Bros. Coffee everyday," "No wonder the West is proud of its coffee!" and "Hills Bros Coffee belongs to the West," it proclaimed, countering directly any claims on coffee by nations of the figurative "East," including Brazil.[108] The harmonic "West" of "Western Civilization," audible within that "West" internal to the United States, surely contributed to the attraction of this slogan, particularly in tandem with the ads' images of coffee served by Chinese and Native American men, the closest domestic iterations of the colonial manservant.[109]

A few years later in the late 1920s, Hills Bros. rewrote its ads again, this time excising all mention of the beans it had previously celebrated and the people who grew them. Instead, it organized an extensive campaign around a procedure the ads entitled "controlled roasting."[110] What "produced" good coffee, this ad series implied, was an industrial process performed in the United States, not agricultural production in Brazil. Hill Bros. joined Hoover in circulating the Fordist fantasy that the United States was the site of both production and consumption, even of products originating beyond national borders. Coffee ads in the wake of the JC's dissolution reveled in the erasures inflicted on Brazil.

The erasure of Brazil from coffee advertisements after the valorization controversy enhanced the domestic erasures at which the ads were already engaged, another instance of global dynamics dovetailing with domestic ones. In ads such as "Mrs. Thomas Was Housecleaning," traces of global hierarchy helped obscure domestic inequality; in post-valorization coffee ads, Brazil's erasure fed domestic forgettings. Forgetting, of course, is key to racial construction, which must erase its process if "race" is to function as natural or real. "Whiteness," a critical innovation solidified as a racial and as a national category in the 1920s, required profound forgetting. It had to overcome the memory, first, of the European immigrants who had previously been categorized as different and inferior to "Anglo-Saxons," and second, of the enormous racial mixture between Euro- and Afro-descended people during slavery and since.[111] These are historical pieces of the literary "absent presence" Toni Morrison has located at the heart of the ideas of "America" and whiteness.[112]

After an orgy of denunciation in the press and by the U.S. government, Brazil's importance in the coffee trade was more rather than less visible, and the country was still the behemoth of coffee production worldwide, making all the more obvious the active choices required to ignore it. Banishing Brazil from the stage on which it had so recently starred, advertisers for the coffee trade planted a complex "absent presence" at the heart of the consumerist fantasies they were working to knit to ideas of the U.S. national self. An ad from a 1931 Hills Bros. series suggests the ways this absent presence haunted the structures it shaped.

The construction of purity out of mixture was the theme of an ad captioned simply "Thoroughbreds," featuring a chilly New England scene of preparations for a steeplechase. A horse, its groomer, a smart female rider, and class-appropriate partner shared a space of aristocratic leisure. Yet the sketch conveys less relaxation than an awkward, stilted stillness on the verge of action. It promises exertion and exhaustion, though from sport,

FIGURE 9. "Thoroughbreds." Hills Bros. ad, 1931. Hills Bros. Collection, NMAH.

not work. Displacing labor from the aristocrats it depicted, this ad, like "Mrs. Thomas," engaged the question of work and ordered it carefully according to race and gender.

"Thoroughbreds" likened coffee and its drinkers to Arabian steeds, their genealogy "as authentic as that of the nobility's most distinguished families."[113] Horse breeding was one of a very few—if not the only—U.S. contexts in which "Arab" connoted aristocracy and purity. Hills Bros.' attempt to upgrade the racial position of its longtime brand icon, the "Arab on the Can," was little and late. Not only had "Arab" long connoted the sinister liminality of Semitic types, but also Hills Bros. ads in the early 1920s had celebrated the brand's excellent blend, "composed of the finest selections from all coffee producing countries."[114] Now the coffee had become "thoroughbred." Like the whiteness of the characters in the scene, coffee's purity emerged from a process of blending that entailed its own forgetting. This ad subtly conjured the quasi-evolutionary process in which many Brazilian and North American proponents of eugenics still placed their hopes. In lauding, paradoxically, the purity of its blend, did Hills Bros. veer perilously, perhaps enticingly, toward recognizing the hybridity of whiteness? If so, all the better to forget it more emphatically.

Like Ordinary Human Beings /
"How Many of Us Are Familiar?"

Coffeemen knew what they were doing, even if they did not articulate it in terms of erasure and forgetting. Industry vehicles carried clear expressions of the privileges of ignorance, as businessmen involved in Brazilian trade extolled the value of visibility. Brazil had "to show the world what she really is to dissipate wrong impressions that all except those who know it, have of this country," advised a well-wisher in 1925.[115] A writer in the advertising industry journal *Printer's Ink* admonished the region: "There is not much hope for South America unless she gets onto herself. . . . She has got to advertise herself to the American mass. She has got to tell us that she has a beautiful climate, and that she isn't totally in the tropics. . . . She has got to tell us that her laws and by-laws are liberal and that she offers sufficient guarantees to legitimate enterprises inspired by foreign capital . . . that these are regular people down there who can think and speak and live just like ordinary human beings we find up in this northern country of ours."[116]

As this condescending advice reveals, while North American business-men may have genuinely believed that distributing such information was in their commercial interests, they also enjoyed being in a position from which to hand down such pearls. On some level, they understood that their nation's "ignorance" of its elsewheres was both sign and vehicle of their advantage, so they worked hard to help their fellow citizens forget.

An illustrative example of the gleeful embrace of ignorance is a *Printer's Ink* reporter's discussion of a 1921 ad campaign on behalf of a loan to Bra-zilian banks. The banking syndicate's half-page ads emphasizing "some outstanding feature about San Paulo" provided U.S. consumers with a "useful geography lesson" that would reflect positively on Brazil.[117] These ads provided our intrepid reporter an opportunity not to learn, but to de-light in U.S. inattention to South America:

> San Paulo! How many of us are familiar even with the name? It is true we ought to know, but no one will take it as a serious reflection on our national instructed-ness if it is said that probably not one in a hundred of us have ever had occasion to recall what teacher told us about San Paulo. Besides, sometimes it is spelled, Sao Paulo, which is confusing, to say the least. And then it is a long way off.
>
> It did not seem a very good prospect. So the bankers decided to advertise to tell about San Paulo, where it is, how large it is, what it does for a living and the kind of character it has for paying up without ugly looks from the sheriff. . . . These bank advertisements showed that the folk down at San Paulo are regular fellows, with automobiles, trolley cars and everything except prohibition.[118]

The writer's glib dismissal of U.S. failings in world geography edged seam-lessly into a dismissal of São Paulo itself. The down-home tone and upright sheriff add local, not international, notes, as if São Paulo were simply part of the U.S. West. Modeling the pleasures of ignorance, the writer invited the reader to share in his condescension as harmless fun, to peer down with him from the heights of U.S. hemispheric dominance onto an ob-ject of mutual disdain, a nation anxious for U.S. attention and a potential playland to boot (no prohibition). This is the stuff an imagined commu-nity is made of: the pleasure of having the "sheriff" on one's side, assured supremacy in relation to an Other.

One proponent of truth in advertising warned his fellow advertisers not to malign the countries whose markets they hoped to court. He reminded readers of *Printer's Ink* that the United States could be as easily misrepresented by a focus on "the white slave trade . . . lynchings . . . sabotage . . . corruption . . . the high figures of illiteracy . . . , etc."[119] North Americans opposed to such evils did indeed garner support by circulating news of them abroad.[120] Yet while such tactics made some headway, the political and economic dominance of the United States gave it a measure of immunity from "misrepresentation," especially in its commercial relations with Latin America. The symmetry this writer summoned, though logical, did not exist. Such "asymmetries of ignorance" are both reflections of power and vehicles for its reproduction.[121]

During the JC's coffee campaign, the power dynamics at play in constructions of U.S. ignorance became glaringly evident. Brazilian observers handily grasped the phenomenon, as their decisions reveal. In 1917, Brazilian participants agreed that the JC's campaign could concentrate on increasing coffee consumption in general, rather than promoting Brazilian coffee specifically. In fact, they had agreed by 1922 that no explicit mention of Brazil need even appear in the ads. This was quite a serious concession, as an observer at the time marveled: "When you consider that Brazil furnishes five-eighths to three-fourths of the total amount of coffee which is produced in the world, and we managed that Brazil should consent that the word 'Brazil' should not be used in the propaganda, but that the money should just be used to increase the consumption of coffee, they have been very good in that, when you consider that Brazil was asked for the money!"[122] Clearly, negotiations of joint advertising included explicit discussion of Brazil's visibility or lack thereof.

The JC tried not to bite the hand that fed it, and it did mention Brazil in many ads. In addition to the common sidebars with small informational tidbits, some ads had offered mini-commercial geography lessons, with import statistics, details of Brazilian urban growth, and reports of the cooperation between U.S. merchants and Brazilian planters.[123] Complementing this implicit instruction were actual geography lessons: curricular material for elementary schools to help teachers spread the word of coffee's fine qualities—in Technicolor. "Every Teacher Should Have This COFFEE School Exhibit," ads proclaimed, for fourth, fifth, and sixth grade "Commercial Geography, and Domestic Science work in higher grades."[124]

Discussions during the NCRA's 1925 mission to Brazil reveal that the question of whether the advertising would necessarily mention Brazil continued pressing. Perhaps the planters had already noticed postvalorization advertisements beginning to shut them out. In any case, a councilman of the São Paulo Institute, Senator Antônio da Silva Azevedo Júnior, put the question in no uncertain terms. "Should there be a pure and simple defense of Coffee? Or should there be a defense of Brazilian Coffee?" he demanded and followed through with a reminder of the bottom line: "São Paulo in shouldering all the expense for this propaganda of Coffee is also rendering a service to other Coffee producing countries. . . . Now, if our interests are linked, and if we, as largest producers, should shoulder the greater part of this expense to the advantage of our product I would inquire: Is there a quota on the part of the American Roasters contributing to this propaganda, or is it to run exclusively for account of the Institute?"[125]

This challenge seemed to stump the NCRA delegates. They requested an adjournment, during which they drafted, in response, a masterful example of evasive equivocation:

> We recommend that any future advertising to consumers should contain diplomatic, frequent, and effective mention of São Paulo or of Santos quality and that a reasonable campaign directed to roasters and dealers through trade Journals and favoring greater use of Santos grade be installed. . . . If the Institute's propaganda is concentrated on Santos only it may tend to embarrass and discourage these individual efforts, and thus materially reduce the total of Coffee propaganda.
>
> . . . a campaign to increase the use of Coffee can create no antagonism in the trade whereas confining the campaign for Santos Coffee alone, might . . . arouse some opposition. . . .
>
> Frequent and effective mention of Santos Coffee should be made in the advertising to consumers while the advertising directed to roasters and dealers should specifically and emphatically exalt the merits and desirability of Santos Coffee.[126]

The roasters' two-step here is dizzying. Their recommendations swung from emphatic affirmations of a Santos/São Paulo–specific campaign to the dangers of such a campaign and back to definitive-sounding endorsements. So much for that famous North American character trait, straightforwardness. No wonder these negotiations reached no accord.

Phoenix: The BACPC

It would take three years for the two sides to come together again as the Brazilian-American Coffee Promotion Committee (BACPC). Rising from the JC's ashes in 1928, the BACPC clearly signified a truce.[127] Coffeemen expressed their hope that "understanding" would heal Brazilian–U.S. trade relations, which, they admitted, "have often been strained to a high degree."[128] Hoover's visit to Brazil as president-elect in early 1928 was a gesture in the same conciliatory direction.[129] Olive branches were extended from the Brazilian side as well. The São Paulo Institute, then running its own ad campaign, directed soothing words to U.S. coffeemen: "The coffee interests of Brazil appreciate the important place you occupy in the distribution of Brazil coffee."[130] As if searching for a formula to steady precarious good relations, a BACPC slogan chided, "Advertising wins new friends. But only taste and quality in the cup can hold friends day-in, day-out."[131] This ad's plaintive note hints at still painful memories of the mid-decade fiasco.

As part of this truce, the new joint advertising offensive once again promised, "Coffee in general, and not Brazil coffee specifically, will be emphasized."[132] The BACPC was determined, its ads insisted, to increase consumption overall, "not by attempted replacement of each other's markets."[133] Yet Brazil was unquestionably the center of the BACPC campaign. Even the group's name revealed its intent to highlight Brazil's cooperation from the outset, settling for none of the JC's ambiguity about just exactly who was joined therein.

"COFFEE is America's favorite drink and practically three-quarters of all coffee consumed in the United States comes from BRAZIL," stated one of the BACPC's first ads to the trade, arranging the words so that "COFFEE" and "BRAZIL," in bold-faced capitals, sandwiched the rest of the text. The ad set up a correlation between the two (Coffee = Brazil), making explicit an equation that in the earlier period they had left unsaid.[134] Perched conclusively at the bottom of every ad, the "Brazil" in the BACPC's name served as a brand repetition, a trusty advertising technique. One chronicler of these events claims that plans for propaganda developed during Brazil's 1927 coffee bicentennial had specified that such reiteration be a sine qua non for further ad campaigns. Agreements reached during that celebration funded the São Paulo Institute to direct propaganda efforts in key consuming countries, securing contracts that required the phrase

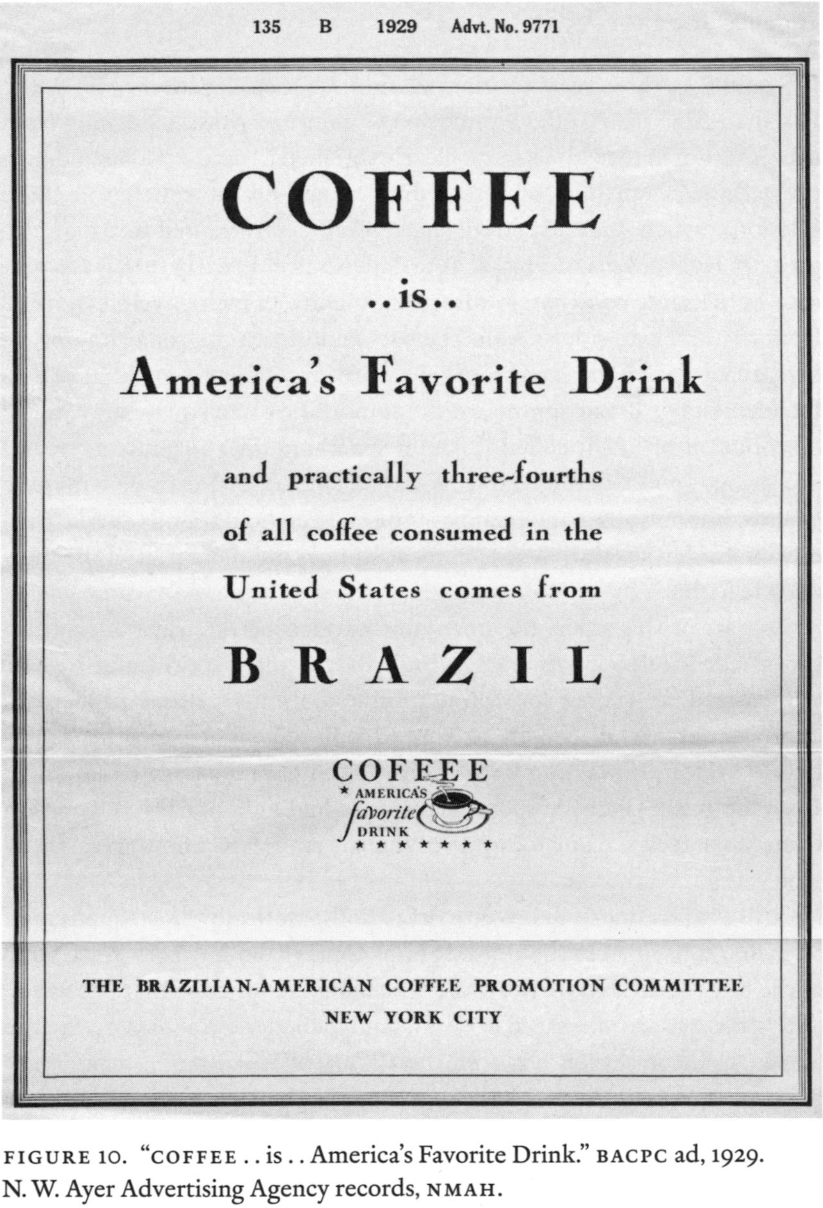
135 B 1929 Advt. No. 9771
COFFEE
..is..
America's Favorite Drink
and practically three-fourths
of all coffee consumed in the
United States comes from
BRAZIL
COFFEE
★ AMERICA'S
favorite
DRINK
THE BRAZILIAN-AMERICAN COFFEE PROMOTION COMMITTEE
NEW YORK CITY

FIGURE 10. "COFFEE . . is . . America's Favorite Drink." BACPC ad, 1929. N. W. Ayer Advertising Agency records, NMAH.

"Brazil Coffee" to appear constantly.[135] Their successful weathering of U.S. anti-valorization pressure had emboldened Brazilian coffeemen to resist their iconic erasure.

"A Romantic Brazilian Background"

Brazilian observers of the U.S. anti-valorization campaign had seen the ways the rhetoric of consumerism could demonize and then erase them. They had also met consumerism's charismatic personification, Mrs. Consumer.[136] Hoover's stalwart defense of his country under siege had cast this figure into the well-worn trope of the nation as woman, updated. She now stood in the company of the motherland and Liberty as metonym for the nation. While at times of crisis, the nation as consumer suggested a fair maiden in need of aggressive protection by a strong state, when the economic situation steadied a little, this metaphor gave a handle to planters looking to make nice. Mrs. Consumer, in a better mood, could again be courted by her Latin lover. The BACPC, to bring Brazil and its coffee back into the good graces of the United States, set out to woo her in style.

Key to this approach was the BACPC's expansion in October 1930 into radio, the nation's "first truly mass medium" and by the 1930s its "favorite leisure activity," a medium that many other advertisers, faced with the belt-tightening of the Depression, would also target.[137] In contrast to the BACPC's textually focused and visually spare ads to the trade, its radio spots showed the committee's lighter side.[138] On its weekly show, broadcast coast-to-coast by NBC, host Will Cuppy kept 'em laughing with his scrambled historical trivia. As he was wont to explain, "Coffee was unknown to the Early Greeks and Romans; they were, however, familiar with the cucumber." Still, "Cuppy" never lost sight of his higher purpose: to sell more coffee. "I really did get a fan letter, though, from a perfect stranger. A lady who says she agrees with me about iced-coffee, and she has Thursdays off. The trouble is, *I* have *Fridays* off. But I'd like to send her a little message today, to show that I appreciate her kind thoughts: DRINK MORE ICED COFFEE LADY. IT'S WONDERFUL IN THIS WEATHER."[139] The sugar-coating on the BACPC's relentless commercial focus worked, at least in terms of entertainment goals. The *New York Times* called the radio program "an 'Outstanding event on the air'" and put the weekly broadcast on its "list of outstanding entertainments."[140]

The radio program claimed to have a double goal: "to increase the present popularity of Coffee—America's favorite drink—and increase the consumption of Brazilian Coffee." But the second goal eclipsed the first; the BACPC's regular broadcast was Brazil-specific to the utmost, carrying the listener all the way to Brazil. "SPEND a Half-hour in Brazil EVERY THURSDAY AFTERNOON," crooned the advance ads.[141] In the age of radio, it was no longer coffee that traveled magically but the consumer herself, absorbing another essential quality of the global commodity: its mobility. Apparently it was quite a trip. "Against a romantic Brazilian background, the entertainment will include Brazilian music played by the Brazilian-American Marimba Band."[142] There would also be "capable vocal soloists," and occasionally "persons prominent in Brazilian political, social or musical circles will be introduced for a brief address."[143]

Brazilian Consul General (and the BACPC's sole Brazilian member) Sebastião Sampaio used the radio program as a platform from which to deliver his characteristic suave boosterism. Sampaio delivered a gracious message in English and then translated it into Portuguese, which he kindly explained was "the national language of Brazil." Sampaio proclaimed himself thrilled to "have the honor of sending my voice in short waves five thousand miles south to Brazil, my beloved country"—but he was probably, and the other BACPC members were surely, more interested in the message his Portuguese speaking could communicate to U.S. consumers.[144] They understood that details about Brazil, especially if they helped U.S. consumers distinguish it from a mass of semi-barbaric peoples, worked like determined reiterations of a brand name.

If the radio show whisked listeners away to Brazil, it made sure to whisk them right back. The exotic may have been tempting, but only as a brief respite from civilization. "Listeners-in are spirited to romantic, southern lands under the spell of Michel Gusikoff's Marimba Band. Then—brought to America to the tune of the latest song-hits." Back in "America," they would find "facts" about coffee and discover the favorite coffee recipes of Hollywood celebrities.[145] Locating "romance" abroad and mass culture and hard science ("facts") at home, the BACPC reiterated, for the consumer's delectation, the pairings of self and Other of the JC's early-decade series. They escorted a global flaneur, or perhaps a world window-shopper (far less macho) on a safely chaperoned journey to an assuredly receptive place.

The BACPC's radio show continued the pedagogical project joint advertising had embraced since its inception. Instructive facts about "coffee-growing, coffee-production, [and] correct coffee-brewing" accompanied lessons on "how to brew good coffee and what good coffee is."[146] The committee fortified its authority to teach by packaging its advice as masculine expertise presented to "the women of America." As a BACPC ad explained, the program was "planned expressly to appeal to housewives, who are buyers for the nation."[147] In this era of scientific homemaking, the show's crafters expected talks on "coffee, its dietetic value, and its correct brewing . . . by dietitians, home-economic experts, and scientists" to be "of special interest to housewives."[148] They set the show to air nationally at five o'clock, the time of day when housewives were most likely to be at leisure. As one announcement related to the trade, "By this time she has completed her housework—it is too soon to prepare dinner. She is 'at home'—ready for new ideas, and entertainment."[149]

This image of a housewife home alone, ready and willing to absorb a message, was a favorite fantasy of advertisers. Their work was many more parts prescriptive (pushing listeners to fit themselves to the normative images distributed) than descriptive. No wonder the BACPC thought it ought to supplement the fatherly instruction of previous campaigns ("Scour the coffee pot!") with "interest and romance in connection with coffee" against the much-touted "romantic Brazilian background."[150] Assigning "romance" to coffee as well as to Brazil, the BACPC reiterated its seductive conflation of coffee and Brazil, multiplying its messages. Coffee, personified as planter, courted "America," in the form of Mrs. Consumer. Equated with romance itself, it offered the consumer a more active subject position. To Brazil, the role of Romeo was preferable to that of Uncle Sam's child ward, a favorite trope in political caricature of U.S. colonies. Romeo provided a neat sidestep around the infantilization of neocolonial subordination.

Crash

Even the BACPC's good showing could not have prevented joint advertising's crash in 1929 along with the coffee exchange and the stock market. The Depression cast Brazil into a crisis its export dependence would not survive. From $445.9 million in 1929, exports dropped to $180.6 million in 1932, while shortages catalyzed industrial production. Increased produc-

BREW YOUR BEST AT HOME

Once you've got the best beans, a few simple steps will ensure that you are brewing your best just like in our stores.

1. Start with the freshest beans from the Caribou Market.

2. Buy whole beans and grind them at home.

3. Use oxygen-bleached or metal coffee filters.

4. Use good-tasting water.

5. Use a coffeemaker with a slow brew time (between 4 and 7 minutes).

6. Use 2 heaping tablespoons of ground coffee for every 8 oz. of water.

FIGURE 11. Caribou Coffee flier. Collection of the author.

tion of coffee elsewhere, in part thanks to the encouragement the United States provided to Brazil's competitors in retaliation against valorization, would multiply the players in the world coffee economy. Brazilians took advantage of the crisis to diversify their economic projects, though their coffee diminution was relative: through the rest of the twentieth century and into the twenty-first, Brazil has continued to occupy the globe's premier position in the coffee trade.[151]

Joint advertising limped along until 1932, riding out its mandate, but its useful life had ended. Other organizations would take on the task of advertising coffee in the years to come, sometimes even in broad, multinational coalitions.[152] They would inherit the world the JC's campaign, including its universe of "tie-ins" and the controversies they accompanied, had helped to shape. Ads would continue to encode and erase the shifting politics of global trade; to naturalize external and internal social hierarchies by linking them; and to promote consumerism as, over the rest of the twentieth century, the world's distribution of wealth has remained unconscionably inequitable. Today, coffees named for their places of production continue to offer consumers tantalizing sips of exotic Guatemala, Sulewesi, or Kenya. For those who notice the scent of violence, these days pointed out by the anti-globalization movement, there is "fair trade coffee" or, for a slightly less affluent niche market, "Juan Valdez." This stalwart peasant and his fuzzy little burro promise that Colombian coffee is grown by happy, autonomous smallholders, the kind of farmers most romanticized by North Americans in the era of agribusiness. For those who prefer to forget the Third World origins of their quotidian luxury completely, Caribou Coffee, a Starbucks-type franchise, touts its founders' inspiration in the Alaskan tundra, recalling nothing so much as Hills Bros.' "Coffee of the West" campaign. Caribou also distributes a didactic flyer listing six rules for making better coffee that could have been lifted directly from the JC files in Smithsonian Institutional archives of advertising history.

Contemporary coffee ads reflect updated versions of the dynamics encoded in their 1920s predecessors. Today's plugs still show the ways U.S. consumers like to think—and to avoid thinking—about the people at home and abroad who provide them with their extraordinary privilege. They transcribe the social phenomena entailed in their production and contribute to the reproduction of those phenomena. In particular, they open a window into consumerism, an ideology of profound importance for lived experience today. Consumerism feeds the categories of social relation that structure the most egregious inequities in the United States and globally. Though it has been seen as a largely domestic phenomenon by its articulate critics, its transnational aspects are vital legitimating supports. These dense nodes of legitimizing cross-references between domestic and global technologies of power construct consumerism as a racialized nationalism, the form in which it can do the greatest damage, outside the United States and within.

ECONOMIC ARENAS were not the only sites to host the process this chapter has detailed, the celebration and then obfuscation of foreign contributions to North American life. Popular cultural realms were equally critical. Chapter 2 delves into one of these: an instance of cultural absorption and erasure involving the Brazilian dance maxixe, hugely popular in 1914. After its moment in the sun, maxixe endured some of the same indignities of erasure and forgetting suffered by Brazil in post-valorization coffee ads. Maxixe's disappearance from songlists and music halls in the United States after 1915 differed in several registers from the removal of Brazil from North American coffee advertisements in the second half of the 1920s. The erasure was less deliberate, with neither agent nor motive; the culture industry's hand was more invisible than the market's in this case. Yet the two are clearly related, guided by the same broad political-ideological currents and moving toward similar ends. Adding one to the other, we begin to fill out the sketch of the workings and consequences of transnational exchange.

CHAPTER TWO

Maxixe's Travels
Cultural Exchange and Erasure

"From the Shores of Costa Rica"?

In 1953, Sammy Gallop, Gil Rodin, and Bob Crosby (Bing's kid brother) saw their rollicking dance tune, the "Boogie-Woogie Maxixe," become a best seller.[1] Featuring bouncy horns and marimba belltones over upbeat percussion, the song was a foot-tapping crowd pleaser, earning repeated recordings by swing orchestras and big bands.[2] The lyrics give a sense of its light-hearted fun:

> It isn't easy to pronounce it/but it's breezy when they bounce it. . . .
> Come a rockin' to the boogie woogie maxixe/that new boogie
>   woogie maxixe. . . .
> From the shores of Costa Rica to the sidewalks of Topeka/You will
>   find it gettin' around
> From the Shenandoah Valley to the beach at Bali Bali/Like a
>   wildfire coverin' ground
> Try it honey/nothing to it/bet yer money/you can do it
> It's a rhythm that's becoming a fad/more popular than rum in
>   Trinidad. . . .
> here's a rhythm that's out of this world.[3]

Without specifying a particular point of origin, the lyrics located maxixe in a realm transcending U.S. borders. The label offered a helpful pronunciation guide, dictionary-style ("ma-*cheech*"), announcing the form as an import before a potential buyer even heard the first note, and the opening line sympathized with fans who found the term perplexing anyway. This was definitely a foreign genre, these hints confirmed, yet enthusiastically available to North Americans. Indeed, in coaxing "honey" to "try it," the singer promised success in the quintessential terms of the Land of Dollars ("bet yer money"). The song's particular foreignness was not clarified by any of its various geographic gestures. Of those who cared to listen to the lyrics at all, some may have assumed that the tune came "from the shores of Costa Rica," but most probably read the line as an invocation of a titillatingly tropical location whose inhabitants had also succumbed to the benign contagion of this captivating beat.

The song's attractions revolved around this seductively accessible exoticism. "Gettin' around" like "wildfire," boogie-woogie maxixe was clearly a world traveler, and it flattered listeners by including them in its cosmopolitan reach. Those partial to literal interpretation could place themselves in a far-flung cultural trend stretching from Latin America to the Caribbean, the U.S. heartland (Topeka) and southland (Shenandoah), points across the Atlantic, and not ten years before the first manned space flight, "out of this world" to boot. But the *feel* of the place names in the jolly swing beat probably displaced their literal meaning for most. Like the harmonic and rhythmic nods to Latin American, Caribbean, and U.S. popular musical genres, surely lost on most listeners, Topeka and Trinidad alike appeal as rhythm and rhyme and as part of the urbane litany of places whose exoticism or cosmopolitanism could be sampled by indulging in the leisure world of popular entertainment.

While fans delighted in the "Boogie-Woogie Maxixe," a new development simmered just beyond their sight. Musicians in Brazil were experimenting with jazz forms, especially West Coast or cool jazz, interesting U.S. musicians in collaborative jazz-samba blends: Antonio Carlos Jobim, João Gilberto, Charlie Byrd, Stan Getz, and others were cooking up the gorgeous harmonies and rhythms of bossa nova. Usually dated to 1956 or 1958, bossa nova is the best-known meeting of North American and Brazilian popular musical styles, and many observers and fans understand it as the first such contact. Such a characterization relies upon the erasure of previous cultural exchange between the United States and Brazil, of which a fine illustration is the "Boogie-Woogie Maxixe." That pop hit was both the product of repeated cultural crossings and an agent of their forgetting. It errs, or dissembles, not only in its generically global self-representation, but also in calling itself "new," and not only because this title had enjoyed its first pressing in 1939.[4] Boogie-woogie, a raggy, percussive piano blues style, had been around as such since the late 1920s; maxixe had appeared in urban Brazil in the mid-nineteenth century, launching its international career by 1890; by the mid-1910s, maxixe had arrived in the United States, where it would enjoy a brief but notable fad.[5] In the "Boogie-Woogie Maxixe," as in most music history and collective memory in the United States today, none of this appears.

The vogue of the "Boogie-Woogie Maxixe" on the cusp of the bossa nova era is good for thinking. It points to a far-reaching dynamic in cultural innovation and evolution: the ways people in global metropoles absorb and forget gleanings from less politically and economically powerful places. Erased in this process are not simply the forms themselves but also the kinds of relations (economic, social, military, etc.) that made those imports possible. To explore cultural exchange and its consequences, this chapter departs from the paradox of bossa nova's appearance as an unprecedented fusion of Brazilian and North American musics, even as it trod on the virtual heels of earlier syntheses. Retreating from this 1950s opening scene by a half-century or more, it follows, back through its erasure, the fertile cultural exchange between U.S. and Brazilian popular music and dance forms in the early twentieth century and the consequences of that exchange in political and ideological realms, all exemplified in that globe-trotting world citizen of dance, the maxixe.

Like many an eyeblink fad, maxixe disappeared from U.S. popular culture and memory when the culture industry turned its attention elsewhere. Later, critics and historians layered their neglect over that of their sources. That is not, however, the extent of the story. Maxixe helps to show how the here today, gone tomorrow quality of popular fashions involves more than meets the eye: even the silliest hiccup in the ceaseless parade of the new finds acclaim for a reason. Maxixe's star rose along the same lines it would eventually descend; following its arc shows some of the mundane ways those underlying structures were continually reproduced and offers some noteworthy details about their consequences. Those structures, in broadest terms, involved a pair of conjoined phenomena key to the structuring of U.S. social relations: U.S. imperialism, at an apex in this period, and anti-black racism.

From the turn of the century to the First World War, U.S. empire was at its most open and avowed. In that era of formal political imperialism, an inescapable vogue for exotic forms characterized U.S. culture. On the stages of popular theaters and the pages of popular magazines, an endless succession of forms, called "Oriental," "Spanish," "Latin," and so on, played and danced together, distinguished barely or not at all. Audiences imbibed a steady diet, as one scholar of vaudeville listed, of "Brazilian Maxixe, burlesques of *The Merry Widow*, Princess Rajah's snake dance, and . . . *Salome*."[6] A French observer noted the phenomenon from a continental vantage point: "The whole world is at our disposition: Hawaii with its nostalgic guitarists, the Orient with its jugglers and disturbing balancing acts, America with its eccentrics, its dancing girls and its dancers, India with its charmers and magicians."[7] Metropolitan subjects joyously, ravenously, sought to consume the colonial world in popular cultural form.

Acquired tastes for the exotic carved out many shallow niches for such forms on Broadway and "Tin Pan Alley," as adepts nicknamed the sheet music publishing industry.[8] These forms' fragile toeholds ensured a quick slip from the public eye, as sheet music and ads for sheet music detail. Maxixe enjoyed its vogue in 1914 (as we shall see below). When publishers stopped advertising maxixes around 1916, they did not simply substitute homegrown forms. Instead, they performed a head-spinning turn to songs invoking Hawaii. Suddenly, Tin Pan Alley was issuing countless Hawaiian waltzes, such as "Myona Waltz," "My Hawaiian Sunshine," "Mo-ana," and comic mix-ups such as "O'Brien Is Tryin' to Learn to Talk Hawaiian."[9] Along the route of this transition, Brazilian and Hawaiian forms overlapped. The back cover of "La Brasiliana—Tango" advertised recent hits for sale, including "My Hulu-Hulu Love" and the "Hula-Hula Intermezzo."[10] Coney Island's Dancing Palace hired a Hawaiian band alongside a Brazilian orchestra, a French review revealed, "to dance the Brazilian maxixe."[11] This succession foreshadowed another Brazil-Hawaii conflation, the 1930s–'40s overlap of the hula and Carmen Miranda phenomena.[12]

After Hawaii's moment in the sun, Egypt had a turn. In one popular music magazine in 1920, Egyptian themes represented a plurality (there was no majority) of place-oriented titles. Music publisher Carl Fischer-Witmark took out a full-page ad for "Bo-la-bo, That Favorite Egyptian Fox Trot" and another for "Alexandria," illustrated with a predictable sketch of a female dancer. Waterson, Berlin and Snyder offered "Desert Dreams," while Jerome H. Remick mixed it up with "The Irish Were Egyptians Long Ago." McCarthy and Fisher featured "(When the Sun Goes Down in) Cairo Town" and "Song of Omar," among others; various other publishers offered titles such as "Kamel-Land," "Mystic Nile," and "On the Streets of

Cairo."[13] A more erudite serial, the *Musical Record*, detailed the "Music and Musical Instruments of the Egyptians."[14]

These crazes fell just before and after the First World War, and Hawaii and Egypt were visible to North American audiences for (different) war-related reasons.[15] But Hawaii had become a U.S. territory much earlier, in 1900, and the United States did not enter the war until April 1917—that is, after the beginning of this Hawaii culture vogue—and the interest in Egypt *preceded* the 1922 discovery of the tomb of Tutankhamen, which sparked a tidal wave of fascination in U.S. popular culture.[16] So exoticist cultural expressions were not simply epiphenomena of political engagements. Nor was there any simple or direct causative effect. These minivogues indexed U.S. involvement with foreign regions and nations in political, cultural, military, or economic arenas but in indirect, uneven, and highly idiosyncratic ways and as inextricable and consequential parts of a multilayered discursive structure that included cultural, political, and commercial phenomena. A literal reading of specific geopolitical relations into exoticist cultural expressions sheds little light on the issue. Brazil, Hawaii, and Egypt were just three of a great many targets of a conflationary imagination that merged the objects of its affection with near-seamless disregard for their enormous differences and distances. Culture and commerce fed imperialist ideology with delicious panoplies of available exotics, kaleidoscopic views of the globe's semi-savage Others, offering counterpoints against which U.S. consumers could posit their nation's unique (and superior) qualities. In this way North American cultural producers and their culture industry followed and led and simply celebrated their state by enthroning and devouring exotic tidbit after exotic tidbit.

The specific mechanisms that fit maxixe into this exoticist hit parade also depended upon one of the critical domestic sides of the exoticist coin: racialized social relations, and anti-black racism in particular. The ongoing Jim Crow violence against African Americans picked up momentum after the end of Reconstruction, continuing a dizzy upward spiral into the 1920s. Maxixe had to thread through the maze of deeply racist cultural and social hierarchies that shaped and constrained Afro-diasporic cultural exchange and innovation. Genres that met with commercial success were usually shorn of their most obvious references to Africa or blackness by producers, performers, and fans, especially white ones. In Brazil, maxixe had undergone a process of whitening before elite social clubs would dance it, but the racial divisions within Brazil that made that distinction possible were difficult to see from afar. Abroad, maxixe's promoters blurred the connection to the South American country most associated with Africa in mores and population. Their work in the United States helped fold maxixe into the culture of empire's benign exoticisms, related to African American forms closely enough to be titillating and at enough distance to be safe.

In the United States, maxixe was not only a black but also a foreign form, and as such it points not only to the links but also to the tensions between imperialism and racism. The two hierarchies overlap imperfectly, leaving stutter space for complex negotiations on the parts of cultural producers in multiple locations. Like so many traveling Afro-diasporic forms, maxixe offered a channel for the cultural exchange at the core of the "practice of Diaspora."[17] Its agents were able to use this practice to wedge open a fraction of space for black performers in Brazil, Paris, New York, and elsewhere, fighting racism in public realms. Yet African Americans shared in the imperial imaginary (as we will see in chapter 4), and African American cultural *forms* reaped some of the benefits of their nation's imperial privilege, though generally without conferring much upon actual African American *people*. When African American cultural forms worked to deepen maxixe's erasure, they fed the exoticist culture of empire, a civilizationist nationalism as potently anti-black as it was exceptionalist in national terms. This paradox is a part of the intensely complex forces that operate to obscure Afro-diasporic elements of U.S. culture and that plant (as noted in chapter 1) an Africanist "absent presence," in the most "American" of cultural forms.[18] Maxixe's fate involved the concrete workings of that confusing process; the light it can shed on them is reason enough to examine its rise and fall.

Fine Traveling Form

Although its U.S. promoters carefully avoided any suggestion of African association, maxixe is unquestionably an Afro-diasporic form. The "oldest of the urban dances of Brazil," it is the "immediate ancestor" of samba, quintessential symbol of the Afro-Brazilian cultural elements at the heart of present-day Brazilian culture.[19] Its precise derivation is inaccessible, as are its early steps, but most accounts place it in the second half of the nineteenth century at the meeting point of three great dance crazes: the Afro-Brazilian *lundu*, danced throughout Brazil by the beginning of the nineteenth century; the polka, which peaked in Europe and arrived in Brazil around 1845; and the Afro-Cuban *habanera*, popular in Brazil from around the 1860s on. As a genre of its own, maxixe entered the dance lexicon in the 1870s or '80s, perhaps simply referring to local ways of dancing these or another Afro–New World regional favorite, the tango.[20] Moving at these intersections, people dancing and playing maxixe incorporated, expressed through bodily movements, a series of Afro-diasporic encounters in the Americas.

Alive and beloved, maxixe was not only a palimpsest of earlier crossings, but also an arena of cultural mixture and an opportunity for ongoing innovation. It was one of many set dance forms that "crossed the Atlantic"—and, we should add, the Equator—"back and forth, not one but many times, invariably altered upon their return and often carrying a new name."[21] Dance historian Curt Sachs granted maxixe a key, catalytic position in the round of exchange initiated at the turn of the century. "Since the Brazilian *maxixe* of 1890 and the *cakewalk* of 1903 broke up the pattern of turns and glides that dominated the European round dances," he charged, "our generation has adopted with disquieting rapidity a succession of Central American [*sic*] dances," including the one-step or turkey-trot, the "so-called 'Argentine' tango," the fox-trot, shimmy, Charleston, black bottom, "and finally the rocking *rumba*—all compressed into even movement, all emphasizing strongly the erotic element, and all in that glittering rhythm of syncopated four-four measures classified as *ragtime*."[22] Maxixe's contributions to ragtime and its heirs, then, may be underappreciated.

What did maxixe look like? What was it like to dance? In many ways, we cannot know. Maxixe's traces in the historical record provide at best snapshots of its various incarnations, freezing a moment framed by word or image. In early periods, when observers were often more concerned to denounce the dance's licentiousness than detail its movements, moral outrage revealed maxixe's close physical contact and the undulating or rippling movement of the hips. Like so many other Afro-diasporic dances and musics, maxixe was condemned by moralists for its uncivilized "choreographic exoticisms" and its "scandalous, improper choreography, with its lascivious, voluptuous, almost acrobatic hip movements."[23] Early twentieth-century caricatures and other sketches show physical contact, including interlaced legs, in the manner of the later *lambada*, and the lead's left and follow's right hands held so far up and away from the body that the shoulders were drawn very close together.[24] These sketches sometimes suggest exaggerated, parodic movements, as in the most mocking tradition of the cakewalk, brainchild of North American slaves and their descendants.

During maxixe's expatriate years in the 1910s, how-to manuals instructed dancers to lean rather drastically from the waist and described stops, checks, and a kick many found difficult to master.[25] One of the only moving image clues, recorded well after maxixe's vogue had subsided, is the "Carioca" in RKO's 1933 *Flying Down to Rio*. That maxixe-derived romp featured pairs glued together at the forehead, undulating sinuously over the parquet. Some couples held rounded arms together at shoulder height and leaned in toward the head, bodies rigid in a perfect A-frame shape; others slithered in directions determined by the lead's hands on his partner's lower back or even a little lower (ahem); still others stretched their straightened arms far out to the side or over the head of the follow, who bent at the waist and dipped deeply back and sideways.[26] *Flying Down to Rio* provides a respite from the endemic problem in dance history (the absence of moving pictures, even after the advent of recording technology) and certainly reveals *a* point along the evolutionary continuum of this live form, but observers must not allow its delight to make us forget our ultimate ignorance of maxixe as played and danced in late-nineteenth- and early-twentieth-century Brazil.[27]

Maxixe is a "set dance," a dance with its own attendant music, though observers tend to privilege the dance. Maxixe was "not a specific rhythm" but a form of bodily movement, writes one commentator; another defines it as "a word with content more choreographic than musical."[28] Musically, maxixe was characterized by a percussion instrument similar to the maraca, the *chocalho*, and its two-four time signature reflected "the fusion of the *habanera*'s rhythm and the polka's tempo, adapted to African syncopation."[29] Beyond this, the form's exact musical characteristics are as difficult to pin down as its steps. The North American jazz pianist Clifford Korman, also a historian of Brazilian music, calls maxixe "a simpler samba" and gives its rhythmic base as dotted quarter, eighth, quarter, quarter, with running sixteenth notes over the top. For reference, he also notes the remarkable resemblance between Brazilian composer Ernesto Nazareth's "Odeon" and Scott Joplin's "Entertainer."[30] Sheet music printed in the United States before the war features similarly dotted rhythms but in two-four time. Highly common was a repeating pattern of sixteenth-eighth-sixteenth, eighth-eighth — a woefully partial description of a fabulously alive, raggy form pulled in and out of the beat by performers' witty syncopations. Few of these made it into long-lived recordings, though there are maxixes available to listeners today thanks to later recreations. They feature wonderful runaway barrelhouse ukelele, gleefully percussive.[31] These recordings, like the "Carioca," are expressions of an ongoing stylistic evolution that reveal of early maxixe only the shape it assumed in later years. Created by bodies in all sorts of motion, maxixe would never come to rest.

When maxixe qua maxixe left Brazil, it journeyed more than several times to France. In the late nineteenth century, according to Jota Efegê, maxixe's most enthusiastic and thorough historian, Brazilian dancers in Paris, along with French and other non-Brazilian dancers who had traveled to Brazil, brought maxixe repeatedly to the French capital, beginning at least as early as 1889, when the Brazilian actress and singer Plácida dos Santos played the Ambassadeur and the Folies Bergères. Jardel Jercolis danced maxixe in Paris before returning to Rio to become an *empresário* of the theater revue; the Brazilian dancer Jenny Cook sang and danced maxixe in 1901 in Buenos Aires, a port city in intimate conversation with Paris (and London); the dancers Derminy and Paule Morly danced at Paris's Alcazar d'Été in 1905; and that same year the ladies Rieuse and Nichette announced the launching of a "choreographic novelty," the "*maxix*," at the Marigny on the Champs Elysées.[32]

By the early twentieth century at the latest, Paris offered some infrastructure to attract and accommodate *maxixeiros*, including Brazilian nightclubs. After building up quite a reputation in Brazil around the turn of the century, maxixeiros Geraldo Magalhães and partner Nina Teixeira, "*mulatos gaúchos*" (mulattoes from southern Brazil), debuted in Paris in 1908. According to an expatriate Brazilian living in Paris who wrote a regular epistolary column home, "the Geraldos," as Magalhães and Teixeira were billed abroad, had become "the *clou* [key] of the nightly parties at the Abbaye de Thélème [nightclub]." The Geraldos made good use of their Parisian fame. They played in England, Spain, and France in a two-year tour the Brazilian press reported as an unqualified success. They launched the song "Vem cá, mulata" (Come Here, Mulatta), providing a vehicle for another pair of Afro-Brazilian performers: two brothers, the "*negros* Alfredo Martins, cellist, and João Martins, fiddler," who toured Europe, then settled in the Paris nightclub Guibout, where they "began to attract great interest, performing Brazilian songs."[33]

Maxixe was a part of the great fad for Afro-diasporic culture that made Paris, like other cities of the European metropole, the sites of intense Afro-*American* cultural exchange, innovation, and transformation.[34] Milan, London, and Berlin joined Paris in adoring maxixe, surely along with other Italian, English, and German citizens and throngs in Spain and Russia as well.[35] We should not be surprised, then, that maxixe traveled to the United States not only from the south but from the east, over the Atlantic. If the paths of its arrival are mostly buried, one clear, wide swath was cut by the hugely successful, widely traveled maxixeiro Antônio Lopes de Amorim Diniz, or "Duque."[36] This Bahian abandoned a career in dentistry to become a dancer and dance teacher, renaming himself, like so many North American jazz musicians, as befit a member of the cultural aristocracy (joining "Duke" Ellington, trumpeter "King" Oliver, and others). Duque went to Paris, London, and Berlin in 1911 or '12, earning broad fame and bringing maxixe to "dominate the French capital."[37] José Patrocinio Filho (son of the great abolitionist of the same name), in Paris at the same time as Duque, sent word to a Rio newspaper that Duque was known there as "the king of the Brazilian tango."[38] The duke had been promoted.

Duque's spark to cultural exchange operated on many levels. He opened several nightclubs in Paris to showcase maxixe, including Chez Duque and La Reserve de Saint Cloud.[39] To Europe, Duque took Brazilian dancer Maria Lina; in Paris, he met and married a French dancer named Gaby des Fleurs and brought her back to Rio de Janeiro. Along the way he stopped by New York City, where dancers were already eagerly moving to the rhythms of his signature form. A woman claiming to be a pupil of Duque's had begun to offer maxixe lessons there in late 1914, promising "Correct notes on his latest successes" and calling Duque, rather audaciously, the "Originator of the Maxixe."[40] Duque had arrived in the Big Apple by December 1914, when he was advertised alongside a vaudeville presentation, *Watch Your Step*, of the renowned husband-and-wife dance team Vernon and Irene Castle. Ads for the Castles' show ran his name in large block letters—"DUQUE—DUQUE—DUQUE"—without further introduction, suggesting supplementary hype in other fora.[41]

Duque was certainly busy in New York. In the afternoons he gave lessons to children, private appearances, and teas at Coney Island's marvelous Luna Park Dancing Palace, where he was artistic director.[42] In the evenings he offered exhibition performances with "Mlle. Gaby" at the chic Club

De Vingt and Hotel Knickerbocker Grille.[43] In February 1915 the pair had moved to the Parisian Café Chantant, which advertised Duque as "King of the Maxixe and World's Most Renowned Dancer."[44] The Café des Beaux-Arts also featured his dancing, accompanying its nightly suppers. Each Thursday, diners there could enjoy "Tango Night: Dance with Duque."[45] The Café Boulevard drew fans to Duque's "marvelous dancing," up until April, when he sailed for Rio de Janeiro. The press reported Duque's intention to return in the fall to tour the United States with a Brazilian orchestra; I found no record of such a trip.[46] After his departure, fans could console themselves by buying sheet music for the "Duque Walk," a one-step published on the eve of Duque's leave-taking from New York.[47]

The publication of the "Duque Walk" reveals Tin Pan Alley's quick response to Duque's presence, but it had actually printed the vast majority of the U.S. sheet music for maxixes and "Brazilian tangos" in 1914, just prior to Duque's New York appearance.[48] As that timing suggests, while Duque boosted maxixe's popularity in the United States as he had in Europe, he was far from the first to introduce it. Maxixe had reached the United States over more routes than the dusty historical record can reveal at this point. Some involved itinerant performers, such as the North American vaudeville troupe Edna and Wood Mysteries and Novelties, on tour in Brazil in the late nineteenth and early twentieth centuries alongside the Dias Braga Company's vaudeville act, "*Cá e Lá*, a compilation of scenes and songs full of maxixes and cakewalks."[49] Modernist musicologist Mário de Andrade claimed to have sent the maxixes, sambas, and *canções* [songs] of Ernesto Nazareth and Marcelo Tupinambá "to friends in the United States, France, and Germany," though he doesn't specify when.[50]

By the 1910s there were exponents of maxixe in the United States just as famous as Duque and in later years quite a bit better remembered than he, including the popular North American dancers Joan Sawyer; Maurice Mouvet and Florence Walton (known as "Maurice and Walton"); and Delirio and Luis. Sawyer had the "Joan Sawyer Maxixe" named in her honor; Maurice and Walton had three between them: the "'Maurice' Mattchiche," "Tango del Maurice," and "Florence Maxixe." The sheet music printed in 1913 for the "'Maurice' Mattchiche" claimed the form had been "introduced by Monsieur Maurice and Miss Florence Walton." A competing claim in Jos. W. Stern's 1914 version of Nazareth's "Bregeiro, Rio Brazilian Maxixe," attributed its introduction to "America" to Delirio and Luis.[51]

Irene and Vernon Castle published a dance manual featuring maxixe

FIGURE 12. Duque at Luna Park. Jerome Robbins Dance Division, the NYPL for the Performing Arts.

in 1914, suggesting that their engagement with the genre preceded their sharing the stage with Duque in *Watch Your Step*. That manual, *Modern Dancing*, included instructions for the "Tango Brésilienne, or Maxixe," which they called the "latest modern dance" and praised as "beautiful" and requiring great grace.[52] That same year, their house orchestra recorded "Creole Girl," the English-language version of "Vem cá, mulata," the song made famous by two pair of Afro-Brazilian performers in Paris, the Geraldos and the brothers Martins.[53]

The Castles were white high-society types with a classy African American band director, James Reese Europe, an important figure in the New York music world in his own right. Europe played maxixes for the Castles—perhaps "Creole Girl"?—and recorded at least one. In 1914, Europe's Society Orchestra recorded "Amapa—Maxixe Bresilien" (with "Irresistible—Tango Argentine" on the other side). Along with his "Too Much Mustard"/"Down Home Rag," these were "the first recordings made by a Negro orchestra," giving maxixe quite an eminent position in U.S. music history.[54] Europe would soon direct the First World War military band that many credit with taking jazz across the Atlantic, revealing maxixe in the musical lexicon of individuals critical to the development of jazz at formative moments in jazz history. Here is another reminder of jazz's "Latin tinge," often acknowledged but rarely with the kind of detail that ruffles its facile celebration as "American."[55]

Maxixe's Moment

As the timing of Europe's recording suggests, 1914 was maxixe's year. For that brief, concentrated moment, maxixe was an inescapable part of the dance craze sweeping the United States. A revue at New York's Winter Garden that year introduced "Brazilian Max-cheese" as one of the great new dance forms of the day:

> The other night a dear, old friend said, "A ball we will attend!"
> Said he'd show me all the latest dances to date
> Promised me he wouldn't keep me out very late,
> So we lost no time at all but we taxied to the hall.
> First we did a "Tango," then did a "Trot," No "Hesitation" at all.
> Then he said, "Now Lilian, Let's do the Brazilian

And I will show you something new."
La-la la (etc.) Oh! what that man did do!
His arm went round my waist/But it wouldn't stay in place.
And every time we bent our knees
'Twas then I felt a run in my silk stocking, how shocking!
While dancing Brazilian Max-*cheese.*[56]

Naming maxixe heir to tango and trot emphasized its salacious daring, gesturing to a class position for the dance, especially for those who heard "No 'Hesitation'" as more than a pun. Audiences of the day were well versed in the distinctions between vulgar trots and upscale genres such as the hesitation.

Though the lyrics didn't mention it, the music of "Brazilian Max-cheese" was that of a song entitled "Dengozo," an Ernesto Nazareth composition. Nazareth, and "Dengozo" in particular, ubiquitous and beloved, seem to have been the central axis of maxixe's U.S. vogue. Many other tunes referred to this song in either music or text. The playful "Dance That Dengozo with Me, 'Oo-La-La'" gestured to Nazareth's piece in both lyrics and principal melody, though the Brazilian musician's name was not to be found in the score:

There's a tune that ev'ry one's dancing,
Slow and dreamy, It's so entrancing,
Oh, that ever fascinating Dengozo strain,
Ev'rywhere you go you hear that haunting refrain. . . .
Grandma's taking her lesson daily, Pa and Ma are dancing it gayly,
In his little high-chair baby Brother so sweet,
When he hears that Maxie [*sic*] how he wiggles his feet. . . .
If they fail to play, Someone's sure to say,
"Please play that Dengozo tune."
[Chorus:] Play it, oh, play it, That Dengozo strain, Oo-La-La. . . .
No more Tango, Trot or Hesitation,
Whirl me, and twirl me, to that melody, Oo-La-La.[57]

This song rejected the trot and tango alongside the hesitation, placing maxixe, supreme, above them all. If this difference from the Winter Garden tune reflected the arc of maxixe's rise, that rise was sudden indeed, for the songs were published at the most months apart, both in 1914.

Another nod to Nazareth, "That Wonderful Dengoza [*sic*] Strain," also

enthused over "that familiar tune they're playing, / You hear in ev'ry cabaret, / That tune that sets your heart a swaying, / Haunts you at night and
in the day." A rhyme helped singers pronounce it—"Daddy's teaching
Clarice/How to do the Maxixe!"—but it might not help dancers move to
it, for the song was a one-step.[58] Still, the enthusiastic celebration left no
doubt as to its appeal:

> Ma hums it when she sets the table, John sings it on his way to
>   school
> Grandma tried hard but was not able, Grandpa keeps acting like
>   a fool.
> Even Bridget, the cook, bought the Castle's new book!
> Oh that wonderful strain! Oh that dreamy refrain! From 'Frisco
>   to Maine
> It just plays tag with your brain!
> It's such a teasing, squeezing, pleasing, little wonderful thing,
> And once you hear it you can't help but sing La la la, Tra la la!
> Ev'ry Tango instructor, Ev'ry street car conductor,
> Does a motion like the ocean to this tune from Brazil,
> That wonderful Dengoza Strain![59]

Both this song and "Dance That Dengozo with Me, 'Oo-La-La'" called the
tune a "strain," as if dealing with a tropical virus, an impression the lyrics
reinforced with their nod to the tune's enormous appeal and its terrific
mobility (both similarly invoked by the "Boogie-Woogie Maxixe"), as well
as its seeming unconcern with social distinctions. Even teachers of the
rival tango, insisted the song, were compelled by a pull as powerful and
inescapable as ocean tides—and by currents as global.[60] From the Castles
to the cook, maxixe was in vogue.

Maxixe's flush faded fast. In the popular music magazine *Metronome*,
advertisers had enthusiastically plugged slates of maxixes in 1914 and
1915.[61] By mid-1916, its pages were nearly clear of them. Music publisher
T. B. Harms did offer two, but he folded them into the category "tango."[62]
Jos. W. Stern, one of maxixe's great exponents in previous years, in 1916
relegated maxixe to motion picture music—sign of a turn in the entertainment industry that would profoundly consolidate North Americans'
grasp of the global cultural center. "At dancing suggestions on screen,"
Stern's ad copy admonished silent film pianists, "proper numbers should
be played"; tangos and maxixes were appropriate "for Spanish, Mexican

or South American Characteristic Numbers." No longer ballroom fare for the Castles, maxixe and tango had both lost their national specificity to a generic Latin-ness.[63] The few maxixes for sale in 1916 included not a single new title. With no new blood forthcoming, maxixe perched on the edge of extinction.

In the 1920s, Brazilian students in the United States still claimed to prefer maxixe to jazz, and in the thirties, Brazilian newspapers continued to celebrate maxixe's success in various European cities.[64] So maxixe continued to be played and danced in Brazil and elsewhere but not in a way that commanded metropolitan attention outside of Brazil. As if underscoring this point, another mini-vogue for "Brazilian" music appeared in the 1920s: a spate of sappy songs published in Chicago and New York that referred vaguely, dreamily, to Brazil. Setting the tone, a 1919 tune entitled "On the Dreamy Amazon" crooned, "Tropical night, filled with delight. . . . / You and I alone are there, / Under the trees, there in the breeze, / Magical charms are everywhere." Singers could express similar sentiments by performing "Brazilian Chimes," "Braziliana," "Dreamy Amazon," "Rio," "Rio Nights" ("When night has fallen down in dear old Rio, down in dreamy old Brazil/The stars begin to shine, and one that I call mine, / Just waits for me, I know she loves me still. . . . / When the tropic moon is in the sky"), "Rose of Brazil," or "Salvador," all issued between 1920 and 1927.[65]

No musician would mistake these songs for maxixe; stylistically, they are all over the map. Some incorporate elements that could be maxixe-esque, such as the sixteenth-dotted eighth-sixteenth pattern against running sixteenth- or eighth-notes; frequent lead-in or pickup notes or phrases (anacrusis); ukelele instrumentation to approximate the *cavaquinho* (another fascinating gesture to the conflation of Brazil and Hawaii in these vogues); or a restricted melodic range (dwelling melodically within a third, occasionally stretching to a fourth). But other directions are equally audible: waltz rhythms (in three); time signatures given as "fox-trot" tempos; long runs of unsyncopated, dot-free eighth-notes; simple "pop" harmonies of tonic-dominant-tonic (1–5–1); and so on.[66] These songs were more like the celebrations of Hawaii and Egypt noted above than the maxixe craze, given their at best faint relation to Brazilian music—maxixe or any other.

The "Brazilianness" this series does evince lies in the lyrics, content, and emotional texture. All reference Brazil explicitly, and all express a sense of loss, perhaps aiming to evoke the ur-Brazilian sentimentalism of *saudade* (nostalgic yearning), but in an imperial inflection. The lyrics personify Brazil (or its regions: Rio, the Amazon, Salvador) as a woman left behind and revel in sweet pangs of nostalgia. Such laments could as easily have been sung to the memory of maxixe, equally loved and as gleefully abandoned.[67] Sung from the perspective of the one who left, the tales are allegories of conquest. The pleasure derived from the power to leave includes the privilege of blithe disregard for both the beloved and the specifics of her country. Cover illustrations sketched the square adobe architecture and desert landscape of the U.S. Southwest or northern Mexico and the lacy shawls and fans of Spanish flamenco dancers. In all these tales Brazil was incidental, a blurry tropical backdrop for the emotional dimension of the white man's burden.

In the United States today, especially if one reads the historical record formalistically or at face value, maxixe appears to have disappeared without a trace. In the turn of the twenty-first-century historical-cultural lexicon of my North American peer group, to take a terribly subjective standard, 1910s and 1920s vogues such as the turkey trot or tango have a place, while maxixe does not. As a measure of the status of Duque and maxixe in a broader collective memory, one swing dance website credits Maurice Mouvet with "creating" Brazilian maxixe in 1913 and doesn't even mention Duque.[68] Even a cultural historian of dance reform, discussing the sanitization of lascivious popular dances, claims that "professional dancers . . . developed elegant versions, such as the 'Castle Walk,' 'Hesitation,' 'Maxixe,' and 'Pousse Café.'"[69] The suggestion that maxixe was an elegant dance developed in the United States as a branch of moral reform would have surprised nineteenth-century Brazilian dance reformers, themselves convinced of maxixe's vulgar immorality. Maxixe has sunk well below memory's horizon.

Mechanisms of Erasure

Without deliberate misrepresentation, simply by accepting and reworking the lingua franca of the cultural hierarchies in place around them, the promoters and performers who introduced maxixe to the United States characterized it in ways bound to erase it. They subsumed maxixe in a broader panoply of indistinguishable exotics, stripped it of its associations with things African—or Brazilian, a category easily conflated with "African" in North Atlantic eyes—celebrated it as kin to tango and to France, and finally absorbed it into jazz as jazz itself was increasingly proclaimed a racially neutral "American" form.

Perhaps the most significant mechanism of maxixe's eventual erasure was the trivializing disregard of its specificity—a key part, too, of its tight embrace. Following Parisian promoters, who sounded Mexican, Incan, gaucho, and other random South American notes in presenting maxixe, U.S. music industry executives, performers, and audiences sanded any Afro-associated edges to fit maxixe to the expected gamut of multiple generic exotics. They declined to notice where it came from (Argentina? Mexico? France?), inflicted endless variations in spelling—matchiche, mattchiche, mattchich, machichi, macheech, max-cheese, maxix, maxie— and reveled in a perpetual confusion over its pronunciation. Reiterations of the foreignness of the word functioned as affirmations of the lack of need to know. They were gleeful reminders of the privilege of ignorance, that unmistakable yet necessarily unarticulated prerogative of power.

Another ideologically revealing mechanism of erasure is the conflation of maxixe with tango. Maxixe was often called "Brazilian tango." The alias made good commercial sense as a frame of reference, but it also suggested that maxixe's distinction from the better-known Argentine referent was trivial. Situating tango as norm and maxixe simply as variant, this comparison set maxixe up to sink back into the matrix that gave it brief life. As dancer-didact Max Rivera declared, "One can say nothing about maxixe which has not already been said about the tango. The two dances have the same exotic origin and the same popular origin."[70] Similar condensations abounded. In the 1910s, some pieces were described as "maxixe or tango" or "tango maxixe," as if the two were interchangeable.[71] Many maxixes were titled in Spanish, even those that referred to some feature of Brazil or the Brazilian landscape.[72] Some songs classified as tangos also referred to Brazil in their titles.[73] In a telling confusion, the Café des Beaux-Arts called its evening with Duque "Tango Night."[74] While it is certainly possible that Duque simply danced tango rather than maxixe in that gig, this was the period of maxixe's greatest vogue, and Duque was its greatest exponent. More likely, the Café expected its patrons to understand what a tango by Duque entailed.

In fact, tango suffered a similar conflationary flattening. Tango and maxixe bled together and into larger generic exotic categories. The "Maori-Tango or Maxixe"; "La Rumba, Tango or Maxixe"; and the sheet music category "Tangos, Ta-Taos, Maxixes etc." brought indigenous Australia, Afro-Cuba, and China into the mix.[75] The forms gained Mexican and generic Latin American affiliations in the "true Tango," "La Bonita: Mexican Intermezzo" and "Manana" (rhymes with banana?), a song its promoters called a "Real South American Tango."[76] Perhaps the price of both genres' U.S. fame was the loss of any specific affiliation with either Brazil *or* Argentina.

In memory and naming, as hindsight reveals, tango had a better footing than maxixe.[77] Part of tango's eventual survival and maxixe's loss may reflect the racial valences of these two South American nations and Argentina's successful self-representation as whiter and more European than its largest near neighbor—a representation that extended even to its Afro-descended cultural elements. A 1938 study of jazz revealed the assumptions of the era about tango: its "rhythms, apparently also originally Negroid, were similarly Latinized by the Argentines"—sweet vindication for the intense labors Argentines invested in the representation of their national racial identity as white.[78] In the mapping of nations onto a continuum from the most African to the most European, Brazil occupied a far less prestigious (more African) position.[79] So while tango's promoters could erase its blackness without deleting its *Argentinidad*, maxixe's advocates had more restricted options. This is part of the reason even maxixe's Brazilian backers collaborated in its alignment with Orientalist, generic Latin American, and other non-Brazilian, non-African cultural or national formations. The representation of maxixe and its most famous Brazilian exponent, Duque, as French is a signal illustration of this representational bent.

Promoters of maxixe in the United States played up its Frenchness and French success with zeal. They advertised particular maxixes as "the Latest European-American Craze," "the Latest Parisian Craze," or a "Celebrated Parisien [*sic*] March."[80] Many offered maxixe titles and descriptions in French or gave the genre name in French (for example, "Maxixe Bresilien" or "Brésilienne," "Tango Argentine").[81] "Dance That Dengozo with Me" winked self-consciously at the genre's French pretensions, adding to its title the flirtatious "Oo-La-La."[82]

Duque allowed himself and his dance to be represented as French, and he probably embraced the opportunity. In New York he surely noted the names of the clubs he played, all angling for the status a Francophone flavor could lend a place of leisure and entertainment: the "Club De Vingt,"

"Café des Beaux-Arts," "Parisian Café Chantant." The first offered "Thés Dansants . . . Under the direction of Duque of Paris, France"; the second billed Duque's appearance as "Paris in New York"; and the third called him the "world's most renowned dancer" and among "Europe's most famous stars."[83] Duque's self-identified pupil (the New York City dance teacher) identified herself as "Back from Paris" and Duque as "late" of the same famous city.[84] With his white-looking features and classy tuxedo attire, Duque's French affiliations often crowded out Brazil entirely. When the *New York Times* reported that "the Parisian dancer" was to "sail for Rio de Janeiro next week to appear in the Municipal Theatre there," it included nothing to suggest that Duque might have been going home.[85]

Duque's success reflected this crowding out of his South American origins by his European experience. Offering the seduction and color of "Brazil," carefully—sometimes completely—sheathed in the sophistication of a Parisian façade, Duque appealed perfectly to audiences reveling in the exoticist culture of empire.

Naming Matters

Presenting Duque and maxixe as French or as tango was not exactly a misrepresentation except inasmuch as any representation is partial. In Brazil, Argentina, Paris, and throughout Europe in the late nineteenth and early twentieth centuries, maxixe and tango shifted in relation to each other, local tastes, and other set dances in vogue at the time. Their companionate travels deepened their connections to each other to the point of indistinguishability. Pieces later scholars would call "maxixes" were called tangos in Brazil before the genre earned a name of its own, and they remained synonymous or contested even in the work of Ernesto Nazareth, probably the best-known composer of maxixes. Many observers cite Nazareth as the quintessential maxixe composer, but he called his compositions tangos.[86] Even Nazareth's compositions published in the United States reflect this confusion; one edition of his "Bregeiro" was called a "Rio Brazilian Maxixe" on the cover and a "Tango Bresilienne" inside.[87] This conflation in naming was substantive as well. Tango and maxixe rhythms, for example, were not clearly distinct. Though it is impossible to define a standard maxixe rhythm, it would be hard to find a more ubiquitous piece than Nazareth's "Dengozo." "Dengozo's" rhythmic pattern of sixteenth-eighth-sixteenth, eighth-eighth, in two-four, characterized several pieces labeled "Argentine tangos" and even one termed a "Brazilian polka."[88] One song labeled "maxixe" gave its time signature as "tempo di tango," using an elongated form of this pattern.[89] U.S. publishers specified some pieces as "Argentine tangos," as if maxixe's visibility as *a* tango in the period of its vogue made such a distinction necessary rather than redundant, as it would be today.[90] Perhaps these various conflations explain dance historian Curt Sachs's double doubt (scare quotes *and* a prose "harrumph") of the "so-called 'Argentine' tango."[91]

Such doubt is a wonderfully eloquent gesture to the complex crossings and mixtures bubbling beneath the surface of genre names. A similar suspicion about "jazz" is justified by the transnational collaborations its supposed "Americanness" can obscure. As scholars of jazz have established, early twentieth-century cultural circuits were critical to jazz's formation. Those global contexts involved the First World War's brisk economy; its boosts to mobility, urbanization, and anti-racist activism; and war-related developments in communications technology and mass culture. Jazz is a product not only of North American versions of these already transnational conditions (layered with the previous contributions of European, African, and Latin American musics), but also of related postwar contexts in Europe, where colonial troops' participation in the recent conflict and their ongoing presence during demilitarization spotlit the cultural productions of colonial subjects, and in the Caribbean and South America, where artists and musicians, in constant contact with their multiple commercial and political metropoles, articulated traveling forms into locally meaningful versions of the primitivist modernism sweeping the rest of the jazz-age world.[92]

That jazz is transnational does not mean that the internal syncretisms and collaborations that went into its creation were either mutual or equitable. The transnational facets of this music were sharply circumscribed by the uneven positions of its agents. Overlapping and conflicting social hierarchies within and across nations, regions, cities, and neighborhoods shaped formations of inequity and privilege, and these exacerbated structures of memory and forgetting, infusing the historical record with silences, gaps, and confusing disjunctures. Breach, disparity, and illogic cannot be resolved by "better" historical research; they are constitutive of cultural formations and expressions of the ways people experienced and understood the possibilities and limits on their lives.

Consider North American musicians' encounters with the music observers subsume under the roiling hybrid of "tango." Garvin Bushell, who toured South America with Sam Wooding's band, remembered such exchange with great pleasure: "I had a ball in Buenos Aires. I loved it, and especially playing beside the great tango orchestras and they're trying to play jazz and we were playing tango."[93] Wooding, too, remembered this mutual exchange: "We used to do tangos. And the funny thing, we'd do a tango sometime, and we got them down pretty good. And the tango band, which was Canero, which was the greatest band there they had at the time, Canero's band was playing 'St. Louis Blues.'"[94] Parisian nightclubs hosted countless similar meetings. Joe Zelli's club in Montmartre alternated jazz and tango in twenty-minute sets; Haitian flutist Bertin Depestre Salnave played in a "tango band at the Apollo Theatre" sometime between 1919 and 1921; trombonist Herb Flemming (né Arif Niccolaiih El-Michelle) and his Plantation Orchestra gigged with a tango band at the Abbaye de Thélème in 1930.[95] Could all these intense encounters have left their participants unchanged?

It is not just that tango's place in jazz is often overlooked—both these genre names place multiple elements under erasure. Recall that the Abbaye had also been the site in 1908 of the triumphant Paris debut of the Afro-Brazilian maxixciros Geraldo Magalhães and Nina Teixeira. Maxixeiro ghosts flitted through the halls of that cabaret, just as maxixe haunted the music played there.

The performance of jazz, tango, and (however spectral) maxixe brought musicians together to exchange, collaborate, and create. We might think of the genres populating the *tumulte noir*[96] as cultural meeting grounds in and of themselves, occasions for syncretism and even engines of innovation proper. Maxixe, tango, jazz, and other Afro-diasporic forms from the Americas, including the Caribbean—beguine, son, merengue, quadrille, danzon, trova, and so on—widened the space for Afro-diasporic cultural exchange, constituting the sites for the "practice of diaspora"—literally, musically.

The transnational spaces of these meeting grounds were as "lumpy" or uneven as any such sites.[97] The Abbaye de Thélème was one of "these establishments [that] gave visitors the impression that they had suddenly stepped into Harlem," as Jody Blake puts it.[98] But remembering the Geraldos' presence at the Abbaye de Thélème reminds us that the club felt like Harlem not because it was patronized by black North Americans, but because people there hailed from throughout the African Diaspora. Paris boasted as transnational a range of black people and cultural forms, as did Harlem, or Buenos Aires, as Sam Wooding's band's experience begins to suggest; or New Orleans, where noted jazz pianist and composer Jelly Roll Morton wrote melodies that incorporated not only blues and ragtime, but also "Creole folk songs, marches, operatic arias, Mexican pop songs, Cuban *sones*, music hall melodies, and of course French quadrille tunes."[99] No wonder so many pieces straddle the borders musicologists attempt to impose over their hybrid, changing forms. History and memory do disservice to the landscapes of dense, scarred layerings of the many cultural forms that wrestled under the signs of the *tumulte noir*'s manifold popular musical forms.[100]

In musicians' discussions of their worlds, a sense of the messy boundaries of genre and its function as meeting ground occasionally emerges. Trumpeter Arthur Briggs described a pianist with whom he played in Paris: "[he] was in an orchestra, not a straight orchestra, they played waltzes, and tangoes [*sic*] and schottisches and things like that, you know."[101] This decidedly "not straight" group filled the marvelous, ample space of Briggs's "things like that" with its musical heterodoxy. This blurriness allowed the pianist, Briggs implied, to play with him—that is, to play jazz (Briggs played with the Southern Syncopated Orchestra, among other early jazz groups). Musicians rarely defined what it was they were playing, but they did express a sense that it was unconventional somehow, and they often conveyed that they understood it as "black." Not in the sense of biology or color or relationship to Africa—there is no consistency to be found here, no stable definition of blackness or diasporic identity. Nonetheless, it is there: salient, central, ambiguous, unavoidable. It is in Briggs's "you know." It is in French pianist Leo Vauchant's description of his arrangement of Cole Porter's "first piano copy of 'Begin the Beguine.' ... I did it in a Latin version. Nobody heard of the beguines there in South America. It was Brazilian and it was also Haitian. I had seen the *Balle Noir* in Paris where they played beguines."[102] Vauchant muddied up nations, continents, "civilizations" ("Latin"), cities, and genres, but his naming of the two American nations imagined as most pronouncedly "African" and of Paris's Negro revue (the *Balle Noir*) made one thing clear: the overarching blackness that framed his understanding of the phenomenon in which he participated.

This understanding, widely shared, gave the cultural forms of the *tumulte noir* a subtle anti-racist charge. This massively popular phenomenon's obvious association with blackness widened the opportunities for Afro-descended cultural producers to claim authorship and public space. Maxixe's effect in this direction should not be exaggerated, but some of its paths are suggestive. As maxixe's star rose, for example, it was increasingly possible, even desirable for Afro-descended maxixeiros to grace Parisian stages. Early maxixe dancers in Paris, such as Plácida dos Santos or Jardel Jercolis, seem not to have identified as black, but subsequent performers such as the Geraldos did, and the Afro-Brazilian Martins brothers even underlined their blackness deliberately by performing at the Guibout "in an *ensemble* with an orchestra of pretty, blond sweet young things, all dressed in white" (the costumes pressing the point).[103] The selection of not just any white musicians but attractive young women as counterpoint to the Martins' black masculinity sexualized the contrast, enhancing it even more, a daring but apparently well-calculated provocation.

This was exactly what elite Brazilians observing maxixe's popularity in France most feared. As a Rio de Janeiro magazine worried, "salons in Rio [might] ease the ban on this arousing dance simply because Paris dissolved the dangers under the misleading appearance of a hyper-civilized dance."[104] This fear, articulated in terms of sexual morality, dreaded above all maxixe in elite social space, and as it turns out, the fear was justified: maxixe did ascend to elite Brazilian stages, as it had outside Brazil.[105] As chapter 3 will detail, the popularity of maxixe, jazz, and the range of black cultural forms in Paris and the United States provided a handle that Afro-Brazilians could and did grasp to claim political and cultural space in Brazil.[106]

In the United States, the process is far less consequential because maxixe was so ephemeral, but the exoticist culture of empire in general gave African Americans similar handles to challenge their stage marginalization; chapter 4 takes this up in depth. Yet even maxixe's blip left intriguing suggestions about its erosion of racism in popular entertainment venues. The *New York Dramatic Mirror*'s vaudeville critic, Frederick J. Smith, criticized a 1915 show that hid its black band: "The left side of the stage, close to the footlights, is thickly banked with palms and a negro orchestra sits in shadowed seclusion. This is, of course, unnecessary after a season of the tango, since we know nearly every ebony musician by sight."[107] In addition to the suggestive evidence here of maxixe as "absent presence" in tango (what else could the "season of tango" in 1914 have meant?), Smith's review reveals that African Americans playing tango(-maxixe) in New York in the 1910s crossed the color line in public with such regularity that they reset expectations for their occupation of public space.

African American commentators in this era often voiced high hopes that just this sort of anti-racist effect would flow from the recognition awarded their cultural production.[108] A *Chicago Defender* editorialist was thrilled that the early recordings (of ragtime, tango, and maxixe!) by James Reese Europe's Society Orchestra would prove that "for talent and ability members of the Afro American race stand as high as any other race" and that Europe's band would change the viewpoint of the "most prejudiced enemy of our Race."[109] But the process through which black cultural popularity undermined racism was not straightforward persuasion through the presentation of evidence of African American ability or excellence. Racism is illogical; it cannot be defeated with logic. Nor was black culture's effect immediate or vast: in the main it did not alter the ways race worked to structure power and allocate state and private violence. What did shift had to do with space and place, the moving of the color line and subsequent possibilities for interracial sociality. Other struggles would start from there, inheriting both the advantages and drawbacks of this cultural politics.

The anti-racist cultural politics of the period just after the First World War was enervated by its embrace of existing discursive elements (such as black sensuality and spectacularity), which other scholars have critiqued. In addition, it failed to wrestle with nationalism, and U.S. American supremacy in particular. Specifically, the U.S. music industry's corporate power gave (and continues to give) North American cultural products disproportionate exposure—even, in some contexts, the African American forms violently marginalized within the nation's borders, though usually not African Americans themselves. As the popularity of jazz exploded in the United States and Europe, the music industry began to fold other forms into jazz, to subsume them under that name. Ronald Clifton Foreman Jr. provides an example from the history of the recording industry: "Borbee's Tango Orchestra recorded for Columbia on February 14, 1917. . . . When copies of Columbia 2233, 'It's a Long, Long Time'/'Just the Kind of a Girl,' reached music stores and record departments, merchants and customers discovered that the performing musicians were members of 'Borbee's Jass Orchestra.' The record label said that they were."[110] Clearly the shift was cosmetic, nothing more than a change of name.

Tango by another name may dance as sweet, but the process of naming is important. Foreman here has documented an occasion on which jazz swallowed up tango(-maxixe)—one small episode in the larger process through which jazz served as patronym, subsuming a vast, transnational musical phenomenon. It was not that jazz was *better* than tango or other Afro-diasporic musics from the Americas and elsewhere, as some music historians sometimes suggest in noting survivals of one form over another. It is that African American music's national affiliation enthroned it above the other forms that had thrown themselves unstintingly into the cauldron of mutual innovation. Jazz's transnationalism, like so many global phenomena, is lumpy—uneven.

In an illustrative example, a Josephine Baker show, probably in the 1930s, absorbed and erased its Brazilian musical content. At the end of the revue, recounted a Paris correspondent for a São Paulo newspaper, "Josephine sings her biggest hit, *Pauvre Noir*. One would never suspect that the song, which in the program and on records lists André Hornez (lyrics) and Barroco (music), is a version of *Terra seca*. Everyone leaves the theatre without knowing that it is a Brazilian song, thinking it's a North American spiritual, as the scene in the play suggests. Maybe Ari Barroso himself doesn't even know that he is currently the composer of the biggest hit in France."[111] Danced by Baker to words by a French lyricist, this piece was hybrid no matter how faithfully it cleaved to Barroso's score. The reporter's point is valid nonetheless: African American culture was so visible and popular that European audiences awarded it ownership of its constituent parts.

The disproportionate naming power African American forms enjoyed during the *tumulte noir* eclipses our view of the fully transnational phenomena of their collective formation. Musicologists have noted that jazz and samba, the two best-known twentieth-century Afro-diasporic forms in the United States and Brazil, emerged together and with much in common—"parallel, simultaneous evolutions," "twin brothers."[112] Parallels and simultaneity, however, imply coincidence. These similarities, instead, are the indices of real relationships. As Eduardo Lis documents, "From the turn of this century, jazz and Brazilian music have influenced *each other*."[113] Lis could as easily have pointed this out about tango or a host of other forms. The intense cross-cultural creativity of this period did not involve jazz borrowing from static forms, and certainly not multiple emergent forms developing chastely in isolation. "We got to know each other very well, you know," Sam Wooding reminded his interviewer about his South American friends.[114]

It is in this sense that maxixe survived: as suggestions about rhythm, harmony, bodily movement, and the like that became part of the palette of possibilities for composers and performers who encountered it. Cultural residues can be disclaimed or ignored, but the contact is, on some level, ineradicable. The run of 1920s pop songs lamenting Brazilian maidens is a perfect record of this; so is RKO Studios' 1933 *Flying Down to Rio*. That movie's maxixe-based "Carioca" (quite a fad in the film's wake) confirms that maxixe had nested deeply in the North American imagination of Brazilian dance.[115] (You, gentle reader, may have heard this song: it is prominently featured in *A Foreign Sound*, the album Brazilian musical superstar Caetano Veloso produced expressly for international distribution in 2004.)[116] Further, in distorted descent from the "Bahiana" played in that film by the African American performer and radio personality Etta Moten Barnett, with white starched skirts and a modest basket of fruit on her head, Carmen Miranda would offer maxixe's legacies to U.S. audiences in the 1940s. As part of the traditions feeding samba, maxixe would echo in the United States during the Miranda-inspired samba vogue, again in the form of boogie woogie, in bossa nova, and surely in countless other musical and dance formations.

In this light, we can reconsider maxixe's erasure and why it matters that the traditions it helped shape do not bear its name. In welcoming Duque and maxixe for fun and profit, North American audiences and performers enriched the palate of cultural elements they used in their negotiations of the social categories that structured their everyday lives. Some, by homogenizing and shuffling musical and dance affiliations with Brazil, Argentina, Europe, and Africa, anchored themselves in an imperial "America." Others drew on maxixe and other Afro-diasporic threads to weave the musical tapestries essential to African American culture and its perception and reception. Their engagement with the form helped carve out collaborative spaces that fed the communal imagination of diasporic commonality and worked in some ways to undermine racism, but the complex vectors structuring Afro-diasporic cultural production in this period—the splintering, shattering intersections of hierarchies among and within nations—mean that African American and Afro-Brazilian popular forms emerged together neither coincidentally nor in jolly cooperation, but in a contested conversation structured by the uneven power relationships between and among various social groups in many countries. Maxixe, tango, samba, and kindred forms are multiply compromised: erased by racism when aligned with the marginalized Afro-diasporic forms grouped under the rubric of jazz, and by nation when perceived as other than U.S. "American."

Yet perhaps the legacies such erasure plants in a collective cultural subconscious are available to us still. Perhaps they lie latent, ready to help revise assumptions about authorship, merit, and debt and to attune North American attention to the subtleties of our relations with the rest of the world.

MAXIXE AND MAXIXEIROS, those generative conduits of Afro-diasporic culture, forged routes that would be traveled by others as maxixe begat jazz and cakewalk flowed seamlessly into samba. Well after the arc of maxixe's fame abroad, for example, Duque still danced and traveled in the grooves maxixe (and he himself) had worn. In 1922, Duque and Gaby danced at the Assírio, a club in the basement of Rio's Municipal Theater, before returning again to Paris, where Duque's dance studio prospered. The band playing for Duque and Gaby at the Assírio was led by a flutist known as Pixinguinha.[117] Pixinguinha already inhabited a world—postwar Rio de Janeiro—marbled through with the eddies of transnational currents, but meeting Duque sparked another round of global cultural exchange, sending Pixinguinha himself into transatlantic motion. That exchange provides the next installment in this story of transnational construction of local definitions of race and nation in the United States and Brazil. In it, we will meet popular and marginal cultural producers in Rio de Janeiro, linked to local elites such as Duque, as well as to elite and popular elements of far-away places and powerful nations. Not only were they linked already in both material and more abstract ways, but they knew it, and knew how to use it, working to extend those lines and to make both links and disconnections work for them—not perfectly but certainly as deftly as coffee advertisers or sheet music publishers did. Moving south and away from the previous two chapters' more elite (and) commercial arenas, chapter 3 adds a third example of people engaged in transnational exchange, negotiating the local and global webs in which they moved and were received, and whose cultural work engaged with and altered lived categories of race and nation.

CHAPTER THREE

Playing Politics
Making the Meanings of Jazz in Rio de Janeiro

"A Truly Herculean Musical Labor"

In 1928, a reporter for the Afro-Brazilian newspaper *O Clarim d'Alvorada* lauded Afro-descended musicians in Paris "in orchestras and jazz-bands" performing "a veritable Herculean musical labor."[1] Like many of his contemporaries among the readers and producers of São Paulo's small but thriving black press, the writer of these words thrilled over the opportunities for cultural expression, political struggle, and personal advancement he saw in the "Negro vogue" abroad. Was this observer unusually far-sighted, or did other Brazilians also come into contact with this distant cultural phenomenon? In particular, did Brazilians of modest means who could not afford to travel encounter the *tumulte noir*? If so, what did they make of it, in both senses of the question: what did they think, and how did they put it to work? How did this "Herculean" labor in the City of Light echo across the Atlantic to Brazil?

Our guide to these questions will be the flutist, saxophonist, bandleader, composer, and multidimensional musical legend Alfredo da Rocha Viana Filho, nicknamed "Pixinguinha." Pixinguinha is an enormously important figure in Brazilian cultural history, author of some of the most gorgeous, enduring compositions and leader of some of the most beloved bands in living memory. This star in the firmament of Brazilian popular music illuminated a range of popular musical spaces beginning in the 1910s and lasting, if in diminished capacity, until his death in 1973. Thanks in part to meeting Duque, in 1922 Pixinguinha would travel to Paris, where he would learn, teach, change, and return to a long life of performance and collaborative innovation. His European travels and his talents make Pixinguinha exceptional, but his experience is illustrative of the social and cultural landscape he shared with fellow residents of Rio de Janeiro in the twenties. That landscape, with Pixinguinha's guidance, reveals aspects of transnational exchange that scholarly and other critical observers have yet to assimilate fully.

Pixinguinha's life and music show that the Carioca (Rio de Janeiro) popular musical scene after the First World War was already profoundly transnational, as it had been for some time. After a brief scene setting to place Rio in its context as one of the 1920s' many scintillatingly cosmopolitan cities, this chapter's first section explores some of the details of Rio's cultural ferment in the 1910s and early 1920s. It confirms that even poor Cariocas did not have to wait for late-twentieth-century "globalization," regardless of their location on the "periphery," to move through global currents. The music they created was in constant conversation across genre, regional and national borders, urban-rural distinctions, and metropole-periphery divides: unmistakably hybrid. The recognition of its hybridity is rare in Brazilian musicology, restricted by the nationalist yearnings of the field. Admiring the still-justified protest animating that nationalism, the chapter heeds its critique of global power differentials but replaces its insistence on purity with analysis of the unevenness of cultural hybridity. Precluding any simple celebration of hybrid forms, this unevenness saturates the historical record, leaving gaps that complicate the tracking of cross-border travels and their consequences. Such lacunae index the disavowals that mark the mutually productive meetings of unequal groups of people such as elite and marginal Cariocas, or Brazilians and foreigners. Like the erasure of metropolitan debts to colonized peripheries (examined in chapter 2), the refusal to recognize the webs of relationships that constitute culture sustains the fiction of bounded and separate cultural categories: "high" and "low," "native" and "foreign," and so on. Charting a few of those meetings, the first section ends with the marvelous savvy of Carioca popular performers, highly aware of the transnational and cross-class circuits their work traversed, nimbly mocking elite Brazilians and Europeans who refused to recognize their debts.

The second section of this chapter departs from the observation that music has lent itself perfectly to the production of "racial democracy," the notion that the Brazilian nation and people do not discriminate by race. This very old idea shifted valence in the first half of the twentieth century as elite Brazilians came to celebrate and proclaim their "tolerance" rather than bemoan the supposedly higher degree of racial mixture this quality had bequeathed them. It is no accident that popular music has offered the grounds for such assertions of racial harmony. The visibility and popularity of Afro-diasporic popular musics during the jazz age or *tumulte noir*, underlined willfully, skillfully, and ceaselessly by popular performers, made it much more difficult for elite Brazilians to deny that the cultural forms delighting the world's paragons of civilization, taste, modernity, and industry were black, though just what "black" meant was often unclear. The ideology of racial democracy today undergirds a reactionary politics. To project back from the present, however, is to fail to understand its emergence as a hard-fought compromise. The history of the idea of racial democracy demonstrates not false consciousness or racial "illiteracy" on the part of non-elites but deft ideological negotiation, transnationally inflected and in cultural realms. That recognition suggests not that the idea of racial democracy should be revered or resurrected but that the popular cultural grapplings behind its production require full contextualizations in order to be seen.

Little Africas, Big Cities: Rio in Context

Although observers at the time and in retrospect tout Pixinguinha's 1922 trip to Paris as an astonishing departure for him and for Brazil in general, Pixinguinha was involved in transnational musical exchange before he ever left his country of origin. By the time he met Duque at the Assírio, Pixinguinha had already established a wide reputation as a flutist and bandleader versant in the several and heterogeneous, already irrevocably miscegenated transnational musical idioms of Carioca popular culture. These overlapping contexts began, for Pixinguinha, in his parents' home.

Pixinguinha grew up in a household of musicians in Catumbi, a Rio de Janeiro neighborhood "that churned with a variety of black-originated musical manifestations," full of migrants from the heavily Afro-Brazilian northeast and southeast.[2] Catumbi was not unique; much of Rio was in great flux at the time. Slavery's abolition and the draw of cities set so many people in motion within Brazil that internal migrants made up more than a third of Rio's population in the census years of 1890 and 1906. In addition, Brazil received three million immigrants from abroad, mostly European, though also significantly Asian, especially Japanese, between 1884 and 1920. Legislators feared labor radicalism and racial degeneration and so encouraged the influx unevenly and with ambivalence (efforts to restrict black and Asian immigrants are discussed in chapter 5). While more immigrants went to São Paulo than any other Brazilian city, Rio's coffee prosperity drew its share, particularly of Portuguese (Italians preferred São Paulo). Migrants and immigrants tripled Rio's population between 1872 and 1906, often outnumbering native Cariocas.[3]

Recent and longtime Cariocas had no easy time in their new urban enclaves, particularly "little Africas" such as Catumbi. The federal and municipal governments were implementing ambitious modernization policies, including disease eradication, urban infrastructural renovation, and port construction. For the most part these reforms only worsened conditions for the urban poor, as they destroyed existing housing and offered nothing in exchange. Aiming to stay near likely workplaces, poor Cariocas crowded into decaying old mansions, the tenements emerging at the time, or in the hills, where the first favelas appeared in the late 1890s. Employment options remained largely confined to domestic labor, artisanal production and vending, dock work, and factory work in Rio's secondary industrial sector. Social conditions had not democratized significantly with the end of the monarchy in 1889 and the establishment of republican government. In fact, political violence rose and the traditional oligarchy grew stronger, not weaker, in the First Republic. Voting, for example, which the 1891 constitution expanded by dispensing with income requirements, still required literacy, functionally restricting formal political participation to less than one-quarter of the eligible (male) population. Revolts and rebellions were far more common modes of non-elite political elocution, and they were brutally repressed. The violence of poverty, exacerbated by endemic racism, shaped social life profoundly.[4]

Pixinguinha's Catumbi, though harshly marked by these inequities, was neither internally homogenous nor separated cleanly from the rest of the city, including its more affluent parts. A cross-class sociality pervaded Rio's leisure space, not only in the city's bohemian and central districts. At informal concerts at the Pensão Viana (Viana Inn), as Pixinguinha's parents' hospitable home was affectionately nicknamed, were members of Rio's lettered elite, including then president of the Brazilian Academy of Letters, Afonso Arinos; the statesman Rui Barbosa; and erudite composer Heitor Villa-Lobos—also all in attendance at the more affluent venues in which Pixinguinha would soon set up his band.[5] Rio's tiny elite and enormous lower class interacted across a political-economic abyss, but interact they did.

In 1919, Pixinguinha's carnival performances prompted the manager of the Palais cinema to ask the young flutist to pull together eight performers from his carnival band to entertain moviegoers in the cinema's chic lobby. The group called itself the "Oito Batutas," meaning eight batons (the kind conductors use) or aces (as in pros, or crack players).[6] The punning name bragged of both excellence and autonomy—not only were all great, but all also personified the maestro's tools; any could lead. This suggestion of disruption to the conventional hierarchy of composer, conductor, and orchestra points to the pleasure the musicians and audiences of the day found in autonomy, improvisation, and innovation.

The Batutas' self-aware formation at a cinema—that epitome of post-war, Hollywood-oriented, urban mass culture—begins to suggest the musicians' agile negotiation of Rio's already transnational entertainment industry.[7] Their repertoire, to please Cariocas' complex, eclectic tastes, included not only the innovations of urban mass culture abroad, but also the full range of local favorites of Brazilian "national" genres. Fans flocked to the Oito Batutas' renditions of *choro* and maxixe, the folkloric "country" *música sertaneja*, pop hits from each carnival season, and "European" styles as favored in the city's cinemas and salons.

Nor were the Batutas solely urban. In 1919, 1921, and 1922, the band visited various Brazilian states on tours underwritten by wealthy nationalist Brazilian music lovers who charged them with the task of identifying and transcribing regional musics. These patrons of the folkloric arts shared the belief at the core of formal Brazilian Modernism and widely shared beyond it that folk culture would found national art as well as national unity.[8] Essentially research trips, these tours required the Batutas to pay very close attention to the diverse genres then played throughout Brazil.[9] Along with the rural forms they sought out, the performers on these tours also encountered, in Brazil's larger cities, the trendy cosmopolitanisms just then coming to call themselves "jazz."

While 1920 may not have been the first year jazz was played and danced in Brazil, the twenties were unquestionably the decade in which jazz caught fire.[10] What jazz meant was as unclear in Brazil as elsewhere.[11] What it was not, clearly, was foreign music played by foreigners. Some of the music called "jazz" was an identifiable genre already in vogue (marches, choros, maxixes, etc.), played with an expanded percussion section. A music magazine complained in 1924 that there was "barely a single little cinema or café-concert band that doesn't call itself, Americanly, jazz-band, simply because it boasts two or three percussion instruments."[12] Other performers "jazzed up" familiar forms more thoroughly. The "triumphant carnival marches" of popular composer Freitinhas (a.k.a. José Francisco de Freitas), "dressed themselves up on records in an entirely Americanized way" so that they all "sounded like authentic Charlestons."[13] Some jazz numbers were renditions of pieces musicians had heard on records, picked up from traveling performers, or gleaned from sheet music. Printed scores for the black bottom, cakewalk, Charleston, one-step, ragtime, and shimmy were all readily available to Brazilian consumers. Record titles reveal that groups that called themselves "jazz-bands" played all genres of music and that plenty of bands with pointedly Brazilian names played jazz.[14]

This intercalation can be difficult to discern through the fog of insistence on Brazilian music's purity or authenticity—the tendency in Latin American musicology Gérard Béhague describes as "the search for 'pure' retention of a given musical trait believed to be attributable without any doubt to a specific primal cultural root."[15] Compounding the confusion is many music researchers' empiricism, which posits social bases for cultural superstructure so that every genre must correspond to a specific social formation.[16] These commitments have suffused the literature with complaints about music "suffering" encounters with foreign genres, "victim" to (North) Americanization, or the suggestion that after such encounters, music could return to its previous pristine state.[17] Such nationalist blinders occlude the fertile eclecticism of the early samba greats, for many of the future pivots of Brazilian musical nationalism cut their teeth on jazz. Pixinguinha and the Oito Batutas played jazz, including Donga,[18] the musician who some claim wrote the first samba, and Batutas percussionist J. Tomás, who formed and directed a group in Rio in 1923 named "Brazilian Jazz." In 1924, Bahian cornetist José Rodrigues led another group, "American Jazz." Ari Barroso, author of the world-famous 1939 samba "Aquarela do Brasil," joined both. Barroso "transformed himself into a jazz-pianist" and supported himself in this way throughout the twenties. Later, chastened by nationalist music critics and wise to who buttered his bread, he would confess having allowed himself to become a "victim of Americanization" and be redeemed.[19] Even "rural," regional music emerged from this ferment, such as the "Turunas Pernambucanos," a group sparked by the Batutas' trip to Recife in 1922, which featured a saxophonist.[20] Brazilian popular musicians played jazz enthusiastically in the twenties, repudiating it, like a romance, after a long engagement.

Much of this musicological nationalism reflects the strong tradition of journalist-historians of early-twentieth-century Brazilian music history (Jota Efegê, Almirante, Ary Vasconcelos, José Ramos Tinhorão, Sérgio Cabral, etc.), and to a certain extent, as José Geraldo Vinci de Moraes points out, their linear model of successive schools and styles still dominates.[21] Yet there is also by now a robust and growing body of music history that beautifully portrays the subtle hybridities of place, space, and genre.[22] This work is faithful in spirit to the anti-imperialist political impetus behind nationalist musicology, for it corrects nationalist musicology's troublesome imputation of integrity to "foreign" music. As noted in chapter 2, jazz too was transnational at its very inception, developed in numerous little Africas in big, cosmopolitan cities swept by global wartime and postwar currents. People at the time and since have certainly perceived jazz as "American," but that reflects global inequities in the music industry and elsewhere, as well as corresponding privileges of naming. In reinforcing the U.S. "Americanness" of jazz, musicology that defends national boundaries for genre defeats its own intent.

What is critical as this field continues to grow is a vise grip on the violent imbalances of transnational and cross-class cultural exchange. Without it, scholars risk lapsing into quiescent celebrations of hybridity or, worse, missing the routes through which the genres belonging to the "Negro vogue" traveled to and from Brazil. Grasping this unevenness means understanding a pair of its structuring paradoxes. The first is that the institutions most likely to spark and facilitate exchange were the least likely to record it. Even more distractingly in many cases, the clearest paths of cultural exchange were those forged by agents also most invested in actively erasing their syncretic pasts. The music industry is a prime example. In the wake of the U.S.-Brazilian commerce in Brazilian coffee and U.S. manufactures that boomed after the First World War (detailed in chapter 1), sheet music publishers and recording companies — Tin Pan Alley and U.S. record producers — established foreign subsidiaries in Brazil. They rarely took South American forms north, and one might note that inequity and then simply stop at the recognition of cultural forms traveling south. That would certainly be the stopping point for music industry executives, since selling music requires the preservation of concepts such as "originality" and the boundaries of genre. Yet this commerce nonetheless clinched genuine exchange in that it followed and paved ways north and south for independent traveling performers in vaudeville, minstrelsy, dance music, theater revue, and the like.[23] Understanding the stakes and structures that conceal such exchange allows one to trust that such movement took place regardless of whether its traces reveal themselves to the retrospective eye.

Postwar inter-American commerce greased the wheels of inter-American and Afro-diasporic exchange in clearly evident as well as murky ways. Early passenger steamship travel between Rio de Janeiro and New York illustrates such assistance, as well as the ways commerce erased even as it enabled cultural exchange. In 1921, the Munson Steamship Line premiered a Rio–New York route. On the inaugural voyage of its flagship, the *American Legion*, Brazilian bandleader Romeu Silva and his "Orquestra Sul-Americana-Brasileira" were aboard to perform.[24] Reports of the trip spotlight the silences and disparities set deeply in the historical record: while several Brazilian historians report that Silva's band entertained the ship's lucky passengers, U.S. researchers do not notice, and the *New York Times* report of the *American Legion*'s inaugural voyage featured only its record time.[25] If Silva's band played on dry land in New York, that event also did not leave a trace. It seems reasonable to expect that Silva played in New York at some point, since he remained there long enough to absorb quite a bit of the jazz scene. Back in Rio, Silva adapted jazz instrumentation and techniques and renamed his group the "Jazz-Band Sul-Americana." He even began to play tenor saxophone himself (badly, remembered composer Ari Barroso, who played with him in the twenties).[26] The 1921 sea voyage was the first of many trips abroad for Silva, who would represent Brazil officially in various capacities and on European stages through the 1940s (as we will see briefly below). Silva's early travels were banked by the Munson Line and a metropolitan imaginary of delicious tropical vacations, neither of which much noticed *him*. Later, when his sponsors included the Brazilian state, he would leave a somewhat deeper impression.

The second paradox structuring Afro-American cultural exchange is that much of it took place outside the Americas. Metropolitan centers mediated exchange between their citizens and visitors, of course, but also among people from colonized or peripheral places. Some places did so lubriciously, Paris being a case in point. The intensity of the Negro vogue in

Paris and the infrastructure it developed to host arts high and low made the French capital a key meeting ground for Brazilian and U.S. musicians, also sparking exchanges elsewhere. Performers who succeeded in Paris often set out from there on extended performance tours of other parts of Europe or points south and transatlantic. Parisian tendrils extended far beyond the people who traveled there themselves.

This geographic unevenness is multifaceted, stamped by relations among different peripheral locations, as well as between metropole and periphery. Here the Rio de la Plata serves as illustration. Like Paris, and much more than other South American capitals, Buenos Aires hosted inter-American encounters. This is both a material question of the Argentine capital's relatively better-developed musical infrastructure in the 1920s and a question of sources—of the ways jazz's uneven transnationalism is inscribed in the historical record. For some of the same reasons that tango eclipsed maxixe in classification and musical memory, Brazilian cities figure even less in jazz history than does Argentina's main urban center. Considering Brazil and Argentina in comparison rather than understanding their interconnections erases the mediation Buenos Aires, like Paris, provided. In Argentina's port capital, traveling Brazilians, North Americans, and other foreigners could take in one another's sights and sounds, whether or not they went on to travel in the United States or Brazil.

Pianist Elliot Carpenter, for example, heard Brazilian music in Buenos Aires when he went there to perform in 1935.[27] While Carpenter appears not to have taken the next step, many performers found Buenos Aires a fine launching point from which to embark upon tours of Brazil and other South American countries.[28] The "colored" North American violinist and bandleader Don Abbey traveled through Argentina to play Rio's chic Assírio in 1922.[29] Five years later, Sam Wooding and his orchestra played in Argentina for six months, afterward passing through Brazil in transit.[30] From Argentina also came the North American bandleader Harry Kosarin, "a sensation, in those years, in the Rio music scene," who also acted as a representative of U.S. music publishers until they fired him in the mid-1930s.[31] When Kosarin came to Brazil, he brought violinist Raul Lipoff and banjoist Eugene Pingatore, brother to Mike Pingatore, the banjo player for Paul Whiteman's band.[32] Pingatore went back to the United States after a few months, but Lipoff stayed and organized his own band, incorporating, along with Brazilian musicians, the members of a chamber orchestra just in to Rio from Egypt.[33] As this wrinkle usefully underlines,

the inter-peripheral unevenness of Afro-diasporic musical exchange includes connections to contemporary Africans, innovating alongside and
in dialogue with their diasporic peers.[34] Inter-peripheral or "south-south"
encounters are the hardest to trace—a situation that justifies greater historical attention to them, not less.

Traveling alongside trade and cultural commerce, via Paris and other
North Atlantic metropolitan cultural centers, through cosmopolitan
peripheral cities such as Buenos Aires, jazz-age popular culture met and
moved Brazilian performers and audiences and set out again on new jour-
neys. In the hybrid musical scene in which Pixinguinha and the Oito Batutas developed, jazz was only one aspect of a panorama whose complexities
were far more than geographic. The multiple contexts of the musicians'
development—little Africa, Rio de Janeiro, urban and rural areas throughout Brazil—brought together people from diverse class, cultural, and regional locations, as well as from far-flung nations. Like Paris, New Orleans,
Buenos Aires, and many others, Rio de Janeiro in the postwar period was a
deeply cosmopolitan city, etched by broad, unequal exchanges of people,
goods, capital, ideas, and cultural forms.

Aces Abroad and the Reverb in Rio

Formed in this milieu, the Batutas were both purposefully national and
thoroughly transnational when they happened across the greatest maxixeiro of their day. Meeting Duque at the Assírio in Rio in 1922 ensured
that the Batutas would continue to be highly active and mindful agents
of cross-class, interracial, transnational cultural exchange. Examining the
texture of that exchange, this section reveals the productive rather than
absorptive nature of such encounters for all involved, as well as popular
performers' roles in sparking further exchange.

Adroitly reading both the Parisian hunger for primitivisms and Brazilian fantasies of national folkloric superiority, Duque decided that the Batutas belonged in Paris. He approached the Brazilian millionaire Arnaldo
Guinle, both a Francophile and a Brazilian nationalist, a frequent traveler
to Paris, and, unsurprisingly, a great fan of Duque. Duque asked Guinle
to finance a Paris trip for the Batutas. Already well acquainted with the
group (he had heard them at the Palais, occasionally had them over to his
apartment to play for parties, and financed their 1919–21 research and performance tour around Brazil), Guinle agreed.[35]

The Batutas spent six months in Paris, February to July 1922. Pixinguinha, fellow Afro-Brazilians Donga, China (Pixinguinha's brother), and
Nélson Alves, and three others who did not identify as Afro-descended —
Sizenando Santos ("Feniano"), José Monteiro, and either José Alves or
Luis de Oliveira (the record is unclear which of the two went to Paris) —
played at the Scheherazade, the "traditional Faubourg *dancing* [club],"
where Duque had assumed artistic direction. They then moved to Chez
Duque and then to an open-air venue also opened by Duque, La Reserve
de Saint Cloud, where they played alongside "Bernard Kay's American
Jazz-Band." They played at a large party at the "Palais des Affaires Publics"
[*sic*] and another one in the boxer Jack Dempsey's house, delighting international Parisian audiences.³⁶

In Paris, the Batutas encountered the *tumulte noir* in full swing. They
well understood the war's role in kicking the jazz age into high gear. "It
was the post-war," Donga recalled, "and the Americans had made [Paris]
their general [military] headquarters. To keep up the morale of those
mutilated in the war, they sowed American music, via four orchestras
paid by the government of the United States."³⁷ Without taking Donga's
count too literally, we can still appreciate his experience of the environment he encountered, enriched by the congregation with musicians from
the African diaspora — including, although none of the Brazilian sources
comment, French colonial subjects. A Paris telegram reported that at the
Batutas' debut, the Sheherazade was "full of people of all social classes, the
presence of many members of the colony being particularly notable."³⁸

Nor did the Batutas simply listen. They jammed, Batutas violinist Nélson Alves remembered: "There was such camaraderie among the musicians of the two nationalities, from this other continent, that sometimes
the North Americans accompanied the Brazilian instrumentalists with
their extravagant, devilishly enchanted 'battery' [percussion section]."³⁹
Sam Wooding's band in Argentina had similar experiences, remembered
reed player Garvin Bushell. "I had a ball in Buenos Aires. I loved it, and
especially playing beside the great tango orchestras and they're trying to
play jazz and we were playing tango."⁴⁰ This is the pedagogic and com-
municative process at the heart of cultural exchange, Afro-diasporic or
other.

Even when the Batutas played alone in Paris, they would have been
challenged creatively — by dancers. In the Afro-diasporic tradition of participatory performance, jazz dance itself moved musicians to innovate, as
"often music was created by the interchange between a group of dancers

and singers." Jazz performers, Kathy Ogren explains, "had to 'make up their own musical variations to fit the dancing.'" Jazz dance in Paris would have been "a central feature of participatory music creation" for the Batutas, just as it was for U.S. musicians.[41]

Their Parisian experiences sparked the Batutas' creativity. Pixinguinha, for example, composed a song, a rollicking *maxixe rebolado*, to which Duque wrote the lyrics in French: "We are the Batutas, come from Brazil . . . to make everybody dance the samba. . . . The music is simple, but very rhythmic. We are sure it will please you."[42] The song offers a trio of insights. First, labeled a maxixe but calling dancers to samba to its beat, it shows the distinction between the two genres in this period to have been of little concern to their performers. Second, the lyrics show the performers' belief that dancing was indispensable to their music and its pleasures. Relatedly, the song's self-description reveals Pixinguinha's and Duque's understanding that audiences would be amenable to music they thought was primarily rhythmic.[43] Finally, this piece shows Brazilian performers working assiduously to convince listeners of the unique and wonderful qualities of their "authentic" national cultural forms—work that paradoxically also ensured those forms' continued evolution.

The Batutas innovated and developed in response to their Parisian conversations. Among the group's more visible changes were shifts in instrumentation. In Paris Guinle gave Pixinguinha a saxophone, which he took up upon his return to Rio with skill and gusto and played for the rest of his career. "Also almost all [the Batutas] changed their instruments," remembered Pixinguinha. "They made violin-banjo, *cavaquinho*-banjo, etc. That was Paris's influence." Their repertoire shifted as well, incorporating an array of jazzy titles, rhythms, and melodies.[44]

The Batutas' evolution and their spark to further cultural exchange continued well after their return to Rio. In 1923, three of the Batutas split off to form the "Oito Cotubas," a group that leaned heavily on fox-trots, balancing out the other half of their programs with waltzes, polkas, tangos, sambas, and música sertaneja. Later in the decade, several Batutas would join jazz bands in Rio and stay with them for years, some traveling back to Europe with them. Still in 1923, the Batutas incorporated "[North] American–style percussion" and billed themselves as the "Bi-Orquestra Os Batutas," announcing their composite choro- and jazz-playing character. The Bi-Orquestra Os Batutas debuted at a Teatro Lírico gala in August 1923 that boasted "the participation of hundreds of Brazilian, French, and North American artists," including the French actress Mistinguette. Around late 1923, the Batutas began to be known as a *"jazz-band sertanejo,"* a term that is almost an oxymoron in its juxtaposition of the extreme urban modern and the rustic rural and nearly paradoxical in emphasizing the foreign and the pastoral for a group rapidly becoming famous as a symbol of Brazil and of urban Rio de Janeiro.[45]

The Batutas' rising star was boosted by their Parisian success, thanks to Brazilians' confidence in French taste. Their new-found prestige won them gigs galore back home, including two particularly fertile spaces of transnational encounter and continued cultural innovation. One was Rio de Janeiro's elaborate Centennial Exposition, under way when the Batutas returned. The Batutas treated exposition audiences, including crowds full of North American tourists at the General Motors Pavilion and the U.S. Embassy, to a heterodox repertoire that included African American and other U.S. genres (Charleston, one-step, two-step, fox-trot, etc.). There were other jazz performers there who probably both heard and entertained the Batutas.[46] In the audiences, besides numerous North Americans at the Expo to enjoy or profit from the festivities, there were Brazilians of all stations, including Villa-Lobos, who would himself soon become a Paris habitué.[47]

The other highly fertile contact the Batutas enjoyed upon their return to Brazil involved impresario Madame Rasimi's famous Paris revue troupe, Ba-ta-clan. The show was in the middle of its Rio run when the Batutas arrived on the scene, and Madame Rasimi hired the band to "play the repertoire that had exploded in Paris the previous month."[48]

Ba-ta-clan itself was a powerful engine of cultural exchange. The troupe's most noted feature was its bevy of dancing lovelies, led by the superstar Mistinguette, in 1922 already a veteran of U.S. as well as European stages.[49] The show toured widely, and during its tours, Madame Rasimi hired local artists, took them with her, dropped them in a new place and hired others, and generally sowed fertile musical turmoil wherever she went. Brazilian jazz aficionado Jorge Guinle documents this dynamic from Ba-ta-clan's first Brazilian appearance: "When, in 1922, Mistinguette and her company Ba-Ta-Clan came to Rio to play the Teatro Lírico, she brought with her an orchestra of American negroes (*"negros americanos"*) whose leader was the percussionist Gordon Straight; with John Forester, trombone, Paul, clarinet, and a trumpet[er] who was later substituted by the Brazilian musician Acioly. This orchestra stayed and played the Assirio"—the theater in which Pixinguinha had met Duque.[50] Straight and his band had probably been playing in Paris when Madame Rasimi hired them—might the Batutas have encountered them there? In any case, in Ba-ta-clan, the Batutas played "alongside French, North American, and Brazilian artists," though it is not clear whether those North American artists included Gordon Straight's band or whether the Batutas replaced it.[51] Whether or not they ever shared a stage, the two groups would have had opportunities to hear each other in the remaining weeks of the company's run.

By bringing Straight and his band to Rio, Ba-ta-clan had planted a productive seed, for those musicians sparked a little transculturation of their own. Trumpet and trombone player John Forester, who had gone to Europe with Will Marion Cook's Southern Syncopated Orchestra in 1919, joined a Brazilian band led by a musician named Andreosi.[52] This group, "already playing 'yankee' music," later traveled to Paris and stayed for over ten years, claimed Guinle. By "yankee" music, Guinle probably meant jazz, although this group's very constitution shows how thoroughly international jazz was by this point. In addition to the North American Forester, Andreosi took along Chamek, the pianist in a group that had just arrived from Egypt, and "Gabriel, cornet; José Arias, alto saxophone; Nelson Roriz, tenor saxophone; Arruda, percussion, and José Andreozzy, banjo," an instrumentation revealing both jazzy interest and experience.[53]

Gordon Straight seems to have stayed in Rio for some time. In 1923 the Rio daily *A Patria* interviewed an authority on jazz it called "Sr. Stretton," who praised jazz in the language of modernity and industry: "Fine fruit of our era of movement, of speed, of dizzying hallucinations."[54] Stretton apparently needed neither introduction nor a first name to identify him to the paper's readers, but the editors did print his photograph, showing, to contemporary eyes, a carefully groomed, light-skinned person of some African descent. The name "Stretton" read by a Portuguese-speaking Brazilian would have come much closer to an English speaker's rendering of "Straight" than "Straight" itself, which would have tongue-tied Brazilians who read its bewildering mess of consonants. That Straight and "Stretton" were indeed the same person appears confirmed by José Ramos Tinhorão's mention of "Gordon Streton," a North American bandleader and percussionist who went to Buenos Aires in 1928 with Brazilian saxophonist Luís Americano, stayed there until 1930, and then returned to Brazil to form a jazz orchestra.[55] To bring this tale full circle, in 1940 Luís Americano played in the band that recorded on board the *Uruguay* for the Good Neighbor visit of North American maestro Leopold Stokowski with—none other—Pixinguinha.⁵⁶

Did Straight/Stret(t)on return with Luís Americano to play with Pixinguinha on the good ship *Uruguay*? Tinhorão doesn't say. If he had, would it have been their second joint gig? Again, unclear. What is apparent is that Straight/Stret(t)on enjoyed years of collaboration with musicians in Brazil and at least one other South American country and that the Batutas continued to feed and feed off the transnational medley of Rio de Janeiro's music scene.

After dropping Forester and Straight/Stret(t)on into Rio's melodious melting pot, Ba-ta-clan continued to mix it up. One contemporary critic remembered that the French revue's 1924 run in Rio included African American performers Will Marion Cook and Louis Douglas.⁵⁷ Cook was one of the foremost theatrical composers of his day and a person with wide European and American experience and influence: he had studied violin in Berlin as a young man and composition with Anton Dvorák in 1895 in the United States, collaborated with Paul Lawrence Dunbar in 1898, and mentored numerous younger performers, including Duke Ellington. His orchestra, featuring such luminaries as Sidney Bechet and Arthur Briggs, became a force "instrumental in creating the vogue for black musicians in England and all over Europe."⁵⁸ Douglas, a bandleader, dancer, choreographer, and co-director of *La revue nègre* (1925), worked in New York, Paris, London, Berlin, other European locations, and Egypt, joining forces with Cook in England (in several ways—Douglas also married Cook's daughter).⁵⁹ If Cook and Douglas did indeed come to Brazil, the elements in their musical palate and their reach would have been notably wider than "England and all over Europe."⁶⁰

Whether or not Cook and Douglas performed in Brazil, their accomplishments were clearly interesting to Afro-Brazilian theater enthusiasts, who took up their suggestions dynamically. When Brazil's first all-black theater revue troupe was founded in 1926 by an Afro-Brazilian veteran of Parisian stages, it explicitly cited Douglas's example.⁶¹ That troupe, the Companhia Negra de Revistas, and its debut play, *Tudo preto* (All Black), marked a transnational, Afro-diasporic milestone in Carioca and Brazilian national culture.⁶² *Tudo preto* placed itself explicitly in the tradition of Parisian Negro revues, overflowing with references to Paris and manifestations of black culture there, as this chapter will explore when it turns to black performers' invocations of the *tumulte noir*. For now I want princi-

pally to note *Tudo preto*'s relation to both the Batutas and Ba-ta-clan, cementing its position in the chain of cultural exchange powered by Afro-
Brazilians' embrace of Parisian cultural conditions.

Tudo preto relied on several members of the Batutas, including Pixinguinha, who conducted the orchestra. Pixinguinha dubbed *Tudo preto* "the
black Ba-ta-clan"; the newspapers loved the nickname and ran it for weeks.
During *Tudo preto*'s opening run, Ba-ta-clan was again in Rio, performing *C'est Paris*.[63] Did the casts of each have a chance to take in the other?
The *Jornal do Brasil* reported that one actress, a Miss "Moons Murray,"
was North American.[64] The musicians accompanying both certainly knew
each other: Ba-ta-clan engaged the "Carlitos Jazz-Band," a local ensemble
headed up by "Carlitos" (nickname of the drummer Carlos Blassifera) and
including Donga, the former Batuta, working with Ba-ta-clan for at least
the second time. Its composer was Sebastião Cirino, flush with the recent
success of several compositions, in particular "Cristo nasceu na Bahia"
(Christ was born in Bahia), composed for *Tudo preto*. In another demonstration of the mobility of the *tumulte noir*'s collaborative stages, Ba-ta-
clan took the Carlitos Jazz-Band, "already playing 'yankee' music," back to
Paris with it when it finished its 1926 engagement in Rio. The band stayed
to tour Europe, including Russia (Moscow) and Turkey, and some of the
members struck out on their own; Cirino, for his part, would work abroad
for fourteen years. Carlitos would be back in Paris in time to accompany
Josephine Baker at the 1930 Colonial Exposition.[65]

Josephine Baker interacted with a range of Rio standouts. In 1931 at the
Paris Casino, Baker played with the already widely traveled bandleader
Romeu Silva, whose band was Baker's favorite (reports Tinhorão, hopefully). Silva would stay in Paris and play with a series of North American performers, including Joe Hayman, Johnny Dunn, Jack Mayes, Billy
Burns, Herb Flemming, Booker Pittman, and Alfred Pratt, who would return to Brazil with Silva in 1936. Flemming would come to South America
soon after 1932 and play the Copacabana Palace along with elite venues
in Buenos Aires.[66] Silva may or may not have occupied a favored place
in Baker's estimation, but she was undeniably a great fan of Brazil and
things Brazilian and, as this already shows, a vector of U.S.–Paris–Brazil
cosmopolitanism and cultural exchange in her own right. Baker would
also travel to Brazil several times, first in 1929, probably bringing with
her a theater full of French, North American, and other performers each
time and picking up local talent while there. Probably commenting on

her 1939 trip, Baker's last husband claimed that "Josephine loved South America and profited from her voyage to stock up on music unknown in France—sambas, macumbas. Her forthcoming revue would have a Brazilian theme."[67]

Those Batutas still back in Brazil would also continue to learn, exchange, produce, and perform their authentic, syncretic, local, transnational, Brazilian, Afro-Brazilian, Afro-diasporic music. In 1927, on a tour of southern Brazil, the Batutas played in the city of Florianópolis with the "acrobatic" North American dancers "Delson and Nata." Their repertoire on that tour included examples of several African American genres. When the group returned to Rio, it played at the Odeon cinema with "Greenlec [*sic*] and Drayton," whom music historian Sérgio Cabral describes as North American, noting they were refused lodging at the Hotel Flamengo "*por serem negros*"—on account of race.[68]

Rufus Greenlee and Thaddeus Drayton, dancers from the U.S. South, went to Europe in 1909 and remained at least until 1914, traveled to Russia, and returned to the United States during the war. Their act peaked in the 1920s, and they again toured Russia in 1926, this time with Sam Wooding's band.[69] U.S. observers such as theater scholar Henry Sampson, a prodigious researcher, or clarinetist Garvin Bushell are interested to note the dancers' Russian tours, but they do not mention travels in South America.[70] These omissions highlight a blind spot in the U.S. accounts that probably obscures other North Americans' performances in Brazil as well—perhaps that of Sam Wooding, who passed through Brazil in transit in 1927; perhaps also that of the Savoy Bearcats, one of the first two Savoy house bands, "a straight-ahead dance band that could keep the dancers happy," who "left for a tour of South America" in 1926 or early 1927.[71]

Greenlee and Drayton infused their brilliant acts with the lessons of their travels abroad, as the next chapter relates. The Brazilian elements in their crucible are not easily identifiable—no observer remembers Portuguese among the dozen or so languages Greenlee spoke, for example—but Thaddeus Drayton pointed to Brazilian elements in a revealing recollection. "You should have heard an Italian orchestra trying to play our special arrangement of 'The Carioca,'" Drayton bragged years later to a pair of jazz researchers.[72] This wonderful mention of the Carioca, a maxixe-derived dance popularized by the 1933 movie *Flying Down to Rio*, proffers a great tangle: Greenlee and Drayton took a Brazilian dance already transnational in circulation and filtered filmically through elite white North

American *and* African American dancers (Ginger Rogers, Fred Astaire, and Etta Moten Barnett); they added elements derived from their experiences all over the world, including Brazil, and took it back to Europe, pushing musicians there once again to attempt it. Woven into that knot of collaborative cultural production among musicians and dancers on both sides of the Atlantic and the equator are strands from a 1927 tour with the Oito Batutas.

In addition to the North American dancers with whom the Batutas performed, the group had further opportunities to play with U.S. bands. The Swiss-born writer Blaise Cendrars described a Rio nightclub, the Diamond's Club, run by a beautiful (judged Cendrars) blonde North American, Edith de Berensdorff. There a group "animated by a prestigious trumpet, the explosive, indefatigable Wild Bird, from St. Louis," played alongside the Batutas. Thanks to their experiences in Paris, São Paulo, Rio, Florianópolis, and elsewhere, the Batutas were prepared for this encounter, which Cendrars described, enraptured:

> the furious struggle that consumed the two groups of black musicians from similar backgrounds but so different in composition and inspiration, in which each sought to best the other, the contrasting rhythms of a "Black Bottom" following the ceaseless, irresistible, enchanting sway of a "macumba," the erotic, restrained acceleration of the "sambas" and "maxixes," trying to supplant the nervous mechanics of the "one"[-steps], the "two-steps" or the delirium of the syncopated slides of the "blues," like the lascivious lundu, concentrated and charged with the melancholy passion of South American blacks, trying to triumph finally over the eccentric "cakewalk," ending up in a hysteric improvisation, executed by the virtuosic Louisiana blacks, leaving the dancing couples in a state of extreme excitement.[73]

Cendrars's breathless exoticization cannot obscure the ways the musicians, collectively and in cooperation with dancers, blurred the line between competition and collaboration. The tension between collective action and individual innovation, so thrilling to hear and move to, is one of the most remarked-upon common threads of Afro-diasporic tradition.[74] In Rio de Janeiro, this tradition found ready ground. The Diamond's Club and similar spaces hosted a musical banter that turned Rio de Janeiro into a cradle of transnational, collaborative cultural production.

The enthusiasm Cendrars expressed in this passage is consistent with his general adulation of Afro-diasporic and Brazilian folk culture. Many of Cendrars's elite and aristocratic Brazilian friends shared his love of the "low," pointing to a critical aspect of Brazilian cultural hybridity: its transnationalism was also a bridging of class positions within and across Brazil. In this period of elite fascination with "folk" on both sides of the Atlantic, Modernists such as Villa-Lobos, Oswald de Andrade, Tarsila do Amaral, and other Francophilic Brazilian literati and artists befriended equally elite Parisian Brazilophiles, including Cendrars, Darius Milhaud, Jean Cocteau, Paul Morand, and their circles, setting out together in search of the popular in their respective national cultural settings.[75] Cendrars famously asked his Brazilian hosts to show him their urban and rural popular culture, prompting claims that he (singlehandedly!) turned Brazilian elites back to their folkloric roots, toward "the valorization of things black," "deciding the game in favor of revindicationist nationalism."[76]

Accounts of these elite collaborations pass roughshod over non-elite agency. It is true that affluent Euro-Brazilians' focus on the folk layered itself over their preexisting enchantment with all things French. Yet to attribute Modernism, futurism, and other 1920s sections of the Brazilian avant-garde to European inspiration is to miss a significant font. In Paris as well as in Rio de Janeiro, elite musical production in this period depended on popular cultural producers.[77]

Villa-Lobos, for example, owes a great, unrecognized debt to the Batutas. This most famous of Brazilian composers had listened to the Batutas (as well as many other popular performers) for years. He heard them again just after their return from Europe at Rio's 1922 Centennial Exposition.[78] In addition to a yawning musical debt, Villa-Lobos also owes the Batutas the price of his steamer passage to Paris. On the floor of Brazil's Legislative Assembly, the composer's supporters secured government funding for his trip to the French capital by arguing that the presence of this genteel, whiter Brazilian was necessary to counterbalance the image of Brazil the Batutas had projected. Congressman Gilberto Amado told his colleagues in July 1922 that Villa-Lobos in Paris would "show that we are not simply the 'Oito Batutas' who sambaed there" and that denying Villa-Lobos the chance to exhibit his work in France "would be to deny that we think, musically, and is an attitude unworthy of the Brazilian Congress."[79] Amado was convincing; off the composer went. Villa-Lobos's debt to the Batutas points illustratively to the class unevenness in Carioca and Brazilian cultural hybridity.

The specific government action of funding Villa-Lobos's transatlantic foray was sparked by elite anxiety over the prospect of the dark-skinned and the popular representing Brazil in Europe. Brazilian governmental cultural policy, as its historians have chronicled, was in flux in this period, swinging between the Eurocentric promotion of Luso-Catholic, Euro-derived, whiter "high" art and romantic, folklorist nationalism.[80] This flux reflects the work of marginal, popular performers, and although it is not always as clear as in the case of Villa-Lobos's trip, their actions sparked policy decisions that shaped cultural landscapes both in Brazil and wherever Brazilians touched down.

Popular culture provoked and inspired elites in this period, and popular performers knew it. Many non-elite, poor, marginal musicians were ideologically agile and perfectly well aware of their work's appropriation by elites and the dynamics of its erasure. When Donga met Cendrars in Rio, he asked Cendrars to give a message to their mutual friend, the French avant-garde composer Darius Milhaud. Milhaud had become enamored of Brazil during a two-year jaunt in Rio de Janeiro as secretary to the French ambassador in 1917–18, and he had met Donga then. Milhaud incorporated Brazilian popular songs, rhythmic styles, folktales, dance genres, and other references into his compositions.[81] His most famous Brazil-inspired piece, "Le boeuf sur le toit," took the title of the popular song that was its basis, "O boi no telhado" (Bull on the roof). This maxixe, which gained renown via the Paris nightclub named after it a few years later and by Ba-ta-clan's incorporation of it into its famous revue, was written by a member of the Oito Batutas, José Monteiro, under his alias, "Zé Boiadeiro" (Joe Cowboy, roughly).[82] Although Milhaud did recognize his debt to Brazilian popular culture, his high-culture colleagues, critics, and audiences read "Le boeuf" as upgrading quaint folkloric tunes, rather than as citing a recent, urban creation.

The message Donga asked Cendrars to give Milhaud played with the values of high and low, metropole and periphery. Tell Milhaud, Donga joked to Cendrars, that he (Donga) intended to write a samba called "Cow in the Eiffel Tower."[83] Reminding his friends that he too had enjoyed international travels, Donga used humor to call Milhaud on the recontextualization his borrowing had inflicted. If in Rio the song invoked regional variation and urban denizens' own beloved antecedents, in Paris the image of a steer on the roof of a peasant's shack became a smug affirmation of the rural backwardness of all of Brazil. Reaching for a comparably ridiculous scene in Paris, Donga protested the ridicule that the song, circulating without qualifier outside the nation's borders, projected onto Brazil. Donga's *bon mot* also claimed an authorial position, reminding his friends who had written "O boi." Behind a generously humorous façade, Donga demonstrated that a "humble" popular musician could be as clever as his most educated peer.

This episode is equally effective as a retort to scholars today who discount the savvy attention of popular musicians to "high" art. Had he listened to Donga, musicologist Bernard Gendron, for example, could not have called twenties jazz musicians "passive recipients" of avant-garde attention.[84] Self-confident and sophisticated, aware of his contemporaries on several social levels and multiple continents, Donga was as sharp as his music was compelling. Evidence that Donga was not alone in his mindful mixings is as close as the person he married, the Afro-Brazilian soprano Zaíra de Oliveira, a versatile, classically trained artist who mixed the erudite and the popular.[85] No wonder Brazilian elites would find themselves forced to compromise with such figures, fortified by Parisian acclaim for themselves and the fruits of their cultural labors.

Donga and the other popular performers whose travels brought them and their music together linked Brazilian popular culture to Parisian–North American–global trends. The consequences of such a feat are manifold—musical, social, political, intellectual, and more. "Influence" flowed in all directions, and while it would be exciting therefore to trace the impact of Brazilian on North Atlantic music, this chapter is interested instead in people and what they did with the global currents they found and helped enhance in their local worlds. What did people make of their transnational encounters at home and abroad? What sorts of personal-political negotiations did they fuel? Taking up these questions, the next section explores the social meaning people made out of the exchange detailed in the section we now close.

Racial Harmony

Writing on "Music in Brazil" in the early 1930s, Mário de Andrade found the occasion to rehearse the classic origin myth of Brazilian nationality: "The Portuguese did not have the same prejudices and color repulsions against the Africans as the English of North America, and all the ethnographers and travelers have agreed that this was a happy chance for us. Instead of the irreconcilable racial problems which so trouble the United States, here a mixed subtype formed, stronger and more resistant, and already perfectly assimilated to the circumstances of our geography."[86]

It is no accident that Mario de Andrade penned this quintessential racial democracy rhetoric (built on a national comparison to the United States and offered up to foreigners!) in order to talk about Brazilian *music*. As the 1920s progressed, whiter North Atlantic *and* Brazilian elites needed less and less convincing to value Afro-diasporic musical culture—less than they required in order to applaud other Afro-diasporic cultural fields (food, say, or collective work strategies or religious formations), and certainly far less than they needed in order to agree that Afro-diasporic citizens ought to have equal political and economic opportunities. As many observers have pointed out, music was a site for the working out of the idea of racial democracy *as* a Brazilian nationalism, a "patriotic" narrative about country and self.[87] Critics of racial democracy today often understand the concept as a cunning imposition from above. It is hard to think about music and not succumb to this assumption: by the end of the interwar period at the latest, music had become a field for the rote reproduction of the idea of racial democracy in the quiescent, reactionary form it still takes today.[88] Yet in the early decades of the century, the political valence of such discourse was an object of lively, even spectacular struggle. Scholars have begun to recognize and document the popular production of the idea of racial democracy, a line of argument that stands to gain from greater attention to the global currents Afro-Brazilians grasped in propounding such an idea.[89]

Brazilians in Rio de Janeiro struggled mightily in the 1920s over the relationship "Brazil" would hold to Afro-diasporic popular musics and therefore to blackness more generally. Whiter and more elite Cariocas were confronted by the conundrum of this obviously "black" formation adored in the globe's premier centers of culture and civilization, according to their own standards, and equally beloved in their "home" milieux. Popular performers and audiences worked joyfully to force this contradiction to the surface. They launched what were undeniably performances of the African diaspora: insistent gestures to the blackness they shared with the objects of the world's adoration. Activists staked claims to political inclusion on the bases of arguments those musics marshalled to their side: Paris loved them, and so did Rio de Janeiro. Elites attempted a range of responses, settling finally on the rhetoric of racial democracy, the very terms in which the demands were made. Those struggles are telling illustrations of the role of the diaspora and, more specifically, the performance of the idea of that transnational formation in shaping ideologies of nation and race.

Cariocas and other Brazilians made different sense of the vogue for black culture that seeped unremittingly into their everyday. The following section listens to the points made by non-elite performers, journalists, and critics as they magnified and reiterated French and North Atlantic negrophilia; the subsequent and final section of this chapter ends with the dilemma this posed to their more elite, whiter fellow citizens and the resolutions they proffered.

"A Little Advantageous '*Quelque Chose*'"

Producers of popular culture made sure their audiences noticed the status of jazz-age culture abroad, pointedly joining Brazil's long love of France to France's ardent "Negro vogue." Using transnational elements of their local cultural environments, musicians, stage performers, religious leaders, and journalists worked to shift the valence of blackness in popular culture in Brazil, claiming the prestige of Parisian cultural authority and metropolitan modernity for previously devalued cultural forms and performers.

The striking Francophilia of three early Afro-Brazilian theater groups is illustrative in this regard. The Companhia Negra de Revistas, the Troupe Negra de Revistas e Variedades, and the Companhia Mulata Brasileira played the cities of Rio de Janeiro, Itapira (in São Paulo state), and São Paulo in 1926, 1929, and 1930 respectively. The Companhia Negra de Revistas, the first to appear and best studied, was full of performers mindful of the nexus of possibility at the juncture of black culture's fame abroad and Parisian cachet at home. Pixinguinha's nickname for the troupe, "the black Ba-ta-clan," was only the beginning.

The Companhia Negra was founded by the Afro-Brazilian impresario De Chocolat, a veteran of Parisian stages (he had been in Paris in 1919). De Chocolat's stage name demonstrated his sharp grasp of the sweetness of things black in France and things French in Rio. Pointing to De Chocolat's mindful Francophilia, black press editor and activist José Correia Leite called him a "*mulato afrancesado*" (Frenchified mulatto) who "made a point of calling himself a '*chançonier*'" rather than a "*cançonetista*," a more Portuguese term for a songster.[90] The revue's cast of characters included a "Jaboticaba Afrancezada" (Frenchified jaboticaba [a tropical fruit]), a sweet young thing who proclaimed in song, "I am the Brazilian Mistinguette." The revue made musical references as well; Mario de Andrade claimed that Cirino's famous tune for the revue, "Cristo nasceu na Bahia," contained "a sly North American melody."[91] Most striking, the revue invoked *La revue nègre* explicitly, pointing to the Negro vogue in Paris to legitimate its existence; a character explained in introducing the troupe, "In Paris, doesn't [Louis] Douglas have his own Black Revue Troupe?"[92]

The Troupe Negra de Revistas e Variedades formed in Itapira and performed the revue *Malandragem* in 1929. The title referred to the quintessentially Afro-Carioca figure, the *malandro*, who conned and flirted his way into the hearts and minds of patriotic Brazilians in this decade.[93] While the members of this troupe did not leave historians explicit discussions of their debts or links to the Paris vogue, they could hardly have avoided such an understanding, as their numbers included more than one actress from the Companhia Negra de Revistas. Cementing the troupe to its more explicitly Francophilic and better publicized precedent, *Clarim* reviewed the Troupe Negra by recalling the Companhia Negra and its nickname, the "black Ba-ta-clan."[94]

The Companhia Mulata Brasileira's play *Batuque, cateretê e maxixe* debuted in São Paulo in 1930 and then played Rio. At Duque's suggestion, one of its lovely stars took on the stage name Jacy Aimoré, an ethereal, French-sounding surname that also belonged to a Brazilian indigenous group. Aimoré revealed to a Rio reporter her understanding of the foreign embrace of Afro-descended performers. "My dream today," enthused the starlet, "is to be a great artist and to go abroad . . . to Argentina, to Europe. They say they really like *mulatas* there, so I want to go see if it's true."[95] Aimoré's confidence echoes in that of the *mulata* character "Francelina" in the mainstream revue *O Rio Agacha-se*, who tells her producer, "See what woke up with the hit I scored there in Paris! When I dropped into the mix those folks practically had a fit! It's not for nothing that they say that Europe bows before Brazil!"[96]

Whether these words belonged to Aimoré or an inventive reporter, the lack of further explanation shows that the paper expected such a sentiment to make good sense to its readers. That suggests a widespread, up-to-date understanding of the status of Afro-diasporic performers abroad, tempered by a keen perception of the eroticizing gaze the metropole turned on the tropics.

In these 1920s theater troupes, surely the tip of the iceberg, Afro-Brazilian performers set themselves in a Parisian tradition, explicitly to identify as "black." Rarely are these groups placed in their proper genealogy as precursors of radical cultural activism, such as that of the 1940s Teatro Experimental do Negro (TEN) (Black Experimental Theater). TEN's most famous exponent, Abdias do Nascimento, is often understood as anomalous in Brazil: an isolated, innovative figure.[97] Even he repudiates any connection to these 1920s racially identified theater troupes, insisting that "a vast, electrified, barbed-wire fence separates my work from De Chocolat's."[98] Yet Nascimento's radicalism—like its transnational context—reaps the legacies of these precursors' cultural politics.

Observers today should take these cultural politics seriously because anti-racist activists at the time did. That is, black-identified Brazilians understood Afro-diasporic cultural production as valuable anti-racist collaboration. They demonstrated this by embracing and magnifying its impact in various ways. The black church in Rio, the Irmandade de Nossa Senhora do Rosario e São Benedicto dos Homens Pretos, approved of the work of the Companhia Negra. Church leaders welcomed members of the company to mass and posed in photographs alongside them.[99] São Paulo black press writers praised the Companhia to the skies.[100] Black press journalists also took glad note of the success of other Afro-Brazilian performers, suggesting faith in the political power of culture overall. They praised specific performers, rejoiced at the blackness of "modern" music, and were glad at the fact that the *negro* was the "great inspiration of ultra-modern choreography."[101]

Black press writers were also overjoyed at non-Brazilian black performers' success, particularly in Paris. The *Clarim* reporter who had expressed pleasure at the "Herculean musical labor" then being performed in Paris (noted at the outset of this chapter) was one of many. "Blacks are in vogue in the City of Light," thrilled a *Progresso* theater critic.[102] As the same paper was happy to remind readers a few months later, Parisians loved the "Negro muse" (Josephine Baker) and her "exotic primitivism."[103] On the occasion of a São Paulo performance by singer Elsie Houston, *Progresso* gleefully reported again: "In civilized Europe the rhythms of Negro music provoke enthusiasm and demand applause," above all in Paris, where audiences loved "Negro music, especially that of North American

Negroes."[104] This love for Afro-diasporic people and culture in France's capital city, black press writers hoped, would somehow benefit them. In 1930, *Clarim* thanked "France, the best friend of the Negro race!" using the European nation as a symbol of a world without racism, in something of the same way African Americans pointed to Brazil.[105] Writers in this forum also suggested Afro-Brazilian music would share some of the same mobility and global popularity. Celebrating the composer "Miss Firmina Rosa de Lima, whose gold medal from the National Institute of Music in 1920 speaks better than we can about this young pianist who brings honor to blacks in Brazil," *Progresso* editor Lino Guedes claimed Lima's compositions would "have a different destiny than that of other songs: they will travel the world; they will fly from mouth to mouth."[106]

Although global mobility, one of the hallmarks of the African diaspora, was a significant part of the radical potential these journalists handily grasped, they did not articulate the object of their hopes as such. That is, they did not pin their hopes on an explicitly or exclusively racial or geographic (African) category. As a *Clarim* contribution claimed in 1926, the Parisian embrace of black artists, along with the fabulous work of the Companhia Negra, proved that "the era belongs to us."[107] This flexible, transnational "us" deftly sidestepped the differences in definitions of black identity prevailing in different places. Similarly, an organizer for the Confederation of Black Youth, a conference *Clarim* had been trying to pull together for years, observed wryly, "Our prestige [abroad] has a little 'Quelque chose' that is advantageous."[108] This clever turn of phrase gestured to the latitude afforded a translator of phenomena on some level untranslatable.

At once pointed and vague, such statements well reflect the nimble ways black press writers used Parisian mediations of the African diaspora to elaborate racial politics. The blurry borders of jazz as category and of the blackness it performed allowed activists to articulate their dissent not as racial identification exclusively but in subtler directions. A *Progresso* writer, probably Lino Guedes, celebrated the black elements in Brazilian culture and encouraged greater attention to them, but he located such elements entirely in the nation's past. His ambiguous, contrasting "we" was alive in an undeniably modern present: "Every day we feel that we are losing this veritable aesthetic treasure brought to us by the *negro*. Hosting a mysterious and superstitious soul, a primitive soul in direct contact with nature, the Negro [*o negro*] infiltrated into our spirit a more colorful, warmer, and more voluptuous vision of things." Brazil should value black culture, Guedes contended, "not because Europe, eccentric and neurotic, values the *negro*."[109] Ostensibly rejecting European fashions, this agile writer simultaneously reminded readers that Europe did indeed value blackness, even as he offered Brazil a way out by consigning it to a bygone day.

Black press writers used the recognition awarded urban Afro-Brazilian culture abroad as both stick and carrot. Emphasizing the European fame of the Companhia Negra's founder and writer, "the applauded De Chocolat, known on all the stages of Europe," *Clarim* editor Jayme de Aguiar modeled a black-based, inclusive nationalism. Aguiar was explicitly optimistic about the company's ramifications for Afro-Brazilians, but he expressed his optimism in terms of nation rather than race. "It is for all of us, this theatrical event," he generously allowed, "yet another firm and victorious step to the temple of progress, in the evolution of our country . . . the fact will, for sure, contribute to the rebirth of the national theater."[110] This solution gave a wide range of Brazilians a chance to share in Paris's reflected glory, as mainstream critics understood. A journalist at the *Correio da Manhã* expressed similar sentiments in reviewing a black actress, Ascendina dos Santos. He wrote hopefully that the actress "promises to cooperate efficiently in the uplift of national theater."[111] Parisian preferences could reflect well on the nation, these writers offered, rather than on a racially defined group, if the nation would embrace the blackness at its core.

"Led by Batutas Such as These"

Elite Brazilians' responses to jazz show that they heard these jazz-based challenges to racial hierarchies, if not in activists' prose articulations, then in the music itself. Such challenges successfully upended the assumptions with which many Brazilians approached race, civilization, and value in the twenties. Clearly the music was black, but there it was, adored and uplifted in the centers of "civilization"—places Brazilians had understood as the antitheses of blackness. This acute dilemma bleeds through the pages of mainstream and elite magazines, newspapers, and other public fora of the period.

Whiter and more elite Brazilian observers in the twenties generally agreed that jazz was North American, European, and "black" in some way

(African, black, Negro, *negro*, colored, or other)—in the anachronistic terms I use here, Afro-diasporic. Their comments on the blackness of jazz revealed the imprecision both concepts demand. Many described jazz as a complex cultural fusion, never failing to underline the "dances of the Negroes of Africa" or the "Negroes drumming, sweating and furious."[112] A music critic trying to define jazz explained the addition of the "blue" note in a Rio magazine in 1924: "The blue . . . is the expansion of the nostalgic sorrow of the Negro expressed through wind instruments. A type of improvisation characteristic to the race where the characteristics of the African are preserved in the strongly syncopated rhythm and in the melismatic groups that characterize the melody."[113] This triple iteration of "character" insistently retraced the correlation between the supposed traits of black people and the specific musical traits in view, while the equation of different racial terms (Negro/the race/African) diffused the referent. Both jazz and race were hard to pin down, as they remain today.

Critics hoping to confine Afro-diasporic popular culture tried strenuously to define it. Launching a pilot issue in 1923, the editors of a new magazine delineated what it was not: "*Brasil Musical* is a magazine that proposes to do Art, and neither politics nor commerce," they proclaimed. "That, clearly, is neither the tango, nor the 'fox-trot' (imitation of the American genre), nor maxixe, very much ours, but barely aristocratic."[114] Repudiating a triplet of Afro-American forms helped these cultural gatekeepers map a transnational cultural hierarchy that could structure their local social landscape. Interestingly, the Afro-Paulista newspaper *O Kosmos* published a piece just a few weeks later moralistically rejecting tango, fox-trot, and not maxixe but habanera.[115] The slight difference between the two lists is striking. *O Kosmos* joined nationalism and moralism in repudiating non-Brazilian Afro-diasporic dances, managing not to reject black cultural formations closer to home. Still, even *Brasil Musical* was unable to practice its proclaimed rejection: just a few pages after the editorial in its pilot issue, it published the score for a popular fox-trot.

A similar sense of jazz as Afro-diasporic was clearly expressed by an *A Notícia* reporter in 1926. Exhibiting a photograph captioned "An orchestra of the eccentric musicians of Rhodesia," the critic asked, "What difference can be observed between this and a 'dancing' salon, at the frivolous and luminous hour in which 'jazz' animates the 'fox' or the 'chimmy' [shimmy] danced by our couples? Not a single one."[116] While no one in Brazil in this period genuinely believed that jazz culture arrived directly, unmediated, from Africa, this vehemence well expressed prevailing assumptions—and fears. For Brazilian patriots in thrall to the idea of "whitening," jazz seemed a backward step toward the blackness they had hoped their nation would surpass.

This vanguard of African culture, as some feared jazz would be, troubled listeners steeped in the civilizationist biases common throughout North as well as South America. Across varied contexts, diverse people shared the view of Africa as the site of backwardness and savagery.[117] How confusing that the most quintessentially modern, industrially productive of nations, the United States, was the "mother-country of 'jazz.'"[118] How treacherously bewildering was Parisian love of jazz for Brazilian elites still enormously enamored of the city that "is and always was a perfect lesson of good taste and excellence."[119] How could Paris, their ultimate cultural arbiter, be "delighting every night in the 'Folies-Bergères,' before a Negro Venus"—the black North American Josephine Baker? The Rio magazine *Careta* reprinted this Parisian description of Baker as an eerie hybrid, a "*mulata* with delicate Anglo-Saxon forms, but whose physiognomy, gestures, dances, and voice preserve all the rhythm and all the strangeness of her originating race."[120] Strange indeed.

On her 1929 voyage to Rio de Janeiro, Josephine Baker traveled alongside the Modernist architect and artist Le Corbusier, who was "inspired by [their] shipboard encounter" to compose a ballet in which Josephine would first enter dressed as a monkey. Le Corbusier revealed the other extreme he also saw in Baker in a sketch he drafted. There, in calm blue lines, Baker stands chic and dignified against the backdrop of Rio's famous skyline.[121] For Le Corbusier and Baker, as for many of their contemporaries, Afro-descended performers embodied the war-torn world's opposite extremes, the savage and the ultra-modern. This projected tension made black performance in this period even more spectacular.

The anguish such contradictions represented to whiter Brazilians overflowed in their comments on African Americans and other Afro-diasporic figures in Paris. Alongside a photo of African American artists Will Marion Cook and Louis Douglas in *La revue nègre* in Paris, sporting feathers, beads, bare feet, and much exposed skin, a critic in *A Notícia* expressed his deep confusion:

> Imagine a revue acted by Negro actors dressed in glaring colors, with an orchestra of lunatics on the set, playing "on-step" [one-step], ac-

FIGURE 13. Le Corbusier drawing of Josephine Baker and Le Corbusier, 1929. Artists Rights Society (ARS), New York/ADAGP; Paris/FLC.

companied by an infernal chorus, amid stylized decorations offering perspectives of "sky-scrapers" seen through drunken eyes, or tropical cabins by the light of an absurd moon; add to that lots of monkey contortions, ebony nudities made up in caricatures, a nostalgic emigrant's song, every contrast, every incoherence . . . and you still won't have conveyed it exactly. But the people laugh and applaud; the artists laugh; everybody laughs. . . .

Twentieth-century, Paris, ultracivilization.

Because it's not a savage look, as one might suppose and as hyperbolic complaints imply. "*The Negro Revue*" possesses subtle refinements, and its jungle has passed through the colonizing melting pot, speaking English; the comedians who take part come down to a few upright individuals with dark skin who rehearse their numbers conscientiously; their extravagant attire is in accord with the most modern aesthetic; the group has a cohesion, a disarticulated [*untrans-adrede*] cohesion, just like "futurist" art. The troupe, the set, the philharmonic instruments, after all, come from New York, city of mechanical and palpable progress. . . .

That, perhaps, denatures the revue, although it gives it a vague aspect of elegance. . . .[122]

Lonely in the face of such derisive laughter, the critic tried to maintain perspective. Was this an incomprehensible joke at his expense? What to make of this visual, musical, logical chaos, in which identity was performative and origin "denaturizing"?

In response to the link Paris forged between modernity and blackness, some commentators preferred to jettison the modern and its mixtures entirely.[123] Others conjured up the same sort of aristocratic contempt heaped upon it in the United States and elsewhere. Reproducing a joky photograph from a U.S. magazine of fifteen chubby white infants entitled "'A jazz-band' of babies," a writer in the conservative women's magazine *Pró-Patria* snorted disdainful accord. Sure—"What little four-year-old brat doesn't know how to break a glass or pull the cat's tail?"[124] Another would-be high-culture vehicle wishfully assured its readers that jazz would not permanently affect "real" music, being just a fad.[125] Band-leader Romeu Silva alit upon a solution that put at least one listener in the mind of Paul Whiteman, softening the offense in the music he performed so that no bourgeois need fear being *épaté*. Silva insisted that his "Jazz-Band Sul-Americana" was "an elegant group, presentable in any salon of Carioca society. No monkeyshines or debauchery, unlike a certain French or [North] American orchestra currently playing here. We are artists, not clowns."[126]

Although Silva's specific referent is not clear, it is fairly obvious that he was making a racially ordered comparison, given the implications of monkeys and moral laxity in the lexicon of his day. Unable or unwilling to distinguish the national origins of the orchestra he disdained (French or North American?), Silva set an exclusive, white Brazilian nationalism against the competing "nationalism" of the African diaspora.

This stance placed Silva on good ground: his group was extremely successful. In 1924 it even made North American coffee merchant William Ukers reconsider his distaste for the quintessential jazz horn:

It was here [in São Paulo] that we finally succumbed to the saxophone, after having fought against it at home for years. But then
one must hear it played by Romeu Silva, "chefe da orchestra," leader
of the "Jazz Band—Sul Americana," really to appreciate its delicate
insouciances, if I may be permitted to transfer the epithet. Yes, I've
heard Paul Whiteman and the rest, but, believe me, until you've
heard Romeu Silva play "That American Boy of Mine" at you from
the music balcony of the dining room in the Esplanada at São Paulo,
you haven't heard a saxophone wail as it should be wailed![127]

Ukers's view of Silva's saxophone playing contrasts with the rather more
sanguine evaluation by Ari Barroso, an irrefutably superb musician. While
the coffee salesman surely did not misrepresent his pleasure in Silva's performance, perhaps we should look for its value outside the quality of the
music itself.

Indeed, music seems to have been secondary to the success of Silva's elegant, sought-after band. "Romeu led the group by demanding discipline
and elegance," claims Sérgio Cabral. "There was no better dressed orchestra in the country."[128] Might the "discipline and elegance" of the audience and musicians in the elevated venue of a fancy São Paulo hotel have
circumscribed, for Ukers, this otherwise vulgar popular form? After all,
Silva's version was still more compelling to Ukers than that of the equally
sanitized white U.S. bandleader Paul Whiteman. Offering a compliment
in French ("insouciances") to joke at the Brazilian's superior performance
of an "American" tune, Ukers tried to stretch his readers' understanding
of America, albeit with a certain smugness at his own well-traveled savvy.
Ukers, too, was selling Brazil along with its coffee, and Silva's scrim of
Brazilian exoticism helped his dinner-music band epitomize the tropical
civilization Ukers wanted U.S. businessmen to perceive in Brazil. Brazil's
Ministry of Foreign Relations agreed, hiring Silva to represent Brazil on a
coffee advertising tour of Europe in 1925, at the Olympics in Los Angeles
in 1932, and at the 1939–40 New York International Fair.[129]

Yet Silva's "classy" band could not divert the current of popular attention, against which the protestations of moralists made little headway.
Even he had to play "uproarious" or "noisy" music to meet the public's
demands, he admitted. Jazz was like popular theater, and as a *Correio da
Manhã* critic begrudgingly acknowledged, it "belongs to a genre that has
no use for the critic; it is the public that accepts or rejects it."[130] The ene-

mies of jazz often found themselves yelling into the wind, as they did, for example, during Josephine Baker's first trip to Brazil.

Traveling to Rio de Janeiro in 1929, Josephine Baker found herself at the receiving end of no little vitriol. The contempt swirling around her persona brought Baker to symbolize, for a certain set of elite cultural critics, the most thoughtless, tasteless popular theater.[131] A reviewer for the Rio daily *A Patria* explained that Baker's dances pleased people "not for their artistic merit, but for the provocative oscillations so unfitting to her tender years."[132] *O Malho* contributor J. A. Baptista Jr. denounced the revealing notices the Odeon theater posted to advertise her upcoming show. Such images might be acceptable "there in Africa, or in the [North] American province where Baker was born: here, no." Baptista used the visibility of African Americans in the world at that moment to link the United States and Africa, decoupling the more often-drawn connection between the "dark continent" and Brazil. Paris remained exempt; Baptista excused Baker's success there by the timing of her arrival during a postwar dance craze and ascribed her continued success to curious tourists, since *real* Parisians, he was certain, had long since become bored.[133] (Ironically, nudity was acceptable on Parisian but not North American stages at the time.) The French capital may have "dissolved the dangers" of that "arousing dance," maxixe, but for critics such as Baptista, even Paris could not "civilize" Baker.[134]

Sweeter than revenge was Baker's runaway success. Baker's records had been advertised in Rio as early as 1927, when the theater journal *A Mascara* excerpted her forthcoming autobiography, complete with photo.[135] As her Rio debut approached and the critics launched their barbs, the daily *O Paiz* ran a photo of Baker in a leopard-print wrap over the caption "Why Paris Fascinates."[136] The Odeon, where Baker would shortly perform, showed the Fox film *Follies* to pique public interest. Full of praise for the film, *O Paiz* published film stills of "Sue Carol and the *Negrinha* [little black girl] *Pickaninny*" and then of the entire cast of the "Celebrated Troupe of American Negroes."[137] There was enough popular support for Baker and these movies to keep the theaters humming for weeks.[138] Meanwhile, the cafés kept their jazz bands strumming, and Carioca feet just seemed to keep tapping.

Elite representational strategies ranging from simple rejections to dainty sanitizations foundered on the shoals of non-elite discursive and artistic production. Rio de Janeiro's cultural landscape and its citizens' awareness of global trends presented incontrovertible evidence that Afro-diasporic cultural forms would continue to attract fans abroad and at home, where the masses led the classes to the city's "jazz-bands" and samba spaces. This was a mountain of popular will with heady implications of cultural relativism and genuine democracy. There was no way around it, so elites went straight in, embracing the idea of racial democracy but articulating it not as a recent innovation demanding attention and change but a longtime trait of the Brazilian nation and self that required only celebration. Brazil was "ahead" of the rest of the world in its tolerant, inclusive stance, they implied, clinging to the filaments of racist discourse that would preserve social inequities more or less intact. One of the many sites of the working out of this line of argument involved Pixinguinha and his valiant troupe of well-traveled aces.

As a symbol of black Brazilian culture reveling in an international gaze, the Oito Batutas provided excellent ground on which to work out some meanings of Afro-diasporic culture at home. Elite Brazilian nationalists seized the platforms of the group's appearance at the Palais cinema and their international debut in Paris to argue that their nation had long had Afro-Brazilian interests at heart. In the tradition of benevolent abolitionism, they represented themselves as defenders of a beleaguered but honorable social inferior. As Benjamin Costallat remembered in 1922, against critics unfriendly to the Batutas' appearance in elite public space, "I had the honor to defend (and this defense was one of the ones I did with the most enthusiasm of my life as a journalist) the 'Oito Batutas'" at the group's Palais debut.[139]

The Batutas' defenders jousted with invisible antagonizers. A satirist in *A Maça* (José Fortunato) justified his piece by noting the "violent debate in the papers," citing none. On the evening of the group's departure, *A Noite* wrote almost hopefully that there "will perhaps be those who, in idiotic affectation, condemn the youths' trip because they are colored." Costallat staged a whole mock battle, ventriloquizing a host of imaginary interlocutors: "There was no lack of censure for the modest 'Oito Batutas.' For the heroic 'Oito Batutas.' . . . The war launched against them was atrocious," he rhapsodized. He had his unnamed objectors protest, "But, they're *negros*," so that he could retort, "So what! They're Brazilian!"[140] It is difficult to imagine that there could have been that much protest over the Batutas, given that they had performed for the visit of the Belgian royal couple in 1920 and by 1922 were widely adored well beyond their home city.[141] That is not to suggest that such protests were never made (two are noted below) but that "patriots" played up anti-Batuta venom significantly in order to magnify the menace of the enemy at the door, which they generously, valiantly, kept at bay.

Such sanction was contingent upon the artists' performance of nation over race. Praising the Companhia Negra de Revistas, journalist Prudente de Moraes Neto insisted that "the *negros* of this company don't perform *negro* art, but Brazilian art of the best sort." Journalist Xavier Pinheiro responded to anti-Batuta remarks by conductor and composer Júlio Reis with, "They are from our *terra* [land], maestro!" Isaac Frankel, manager of the Palais cinema, channeled interpretation of the Batutas' identity at their very first appearance, affixing a sign labeling them as "the only orchestra that speaks directly to the Brazilian heart."[142]

Clearly, any performance of non-national Afro-diasporic culture would fall outside the circle these writers were willing to endorse. Costallat predicted, with overtones of admonition, that the Batutas "will take [to Paris] genuine Brazilian music, that which has not yet been contaminated by outside influences." He reminded his readers of what the North Americans, those "declared racists" (an interesting choice of modifier), had done:

> [They had exported] a great [North] American orchestra of blacks, The Syncopated Band [surely a reference to Will Marion Cook's Southern Syncopated Orchestra], who played Beethoven and all the classics, accompanied by car horns, train whistles, bells, old tin cans, and the most infernal and prosaic noises the morbid imagination of the jazz-band could possibly invent. . . . Paris, which went en masse [*em peso*], in evening dress, in luxurious gowns, to listen religiously to all that ridiculous noise in the Théâtre des Champs Elysées, will naturally understand the distinction between our musicians and those [North] American clowns, those tin-can men, with their car horns and train whistles. . . .

> The [North] Americans took noise [to Paris]. Ours will take sentiment. What emerged from the tin cans will now emerge from the hearts. The difference is great.[143]

Eurocentric cultural hierarchies (and self-image) intact, Costallat implied that *those* were some crazy Negroes, unlike his home-grown variety—as long as they kept themselves clean of "foreign influences." Elite emphasis on the national contours of the cultural phenomena in question aimed to channel Afro-diasporic cultural politics away from the race-oriented subject positions that elsewhere, they knew, kindled militant anti-racist dissent.

Pointing to an outside gaze, elites claimed racial tolerance as a Brazilian national trait. Floresta de Miranda, millionaire Arnaldo Guinle's private secretary, published an open letter to a Frenchman living in Brazil who had suggested the Batutas were a poor choice to represent the nation. Emphasizing his opponent's Frenchness, de Miranda confidently spoke for his entire nation: "The fact of their being black has no pejorative significance for Brazilians," he chided.[144]

Their insistence on the Batutas' "Brazilianness" did not prevent some elite fans from celebrating the musicians' similarity to successful African Americans in Paris. They quickly realized that the Batutas could be used to set Brazil and the United States on the same plane, a prestige-winning comparison long a treasured project of Brazilians seeking to coax from foreigners the recognition they thought warranted by Brazil's dominance in the Southern Cone. A journalist from *O Paiz* made the connection: "These countrymen of ours went to Europe, as [North] American musicians of their genre frequently do, attracted by the natural desire to earn money, thanks to the accessibility of a public as avid in general as the European public is for exotic novelties, principally in dance."[145] So did de Miranda: "The great orchestras in Paris . . . are the jazz-bands of black North Americans, and it doesn't seem to me that the great republic suffers any eclipse as a result."[146]

After the First World War, in a period when black activism was visibly challenging white supremacy in European colonies and other American nations, many Europeans hoped that cultural approximation would diminish the hatred that had ignited that devastating conflict. When George Lansbury, British editor of the *Daily Herald* and later the leader of the Labour Party, introduced the Southern Syncopated Orchestra in London in August 1919, he pinned upon it what would become fairly widespread utopian hopes: "He said that 'we were now being given an opportunity to study and enjoy the ideas and cultures of other people. . . . One day there would be an end of hatred, and barriers of race and creed would be broken down, for at the bottom we were all merely men and women.'"[147] António Ferro, a Portuguese poet on a speaking tour in Brazil, called the jazz band "the siren of Peace . . . the dogma of our Hour."[148] Brazilians took up this rhetoric aptly, particularly concerning the Batutas abroad. The Brazilian ambassador in Paris, Reis Velloso, wrote in Donga's travel album, "Led by Batutas [batons] such as these, the world would not need Geneva to resolve the question of peace."[149]

The European embrace of multiculturalism as the solution to war, expressed specifically as approbation of Afro-Brazilian performers, pushed Brazilian elites to accept the idea that their nation ought to be represented as racially and culturally mixed. It gave them a graceful way to accede to the arguments proffered in popular venues and even to claim them as their own, soothing the nationalist ache for "our own voice" or "a music 'genuinely ours.'"[150] "We should seek to be known in Europe as we are," affirmed Costallat. "We have an international personality as worthy as others', and we ought to affirm it at all times." Brazilians had placed hopes in culture as an ambassador since the days of maxixe's global vogue. "If the tango has already achieved immortality, bringing Argentina greater fame than all the cattle and all the fruit she has exported," wrote a journalist in 1914, "we must continue to hope to see maxixe collaborate in the service of our European propaganda."[151] The warm postwar reception given Afro-diasporic culture expanded the opportunity for Brazil's Afro-American cultural mixture to garner favorable attention, as Brazilians well understood.

As the decade wore on, elite Brazilian representations of jazz moved increasingly toward the positive potential of this sort of cultural syncretism. "What is being done in Paris in this regard results from an imposition of modern conscience," the prominent São Paulo paper the *Diario Nacional* reported in late 1928. "Nostalgia for syncopated rhythms, for Negro rhythms, laments from the Russian soul . . . Argentine tangos . . . Portuguese fados, all peoples sing the same emotions, the same afflictions." Perhaps, the author sighed, "the approximation of peoples through art" would prevent some of humanity's destructive squabbles.[152]

Elites explored the representational strategies available given the limits imposed by their non-elite peers and international attention. In a lecture at the Teatro Lírico in Rio in 1922, António Ferro embraced this synthesis while offering another way to divert the subversions of jazz, by circumscribing the music with a clear and comforting race-based division of labor: "In souls, in bodies, in books, in statues, in houses, onscreen—there are Negroes drumming, sweating and furious, Negroes in red, Negroes full of life. The moment is a Negro. The jazz-band is the mosaic of the Hour.

Jazz-white; band-Negro. Pale bodies—dancing; ebony bodies—playing. The jazz-band is the ex-libris of the century. May your souls dance to the rhythm of this jazz-band of whites masked by the coal of my words."[153] The relentless physicality of "Negroes" in this quote and the clean separation of blacks at work and whites at leisure preserved racial hierarchies, again in the form of a claim to repudiate them.

Introducing Ferro in São Paulo before a lecture a few weeks later, the Modernist poet Guilherme de Almeida embraced jazz in a way that shied entirely clear of blackness. Ferro was like a jazz-band himself, de Almeida offered: "a complete jazz-band, an authentic jazz-band, a jazz-band from Hawai [*sic*]; but a civilized, modernized, stylized, Broadway-filtered jazz-band, really *Uncle Sam*, really *grill-room*, with straw petticoats, and the vulgar shenanigans of a Jig."[154] Lest the connotations of "complete," "authentic," or "Hawai" darken Ferro himself, the presenter provided listeners with these filters of North American civilization and modernity. The coal of *his* words would wash off with Gold Dust Twins soap.[155] Ferro and his presenter both took jazz as an opportunity to make a boisterous poetic mess of the world, in a cadence almost beat. Yet their nods to miscegenation were well contained—for Ferro by a stark division of labor; for his host, by the startling absence of blackness at all.

As this confirms, Brazilian elites found ways to reconcile this embrace of cultural and racial mixture with racist social hierarchies, as so many critics of racial democracy have explained. Derogatory implications could be remarkably overt. Discussing the Companhia Negra de Revistas, a *Careta* reviewer who understood that the group's "example, as always, came to us from Paris," nevertheless sneered, "in Paris, the appearance of the Negro 'stars' of the 'Folies-Bergères' didn't cause, as it did among us, a critical shortage of cooks."[156]

In this vein belongs the satirical take by *A Maça* columnist José Fortunato, who reported that he had interviewed the Batuta who did not go to Paris in 1922, "Antonio Feliciano do Espirito Santo, retired dockworker, knight of the order of Leopold and official in the Legion of Honor, who, receiving us in his office, generously furnished us with a kerosene can for a chair." The musician had been forced to wear shoes to perform for a visiting official (unnamed but presumably the King of Belgium), after which his feet hurt so much that he was unable to stand for any length of time. "Running his fingers through his toes," the Batuta explained that his footache prevented his accompanying his fellows to Paris. The interview was pure fabrication, its subject invented for a jolly round of ridicule. The piece mocked the Batuta's presumptuous name and noble title, contrasting them with his humble occupation and office furnishings. It imputed simian proportions to his pedicular digits. It narrated the following dialogue:

> —And what do you think of this mission, we asked? Is it in the national interest?
>
> Antonio Feliciano gazed at the roof unworried, like someone searching casually for a rat, or an idea, and gave his opinion:
>
> —I think, frankly, that the results for Brazil will be excellent. The fellows who went are really *batutas* [batons/aces]. . . .
>
> —Do you think, then, that France will send us, in return, a delegation of musicians, we inquired?
>
> —No sir.
>
> —A great literary mission . . . ?
>
> —Not at all!
>
> —A political embassy . . . ?
>
> —Nor that.
>
> —Well then, we exclaimed, upset,—what will we get out of the Batutas' trip to Paris? . . .
>
> —In a few years, you know what? He leaned toward us, and concluded:
>
> —France will be like this, full of little mulattoes!
>
> And he grouped his fingers together in a bundle, to give an idea of the multitude.

Sealing its message, the magazine adorned this lesson in racial character with a cartoonish ink sketch of a blackface clown holding a banjo.[157]

Fortunato's column and cartoon suggested that cultural travel would spread to the metropole the biological contamination that had already infested Brazil (blackness or race mixture).[158] The Batuta's biologistic opinion was set up for ridicule along with the rest of his person, allowing the author both to disclaim the biological view of race increasingly displaced by the enthusiasm for culture in this moment and to reinforce it by painting his subject as ignorant, prehensile, bestial. Reproducing racial hierarchy via a claim to reject it, Fortunato had hit upon the double move the ideology of racial democracy would strew throughout Brazilians' everyday.

Os «Batutas» em Paris

Embarcaram ha dias para a Europa, com destino a Paris, os oito cantores e musicos bra ileiros que fizeram epoca, entre nós, com os seus «maxixes» e modinhas nacionaes. Foram, diz-se, fazer propaganda da arte indigena, tão menosprezada pelos nossos maiores escriptores e artistas.

A partida desses propangandistas foi objeto de violenta discussão nos jornaes. Para uns, a nossa missão musical vae redundar em prejuiso para os nossos creditos de povo culto, de que os Oito Batutas não podem ser a expressão mais legitima. Para outros, porém, os francezes saberão o que essa missão exprime, tomando os nossos oito graúnas como authenticos representantes do genio popular, e não como delegados do Club dos Diarios, da Associação Commercial ou da Academia Brasileira de Letras.

Indifferentes a essas duas opiniões, tomámos um alvitre: consultar, a respeito, o nono batuta, o sr. Antonio Feliciano do Espirito Santo, estivador aposentado, cavalleiro da Ordem de Leopoldo e official da legião de Honra, o qual com a maior gentileza, nos forneceu, no seu gabinete de trabalho, um caixão de kerozene para nos servir de cadeira, e nos foi, logo, dizendo:

— Eu, como a imprensa não ignora, não quiz ir á Europa com os meus companheiros. Isso não significa, entretanto, que eu tenha divergido delles em relação á embaixada, mas, simplesmente, uma indisposição de saúde, que me impediu de embarcar.

Cuspiu longe, na parede, e esclareceu:

— Quando o marechal Mangin esteve no Rio, o sr. ministro da Guerra forçou-me a tomar parte em uma festa ao glorioso militar. Calcei as botinas, e fui. Tamanho foi, porém, o supplicio do calçado, que ainda hoje não me posso ter em pé por muito tempo.

E passando os dedos da mão entre os do pé:

— Foi por isso, apenas, que eu não embarquei.

— E que nos diz o senhor dessa missão? — perguntámos. — Acha que ella convém aos interesses nacionaes?

Antonio Feliciano olhou o tecto com despreocupação, como quem procura casualmente um rato ou uma idéa, e opinou:

— Eu acho, com franqueza, que os resultados para o Brasil vão ser os melhores. Os companheiros que seguiram, são, realmente, batutas. E' gente escolhida a dedo.

— Acha então, que a França nos mandará, como retribuição, uma embaixada de compositores? — indagámos.

— Não, senhor.

— Uma grande missão literaria, com Anatole France, Paul Bourget, Henri Barbusse, Frederic Masson...

— Absolutamente!

— Uma embaixada politica, chefiada por Briand?

— Tambem, não.

— Então, — exclamámos, arreliados, — que vamos tirar nós da ida dos Oito Batutas a Paris? Que é que isso nos vae adiantar?

— D'aqui a alguns annos, sabe?

Chegou-se mais para nós, e concluiu:

— A França está assim, de mulatinhos!

E juntou os dedos em feixe, para dar uma idéa de multidão.

José Fortunato

FIGURE 14. José Fortunato, "Os 'Batutas' em Paris." *A Maça*, 1922. Reproduced in Cabral, *Pixinguinha*.

This carefully circumscribed version of racial "harmony" would be the image of Brazil that elites would offer for the rest of the century. The world would come to agree, fascinated, after the Second World War. The 1920s were the years in which elites were compelled to accept parts of a world-view that they had encountered in popular culture and non-elite discourse for some time. Cultural workers used Parisian accolades to boost the cultural capital of Brazilian popular music, including jazz, bringing elites to the local negotiating tables of café-concertos and cinemas, "dancings" and salons, where non-elites staked claims for the full rights of citizenship. The compromise worked out in these spaces would set this "harmony," for better and for worse, at the foundation of a lasting Brazilian nationalism.

WHEN GREENLEE AND DRAYTON played their gig at Rio de Janeiro's Odeon cinema alongside the Oito Batutas, they were in for an unpleasant surprise. Irony of ironies, as noted above, in the land of "racial harmony," the African-American dance team was refused lodging in the Hotel Flamengo. Garvin Bushell, clarinet player in Sam Wooding's band, also in Rio de Janeiro in 1927, took home a similar memory. "I could live in Rio and enjoy it," he confessed, "if I could speak the language. But they had segregation there. We went to a fun house once, and they wouldn't let us in."[159] These experiences were in marked contrast to the adulation awarded (most of the time) to wealthy African American travelers, whose subsequent celebrations of Brazil helped circulate misleading optimism about conditions there. Still, African American performers' travels brought their popular-cultural forms into contact with the global phenomena just then providing black Brazilians with their powerful anti-racist arguments. As chapter 4 explores, even in the context of the violent disdain that circumscribed jazz culture in the early postwar years, some North American cultural workers would put these ideas to use, crafting some deft cultural interventions of their own. To follow these vaudeville and other popular performers in the United States, themselves vectors of transnational exchange and savvy agents of change to local and broader definitions of race and nation, our story now moves north once again.

CHAPTER FOUR

Nation Drag
Uses of the Exotic

Introducing: Jones

In his 1919 *As Nature Leads: An Informal Discussion of the Reason Why Negro and Caucasian Are Mixing in Spite of Opposition*, the erudite antiracist philosopher and historian Joel Augustus Rogers introduced readers to his friend "Jones," no first name given. Jones, it seems, was quite adept with the ladies. He struck up a telephone flirtation with a young woman, and "soon she wanted to meet him. Jones objected that she might not wish to meet him as he was a Brazilian and rather dark. If Jones has ever been to Brazil, it must have been that in Indiana. Jones then learnt that she had a violent antipathy for Negroes, why it was she did not know, but she hated them, and would never sit by one in a car—but, of course, according to American notions, Africans from Brazil and the West Indies are not Negroes, only those of the United States are."[1] Rogers went on to relate the successful progression of this romance through the couple's meeting, and a few steps beyond.

Rogers was happy to report that among the other results of their relationship, the lady's "antipathy for the Negro race is quite gone."[2] Few observers today still think of interracial romance as a route out of racial thinking, and most would probably take Rogers's moral as just that, and apocryphal. But the dynamic at play is noteworthy. Jones played to the woman's yearning to engage the prohibitions that simultaneously shaped her desire and denied its fulfillment. His profession of Brazilian darkness was not a simple detour around his interlocutor's racism, but a deft way to pique her romantic curiosity. A late-nineteenth-century innovation in

communication technology, the telephone, framed a meeting ground unencumbered by the body, where the woman's projections could find free
rein. In that space Jones nimbly manipulated desire, its deferral, and the
bewildering intermediacy of a foreign racial system. Freed from familiar
bearings, the woman reeled in Jones's subterfuge, his eager partner in their
improvised dance.

Jones's strategy reveals one of the facets of Brazil's usefulness to anti-
racist argument in the United States: the aura of sensuality it mustered
in North Atlantic imaginations, as one of any number of ill-distinguished
exotic, peripheral places. The seductions of its exotic *sexuality* number
among the reasons Brazilian *racial* categories did not fit the black-white
schema supposedly prevailing in the United States. This sort of statement
should increasingly be losing any sense of paradox as consensus accumu-
lates around the insight that social categories make meaning in conjunction
with each other. What has not been as fully articulated is the other buttress
of this strategy: the multiple racial schemas that exist alongside each other,
in tension and contradiction, all the time. Then as now, people constantly
threaded their way from dichotomous to plural racial schemas and back
again.[3] To mollify the black-white dichotomy of his lady's expressed hatred,
Jones conjured up and superimposed a multi-category system. Such a system was clearly in the air: for all that "Brazilian" was not supposed to be a
meaningful category in the woman's world, she understood it immediately.
The mismatches between the two schemas revealed the fissures in both;
Jones did not so much substitute his vision for hers as invite her into its
liminal space. She apparently found that quite . . . comfortable.

Jones may be a figment of Rogers's bountiful, eclectic imagination,
but truth is more wonderful than fiction. Many real people act in ways
that dramatize the ill fit of racial categories, those untenable attempts to
classify and contain the infinite gamut of human difference. Some people
"pass" from one to another, or repeatedly back and forth between them,
or achieve recognition for an intermediate category such as "mulatto" or
"biracial," and many people fall perilously, tragically through the cracks.
Others are quite content to occupy the uncharted gaps between categories, among systems. The historical record is full of resourceful people
who, like Jones, have invoked the fluidity of race by pointing to its variation elsewhere, especially those elsewheres with as generously sensual
connotations as Brazil. In a fascinating and ill-understood move, closer
in some ways to drag than passing, they have animated and occupied an

eroticized, quasi-racial national category that at times escaped the confines of the starker category "black."

This chapter explores the multiple permutations of this strategy as deployed by a handful of early-twentieth-century figures, mostly African American vaudevillians, musicians, and dancers, who operated within the exoticist culture of empire. That is, as chapter 2 set forth, at the turn to and during the early twentieth century, an apex of formal U.S. imperialism, popular culture engaged widely and joyously with "exotic" cultural forms. North Atlantic audiences gobbled up the music and dance of colonized places, homogenized and ill distinguished, reveling in their supposed primitiveness, spirituality, and sensuality.

Mainstream North American performers of the exotic largely invoked the familiar rubric of Orientalism that Edward Said and subsequent exegetes have so deftly interpreted.[4] African American performers, however, were not always afforded the distance necessary to sustain that condescending relationship. As objects of exoticist projections within the United States, as well as subjects of an imperial state in relation to the world, African Americans navigated the riptides of internal colonialism.[5] For the most part these were dangerous currents; the fetishization of Afro-primitivism worked primarily to demean and diminish Afro-diasporic art of all sorts. It helped disfranchise African Americans and undermine black commercial and intellectual ventures, ideologically and materially. But that is not the end of the story. Black performers also found ways to ride the waves of the jazz age's global primitivist vogue. Some played (along) with exoticization by performing foreign cultural forms such as tango, hula, or "Brazilian dance"; some claimed identity with far-flung nations and peoples, pretending to "be" from places in which they had never set foot.[6] Some steamed across the Atlantic to entertain other imperial powers fascinated by the cultural production of colonial subjects, revealing another reason exoticist culture was compelling in the United States: it was beloved in Europe. Ah, Europe, still the site of the citadels of culture for North American elites! Echoing Afro-Brazilians' citation of European, particularly Parisian, love for their cultural production, African American performers capitalized on primitivist and jazz adulation in London, Paris, and other European centers. In mindful performative gestures, travelers trumpeted their warm receptions or demonstrated their acquired skills. Tacking between exoticism and Europe, individuals sampled and mixed these strategies as their contexts and talents allowed.

Historians of African American performance in this period have documented the ways black performers worked to refuse the exoticism projected onto them, focusing on the dangers of this ideological landscape. As one such observer writes, "Because of the rising interest in 'primitivism' (the so-called link between black people and subconscious nature), black artists and performers had to walk the tightrope bridging the mainstream and the 'exotic.'"[7] Certainly the dangers were real, as this chapter encounters again and again, but many performers nonetheless jumped willingly off the rope and into the realm of the exotic, reaping meaningful, if often fleeting, personal and collective gain. Those scholars who find advantages for black performers in negotiations of primitivist-exoticist terrain (often in terms of the power of black female sexuality) have rarely considered the ways African Americans performing the exotic invoked foreign national or cultural categories.[8] For the most part they pay little heed to the transnational context of imperialism and the exoticist culture it spawned in the United States, portraying black eroticization as a purely domestic tradition. They have understood what Caribbean postcolonial intellectual and poet Audre Lorde called the "uses of the erotic" but not the related "uses of the exotic," as this chapter is therefore subtitled.[9]

African American exoticist performance was heterogeneous in every way. Given variations in class, region, gender, sexuality, looks, talent, field, and so much more, African Americans held no single relationship to the exotic, just as they espoused no predictable politics on the issue of U.S. imperialism. On that question some endorsed the notion that a "badge of color" united subjects of formal and internal colonialism, while others rejected any suggestion of similarity, claiming a full and simple "American" identity.[10] Politics on that level, in any case, only roughly translate into stage or bandstand practice. Some performers had no political goals in mind at all. Jones and his Gepetto demonstrate two points along this range. Jones's performance of Brazil was fairly straightforward: he aimed to get the girl. Rogers's performance of Jones, in contrast, was profoundly political; this explicitly activist and anti-racist scholar ventriloquized his clever "friend" to build momentum for social transformation.

The uses of exoticist performance, as Jones and Rogers show, begin with the mundane and run the gamut to the radical. Performers put on the exotic to get hired, get paid, and get famous. Sometimes exoticist performance chipped away at racist expectations, as when it allowed performers to cross the color line and perform in segregated venues or to perform genres previously deemed inappropriate for black artists. Evidence presented below will suggest that exoticist performance, including the performance of European love for the exotic, was part of what allowed black performers to expand beyond minstrelsy. This was a shift of no little political import, for minstrelsy was the reigning paradigm of popular entertainment until the end of the nineteenth century.[11] In the 1880s, the multigenre, skit-based form of vaudeville emerged. Vaudeville staged the debate over cultural hierarchy that by the end of the century would confirm distinctions between "high" and "low," distancing opera, for example, from slapstick.[12] Vaudeville's star would eclipse minstrelsy in the new century before fading in turn in the stronger glare of motion pictures. The 1920s, one researcher argues, were the "golden era of African American vaudeville."[13] Is it merely coincidence that this exoticist decade elevated vaudeville to such heights? Historians of minstrelsy and vaudeville rarely gaze beyond U.S. borders, despite the fact of the two genres' convergence at a moment of great and public controversy over U.S. empire.[14] This chapter argues that the 1920s were gilded for black vaudevillians in part because exoticism offered such tantalizing and delicious performative opportunities. Wielded by savvy performers, the exotic provided tools with which to renegotiate the valence of black popular performance.

Still more overtly political reasons motivated some performers, such as those who launched cultural ventures to nurture black artists, prove the worth of black art, promote black self-esteem, or forge coalition with African or other Afro-diasporic communities. These performances could be mindfully anti-Orientalist, but black exoticism was not automatically so. African Americans were not immune from Orientalist seductions. As cultural producers in an affluent nation, African American performers could also be authors in exoticist fields, reproducing some of the elements of their own and others' subordination.

This chapter explores the phenomenon of black exoticist performance over the (long) 1920s. The first part considers the uses popular entertainers found in the transnational cultural currents suffusing their local worlds, particularly the conjoined streams of the exotic and Europe. Surveying a number of cultural workers, each rather briefly, this section compiles the ways they used those currents: they pointed out foreign opinions of U.S. affairs, drew on the prestige of foreign recognition, and engaged in exoticist performance. It closes with reflections on the ways black performances of the exotic and of Europe complicate notions of "passing" and "drag," discussions of which tend not to take the two concepts' complex relationship into sufficient account. Having offered a sense of the range of possibilities and intentions within and behind exoticist performance, the chapter next introduces the scintillating Olive Burgoyne, specialist in "the Brazilian dance," despite little or no Brazilian experience. Delving into the life of this gorgeous, self-made dancer gives a more textured sense of the possibilities and pitfalls of black exoticism. The chapter closes with another biographical section, this one on an astonishing musicologist and performance artist named Elsie Houston, of ambiguous race and nationality, whose choices and constraints foreclose celebration of black exoticism and undermine notions of stable identity in thoroughly discomfiting ways.

Exotic Affairs: Nation Drag

In the late nineteenth century and turn to the twentieth, North Atlantic audiences "discovered" the exotics in their midst. The African American opera and concert singer Matilda Sissieretta Joyner Jones, known as "Black Patti," was one unwitting object of such revelation. Jones was cause for epiphany for a reporter for the Toronto *Empire*. "As she stands before her audience," the writer revealed, "we understand *for the first time* something of the fascinations of the dark-hued women of the Orient."[15] This backhanded compliment clearly conveys the context of empire and its implications for African Americans' (self-) representations onstage. The remark, one of the many impositions of exoticist representation with which Jones was forced to wrestle in her public life, was probably made on the occasion of her performance at the Toronto World's Fair in 1892, one of at least four international fair engagements Jones would accept.[16] Jones likely found herself the object of similarly exoticizing gazes at all of them, for world's fairs in this period were potent lenses for the conceptualization of empire. They spread panoramas of exotic and civilized peoples before eager visitors, offering comparative vistas that near-invariably resolved into imperial perspectives.[17] In such a frame, even Jones, with a signal demonstration of African American accomplishments in the arts (by every measure—at the Pittsburgh fair she was paid $2,000, the highest salary earned to that date by an African American artist) could be reconciled, in the pages of a paper entitled *Empire*, into a naif, sensual exotic.[18] The reporter's praise of Jones as Oriental, the representational logic of the fairs, and even the newspaper's title all faithfully reflected the emerging tenor of the times.

Jones also encountered other, more welcome aspects of the imperial era's transnational cultural circuits, such as the enthusiasm for black artists abroad. On several tours of the Americas and Europe, including an appearance for the Prince of Wales, her breathtaking voice earned great kudos, helping to establish the reputation that would secure her world's fairs showcases, earn her star billing at Madison Square Garden during a "Grand Negro Jubilee" in 1892, and provoke an invitation to perform for the President and Mrs. Harrison at the White House that same year.[19] There is no question that her European fame was the underpinning to her U.S. success. Indeed, as it was that success that made the *Empire* reporter notice her in the first place, this exotic was constituted by Europe. The exotic and Europe were not opposites, save as sides of a single coin.

Jones used her European experience to undergird a modest activist intervention. Perhaps racial hatred was not completely necessary, she chided her fellow citizens with gentle decorum. "I of course enjoy singing in this country more than any other," she graciously assured the *Pittsburgh Post* when she returned from England in 1896. "But outside of America I think England and the English provinces of India and Australia and South Africa are the places I would prefer visiting were I to start on another world-girding tour. There is not the slightest antipathy in the matter of color in England or in the provinces."[20] This anti-racist lesson hinged on the authority of Jones's travels, especially to Europe; she used her own movement over the global currents of black performance to challenge social relations at home.

As her beautiful elocution makes clear, Jones did not want the role of black exotic, primitive and sensual. She attempted to refuse those imposed frames and choose only Europe's shadow, but as exoticist tastes spread after 1898 and as the century turned, such an evasion grew more difficult. Despite her success and acclaim as a concert soprano abroad, in the United States Jones could not confine her career to the "high" musical arts. She turned to vaudeville, first in 1896, when she briefly joined the cast of manager John Isham's "Oriental America," and later as leader of her own "Black Patti's Troubadours." That mix of comedy and classical music, reports Henry Sampson, was the "first successful black road show to tour the East and South."[21] Jones would mentor and support black performers for nearly twenty years, retiring to her hometown of Providence, Rhode

Island, around 1920. In a bleak illustration of the meager fruits of stage success for African American performers, any savings she might have had melted during the Depression; Jones died in 1933 in poverty and obscurity.[22] In the 1890s, however, the arc of her fame cleaved to the Orientalist surge.

From its very name, Oriental America (1896–1899), one of several similarly named companies at the time, signaled the vogue for Orientalist performance.[23] It was also a landmark in the evolution of black performance, opening new locations to and shifting prevailing standards for African Americans onstage. The pioneer historian of black music, Eileen Southern, credits the company's 1896 production with being "the first show with an all-Negro cast to play Broadway and the first all-Negro show to make a definite break with minstrel traditions and the burlesque theaters where minstrel shows were customarily presented."[24]

This was a critical break, given the status of minstrelsy at the outset of the imperial era. Why was Oriental America able to buck its reins? The answer lies in its gentle substitution of exotic performances. The troupe did not refuse blackface entirely and retained a minstrel pattern, layering exoticisms over that base: "a Japanese dance, cleverly rendered" by four women (perhaps the famous quartet of Dora Dean, Mattie Wilkes, Ollie Burgoyne, and Belle Davis); a piece billed as "the maids of the Oriental Huzzars"; and then—strikingly—an operatic medley as finale, likely the showcase for Sissieretta Jones.[25] The show progressed from Orientalisms to opera as if the expansion into exoticist terrain generated the momentum to fuel that daring step and, most important, the departure from minstrelsy. Exotic skits and scenes provided entertaining alternatives to the expected slavish jester figures, while still meeting and catering to projections of African Americans' shared cultural legacies with other "uncivilized" peoples.

The extent to which performers of exotic forms understood themselves as like their objects is unclear. Jones may not have wanted the role of black exotic, but clearly other performers did, and it is important not to jump to anachronistic conclusions. Eric Lott's wonderful work complicating the racism behind minstrelsy is useful to remember here.[26] Just as white minstrels and their white audiences held complicated relationships to the forms and people they impersonated, mocked, envied, desired, and understood themselves as profoundly *like*, so black exoticisms may have involved identification, self-projection, and desire. Consider two well-known players, Aida Overton Walker, star of Williams and Walker's famous vaudeville productions, and the renowned "Blackbird," Florence Mills. Walker did a "Spanish song and dance" in the New York production of *His Honor the Barber* in 1911; evoked a more intentionally African exoticism in 1911–12 with "Aida Walker and Her Abyssinia Girls"; and led the "Porto Rico Girls" from 1912 to 1914, the year of her death at the age of thirty-four.[27] Mills (who would die even younger, at thirty-one) traveled with groups named to evoke Latin themes, from the "Bonita Company" to the "Panama Trio" (with future Paris nightclub maven Ada "Bricktop" Smith), and in New York, as a fellow performer remembered, she "used to do [a jungle number] called 'Hawaiian Night in Dixieland.'"[28]

Walker and Mills were anti-racist artists who cared about the politics of culture, making it unlikely that they played exotic Others as distant and strange. Walker, for example, crafted performances to contest the sexualization and corresponding denigration of black women, as in the version of *Salomé* she performed for both black and white audiences. *Salomé* was popular enough to have a name coined for its vogue—"Salomania"—and its fame hinged precisely on the eroticism of this dance combined with its classical allusions.[29] Walker, however, skirted its notorious naughtiness; according to historian David Krasner, her version was "classy," relatively chaste, and surpassed white contemporaries in grace and skill.[30] Walker's *Salomé* intervened in white assumptions about African American primitivism and rejected the excessive sexuality projected onto the black exotic.

Walker's cultural politics included mentoring young artists, Florence Mills among them. As a child performer, Mills learned one of her first hit songs from Walker.[31] Mills too was known to be race-conscious and activist, refusing demeaning roles and segregated performance venues when her fame allowed.[32] Walker's and Mills's performances of Spanish, African, Latin American, and Hawaiian forms, then, must not have offended their anti-racist sensibilities. Perhaps they felt the elision white audiences projected onto black and brown as a sort of kinship, understanding their stage work as celebrating non-white culture broadly. This empathy must be part of what made Okeh, a "race" record label, market "Hawaiian" numbers to its black-identified audience or why African American consumers bought fashions, magical amulets, beauty products, and other items that in some way invoked Egypt or Tut, from Claude Barnett's "Nile Queen" cosmetics to the hieroglyphically adorned "Madagasco" hair straightener.[33] This was consistent with mainstream advertising, in which by 1925 "Oriental themes [had become] predictable."[34] Tut's Egypt, however, represented a compellingly anti-racist version of the black exotic, with its evidence of early, sophisticated African civilization. Woven into product logos in a realm not so far from popular performance, these commodities and their advertisements—like performances of the exotic by artists such as Walker and Mills—rearticulated African Americans' supposedly privileged relationship to the exotic in a way that reproduced the letter but undermined the spirit of Orientalism.

If this anti-Orientalism seems but minimally "anti," remember the limits of context. Later, after the First World War, struggles for racial justice and self-determination for colonized peoples both intensified and converged. In that context, the radical seeds in black exotic performance would blossom. The career of the dramatic actress Laura Bowman, for example, began with exoticism and proceeded to a mindful forging of Pan-Africanist solidarity.

During the war, Bowman and her husband, fellow actor Sidney Kirkpatrick, performed as a "Hawaiian" duet in Indianapolis. In 1923 they moved to New York City with the Chicago-based "Ethiopian Art Players," presenting Wilde's *Salomé* and a jazz version of *The Comedy of Errors*. Bowman organized a drama school in Harlem, the National Art School, and did *Salomé* there again in 1928.[35] After Kirkpatrick's death and Bowman's remarriage to Haitian actor LeRoi Antoine, Bowman traveled to Haiti, bringing back drums and music for a 1938 production at the Lafayette Theatre in Harlem.[36] Bowman's career phased through exoticism (Hawaii, *Salomé*), primitivism (jazz Shakespeare), assimilationist didacticism (the "National" art school in Harlem), and Pan-Africanism in practice. Exoticism grounded both the explicitly activist, black-oriented theater work in the late 1920s and her Afro-diasporic community building in the decades to follow.

Bowman wasn't braver than Walker or Mills, just luckier; she worked at a time when other cultural workers were making similar moves. There were in the 1920s and '30s, for example, several dancers in New York teaching dances from Nigeria and Sierra Leone.[37] Cultural workers took the exoticist interest in Africa as primitive and savage from the century's first decades and turned it, in the postwar period, toward respectful encounters with actual people and live, co-evolving cultural forms. They had parlayed exoticist and primitivist vogues into pan-Africanist endeavors, and their travels and collaborations reinforced the interpersonal web as well as the abstract idea of the African diaspora.

African American engagement with exoticism could also move in the opposite direction, rejecting the Afro-diasporic commonalities embraced by Bowman through her Haitian drums. Until well after the Second World War, after all, many more people agreed with E. Franklin Frazier's rejection of Africa in America than with Melville Herskovits's defense of African cultural continuities.[38] The debate, like other controversies about exoticism and empire, received its literal stagings. A series of black-cast shows in the late twenties and thirties, for example, wrestled with the relationship African Americans ought to hold to the exotic or to primitivism. *Earth* (New York, 1927); *Savage Rhythm* (New York, 1931); *Run, Little Chillun!* (New York, 1933); *Louisiana* (Brooklyn, 1933), which became a movie, *Drums Of Voodoo* (1934); and *Conjur* (New York, 1938) are probably part of a longer list.[39] The much-publicized *Run, Little Chillun!* gives a sense of these collective workings-out. The play explored a conflict between two black groups in the U.S. South, one a nomadic pagan cult, the other a stable but poor agricultural community, more or less faithful to the Christian church. As its stage directions specified, the set was to give an impression of "something approaching voodoo—not too directly African, but with a strong African flavor. . . . The whole betokens and partly expresses a religious attitude of joy and freedom toward life, in sharp contrast to the well-known spiritual joy in suffering which characterizes the more orthodox religious services of Negroes."[40] The plot unfolds when the proselytizing travelers conscript members of the struggling rural community, threatening to decimate its already thin ranks. In the dramatic climax, the primitive pagan princess is killed off, and the preacher's prodigal son, whom she had tempted, returns to the fold. Foregoing any critique of the forces that impoverished rural black hamlets, the play ended by handing a clear win to the traditional authorities of church, family, and state.

The other shows on this list apparently featured a similar conflict between Christianity and "voodoo," confirming that black thespians repeatedly chose to stage this sort of conflict and resolution in a black public sphere visible to many whites. All the plays resolved the question with an affirmation of distance from pagan barbarity, perhaps after pausing for a moment to relish the possibility of proximity in the acts before the final resolution. That moment would have provided different pleasures to white and black audience members, as African American producers, actors, and directors well knew.

Staging exoticism was only one part of the performative politics made possible by the transnational currents present in North Americans' local worlds during the imperial era. The other transformative performance, as noted, involved Europe. European desire for the exotic and the primitive, which extended to the African American arts, was a critical spark to the jazz age. Performers drew actively and strategically on European recognition, spinning it several ways.

When Sissieretta Jones proclaimed the supposed lack of racism in the United Kingdom ("not the slightest antipathy in the matter of color in England or in the provinces"), she was working to denaturalize racism— to show that racial antipathy was not a natural or necessary facet of social relations in heterogeneous societies. This attempt to convince, cajole, and shame North Americans into better behavior by gesturing to a place supposedly racism-free is a time-tested strategy.[41] In this chapter I am less interested in such logical arguments than in performative and cultural politics, but it is worthy of note that cultural workers not only made the point but seem also to have brought it to the attention of activists in more traditionally political arenas. That makes sense, since it was mostly cultural workers for whom primitivism generated steamship and railway passage. Josephine Baker's reception in Paris, for example, provided terrific evidence for the *Chicago Defender* to argue that "the narrow customs which prevail in America are known and condemned everywhere."[42]

Another useful figure in this regard was Sissieretta Jones's slightly younger colleague, the coloratura soprano Anita Patti Brown, who toured the Americas during the First World War. The *Chicago Defender* made a special arrangement with Brown for her Brazilian stay, so that covering her travels became an occasion to present Brazil as a site for African American emigration.[43] A "special correspondent" writing during Brown's engagement in Brazil (perhaps Brown herself?) called the South American country the "elysian field of the Black people," where black men owned the wealthiest corporations, governed the country, and lived in harmony with their white fellow citizens. A week later the *Defender* proclaimed in two-inch-high block letters across the top of its weekend-edition front page, "Brazil Wants Educated Black Men."[44] The *Defender* would make Brazil the centerpiece of a long-running anti-racist campaign in the years to come, as the next two chapters of this book will elaborate; Anita Patti Brown deserves pride of place in the history of that campaign.

The strategy of pointing to foreigners' embrace of African American artists, in addition to denaturalizing racism and shaming U.S. racists, also simply conferred prestige. The *Defender* clearly put stock in recognition from abroad. In its ongoing campaign to get phonograph companies to sign "race artists," the paper spotlit global interest. "Reports have come to this office that records of race artists are in demand at British West Indies, South America, and other foreign countries," it wrote.[45] Something in the strategy worked, for soon after Brown's "triumphant" tour, Victrola and Edison contracted her to record.[46]

Artists acted on the prestige bestowed by European success—literally. The full extent of Europe's potential as performance is evident in the work of Rufus Greenlee and Thaddeus Drayton, two vaudeville dancers who formed a team around 1909. This "big-time vaudeville act" used their experiences in both exotic and European forms to choreograph a radical innovation in black performance. Departing from the conventions of African American dance teams made up of a straight man and a blackface comedian, Greenlee and Drayton both sported immaculate black tie, forming a "class act" (precise, graceful dancing in formation). Pointing proudly to the space carved out by his "pioneering team," Greenlee claimed that following their example, "everybody washed off the burnt cork and tried to do a *neat* act—we paved the way for the class act."[47]

Greenlee and Drayton's innovative performance of "class" in a European inflection relied on the interlinked transnational currents of the exoticist culture of empire in the Western hemisphere and jazz-age primitivism across the Atlantic. Born in the South, both went to New York as children with their relatively well-off families. Drayton worked in white acts as a "pick," the stock role for African American child dancers.[48] "Pick" is short for "pickaninny," from the Portuguese or Spanish words for small fry, *pequeninho* and *pequeniño*.[49] The word's ugly derogatory implications in the United States have clouded its derivation and hid the phenomena it indexes: cultural contact, borrowing, and the conflation of African America and Latin America. These dancers were agents of continued cultural synthesis, bringing together local and transnational trends in spirited, crazy-quilt collage. They would juxtapose folk traditions of the United States and elsewhere over steps that sounded out the rhythms of the industrial age. As another self-described former "pick" remembered, "We'd go from plantation to Russian to the time step." What mattered to audiences was that it be fast. The "stereotype of rhythm and speed was expected of [these young] black performers, regardless of the style and category of their work."[50] This combination of freedom and limit, especially imposed on young dancers, practically ensured innovation.

This simmering mixture of minstrelsy and the exotic was part of Drayton's training when he teamed up with Greenlee for a European tour. Returning to the United States at the outset of the First World War, Greenlee and Drayton used what they had learned abroad—particularly the remarkable fluency Greenlee had gained in over half a dozen languages—to angle for bookings. "'We spend days walking up and down Broadway, all dressed up and twirling our canes,'" Drayton related, "'and Green asking me questions loudly in different foreign languages.' . . . Told that they had just arrived from Europe—were they famous foreigners?—[Al Jolson] sent them to Shapiro and Bernstein, who had them booked."[51] The agents were probably not convinced that they had a pair of "famous foreigners" on their ticket, but it was clear that this was an act capable of stirring up quite a buzz with its intriguing masquerades.

Once booked, Greenlee and Drayton moved their performance of accomplished urbanity from street to stage. Their "class act" cultivated a genteel polish in dress as well as dance style, based on the prestige of their European experience. Billing themselves as "Those Two Colored Fashion Plates" in the mainstream entertainment weekly *Variety*, they boasted of their recent engagements in "Wintergarten, Berlin, and Orpheum, Budapest, Austria-Hungary."[52] They also preserved the language schtick. As clarinetist Garvin Bushell recounted in his memoirs, the team "had an international act where they'd come out dancing and talk in all these different languages. They'd start with Hungarian, then they'd speak Russian, then French, Yiddish, English, and finally wind up in German"—and Italian and Gaelic, in other reports.[53]

Producers often balked at this aspect of their performance. "Agents were always trying to get us to cut out the talking," remembered Drayton. Jazz historians Marshall and Jean Stearns explain that talking acts earned more, but while the extra expense was surely part of the reason the dancers were asked to excise this aspect of their act, the obvious erudite cosmopolitanism of these African American performers probably rubbed white viewers uncomfortably against the grain. The pair understood this discomfort perfectly and flaunted their refusal to soothe it: in response to demands that they silence their voices, "Greenlee added a lot more and started singing, too."[54] The duo's insistence on maintaining this facet of their performance despite their agents' subsequent change of heart reveals the disguise to have been more potent than expected. Greenlee and Drayton refused the ridiculous roles of blackface, staking claims to speech, intellect, elegance, and affluence on the grounds of their international travels.

Greenlee and Drayton's New York success would spark further motion, as readers may recall from chapter 3; in the 1920s their travels included Brazil, and in the '30s their repertoire featured the Carioca, the "Brazilian" dance from *Flying Down to Rio*. Surely Greenlee picked up some Portuguese for his next round of Broadway patter?

That Greenlee and Drayton were able to use Europe and language so successfully in their refusal of debased performance has much to do with gender. The distinctly feminine sexuality of the exotic was not such a minefield for them. What they most needed to conquer were the usual representational possibilities for African American men. Playing dandyish European sophisticates helped them steer clear of the Scylla of the minstrel fool and the Charybdis of the buck. The performance of "Europe" was harder for African American women to pull off, requiring the transcendence of not one but two qualities, "black" *and* "female," which distanced their designates from the heights of European status. No wonder, then, that in contrast to Greenlee and Drayton, many African American women who broke into the world of "high" art dance in the twenties often did so via ever more thorough performances of the exotic. As the constraints of Jim Crow consolidated and the seductions of the exotic continued to glow, some rose to a level of exoticist performance so thoroughgoing that they practically qualify as "passing."

The concert dancer Margot Webb, for example, had worked the multiculti repertoire of a "pick" as a child, as had Thaddeus Drayton. Her adult routines are an illustrative index of the exoticist twenties, including rumba; bolero; tango; waltz; novelty dances such as the Apache; fleeting fads such as the Continental and the Carioca; and "'Oriental' numbers, Egyptian dances, Gypsy routines with tambourines, scarf dances, Grecian dances—basically, all kinds of ethnic dances distilled into [a] catchall style."[55] Graduating from "pick" routines to exoticist programs was a step Webb took alongside many others; her endpoint, however, was audacious. "Norton and Margot," as Webb and her partner named their duo, became "one of the few Afro-American ballroom teams in history."[56]

As Webb's biographer, Brenda Dixon Gottschild, observes, Norton and Margot's significant, even striking, success was still always tightly constrained by racism.[57] When skill and will were not enough to propel Webb over the barriers racism threw in her way, she deployed her exoticist training to move up the cultural hierarchy into the realm of the dances she wanted to do. To break in to the white world of ballroom dancing, Webb engaged in masquerade. Adroitly reading her ideological environment, in which African American dancers could not be hired but "Latin" ones sometimes could, she modified her first name from Marjorie to Margot, sometimes dropping the final "t" for an even more Latin effect. Norton and Margot presented themselves as "Spanish" to work a Jewish summer camp in 1936 and as natives of the "South Seas" in a 1941 show in Montreal, a double drag in which they first had to feign Francophone affiliations. Norton, who spoke no French, simply refused to speak.[58]

With these masquerades, the couple elevated their performance to the level of genuine identity. This fully deliberate, acknowledged exoticism helped some performers, unlikely to be able to claim themselves white, to sidestep the strictures of anti-black racism. The tactic has a long tail, evident in literature and beginning to be documented historically.[59] Those who wielded it, like Norton and Margot, were not exactly passing as white. They were not exactly passing at all, necessarily. They were raising an alternative racial schema—a system in which there were not two but many racial categories—to displace the black-white dichotomy constraining their skills and ambitions. Rogers's Jones would have approved.

Another way in which Norton and Margot were not passing involved their disguises' sitting lightly upon them, only nominally threatened by the possibility of revelation. Gottschild notes that "what was required of Webb was simply stating that she was Latina. She was not obliged to feign an accent or give proof of her country of origin. 'They just took me at face value'" in Webb's ironic phrase. In Canada, similarly, Webb remembered the absolute openness of the farce, suggested by the booking agent herself. She "told us they weren't going to hire blacks so we'd better be something else. 'It says here,' [the agent] observed, pointing to a clip from the Montreal paper, 'featuring a real South Sea Island dance team.'" Dancer Edna Guy had a similar experience when applying to a dance camp. The director "recommended that Guy send a photograph and perhaps pass as East Indian. Guy easily recognized the hypocrisy: 'They will let every other foreign nationality come in their classes expect [*sic*] an American colored girl. Oh! Why are they like that.'"[60]

Nor were these ballet-trained dancers required to perform "Latin" styles. Margot Webb's specialty remained a toe dance, and her favorite couple dance was always the waltz, "the dance most reminiscent of ballet adagio work and the lightest, whitest part of their repertory." Perhaps their performance of balletic whiteness shifted the perception of their skin color toward the lighter end of the scale, enhancing their opportunities to pass as foreign. As dance historian Julia Foulkes has observed, "Lighter-skinned African Americans had less trouble because passing as white or foreign was another way to enter white dance studios."[61] Gottschild agrees that Norton and Margot's co-workers in Montreal "had caught on to the team's masquerade but chose to treat them as pariahs rather than fire them."[62] More important, audiences chose not to react. Those who "knew," on whatever level, preferred the masquerade to losing the opportunity of this spectacle, whose pleasure hinged on the blackness of its objects but whose possibility required its denial.

The same setting presented itself to Laura Bowman, the dramatic actress we met above. In 1916, she and Sidney Kirkpatrick moved to Indianapolis, "rather a prejudiced town with disadvantages for colored performers," she mildly put it. The couple decided to claim to be Hawaiian, a transparent sham that nobody protested. Bowman again: "Although it was Sidney's home and everyone knew his family, we billed ourselves as a modern Hawaiian Duet and got by with it. We often played in theatres that did not allow colored patrons or performers."[63] Black exotic masquerades, therefore, allowed black artists to desegregate not only white-dominated performance genres, but white-only performance spaces as well.

This was the case of the 1914 fad for Brazilian-Argentine-French tango, as readers may recall from chapter 2. African American instrumentalists dominated tango bands, crossing a color line, we learned from a vaudeville critic who mentioned it in 1915. Hiding a "negro orchestra" behind a bank of palms, he pointed out, was "unnecessary after a season of the tango, since we know nearly every ebony musician by sight."[64] African American musicians had played tango in white venues openly, though whether they could continue to do so with other genres was an unsettled question. Why? What was happening that allowed black musicians to appear openly in white clubs? Were they "passing" as Argentine or Brazilian? If so, did they do so mindfully, or was it inadvertent, the music their only disguise? Whatever the details, it is clear that in the liminality of tango's exoticism, the performers moved beyond the binary of black and white for a fleeting moment. This subtle movement was less a loud crack than a small crevice, part of a network of similar fissures in the ideological terrain opened up in front of performances of exotic forms by African American artists.

White producers and audiences cooperated in the charade—they wanted, on some level, to enjoy the tanguistas', or Bowman and Kirkpatrick's, or Norton and Margot's several performances.

Such manipulations of racial and national categories were not confined to the United States. Information gathered from travels and fellow cultural workers gave performers finely tuned understandings of the precise masquerades required elsewhere as well. Europe had a widely known reputation as a place "free" of racism, for example, which meant African Americans could perform as such. South Africa, in contrast, was reputed to resemble the United States in its anti-black racism. "South Africa was known as a destination with severe race prejudice," writes a biographer of a family of black women in vaudeville, "so severe that when the Meredith Sisters toured the area they billed themselves as American Indian Squaws."[65] To evade South African racism, the Meredith Sisters clearly saw, they needed a category that would stand on its own and avoid being collapsed into a subordinate local one.

White views of this phenomenon could be as clear as the masquerades were transparent. In 1899, a white minstrel quipped, "Der ain't no niggers since de war broke out;/'I'm a Cuban now,' you'll hear them shout."[66] The author of this taunt had clearly registered the solidarities imperial engagements made possible between subjects of internal domestic and formal political colonialism. In particular, he had noted African American admiration for and identification with the Cuban, particularly Afro-Cuban, soldiers just then visibly and valiantly resisting U.S. occupation. This taunt also highlights the axis of these charades: the parodied speakers did not renounce one nationality for another or pass from black to white; they substituted a national for a racial category. More precisely, they refused an inherently demeaning racial category by gesturing to a national one that was both dark and dignified. "Cuban" was incompatible with "n——," not blackness.

Understanding, of course, implied neither sympathy nor support. White willingness to go along with national masquerade was highly contingent. In many cases the revelation of a person's "real" identity would have mattered—a lot. Masquerades in those contexts could be breathtakingly audacious. In the late 1930s (a date that makes this story all the more remarkable), Herb Flemming returned to the United States from many years in Europe, mourning the feeling of freedom he left behind. During a tour of the South, in Macon, Georgia, he used his language skills in a convincing nation drag: "There were no hotels (colored) available at the time of my arrival (11:30 P.M.). So, playing dumb, I walked into a white hotel and spoke only German. A man offered to help the desk clerk to find out what I wanted (the man was American, born in Hamburg, Germany). When he learned of my desire he was overjoyed to be able to prove there were colored people from his country who only spoke German. He told the hotel manager: 'This is a countryman of mine and I want him respected.' I got a room in a white hotel in Macon, Georgia, believe it or not!"[67] Flemming's narration suggests he was performing near or in Macon, perhaps the very next day. Why, then, was he not more concerned with being "discovered"? Flemming read the landscape of social possibility through his own frustration with U.S. racism and reached a conclusion that, for reasons that must remain elusive, did not bring white wrath down upon his shoulders. Not every careful player of this outside chance was so lucky.

Flemming's nerve is all the more striking when placed beside failed attempts to use national masquerades. Whites were not always willing to tolerate the border crossings such disguises reflected and enabled. The experience of Caterina Jarboro, born Catherine Yarborough in Wilmington, North Carolina, in 1903, suggests that whites policed the boundaries of race more intently in elite cultural realms than in vaudeville; it also may point to the diminished space for such moves during the Depression.[68] Jarboro "passed" as Italian to earn a principal role with the Chicago Opera Company in 1933. The *New York Times* raved about her "vivid dramatic sense" and "remarkably pure and distinct" Italian pronunciation. Alas, Jarboro was revealed to "be" African American and was dismissed. She turned to the National Negro Opera Company and a segregated career as a concert singer.[69] The crest of the exoticist wave that pulled Sissieretta Jones out of opera to her second-choice venue of vaudeville rolled Jarboro hard into the undertow of Jim Crow social codes, increasingly consolidating as the 1920s drew to a close.

The reasons Flemming pulled off his charade while Jarboro did not include the one-time nature of his attempt versus the sustained effort of hers, as well as, again, gender. Gendered ideas about which sorts of subjects ought to speak helped make Flemming's words (like Greenlee's) compelling and Jarboro's gorgeous pronunciation unbearable. Masculinity was far from sure-fire protection, and in fact racially marked subjects attempting to assume the prerogatives granted its white claimants could face even more bitter consequences. A tragic illustration is a 1916 lynch mob that murdered an African American minister on a train for "fraudulent impersonation of a Frenchman"—a luggage tag revealed he had traveled to France.[70] Pasted over the "skin" of a suitcase, the tag indexed the minister's various mobilities (economic, social, geographic) and recalled all sorts of passings, including the possibility of national masquerade, as the accusation specified.[71] The extreme brutality with which it was met confirms the potential power of this representational stance.

As the Depression receded, and as there was less encroaching on white privilege in "low-culture" venues, black exoticist masquerades continued. Lavinia Williams, one of the dancers from Katharine Dunham's original company, adopted nation drag during the filming of the 1940 *Carnival in Rhythm*, as did her fellow cast members, in a permutation that indexed the samba craze accompanying Carmen Miranda. "We were [passed off as] Brazilians," she recalled, "anything but black Americans."[72] People discussing this chapter with me have offered anecdotal musings about similar charades by baseball players, activists, job seekers, pleasure shoppers, and more; clearly the phenomenon is ongoing, though its specifics will change over time.

Scholarly observers have not fully recognized this shifting between two kinds of racial schemas, one with multiple intermediate racial categories and the other predicated upon the duality of black and white. Margot Webb and her biographer, Brenda Dixon Gottschild, perceptive social critics who offer an unusually explicit discussion of national masquerades, illustrate the dilemma. "Back then, performers in the United States who were Spanish- or French-speaking and claimed to be from another country were treated as honorary whites and were not subject to antiblack discrimination," Gottschild glosses, agreeing with Webb: "They called Spanish 'white' then. . . . Today they lump the two groups [i.e., 'Spanish' and 'black'] together, but in those days if you spoke Spanish and were from any country speaking Spanish—you were considered white, whether you were dark-skinned or not."[73] Yet as Gottschild also explains, "Norton was noticeably darker than Margot and looked Spanish, a connotation that allowed for a broader range of skin color than the white category."[74] The contradiction between the suggestion that Spanish *meant* white and that Spanish was a category *broader* than white is precisely the tension so productively mined by African American masquerades of nation and performances of the exotic. It is the tension generated by multiple, competing racial schemas—some dichotomous, some plural—operating simultaneously.

A similar misconception characterizes scholars' discussions of one of the incidents of national masquerade in *Uncle Tom's Cabin*: George Harris's escape from slavery by pretending to be "Spanish." Presenting a collection of essays on passing, one scholar writes, "George's masquerade exposes the inability of his audience—representative of the rural antebellum South—to read 'otherness' in anything but black/white terms."[75] Yet while "black" and "white" were certainly dominant terms in Harriet Beecher Stowe's day, they were not the only ones available. A more nuanced observer sees in Harris's Spanish masquerade an "important alternative vision to the manichean allegory at work in his culture," existing *alongside* the dualistic division of black and white, the author's prose implies.[76] As she continues, "the nonblack, nonwhite other passes precisely because such otherness remains relatively unintelligible in the terms of a manichean hierarchical system."[77] The word "relatively" is critical, for Harris's masquerade would have floundered had he assumed a character that was entirely unintelligible to his peers. Harris's category made sense: "Spaniards" inhabited North American imaginations in the nineteenth century, representing "power" when figured as lighter-skinned and "difference" when darker.[78] As the Meredith Sisters, performing as "Indian Squaws" in South Africa, well understood, a successful masquerade had to embody a *relatively* un-*familiar* category, recognizable as kin to but obviously outside the family of local possibilities.

Observers of national masquerades have often understood them as instances of "passing." As Margot Webb explained about an actor of her acquaintance, "That's why Frank Silvera made so much money—because he was really passing, in a way. He was always playing foreign people. He was either Jewish, Greek, Spanish—anything but black."[79] Webb understood "passing" in its usual sense of a foray into whiteness, as in the definition ventured by another scholar: "light-skinned black Americans who shed their blackness in order to assume the social, legal, and economic privileges of whiteness in America."[80] As this definition suggests, passing as conceptualized in most cases invokes only the racial categories of black, white, and in between. While such a process can wreak wonderful havoc on the schema of black and white, undeniably a controlling fiction of U.S. life, it stops short of the more profoundly disruptive transformations. So thoroughly does passing invoke this simplistic schema that its most brilliant scholars obediently confine themselves to it, even as they critique its reinforcement of "an archaic notion of identity" or point out that "one cannot pass for something one *is not* unless there is some other, prepassing, identity that one *is*."[81]

Might "drag" be a better description of these national masquerades than passing? Drag is often understood as a more explicitly acknowledged performance. "In contrast to passing, drag calls attention to the act of impersonation and foregrounds its status as imitation."[82] Because drag is explicitly conceptualized as a performance, it holds out the promise of entertainment—drag is fun. Drag "describes discontinuities between gender and sex or appearance and reality," in which, rather than constituting a problem, "incongruence becomes the site of gender creativity."[83] Drag is a fabulous parody that "mocks . . . the notion of a true gender identity" and "implicitly reveals the imitative structure of gender itself," in Judith Butler's resonant terms.[84]

Most theorizations of drag have confined themselves to gender, and discussions of passing tend to focus on race. Yet the determination of a given performance as drag or passing is less about the category it negotiates than the eye of the beholder. A masquerade can shuttle between drag and passing as context shifts the act's reception.[85] When performers such as the stars of this story mounted their transparent but necessary charades, some in their audience chose ignorance's bliss; to those fans, the performers were passing. Others enjoyed the performance enhanced with performance, the play within a play. Neither passing nor drag describes these phenomena precisely; they exceed language in a way that burlesques the desire to define them. If the masquerades discussed here passed, it was from binary to plural (two-category to multi-category) racial schemas, but they never came to rest in either. They pointed out the coexistence of both, highlighting the shifting social landscapes that are not the exception but the norm, mocking our ceaseless struggles to make them hold still.

PAN-AMERICAN COMMERCE boomed during and after the First World War, as we have seen above, offering many a handle to popular performers. In a nod to importers who marketed Brazilian products in the United States, a series of performers shared the same sweet, stale pun: a New York vaudeville singer known as "the Brazilian Nut"; a traveling theater troupe named "Valyda and Brazilian Nuts"; a Hardtack Jackson show called "Two

Nuts from Brazil"; the comedy troupe "Marshall Rogers' 'Brazilian Nuts'";
and *Charley's Aunt*, a Broadway farce that played for laughs with the title
character's repeated, apparently hilarious reminder that she hailed "from
Brazil where the nuts come from."[86] Perhaps these acts incorporated
actual performers from Brazil; perhaps they simply added the carryover
publicity of importers' ad campaigns to the connotations Brazil held for
North American audiences in general—far, strange, semi-savage, vaguely
sensual. But the performances produced by and for African Americans
(Valyda, Jackson, and Rogers, at least) contained something more. The
pleasures of its exoticism, to which African Americans were not immune,
enhanced Brazil's seeming promise of a less racist place, a reputation African Americans helped distribute and promote. Sensuality and spectacularity, tinged with overtones of political advantage, proved an enticing
attraction.

Perhaps Brazil's multiple gifts to performers of exotic subjects explains
its attraction to the dancer Olive Burgoyne. Burgoyne performed countless exotic forms over her long and active life, eventually settling on a specialty, "the Brazilian dance"—despite the lack of any evidence that her
travels included Brazil. Indeed, South America was the rare omission in
a life that seems to have touched down nearly everywhere else. Examining Burgoyne's career in slightly more detail will help elucidate the dynamics at play in African American performances of "Brazil" and other
exotics. The task involves some speculation, not only because, like most
early-twentieth-century black performers, Burgoyne never earned the attention she deserved. The details of her life are also difficult to discern
because this quintessential performer was never out of character, and her
characters often changed. As the author of multiple, competing stories
about herself, Burgoyne would surely be pleased to see how blurry she
succeeded in leaving the historical record.

Ollie Burgoyne's "Brazilian Dance"

In 1896, a winsome Chicago-born dancer, still a teenager by most accounts,
joined Isham's Oriental America. With this step, Olive Burgoyne began a
theatrical career that would span decades, continents, and too many cultures and nations to list. Burgoyne was as adept in picking up identifications as Rufus Greenlee was in languages; she layered affiliations over

each other in both stage and everyday performances. Perceptively reading the world around her, Burgoyne placed herself determinedly at the fertile interstices of the exotic, the primitive, and Europe's "Negro vogue."

As a result of Burgoyne's nimble transubstantiations, there are multiple, competing accounts of the landmarks of her life. She herself changed the spelling of her last name, leaving at least three competing versions to knock about the corridors of history, and her own interventions and her adaptations to her travels pulled her first name back and forth from Olive to Ollie to Olga. Unsurprisingly for an actress, she altered the date of her birth so effectively that biographers are still not sure whether she greeted Chicago in 1878, 1880, 1885, or even 1895.[87]

Burgoyne spent anywhere from a few months touring Germany, Poland, and Russia to several years touring both Europe and the United States (depending on the source), finally settling into a two-year gig in St. Petersburg at a nightspot variously listed as the Kammernestrosky or Christoph Gardens.[88] When it was up, she stayed in Russia, performing and running a small business—a lingerie boutique—for some time (one year to several, different sources say). While most reports, including those in Burgoyne's own voice, portray her Russian stint as stationary and as beginning around 1902, Sampson claims Burgoyne performed in a 1903 production called *Uncle Eph's Christmas*, probably in the United States, and Helen Armstead Johnson placed Burgoyne in the operetta *In Dahomey* in London in 1903. When the show closed, Johnson noted, "many of the performers created their own teams and individual acts and traveled imaginatively. One of them was Olga Burgoyne who, with her partner, Usher Watts, formed the *Duo Eclatant*."[89] Elsewhere Johnson places Burgoyne and Watts in Russia in 1902, the year *before* the Shaftsbury run of *In Dahomey*.[90] Burgoyne neglected to mention Watts in the existing accounts she gave of her own life; she also did not refer to D. C. Nelson, the musician she had married in 1928 according to a 1932 newspaper article.[91]

Burgoyne lived in Russia until the outbreak of war—which war, however, is unclear. Some accounts suggest the 1905 Russian Revolution sent her home; others blame the First World War.[92] The finding aid for her papers at the Schomburg Branch of the New York Public Library even reports that she moved *to* Russia in 1930. Secondary sources all accept Burgoyne's claim that when hostilities began, she was taken by surprise while tending to her health at an Austrian spa ("The Russian Revolution had been raging, but Olga had not read a newspaper in three days").[93] Unable to return to gather her things, all evidence of her activities there, such as the imperial certificate issued by the tsar, were (conveniently, a cynic might mutter) lost.

These confusing details are not necessarily inconsistencies. Burgoyne could certainly have been in several productions and two continents in a single year, *Uncle Eph* could have been staged in Europe, and there are many reasons a person might omit a husband or male partner from a story she wanted to tell about herself. Burgoyne often crafted her life story as a tale of a powerful, talented individual, forging her path alone. In addition to overlooking her husband and partner, she left out her cousin, the dancer Ida Forsyne, a long-time resident of Moscow who must have been there at the same time as Burgoyne.[94] She also neglected to credit any of the shows that trained her or brought her to Europe. Perhaps she kept silent about her collaborators because they interfered with her constant self-reinventions, particularly her regular updates of her age.

Burgoyne's individualist emphasis is evident in her presentation of her return to the United States in 1905 or 1914. "It was the worst time of my life," she remembered in 1967 in a discussion with a reporter for the Ventura, California, *Star Free Press*. "No one would hire me, and I didn't care what I had to do. But I didn't know anything about housework—I never did any. I had no education, so I couldn't teach school. What was I going to do?"[95] This perceptive evaluation of the options available to African American women (including perhaps a muted reference to the underground economy—"I didn't care what I had to do") explains why Burgoyne despaired. Its astuteness also illustrates the deft grasp of social conditions that underpinned her solution. Burgoyne took the pulse of her moment and made a decision: to cultivate, for public exhibition, multiple, competing allegiances, affiliations, and identifications, extending a tactic at which she was probably already quite adept.

Burgoyne's multiple exoticisms flowed logically from her early, formative work with the Oriental Americans, her training in "the Oriental art of Delsarte" (a French technique of expressive movement and dance popular in the 1900s and 1910s), and her travels in "Germany, Denmark, Sweden, Hungary, France, Switzerland, Egypt and Turkey where she mastered the oriental dances."[96] Over the Orientalism instilled early on, she layered what she learned on her travels—not just the fluent Russian, German, and French this keen student of languages and cultures acquired.

Burgoyne put the various traditions she "mastered" to different applications. She used Afro-Francophonic affiliations, for example, to raise the prestige of her sensual cachet. She used a French title for her partnership with Watts (the Duo Eclatant) and called her St. Petersburg lingerie boutique the "Maison Creole," and in 1920s vaudeville circuits, she billed herself as an "Algerian Girl."[97] This last may have felt like the truth rather than a pose to Burgoyne, who told a reporter in 1967 that her father was Algerian (something other sources do not confirm). Yet even if her parentage did give her some lien on this self-presentation, as someone who grew up in Chicago, Burgoyne was "American" enough to be able to embrace or leave Algeria behind. She chose it and the other black French titles because she understood how Frenchness enhanced her prestige and blackness, her sensual attraction. Demonstrating the success of this aware self-representation, a St. Petersburg paper in 1907 praised the "Creole girl Bourgogne, an exotic beauty with sparkling eyes, a teint of soft bronze and dazzling white teeth."[98] Though the term "Creole" meant different things in the United States, Burgoyne still used it upon her return from Russia to evoke a deliciously foreign female sensuality, suggests a show she illuminated in 1920, *Town Top-Piks*, which included a song entitled "Land of Creole Girls."[99]

Burgoyne used her color in primitivist Europe to set herself apart from white showgirls, fully aware of the representational impact of blackness in her pretty, female form. She articulated this understanding to a reviewer of *Run, Little Chillun!*, probably when the show was first produced in 1933. In Russia, she reported, she "had been taken in by an American with several other colored girls from a show in Leipsig," all left stranded by poor management. Happily, "with youth and courage, and because of the fact that black girls were a novelty, I found no difficulty in getting a place singing and dancing."[100] For the California reporter with whom she reminisced thirty-four years later, she also remembered that in Warsaw, where she designed her own act before heading on to Russia, "I was the only black face in town. I had costumes made and was doing very well." In St. Petersburg, too, she explained her success as in part a reflection of her being, again, "the only 'black face' in town" (an individualist framing she chose despite her cousin Ida's probable presence).[101] To enhance this aspect of her identification in Russia, she placed black models in the windows of her chic boutique.[102]

Burgoyne understood some of the pitfalls of presenting herself as an erotic subject—not just a young black woman, but an actress to boot. To ward off the "shame" that could easily adhere to such a figure, she carefully emphasized her propriety. Even in her older age, when discussing with a North American reporter the invitations to dinner she received after her St. Petersburg performances, she insisted these had been "the most dignified of arrangements."[103] In 1933, closer to the dilemma, she offered an even more detailed version of these invitations, portraying them as encounters with foreign mores. Offered monetary gifts by admiring men, she refused:

> I was still almost a child and had my own ideas of what was proper.[104] When the offending gentleman called me "Durotchka!" I just knew I was insulted. "What does he call me," I asked tearfully. "Little Dummy," replied my friend, "but you are a big one. It is the custom of the Russians, if you please them, to give a gift for your flowers, your carriage, or little needs. They do not expect to buy your kisses, take it graciously." I worked hard and saved and soon found myself owner of a lingerie shop which I called Maison Creole, where I employed twenty-seven persons, meanwhile continuing my theatrical career. My clientele included ladies-in-waiting and many of the nobility. Some gave me personal gifts.[105]

The morality tale ends happily in this 1933 version, with Burgoyne successfully negotiating the foreign cultural landscape to financial success and acceptance into an aristocratic social circle.

The passage above begins to suggest the ways Burgoyne used her Russian affiliations to buttress later social mobility. Upon her return to the United States, Russianness was one of her favorite performances. She presented herself as "Olga" rather than "Olive" or "Ollie," inconsistently, for the rest of her life. She taught Russian dancing and was remembered as "the well-known black exponent of Russian dancing" regarding her work with the New Negro Art Theatre Dance Company in 1931.[106] Burgoyne's reasons for this reiterated Russianness emerge in a revealing anecdote she liked to tell about a fur coat she salvaged from her days in St. Petersburg. The coat was "of the most beautiful Persian lamb, lined with Siberian squirrel. 'Oh,' said her friends on her return to America, 'why not have two coats, one of squirrel?' 'Squirrel, indeed,' she replied. 'In Russia we think that is only fit for a lining.'"[107] Burgoyne told this story to emphasize her financial success and entrance into the social circles of the Russian nobility, her amply royal "we" demonstrating an easy assumption of Russianness.

To North American peers, who would have been unlikely to hear it as a claim of Russian citizenship or origin, Burgoyne mobilized a Russian affiliation in order to translate a self-proclaimed *class* position over to the other side of the Bering Strait.

Upon her return to the United States, Burgoyne developed further layers of exoticist performance. In *They're Off*, a 1919 racetrack drama put on by the Billy King Stock Company, an Atlanta-based group with which she performed from 1915 to 1923, Burgoyne performed "a classic dance called 'Brazil.'"[108] This production fell near the early part of her years performing in the United States, and it seems that its success was instructive to Burgoyne. As Sampson reported in summary of her career, "Miss Burgoyne's specialty was dancing and her forte was the Brazilian Dance, the Snake dance, and the famous Spanish dance. Her arms, hand motions, and the swing of her graceful body in doing these dances caused the theatrical critics to rate her the peer of any dancer in the world."[109] The slightly jarring syntax of this sentence, claiming Burgoyne's (singular) strong point to have been threefold, points to a truth stronger than grammar: Burgoyne's specialty was the performance of multiple identities and exotic forms.

While Burgoyne's own experience and training would have allowed her to recognize a wide range of genres and styles of dance, the "Oriental," "Russian," "Algerian," "Creole," "Brazilian," "snake," and "Spanish" dances she performed in the United States were probably less reflective of her expertise in "genuine" versions of those forms and more signs of her keen understanding of her audiences' projections and desires. Burgoyne did study dance in Russia, but my guess would be that the dance she studied only faintly resembled what she danced for U.S. eyes. In Russia she probably studied formal ballet, a prized tradition there, especially prior to the folk culture revival of the revolutionary periods, and closest to the aristocratic social position Burgoyne cultivated for herself in Moscow. The "Brazilian dance" could have had elements of maxixe, a notable fad in the United States five or fewer years before *They're Off*, just as the "famous Spanish dance" may have glossed flamenco or tango. The "snake dance" surely borrowed from the Salomé craze, but regardless, it unmistakably invoked the full charge of Orientalist, not-quite-human attraction and danger, overtones of Edenic expulsion. Regardless of their faithfulness to any identifiable referents, the versions Burgoyne performed all shared an unequivocal evocation of exotic sensuality. They varied from each other somewhat—images of Spain or Spanish America may have been an inch

lighter in skin tone and in scale of civilization than ideas about Brazil—
but to audiences in the era of U.S. imperialism and its exoticist cultural
expression, all were gorgeously murky and mysterious. The placement side
by side of "Brazilian," "Spanish," and "snake," especially in the person of
a Russian-speaking, "Algerian," "Creole" woman, ironed over the niceties
of all their distinctions, pulling the adjectives into a smooth suggestion of
multiply-exotic Otherness. Burgoyne's performative categories ought to
have been in contradiction but seemed instead to build upon each other.

In terms of representation in U.S. popular fields, there is a significant
distance between this "mysterious" exotic, amply available for the viewer's
own projections, and an African American's far more familiar figure. Burgoyne's gesture to Brazil and to "Spanish" traditions substituted a racially
intermediate exoticism for, and overlaid it upon, the starker category of
blackness. Her strategic self-placements bowed to North Atlantic audiences' expectations of the pleasurable spectacle at the intersection of
blackness, performance (especially dance), and exotic sensuality. But she
bowed *out* of U.S. racial schemas by invoking foreign titles repeatedly.
She drew pleasingly on the multiple racial categories in use at the time,
some national, some cultural, some regional, some color-based, and so on.
Her life calls attention to the ill-understood relationship of simultaneous,
competing schemas of racial categorization, which existed then as they do
today, slipping over each other into foreground or background as context
compels. Burgoyne and her colleagues performing exoticisms disrupted
the simple division of black and white, casting wrenches of multiplicity
into the machinery of binary distinctions upon which Jim Crow relied.

Burgoyne's brilliant application of the strategy of multiple national
masquerades worked only for a while. When possibilities for touring dried
up in the mid-1930s and Burgoyne ceased her European excursions, she
fell back under the shadows of starker racial classifications. She played
mostly maids in white-dominated movies and theatrical productions, and
her career as a concert dancer was constricted in ways that did not do justice to her talent. Even by 1933, Burgoyne's onstage presence had begun to
shift. In that year she premiered the role of Mother Kanda, the "voodoo"
elder, in the original New York production of *Run, Little Chillun!* In
Kanda, Burgoyne explored a character new to her: a powerful black exotic
figure, primitivism unassuaged by a prestigious foreign nationality, who is
mature, dangerous, and doomed. The rave reviews for her commanding
stage presence suggest this was a role she animated with feeling.

FIGURE 15. Stella F. Simon, Olga Burgoyne as Mother Kanda in a scene from *Run, Little Chillun!*, 1933. Photographs and Prints Division, Schomburg Center for Research in Black Culture, NYPL.

Perhaps Burgoyne's exoticist performances worked only during the period of the Negro vogue and the height of the imperial era, faltering as the global Depression ground its terrible wheels. Perhaps her aging body could no longer convey the sensual exoticism of her earlier attractions. Perhaps "Russia" after a round or two of Red Scares no longer invoked aristocracy in sufficiently obvious ways. In any case, a few months after a stint in the New York production of *The Willow and I* in late 1942, Burgoyne took a trip to Oxnard, California, to visit a friend, and the visit stretched out into a stay.[110] Incapable of inactivity, Burgoyne accepted a supposedly short-term job as a "hat-check girl" at a local restaurant-cabaret. Though it was far from the public eye, she apparently enjoyed the place and made it her own; she would wait tables, check coats, and (when the management discovered her abilities) perform a little as well, essentially up until her death in 1973.[111]

The obscurity in which Ollie Burgoyne ended her life, like the similar fate of Sissieretta Jones and the tragic early deaths of Aida Overton Walker and Florence Mills, points to the brutality constraining the most successful African American performers, no matter the triumphs secured through exoticist performance. African American performers used the exoticist hungers excited by colonial engagement to wedge open spaces for their activity, but even their skillful negotiations expanded ideological contexts still constrained within razor-sharp limits.

No single individual illustrates the tyranny of exoticist projections more acutely than our last subject, a figure who confirms acutely that "all race identity is . . . the product of passing" and whose life performance, like a deliberate drag, "reveals the imitative structure of gender itself"— and of race and nation, we might add.[112] This is Elsie Houston, a diva who toyed with the borders of mere human social categories, though her brilliant settings of the ideological elements in her reach ended in tragedy.

Untranslatable: Elsie Houston

Singer, writer, composer, scholar, folklorist, drummer, dancer, and more, Elsie Houston belies categorization. Her life was a surreal transnational performance of the possibilities and pitfalls for a female artist sometimes read as black during the global exoticist Negro vogue.

Houston was born in 1902 in Rio de Janeiro, the second of three girls.

There are some wrinkles in the timing of her life story (as in Burgoyne's); in one oft-told version her father, James Franklin Houston, was a dentist from Tennessee. He had gone to Brazil after the U.S. Civil War with the disaffected confederates who established the town of Americana in the Brazilian interior. Houston, *père*, left Americana for Petrópolis, where he met Arinda Galdo, settling with her in Rio to practice dentistry.[113] The timing of this narrative is confusing; either Houston was very old when he began a family or a generation slipped through a gap. We must read the story for its large structures rather than try to pin down specific details.

Houston's parentage raises fascinating questions about her life from its beginning. How did the Houston family understand their nationality? What was their racial self-categorization? The ex-confederates may have taken slaves with them, but few could have been dentists; James Franklin Houston was surely "white" in U.S. terms. Yet in Brazil he became husband to a woman of African descent, we must conclude from Elsie Houston's complex(posit)ion. Did he believe his Brazilian stay had changed his standards, or did he absorb and diffuse his life's internal contradictions before they reached his conscious mind? These are questions I cannot answer, though it is likely that as North American transplants taking their rightful place among Rio's cultural elites, the Houston family's highly privileged social location kept them from having to identify with subordinate positions of any sort.

As befit the child of such an august family, Elsie Houston traveled to Europe in her twenties for classical music training and the Parisian finish so highly valued by her class compatriots.[114] In Paris she encountered the mania of futurism, surrealism, and primitivism for authentic "folk" culture. Like many other elite Brazilians with Modernist leanings in the twenties, Houston's European stay turned her attention back to the folkloric forms of Brazil.[115] Houston came to love Brazilian popular music and would devote the rest of her life to its exposition.

Most of the 1920s found Houston in Paris, though she continued to travel widely. The record of her travels and studies includes encounters with a star-studded list of Modernist artists from two continents. In 1922 she met the Brazilian composer Luciano Gallet, one of the first people to spark her interest in folklore. After vocal training with Lilli Lehmann in Germany in 1923, she recorded some of Gallet's songs in 1924 and more in '25 (probably back in Brazil). She met and formed a friendship with Brazilian Modernist Mário de Andrade (on which side of the Atlantic is

unclear). Her Paris debut was managed by the French surrealist Aurélien Lugné-Poe, whom she also befriended. In 1927, Houston studied in
Argentina with French soprano Ninon Vallin, who had begun regular performing trips to South America in 1916 and loved South American music.
Houston would resume lessons with Vallin later that year in Paris. Also in
1927, Houston performed in Villa-Lobos's Paris premiere, together with
the then already well-known Polish pianist Artur Rubinstein, who would
go on to international stardom a decade later.

For Houston, 1927 was a busy year indeed, for it was also then that she
met and married the French surrealist Benjamin Péret. Houston changed
her name only from "Mlle." to "Mme." after her marriage, though at times
she used a composite last name.[116] In 1928 "Mme. Elsie Houston" authored
a paper (in flawless, erudite French) on Brazilian popular ceremonies,
music, and dance to deliver to the First International Congress of Popular
Arts in Prague, perhaps drawing from the research for that paper to prepare the collection of scores of Brazilian popular music she would publish
with the Librairie Orientaliste Paul Geuthner in 1930.[117] In 1929, Houston
and Péret left Europe for Brazil, where they would spend the bulk of the
next two years. A photograph dated September 1930 shows the couple
smiling shyly in São Paulo's Place de la République.[118]

In Paris and Rio in the 1920s, Houston ran with a group of high-
powered intellectuals and artists. As she traveled, studied, researched,
wrote, performed, recorded, collected, arranged, and interacted with her
equally brilliant and talented colleagues, she must have sustained a thrilling sense of promise—her own and that of art itself. Primitive and modern
art shouldered a heavy load of humanitarian and radical hopes in that era.
After the First World War, many people yearned to entrust cultural approximation with the task of diminishing the hatred that had ignited that
devastating conflict. Like the many Modernists who set their art to liberal
humanist politics, Houston would express a similar sentiment years later,
in a Pan-American version appropriate to that wartime and Good Neighbor context.[119] For both personal and political reasons, the twenties must
have been a heady time for Houston.

I suspect the 1930s may have been less joyous. Perhaps not—perhaps
Houston was among those surrealists who were deeply radical, committed
anti-imperialists, for whom the 1930s were a decade of great activism and
hope.[120] I have no evidence that she leaned that far left, however, and in
her personal and professional life, signs were certainly less auspicious. Her

relationship with Péret was rocky. Friends of Houston's remembered Péret as eccentric and always financially unstable. Houston's sister claimed that "the marriage got in the way of [Houston's] career" and that "Benjamin didn't like music. He got in the way of her studies."[121]

I wonder whether there were other areas of misunderstanding. Péret's politics "follow[ed] the increased social concerns of the latter phase of Modernism itself," M. Elizabeth Ginway has written in her study of Péret's relationship to Brazilian Modernism. "Like Breton, Péret joined the Marxist cause in 1927, extending the surrealist revolution to the political arena." He arrived in Brazil a firm Trotskyist and co-founded the Trotskyist Liga Comunista (Communist League). For Péret, these left politics included an intense interest in Afro-Brazilian culture and history. He authored a study, "O almirante negro" (The Black Admiral), on the Afro-Brazilian leader of the 1911 naval revolt and wrote about quilombos and the Afro-Brazilian religious traditions of candomblé and macumba.[122] Péret was among the few intellectuals in this period who "did recognize the actual oppression of blacks in Brazil," claims Ginway, but in tune with the broader surrealist embrace of the exotic, Péret's frames for appreciating Brazilian culture seem to have aestheticized the exoticism he perceived in Afro-Brazil. Péret gave an interview to a local newspaper explaining that "he was more interested in the exotic elements of Brazilian culture and therefore was less interested in contacting the members of the country's cultural elite."[123]

Where did Péret's appreciation for the exotic and disinterest in the country's cultural elite leave Elsie Houston? What did Péret expect from Houston, and how did she respond to his expectations? Houston's views and politics are far more difficult to discern than her husband's. Later in her life she would perform benefit concerts for liberal and leftist causes, but she always remained guarded about her own opinions.[124] She certainly appreciated macumba (her son even claims it was the source of some of her music) at a time when it was officially prohibited and often violently policed.[125] But there is no indication that she identified racism in Brazil, nor that she valued Afro-Brazilian more than other popular Brazilian folk forms—nor, no matter what one makes of her photographs, that she identified as "black." In her 1928 paper at the Prague conference, for example, she treated Afro-Brazilian traditions, along with the other folk traditions catalogued, with the enthusiastic distance of an amateur and with clear elitist inflection. "Recently it has again become clear," she wrote, "that the Brazilian intellectual elite maintains an ever-growing interest in all things having to do with popular art, and we hope that a campaign will be undertaken to produce some of the shows . . . discussed here, not only for the people of our capital, but in other countries as well."[126] Articulating a hopeful sense of the growth of her field, she placed herself firmly among an artistic vanguard—precisely the "cultural elite" in which Péret claimed disinterest.

If Péret did project qualities onto Houston that she herself did not believe she possessed, it was not the first time for this habituée of the exoticist *tumulte noir*, nor would it be the last. Houston well understood this dynamic. She had just finished preparing a manuscript for the Librairie Orientaliste, after all. Speaking to a Brazilian press representative in São Paulo during a stay there with Péret in 1929, she offered a clear-sighted explanation of the reasons for her success abroad, including the conflation, in Europe, of "Brazilian" and "black" ("*negro*" is the Portuguese word she used): "With a repertoire that is distinctly regionalist and in large part made up of African rhythms, it was to be expected that I would arouse some interest. Parisians are accustomed to black music, especially that of North American blacks. . . . It would not be too much to expect my initiative to be well and enthusiastically received. What is more, I found the path already laid out by the musical successes of Villa Lobos, to whom Brazilians owe much of the interest and real curiosity now being awakened, in Europe by our music."[127] Houston's "our" seems fairly clearly to indicate a racially "neutral" Brazilian national identification, though the editors of the Afro-Paulista newspaper *Progresso* who reprinted her remarks may have intended their readers to hear otherwise.

If Houston felt that her insights about her reception as an artist were relevant to her personal life, she did not divulge. In 1933, after the birth of their son, Houston left Péret and returned to France.[128] I lose track of Houston then until November 1937, when she and her son had arrived in the United States, where she would spend most of the rest of her numbered days.

In the United States, Houston led a very different sort of life than she had in Paris. Foregoing the authorial stance of composer or intellectual, Houston became a performer, a role more feminized than those she had previously been interested to play. More feminized, but not necessarily more passive: Houston was an energetic and dedicated performer, sustaining a calendar impressive both for its intensity and for the range of programs offered.[129] She appeared in formal, classical music concert halls in solo recital or with elite orchestras such as the NBC Symphony Orchestra, the Kansas City Philharmonic, the Rochester Philharmonic, and more.[130] She performed for charity benefits.[131] She could frequently be heard, live, on the radio.[132] Her longest-running engagements were in New York's lush nightclub scene, such as the "chichi" upper East Side Le Ruban Bleu and the Rainbow Room.[133] Finally, Houston became a favorite ingredient in the saucy Pan-American programs that crossed high/low cultural divides, from the Brazilian Music Festival at the Museum of Modern Art, to the Pan-American Union's free outdoor concerts in Washington, D.C., to the New York World's Fair.[134]

This last category of performance is the most revealing of the context for Houston's U.S. stay. As the deep shadows of the Depression, the Third Reich, and increasingly rigid Jim Crow segregation lengthened, the United States worked to bolster its place in the hemisphere with the Good Neighbor Policy, a "passionate courtship of Latin America," as a Houston admirer described it.[135] "Latins Take Broadway by Storm," the press reported, celebrating trade pacts translated into "the universal language of the conga drums."[136] Houston was received as part of this popular influx. In this political and ideological context, her expertise in Brazilian folklore did not grant her the status of vanguard intellectual. Instead it framed her as a native informant, an "authentic" representative of a fascinatingly exotic form.

Houston found herself drawn into the intense reproduction of this discursive framework and worked to make it her own. In the glare of Good Neighbor footlights, Houston performed an "authentic" Brazil. In her first year in the United States, she usually programmed French and Brazilian songs. North American audiences quickly demonstrated their preferences. In February 1938, not three months after the first public notice of her presence in New York, Houston gave a solo recital to a "sizable and enthusiastic audience." The *New York Times* observed that "Particularly in the songs of her own land, Miss Houston's singing was cordially received."[137] A month later, commenting on her performances of Brazilian and French songs at Le Ruban Bleu, the same paper revealed that Houston's fans knew what they wanted to hear from her. "In Paris and New York she has quite a following which is not shy in asking for its favorites, including her unusual Brazilian incantation."[138]

These quasi-religious "incantations," Houston discovered, were particularly intriguing to her U.S. fans. She adapted her repertoire, and reviewers began to praise what they called her "voodoo songs." In an otherwise biting 1940 review of a multi-artist show, a critic for *Modern Music* found "the one bright spot" in Houston; "her Voodoo songs supplied the only pleasurable event of the series. They had definite musical interest, and she sang them with her familiar but unforgettable magic."[139] Another dour *Modern Music* critic found an entire Museum of Modern Art (MOMA) concert series lifeless, "Except for one inspired moment on a League [of Composers] program when Elsie Houston went into her Voodoo act by candle light."[140] In early 1943 Houston was hired to perform at the Monte Carlo to do "native folk melodies and an interpretation of voodoo music."[141] Upon her death both the *New York Times* and the *Washington Post* would call her specialty "Brazilian folksongs of the voodoo variety."[142] Houston must have grimaced and sung loudly to drown out her own highly precise understanding of distinctions among the various popular forms she had studied. Yet perhaps the word was her own aware compromise on the closest possible translation of "macumba." "Voodoo" did circulate in the United States with some of the connotations of "macumba" in Brazil: a magical, very powerful Afro–New World religion, feared and despised by outsiders.[143]

As Houston put "voodoo songs" in her programs, the word "exotic" began to appear to describe her. She programmed such songs for her solo appearance with the prestigious National Symphony in Washington in 1941, and in a radio interview there a year later, the host advertised her as the "exotic Brazilian soprano and voodoo singer, soloist with the National Symphony Orchestra at the Watergate Pan-American program."[144] One reviewer called her *intervals* exotic; another described a colleague, Olga Coelho, as "less exotic, less colorful" than Houston, though "a singer of subtlety and grace."[145] As one might imagine, Coelho's looks tended to the fair, spare, angular end of the spectrum.

Houston seems to have resented Coelho. One night while performing at the Rainbow Room, Houston spied, in the audience, an acquaintance who worked for CBS Radio. After the show, this man remembered, Houston "came to our table and assailed me because CBS was broadcasting another Brazilian, Olga Coelho. She had nothing against Olga, except that Coelho was not Houston. Elsie regarded herself as *sui generis*."[146] This anecdote exposes a telling contradiction in Houston's self-presentation in the United States. She wanted to be *the* premier Brazilian performer in the country and, at the same time, to be celebrated as the unique individual she was, as everyone is. She understood that she would have to cater to North American expectations of Brazil by playing to type, yet she wanted to remain, as her fan aptly put it, "*sui generis*," one of a kind. Something of this dilemma confronts every person who finds him or herself slotted into a stereotype. Houston's relationship to Carmen Miranda elaborates.

Houston preceded Carmen Miranda to New York, but Miranda's star took off on a far steeper curve. In response, Houston adopted and outdid the hairstyle, lipstick, and haberdashery of her more famous contemporary. This same former CBS employee remembered the outfit she wore to a lunch date with him, the hat above all: "She had constructed a truncated conical hat of artificial fruit which outrivaled Miranda; it was chic."[147] Her darker skin made Houston's representation of Brazilianness a shade truer to Miranda's Bahiana look (a look Miranda also emulated, since she was also more than simply Brazilian, given her birth in Portugal and brilliantly quick adaptation to her U.S. context). Houston's Brazil was also a shade less compelling, Houston's lesser fame confirms, perhaps due to white-leaning beauty standards; perhaps because she was now older; perhaps for political reasons, if she did indeed audibly embrace leftist causes; or perhaps simply because her intellectual, "high art" approach could not reach the popular arenas Carmen charmed. "She was too highly seasoned for the popular American taste," offered her lunch companion. Hmm.

Houston parodied Miranda's fruit-top and carried it off, but she refused her kittenish sexuality. While it is difficult to find a photograph of Miranda *without* that gorgeous grin, Houston never smiled for the camera. In photo after photo, she peers out from heavily kohled lids, with lips pressed firmly together, as if immobilized by the weight of the jewels in her ears and the wisdom of the ages. Houston was not asexual—not at all. In her candlelit "voodoo act," drumming to accompany her own singing, Houston smoldered with the self-aware maturity of the priestess long past the stage of the virginal novice. This stance was consequential for Houston's U.S. reception. It was no coincidence that the fan who remembered his first contact with Houston at an official function "during this country's early passionate courtship of Latin America" discussed international relations in such sexual terms. The Good Neighbor Policy relied on and fed this vision of nations as sexed and as engaging in lubriciously anthropomorphic "relations" and expected representatives of those nations to resonate according to the simplest heteronormative gender conventions.

Along with her refusal of the infantilization of a conventional femininity, Houston refused to be treated as a social inferior. As a deeply aristocratic person, she may have been unprepared for the social reevaluation her "voodoo act" imposed, but she quickly grasped its effect and responded. By 1941 Houston was no longer content with her father, the dentist of the Tennessee Houstons, or her mother, "a Brazilian girl" he married. Modifiers in captions and press coverage of Houston began to ratchet up her class position. A *Theatre Arts* photo caption introduced her in a stunning reincarnation: "Elsie Houston, singer ambassadress between the Americas, is a Brazilian by birth, Baroness Marcel de Courbon in private life and a great-great-grandniece of Sam Houston, first president of Texas."[148] The Sam Houston affiliation began to crop up regularly, and her mother became a member of "a distinguished Spanish family" or from "Portuguese aristocrats who settled in Brazil 300 years ago."[149]

One anecdote suggests another way in which Houston refused the condescension of white North American "patrons" of the arts. At a party at a socialite's apartment, the hostess asked Houston to sing. "Elsie borrowed a man's hat and took a collection. 'I sing for money,' she said. 'No silver, please.' Then she turned off the lights, and with a card table substituting for drum, created an incantation."[150] Nonplussed at discovering the hostess's less than friendly reasons for inviting her, Houston took the implication to its fullest realization, making explicit her exchange value on the cultural market. Perhaps Houston had witnessed this dynamic at work in Paris. African American jazz musicians in Paris often received invitations to the parties of white U.S. expatriates, where it was understood they would enter through the service door and at some point in the party, perform. Houston's response to being exhibited for the pleasure of the other guests must have made the hostess squirm. I imagine she was not invited back.

Houston's deepest rejection of expectations was a refusal to be any single thing at all. If Ollie Burgoyne's identity was unclear, Elsie Houston was literally a changeling. A writer who likened her to "an African queen" also characterized her features as "Mayan" (any American indigenous group in a pinch) and described her skin as "oily and watery," combining two things that notoriously do not mix. Then again, he remembered her appearance with difficulty. It "changed from time to time," he observed, flagging Houston's fluid self-presentation.[151] She often earned oxymoronic accolades, such as the praise of one reviewer for her "familiar but unforgettable magic."[152] Another reporter sounded similar notes in a

1940 review: "One cannot discuss Miss Houston's songs in detail, though they were very striking in most instances. Nor is her remarkable delivery of them easy to describe."[153] Houston defied description. Words could not capture this figure, who slipped into the space of *différence*.

It is important that Houston was not locked into the social category one might expect from "an African queen" in the interwar United States. Houston surely understood the social and professional consequences of the label "black," and her determined fluidity and elitism probably intended to keep it off her back. Most of the time, Houston succeeded, by performing a category ("Brazil") that could refuse U.S. racial categories. Reviewing Le Ruban Bleu, a *New York Times* writer listed "Elsie Houston, Brazilian singer; Marie Eve, Swiss mimic, and Jimmy Daniels, Negro, singer, late of Paris."[154] Something about Houston—perhaps simply the "Brazilian" taking up the space where another adjective might have fit—held the reviewer's pen. There were, however, telling exceptions.[155] On the occasion of the 1940 Festival of Brazilian Music at MOMA, a nationalist Euro-Brazilian music critic denounced her as "the American mulatta Elsie Houston, born in Brazil by chance, but who gave interviews speaking in the name of Brazilian music and singing folk and popular songs."[156] This little bullet of vitriol, intended primarily to insult, parts the curtains of the codes of politeness that kept the blackness of this daughter of the elite unspoken. It would be fascinating to know what prompted it, beyond resentment of Houston's transcendence of national boundaries, which this critic devoted his life to reinforcing.

In one sense, this ill-intended notice was correct: Houston made her career by performing, for elite North American and European audiences, "authentic" Brazilian folklore when her claims to authenticity were threadbare. Not only was she born in her nation's capital, a most urban locale from which to launch an exploration of the rural forms of folklore, but also it was Houston's experience of Paris in the 1920s that catalyzed her turn to Brazilian popular forms: her Brazilianness was mediated by Europe. What is more, Houston had U.S. nationality through her father and probably French through Péret.[157] Still, it would be difficult to imagine a more faithful or expert elite exponent of these forms. Houston's "inauthenticity" proves primarily the impossibility and irrelevance of authenticity itself.

Houston's determined fluidity refused, overall, to fit expectations dumped onto the shoulders of dark-skinned women associated with exotic elsewheres. She knew perfectly well what those expectations were, all her careful self-presentation confirms, and she probably articulated a broad social critique to herself, though she kept it under wraps. "She has some very sharp opinions on foreign affairs which she wouldn't divulge," the *Washington Post* once complained.[158] In one revealing comment, she tried to bring the United States to a more honest accounting of its own cultural hybridity. Making a point similar to that made by French composer Darius Milhaud many years before, Houston placed an Afro-diasporic popular form at the heart of "America": "Jazz has done much to help South Americans understand people here, and South American music played in the United States is helping you to know us."[159] She elevated jazz over classical music, mainstream pop, or a Hollywood product, all associated with white North America, while claiming for herself the broadest possible speaking position, a collective "us" not just from Brazil but from all of South America.

Houston's broad and mobile identifications seem to have left her, ultimately, no solid ground. As one of her fans wrote, when Houston left Paris for New York, "she turned back to her hemisphere, not wholly home."[160] For Elsie Houston, there *was* no place called "home." In early 1943, with a brace of concerts recently completed and more in the works, Houston took her own life. Friends blamed financial concerns and the "humiliations" of nightclub work, ways of noting that conditions in New York during the war ultimately prohibited Houston from carving out the elite concert space she wanted for her folkloric interpretations. The stresses of her multifaceted exile, supposedly the postmodern condition, layered impossible pressures onto this most modern figure.

When she performed at the behest of the Department of State, Houston insisted on near-darkness, lighting huge candlesticks to draw her audience, like moths. It is only through a similar dimness that we peer at her life. While the real reasons for Houston's final decision may never come to light, the tragedy of her suicide forecloses any understanding of her ideological negotiation as triumphant. Still, her life performance highlights the possibilities she saw and bet on—and lived off for a while—over various continents and decades. She understood the changing spectacularity of her self-presentation and milked her appeal and authority as a citizen of Brazil with claims on North America, a foot in the African diaspora, knowledge of "civilized Europe," and an authentic and expert vehicle for the vicarious experience of the exotic.

FIGURE 16. Carl Van Vechten, Portrait of Elsie Houston. Library of Congress, Prints and Photographs Division, Carl Van Vechten Collection.

"If ever we come to understand the Americas for what they really are, we shall become aware of our debt to Elsie Houston."[161]

WHILE ELSIE HOUSTON'S AND OLIVE BURGOYNE'S talents were undeniably exceptional, the fluid complexity of their racial and national positions was not. It is just that their lives in the public eye left traces easier to discern in historical record, permitting a glimpse of processes not otherwise visible for people on the dark side of the footlights. Happily, though, exceptional sources can open windows onto those everyday processes for the rest of us. One such source is the São Paulo black press, which undergirds the rest of this book. The pages of that press convey a sense of the fluidity and complexity of racial and national definitions levied upon and invoked by modest and middling people going about their lives. As well they must, given equally transnational contexts, even for those whose physical bodies stayed within city limits.

The next two chapters explore not only the transnational contours of black press communities in São Paulo, Chicago, and elsewhere, but also the ways the resultant categorical fluidity was invisible or, worse, anathema— inadmissible—to contemporaries as to historical interpreters. Newspaper editors and reporters worked as hard in some cases to "forget" the lessons of their contact as coffee advertisers worked to erase Brazil or sheet music publishers to bury maxixe. The forgetting in the pages of the black press, of course, worked not for profit but to create solidarities of use in antiracist struggle, namely, black and Brazilian nationalisms. To analyze the construction of those ideas denaturalizes them, and while it may disarm some of the big guns they rally to the struggle, it fashions other tools, better for our day.

CHAPTER FIVE

Another *"Global Vision"*
(Trans)Nationalism in
the São Paulo Black Press

In 1923, thrilled with a recent trip to Brazil, a prominent African American journalist made plans to send black farmers from the U.S. South to expand Brazilian cotton growing. His resources, he revealed, included a capital contribution of "no less than 10,000,000 (ten thousand dollars) [*sic*]." He promised to begin organizing the company within two or three years. "I plan to carry out my expectations in 1924 or 25. I will call it *The National Negro Business League of the Nort America* [*sic*]." As the milreis zeroes confusing the dollar amount and other errors in orthography suggest, this account is from a Brazilian source.[1] A São Paulo newspaper broke the story, provoking not gratitude but alarm, even in the Afro-Brazilian press. Little did the well-intentioned Chicago newspaperman anticipate the firestorm this fine-sounding business venture would spark, nor would he ever understand the reasons his "racial brothers" in Brazil did not flock to his defense.

This story is worth revisiting in detail, for it is an early expression of a misinterpretation that continues to be widespread today. Scholarly as well as non-academic observers continue to misconstrue Afro-Brazilians' expressions of national loyalty or denials of racism as a "lack" of racial identity, "absence" of racial consciousness, or "inability" to understand their own society (among other things).[2] These are part of a long tradition of comparative scholarship characterizing Afro-Brazilians as provincial, insular, and individualistic rather than collective in their responses to racism; deceived by false consciousness; and unaware of the "truth" of racial hierarchy in Brazil.[3] The tradition continues in recent work, as in that of the North American scholar who charged all Brazilians with "a re-

tarded level of racial literacy" and subalterns with complete "racial illiteracy."[4] Like the African American journalist full of good intentions, these
observers leave no room for the possibility that *they* have failed to understand Afro-Brazilian identification—that it might be different from the
sort they have come to expect. The problem lies not so much in individual
error as in the unthinking acceptance of comparison as method. Comparative method seeks to give an account of two things as they are and
to learn from their differences and similarities. In order to do so, it must
imagine them as distinct and well-bounded. Race, a social construction
that emerges in relation to other social categories (race, gender, nation,
and so on) is not such a beast. Students of race must devise methods that
can elucidate relations or connections. I have discussed this in more theoretical detail elsewhere.[5] The transnational approach in this book is my
applied suggestion, one of many possible solutions.

This chapter places one group of Paulistas who identified as Afro-
descended in the transnational frames in which they lived and saw themselves and considers their connections to some U.S. contemporaries. It
does so by exploring one of the clearest routes of Afro-diasporic communication in the 1920s, still one of the best windows onto black-identified
experience for historians today: the black press. After a brief introduction
of that medium, the chapter reads the São Paulo black press's transnationalism and then explores the connections between black Chicago newsmen
and Afro-Paulista expressions of national loyalty, anti-racism, and black
solidarity. What emerges is a picture of a cosmopolitan group of people
with an impressive awareness of global conditions and current events
who formulated pointed, anti-racist strategy with tools drawn from every
facet of their multidimensional context. Their work is an unacknowledged
chapter of the intellectual history of the idea of racial democracy.

The Black Press as Avenue of Transnational Exchange

Given the importance of newspapers as sites for the imagination of geo-
graphically dispersed community, it is no surprise that among the most
powerful engines of transnational exchange between African Americans
and Afro-Brazilians after the First World War was the black press in both
places.[6] By the 1920s, both Afro-Brazilians and African Americans were
publishing newspapers aimed at racially defined groups of readers, in out-

lets that reflected their nations' respective affluence. The U.S. black press was extensive and substantial, with larger papers enjoying fair financial stability and regular publishing calendars. They were linked formally and informally to African American educational, financial, and legal institutions, constituting a network of race-based organization, and their editors were often public figures, enjoying recognition, respect, and sometimes personal fortune. As befits a phenomenon of this import, the U.S. black press has enjoyed careful scholarly attention.[7]

Far less well studied and much smaller, the Brazilian black press consisted of fewer than twenty mostly monthly or bimonthly titles concentrated in the state of São Paulo, mostly in the capital. The publications blinked in and out with the state of their editors' meager finances; never were more than four in existence in any given calendar year.[8] During the war, three opened and folded: *O Menelick*, *A Rua*, and *O Xauter*. In the years 1918–19, only *O Alfinete*, *O Bandeirante*, and *A Liberdade* were in circulation. *A Sentinella* printed its only exemplar in 1920. *O Kosmos* began to publish in 1922 and probably folded in 1925; *Getulino*, from the smaller São Paulo city of Campinas, ran from 1923 to 1926; *Elite* started and stopped in 1924, the year *O Clarim* began. *Clarim* ran longer than any of the others, putting out its final issue in 1935, but with several interruptions and new starts along the way.[9] *Auriverde*, *O Patrocinio*, and *Progresso* all began in 1928. *Auriverde* seems not to have survived into the new year, while *O Patrocinio*, from Piracicaba, continued publishing until 1930, and *Progresso*, to 1933, the year *Evolução* began and the date of its only microfilmed copy. In the 1930s, some of the papers generated political parties or affiliated themselves with existing ones; papers also began to be published in other Brazilian states.[10] At the authoritarian constriction of the Estado Novo in 1937, when dictator Getúlio Vargas outlawed political parties, the entire press went underground, reemerging only after the Second World War.[11]

Despite the brief lives of many of these papers, they reached a surprising range of readers. The precise number can be gauged only roughly, for it exceeded circulation figures (1,000–2,000 printed each month, one scholar estimates in *Clarim*'s case) by an unknowable amount.[12] The geographic range is equally blurry, though there are some good clues. Readers were concentrated in the city of São Paulo, but the papers circulated far beyond. *Clarim* had representatives in the cities of Santos, Rio, and Salvador.[13] Individual journalists traveled, such as the poet Cyro Costa, or the peripatetic Vicente Ferreira. The Rio de Janeiro Federação dos Homens de Côr (Federation of Colored Men), an Afro-Brazilian mutual aid organization, had a journal and maintained contacts with various São Paulo papers.[14] Mainstream papers in both Rio and São Paulo paid their respects.[15]

The press's "community," if it can even be called that, exceeds categorization in terms of class, geography, and certainly race. Its blurry boundaries point to the heterogeneity of Afro-Brazilian experiences in São Paulo and nationwide and the impossibility that any single source could "represent" such a large and diverse group. The press's heterogeneity—its multiple opinions, its internal contradictions—makes it a rich and revealing historical source. Yet students of this press, perhaps because they have underestimated the numbers of people it reached, have generalized unnecessarily about its representative power. Historians have made sweeping claims that this press reflected "the mentality of a race" and differed little from journalistic endeavors in other regions of Brazil or other countries in the Americas. As a supposed window onto "Afro-Brazilian psychology," the papers have seemed to many observers signal proof of Afro-Brazilians' "essentially assimilationist" and "integrationist" tendencies.[16] Such projections reflect insufficient understandings of how broadly and strategically black press writers formulated their activist positions.

The Afro-Paulista press enjoyed far-flung interlocutors in the city of São Paulo, São Paulo State, Brazil, and beyond. Outside of Brazil, in addition to Italian newspapers, editors and writers from the African American press noticed and engaged its work. This engagement was reciprocal, though imperfectly so: the U.S. and Brazilian black presses reached out to each other in an irregular, uneven embrace, reading and reprinting material from each other's pages and sometimes entering into more direct communication. *Clarim* published U.S. black press articles on Marcus Garvey and "the Negro movement in the U.S. and elsewhere," translated by a Bahian polyglot of its acquaintance named Mário de Vasconcelos.[17] The largest African American newspaper, the *Chicago Defender*, reported on Brazil from the United States and even sent emissaries to explore conditions for black people there as early as 1916.[18] After a visit by the *Defender*'s editor to Brazil in 1923, the Chicago paper entered into direct exchanges with Brazilian papers, most intensely *Clarim* but also at least one other organ of the Afro-Paulista press, *Progresso*, and one mainstream newspaper, Rio de Janeiro's *A Notícia*.[19] (These exchanges are covered in chapter 6.)

While the black press boosted Afro-American exchange by an order of magnitude, it did so neither mutually nor equally. The social boundaries of the U.S. and Brazilian black presses did not allow their representatives to interact on a level footing. Global power imbalances in the news and entertainment industries, publishing, foreign language acquisition, and raw wealth structured even the press, this widest of communication channels. The asymmetry of inter-American relations kept Afro-Brazilians from the liquid clarity of empathic Pan-African solidarity. Like the transnational circuits of black literary Modernists, the "often uneasy encounters of peoples of African descent with each other" frequently evinced "unavoidable misapprehensions and misreadings, persistent blindnesses and solipsisms, self-defeating and abortive collaborations, a failure to translate even a basic grammar of blackness."[20] The journalists found ways to imagine racially inclusive national communities and broader diasporic identity formations nonetheless. Indeed, inequity is the mother of utopian collective invention—not a barrier, but the very condition of transnational exchange. The U.S. and Brazilian black presses defined a space, collective though not evenly shared, where writers and readers in conflict and in cooperation (re)shaped global and local imagined communities.

Afro-descended journalists in both the United States and Brazil cultivated the seeds sown at such crossings. On the U.S. side, as other scholars have documented, they provided powerful ammunition with which to denaturalize white supremacy, enriched the transnational dimension of U.S. black nationalism, and framed black North Americans' "global vision."[21] Less attention has been paid to global perspectives held by Brazilians of African descent, although their local landscapes were equally swept by the world's winds and their perspectives equally capacious. The next section explores the marvelous range of scales invoked in the São Paulo black press and the uses its writers found in those scales for strategic representations of self and society.

Cosmolocopolinationalitan

Emerging in the city of São Paulo at the intersection of global and local spheres, the Afro-Brazilian press was a transnational phenomenon from the moment of its formation. São Paulo in the 1920s was a city animated by industrialization, urbanization, the simmering coffee trade, and technological development. Its social fabric was criss-crossed by immigration and migration as waves of rural migrants and European and Asian immigrants made the place their home.[22] The papers' infrastructure and membership reflected social phenomena particular to that ferment, including one quite concrete: many were based out of the recreational societies, cultural centers, and mutual aid organizations Afro-Brazilians had organized there since at least the first decade of the twentieth century.[23] As cross-fertilizations of African associational traditions and immigrant mutual aid organizations, these were bodies formed at the junctions of transatlantic migrations both recent and remote.[24] The close ties between the societies and the papers blur neat lines between social and political realms.[25]

In homage to their complex matrix, black press writers embraced São Paulo, constantly reiterating their Paulistano (from the city of São Paulo) and Paulista (from São Paulo state) loyalties. "São Paulo progresses step by step," exulted *Clarim* in 1924; "we observe its superiority in everything: industry, commerce and agriculture."[26] Placing themselves in Brazil's most cosmopolitan, industrialized, and populous city, black press writers gained access to all the qualities they most wanted to claim for themselves. Urban identity was solid ground for claims of citizenship, which black press writers often staked on declarations of Paulista pride; that it was São Paulo in particular that gave that citizenship a decidedly modern, industrial, progressive cast.[27] These were paramount representational goals, black press writers confirmed, ceaselessly reiterating their own "progress" and "evolution" in images, words, and even newspapers named precisely that.[28]

Black press writers' self-presentations aimed overwhelmingly at one or another mutually reinforcing aspect of this multifaceted concept. Modernity, industry, urbanity, citizenship, and masculinity were resounding retorts to the discursive structures of anti-black racism in Brazil: eugenic hopes for the "whitening" of the population; "scientific" racism; and the alignment of dualistic distinctions between civilization and barbarity, progress and backwardness, West and East, Europe and Africa, male and female, and white and black, in jumbled combinations.[29] These amorphous prejudices called for just the sort of blunderbuss response the journalists used against them, insisting in every way that they were progressive, modern, patriotic Brazilian men.

São Paulo may have conveyed precisely those qualities the journalists most wanted to imply about themselves, but they did not restrict themselves to its scale. They narrowed their gaze all the way down to the smallest and expanded it to the broadest global view. At the most intimate, minute level, the press featured the black body in modern, productive, powerful, masculine strokes. Dignified sketches represented "the black race" as individual strong young men, progressively angrier and less humble from mid-decade on.[30] Even enslaved bodies were rendered technological and efficient, a "fleshly machine" or "formidable producing machine."[31] The 1933 cover of *Evolução* conveys perfectly the range of argument the black press placed upon the body. In bold, stylized strokes, two powerful, bare-chested men, one black and one white, shook hands, both gigantic across a background of skyscrapers, smokestacks, and fields of coffee plants. The image joined industry, the high-art innovations of Modernism, the urban contours of the "modern," racial equality among men, and the agricultural basis of São Paulo's prosperity. Likening the bodies to the buildings, it emphasized their size, strength, power, masculinity, and angular, "modern" lines. These bodies, it argued wordlessly, were both as modern as the skyscrapers, working and growing together.

The most common representations at the individual scale were not drawn, however, but photographed. Photography held out the promise of unmediated communication, invulnerable to exaggeration. Photography, "contrary to North American movies, does not expose the *negro* to ridicule," insisted a *Progresso* theater critic. In the camera's eye, these journalists trusted, the real self emerged: "Photographed. Nothing caricatured."[32] Throughout the black press's pages, sober young men in suits gazed unflinchingly into the camera. Author photos, group shots, regular "photo album" features, and occasional portraits of great men of color (sometimes alongside great white friends, all men save Princess Isabel) made the pages a collage of respectable black masculinity.[33] The bourgeois conventions of portraiture; the subjects' fashionable, modern dress; and this evidence of the press's proficiency with the technology of photography all positioned it and its constituency squarely in the "modern" age.[34]

From the micro to the macro, black press writers chose images to contest black marginalization. They anchored the bodies they featured in local, urban, or broader contexts or mixtures of several at once. Close behind Paulista locales in frequency and adamance of mention were Brazilian national sites. Paeans to "the sacrosanct name of Brazil," "our beloved homeland," and "the greatness of the beloved Brazilian homeland" were endless and expected, so common as to function at times as mere rhetorical flourishes.[35] Fervent nationalism even suffuses many writers' dis-

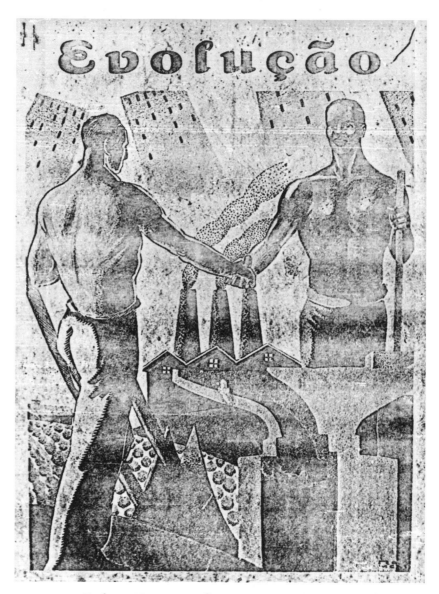

FIGURE 17. *Evolução*, May 13, 1933, front cover. Jornais Negros Brasileiros—
Arquivo do Instituto de Estudos Brasileiros [Brazilian Black Newspapers—
Archive of the Institute of Brazilian Studies], University of São Paulo.

cussions of slavery, producing apologies for the institution or commemorations of slaves' contributions to the nation's growth that sound almost celebratory.[36] In the pages of this press as in so many other public fora in Brazil after the First World War, Brazilian national identity enjoyed the status of a self-evident, highly ideologically rewarding affiliation.

Other large-scale identifications that have tempted Afro-Brazilians at other moments or in different places were less compelling in São Paulo in the 1920s. While some reporters articulated a Latin American or Pan-American consciousness, few suggested an African association, though there were exceptions.[37] Even Africa as a place was virtually absent from their writings. No wonder, since in the scale of more modern and more backward peoples and nations posited at the time, Africa sat solidly at the far savage end. When Africa appeared at all in these journalists' reporting (really only in the last two years of the decade), it appeared as barbaric, rural, or beautiful and spiritual but belonging to the past: "backward," "uncivilized" "the cradle of humanity's birth," and so on.[38] This was a particularly Paulista position, for African identities were apparently present and powerful for many Afro-Brazilians in Rio de Janeiro, Bahia, and elsewhere.[39] São Paulo's unique cosmopolitanism dislodged Africa from these journalists' identities, and they, in turn, minimized their imagined connection to Africa, steering wide of its unavoidable evocation of black anachronism.

Africa's absence points to the complex ways these writers expressed racial identification. Their participation in the press's explicitly racialized forum indicates that they all identified as Afro-descended in some way. Yet the words they used for race shifted carefully out of any specific racial position. The journalists variably named themselves *de côr*, *da classe*, *preto*, and *negro*. Their terms for race could change from article to article by the same author and even within a single piece.[40] Such shifts might have been tethered to skin shade, class or social status, profession, gender, age, neighborhood, or a genuine belief in the noble rhetoric of whitening, but they all reflect an ample understanding of the consequences of racial identification. Users of these terms understood full well the political implications of choosing between race-conscious collective terms and more fluid and incidental words for shade or status. Such understanding is explicit in an attempt in 1927 by *Clarim* editors to impose the term *negro* uniformly. "Any colored, black, mulatto, brown, etc., descendant of an African or indigenous person is NEGRO," they insisted, following with a transparently cryptic refusal to elaborate: "There is no room here to explain the premises of this conclusion we have reached."[41] Their vehemence is ample evidence that much of their audience disagreed in practice.

This striking combination of obvious racial identification and absolute refusal to occupy a defined racial position constitutes the crux of black press writers' anti-racist strategy. This seemingly paradoxical tactic reveals its compelling logic as we continue to consider the transnational context in which the Afro-Brazilian press developed and resoundingly placed it, the final piece of which involves the United States.

At the other end of the scale that consigned Africa to yesterday stood the United States. No wonder that of all the distant lands the Afro-Paulista press considered in its ample, inquisitive reporting, the United States was far and away its favorite foreign subject. In part the U.S. position in the pages of the São Paulo black press reflected the North American nation's presence in the hemisphere: as an imperial power, an exporting cultural producer, and the strongest trading partner in the region, it was unavoidable. To many Brazilians it also seemed an icon of modernity and progress, a beacon to follow down the righteous path to prosperity and happiness. Afro-Paulista journalists often voiced such views, characterizing the United States as fast-paced and powerful, "the *leader* of progress"; "the immense and formidable country of Washington . . . thinking brain of the Universe . . . formidable country of Lincoln . . . solid and virile nation, of iron economic vitality," reminding readers that "the entire world admires the rapid improvements of that extraordinary country."[42]

As a symbol or model of national progress, the United States offered a perplexing combination of extremes, for it was also the epitome of racial hatred. Readers of the gamut of the Brazilian press were well acquainted with the terrible racial conflicts there.[43] Particularly as the twenties progressed, the hopes inspired by postwar activism foundered amid news of continued or renewed Ku Klux Klan (KKK) violence, lynchings, and the consolidation of Jim Crow. The United States therefore encompassed both "modernity" and racism so quintessentially as to give the impression that the two might be identical, causal, or in some other way related, reinforcing the alignment of whiteness and progress key to racism in Brazil.

Afro-Brazilian journalists in São Paulo confronted this nexus of racism and modernity aggressively and in various ways. One interesting choice involved emphasizing metropolitan blackness. They spoke of athletes frequenting the "most aristocratic clubs" of the "land of dollars" or lawyers testifying before the French Parliament as *"negros retintos."*[44] *Retinto*, literally "redyed," designates the darkest shades of skin. Blackening the epitome of modernity, a *Progresso* book reviewer reminded a foreign observer that "there is, in the U.S., an Africa of 10 million blacks (absolutely *retintos*)."[45] Another *Progresso* writer emphasized that the U.S. dances he saw in Paris were performed "by *pretos retintos* of [North] American origin."[46] These and other black press writers drew comparisons in order to mark African Americans as dark*er* than they. *O Alfinete*'s Oliveira explained that the United States was the place in the world where "the *mestiço* population is the most dense."[47] The African American athletes in prestigious clubs, assured the *Evolução* reporter, were "much deeper black than São Paulo *negros!*"[48] Such gestures unraveled the civilizationist logic of "whitening" (the whiter the people, the more civilized the place), pointing out shadows in societies whose progress or culture was supposed to reflect only light. Like the projection of blackness into a shared national past (the "folkloric" approach), these comparisons helped black press writers narrow the divide whiter Brazilians too often cast between them.

Another way these journalists found to worry the knot the United States tied between racism and modernity was to attack the link directly, arguing that racism was *not* modern. They insisted, for example, that racial prejudice "doesn't fit the spirit of modern times" or that *"lynchamento"* was an aberration, out of synch with the era.[49] Occasionally they attempted to diminish their fellow citizens' hunger to be modern, offering nostalgic rhapsodies to monarchy or empire or reminding readers of the general greatness of the past.[50] But modernity was too widely embraced as a goal of Brazilian development and the infamy of the United States as both modern and racist too potent; direct denial could make little headway against the northern nation's signifying punch. So these journalists developed sideways approaches, drawing stark national(ist) contrasts to try to guide their worlds along a different course. What they developed was a form of the rhetoric later observers would call "racial democracy" but in a distinctly anti-racist, hortatory or utopian vein.[51] Not only was the São Paulo black press dedicatedly activist, but it also articulated a rhetoric of racial democracy right alongside the critiques that would come to be leveled against elite articulations of this idea. One site for the elaboration of this notion was a debate ostensibly about the United States and African Americans, mounted in heated disputes over the course of the postwar period.

An early episode of this debate began to churn in September 1918 in a pair of editorials in *O Alfinete* by its director, A. Oliveira. Oliveira denounced racism in Brazil in unequivocal terms: "The equality and fraternization of races . . . which the Republic installed as symbol of our democracy, as regards *negros* is a fiction and a lie."[52] Praising African Americans' "solid intellectual culture," Oliveira admired that "race's" progress, commerce, and the way it asserted itself "with respect to its rival, the white [*sua rival, a branca*], with which it treads, in parallel, the path of civilization." This extreme black-white separation ("parallel" paths, which of course never meet) found favor in Oliveira's eyes. "Let us strive," he urged his readers, "to eradicate our illiteracy and see whether or not we can imitate the North Americans."[53]

"Grave Error!" screamed a headline in *O Bandeirante* over a response by literary director J. D'Alencastro. His adamant repudiation of U.S.-style racial relations begins to suggest the strategy black press writers would embrace and refine over the next few years, wrapping the rejection of both racism and the United States into a single tenet of patriotic common sense:

> There are many among us who have formed a mistaken idea about what will constitute the uplift of our class [*classe*]; many who, completely corrupting the elevated goal that we should all keep in view, who think and preach, without any basis, simply, racial separation [*separação de raças*], selecting ours from the white race [*da raça branca*]! . . . This is the height of folly! It is a grave error, if not an actual crime of treason! To intend to establish here the same parallel between us and North American blacks [*pretos*] is only to ignore the atmosphere of prejudice, of enmity, of contempt and of persecutions in which live those, our brothers in color [*irmãos na côr*]; it is to demonstrate the most crass ignorance on the subject. If our ancestors had as cradle the land of Africa, we must note we have as cradle and homeland this great Country. . . . We are not Africans, we are Brazilians! . . . If in the United States there exist racial prejudices [*preconceitos de raça*], here, happily, there is none of that tremendous scourge. . . . Anywhere a white [*branco*] may be, there very calmly a black [*preto*] can go. . . . To provoke the utopian separation of the races would be to bring down upon us a war without truce [a war to the end]—in which we would be fatally defeated. . . . What we

must do is . . . not attempt to perpetuate our race, but instead to in-filtrate ourselves into the bosom of the privileged race—the white [*a branca*]. It's not the fault of the whites [*brancos*], but ours! . . . Let us be Brazilians and remember Roosevelt's words on the occasion of his visit to our country. To elevate our character . . . Brazil first and foremost, above all![54]

Comparing an infernal United States to an Edenic Brazil, D'Alencastro rejected Africa, North America, and racial consciousness as such. What sweeter paean could one pen to the promise of whitening than to "in-filtrate ourselves into the bosom" of a feminized, receptive, "privileged race"? Yet this condemnation was full of tension, even from the vantage point of prose: D'Alencastro based his call for national autonomy on the authority of a foreigner (Roosevelt) and described the separation he de-nounced as "utopian."

The tensions within the posture D'Alencastro modeled in 1918 explain much about the black press elaboration of the notion of Brazilian "racial democracy" over the decade and a half to follow. Understanding them is therefore vital. Most important is the paradox of a nationalist denial of Brazilian racism by an anti-racist Afro-identified subject. Key is the real-ization that a subject can be Afro-identified and anti-racist only if shaped, consciously, by racism. To quiet the confusion with which many observers (especially those steeped in the U.S. context) have received black Brazil-ian professions of racial democracy, it is crucial to see this: the São Paulo black press's emphatic discursive downplaying of race contains its ma-terial converse. In order to argue so vehemently against the value of race in ordering social relations in Brazil, Afro-Brazilians had to understand race as the very substance of their collective subordination, the very thing they would need to transcend in order to participate fully in the antici-pated windfall of Brazil's post–Great War political and economic growth. Consider the terror in this rant of the consequences of committing "an actual crime of treason" or encountering "a war to the end in which we would be fatally defeated." D'Alencastro defended a system whose failings he knew too well. Indeed, the previous issue of his own paper had pub-lished a piece denouncing "the vile and inconceivable racial prejudice that unhappily exists in our country," and the subsequent issue criticized the police for abusing black mourners, denounced prejudice, and called "men of color" to organize in response.[55] This is consistent throughout the São

Paulo black press; alongside every profession of patriotism and praise for Brazil's lack of racism ran denunciations of perfectly concrete instances of prejudice. The papers raged against black exclusion from (among other places and groups) certain neighborhoods via rent discrimination, certain religious congregations, public parks, the Civil Guard, a movie theater, public space, higher education, an orphanage, a barbershop, Catholic high schools, the Rio School of Nursing, a restaurant in Rio, and domestic employment in white or aristocratic households—and that list is from but a small sampling of black press pieces.[56] Like his fellow journalists writing over the subsequent decade and a half, D'Alencastro's insistence that Brazil harbored "none of that tremendous scourge" was based not on blithe ignorance of racism but an all too acute awareness.

The heat of the D'Alencastro-Oliveira debate of 1918–1919 was in part a product of the First World War. Black troops had been highly visible in the war and just after, as had black activism and then backlash, heightening the visibility of questions of racial relations and African America. After 1919, comparative or other mentions of the United States subsided for several years, though they never completely disappeared from the press's pages.[57] The next noteworthy provocative instantiation of global currents registered in the São Paulo black press was the 1923 visit of *Chicago Defender* editor Robert S. Abbott, the African American journalist whose colonization venture opened this chapter. There is no clearer demonstration of the complex comparative anti-racist strategy developed in the Afro-Paulista press than the responses elaborated to contain his intervention.

"Teaching the 'Our Father' to the Vicar":
Robert Abbott's Brazilian Lessons

The editor of the "World's Greatest Weekly," the black newspaper of greatest circulation in the United States, decided to travel to Brazil after many years of admiring it from afar. Since at least the 1910s, Robert Abbott had been enamored of Brazil and convinced that its people were free of the racism plaguing his native land. He finally toured South America in 1923, making himself into a highly effective engine of transnational exchange. He gave lectures during the trip, wrote an extensive series of articles upon his return, sparked much reporting in other venues, and continued to translate and publish articles from both mainstream and Afro-Brazilian newspapers in subsequent years. While in Brazil, Abbott met a host of Brazilian dignitaries of all shades of skin color and political affiliations. In Rio de Janeiro he was invited to speak before the "Press Association of Rio" (probably the National Press Association) and was made an honorary member. He spoke to the Federation of Colored Men and to groups he called "the Democratic Conference of Brazil" and "the Progressive Union." Each lecture was followed by speeches by his hosts, receptions, interviews, and the like.[58]

The impressions Abbott took away from all these meetings with articulate, accomplished Brazilians were the ones he knew he would gather before his steamer left its U.S. port. Abbott loved Brazil because he had fully swallowed its claim to be a place free of racism. In fact, South American conditions were not what he expected. Abbott encountered a great deal of racial discrimination. He had a terrible time obtaining his visa, prevailing only after his congressman and senator sent repeated letters to the Brazilian Embassy in Washington. The Hotel Gloria in Rio de Janeiro refused him a room; the São Paulo Palace Hotel asked him to leave after just one night, blaming American tourists; and the Hotel Odeste would not let him eat in the dining room, nor would the porters there carry his bags.

Abbott drew the conclusions from his experiences in Brazil that he wanted to draw, regardless. For the most part, he remained firmly oblivious to anything contrary to his hopes. He wanted to see the lack of racism as a national trait, shared uniformly across Brazil's scattered and diverse regions, so he judged the status of the "thousands of Negroes" he saw in São Paulo as "about the same as those of Rio de Janeiro," an evaluation few contemporaries or historians have shared.[59] When Abbott was forced to recognize prejudice, he blamed it on North American travelers or treated it as an aberration. He characterized the consular obstacles he encountered, for example, as "entirely contrary to the Brazilian National Constitution and shamefully at variance with the finely democratic temper of the Brazilian people."[60]

Abbott's wife Helen, traveling with him, was far more attuned to the racism they met. She was light-skinned enough to pass (she bought their first-class steamer tickets, for example) and could eavesdrop on conversations people wouldn't hold in Abbott's earshot. She was painfully uncomfortable that Abbott "had been pushy and had often sought to go places he was frankly not wanted," a discomfort for which Abbott's biographer, Roi

Ottley, had no patience, painting her as a wet blanket and a nag.[61] Helen Abbott's story remains to be told.

Robert Abbott's lectures in Rio de Janeiro managed to rub a large number of well-disposed listeners the wrong way. Unsurprisingly: Abbott was, forgive the anachronism, ethnocentric. He spoke in English and encouraged Afro-Brazilians to learn English so that *they* could better understand black North Americans. During a public campaign to commemorate a certain Afro-Brazilian figure three years later, he urged Brazilian politicians to organize a ceremony and invite important black men, particularly North Americans.[62] Most important, he dared lecture Brazilians on Brazilian conditions, an affront his listeners resented for its arrogance as well as for its content.

Many Afro-Brazilians were unhappy with Abbott's myopia about Brazilian racism and criticized him for it in the black press and elsewhere. In an article in the mainstream daily *A Patria*, for example, José do Patrocinio Filho, son of the well-known abolitionist of the same name, protested that Abbott should have offered Brazilian audiences less flattering, more realistic and productive words. He lamented the deception he feared Abbott's words would only deepen: "That this equality exists for blacks here — fantastic — purely fantastic. . . . The data gathered by Dr. Abbott will produce among North American blacks a sign of evident happiness, but for those from Brazil, it will be a genuine letdown, keeping them under this illusion of equality in which they remain suspended. . . . Resigned to the white's pious contempt, making him believe the racial struggle doesn't exist among us."[63] This clear-sighted critique of the idea of racial democracy, fully aware of its differential significance abroad and in Brazil, predates by ten years the book by Brazilian sociologist Gilberto Freyre that would supposedly "introduce" this myth, *Casa-grande & senzala*. Afro-Brazilians generated the idea of racial democracy right alongside its critique.

Even more vehement was a piece in the Afro-Paulista *Getulino*, angry that Abbott and others had allowed themselves to be swayed by appearances. The *Getulino* writer drily compared Abbott's denying racial prejudice in Brazil to denying the defeat of Germany, and he compared Abbott's lecturing Afro-Brazilians on their own racial situations to "teaching the 'Our Father' to the vicar."[64] Blinded by an arrogance that made him feel he could speak authoritatively after only shallow investigation, Abbott, such authors charged, misunderstood the nature of racism in Brazil and harmed the very cause he thought he was helping.

When Abbott left Brazil, he stepped unknowingly even deeper into the mire. During his journey home, Abbott wrote a letter to the president of the Brazilian Press Association, the satirist Raul Pederneiras. Once back in the United States, he promised, he would gather funds to send African Americans to Brazil. This letter, eventually published by the *Jornal do Commercio*, made the promise that opened this chapter.

With the best of intentions, Abbott had blundered into a debate about Brazilian immigration policy that had been boiling for years. Brazilians had contemplated the possible arrival of African American colonists since at least the mid-nineteenth century, when African Americans and North American white supremacists both considered it.[65] It was in part the threat of black North American migration that prompted Raimundo Nina Rodrigues to pen his influential *Os africanos no Brasil* (1905). His "immediate justification," historian Dante Moreira Leite explains, "was to prevent a plan then under discussion, to bring North American *negros* to Brazil, which would be, he thought, an 'assault on our nationality.'"[66] Nina Rodrigues himself placed the offending proposal about "ten or fifteen years ago"—that is, around 1890–95—placing it intriguingly near the formulation of Brazil's 1890 restrictions on African and Chinese immigration.[67]

A Lombrosian criminal anthropologist, Nina Rodrigues worried about African "inferiority" and urged his countrymen to take all possible steps to ensure Brazil's continued whitening. *Os africanos no Brasil* and Nina Rodrigues's oeuvre in general shaped elite views of the relationship between race and national progress, with great consequence for Brazilian domestic and foreign policy. He fanned fears of the debilitating African presence then weakening Brazil, and opinions such as his prevailed, preventing such settlements from taking place.[68] This is a clear instance of connections between the social positions of African Americans and Afro-Brazilians. In the century's first moments, African American actions, prompted by ideas about Afro-Brazilians or race in Brazil, shaped Brazilian state policies critical to questions of nation formation and generated anthropological "knowledge" of local racial truths.

As the century progressed, Brazilian elites largely relinquished biological determinism in favor of environmentalist and culturalist paradigms that spelled a brighter future for their nation.[69] Neither innovation served to dent the widespread faith in "whitening," however, nor the concomitant determination to restrict the immigration of those of African descent.

Especially resolute was the determination to rebuff African Americans, whom most perceived as a particularly noxious population of aggressively race-conscious activists. When the issue returned in 1920 with the formation in Chicago of a black emigration society (the Brazilian American Colonization Syndicate [BACS]), alarmed legislators introduced a bill to exclude immigrants of African descent, provoking a raging debate in the Brazilian Congress.[70]

Though many legislators expressed themselves in favor of such a prohibition, more were invested in promoting Brazil's international reputation as a country without racism. Luckily for them, there were informal means to the same ends. By the time the immigration bill was introduced, the Brazilian consul in St. Louis had already requested and received permission to deny visas after alerting the Ministry of Foreign Affairs in Rio de Janeiro of "the organization of a syndicate for the emigration of *negros*" to Brazil.[71] The president of the state of Matto Grosso, where the colonists hoped to go, had simply refused to grant an extension on their contract for the land, as one of the bill's sponsors informed his colleagues by reading them the state president's reassuring telegram.[72] Debate in the Congress, then, was essentially only about the Brazilian state's right or need to codify a restriction already in place. Lawmakers nixed the bill.

The Ministry of Foreign Affairs quietly advised its representatives to put the unlegislatable exclusion into practice, and Brazilian consuls throughout North America and the Caribbean began (or continued) to deny visas surreptitiously.[73] Brazilian politicians' overt acknowledgments of this subterfuge show how very actively the Brazilian state discriminated. It may never have legislated racism, as comparers so avidly note, but in many cases it worked no less hard to enforce it.[74]

Somehow the telegrams the Brazilian government sent to consuls in St. Louis, Norfolk, New York, New Orleans, Baltimore, Chicago, San Francisco, and Barbados regarding BACS were intercepted.[75] The response was furious and immediate. Attorneys for BACS brought a legal challenge, citing international treaties and the Brazilian constitution.[76] The NAACP sent a challenging letter to the Brazilian consul in New York.[77] Brazil did not substantially alter its policies, so over the course of the 1920s, civil rights groups, community organizations, and congressmen whose constituents had been offended staged letter-writing campaigns, filed legal actions, and registered plentiful complaints with representatives of both the Brazilian and the U.S. states.

When Abbott encountered this obstacle, he put his powerful shoulder to the wheel. He wrote to the Brazilian ambassador, and when the ambassador's response did not satisfy him, he approached the U.S. State Department. There seems to be, Abbott charged, "a secret understanding between the Brazilian Consuls in their country to not vise passports for Negroes," he charged, warning of significant public concern and urging that "appropriate diplomatic action [be] taken by the United States to protect the rights of . . . its citizens." Abbott menacingly insisted that he was "not willing to let this matter drop."[78]

Abbott's colonization plan terrified whiter Brazilians, and his challenges to their government made many Brazilians see red. The major urban newspapers reported on the "Effects of Mr. Abbott's Visit to Brazil: American Negroes Intend to Provoke a Diplomatic Intervention to Force the Brazilian Government to Permit Their Entry and Permanence in National Territories."[79] The foreign "*elemento negro*" would bring nothing but discord, "backwardness and retardation," they warned. In the national press's view, African Americans brought the indignities they suffered upon themselves with their greed and belligerence and would do so wherever they went. They were "sons of Ham born in other lands, full of hatred for whites, battling them with iron and fire and desirous of the advantages offered by Brazilian lands."[80] A Brazilian government official discussing the prospect two years prior had likened this would-be migrant group to immigrants inadmissible based on "the corrosive principle of their tendency to crime." These were "undesirable negroes [*negros indesejaveis*] who in the United States feed prejudice and perturb the peace of the American family."[81] Such restrictionists took the prospect of African American immigration as an opportunity to express and legislate the kinds of racist sentiments (e.g., black backwardness, Brazil's necessarily white future) that otherwise remained under cover or disavowed.

Black press writers shifted their stance in an attempt to contain this outburst. During Abbott's visit, black press protests over his inappropriate intervention fully acknowledged Brazilian racism—as obvious as Germany's defeat, denials "purely fantastic." In response to his colonization plans the writers toed the state line, leaving Brazilian racism entirely out of the picture. *Clarim* writer Gervasio Moraes charged Abbott with scheming to spread racial separation. Moraes didn't deny Abbott's observation that Brazilians lived in "the most sainted and significant fraternity," but he sarcastically rejected Abbott's "offer" of inappropriate, even disastrous, "social imports from our Sister America."[82] A *Getulino* editorialist reported the non-black press's notice of a diplomatic incident then being provoked by "the *leader* of the black race in the United States." Expressing no opposition to the racist immigration provision, this journalist sympathized only with his fellow Brazilians' concern for the damage Brazil would sustain in a conflict with "a nation as powerful as the 'American colossus.'" Furious at the "pretension" with which the "*millionario negro*" repaid the kind hospitality he had enjoyed in Brazil, he called African Americans "our brothers [*irmãos nossos*], to be sure, but of different habits, sentiments, and religion. If the *general in charge* is doing what the newspapers laconically say he is, what won't the *bulk of the army* do?"[83] This writer imagined a transnational diasporic community without losing sight of its important internal differences, a deft stance still often difficult to maintain.

Black press writers took Abbott's performance of racial identity as an opportunity to demonstrate elite and state interest in organizing Afro-Brazilian loyalties around shared "habits, sentiments, and religion." This claim to equal citizenship, contained within an offer of national loyalty, drew force from Abbott's threat of social disruption, which he generously demonstrated with his protests over visa denials. Afro-Brazilians offered national loyalty as a bulkhead against a wave of militant, black-identified immigration. Rather than feeding transnational diasporic solidarity, then, North American activism, though transnational and anti-racist, helped push Afro-Paulista writers away from denunciations of Brazilian racism and toward professions of loyalty to the Brazilian nation.

After Abbott's visit, nationalist denials of racism in the São Paulo black press increased in all arenas.[84] Such statements still managed to move in pointedly anti-racist directions, as is clear when one keeps in mind the transnational counterpoints structuring, sometimes implicitly, their logic. Consider a history lesson in *Clarim* in 1925, written about the past to stake a claim to the future. Brazilian slaveowners, the writer explained, were "not always benevolent, but, in any case, less barbaric than those of other countries, especially those from the United States. . . . They [slaves] contributed so much, so that Brazil would never have color prejudice [*preconceito de cor*]. . . . In the United States, even now, the inequality between blacks and whites [*pretos e brancos*] survives even after death; in some places there are different cemeteries for each!"[85] Denying Brazilian elites the treasured representations of their antecedents as benevolent, the writer granted them but a scant remove from barbarism ("less barbaric").

Yet he made his words palatable with a familiar and comfortingly nationalist comparison. The piece continued with an additional, radical note: listing a number of prominent Afro-Brazilians as proof of the possibility of social mobility in Brazil, the writer rhapsodized, "What a beautiful gallery of illustrious Negroes and sons of Negroes [*negros e filhos de negros*] Brazil presents!"[86] This distinction between a *negro* and his children, notoriously impossible in the United States, turned a hint of black disappearance into a celebration of Afro-descended elements in the national present. Revising the ideology of "whitening," it modeled a patriotic refusal to hope that Afro-Brazilians would disappear.

Rejecting the United States to embrace Brazil allowed black press writers even to broach the subject of racism, often otherwise taboo. José Correia Leite demonstrated in 1926: "There in North America, where prejudice is a fact, what belongs to the Negro belongs to the Negro, what belongs to the white belongs to the white; here, no; everything Brazilian is ours with the exception of some tiny little things that cannot qualify as prejudice."[87] Leite's exception, a sheathed accusation, called on the perpetrators of those "tiny little things" to clean up their act, but it was sweetened with a demonstration of Afro-Brazilian willingness to reproduce Brazil's good reputation.

Comparative denunciations of Brazilian racism allowed not only the discussion of racism, but also its denunciation in no uncertain terms. The violence of U.S. racial relations put teeth in these pointed exhortations. Gervasio Moraes, for example, conjured up a powerful black warrior in an audibly threatening U.S.-Brazil comparison: "While the North American Negro [*negro*] girds his chest and flings himself against the white [*branco*] in a barbaric and bloody war of extermination, dragged down by mortal hatred; while boiling gushes of brothers' blood run in the sewers, the Brazilian Negro extends a fraternal hand to his white brothers, and they strengthen the characteristic friendship that unites them."[88] De Moraes's violent images pointed out the ravages of white-supremacist racism on whites as well as on blacks. Whether he expected to reach whiter readers directly or in some more attenuated way, the menace of his prose is unmistakable. Note whose helping hand is extended in this formulation: this is an offer proffered from a rhetorical position of some strength.

Mentions of lynchings in the pages of the black press functioned in similar ways. Reporting on lynchings and the KKK accelerated over the decade, as did the use of the catchword "hatred" to characterize North

American racial relations.[89] The effectiveness of lynching as terrorism in the United States built on the performative qualities that made it so very mobile.[90] When it traveled outside the U.S. South, its symbolic potential moved in directions white supremacists did not anticipate. Afro-Brazilians borrowed from the force of lynching's horror to strengthen their anti-American nationalism, core of their transnational anti-racist posture.

While not nearly as striking, everyday aspects of their urban environment also produced abundant material with which black press journalists could elaborate their subtle anti-racism *qua* anti-Americanism. Their discussions, for example, of "modern" fashions, dances, and cinema attendance were resoundingly critical, especially when such fashions implied women's liberation in dress and sexual behavior.[91] These are some of the black press's most open rejections of the modern. Perhaps cultural expressions were among the less risky modern developments to critique, given the popularity of a postwar moralism anxious over urban youth culture and its challenges to gender conventions. In Brazil this anti-moralism was a position already marbled through with nationalism, since youth culture and changes in gender conventions, from risqué fashions to formal feminisms, were associated with the United States.[92] Mainstream papers decried the "invasion of American films, harmful to the purity of our simple and honest traditional customs" and worried at the lessons learned there, "condemnable Yankee attitudes, liberties that corrupt the decency and the modesty of our homes."[93] Black press writers found in bourgeois moralism, therefore, another arena in which the U.S.-Brazil contrast could underline Afro-Brazilians' patriotism and overall respectability.

Rejecting the forms of U.S. youth culture more associated with African Americans gave São Paulo black press writers another opportunity to perform the repudiation of Afro-diasporic racial identification. *Clarim* contributor Horacio da Cunha called the Charleston a "creation of North American blacks," "noxious for one's health," and urged his "fellow citizens of color" to take "severe and energetic measures against this dance of death."[94] His colleague "Tuca" denounced the "introduction of the jazz band, of futurism in our midst . . . a veritable disaster for our youth," explaining his distaste as a function of his patriotism—he was "nationalist down to his toes."[95] Rejecting these cultural forms allowed these writers not only to reject the stereotypes of excessive sexuality, immorality, and hedonism that circulated around jazz culture, just as many African Americans also strove to do.[96] Afro-Brazilians' use of this tactic also added the repudiation of African American choices and the patriotic performance of nation over race.

This double move—the simultaneous citation and disavowal of foreign cultural trends—is the posture analyzed in chapter 3 as the basis of the racially inclusive nationalism built on the strength of the "Negro vogue" by popular performers and others in Rio de Janeiro. When one considers the particular foreign qualities this nationalism was invested in rejecting, it is clear that such nationalism did not preclude a racial identity but made race a virtual condition of its expression.

These takes on hairstyles, the Charleston, and jazz also reflected the ways gender interacted with race, class, sexuality, and other social categories, seen in the overlapping frames of local, national, and transnational contexts. In one demonstrative take, *Auriverde*'s Luiz Barbosa ran modernity's various hazards together in an affront on the subtly but invariably gendered concept of "morality": "With effusive pride people refer to 'jazz,' 'á la garçonnes,' [and] skyscrapers as Progress!" Barbosa harrumphed, "And morality, gentlemen?"[97] Rolling one black American music, one Parisian fashion, and one icon of North American technological wizardry into a single emblem of modernity's rancid decay, Barbosa rallied the "gentlemen" to his unimpeachably high ground.

Part of this moralism involves the journalists' fear that their community's flouting of bourgeois gender conventions would increase racism. A *Kosmos* music critic entreated dance hall patrons to accommodate existing mores: "Let us be compliant," he begged, "so as not to be labeled uncivil and violators of social laws."[98] This worry was justified in a way. Whiter Brazilian elites did take Afro-Brazilian women's participation in youth and leisure culture in the recreational societies as opportunities to express dismissive contempt, in part finding useful outlets for their own anxiety over the social transformations of the 1920s.[99] Some Afro-Brazilian men attempted to deflect this censure by participating in the policing of black female sexuality.[100] Such repression did not go nearly as far as it might; many men in this group were willing and able to collaborate with women in running mutual aid associations, societies, and newspapers, as the pages of the press reveal. Women sold newspapers in the city center, organized supporting businesses and advertisers, and sat on the committees that planned the societies' social and cultural events.[101] This is unsurprising, given other researchers' conclusions about Afro-Brazilian women's prominence in family and community affairs.[102] Further, although there were authors who reproduced the most trite expressions of female vulnerability to sexual temptation, others offered, with empathy and solidarity, quite sophisticated analyses of the particular difficulties Afro-Brazilian women encountered in the labor market.[103]

Misogyny was not, in the end, the discursive nexus of black press solidarity with the whiter Brazilian elite, though it could have been. Rather than distinguishing themselves from women or femininity, black press journalists preferred the counterpoint of a North American modernity, appreciating the way rejecting the United States permitted the articulation of an unequivocal anti-racism.

This complex denunciation of U.S.-associated social trends, in Brazil or outside it, largely characterized the strategy of the Afro-Brazilian press in the 1920s. Toward the end of the decade global currents of Pan-Africanism and radicalism would support radical and even militaristic racial identification in São Paulo, visible in such groups as the Frente Negra Brasileira (Brazilian Negro Front) and the Legião Negra (Negro Legion or League) in the 1930s.[104] These formations reflect in part the critical mass convened in the small counter-public sphere of the black press, enabling readers and writers to imagine themselves as belonging to an identifiable cohort. The press facilitated a collective experience of discrimination, as it showed the inequalities that optimists hoped to change after the war instead entrench themselves ever further in urban occupational and demographic patterns.[105]

In this atmosphere, the journalists increasingly let their social critique rise to the visible surface, crafting expressions of racial identification that pointed out the rigid classifications in operation locally. "We Negroes," Jayme de Aguiar observed in 1928, "are nothing more than Negroes, although our skin may be darker or lighter [*um tanto mais parda o morena*], for many of our fellow countrymen." Blacks and mulattoes, wrote his colleague "Mathias" in 1933, "are the closest of brothers [*irmãos chegadinhos*]. . . . If they don't say it right to our face, it will be said behind our backs as soon as we begin to leave."[106] No less aware of the world beyond at this moment than at any other, these statements too were often penned as comparisons or citations of a northern model.[107] In 1933 Leite preferred the African American who "lifts up his head, is confident and self-possessed," to the Afro-Brazilian, who "drinks cane liquor and dies": "Pretending to be more humane than the [North] Americans, we don't lynch Negroes, but we do more than that and completely extinguish the Negro race, abandoning it to syphilis, to idleness. Which is preferable—Brazilian sentimentalism or American brutality? Isn't our sentimentalism murder? The Americans lynch fifty Negroes a year. We kill the entire Brazilian Negro race."[108] This militance is not new but a reminder of the radical rhetoric penned in the wake of the First World War, and it reflects continuity with the positions black press writers took throughout the twenties, even those that appeared conciliatory. Clearly its seeds lay in its author's earlier nationalism, radical in its transnational context, just as this radicalism did not cease to be nationalist. Case in point: even in this devastating critique, Leite included himself in his circle of "we." The national contrast functioned here, as it had earlier in the decade, to denounce Brazilian racism and spur Afro-Brazilians on to energetic action.

Intriguingly, African Americans in São Paulo seem not to have shared in the Pan-African consciousness then on the rise or simply not to have been particularly interested in their Brazilian "racial brothers." Horacio da Cunha complained in 1928 that "there exist, in this capital, many North American blacks [*pretos da America do Norte*] who unite only with their countrymen [*conterraneos*] and who relate only to each other." Cunha fumed over these African Americans' self-segregation, not from North American whites, but from Afro-Brazilians (and over their arrogant disinclination to learn Portuguese).[109] So much for North Americans' vaunted racial consciousness. Cunha took the opportunity of his displeasure with these North American representatives to take a position readers by now will recognize. He did not mean to antagonize "a race, our sister in color; but neither do we care to be antagonized by them. Thank God we are Brazilian and in our land, and I say with enthusiasm, 'let us go together, united, separated in nothing.'"[110] Afro-Brazilians' strategic, comparative nationalism was provoked not only by images of or news from the United States, but also by African Americans actually *in* Brazil, including but not limited to the Chicago newspaperman whose memory simmered within Cunha's displeasure.

Though there is no evidence that Abbott learned of the opposition his actions provoked, I imagine he would have been chagrined to discover criticism from Afro-Brazilians, especially those who identified as "black" in some way. Then again, Abbott did not see that some Brazilians of African descent refused to choose such an identity, whether they succeeded in avoiding its imposition by others or not. Abbott assumed that race would be the primary category of any Afro-diasporic identity. Ironically, proof to the contrary was close at hand: Abbott himself appeared to many Brazilians as something other than black, owing to his personal affluence and his nation's wealth. Abbott's biographer notes that the racial identity Abbott assumed he shared with Afro-Brazilians was often displaced by his national and class status. "Because of his wealth and his recognized position as a North American publisher, Abbott was given upper-class status; or, to use the Brazilian saying, 'A rich Negro is a white man, and a poor white man is a Negro!' His mulatto wife was . . . icing on the cake."[111]

Misunderstandings, of course, flowed in all directions. Just as Abbott sometimes wrote as if all Brazilians were black, the Afro-Paulista press fantasized that all African Americans were rich. "Everyone talks enthusiastically about how North American blacks are millionaires, industrialists, doctors, pharmacists, engineers, etc.," wrote Horacio da Cunha.[112] If not "everyone" did so, Cunha's fellow journalists certainly did, marveling at the supposed "colossal fortunes" of Josephine Baker, Jack Johnson, "Stephin Fetchit," Abbott, and others.[113] These exaggerations reflect the great distance between even meager success in U.S. terms and the possibilities for financial mobility in the writers' communities, along with a dose of earnest desire for the United States to *be* the meritocracy of its claims. Projections of "racial paradise" were cast both north and south.[114]

São Paulo black press writers often expressed frustration that African Americans could overlook their relative power. Noting the NAACP's successful litigation against the grandfather clause in the U.S. Supreme Court in 1929, a *Progresso* contributor chided "North American Negroes and other NAACP allies": "Unfortunately, they do not realize their prestige, which is much greater than they think."[115] While unconcerned with the class distinctions that made this statement true for only certain African Americans, this writer portrayed the impact of national location clearly. In relations with subjects of subordinate nations and when seen as acting in tandem with their state (as Brazilian observers at the time wrongly assumed about visa protestors), even disfranchised citizens of an imperial power would refract their nation's might.

Unaware of the ways Afro-Brazilians tailored their interventions to their specific ideological contexts, African American visa seekers chose head-on confrontation to fight Brazilian racism. Most did not realize that their bluntness would play to a venerable tradition of national contrasts, helping to push Afro-Brazilians away from the Afro-diasporic sensibility they expressed at other times into a defensive posture that looked from afar like conciliatory Brazilian nationalism. They could not have predicted that their challenges to Brazilian visa policies would align protests against racism with disloyalty to the Brazilian nation, lending the rhetorical crutches of nationalism to such vehicles of white supremacy in Brazil as immigration policy, health care priorities, urban reforms, and more. Nor could they see the anti-racist militance in the nationalist rhetoric articulated by Afro-Brazilian activists. The apparent affront to Brazil's national autonomy made some black press writers, readers, and sympathizers less willing to put into practice the fellowship they otherwise sometimes expressed regarding the African diaspora. That hesitation should not be misinterpreted as a "lack" of politicized racial identity. It is instead a position taken to address the exigencies of a world in which some people can claim themselves whole by casting others as apparently lacking. It is a sign of some of the concrete ways in which Brazil and the United States, like so many of the units that make up our interdependent world, are intimately and directly connected.

ABBOTT'S PARTING SHOT upon leaving Brazil in 1923 was far from his final salvo. This determined anti-racist activist would continue, throughout the 1920s, to broadcast his ideas of Brazilian virtue, convinced of their utility in his corner of the world. Despite the contradictions of squeezing anti-racist lessons from a profoundly racist society, it was a pretty good strategy. It made sense to many people on both sides of the Equator at the time, and historians today can lean on the tensions within it to draw out some otherwise inaudible aspects of the social phenomena that made it possible. The next chapter therefore takes up another moment of black press activism in transnational context, an initiative to build a public monument in 1926. Zeroing in on a single sustained campaign, this final piece of our story apprehends people in the act of forging links across seemingly insuperable chasms of class and geography. One favored tactic, it discovers, was translation, easily skewed to particular purposes and usefully dispensing with the need for actual travel. One of the imaginative pieces so hopefully applied to constructions of both national and racial communities was another social category altogether: gender, invoked to magnify here its subsidiary, there its sustaining relationship to nation and race. And because this monument initiative centered a figure from Brazil's hallowed past, everybody involved—black and white, north and south, in conversation and in conflict—was sculpting the world he or she wanted to imagine out of that most malleable political clay, history.

CHAPTER SIX

Black Mothers, Citizen Sons

The Black Mother: perhaps the most moving evocation of our soul; symbol, in truth, of the Brazilian family environment, which formed under her influence, under the influence of her example of immense and heroic dedication; symbol of her own race, which from her fecund flanks issued forth, and of a past that is already wafting away in delicious legend; symbol, finally, of her own superior sentiments, which, with her blood and her moral contact, she transmitted to us, to our great pride and joy.

With this ode to the Mãe Preta, Candido Campos, editor of Rio de Janeiro's *A Notícia*, urged Brazil to erect a monument to the Black Mother of slavery times. It was 1926, less than three years after the North American United Daughters of the Confederacy (UDC) had proposed that a statue to "Mammy" be built in their nation's capital.[1] While vehement African American protest effectively killed the Mammy monument movement in a matter of months, today Mãe Preta statues grace plazas in São Paulo, Campinas, and other cities throughout Brazil.[2] The Mãe Preta monument proposal won support from a wide cross-section of the population of Rio de Janeiro and then much of Brazil, from individuals of means to the humble attendees of public rallies in support; from the nation's next president to Campos's journalist colleagues to local and national politicians; from enthusiastic Afro-Brazilian journalists, clergy, scholars, activists, and performers in Rio to their journalist "racial brothers" as far afield as São Paulo and Bahia and beyond. Afro-Brazilians embraced the proposal and even championed the monument's construction when politicians' interest flagged.

FIGURE 18. Mãe Preta statue, São Paulo. Photo by Denise Botelho.

How tempting it is to compare the Mãe Preta monument initiative to the strikingly similar North American version. Afro-Brazilians' embrace of this humiliatingly debased figure seems conclusive proof of the mistaken notion that in comparison to activist African Americans, Brazilians of African descent lack a politicized racial consciousness or accept Brazilian national ideology unthinkingly, against their own best interests. Yet the Mãe Preta monument movement is a better occasion for an exploration of the connections between the United States and Brazil than for a comparison of national differences. As the first section of this chapter will detail, the movement spilled over national borders from its inception, when it was conceived as a performance on a global stage to demonstrate Brazil's

racial harmony and spiritual superiority. Afro-Brazilians embraced it because they found in its transnational staging a valuable goad with which
to prod Brazil closer to that vaunted reputation. When the U.S. black press
picked it up, as this chapter's second section elaborates, African Americans began to use it to call upon *their* government to live up to its democratic ideals. All these groups set the Mãe Preta as a prism through which
to refract an imagined global gaze. Though groups of supporters imagined international opinion differently, each hoped it would sanction their
particular vision of their nation's modern body politic. The extraordinary
range of the Black Mother's travels crystallizes a view of the marvelously
complex ways people actively engage the transnational elements of their
local, everyday lives.

Key to the ability to transcend the various distances involved was the
gendered charge of the rhetoric around this event. Afro-Americans north
and south took the Mãe Preta monument movement as an occasion to
make common cause with their "racial brothers," echoing Brazilians black
and white who invoked Brazil's "national fraternity" to unite disparate
groups within Brazil. Through translation they mediated their differences
in highly selective, active ways, coaxing disparate qualities into alignment
and unbalancing others apparently already aligned. Within Brazil, as between Brazil and the United States, monument supporters reiterated the
gendered quality of citizenship, invoking a masculine fraternity of citizens
to bridge their various gaps.

The Mãe Preta at Home

As a vector for the imagination of Brazilian national community, the Mãe
Preta was the object of much rhetorical struggle. Was her legacy a peaceful, unified nation, fully perfected in moral terms, or did Brazil's debt to
her and her descendants require social change? The public debate shared
one universal front: virtually all the monument's champions—black and
white, home and abroad—rejected the notion that racial mixture in Brazil's past had weakened the nation. Embracing one of the critical ideological innovations under way at the time, they championed this history as
the nucleus of Brazilian moral superiority. The monument movement was
therefore one of the sites of elaboration of what would come to be termed
"racial democracy," the celebration of racial mixture increasingly impor-

tant to Brazilians' sense of their national identity in the 1920s, replacing a more biologistic and openly racist paradigm associated with the ideology of "whitening."[3] Today most observers see the idea of racial democracy as a reactionary erasure of racism and social inequality, but in the twenties its final valence was far from clear.

As an early staging of racial democracy, the Mãe Preta monument movement highlights the importance of this ideology's global audience. The journalists and politicians who first advanced the monument idea framed their suggestion in broad transnational strokes, following Campos's lead. Campos pointed to the famous statue of the Redeemer, just then under construction atop Corcovado mountain. With that monument, Campos argued, "we will have demonstrated the depth of our religious sentiment. It is via such actions that a country's people [*povo*] truly 'express' their soul, revealing its intimate structure and affirming its particular individuality in foreigners' eyes."[4] This international terrain would be the backdrop for the rest of his essay; "foreigners' eyes" would be followed with mention of the demonstration the nation "owed to the world," the way Brazil's history had placed it "in the world, in a unique position," and Brazilians' dissimilarity to any "other people on the planet."

The performance Campos wanted Brazil to offer this global audience involved its unique national identity. Despite the statue of the Redeemer, he argued:

> We still have not expressed one of [our soul's] most moving and palpable and certainly most characteristic sentiments: that of the love and gratitude for the mournful race brought from Africa, and which the mysterious laws of life made one of the most dynamic elements in our racial and spiritual formation.
>
> This fact of transcendental significance has placed us, in the world, in a unique position vis-à-vis the black race. Acting on the profound chimera of our sentiments, it stripped us of racial prejudice, as it did no other people on the planet.

Brazil's uniqueness, Campos offered, was its racial harmony, a trait that had already been catalogued for at least a century when Campos wrote. Like all aspects of national identity, Brazilian racial harmony depended on contrast with other nations to make sense, and monument proponents invariably bolstered their avowals of patriotic pride by contrasting Brazil with other places. As a Mãe Preta supporter explained, "There exists today in all of Brazil a very sound sentiment that seeks to integrate blacks into Brazilian social communion even more, without a single hateful prejudice. . . . In the soil of Brazil, great in everything, the ideas most nourished by other arrogant, ungodly peoples did not take root."[5]

The Black Mother's narrative of racial democracy as national history seemed to demand transnational frames, as if she—like the idea of racial democracy itself—made no sense without them. Indeed, without its global framing, the idea of racial democracy would not have been able to resolve its structuring internal contradiction: high-minded anti-racist rhetoric plastered over reactionary positions on race and social hierarchy. Global frames allowed proponents to shift the focus from a local stage with differentiated social actors to an international setting in which "Brazilian" was a singular, monolithic category. This is evident in the support voiced by the journalists, politicians, and "men of affairs" at the elite end of the range of monument proponents who praised the Mãe Preta in the quintessentially culturalist terms of morality and spirituality, refusing to center racial mixture in their own individual and national identities. Their elegies did not interrupt prevailing disparaging images of black female ignorance, criminality, and licentious sexuality, which figured prominently in the background and occasionally rose to the fore even in the media that most supported the monument.[6] They clung to racial hierarchies even as they loudly repudiated racism. For example, when politician Gilberto Amado, commending the monument idea, called Campos "pure white" and of laudable "Aryan temperament," Campos placed the comments among the columns of adulation and flattery he regularly typeset, revealing that he had received this avowal of whiteness as praise.[7]

Black Extinction and the Construction of Whiteness

Campos suggested that the Black Mother encapsulated "two different, equally profound meanings: that which sums and symbolizes the Black Race and its 'works,' and that which points to the intimate and indestructible link of its/her soul with that of the white."[8] His prose distinction, echoed also in the call that opens this chapter, separated the Brazilian people from "the Black Race." This distancing depended on a temporal separation, a popularized evolutionism confining the Black Mother to the previous century. Campos's elite peers followed him overwhelmingly in this distinction between a modern Brazilian whiteness and an increasingly distant black past, constructing whiteness in the transnational frames of racial democracy rhetoric. As movement adherent Conrado Carneiro wrote to *A Notícia* to explain his support for the monument, "I, being white [*sendo branco*], sucked from ebony breasts [*seios de ebano*] the vital liquor and with it the 'energy of kindness . . . that above all distinguishes us among the nations of the Earth.'"[9] The full personhood of Carneiro's "I" contrasted strikingly with the Mãe Preta's disembodied breasts, formed not of flesh but of ebony, as if a trendy piece of primitivist sculpture. *Being* white, Carneiro demonstrated, literally fed upon the (tradition of the) Black Mother, whose generosity raised Brazil up in the family of nations.

For commentators intent upon an ever-whiter Brazil, the Black Mother's confinement to the past was key. For the *Diario da Noite*, the Mãe Preta was "a symbol [that] evokes that extinct figure of a woman," not just past but extinct; not a woman but a figure of one—and a symbol of a figure, at that.[10] At multiple removes and safely extinct, the Black Mother could be idealized—"a sort of guardian angel," this article concluded—and mourned in a delicious rehearsal of the fittest's own survival. In similarly saccharine tones, popular Rio de Janeiro novelist and essayist Benjamin Costallat directed the development of collective memory. "Can't you see her?" he demanded.

> . . . There she is, in the back of our memory and our melancholic longing [*saudade*], leaning against a corner of the kitchen, very clean in her *encarnada* skirt, new sandals, her kinky head all white. . . . She was part of our world, one of us.

> Where had she come from? No one knew. African or the daughter of slaves, she was one of us, part of our family. And she loved us, a lot, really, a lot. . . .

> One day, she died. It was as if one of our own had died. A very close relative. And she who was black [*negra*], who didn't have our blood, who was poor and old, and who wasn't anything, was, for all that, everything, everything, in our house, our family, in our friendship, everything. . . .

> Thus the last "Black Mothers" died.

> Today they're very rare. The century belongs to the "nurses," to the "frauleins" and to the governesses [*governantes*]. Our poor children

[sons: *filhos*]! Let there be, then, engraved in bronze, the immortal physiognomy of the goodness and sweetness of the "Black Mothers" of the past, of other, happier times![11]

With great blocks of elliptical space strewn about his sentences, Costallat textually performed the distancing he discussed between his readers and his topic. His nostalgia, fading easily into derogatory stereotype, was pronouncedly resigned, encouraging his readers to accept as inevitable a trend just then under way: the replacement of black child-care workers (and other black workers) by European immigrants. Leaving "nurses" and "frauleins" in their original languages, Costallat boasted of his own good fit with the European cosmopolitanism he proclaimed, sprinkling his chronicle with exclamation points as if with delight. His sugar-coating of post-abolition labor patterns absolved sympathetic readers of discriminatory hiring practices and other vehicles of the active reproduction of racialized poverty and class distinction in urbanizing Brazil.[12]

Celebrating the Black Mother's self-sacrificing dedication to the well-being of her master and his family, these supporters buried any discussion of the present under an unctuous nostalgia. Like all historians, these memorialists were talking about their present, when a series of related demographic, economic, and social changes appeared to threaten existing authority. After the First World War, urbanization, industrialization, the growth of mass culture, and attendant changes in patterns of work and leisure brought women in public space to the city's attention, while changing fashions revealed more of women's (and men's) bodies than memory could fathom.[13] As "fashion, leisure, the labor market, and the communications media were swiftly and dramatically transformed," observers feared "unprecedented changes in gender norms."[14] Horrified critics denounced the contamination of "family": "Nowadays, the traditional modesty . . . of the Brazilian family is no longer preserved. With football, modern dances swinging to jazz bands, [and] movies without the treasure of censorship, the germ of dissolution has found an environment for its proliferation, and the family, the very foundation of society, has not been exempted from its terrible and prejudicial contagion."[15] Amid echoing denunciations of the patriarchal family's dislocation from its proper place as the anchor of Brazilian national life, Brazilian legislators revised scores of laws regarding health and hygiene, divorce, labor, age of consent, and more.[16]

The Mãe Preta's narrative offered eloquent avenues of resistance to these changes. Her rural family, black and white, inhabited a web of agricultural interdependence presided over by benevolent patriarchal authority. Commemorating the Black Mother allowed critics to rail against threatening specters of female sexual agency, ongoing racial mixture, upset racial hierarchies, the dissolution of the patriarchal family, mass culture's reconfiguration of public space, and non-market labor practices. The version of gender conventions she modeled proposed a bulwark against both foreign encroachments on Brazilian cultural territory and internal dissent, for her quintessential "Brazilianness" allowed the Mãe Preta to chide the U.S.-focused "modern woman," gaga over Hollywood, practically naked, and jiggling scandalously with the steps of the Charleston, while her faithful obedience and authentic darkness rebuked the *mulata*, crux of some of the most visible sorts of resistance to consolidating urban capitalism.[17] Whiter, more privileged proponents of the Mãe Preta campaign made her image into a highly expressive representation of white patriarchal authority.

Critics interested in challenging that authority, however, also found Campos's proposal attractive.

Modernity and Nostalgia: Suggesting an Alternate Extinction

Brazilians who actively self-identified as Afro-descended, including the leadership of the black church; the cast of the black theater revue *Tudo preto* in Rio de Janeiro; and the editors, contributors, and primary readership of the black press of São Paulo, supported the Mãe Preta monument as well.[18] These activists took up her symbol to proclaim the unequivocal centrality of blackness in Brazilian society, trusting symbolic centrality to presage material inclusion. Balancing carefully amid the tectonic flux of social categories, these subtle thinkers crafted their support to fit and to expand their ideological context, sometimes challenging their fellow citizens in absolutely explicit tones, sometimes hugging the contours of the original proposal in ways that might appear acquiescent. Their reworkings of white supporters' nostalgia is a fine example.

Some black press writers rejected nostalgic postures out of hand. *Clarim* collaborator Antunes da Cunha, for example, called the Mãe Preta a "figure evocative of our fatherland's past" but one for whom no longing was necessary, for she lived on in her contemporary counterparts. "Black ladies today are fragments who recall the docile, martyr mother," he contended, calling her descendants to the task at hand: "Now in this day, in the century of light and right, the somnolent soul of the Black Race must awaken to a new era of intellectual tasks to complete the liberty that the law of May 13 merely sanctioned."[19] The Mãe Preta's memory, he charged, should fuel a determination to finish the job and realize the full potential of Afro-Brazilian liberation. The black press also appreciated the anti-nostalgic call to action of Dr. Julio Prestes de Albuquerque, president of the state of São Paulo. "We must live in the present and interpret the future in powerful action; of the past, awareness, but not *saudade*."[20]

Even more vehement was an author who signed himself simply "Raul." "Yes, There Are Negroes in Brazil," Raul proclaimed, setting out "once again to undo the weak argumentation of an illustrious scientist and fellow citizen who attempted in an article published in a great daily [newspaper] of our opulent capital to deny the capable valor of the African race in the formation of our great and proud mestizo race."[21] Although Raul did not name his adversary, the offender could very well have been Dr. Couto Esher, who had written such a piece in the *Diario Nacional* of São Paulo two months prior to the publication of Raul's denunciation. Esher apparently objected that the monument would entrench an undeserved reputation: "Such a monument, in a public plaza in Rio or in São Paulo would only serve to allow a visiting foreigner to convince himself that the notoriety we have in Europe and America, of not being legitimate whites, is well founded. Everyone who has traveled abroad knows this. It's a surprise when we declare that we are white! . . . What a struggle we have had, we Brazilians, to convince foreigners that we are neither Negroes nor mulattoes!"[22]

Exercised over the essay's willful excision of Afro-Brazilians from the national body, Raul responded sharply. The "truth" of Afro-descended people's presence and valor, he argued, "will not appear only in the monument 'To the Black Mother'" but in any gathering of Brazilians, where "the Black and mixed-race element [is] in the majority, because this purely national element is formed in the vanguard of the great Brazilian people." Raul positioned his opponent against white Brazilians of good conscience, who would not worry what foreigners thought—paradoxically reminding readers of international attention even as he denounced those who kowtowed to it:

> This act of reparation that a handful of noble Brazilians proposed . . . is happening because they can count on national conscience, on the

support of Brazil and of Brazilians who don't care about the gazes of visiting foreigners, those strangers who live to say that we are not white, purely white; well in fact we're not, with or without the monument "To the Black Mother," and whoever is ashamed should set out for an uncivilized region, where there exists no kind of crossing. . . . [Brazilians] belong to a single race, a mestizo race, and it is not the monument in question that will prove this great reality; the real truth is here.[23]

Making "civilization" the site of racial *mixing* rather than racial purity, Raul laid out the substantial—to some, shocking—implication of the revision in racial ideology visibly under way in the Mãe Preta monument movement.[24]

Insisting that black people had survived in Brazil and that the Black Mother lived on in modern Afro-Brazilian women, these proponents of the monument proposal called for a different extinction. For them it was the social relations of the Mãe Preta's era—namely, racism—that had no place in the modern era. Among their colleagues, however, were many willing to work with some notion of black extinction, the aspect of the Mãe Preta's narrative that most upheld the idea of whitening.

Many monument supporters in the São Paulo black press drenched themselves in nostalgia. A *Getulino* writer who called himself "Ivan," for example, allowed that "the Mãe Preta, today an entity whose influence is dying away and vanishing in the changes of life and customs, had a widespread and significant role in days of old."[25] José Correia Leite indulged in over-the-top sentimentalism: "In the thousands of lost graves throughout Brazil, we scatter an armful of flowers and a deeply felt prayer of sweet nostalgia!"[26] Reeling at the unfathomable number of graves and the depths of his feeling, Leite dramatized the separation between his modern cohort and the Black Mother of days long ago. Many other writers echoed this pair.[27] These writers embraced the hopes for Brazil's racial evolution that structured their ideological firmament, and they worked to periodize it in a way that would tether their own survival. Drawing upon nostalgia to underline the difference between the Mãe Preta's past and their present, black press activists staked out the distance between her submissive figure and their ambitious, patriotic, modern selves.

As chapter 5 emphasized, black press writers were deeply invested in establishing themselves as "modern." So were elite Brazilians and many others, in tune with the ideological thrust of the postwar period well beyond Brazil.[28] The monument movement caught on in part because it offered an opportunity for a contrast to a quintessential non-modern other. Not only does a dead black mother, formerly a slave, combine all the key counterpoints to modernity's futurity and social value, but the maternal also offers an extra psychological component. In many cultural figurations of modernity, argues critic Rita Felski, nostalgia is a central theme: "the redemptive maternal body constitutes the ahistorical other and the other of history against which modern identity is defined."[29] Though Felski does not consider 1920s Rio de Janeiro and São Paulo, her analysis certainly appears to apply. It is important, though, not to assume that modernity entails any particular set of qualities and thereby fail to distinguish between categories of practice and categories of analysis. As thoughtful critics of the concept of modernity have pointed out, modernity is an important category of practice precisely because actors can fill it with such a range of content.[30] The Mãe Preta did not just lend precast building blocks to people looking to define themselves as modern; the discursive negotiation around her person reveals the process of imbuing modernity itself with meaning. Actors in the Mãe Preta drama triangulated all these social categories—race, gender, nation, modernity—moving them around in relation to each other in order to position themselves. Whiter Brazilians, reacting to European disdain for the backward tropics, imposed the ascription of archaism on black Brazilians, who then in turn ascribed it to a female figure literally confined to the past. Black press reworkings of nostalgia displaced the implications of barbarism from actual, living Afro-Brazilians male and female, a deft imaginative move.

Nonetheless, for Brazilians of all sorts the celebration of black Brazil in female form posed a dilemma that the scrim of nostalgia only partially resolved. Many black press supporters would have preferred to skirt the issue entirely, and to that end they repeatedly circulated proposals to monumentalize a great Afro-Brazilian man.[31] Others took the opportunity of the monument's popularity to attack racist misogyny directly, turning the ubiquitous rehearsals of the Mãe Preta's virtue to challenge the widespread disparagement of black women.[32] Most widely, in the end, Afro-Brazilian supporters stitched a silver lining into the proposed monument's gendered invocations. Critical to their work were the masculinist assumptions that structured the Brazilian constitution's definition of an active citizen as a literate adult male, just as they underlay the visual trope of a Black Mother raising boy children, black and white, a figure by then long in circulation in Brazilian high art.[33] Monument supporters leaned into these assumptions to make the movement an occasion for the reinforcement of one of the era's most powerful metaphors of Brazilian citizenship: the idea of a national fraternity across race and class.

A Genuine Lesson of National Fraternity

Invocations of national fraternity in São Paulo's black press overflowed. *Progresso* printed the opinion of a traveling Hindu Theosophist who affirmed that Brazilians exhibited more *fraternidade* than anywhere else he knew; Gervasio Moraes of *Clarim* decried the KKK and U.S. racial hatred, extolling his homeland, whose black citizens extended to their white fellows "the hand of *fraternidade*."[34] Lynching and the other horrors of U.S. race relations, reminded a *Progresso* author in 1929, were distinctly not fraternal.[35] Invariably the reiteration of fraternity located Brazil in relation to other nations, drawing meaning from this placement in transnational context.

Monument supporters from all social positions agreed that the monument proved Brazilian fraternity. The humbly named Simão de Laboreiro (Simon the Laborer) cited the Mãe Preta proposal as evidence that all men were "children/sons of the same God."[36] President-elect Washington Luis picked up the theme, claiming that "such a monument would be yet another demonstration of fraternity," as he began a letter to *A Notícia*:

> "Fraternity, the sentiment that unites all men as brothers, with no distinctions whatsoever, will be the work of the South American peoples." And because, among us, there is no racial superstition, color prejudice, or exclusiveness over origins, in "South America, Brazil is the country foreordained to make this fraternity real." In the work of moral and material progress we are accomplishing, it is easy to see that racial differences don't count. In the world, the only thing that matters are climates, and these are modified by the work of men.[37]

Washington Luis's ringing reiteration of the masculinity of citizenship rested its case by pointing to the international context. So too did Afro-Brazilian articulations always contrast fraternity in Brazil with its lack in other nations, particularly the notoriously racist United States. The profound relation of the Mãe Preta monument's transnational orientation to its reworking of the idea of Brazilian national fraternity emerges in piece after piece by Afro-Brazilian supporters, always intent on reminding readers that commemorating the Black Mother was "the best way to show clearly *to the world* our policy of human fraternity."[38] This worldview steadied itself against the point of comparison provided by the United States. As the carnival society União da Aliança (Alliance Union) explained in support of the statue, "One of the high and dignifying virtues of our people has been, and continues to be, except in the rarest cases, esteem for blacks, there being little here of the extreme caste spirit that, for example, in another great American Republic, threatens to make permanent a feature solemnly antipathic to its material and moral progress."[39]

A *Getulino* monument supporter agreed, pointing out that "North American men, ignoring the terrible phenomenon they would leave to their descendants with their ethnographic prejudices, separated themselves, letting two opposing races evolve in their country, one scorned, one scornful, [while] we, colored Latins [*latinos de côr*], realized the most thrilling fraternal work of all time."[40] Afro-Brazilian celebrations of Brazilian national fraternity made U.S. racial violence, especially the explicitly performative and easily communicated horrors of lynching, into an argument against racism at home. Celebrating the perfect absence of prejudice in Brazil reminded listeners of the consequences of racism, dreadful for those on the receiving end or who feared the vengeful reactions against it.[41]

In an illustrative reed of this switch, the black church in Rio de Janeiro, the Irmandade de Nossa Senhora do Rosario e São Benedicto dos Homens Pretos (Brotherhood of Our Lady of the Rosary and Saint Benedict of the Black Men) sent a letter to *A Notícia*:

> In the cradle of democracy that is the blessed land of the Southern Cross, in the land consecrated by the Lord because its primitive name was Sacred Cross, will be a great and noble proof of the sentiments of the Brazilian people, and, perhaps, *a genuine lesson*, this sovereign demonstration *to the entire world* that in Brazil color prejudice finds no shelter. . . .
>
> How your exceptional initiative defines perfectly the greatness of heart and good manners of the Brazilian people! . . .
>
> How you make us worthy of the veneration of this people, pro-

moting a monument to the Black Mother, when *in other parts of the world* is sought the extinction of the black race![42]

Echoing the biblical vision of Brazil as a holy land, which Campos also remembered in his proposal, Irmandade elders synthesized the national and the divine, juxtaposing the gendered universalisms of Catholic and democratic doctrine. Joining spiritual fraternity to political, the Irmandade prayed for the monument proposal's success, underlining the ubiquity and consequence of divine surveillance. Under the watchful eyes of God and the rest of the world, these writers seem to have hoped, Brazilians would be on their best, most harmonious behavior. Perhaps the "genuine lesson" the monument would teach the rest of the world could serve to instruct students inside Brazil as well.

The Irmandade also performed its support by celebrating a Solemn Mass "in thanksgiving for [the monument] initiative," as *A Notícia* explained. A sign of the crucial role of non-elite and Afro-Brazilian backing for the movement, the mass was enormously public; hundreds of people attended and countless others read about its details. With this event the church both drew on public support and strove to form public opinion, both in its large, diverse, heavily Afro-Brazilian membership and among the whiter elites invited.

The mass organizers chose their tactic well. *A Notícia* gave the mass generous exposure, mentioning it repeatedly in the planning stages, as news when it happened, and in retrospect as a social event of note. The attendees, we learn from this coverage, included white and black political and social elites, as well as church regulars, members of Rio's black theater revue *Tudo Preto*, and a crowd of interested others.[43] The theater troupe also celebrated the Mãe Preta in the grand finale of its debut, but alas, the details of that scene, surely another public and influential performance of support, were not preserved in the historical record.[44]

Campos was happy to recognize these Afro-Brazilian contributions, and he welcomed black support—if it fit his terms. Those terms were often decidedly different for Afro-Brazilian support than for more elite expressions. When *A Notícia* reprinted the church's letter, it praised its warmth and the "spontaneity of the support that the idea of the erection of a monument to the Black Mother found in the breast of that traditional Brotherhood," rather than the thoughtfulness or erudition awarded to more elite affirmations of support.

More strikingly, among the vast column inches of reprints with which he filled *A Notícia* during the campaign, Campos chose not to typeset a letter from Jayme Baptista de Camargo, president of the Rio de Janeiro–based Federação dos Homens de Côr. He reprinted a small excerpt of the letter, in contrast to his usual practice. Nor did he reprint the articles Camargo sent him from the federation's newspaper, despite Camargo's specific request (which Campos included, turning his refusal public). The decision Campos made about what would circulate in his paper had lasting ramifications, for the federation's paper seems not to have been preserved at all for later generations of readers.[45]

In the reprinted piece of his letter, Camargo sent praise and good wishes. His group, Camargo explained, "has always followed with great interest all civic movements that affect either the homeland or Humanity and some time ago even floated the idea of erecting a monument to the Black Race." Perhaps Campos published no more than this because he was unwilling to bring to light evidence that he was not the first to propose this sort of monument. Surely it also had something to do with Camargo's tone, which even in this brief excerpt was determined, self-aware, and bitter. How could he and his colleagues not applaud this brilliant suggestion, Camargo continued, "Registering our gratitude for a just step toward recognizing the conscription of slaves, uprooted from African soil, from the free homeland, and brought shackled to inhospitable American shores, where little by little, with unheeded sacrifices, unspeakable suffering, they saw prosperous cities rise whose white sons had been nursed by the 'Black Mother.'"[46] Over a foundation of racial neutrality, Camargo layered a deep identification with slaves and their descendants. Though few of his fellow activists were as explicit, Camargo was far from alone in his critical stance.[47]

A measure of the success of such strategies is the reverberation in the national media caused by *Clarim*'s entry into the Mãe Preta debate. One of the longest-lived papers of the São Paulo black press, *Clarim* reported enthusiastically on the Mãe Preta movement for at least two years before a watershed: an issue devoted entirely to the monument, released on September 28, 1928. The decision was sparked both by the Carioca orator Vicente Ferreira's suggestion to celebrate "the Day of the Mãe Negra" every year on that date, the anniversary of the Lei do Ventre Livre (the Free Womb Law, which freed all children of enslaved women born from then on, an unmistakable step toward abolition) and by disgust at the entropy that had bogged the monument proposal down. As poet and

Progresso editor Lino Guedes complained in *Clarim* in 1927, monument supporters' enthusiasm lasted just until the time came to pledge funds.[48] Later *Clarim* would object that "the victorious and magnificent nationality consigned her to oblivion just at the moment when they had promised to raise her a monument," and it would denounce the "condemnable lethargy" of the "somnolent" monument commission.[49] But in 1928, *Clarim* successfully woke every slumberer.

Clarim supporters worked overtime to publicize their Mãe Preta theme issue, carrying it personally into the editorial offices of at least fourteen São Paulo papers, all of which carried commentary thereafter, as did "many others from the interior and other States" that *Clarim* claimed it could not list "for absolute lack of space."[50] Mainstream newspapers called *Clarim* "the excellent and vibrant organ of the black race of S. Paulo" and "a worthy representative, a legitimate spokesman for the black race"; they noted that "the Day of the Black Mother is today—and for that reason, the black youth of S. Paulo will circulate another issue of 'O Clarim d'Alvorada'" and that "Tomorrow a newspaper will circulate in this capital that is, in all, a great appeal on behalf of the handsome initiative; 'O Clarim d'Alvorada' is its name. It fights ardently for the causes of black men and loses no occasion to glorify the great figures of abolitionism."[51] Candido de Campos at *A Notícia* received a complimentary copy of this issue, of course, and *Clarim* printed the entire letter he wrote back in thanks. *Clarim*'s focused 1928 issue extended and perhaps even shifted the axis of Mãe Preta publicity from *A Notícia* to *Clarim* and, correspondingly, from Rio to São Paulo and from whiter, more elite journalists to Afro-Brazilians of more modest means. A shift in black press terminology from Mãe Preta to Mãe Negra around the same time offered linguistic confirmation of an increasingly visible, inclusive Afro-Brazilian identity.

It is difficult to gauge the effectiveness of black monument supporters' reframings of the Black Mother's tale, for Brazil's Revolution of 1930 disrupted the monument plans. The monuments now visible in Brazilian city centers had to wait almost thirty years for their public places in the sun. São Paulo's version, executed by sculptor Júlio Guerra, did not appear until 1955.[52] Still, while monument supporters did not succeed in the 1920s, they had nonetheless hit a vein. The 1930s work of Brazilian sociologist Gilberto Freyre, too often credited (or blamed) with the stunning paradigm shift from whitening to "racial democracy," revolved centrally around the role of enslaved women in the foundation of the nation he adored, "concrete" evidence of the compelling arguments marshalled by Afro-Brazilian activists and the wide exposure they managed to give their views. Magnifying the transnational scope of the discourse of racial democracy, they gave it a radical charge—and wings. Afro-Brazilian support would catapult this already transnational issue into the purview of readers outside Brazil.

The Mãe Preta Abroad: The Bridge of Her Back

It was the *Chicago Defender* that aired the monument to a mass audience outside of Brazil, thanks to its editor, Robert Abbott. Long a fan of Brazilian race relations, Abbott was ever eager to showcase Brazil in his paper, offering its supposed lack of racism as a goad and a model to his truculent countrymen. Involving the *Defender* in building awareness of a transnational Afro-diasporic community, a resource and potential ally in the fight against racism, domestically or globally, Abbott was in tune with the increasing internationalism of many African Americans after the First World War.[53]

Abbott learned of the Mãe Preta from contacts he had made during his visit three years prior. He mentioned his interest in the movement to a priest he had met in Rio (perhaps the Irmandade's Olympio de Castro?), who sent him some of *Clarim*'s coverage, generating an ongoing exchange between the two papers.[54] In May 1926, he splashed a page-wide headline across the *Defender*'s front page trumpeting the monument initiative. Underneath the headline he ran a clip from a mainstream Brazilian paper enthusiastic over the opportunity to honor formerly enslaved "Colored women who have generously given their nourishing milk and their resistant blood . . . the wet-nurses [who] unselfishly transmitted the vigor of their own red blood from their veins to the veins of the dominating white race." The *Defender* printed fervent compliments to the white journalist who had suggested "that a statue be erected 'to do honor to the Colored mothers of the country'" and to the citizenry that would embrace such a suggestion. "Men and women of all races and in all ranks of life," the *Defender* trilled, "are joining in the movement to pay tribute to the women of the Race."[55]

Abbott's interest and the structural platform provided by the black presses in both countries made this event, already stamped by long-extant

FIGURE 19. Front page of *Chicago Defender*, May 22, 1926.
Courtesy of *Chicago Defender*.

patterns of transnational exchange, the occasion for another round of
Brazil-U.S. conversation. Campos was thrilled to have drawn North American attention, particularly given its positive terms, and he too reached
transnationally, translating and reprinting Abbott's raves in *A Notícia*.
So the Mãe Preta monument movement generated two journalistic ex-

changes, one between the *Defender* and the whiter Rio de Janeiro paper *A Notícia*, and one between the *Defender* and the Afro–São Paulo *Clarim*.

Throughout this sustained transnational conversation, astonishingly, nobody mentioned the UDC's "Mammy." Not a single writer discussed the monument proposal that had gripped the United States three years earlier. While it is possible that news of the U.S. statue proposal simply did not filter through to Brazilian ears, it seems unlikely. U.S. news and current events were hyper-visible in Brazil in the 1920s, especially news of the U.S. "racial problem." AP and UPI wires were regularly reprinted in the Brazilian press, as were pieces gleaned from U.S. newspapers, including African American ones such as the New York *Amsterdam News* and the Baltimore *Afro-American*. Perhaps as a result, Brazilians knew at least a little about "Mammy" and her place in U.S. race relations.[56] The Mãe Preta monument drive was launched by a Rio newspaperman whose paper covered U.S. racism and issues relevant to Afro-Brazilians a degree or two more than the journalistic average. Plus, Abbott had been visiting Brazil during precisely those months (March and April 1923) that his paper, and the U.S. black press in general, had most raged against the Mammy monument proposal. Since comparisons between Brazil and the United States underlay discussion of the monument in the Brazilian press, whose members were happy to highlight the difference it ostensibly showed between their nation's racial harmony and North American racial antagonism, one would think that the U.S. Mammy monument movement would have made it into print in Portuguese.

Even more curious is a similar refusal by the *Chicago Defender* to make comparisons; it had discussed the 1923 movement extensively. The Senate bill granting land for the statue had raised the *Defender*'s ire, along with the that of many other African American newspapers, organizations, and women's clubs. The *Defender* had caricatured the idea mercilessly, portraying it as a rotten egg, a "mockery," and a "humiliating and insulting" idea. It highlighted not the supposed altruism of enslaved women, but the sexual abuse they had been forced to endure and the injustice and violence still meted out to their descendants.[57]

How could Abbott praise the Brazilian movement so enthusiastically when his paper had so recently, and with such vehemence, attacked the U.S. version? Why didn't he explain to *Defender* readers why the Brazilian monument honored that country's black citizens while the U.S. proposal humiliated theirs? Abbott's interest in Brazil, the suggestive timing of his visit, and the uncanny similarity of the monument movements—on face so alike, yet read as polar opposites by the different national groups of Afro-Americans—would seem to demand comparison, all the more so given that Abbott's every mention of Brazil, including his coverage of the Brazilian monument movement, was constantly comparative, always seeking to throw into relief U.S. racism's unnatural, unnecessary illogic.

Reiterated national comparisons underlay the meanings observers in both countries hoped to squeeze out of the Brazilian monument, yet they scrupulously avoided the most striking comparison of all. Had the *Defender* stirred the embers of the Mammy monument controversy, African Americans would have been hard pressed to see the Brazilian movement in the positive light Abbott wanted to shed on all aspects of Brazilian race relations. Such a reflection would have robbed the monument of its potential to build solidarity among "racial brothers" in the Americas and diasporic support for black struggles against racism within the United States and without. This should confirm a suspicion many historical observers increasingly voice about comparative method: even determinedly comparative observers of race in the United States and Brazil dispensed with comparisons when another approach better fit their goals. Comparison is not a neutral analytic method but a highly pointed claims-making device. In the case of the Mãe Preta monument movement, black activists' goals were less suited to comparison than to another potent vehicle of transnational approximation: translation.

Acts of Translation

Mãe Preta supporters found in translation, as in comparison, another tool with which to advance the broadest arguments they made through the shape of their monument support. Like comparison, translation sets two social bodies (textual, national, etc.) alongside each other, relying upon and feeding ideas of their equivalence. Such direct correspondence is a cipher, of course, since words are poorly patched to their object pairings even within a single sign system. Bridging different languages requires an even more laborious mediation.[58] As *A Notícia* and the *Chicago Defender* sent each other, translated, and published their celebrations of the movement, they tweaked the language used by the other into line with their view of the movement and the society they understood it to represent. Setting these articles and their translations alongside each other reveals a fascinating series of inequivalences. Many are simply signs of a translator's perhaps hurried process or renderings of idiomatic expressions. The gaps across racial terms, however, allowed for some more creative acts of interpretation.

The *Defender*'s initial headlines, "Brazil Pays High Honor to Dark Citizens" and "Brazil To Honor Her Women," already mined the gaps between Brazilian racial classifications and U.S. English.[59] Note, first, the lack of racial specificity of the Brazilians honored, rendered either "Dark" or simply belonging to Brazil. This omission suggested that all of Brazil's citizens were "dark," all honored by the monument. Note also the verb tense: the subjects thus honored existed in the present. The headlines portrayed Afro-Brazilians' present-day inclusion in their national body politic: "dark" people were "citizens," and the women honored required no other adjective than the "her" designating them as belonging to the Brazilian nation.

In its monument movement coverage, the *Defender* dedicatedly refused to call Afro-Brazilians "Negro" or the less common "Black" or to characterize the movement as racially particular. "Men and women of all races and in all ranks of life" were supporting the monument, it related, putting to shame evil North American treatment of the "darker races." "Dark-skinned peoples" mingled freely; there was no "color" barrier; the whole country enthusiastically honored "the women of the Race."[60] All of the categories of racial differentiation named were plural, consistent with the general practice of the African American (and much of the mainstream) press in this period. Abbott's decision never to use the word "black," capitalized or not, preferring "Race" with a capital R, was his contribution to the explicit debate raging in the United States over racial terms, including their capitalization.[61]

These articles did not envision race in Brazil as a black-white dichotomy. Their success in avoiding such a mischaracterization, however, involved a different sort of "mistake": Abbott and his translators and reporters often portrayed the entire population of Brazil as (various shades of) black. Their prose describes a continuity of color in a mixed-race population that would probably have fit, under a "one-drop rule," into the "Negro" category. (Abbott himself knew this wasn't quite the case—indeed, his pleasure in his 1923 visit to Brazil had much to do with his reception there by people he considered "white.") As in its original reporting, when the *Defender* translated Brazilian newspaper pieces, it maintained the vision of

Brazil's racial panorama as a range of gray and continued to avoid the category "black."

The terms specific to the U.S. context were not ones the Brazilian papers used, so the language the *Defender* preferred had to be imposed. Where the Brazilian journalists wrote "*preto*" or "Mãe negra," the closest translations of which, with capitalizations preserved, would have been "black" and either "Black Mother" or "negro Mother," the *Defender* opted for "Colored," capital C, and "mother," small m. For "*brancos, pardos e pretos*," in the letter from the black church, the *Defender* substituted "whites, mulattoes and colored people," uninterested to note that in Brazil "*pardo*" was a wider term that included "*mulatos*" along with many others and that "*pretos*" designated darker black pigmentation, entirely different from the wide range suggested by "colored people." The Portuguese phrase gave a sense of a color range (from light to medium to dark) while the *Defender*'s English translation listed two categories of racial mixture, neither of which designated a color.[62]

The *Defender*'s "mistranslations" could be quite amusing, as in its report that "Mr. Abbott was made a member of the Federation of Men of the Brazilian corps."[63] The *Federação dos Homens de Côr* became in this slip a racially neutral organization, distinctly martial, extremely nationalist, and probably unrecognizable to its members. The *Defender* also misgendered the friendly mainstream newspaper *A Noite*, calling it *O Noite*— probably a less egregious error in the editors' eyes, given the laudatory context in which the mistake was made.[64] This could simply be one of the frequent typographical errors gracing any given page of the black press in this period. It is tempting, nonetheless, to read this masculinization of the word "night" as the sign of someone's desire to revise the connection its grammatical gender implies between darkness and femininity.

Interestingly, Abbott himself gestured to the difficulties of translation between divergent racial schemas, although not in a way that revealed his wishful thinking on race in Brazil to himself or his readers. He knew that aspects of the racial schemas prevailing in the two countries did not travel well, but he poignantly hoped that what failed to travel were those aspects related to violent racism in the United States. "The white South has made one original contribution to human thought . . . the one word, 'lynch,' which is untranslatable."[65] In fact the Brazilian *lynchamento* (today more often spelled *linchamento*), a simple Lusification of the English word, communicated profoundly. Not only were there lynchings in Brazil, but also the terrorism of the act heightened lynching's symbolic mobility, allowing it to police behavior far beyond the national borders of the country that coined the term.[66]

A Notícia's renderings of *Defender* articles reveal that Brazilian translators took similar ideologically significant liberties. They neglected the English texts' capitalizations, leaving "*negro*," "*preto*," and every other racial term uncapitalized. This move, consistent with the practice of the Brazilian press even today, minimizes the importance of these categories, as if reluctant to concede them the status of proper names. That move recalls many Brazilians' wishful insistence that Brazil had successfully escaped a social system ordered by race—a claim the monument movement explicitly fed. Left out entirely in the *A Notícia* translation was the *Defender*'s statement, "No thought of any 'color line' will enter." Arguably, "color line" was idiomatic, perhaps prohibitively so. But the translator had not shied from translating the similarly idiomatic "fair play" as "*igualdade de raças*" (racial equality). Perhaps rather than being bewilderingly foreign, the flexibility of the concept of a movable color line made it uncomfortably applicable to a Brazilian context. Finally, when Abbott called *A Notícia* a "local" paper, Campos printed "Carioca," a person or thing from Rio de Janeiro. Exaggerating North American familiarity with Brazilian culture, Campos magnified the compliment Abbott paid his city and country. The ambiguity of language allowed *A Notícia* not to perceive the *Defender*'s slant, enabling Campos to celebrate the *Defender*'s attention as North American honor and praise, with only minor adjustments.

One such small adjustment involved bleaching the *Defender*. *A Notícia* introduced it as "one of the most important dailies of that country, with a circulation of tens of thousands of issues" and claimed it was "read by tens of thousands of people of all types" (*de todas as classes*).[67] Pushing the *Defender*'s race to the background, Campos portrayed it as an organ of a powerful nation, hoping to increase the prestige of his cause, his newspaper, and, likely, himself. Campos's self-aggrandizement is useful in hindsight, for it reveals the hypocrisy of claims of racial tolerance in a system where high status and blackness were rarely aligned. It was also useful to Afro-Brazilian monument supporters in a way. Pointing out to readers in Brazil the North American gaze that had alit, in the form of the *Defender*, upon Brazilian current events, Campos contributed to the black press's project of pushing whiter Brazilians to live up to their nation's international reputation of racial harmony.

Another telling mistranslation was Campos's version of Abbott's praise, "Brazil will do whole-heartedly what the United States has grumblingly refused to do." This hint that the United States had refused to do *something* might be Abbott's shadow of a bow to the U.S. Mammy monument movement. Abbott probably did not intend to refer explicitly to the 1923 Mammy monument proposal but rather to the broader U.S. failure to commemorate patriotic African Americans in sculpture in any dignified way. The *Defender* was exceedingly interested in monument building in this period, in the United States and abroad, and Abbott's missives from his 1923 tour had reported on the various other South American countries' monuments he considered suitable.[68] In the Portuguese translation, Campos's paper rejected "whole-heartedly" in favor of "merely" (*apenas*) and for "grumblingly" substituted "*rancorosamente*," a word more vehemently hateful than its referent: "O Brasil deseja realizar apenas o que os Estados Unidos rancorosamente se têm recuzado a fazer" (Brazil hopes to do merely what the United States has bitterly/hatefully refused to do). "Merely" minimized the deed, reassuring readers that the statue would bring about no drastic change. "Hatefully" maximized Abbott's criticism of the U.S. government to bring it into line with the Brazilian understanding of U.S. racial hatred, changing a mild "grumbling" into the fierce racial animus Brazilians so often told each other was the distant, different situation in the United States.

Like their *A Notícia* colleagues, writers in the São Paulo black press made similar "mistakes" when they discussed race in the United States. Some slotted Lincoln into the role of benevolent "liberator," played in Brazil by the Princess Isabel ("*a Redemptora*"), almost a cult figure in their collective pages.[69] Others optimistically tried to make the United States fit their formulation of a national brotherhood across race. *Clarim*'s Gervasio Moraes criticized the racism that made the blood of brothers flow together, and similarly a *Progresso* writer lamented that the racial question in the United States "went so far as . . . to ignite mortal hatred among brothers" (chegou . . . a accender odios de morte entre irmãos).[70] While there was a powerful discourse of a foundational national brotherhood circulating in the United States in this period, it did not resemble the inclusive fraternity of nation across race articulated by these Afro-Brazilians. To the vast audience of D. W. Griffith's enormously popular 1916 film epic *Birth of a Nation*, the blood "the racial question" tragically shed among brothers was that of Northern and Southern *whites*. Griffith's vision, widely shared before his film and given ever greater visibility by his cinematic innovations, was a fraternity of race across region—entirely different from the Brazilian conception.

When black press writers wanted to express solidarity with African Americans, they often got around the bad fit between the definitions of their two groups by leaving those definitions open. The phrase "*nossa raça*" (our race), for example, deftly posited a U.S.-Brazilian racial solidarity that did not specify color, indicate a degree of African descent, or in any other way fix the contours of that group. It thereby avoided the problems of translation between divergent systems of racial definition, embracing the transnational category now often named the African diaspora.

These inexact translations reflected larger differences in the definition, perception, and lived experience of racial categories. They point to the impossibility of perfect understanding and show the concept of equivalence in translation to be an ever-retreating ideal. They also show the ways the yawning gap in the racial schemas prevailing in the two places allowed all involved to skew the translations toward the meanings they preferred. For in the midst of all these misses, the Mãe Preta monument's supporters in both countries did find some linguistic common ground. If race was ambiguous, masculinity seemed rewardingly concrete.

The Misleading Transparency of Masculinity

If their treatment of racial terms was strategically inexact, *Defender* and *A Notícia* translators moved closer with words for gender—especially words male in gender. They rendered "fraternity," "brothers," "sons," and "citizens" into their closest phonemic equivalents, as if the masculinity cherished by all involved were similar in the two contexts. Perhaps Abbott had gleaned the rhetorical value of Brazilian national fraternity during his trip in 1923. Certainly he had already adopted the language of brotherhood (though not Portuguese) by that time. A reporter from the Rio newspaper *A Noite* who met him reported, "We had not had the time to shake hands or visit with him before he complimented the city. 'What a beautiful city!' he exclaimed. 'What cordiality I find here. How all the races of men shake hands as brothers. Pardon me, senor [*sic*], but I cannot find words to express my admiration for the people here.'"[71] In his talk to the Federação dos Homens de Côr, Abbott praised "your sublime example of fraternity," and if any doubt remained in his mind about the appropriateness of this trope, his hosts removed it: "Following Mr. Abbott, Dr. Tito Carlos spoke in English. . . . 'Brazil has always and always will stand for the spirit of fraternity,' he promised. 'We shall always say that all men are born FREE and EQUAL and we shall always be brothers to all!'"[72] Regardless of whether Abbott had embraced the rhetoric of fraternity before his Brazilian sojourn, the intensely positive response it provoked among his Brazilian listeners would have been amply instructive.

Abbott's *Defender* articles about his trip praised Brazil in terms redolent of the fraternity he observed, emphasizing the masculinity of citizenship. In screaming capitals, Abbott reported his speech admiring Brazilians who "RECOGNIZE AND APPRECIATE THAT ALL MEN ARE EQUALS."[73] Upon his return, Abbott wrote, "In Brazil there is a feeling of common brotherhood," and in its homage to the Mãe Preta monument movement, his paper included president-elect Washington Luis's proclamations of Brazilian fraternity.[74] *Defender* columnist Roscoe Simmons agreed that masculinity, qua humanity, was the essential point of contact: "This writer doesn't know what the great editor-thinker found, but South Americans found in Mr. Abbott a man."[75] Simmons reprinted Abbott's capitals as the nucleus of his speech: "'It would not be hard for Brazilians to understand the American Negro—it is so hard for white America. Now why do you understand us? The answer is simple, friends. Because you recognize and appreciate that all men are equals.'"[76] Other African American fans of Brazil made similar rhetorical choices. R. W. Merguson, for example, revealed how sorry he and his fellow travelers had been to leave the country "where for once, at least, in our lives we were *Men* and treated as such."[77]

Despite their shared embrace of "masculinity," it is not at all clear that Brazilians and North Americans understood entirely what each other meant by that quality. That they should have held different definitions of gender makes sense if social categories such as race and gender make meaning in relation to each other.[78] Since race varies over time and place, related categories should show corresponding variation. Those differences emerge in some of the mistranslations we have already seen and in the shapes masculinity took in each Afro-diasporic community.

Brazil's black press set the strong, productive slave as quintessential male figure. Writers in that forum praised "the formidable producing machine" the enslaved worker had been, "the Ebony Hercules." They lauded the contributions of "the heroic race," "the active and strong race," "the most solid trunk in the formation of our great nationality," and they celebrated the fidelity and valor of Afro-Brazilian soldiers.[79] Though the young, productive male slave was a minority in the slave population, as an icon he was symbolically useful in his correspondence to a 1920s' view of the quintessential citizen of the Republic, typically male and "valuable" to the Brazilian economy (closer to representative, given legal restrictions on electoral participation). The press's reiterations of such images were pointed reminders of the nation's reliance on Afro-Brazilian productivity and of the gender identity the great majority of these Afro-Brazilian journalists shared with the nation's ruling elite. As discursive intervention, they worked to buttress the "fraternity" underpinning the imagined community they wished for and worked to produce.

Acceptable images of slaves, however, were carefully drawn to fit only the most heroic molds. This was no celebration of enslaved masculinity as submissive. The treatment of the Mãe Preta's rough counterpart, Pãe João (Father John), well illustrates this direction. In the press's frequent suggestions of Afro-Brazilian men, real or "typical," worthy of monumental commemoration, Pãe João never came up, though he did earn mention in other contexts in the pages of these papers.[80] Pãe João was a tired old man, weak and resigned to his condition, and unredeemed by the implications of racial or cultural intermixture called up by the Mãe Preta. This was not the image Afro-Brazilian activists were interested in portraying to their fellow citizens or anyone else.

The particular cast of this powerful masculinity involves the religious dimension of the ideological context in which these activists wrote. Exceedingly rare in the São Paulo black press's pages were images of slaves as fathers, husbands, lovers, or any other implicitly sexual or familial identity. Instead, emphasizing Afro-Brazilian soldiers, slaves, and laborers' resignation and dedication, the journalists emphasized notions of sacrifice. Consider a poetic passage in *Clarim* likening slaves first to saints and then, with the addition of a suggestive celestial indication, to Christianity's messiah. Our ancestors, claimed the writer, "sacrificed themselves laboring with saintly ardor and a thousand mishaps, overcoming obstacles modestly until they almost became slaves, but a star every so often appeared in the cloudy sky—it was that of an ancient hope that remained, which would redeem their afflictions."[81] The star, he explained, was abolitionism, in an unmistakable messianic inflection. Although it is true that emphasizing sacrifice might also have diffused any threatening implications black manhood might otherwise have carried, I suspect that was less important than the way the masculinity articulated by these writers was tailored to the hierarchical Catholicity of their context.

In the United States, though some African Americans were willing to commemorate enslaved ancestors as symbols of their modern selves in the early twentieth century, by the 1920s that strain of thinking had been overwhelmed, replaced by the unflinching "New Negro." Slaves were not paragons of masculinity in African American discourse by the 1920s but nearly the opposite.[82] North and South Americans held quite distinct conceptions of the grounds they believed they had in common.

The different boundaries of gender conventions emerge in the *Defender*'s and *A Notícia*'s different translations of female gender categories. Femininity enjoyed none of masculinity's seeming transparency. In the *Defender*'s reprints, the Mãe Preta lost the capital "M" her Brazilian devotees awarded her. In the other direction, where the *Defender* praised the monument "to do honor to the Colored mothers of the country," *A Notícia* translated "em honra das mulheres de côr do paiz," substituting "*mulheres*," "women" for Abbott's "mothers." Perhaps this switch was related to the predication of support for the monument by Brazilians of all colors on the Black Mother's consignment to the past. Abbott's word choice clearly implied that homage was rendered to living beings. The translator intervened, correcting Abbott's "mistake."

In this case, the translator needn't have worried. Abbott's "mothers" reflected his mischaracterization of Brazil as *all* "Colored," rather than a suggestion of black-white contact there in his present day. In fact, Abbott avoided all discussion of interracial sex—or, for that matter, women at all. In his travel narratives Abbott wrote of "the races," Afro-descended people, and "Negroes" in high places, mentioning women only in passing.[83] Strikingly, the process of racial mixture in the present seems to have been beyond the purview of his pen. This held true even in his discussions of the Mãe Preta, where his prose resonated most with that of the culturalist, whitening-committed monument supporters equally wary of the topic.

The *Defender*'s discomfort with discussions of racial mixture allowed the paper, as it allowed its Brazilian counterparts, to avoid explicit discussions of interracial sex. Noticing this discomfort and its implications allows us to complicate our understanding of the reasons it was inconceivable for commentators in 1926 to mention the U.S. Mammy monument movement. The U.S. movement had provoked uncompromising denunciations not only of interracial sex in general, but of the coercion and violence in most sexual relations between white men and women of color, most glaringly during slavery. Recognition of this violence would have perverted the Mãe Preta narrative, robbing it entirely of the implications of fraternity and black citizenship commentators on all sides of the color line and the Equator, despite their varying ultimate intentions, wanted the tale to carry.

What the proximity of translations of masculinity suggests, then, is not that the contents of the category "masculine" were identical, but that the weight and value of masculinity were powerful in both places. Afro-Brazilian and African American men both saw the social category they shared with their nation's political and economic elite as filigreed political capital, and tried nobly to use it in their favor.

THE MÃE PRETA monument movement allowed far-flung activists to negotiate gendered concepts of citizenship in several imagined communities, from the Brazilian nation to the African diaspora. They magnified the distorted echo gender and race generate in overlapping transnational and local contexts, taking good advantage of the ways that categories of social relations, like all socially constructed ideas, vary from place to place, revealing their fissures when they meet. To negotiate their social position, structured as it was by ideas of race and nation, they spun the Mãe Preta narrative to point to U.S.-Brazil variation in some cases and sameness in others, building their comparisons onto already deeply piled layers of repeated contacts and connections. While monument proposal activism did not single-handedly install racial democracy at the heart of Brazilian national identity, it was part of the broad fabric of interventions working in similar directions. This same transnational tangle calls for equally deft strategic solutions today, fortified by the light their work can shed on ours.

Conclusion

Is it the highly visible or the less visible encounters that shape our inter-connected world? Each have their power; this book concerns the latter. Its protagonists' names cannot be found in textbooks. They are musicians and entertainers of middling fame, chorus girls and band members, bit-part vaudevillians, songwriters with maybe a hit or two. They are the people whose lives are refracted in archetypes such as "Aunt Jemima," "the Brazil-ian mulatta," "the Arab on the Can™"; they are stevedores, seamstresses, postal workers, and housewives; people who play music on the weekend, listen to the radio while they work, or pen a newspaper article in stolen time. The travels that bring them into contact are more likely to be flights of fancy than travels by land or sea, and their communication therefore is often mediated by the culture industry rather than direct. They are con-sumers and producers of culture, North American dancers of maxixe or "the Brazilian dance," readers of popular magazines, radio audiences, or grocery store customers happening across images of Brazil in coffee ads. In so doing, they were engaging in transnational encounter, as were Brazilian journalists, churchgoers, performers, and songwriters playing jazz, writ-ing articles about Marcus Garvey or the KKK, enjoying Parisian revues, making tacit that awareness in their own compositions.

Although participants in this sort of exchange reach and even yearn for each other across great distances, they do so not necessarily because they have anything in particular in common. They sometimes hope they do and sometimes make it so with that hopeful reaching, but for the most part they come to these imaginative meetings on uneven ground and with grossly uneven resources—so much so as to be virtually untranslatable into each other's terms. This unevenness and its untranslatability are cru-cial to the ways these encounters matter. It is precisely because the United

States was (and is) so much richer than other American nations that North Americans could sustain the unfamiliarity necessary for their projections. (Too, at least one reason for U.S. affluence is precisely this field of un-even, exploitative interactions.) Economic and cultural unevenness feed off each other to the point of indistinguishability. Coffee advertisers and their audiences could literally afford to flatten Brazil's vast territory of di-verse people into a metaphor for the opposite of their own imagined com-munity—and compel Brazilian growers to foot the bill. First World claims on monopolies of knowledge production ought not to survive the obser-vation of this privileged production of ignorance. North American dance fans could lose their cares in the titillating exoticism of maxixe's promis-cuous beat, all the while preserving their choice to keep or to revise their sense of a modern, civilized self (anti-modernism has its uses too). Per-formers could drench themselves in a marketable "Brazilian" sensuality and cloak themselves in the confusions of a racial order just slightly out of local kilter. Equally important was unevenness on other planes: uneven re-lations of race and gender are precisely what allowed sensuality to sell and what pushed performers of color to want and need to engage in this sort of cloaking. Those uneven relations are, further, what allowed coffee adver-tisements to naturalize global disparities; that naturalization then let the ads portray domestic racial and gender hierarchies as natural in return.

A similar set of uneven relations, including French colonialism, brought a primitivist frenzy to 1920s Paris, bestowing love upon another product of uneven encounters in and across the black Atlantic: jazz. The cultural currents of the *tumulte noir* were put to wonderful use by performers in Rio de Janeiro, motivated to notice and care by related disparities in their local exercise of class, race, and urban geography. Like all the encounters narrated in this book, they were based as much on ignorance as famil-iarity or comprehension. Key to their success was an incommensurability: the failure of French racism to translate into terms legible to Carioca ob-servers, and an unevenness: Brazil's relatively modest status in global geo-politics, which elite Brazilians profoundly desired to improve. That un-evenness allowed a range of black and brown Brazilians to make a play for social justice by calling attention to international interest in race in Bra-zil. The journalists animating the black press of São Paulo were one such group, powered by their encounters with each other, European migrants, other Brazilian newspapermen and women, and African American jour-nalists and would-be travelers from the north. That popular musicians and journalists in Brazil were able to articulate not just the nineteenth-century notion of racial harmony but a political notion of racial inclusion—a version of the idea we now call "racial democracy" before the intellectuals supposedly responsible for its creation and before it came to serve as a racist nationalism—rests on these many uneven transnational and local encounters.

Unevenness characterizes meetings across borders of all sorts, including those that constitute the African diaspora, not despite but through the very process of shared, determinative experiences. The meetings narrated in the preceding pages between black Brazilians and North Americans were strikingly uneven encounters, even as the participants embraced hopes for solidarity and coalition. The uneven power of the two states, despite their mutual refusal to confer the benefits of belonging upon black citizens, stamped black journalists' interactions. The very site of their meetings reflected disparate nation-state wealth: *Chicago Defender* staff could travel abroad while the Afro-Paulista *Clarim* editors stayed home. Afro-Brazilians perceived African Americans as backed by their state when they were not, a misperception that went unrecognized and therefore uncorrected.

Part of the impossibility of correcting such misperceptions is that their authors hold such stake in them. Sometimes this is on the part of those perceived, as when African Americans fighting visa denials wanted their opponents to think the U.S. state was in their corner. Sometimes it is on the part of the perceivers; imperfect understanding is often necessary to the lessons people hope to draw from their contemplations of each other. Afro-Brazilians wanted very much to think that African Americans were reaping the rewards of their nation's vaunted modernity, since their nation's leaders clearly hoped Brazil would follow in U.S. footsteps. Still, Afro-Brazilians recognized racism in the United States far more than African Americans could see its operations in Brazil. African Americans' skillful and determined use of Brazil as an argument against U.S. racism relied upon the failure of Brazilian racism to translate into terms North Americans might recognize as their own. Far more often than we think, "mistakes" in understanding are not simple oversight or ignorance but energetic, strategic refusals to know.

The people engaged in the encounters narrated in the preceding pages produced and refined some of the critical defining concepts of their day and ours. In particular they reworked the understandings of race and nation that shaped lived experience and a sense of self for many residents of the United States and Brazil after the First World War, especially in some of these countries' larger cities. There were other factors involved in constructing those nationalisms and racisms, of course; this book claims not to be exhaustive but to point to an underappreciated aspect of the process of ideological construction and therefore to discursive formations not usually considered when scholars contemplate race and nation. To see consumer citizenship, the deeply hybrid whiteness of the United States, or the idea of racial democracy as racialized nationalisms helps immeasurably to grasp the transnational processes through which national and racial ideology emerge. One such process involves the ravenous U.S. culture industry digesting the products of colonized places to feed the white imperial body of state and elite fantasy. Another entails utopian proclamations of solidarity and coalition across national and many other borders, while a third concerns the machinations of elite and state actors to contain the implications of such transnational connections. Finally, there are the subtler, strategic reworkings of apparent connection, so easily overlooked in the absence of multi-scale contextualization. Methods such as comparison that leave aside these formative connections will not suffice. At the very least, this book has spotlit some of the ways both scholarly and non-academic comparisons function as active, argumentative subject formation.

To see the transnational connections stitching together racial and national schemas throughout the Americas entails a serious reworking of historical method. To historicize—or indeed to understand in any way— the grand concepts of race, nation, and the Others that shape the most trivial everyday experience and the broadest contours of a life requires both an expansion of perspective to a scale often considered prohibitively daunting and a leaning in tight to see agency well beyond the privileged. The shift in perspective that offers this vision to academics such as myself doesn't come from academic history. The impetus to launch this experiment in method comes from anti-imperial, anti-colonial and postcolonial struggle, translated into those fields of thought. It is no wonder, then, that the implementation of this experiment in historical practice generates evidence to fill in and flesh out the grand dynamics diagnosed by scholars in those fields. Here history, the painstaking craft, has something to offer, for where the big stories are the stuff of tragedy and horror films, the small ones are the sites of hope.

The tales of uneven encounter recounted in this book are microhistories of larger, bolder stories. Their specific, particular unevenness reflects the grand unevenness of capitalist development.[1] It reflects the unevenness of so-called "modernity," the idea and practice that conceals place behind time—that is, site specificity behind an epochal label—incommensurable inequity behind imagined singularity, and direct engagement behind façades of belatedness or futurity.[2] These encounters are the local encounters of global empires, characterized by violence at once banal and shocking.[3] They are the encounters of development: the maintenance of coloniality in a postcolonial world, the refiguring of exploitation as altruism, and the making of the world as ever more unequal.[4] Yet at the same time and without contradiction, they are pregnant and wonderful. The transnational lens that reveals the uneven encounters shaping repressive notions of race and nation also spotlights another dynamic: the ways such encounters arm determined and brilliant people, allowing them to occupy the interstices of constricting conceptual structures, scrabble at the mortar, and break out into new ground.

Abbreviations

ACI   Associated Coffee Industries
AHI   Arquivo Histórico do Itamarati (Ministry of Foreign Affairs)
AHR   *American Historical Review*
AN   Arquivo Nacional (National Archives), Rio de Janeiro
ASR   *American Sociological Review*
BMRJ   *Black Music Research Journal*
Clarim   *O Clarim da Alvorada*, *O Clarim d'Alvorada*, or *O Clarim*.
EPM   Kinkle, *Encyclopedia of Popular Music and Jazz, 1900–1950*
GPO   Government Printing Office
HAHR   *Hispanic American Historical Review*
HAJ MTC   Helen Armstead-Johnson Miscellaneous Theater Collections, NYPL.
JC   Joint Coffee Trade Publicity Committee
JNH   *Journal of Negro History*
LC   Library of Congress
LCDRS   Library of Congress, Division of Recorded Sound
NA   National Archives and Records Administration
NA A2   National Archives and Records Administration, College Park, Md., facility
NMAH   Smithsonian Institution National Museum of American History, Archives Center, Washington, D.C.
NYPL   New York Public Library
NYT   *New York Times*
PI   *Printers' Ink*
RG   Record Group
SDVC   Samuel DeVincent Sheet Music Collection, Archives Center, NMAH, Smithsonian Institution

SI	Smithsonian Institution
SIBL	Science, Industry, and Business Library (branch of the NYPL)
SM	*Spice Mill*
T&CTJ	*Tea & Coffee Trade Journal*
UFF	Universidade Federal Fluminense (Fluminense Federal University), Nitteroi, Rio de Janeiro
UFRJ	Universidade Federal do Rio de Janeiro (Federal University of Rio de Janeiro)
UNICAMP	Universidade de Campinas (University of Campinas)
USP	Universidade de São Paulo (University of São Paulo)
WBR	*Wileman's Brazilian Review*

Notes

Preface

1. A longer exegesis is Seigel, "Beyond Compare"; see also Seigel, "The Point of Comparison."

2. Stolcke, "Brasil," 216; see also D. Silva, "Facts of Blackness," 207.

3. Du Bois, "The Negro Race in the United States of America"; Rogers, *As Nature Leads*; Rogers, *Nature Knows No Color-Line*; Ardizzone, "Red-Blooded Americans"; Joel Williamson, *New People*; Mencke, *Mulattoes and Race Mixture*; Sollors, *Beyond Ethnicity*; Toplin, "Reinterpreting Comparative Race Relations"; Skidmore, "Toward a Comparative Analysis of Race Relations since Abolition in Brazil and the United States"; Skidmore, *Black into White*; Skidmore, "Bi-Racial U.S.A. vs. Multi-Racial Brazil." White-supremacist racial "scientists" corroborate this work, despite quite the opposite intent; see the likes of E. Cox, *White America*; E. Cox, *The South's Part in Mongrelizing the Nation*; Reuter, *The Mulatto in the United States*; Shannon, *The Racial Integrity of the American Negro*; Stone, *Studies in the American Race Problem*.

4. The literature on racism in Brazil critiquing the myth of racial democracy is far too extensive to list here, for it could include nearly every academic book on race since 1950. A good review of the earlier material is Costa, "The Myth of Racial Democracy," and more recently, J. Dávila, "Expanding Perspectives on Race in Brazil."

5. Singh, *Black Is a Country*, 44.

6. Kelley, "How the West Was One," 124; my emphasis; see also Kelley, "'But a Local Phase of a World Problem'"; Gilroy, *The Black Atlantic*; Kelley and Lemelle, *Imagining Home*; R. Thompson, *Flash of the Spirit*; Edwards, *The Practice of Diaspora*; Mann and Bay, *Rethinking the African Diaspora*; and Matory, *Black Atlantic Religion*; see also Matory, "The English Professors of Brazil."

7. So does Mintz, "The Localization of Anthropological Practice"; see also Matory, *Black Atlantic Religion*, 268–69, and passim.

8. Seigel, "Beyond Compare"; Seigel, "World History's Narrative Problem."

9. Some of these debts I reference in titles and subtitles, such as those in chapters 4 and 6, invoking Lorde, *Uses of the Erotic* and Moraga and Anzaldúa, *This Bridge Called My Back*. See also Brown, "'What Has Happened Here'"; Higginbotham, "African-American Women's History and the Metalanguage of Race"; Fanon, *Black Skin, White Masks*; Said, *Orientalism*; C. Robinson, *Black Marxism*; further debts are owed to Rubin, "Thinking Sex"; Sedgwick, *Between Men*; J. Butler, *Gender Trouble*; J. Butler, *Bodies That Matter*; Halberstam, *Female Masculinity*; Wiegman, *American Anatomies*.

10. Joseph, LeGrand, and Salvatore, *Close Encounters of Empire*; A. Kaplan and Pease, *Cultures of United States Imperialism*; A. Kaplan, *The Anarchy of Empire in the Making of U.S. Culture*; McAlister, *Epic Encounters*; Klein, *Cold War Orientalism*; Renda, *Taking Haiti*; Fein, *Transnational Projections*; Fein, "New Empire into Old"; Jacobson, *Barbarian Virtues*; Briggs, *Reproducing Empire*; Findlay, *Imposing Decency*; Rafael, *White Love and Other Events in Filipino History*; Burnett and Marshall, *Foreign in a Domestic Sense*; Wexler, *Tender Violence*; Striffler, *In the Shadows of State and Capital*; Streeby, *American Sensations*.

11. A. Kaplan, "'Left Alone with America'"; A. Kaplan, *The Anarchy of Empire in the Making of U.S. Culture*, 12.

12. Klein, "*Crouching Tiger, Hidden Dragon*," 20–21.

13. Fein, "Culture across Borders in the Americas," para 1 (no page number). Emphasis in orginal.

14. Anderson, *Imagined Communities*, xii; Fein, "New Empire into Old," citing (among other sources) Ferguson, *Colossus*.

15. Matory argues for "dialogue" as analytic metaphor in *Black Atlantic Religion*, ch. 7.

Introduction

1. J. Leite and Cuti, —*E disse o velho militante José Correia Leite*, 38, 40.

2. Gabaccia, "Is Everywhere Nowhere?," 1116.

3. Hanchard, *Orpheus and Power*, 95.

4. Frederickson, "Race and Racism in Historical Perspective," 13.

5. Excellent critiques of the globalization paradigm include Cooper, *Colonialism in Question*, esp. "Globalization," 91–112; and N. Smith, "The Satanic Geographies of Globalization."

6. There are many versions of this disdain in circulation today; Elizabeth Chin refutes one operating in the United States, the notion that the poor cannot "understand and manipulate the symbolic world around them"—in *Purchasing Power*, 28. On cultural politics, see Kelley, *Yo' Mama's Disfunktional!*; Lipsitz, *Time Passages*; Lipsitz, *A Life in the Struggle*; Lipsitz, *Class and Culture in Cold War America*; Moore, *Nationalizing Blackness*; Blake, *Le tumulte noir*; Witt, *Black Hunger*; Stam, *Tropical Multiculturalism*; Perrone and Dunn, *Brazilian Popular Music and Globalization*; Dunn, *Brutality Garden*.

7. J. Scott, *The Common Wind*; see also Dubois, *A Colony of Citizens*; Linebaugh and Rediker, *The Many-Headed Hydra*; Carelli, "Les Brésiliens à Paris de la naissance du romantism aux avant-gardes"; Carelli, "Deuxième partie."

8. In the Brazilian context, see K. Butler, *Freedoms Given, Freedoms Won*; Carvalho, *Os Bestializados*; Slenes, *Na senzala, uma flor*; and Sidney Chalhoub's work, such as his *Trabalho, lar e botequim*; see also Karasch, *Slave Life in Rio de Janeiro, 1808–1850*; Metcalf, "Millenarian Slaves?"; Graden, "An Act 'Even of Public Security'"; F. Gomes, *Histórias de Quilombolas*; J. Reis and Gomes, *Liberdade por um fio*; J. Reis, *Slave Rebellion in Brazil*; Harding, *A Refuge in Thunder*; Burdick, *Blessed Anastácia*.

9. "Global vision" is from Kelley, "'But a Local Phase of a World Problem,'" the subtitle of which is "Black History's Global Vision, 1883–1950."

10. The wonderful and growing body of academic literature on the relationship of nation and race includes Balibar and Wallerstein, *Race, Nation, Class*, esp. Balibar, "The Nation Form: History and Ideology"; Applebaum, Macpherson, and Rosemblatt, *Race and Nation in Modern Latin America*; Bederman, *Manliness and Civilization*; A. Marx, "Race-Making and the Nation-State"; Mosse, *Toward the Final Solution*; Torgovnick, *Gone Primitive*; and McClintock, *Imperial Leather*. Scholarship that focuses primarily on race, however, tends to hold nation static, usually by allowing the research project to rest within (or compare more than) one simply bounded nation-state. The field has yet to integrate nation into its breathtaking analysis of the ways race is forged, both in tandem with other social categories (gender, sexuality) and in relation to opposite racial categories (black/white, indigenous/mestizo, creole/peninsular). Scholars of both race and nation, on the other hand, have focused amply on gender and sexuality, as do I in the chapters that follow. The scrutiny other scholars of race and/or nation have awarded gender and sexuality allows me not to privilege these at the level of argument. On gender, sexuality, and nation, see Diana Taylor, *Disappearing Acts*; Gilmore, *Gender and Jim Crow*; Duggan, *Sapphic Slashers*; Wiegman, *American Anatomies*; Fiol-Matta, *A Queer Mother for the Nation*; Caulfield, *In Defense of Honor*; Mosse, *Nationalism and Sexuality*; Parker, ed., *Nationalisms & Sexualities*.

11. Black nationalism, when not U.S.-bound, can be a different case, often anti-nationalist in its transnational solidarities. See Singh, *Black Is a Country*.

12. Azevedo, *Abolitionism in the United States and Brazil*; L. Vianna, "As dimensões da cor"; Schwarcz, *Retrato em branco e negro*.

13. E. Cox, *White America*; E. Cox, *The South's Part in Mongrelizing the Nation*; Reuter, *The Mulatto in the United States*; Shannon, *The Racial Integrity of the American Negro*; Stone, *Studies in the American Race Problem*; Stepan, *"The Hour of Eugenics."*

14. L. Hill, *The Confederate Exodus to Latin America*; Hill, "Confederate Exiles to Brazil"; see also J. Dawsey, "O espelho americano," and C. Dawsey and Dawsey, *The Confederados*. Woodward counts "eight to ten thousand voluntary Confederate exiles" throughout Latin America, the majority in Brazil, in *American Counterpoint*, 67.

15. LaFeber, "United States Depression Diplomacy and the Brazilian Revolution, 1893–1894."

16. José Correia Leite, "E, apoz *A Liberdade* . . . ," *Clarim*, August 30, 1925, 1; Horacio

da Cunha, "Os pretos da America do Norte e os pretos da America do Sul," *Clarim*, February 5, 1928, 1.

17. Margolis, *Little Brazil*; Margolis, *An Invisible Minority*; Goza, "Brazilian Immigration to North America"; Beserra, *Brazilian Immigrants in the United States*; DeBiaggi, *Changing Gender Roles*.

18. Bolster, *Black Jacks*; Linebaugh, "All the Atlantic Mountains Shook"; Gilroy, *The Black Atlantic*; Linebaugh and Rediker, *The Many-Headed Hydra*; Cruz, "Virando o jogo."

19. Freyre's encounter with the sailors in Brooklyn is something of a primal scene, replayed endlessly by Freyre scholars; see Araújo, *Guerra e paz*, 40; Woodward, *American Counterpoint*, 56; see also "Brazilian Visitors in Norfolk," *Colored American Magazine* 9 (August 1905): 406–7; quoted in Hellwig, *African-American Reflections on Brazil's Racial Paradise*, 21–34; James N. Green, slide show and lecture, Emory University, Atlanta, Spring 2001, accompanying Green, *Beyond Carnival*; Morris, "Rolling Down to Rio with Hughes"; Ukers, *A Trip to Brazil*.

20. Cooper, "What Is the Concept of Globalization Good For?"

21. Hellwig, *African-American Reflections on Brazil's Racial Paradise*; see also Guimarães, "Brasil-Estados Unidos"; Hellwig, "Racial Paradise or Run-Around?" Hellwig, "A New Frontier in a Racial Paradise."

22. Rosenberg, *Spreading the American Dream*; Rosenberg, *World War I and the Growth of United States Predominance in Latin America*, 77–111.

23. Anzovin and Podell, *Famous First Facts International*, 299; Innis, "Technology and Public Opinion in the United States," 16; "The Associated Press in Central and South America," *Traffic Bulletin of the Associated Press* 5 (April 1919): 1–4.

24. Leite in Bastide, "A imprensa negra do Estado de São Paulo," 131; see also Edwards, *The Practice of Diaspora*, 3.

25. Tuttle, *Race Riot*; Painter, *Standing at Armageddon*; Kelley, *Hammer and Hoe*, 228–31; Du Bois, "Returning Soldiers," *The Crisis*, May 1919; in Du Bois, *The Emerging Thought of W. E. B. Du Bois*, 245; "Barred from French Fine Art School," *Afro-American* (Baltimore), April 27, 1923, 1.

26. Tuttle, *Race Riot*.

27. Du Bois, *Black Reconstruction*, 15; Stoddard, *The Rising Tide of Color against White World-Supremacy*; on these, see Guterl, *The Color of Race in America, 1900–1940*; on black internationalism, see Von Eschen, *Race against Empire*; Plummer, *Rising Wind*; Gallicchio, *The African American Encounter with Japan and China*; Brock and Castañeda, *Between Race and Empire*; Gatewood, *Black Americans and the White Man's Burden, 1898–1903*; J. Harris, *African-American Reactions to War in Ethiopia, 1936–1941*; Hellwig, *African-American Reflections on Brazil's Racial Paradise*; Hellwig, "The Afro-American Press and Woodrow Wilson's Mexican Policy, 1913–1917"; Hellwig, "Afro-American Reactions to the Japanese and the Anti-Japanese Movement, 1906–1924"; W. Scott, *The Sons of Sheba's Race*; Watkins-Owens, *Blood Relations*; Edwards, *The Practice of Diaspora*.

28. Cobbs Hoffman, *The Rich Neighbor Policy*.

29. D. Williams, *Culture Wars in Brazil*; Needell, "The Domestic Civilizing Mission."

30. Von Eschen, *Satchmo Blows up the World*.

Producing Consumption

1. Butter-Nut ad, 1922, Series 3, Box 11, Folder "1922 Fall Campaign," Hills Bros. Collection, National Museum of American History Archives Center, Smithsonian Institution, Washington, D.C. (hereafter NMAH). My understanding is that Butter-Nut is a subsidiary of Hills Bros., although there may be some more formal corporate relation.

2. The irony of this language in a period in which Brazil was also a federation of "United States" (*Estados Unidos do Brasil*) would have been lost on most North Americans, who still claimed for their country the name of the entire continent—as they continue to do today.

3. A. Kaplan and Pease, *Cultures of United States Imperialism*; di Leonardo, *Exotics at Home*; Rydell, *All the World's a Fair*; Streeby, *American Sensations*.

4. This definition of consumerism is from Cross, *An All-Consuming Century*, 1; see also Baudrillard, *The Consumer Society*.

5. Bederman, *Manliness and Civilization*, ch. 3; Rotundo, *American Manhood*, ch. 11, esp. 248–51; S. Davis, *Living up to the Ads*, 50; Marchand, *Advertising the American Dream*, 14, 414n12, citing Lears, *No Place of Grace*, 47–51; Lears, *Fables of Abundance*, esp. "The Pursuit of the Real," 357; Jacobson, *Barbarian Virtues*, 129–36; Cohen, *A Consumers' Republic*; Leach, *Land of Desire*; Horowitz, *The Morality of Spending*; Donohue, *Freedom from Want*; Richards, *The Commodity Culture of Victorian England*; Mosse, *Nationalism and Sexuality*; Mosse, *Toward the Final Solution*.

6. Marchand, *Advertising the American Dream*, 63–66, on consumer citizenship; Baudrillard, *The Consumer Society*; Lears, *Fables of Abundance*; Cross, *An All-Consuming Century*; Ewen and Ewen, *Channels of Desire*; Ewen, *Captains of Consciousness*; Lears, "From Salvation to Self-Realization"; see also the other essays in Fox and Lears, *The Culture of Consumption*; Leach, *Land of Desire*, 386, for a strong critique of the myth of consumption as freedom; Boorstin, *The Americans*; Donohue, *Freedom from Want*; Horowitz, *The Morality of Spending*; E. Martin, *Flexible Bodies*; McGovern, "Consumption and Citizenship in the United States, 1900–1940"; Susman, *Culture as History*, esp. "'Personality'" and "Culture and Civilization: The Nineteen-Twenties"; García-Canclini, *Consumers and Citizens*; Stychin, *A Nation by Rights*, 15; Cohen, *A Consumers' Republic*; Falk, *The Consuming Body*.

7. On the racialized and racist aspects of consumer citizenship, see Marchand, *Advertising the American Dream*; Frazier, *Black Bourgeoisie*; Chin, *Purchasing Power*, 7; A. Dávila, *Latinos, Inc.*; Ownby, *American Dreams in Mississippi*; Marable, *How Capitalism Underdeveloped Black America*; D. Baldwin, "Out from the Shadow of E. Franklin Frazier?"

8. The excellent books in the previous two footnotes for the most part either analyze consumption in the abstract, unconcerned with its relationship to nationalism (Baudrillard is the prime example) or restrict themselves to "America," as many delineate clearly in their titles (the historical approaches mostly fall into this category). Even comparative perspectives find parallels rather than connections, as in Strasser, McGovern, and Judt, *Getting and Spending*. Exceptions include work that focuses on the context of empire, which identifies consumerism as transnational in its formation, and studies of consumerism in Latin America—for example, García Canclini, *Consumers and Citizens*; Rydell, "The Culture of Imperial Abundance"; Moreno, *Yankee Don't Go Home!*

9. Gereffi and Korzeniewicz, *Commodity Chains and Global Capitalism*; Topik, "Historicizing Commodity Chains"; Topik, Marichal, and Frank, *From Silver to Cocaine*, esp. Topik and Samper, "The Latin American Coffee Commodity Chain"; Baudrillard, *The System of Objects*; Appadurai, *The Social Life of Things*. The classic, model commodity history is Mintz, *Sweetness and Power*; on the genre's expansion and popularization, see Robbins, "Commodity Histories."

10. Pomeranz and Topik, *The World That Trade Created*, 80–87.

11. Mokyr, "The Second Industrial Revolution, 1870–1914"; Atkeson and Kehoe, "The Transition to a New Economy after the Second Industrial Revolution."

12. Roseberry, introduction to Roseberry, Gudmundson, and Samper, *Coffee, Society, and Power in Latin America*, 10; Jiménez, "'From Plantation to Cup,'" 48; Halperin-Donghi, *Contemporary History of Latin America*, 158, 169–70; J. Love, *São Paulo in the Brazilian Federation*, 38; Pomeranz and Topik, *The World That Trade Created*, 106; see also Topik, "Coffee"; Baer, *The Brazilian Economy*; Bulmer-Thomas, *The Economic History of Latin America since Independence*; Mahony, "The Local and the Global." The contemporaneous rubber boom, at its height in the 1910s, was also significant; see Weinstein, *The Amazon Rubber Boom*; Z. Frank and Musacchio, "Brazil in the International Rubber Trade, 1870–1930."

13. Cobbs Hoffman, *The Rich Neighbor Policy*, 5; Burns, *The Unwritten Alliance*; Burns, "Tradition and Variation in Brazilian Foreign Policy," 198–99; Halperin-Donghi, *Contemporary History of Latin America*, 159; Roseberry, Gudmundson, and Samper, *Coffee, Society, and Power*, esp. Jiménez, "'From Plantation to Cup'"; Topik, "Coffee"; Delfim Netto, *O problema do café no Brasil*; Peláez and Instituto Brasileiro do Café, *Essays on Coffee and Economic Development*; Pendergrast, *Uncommon Grounds*; Stein, *Vassouras, a Brazilian Coffee County, 1850–1900*; Stolcke, *Coffee Planters, Workers, and Wives*; Wickizer, *The World Coffee Economy*; W. Williamson and National Coffee Association of USA, *The Retail Market for Coffee*; Uribe-Compuzano, *Brown Gold*, 90–91, 174, cited in Brandes, *Herbert Hoover and Economic Diplomacy*, 130; Jacob, *The Saga of Coffee*; "Flavor it with Coffee," JC ad no. 44D, in *The Coffee Club*, 1921, Series 1, Box 28, Folder 3, Ayer Collection, NMAH.

14. Rosenberg, *Spreading the American Dream*; B. Levine et al., *Who Built America?*; Painter, *Standing at Armageddon*.

15. Jacobson, *Barbarian Virtues*.

16. Bandeira, *Presença dos Estados Unidos no Brasil*; Black, *United States Penetration of Brazil*; Cobbs Hoffman, *The Rich Neighbor Policy*; J. Smith, *Unequal Giants*; Topik, *Trade and Gunboats*; Valla, *A penetração norte-americana*; Valla, "Os Estados Unidos e a influência estran[j]eira"; Aita, "Discurso político e relações internacionais"; Wesson, *The United States and Brazil.*

17. J. Smith, *Unequal Giants*; Vinhosa, "As relações Brasil–Estados Unidos durante a primeira república"; Topik, *Trade and Gunboats*; P. Smith, *Talons of the Eagle.*

18. Marchand, *Advertising the American Dream*; Lears, *Fables of Abundance*; Olney, *Buy Now, Pay Later*, 169; Scanlon, *Inarticulate Longings*, esp. ch. 1. The 1920s and '30s, Marchand contends, are privileged moments for the use of advertising as cultural historical source material not only because of the sheer volume produced, but also because of the "detailed vignettes of social life" that ads offered as they shifted from portraying primarily the product to narrating consumer behavior (xxi). See also Barton, *The Man Nobody Knows*, and Fried, *The Man Everybody Knew*; Woodard, "Marketing Modernity"; Padilha, *A cidade como espetáculo.*

19. For example, one source referred to "that belated contribution to the American coffee propaganda which the São Paulo Minister of Finance in 1912 promised." Ukers, "A Dark Man with a Bundle," in "The Trade Oracle," *Tea and Coffee Trade Journal* (hereafter *T&CTJ*), February 1916, 135–36.

20. Dr. Murillo Mendes (director of publicity for the São Paulo Coffee Institute), reported in "Brazil Coffee Propaganda in 1931: A Survey of the Advertising Activities of the São Paulo Institute in Europe and Japan and the United States," *T&CTJ*, December 1931, 627–29; "São Paulo News Letter," *T&CTJ*, December 1932, 549; "Coffee Association Activities: Colombia Will Cooperate in National Coffee Publicity Program," *T&CTJ*, December 1932, 548; "Brazil Planters Organize: They Form a Company to Collect a Surtax of 5 Cents per Bag to Advertise Coffee in America," *T&CTJ*, June, 1917, 512–13.

21. *A Copy Writer Speaks.*

22. "Analysis of 1923 Coffee Advertising That Will Reach 65,000,000 People," *Spice Mill* (hereafter *SM*), January 1923, 34–36.

23. Coste, "A Guide-Post," 158–68; esp. 162, 164, and 167; "Analysis of 1923 Coffee Advertising That Will Reach 65,000,000 People"; "All of these Magazines will be used to advertise COFFEE," JC ad, *SM*, December 1922, 2137; "One Billion Coffee Advertisements," *SM*, January 1923, 37, which offered the following JC claim: "Since our campaign began the per capita consumption of Coffee has increased between twenty and thirty per cent." A slightly grander version of the ad campaign's details appears in "Parecer do Deputado Sampaio Vidal sôbre a mensagem envida à Camera dos Deputados pelo Presidente da República Epitacio da Silva Pessôa, em 17–10–1921 (do 'Jornal do Commercio' de 21–1–1921)," in Vidal, *Defesa do café no Brasil*, 32–53.

24. Ukers, *All about Coffee*, 490; Coste, "A Guide-Post," 162.

25. Ewen and Ewen, *Channels of Desire*; Cross, *An All-Consuming Century*; Marchand, *Advertising the American Dream*; Judith Williamson, *Decoding Advertisements*; Scanlon, *Inarticulate Longings*, 172; S. Davis, *Living Up to the Ads*; see also the won-

derful ethnographic take on advertising as a site of social struggle over meaning and power in Mazzarella, *Shoveling Smoke*.

26. Coste, "A Guide-Post," 168. While JC claims were undeniably hyperbolic, coffee consumption did rise remarkably in this period. See Roseberry, Gudmundson, and Samper, *Coffee, Society, and Power*.

27. Coste, "A Guide-Post," 158; Howard Henderson, "Account Histories: Cheek-Neal Coffee Company," Box 5, Folder "Coffee Accounts 1914–1960," 7, John W. Hartman Center for Sales, Advertising, and Marketing History, Duke University (hereafter HC); "Correspondence with Australia on Experience in Marketing and Advertising of Coffee of the J. Walter Thompson Company," Box 1 Information Center, Folder "Case Studies—Coffee 1912–1962," unpaginated, HC; "Cooperative Advertising: The Work of the Joint Coffee Trade Publicity Committee Cited in Metropolitan Life Insurance Company's Review," *SM*, November 1926, 2110–12.

28. JC ad, 1919, Series 1, Box 28, Folder 1, Ayer Collection, NMAH.

29. "Who now is afraid of COFFEE," JC ad, 1919, archived in Ayer for 1920, Series 1, Box 28, Folder 1, Ayer Collection, NMAH.

30. "My reputation depends on COFFEE," "A life saver among life-savers," and "When your collar starts to wilt," all 1920, Series 1, Box 28, Folder 1, Ayer Collection, NMAH.

31. "Flavor it with Coffee," JC ad, 1921, Series 1, Box 28, Folder 3, Ayer Collection, NMAH; "Six Rules for making BETTER COFFEE," JC ad, 1923, Series 1, Box 28, Folder 3, Ayer Collection, NMAH. The advertisers ignored the tilde ("~") in "São," consistent with a fairly common North American disregard for characters not used in the English language.

32. "Brazil is doing its part," JC ad, 1919, Series 1, Box 28, Folder 1, Ayer Collection, NMAH; "A life saver among life-savers" and "When your collar starts to wilt," JC ads, both 1920, Series 1, Box 28, Folder 1, Ayer Collection, NMAH (my emphasis); "Flavor it with Coffee" and "Scour the Coffee Pot!" both 1921; "Six Rules for making BETTER COFFEE" and "Mrs. Thomas Was Housecleaning," both 1923; all four in Series 1, Box 28, Folder 3, Ayer Collection, NMAH. Interestingly, the distinction in English between agriculture and industry was moot in Brazilian Portuguese, in which *industria de café* described coffee's production anyway.

33. Bederman, *Manliness and Civilization*; Torgovnick, *Gone Primitive*; Jacobson, *Whiteness of a Different Color*; Jacobson, *Barbarian Virtues*.

34. "The COFFEE House is coming back," JC ad, 1919, Series 1, Box 28, Folder 2, "Book No. 130: JCTC, 1919–1920," Ayer Collection, NMAH; "Address Delivered by the Honorable Sebastião Sampaio, Consul General of Brazil, at the Annual Convention of the Associated Coffee Industries of America, Denver, Colorado, September 12, 1932," [Associated Coffee Industries] *Convention Report*, September 12, 1932, 19–20, New York Public Library (hereafter NYPL).

35. "Time dispels our old illusions" and "Wild and weird were our old delusions," both JC ads, 1920, Series 1, Box 28, Folder 2, "Book No. 130: JCTC, 1919–1920," Ayer Collection, NMAH; "Who now is afraid of COFFEE," JC ad, 1920, Series 1, Box 28, Folder 1, Ayer Collection, NMAH.

36. "Coffee History by Radio: How Will Cuppy Scrambles It for the Edification and Delight of Listeners-in on The Coffee Matinee," *T&CTJ*, August 1932, 134–36; quote on 134.

37. Smith, *Unequal Giants*, chs. 4 and 5.

38. "Report of the 1925 Conferences"; Pendergrast, *Uncommon Grounds*, 157.

39. "Coffee—the American Drink," JC ad, 1919; in Ukers, *All about Coffee*, 476; "The sovereign drink of pleasure and of health" (bottom bold text reads: "Coffee—the American drink"), JC ad, 1919, Series 1, Box 28, Folder 1, Ayer Collection, NMAH.

40. Cited in "Report of the 1925 Conferences," 23.

41. "Coffee increases factory efficiency," JC ad, 1921, 1, Box 28, Folder 3, Ayer Collection, NMAH; "Coffee Week. March 29 to April 3," JC ad, 1920, Series 1, Box 28, Folder 1, Ayer Collection, NMAH.

42. This figure is a rough Brazilian equivalent to Juan Valdez, despite Topik's claims that there is no such figure ("Zé Prado," as Topik names him); see Topik, "Representaçoes nacionais do cafecultor."

43. Anderson, *Imagined Communities*; Cooper, *Colonialism in Question*, esp. "Identity," 59–90.

44. "Mrs. Stevens Makes a Discovery," JC ad, 1923, in *SM*, January 1923, 34–36; "Flavor it with Coffee"; "Scour the Coffee Pot!" JC ad, 1921, Series 1, Box 28, Folder 3, Ayer Collection, NMAH; "Six Rules for making BETTER COFFEE," JC ad, 1923, Series 1, Box 28, Folder 3, Ayer Collection, NMAH; "Cooking food and roasting coffee are closely related," Hills Bros. ad, 1927, Series 3, Box 16, Folder 1, Hills Bros. Collection, NMAH. Black domestic labor: "Mrs. Thomas Was Housecleaning," JC ad, 1923, Series 1, Box 28, Folder 3, Ayer Collection, NMAH; "Back you will come for more Hills Bros. Coffee," Hills Bros. ad, 1927, Series 3, Box 16, Hills Bros. Collection, NMAH; "Griddle cakes are best when the flour and milk are mixed *a little at a time*," Hills Bros. ad, 1928, Series 3, Box 57, Folder 1, pamphlet: "Advertising for the First Half of 1928," Hill Bros. Collection, NMAH.

45. "Back you will come for more Hills Bros. Coffee"; "Griddle cakes are best when the flour and milk are mixed *a little at a time*."

46. Scholarship on "Aunt Jemima" is wonderfully digested in Witt, *Black Hunger*, esp. "'Look Ma, the Real Aunt Jemima!' Consuming Identities under Capitalism," 21–53.

47. Rogin, "'The Sword Became a Flashing Vision'"; Kirby, "D. W. Griffith's Racial Portraiture"; Tyler, "Racist Art and Politics at the Turn of the Century"; Cripps, "The Birth of a Race Company."

48. Pendergrast, *Uncommon Grounds*, 170–71; Henry T. Stanton (vice-president, J. Walter Thompson Company, Chicago), "How Maxwell House Hooks Its Advertising to Sales Potentials: The Cheek-Neal Coffee Company Operates a System of Sales Analyses That Are Used as the Basis of Its Advertising Plans," *PI*, September 22, 1927, 165–74; "Maxwell House Coffee—an Advertising Success," *PI*, October 11, 1928, 131–32 (claims the Maxwell House campaign was "unusually successful," multiplying its sales four times over the period 1922–27); "Account Histories: Cheek-Neal Coffee Company."

49. Postum used a "mammy" image in 1927, reports Pendergrast, *Uncommon Grounds*, 172n9. See also W. Livingston Larned, "Is 'Mammy' Telling Too Many Ghost Stories? Modern Advertising Throws Fear into the Hearts and Minds of the Multitudes," *PI*, September 23, 1926, 57–60. Brazilians too would have found entirely legible this image of an African American employee, content, cooperative, and successfully confined to the domestic sphere, if they were following the JC campaign this closely, though their readings would have revised it to fit their own social context. The figure of an enslaved black woman ("Mammy's" referent) was a favorite among Brazilian elites, as would become publicly clear in 1926, when many jumped eagerly to commemorate "a Mãe Preta," the Black Mother of slavery times. See chapter 6.

50. "Mrs. Thomas Was Housecleaning."

51. Brown, "'What Has Happened Here'"; Higginbotham, "African-American Women's History and the Metalanguage of Race." Notably, this is the JC's only image of white female labor; the other ads featuring white women making coffee as part of entertaining friends or caring for a husband chose not to picture the more onerous tasks those processes might involve: "Serve COFFEE when you entertain," Ukers, *All about Coffee*, 475; "Any Time is COFFEE-time," Ukers, *All about Coffee*, 475; "We'll never disagree, dear—well anyway not about the coffee!" Ukers, *All about Coffee*, 498; "Mrs. Stevens Makes a Discovery"; "Flavor it with Coffee"; and especially the celestially serene white maiden in "Scour the Coffee Pot!"

52. See "Modern Woman as Businesswoman: 'The Little Woman, G.P.A.'" in Marchand, *Advertising the American Dream*, 167–71. Also: "To foster a scientific approach to advertising the [JWT] Company established a Research Department in 1915 and hired eminent academics such as John B. Watson, the founder of behavioral psychology." "The J. Walter Thompson Company," http://scriptorium.lib.duke.edu/hartman/jwt/history.html, HC. For its part, the JC went directly for scientific appeal by establishing a home economics service and appointing Helen Louise Johnson its director. See Johnson's report to the 1924 NCRA convention, "The Prescott Report in Home Economics," *SM*, October 1924, 2250–52; cited in Jiménez, "'From Plantation to Cup,'" 61–62nn88–89.

53. Pomeranz and Topik, *The World That Trade Created*, 83–87. While Pomeranz and Topik recognize the historical changes behind coffee's shifting meaning, they sometimes succumb to the temptation to attribute causative or essential qualities to coffee directly, as in the claim that "rulers were right to fear the sociability of coffee" (83).

54. Flexner, *I Hear America Talking*; Pollan, *The Botany of Desire*; Hart, *Diamond*; E. Epstein, *The Diamond Invention*. North Americans still cherish this coffee-tinted image of their national selves as independent, productive, and industrious, despite the global labor restructuring that has made it more than ever a hollow claim. See Jacob, *The Saga of Coffee*, 327; Pendergrast, *Uncommon Grounds*, 44; 50; ch. 3, passim; Gladwell, "Java Man." Historian Michael Jiménez, a thorough analyst with an eye for nuances, also believes coffee in the workplace boosted productivity. He describes the measures the industry pursued to make coffee available in factories, concluding, "Coffee thus effectively became a handmaiden in the making of the

new industrial order which emerged in this period." Jiménez, "'From Plantation to Cup,'" 49. I would only caution that if coffee buttressed industrialization, it did so at least in part discursively, thanks to coffee promoters' success in getting workers, employers, and consumers in general (including hopeful historians such as Jiménez and myself) to believe that coffee makes one work harder. Verena Stolcke maintains a wise skepticism in "The Labors of Coffee in Latin America," calling coffee "a beverage that was endowed with social meanings and believed to contain a stimulating quality" (67).

55. Jiménez, "'From Plantation to Cup,'" 49, 61n83; "Some Coffee Drinking!" and "Hot Coffee for Steel Workers," *The Coffee Club* 4, no. 4 (February 1924): 2–3

56. Leach, *Land of Desire*, 271; Weinstein, *For Social Peace in Brazil*, discussion of Fordism (or Americanism) and Taylorism, 4–8; Fones-Wolf, review of James Hoopes, *False Prophets*.

57. F. Taylor, *The Principles of Scientific Management*. On the "identity-of-interest" of workers and managers before Taylor or Ford, see Painter, *Standing at Armageddon*, introduction. Brazilian elites were equally interested in rationalizing factory production, as much to remake their own self-image and claim professional authority and technical expertise as to control workers and craftsmen. Weinstein, *For Social Peace in Brazil*; see also José Bento Monteiro Lobato's translations of Ford and his own *How Henry Ford Is Regarded in Brazil*.

58. "These Advertisements will help you to sell more COFFEE," JC ad, 1923, Series 1, Box 28, Folder 3, Ayer Collection, NMAH.

59. "On bended knees the black slaves served COFFEE," JC ad, 1919, Series 1, Box 28, Folder 1, Ayer Collection, NMAH; "The sovereign drink of pleasure and of health," JC ad, 1919, Series 1, Box 28, Folder 1, Ayer Collection, NMAH; "'Coffee the Drink of Intellectuals' Says Million Dollar Campaign Copy: Advertising in 306 Newspapers to Begin April 21—National Magazines to Follow in June," *PI*, April 17, 1919, 17–18. See also "Iced Coffee," JC ad, 1924, Series 1, Box 28, Folder 1, Ayer Collection, NMAH: iced coffee "is less sugary than the average warm weather drink and for that reason generally popular with men."

60. "The robust West loves its vigorous drink," Hills. Bros. ad, 1925, Series 3, Box 16, Hills Bros. Collection, NMAH; "The Story of Controlled Roasting," *PI*, July 29, 1926, cover.

61. "Café—Cawfee/COFFEE," JC ad, 1919; reproduced in Ukers, *All about Coffee*, 476.

62. JC ad, 1919; reproduced in Ukers, *All about Coffee*, 476.

63. "Coffee Propaganda Progress: A Digest of the Report Made by the Joint Coffee Trade Publicity Committee at the NCRA Convention," *T&CTJ*, December 1918, 620 (calls beginning of Prohibition "a time that the committee considers most auspicious to push coffee, and to push it *hard*, as a substitute for intoxicants"); McCreery to Director of Military Intelligence, "American Coffee Propaganda," and "Will This Million Dollar Coffee Campaign Materialize? After Repeated Postponement, Plans Now Call for Advertising to Start in April," *PI*, February 6, 1919, 28–31.

64. "'Coffee the Drink of Intellectuals'" (the internal quote is the ad copy discussed); "Quaker City Yale Grads Popularize Coffee Club: Philadelphia Public Ledger Tells How College Men Make Beverage a Feature of Every Meeting"; ad no. 11 in *The Coffee Club* 4, no. 4 (February 1924): 1–2; preserved in Series 2, Box 6, Folder 6, Hills Bros. Collection, NMAH.

65. "The drink of Democracy," *The Coffee Club* 4, no. 4 (February 1924): 4, opposing "Coffee speakeasies"; "The sovereign drink of pleasure and of health."

66. Alcohol's masculine aura was constructed in part by its principal foe, the temperance movement. See Ginzberg, *Women and the Work of Benevolence*; Bordin, *Woman and Temperance*; B. Epstein, *The Politics of Domesticity*; Giele, *Two Paths to Women's Equality*. On the connection between fears around African Americans and alcohol and the success of female reform movements, see Crowe, "Racial Violence and Social Reform," esp. 235–36, and Bederman, "'Not to *Sex*–But to *Race*!' Charlotte Perkins Gilman, Civilized Anglo-Saxon Womanhood, and the Return of the Primitive Rapist," ch. 4 in *Manliness and Civilization*.

67. "Quaker City Yale Grads Popularize Coffee Club"; "On bended knees the black slaves served COFFEE."

68. "Quaker City Yale Grads Popularize Coffee Club"; "'Coffee the Drink of Intellectuals,'" which also reported "The Coffee House Is Coming Back," "where men may meet and mingle with the freedom of a club."

69. Terry Gilkiron [illegible—Gilkirov?], "Kernel Koffee" (cartoon), *The Coffee Club* 4, no. 4 (February 1924): 1. Series 2, Box 6, Folder 6, Hills Bros. Collection, NMAH.

70. *T&CTJ*, August 1918, 165.

71. *T&CTJ*, October 1921, 18a; *SM*, January 1924, 59; *T&CTJ*, September 1920, 273.

72. *T&CTJ*, April 1918, 316.

73. Jacobson, *Barbarian Virtues*; see also Roediger, *The Wages of Whiteness*.

74. Linebaugh and Rediker, *The Many-Headed Hydra*; Bolster, *Black Jacks*; Gilroy, *The Black Atlantic*.

75. As U.S. state representatives did, for example, in the Philippines. See Rafael, "White Love: Surveillance and Nationalist Resistance in the U.S. Colonization of the Philippines," 189.

76. Bacha and Greenhill, *150 Anos de café*, 45.

77. Delfim Netto, *O problema do café no Brasil*; Jiménez, "'From Plantation to Cup,'" 44, 59n41; Roseberry, introduction to Roseberry, Gudmundson, and Samper, *Coffee, Society, and Power*, 11; Holloway, *The Brazilian Coffee Valorization of 1906*; Topik, *The Political Economy of the Brazilian State*, ch. 3. See also Sensabaugh, "The Coffee-Trust Question in United States–Brazilian Relations, 1912–1913."

78. Vidal, *Defesa do café no Brasil*, vols. 1–2; Thorp, *Latin America in the 1930s*; Topik, *The Political Economy of the Brazilian State*; Fritsch, *External Constraints*; J. Love, *São Paulo in the Brazilian Federation*; I. F. Marcosson, "The Crisis in Coffee," *Saturday Evening Post*, October 3, 1925, 130; "The Future of Valorization," *T&CTJ*, June 1929, 866; Delfim Netto, *O problema do café no Brasil*; Bates, *Open-Economy Politics*. The great lacuna in all these works, of course, is the harsh toll valorization exerted on plantation laborers.

79. D. Frank, *Buy American*; Topik and Wells, "Epilogue," 230; Jacobson, *Barbarian Virtues*; Eckes, *Opening America's Market*; Cárdenas, Ocampo, and Thorp, "Introduction: The Export Age"; Hurt, *Problems of Plenty*; E. Kaplan, *American Trade Policy*. For 1920s accounts, see the series of *Saturday Evening Post* articles by I. F. Marcosson on "alien commodity control," including "The Crisis in Rubber," June 5, 1926, 12–13, 140, 145–46, 149–51; "Brazil in Evolution," September 19, 1925, 30–31, 206, 209–10, 213–14, 217; and "The Crisis in Coffee," October 3, 1925. See also "Coffee Situation Subject of Newspaper Editorial," *SM*, Feburary 1925, 260, reprinting an article in the *Evening Post* (Chicago), December 26, 1924.

80. Hurt, *Problems of Plenty*; E. Kaplan, *American Trade Policy*, 2, 18.

81. Critics readily pointed out the contradictions—for example, "Monopolies," *Wileman's Brazilian Review* (hereafter *WBR*), February 4, 1926, 141–43; "United States and Rubber," *WBR*, February 11, 1928, 174.

82. In 1926, the NCRA and the Green Coffee Associations of New York, San Francisco, and New Orleans formed a coalition, the National Coffee Trade Council. Jiménez, "'From Plantation to Cup'"; "A Call for Roaster Co-operation: Current Conditions Test for National Organization—Value of Word-of-Mouth Publicity," *SM*, March 1925, 442; Font, *Coffee, Contention, and Change*, esp. ch. 3.

83. "Report of the Mission to Brazil: To the Executive Committee of the NCRA," *SM*, December 1922, 2148–68; "The U.S. and Coffee Stabilisation," *WBR*, January 21, 1925, 84.

84. "Report of the 1925 Conferences," 4, 7, 9–10, 13, 26; NCRA, "Salutation," in "Report of the 1925 Conferences," 4.

85. Schurz, *Valorization of Brazilian Coffee*; "Offer Plan to Remedy Coffee Situation: NCRA Make Four Recommendations in Statement Submitted to Secretary Hoover," *SM*, January 1925, 18–24; U.S. Congress, *Preliminary Report on Crude Rubber, Coffee, Etc.*; U.S. Congress, *Hearings on Crude Rubber, Coffee, Etc.*; U.S. Congress, *Crude Rubber, Coffee, Etc.*, 290. See also "Hoover Sees Threat to Foreign Trade," *NYT*, November 1, 1925, 22.

86. Brandes, *Herbert Hoover*, 135, citing Klein to Schurz, 14 November 1925, RG 151:351.1 (Brazil), NA and *NYT*, November 14, 1925; Fritsch, *External Constraints*, 115.

87. Brandes, *Herbert Hoover and Economic Diplomacy*, 134, citing Montgomery to F. E. Norwine (president, NCRA), May 22 and June 2, 1928, in U.S. Congress, *Preliminary Report on Crude Rubber, Coffee, Etc.*

88. Brandes, *Herbert Hoover and Economic Diplomacy*, 134, citing Klein to Friele, March 19, 1928, and Klein to Coste, April 2, 1928, in U.S. Congress, *Crude Rubber, Coffee, Etc.*, 10.

89. Topik, *The Political Economy of the Brazilian State*, 88; Fritsch, *External Constraints*, 113–15, citing W. L. Schurz's *Final Report on the Work of the Coffee Mission*, dated July 8, 1925, in Haeberle to Secretary of State, November 7, 1925, RG 59, NA, 832.61333/220; National Roasters Association to Secretary of State, August 31, 1925, RG 59, NA, 832.51/20, /21, /23, /24, /29, /30; for a more general view, see Becker, *The Dynamics of Business-Government Relations*. Nor was the U.S. coffee industry itself unified in its views. See "Brazilian Coffee in the United States," *WBR*, February 18,

1925, 217–219; Bert Halligan, "Meeting of Mid-West Section of the NCRA, Chicago, March 17," *SM*, April 1925, 632–45; "Propaganda for the Trade Can Be Easily Reflexed," *SM*, February 1925, 332; "The Future of Valorization: A Skillful Defense of the Institute by a Brazilian, and a Londoner's Skepticism as to Price Maintainance," *T&CTJ*, June 1929, 866; "Labor Conditions on Brazil's Coffee Plantations," *SM*, June 1926, 980; "Joint Meeting of Committee Representing Roasters," *SM*, December 1922, 2180–90; "Impressions of Conditions at Santos: Peter Eiseman Back from Brazil, Reviews the Coffee Situation as He Observed It," *SM*, November 1926, 2127; John J. Thaden, "An American Looks at Brazil Coffee Control," *T&CTJ*, January 1929, 92–93; "Brazil Coffee Control Misconceptions," *T&CTJ*, February 1929, 259; "Coffee Trade Attitude toward Brazil's Policy and the Hoover Movement," *SM*, January 1926, 106; E. A. Kahl, "Year 1924 Baffling to the Coffee Trade," *SM*, January, 1925, 21, Kahl, "Review of Coffee Prices and Tendencies: Pamphlet Just Issued by Coffee Department of W. R. Grace & Co.," *SM*, June 1926, 1104–5; Kahl [?], "The Coffee Situation as Viewed at San Francisco," *SM*, February 1924, 338.

90. Leff, *Reassessing the Obstacles to Economic Development*, 81; Marcelo Abreu, "Argentina and Brazil during the 1930s"; Topik contends, in "Historicizing Commodity Chains," and in Topik and Samper, "The Latin American Coffee Commodity Chain," that Brazilians were active "price makers" in the relationship with North American coffeemen and urges historians therefore to complicate ideas about "producers" and "consumers."

91. "New Coffee Advertising Campaign: To Show That Coffee Is Still Cheap—Ads Will Be Read by More Than 15,000,000," *SM*, March 1925, 468–69; "New Coffee Advertising Shows that coffee is still cheap," JC ad, 1925, *SM*, March 1925, 443. "Coffee Growers Invest $1,028,015.17 in Advertising," *PI*, October 30, 1924, 147–48; quote on 148. The São Paulo Institute sent only one installment of funds; unable to elicit a response to its letters, the U.S.-based staff of the JC was stymied, according to Ross W. Weir, "The Coffee Advertising Contract," *SM* Convention Extra Edition, November 1926, 2252–53. On these contract negotiations, see "Report of the 1925 Conferences."

92. Emmet Beeson, "American Coffee Drinker at the Mercy of Brazil: South American Republic Controls Price and Quality and Manipulates Crops and Exports to Advantage, Asserts New York Broker," *NYT*, June 29, 1924, x4.

93. "International Drama of a Cup of Coffee," *NYT*, January 11, 1925, sec. 4, 7. Note also that the *Times* augmented Hoover's voice by filling a Sunday section front page with his tirade; Richard V. Oulahan, "Hoover Warns World of Trade Wars," *NYT*, January 10, 1926, sec. 8, 1.

94. R. D. Fleming, "Brazil's Corner in Coffee," *Industrial Digest* 5, no. 1 (January 1926): 18–19, 64–65; quote on 18. Fleming also gleefully reported that Hoover had encouraged New York bankers *not* to lend to Brazil in case the money might support valorization and increase coffee prices to the U.S. consumer (64). I. F. Marcosson also cheered that the "North American housewife, alarmed at the increasing cost of the favorite family breakfast beverage, has cut down her purchases to such an extent that

the whole coffee market has been affected." "The Crisis in Coffee," *Saturday Evening Post*, October 3, 1925, 38.

95. "Fathering" in Oulahan, "Hoover Warns World of Trade Wars"; "International Drama of a Cup of Coffee."

96. Oulahan, "Hoover Warns World of Trade Wars"; Herbert C. Hoover, "The Questions Mr. Hoover Asks: He Sees Grave Problems Arising from Government Trade Control," *NYT*, January 10, 1926, sec. 8, 1; Hoover's use in this article of a world trade map with the United States at the center was a common illustration of this perspective in this period, writes Schulten in *The Geographical Imagination in America*.

97. Hoover's philosophy of business articulated in Hoover, *The Memoirs of Herbert Hoover*, cited in Brandes, *Herbert Hoover*, 63; "enterprising" and "manufacturing" in Aughinbaugh, *Selling Latin America*, 358 and 11.

98. Topik and Wells, "Epilogue," 230; Becker, *The Dynamics of Business-Government Relations*; E. Kaplan, *American Trade Policy*.

99. Beeson, "American Coffee Drinker at the Mercy of Brazil"; Roosevelt quoted in Jacobson, *Barbarian Virtues*, 3, 109–10.

100. December 26, 1924; reported in "Coffee Situation Subject of Newspaper Editorial." During the 1917 valorization, similar plans had hatched; see "Plans Maturing for Development of Porto Rico Coffee Industry," *SM*, January 1917, 31.

101. Delfim Netto, *O problema do café no Brasil*, 90. See also the discussion of the "all-out boycott by American roasters of Brazilian coffee" in 1925 in Fritsch, *External Constraints*, 112.

102. "International Drama of a Cup of Coffee"; see also Brandes, *Herbert Hoover and Economic Diplomacy*, 136. The reference to rubber is not coincidental. The collapse of the Amazon rubber boom was an event of recent memory (the first two decades of the twentieth century); it is reasonable to think Brazilians would have smarted at this reminder. See Weinstein, *The Amazon Rubber Boom*.

103. Delfim Netto, *O problema do café no Brasil*; Jiménez, "'From Plantation to Cup,'" 45, 60n52; Topik, *The Political Economy of the Brazilian State*, 89; J. Love, *São Paulo in the Brazilian Federation*.

104. *The Story of Coffee and How to Make It*, 1.

105. "Coffee . . is . . America's Favorite Drink" (two-dot ellipses in the original), BACPC ad no. 9771, 1929, Series 1, Box 28, Folder 3, Ayer Collection, NMAH.

106. "This Time Try Coffees From Central America. Twice the richness . . . twice the flavor. Never 'thin' or 'flat' or bitter," Folger's Coffee ad, n.d.; in Ukers, *All about Coffee*, 480.

107. "Twenty million bags a year but only a limited amount can qualify," Hills Bros. ad, 1922, Series 3, Box 11, no folder, Hills Bros. Collection, NMAH.

108. "There's a heart-deep western welcome *in every savory sip*"; "Western hospitality knows no half-measures"; "The robust West loves its vigorous drink"; "From the land of the purple sage"; "No wonder the West is proud of its coffee!" "Hills Bros. Coffee belongs to the West"—all Hills Bros. ads, 1925, Series 3, Box 16, Hills Bros. Collection, NMAH.

109. "From the West's homes of wealth and discrimination comes a tradition of wonderful coffee," 1924, and "What wonderful coffee you have out here!' Eastern visitors exclaim," n.d., both from Series 3, Box 11 (1922–24), Hills Bros. Collection, NMAH, and "No wonder the West is proud of its coffee!," 1925, ad no. 16, Series 3, Box 16 (1925), Hill Bros. Collection, NMAH.

110. "Cooking food and roasting coffee are closely related" and "Back you will come for more Hills Bros. Coffee," both Hills Bros. ads, 1927, Series 3, Box 16, Hills Bros. Collection, NMAH; "Griddle cakes are best when the flour and milk are mixed *a little at a time*," 1928, and "Why does the coffee-loving West look for Hills Bros. Arab?" 1929—both Hills Bros. ads, Series 3, Box 57, Folder 1, Hills Bros. Collection, NMAH; other ads from late 1920s through early 1930s in Series 3, Box 57, Folder 1, Hills Bros. Collection, NMAH.

111. Du Bois, *Black Reconstruction*; Roediger, *The Wages of Whiteness*; Roediger, *Black on White*; Guterl, *The Color of Race in America*; Jacobson, *Whiteness of a Different Color*; Haney López, *White by Law*; Hale, *Making Whiteness*; Saxton, *The Rise and Fall of the White Republic*; Ignatiev, *How the Irish Became White*. On forgetting, see also Renan, *Qu'est-ce qu'une nation?*; Trouillot, *Silencing the Past*.

112. Morrison, *Playing in the Dark*.

113. "Thoroughbreds," Hills Bros. ad, 1931, Series 3, Box 20, folder for 1931–32, Hills Bros. Collection, NMAH; "O cavallo arabe," *Sport Illustrado*, January 8, 1921.

114. "Where the finest coffee FLAVOR comes from," Hills Bros. ad, 1923, Series 3, Box 11, Hills Bros. Collection, NMAH.

115. "Dr. Arthur Neiva," *WBR*, August 1, 1925, 415–17; see also James S. Carson, "Some Special Present Day Foreign Trade Problems and How the Coffee Industry of the United States Can Help to Solve Them: Sum of Address Delivered by Mr. James S. Carson, Vice-President of American and Foreign Co., Inc.," (*ACI*) *Convention Report*, September 12, 1932, 23–26.

116. A. A. Preciado, "Come Out of It, South America; Wake Up! Why South America Should Advertise Here to Correct False Impression," *PI*, October 23, 1919, 45–48. Even if Preciado was himself South American (which I do not know), the publication of this piece in a U.S. trade journal offered North American businessmen the condescending view I am describing.

117. "Selling San [*sic*] Paulo Loan Here by Advertising: Bonds, Hitherto Usually Sold in England and France, Now Find a Ready Market in This Country," *PI*, April 28, 1921, 42–44.

118. Ibid.

119. Samuel Phillips, "Beware the Unconscious Propaganda of the Jokesmith: Don't Poke Fun at South America in Your Light Fiction and Then Expect Them to Buy Our Goods," *PI*, July 17, 1919, 65–66.

120. Bederman, *Manliness and Civilization*, esp. ch. 2 on Ida B. Wells.

121. Chakrabarty, "Postcoloniality and the Artifice of History."

122. "Discussion on Advertising Campaign [NCRA annual meeting, 1922]," *SM*, December 1922, 2208–10. Brazilian input was compromised by the fact that although the bulk of funds came from the planters, Brazil was represented on the JC by a single

member; see Coste, "A Guide-Post," and "Will This Million Dollar Coffee Campaign Materialize? After Repeated Postponement, Plans Now Call for Advertising to Start in April," *PI*, February 6, 1919, 28–31. It is difficult to measure the input of the JC's Brazilian member or the bloc of planters he represented since I have not discovered minutes of negotiations over the content of advertising. Congressman Sebastião [Rafael de Abreu?] Sampaio Vidal describes the JC as working in "daily and dedicated cooperation" with the Sociedade Promotora da Defesa do Café; see Vidal, *Defesa do café no Brasil*, 45. Besides this perhaps exaggerated claim, the only element of negotiations on content I can glean is this discussion of whether the word "Brazil" would appear in the ads.

123. "Coffee—the universal drink," JC ad series, including "My reputation depends on COFFEE," "A life saver among life-savers," and "When your collar starts to wilt"—all 1920, Series 1, Box 28, Folder 1, Ayer Collection, NMAH; "Quaker City Yale Grads Popularize Coffee Club" and "São Paulo's Growth," both in *The Coffee Club* 4, no. 4 (February 1924): 1–2; preserved in Series 2, Box 6, Folder 6, Hills Bros. Collection, NMAH; "Flavor it with Coffee," JC ad, 1921, Series 1, Box 28, Folder 3, Ayer Collection, NMAH; "How to make GOOD COFFEE"; "Serve COFFEE when you entertain"; "Any Time is COFFEE-time"; "I drink it every afternoon"—all JC ads, 1922; in Ukers, *All about Coffee*, 475.

124. "Picking Coffee on a Brazilian Plantation," JC ad, 1923, Series 1, Box 28, Folder 3, Ayer Collection, NMAH.

125. Cited in "Report of the 1925 Conferences," 33.

126. Ibid., 45–46.

127. "Review of Work of Brazilian-American Coffee Promotion Committee," *SM*, February 1930, 198–200.

128. *T&CTJ*, January 1929, 134. See also BACPC agreement in that same article.

129. "Welcome Hoover!" and Bezerra de Freitas, "A civilização norte americana," both in *Crítica*, December 21, 1928, 1–2. These articles, like much coverage of Hoover's 1928 visit, were admiring and positive.

130. Bureau of Information of the São Paulo Institute, "Feature BRAZIL COFFEES," ad, 1928, *T&CTJ*, July 1928, 63; January 1929, 153; April 1929, 581; June 1929, 867; "To The Grocery Trade of the United States," ad, 1929, *T&CTJ*, January 1920, 19; "It will pay you to use more BRAZIL COFFEE," ad, 1929, *T&CTJ*, 1929, passim.

131. "It's Cup-Quality that counts with coffee drinkers," BACPC ad no. 12295, 1929, Series 1, Box 28, Folder 3, Ayer Collection, NMAH.

132. "Brazil Publicity Launched: Committee Approves Program for Coffee Advertising Campaign to Start Immediately; Spending $160,000 First Year," *T&CTJ*, April 1929, 580.

133. "Happy New Year!" BACPC ad, 1932, *T&CTJ*, December 1932, 583.

134. "COFFEE . . is . . America's Favorite Drink"; also *T&CTJ*, April 1929, 583, and June 1929, 802–803; an ad the São Paulo Institute circulated in Budapest wrote the equation out: "Brazil = kávé." "Brazil Coffee Propaganda in 1931," *T&CTJ*, December 1931, 629.

135. Ukers, *All about Coffee*, 491.

136. Personified in Christine McGaffey Frederick's 1929 *Selling Mrs. Consumer*; about it, see Rutherford, *Selling Mrs. Consumer*.

137. Marchand, *Advertising the American Dream*, 311; B. Savage, *Broadcasting Freedom*; Spalding, "1928"; Lears, *Fables of Abundance*, 334.

138. The BACPC's 1929–30 trade journal series was devoid of images save the coffee cup logo, a departure from both its radio spots and the cheery family narratives of the JC's campaign. This is a distinction advertising historians note between feminized "uplift" copy and the masculinized "bottom-line" approach. See S. Davis, *Living up to the Ads*, ch. 1; on the distinction during the Depression, see Marchand, *Advertising the American Dream*, 306, 353–55.

139. "Coffee History by Radio," *T&CTJ*, August 1932, 134. "Thursdays off" marked this "lady" as a maid; "Cuppy" was drawing on the low social position of domestic labor to construct an object for ridicule.

140. "Coffee Matinee, an 'Outstanding event on the air,'" *T&CTJ*, November 1931, 461.

141. *SM*, September 1930, 1357.

142. "America's Favorite Drink goes on the air," BACPC ad, *SM*, August 1930, 1199.

143. "SPEND a Half-hour in Brazil EVERY THURSDAY AFTERNOON."

144. "Consul General Sampaio's Message," *T&CTJ*, August 1932, 136.

145. "Coffee Matinee, an 'Outstanding event on the air'"; "'Everybody's brewing it': A Midsummer Serenade to Iced Coffee," BACPC ad, 1932, *T&CTJ*, June 1932, 575.

146. "'Everybody's brewing it'"; "Coffee Matinee, an 'Outstanding event on the air'"; "Brazilian-American Coffee Promotion Committee Using Radio," *SM*, October 1930, 1510.

147. "SPEND a Half-hour in Brazil EVERY THURSDAY AFTERNOON."

148. "And here's what we'll do for you during the coming year!" *SM*, July 1930, 1037.

149. "America's Favorite Drink goes on the air, over a nation-wide net-work!" *SM*, August 1930, 1199.

150. "Brazilian-American Coffee Promotion Committee Using Radio"; "America's Favorite Drink goes on the air."

151. Topik and Wells, *The Second Conquest of Latin America*, 229; Topik, *Trade and Gunboats*; Rocha and Greenhill, *150 anos de café*; J. Love, *São Paulo in the Brazilian Federation*; Topik, *The Political Economy of the Brazilian State*, 84; Fritsch, *External Constraints*. Thanks very much to Steven Topik for helping clarify to me Brazil's position in the world coffee trade after 1929. On the effects of the Depression in Brazil, see Hilton, *Brazil and the Great Powers*, 19; Leff, *Underdevelopment and Development in Brazil*; Thorp, *Latin America in the 1930s*; Thorp, *Progress, Poverty and Exclusion*; Lee, "The Effects of the Depression on Primary Producing Countries," 148; Baer, *The Brazilian Economy*, 37–38 (dollar amounts of exports on 35); Prado Júnior, *História econômica do Brasil*, 292; Dean, *The Industrialization of São Paulo*.

152. Bates, *Open-Economy Politics*.

Maxixe's Travels

1. Advertisement for Liberty Music Shops, *NYT*, December 20, 1953, 57.

2. Sammy Gallop, Gil Rodin, and Bob Crosby, *Boogie-Woogie Maxixe*; recorded by Jack Richards and the Night Winds, Dick Jacobs, director, Coral 9–61063, 45 rpm (n.d.); Gil Rodin and Bob Crosby and his orchestra, Decca 9–25114 (n.d.); the Ames Brothers with the Hugo Winterhalter Orchestra and Chorus, Victor 20–5530 and Victor 47–5530 (n.d.); and Armed Forces Radio and TV Series P-3407, 16" (n.d.); all Library of Congress, Division of Recorded Sound (hereafter LCDRS).

3. This transcription from Coral 9–61063.

4. Garrod and Korst, *Bob Crosby and His Orchestra*, 14; Shapiro and Pollock, *Popular Music, 1920–1979*, 253; Gama Gilbert, "Records: New Venture," *NYT*, November 21, 1940, 122.

5. "Boogie-Woogie," in Kernfeld, *New Grove Dictionary of Jazz*, 135–136. Sources on maxixe detailed below.

6. Daly, *Done into Dance*, 107; on Salome, see Walkowitz, "The 'Vision of Salome.'" On the imperialism expressed gleefully on Tin Pan Alley, see Dennison, *Scandalize My Name*.

7. Léon-Martin, *Le music-hall et ses figures*; cited in Rose, *Jazz Cleopatra*, 94.

8. Like the metonymies of Broadway or Hollywood, Tin Pan Alley may at one point have been an actual street, perhaps a section of Twenty-eighth St. in New York City, where many late nineteenth-century music publishers worked.

9. Advertisements for Jos. W. Stern and Carl Fischer-Witmark, *Metronome* 33, no. 4 (April 1917): 6, 12.

10. "La Brasiliana—Tango by Sylvester Belmonté" (New York: Jerome H. Remick, 1913), Box 50, Series 8.62 (Geography: Brazil), Folder C ("Instrumental, 1876–1941; n.d."), Samuel DeVincent Sheet Music Collection, Archives Center, NMAH (hereafter SDVC).

11. "'Dancing Palace' de Luna-Park," unattributed journal article, n.d., n.p. In French. In "MGZR Maxixe (Dance)," clippings file, Jerome R. Robbins Dance Collection, NYPL, Performing Arts Division.

12. Imada, "Binding Hawai'i and New York in the American Empire." References to Hawaii in discussions of jazz are fairly frequent; see Léon-Martin, *Le music-hall et ses figures*; Guilherme de Almeida in Ferro, *A idade do jazz-band*, 19.

13. Advertisements, *Metronome* 36, no. 4 (April 1920): 4, 6, 14, 22, 24, 63, 77, 83, 98.

14. Lolligo, "Music and Musical Instruments of the Egyptians," *Metronome* 36, no. 4 (April 1920): 39–40.

15. Egypt was a site of fighting, of course; Hawaii was not until the Second World War, though it was of note as a Pacific outpost. See "Armed Volcano Is Part of our Pacific Gilbraltar," *NYT*, January 11, 1914, SM7; "Japan Could Take Philippines Easily . . . Hawaii Could Be Held," *NYT*, January 29, 1914, 2; "Army in Hawaii to be Increased," *NYT*, March 4, 1914, 10.

16. On Hollywood Orientalism in the period of the discovery of Tut's tomb, see Karnes, "The Glamorous Crowd."

17. Edwards, *The Practice of Diaspora.*

18. Morrison, *Playing in the Dark*; see also Quintero-Rivera, *A cor e o som da nação.*

19. Duran, *Recordings of Latin American Songs and Dances*, 21; Needell, "The Domestic Civilizing Mission," 9.

20. Alvarenga, *Música popular brasileira*, 335–36; Efegê, *Maxixe*; Almeida, *História da música brasileira*; Sandroni, *Feitiço decente*; Béhague, *Musiques du Brésil*, 76; N. Lopes, *O Negro no Rio de Janeiro*, 41; Vasconcelos, *Panorama da música popular brasileira na Belle Époque*, 25–26; Andrade, "Ernesto Nazaré"; Andrade, *Ensaio sobre a música brasileira*; Chasteen, "The Prehistory of Samba"; Fryer, *Rhythms of Resistance*, 154.

21. Chasteen, "The Prehistory of Samba," 33.

22. Sachs, *World History of the Dance*, 444–45.

23. N.a., n.t., *Revista da Semana*, March 7, 1913; cited in Efegê, *Maxixe*, 152; Efegê, *Maxixe*, 157, citing Almeida, *História da música brasileira*, 15; see also Vasconcelos, *Panorama da música popular brasileira na Belle Époque*, 15.

24. Efegê, *Maxixe*, sketches throughout; Fryer, *Rhythms of Resistance*, 154–55.

25. Castle and Castle, *Modern Dancing*, 107; Kinney and West, *Social Dancing of Today*, 45–47; Giovannini, *Balli d'oggi*, 143–49.

26. Freeland, *Flying Down to Rio.*

27. On the "ephemerality of dance" and corresponding difficulties for dance history, see Foulkes, *Modern Bodies*, 6; Browning, *Samba.*

28. Efegê, *Maxixe*, 47; Chasteen, "The Prehistory of Samba," 39. On set dances, see Szwed and Marks, "The Afro-American Transformations of European Set Dances and Dance Suites."

29. Efegê, *Maxixe*, 43–46.

30. Korman, roundtable talk on Brazil and jazz.

31. The CD recording *Carinhoso* (Paradoxx, 1996) has Nazareth's "Apanhei-te, Cavaquinho" and "Odeon," for example.

32. Efegê, *Maxixe*, 142–44. Cook's English name reflects Brazil's diverse immigrant population in this period, a quality it shared with other parts of the New World's Atlantic coast.

33. Jota Efegê, "Geraldo Magalhães terna reliquia dos velhos cafés-cantantes," *O Jornal*, October 25, 1964; reprinted in Efegê, *Figuras e coisas da música popular brasileira*, vol. 1, 118–20; Efegê, "O mulato que foi cantar lundus e dançar maxixe na Europa," *O Globo*, September 21, 1972; reprinted in Efegê, *Figuras e coisas da música popular brasileira*, vol. 2, 106–8; Efegê, *Maxixe*, 141–52; on 146 citing *Gazeta de Notícias*, January 31, 1909, on Magalhães and Teixeira at the Abbaye de Thélème; on 148 citing "O Brasil em Montmartre: O sucesso do *Vem cá, mulata*," *Gazeta de Notícias*, April 28, 1913; on 151 noting one Brazilian nightclub in Paris, the Ideal, which prohibited maxixe in 1914, suggesting that the dance must have been in vogue indeed to have incited such opposition.

34. Blake, *Le tumulte noir*, 27, 62; Dewitte, *Les mouvements nègres en France pendant les entre-deux-guerres*; Dewitte, "Le Paris noir de l'entre-deux-guerres"; Stovall, *Paris noir*; Stovall, "Music and Modernity, Tourism and Transgression"; Edwards, *The Prac-*

tice of Diaspora; Edwards, "On Critical Globality"; Fabre, *From Harlem to Paris*; Riis, "The Experience and Impact of Black Entertainers in England, 1895–1920." Riis calls London "Ragtime Crazy" by 1912; Rye, "The Southern Syncopated Orchestra"; Lotz, "The 'Louisiana Troupes' in Europe"; Lotz, "Will Garland and His Negro Operetta Company."

35. Giovannini, *Balli d'oggi*; Rivera, *Le tango et les danses nouvelles*; see also "The Pavlowana, the First of a New Series of Social Dances by Mademoiselle Anna Pavlowa," article in an unidentified magazine, n.d., pp. 10–11, in MGZR Maxixe (Dance), clippings, NYPL, Performing Arts Division. On maxixe in Berlin, see "Die Matchiche ein neuer tanz," photographs, n.p., February 15, 1906 [handwritten date], in MGZR Maxixe (Dance), clippings, NYPL, Performing Arts Division.

36. Dancer and dance historian Eduardo Sucena mentions Duque's success in Berlin in the 1910s, claiming that he and his partner "snatched first prize in the dance contest held in Berlin in the Admirals-Palast"; see Sucena, *A dança teatral no Brasil*, 123. Duque's presence in England is reflected in the 1913 promise of a London dance teacher to teach "Brazilian Maxixe, as introduced by Duque"; Efegê, "Inglêsa dava lições de maxixe brasileiro," *O Jornal*, March 6, 1969, 3; Fundo João Ferreira Gomes (Jota Efegê), Arquivo Nacional (hereafter AN); Duque's presence in Spain is reflected in King Afonso XIII of Spain's bestowal upon him of the Cross of the Knights of the Order of Isabel in 1915; Efegê, *Maxixe*, 148, 153; see also Jota Efegê, "Quando o maxixe era moda," *O Jornal*, April 14, 1968, 3, 4th notebook (^{40} caderno), Fundo João Ferreira Gomes, AN; and Pierre, "Maxixe—1910, samba—1920, caterête—1930," *Amateur Dancer* (London), no. 5 (February 1931): 17–19.

37. Efegê, *Maxixe*, 141, claims Duque went to Europe in 1911 or 1912, but then on 147, claims he arrived in 1912–13; "dominate" on 147.

38. The newspaper was the *Gazeta de Notícias*, according to M. Silva and Oliveira, *Pixinguinha*, 50.

39. Cabral, *Pixinguinha*, 45–46.

40. "Back from Paris" [advertisement], NYT, October 4, 1914, 15; "Authorized teacher" [advertisement], NYT, December 13, 1914, RPA7.

41. Advertisement for "Watch Your Step," NYT, December 11, 1914, 20.

42. "'Dancing Palace' de Luna-Park," unattributed journal article, n.d., n.p. In French. In "MGZR Maxixe (Dance)," clippings file, Jerome R. Robbins Dance Collection, NYPL, Performing Arts Division. I am not sure of the dating of this piece nor, therefore, of Duque's work at Coney Island. It could conceivably have been as early as 1904, when the park opened, or as late as 1924, when Duque retired from performing. My research did not uncover evidence that Duque appeared in the United States other than on the 1914–15 trip detailed here.

43. Advertisement for "Watch Your Step," NYT, December 11, 1914, 20; advertisement for "The Club De Vingt," NYT, December 18, 1914, 20; advertisement for the Hotel Knickerbocker Grille, NYT, December 18, 1914, 4.

44. "With Europe's Most Famous Stars" [advertisement], NYT, February 7, 1915, X6; same ad in NYT, February 5, 1915, 18.

45. "Every night, at Supper, the celebrated Duque of Paris. Assisted by Mlle. Gaby" [advertisement for the Café des Beaux-Arts], *NYT*, February 18, 1915, 20; same ad in *NYT*, February 8, 9, 11, and 15, 1915; similar ads, *NYT*, February 19, 23, and 25, and March 4, 8, 9, and 11, 1915.

46. Advertisement for Café Boulevard, *NYT*, March 30, 1915, 20; similar ads in *NYT*, April 4, 1915, X6, and April 7, 1915, 22. Notice of his departure in "Theatrical Notes," *NYT*, April 23, 1915, 13.

47. Advertisement for Jos. W. Stern, *Metronome* 31, no. 3 (March 1915): 2; same ad in *Metronome* 31, no. 4 (April 1915), inside front cover.

48. The publisher of "Duque Walk" had the previous year issued Nazareth's "Bregeiro" and "La Cumanda (My Beloved) Maxixe." Fellow music publishers in New York, Detroit, Battle Creek (Michigan), and Chicago—Tin Pan Alley in the broadest, metaphoric sense—offered many more. The following were all published in 1914: "Dengozo" (another Nazareth composition); "Roguish Eyes"; "Graciosa, Maxixe"; "Lobster à la Newburg"; "Maxixe Briolette"; "Buenos Dias (Good Morning) American Maxixe"; "Brazilian Love"; "La Belle Sevilliene: International Maxixe"; "A Brazilian Gem"; "The Uriel Maxixe"; and the "Castle Square Maxixe." "La Brasiliana—Tango by Sylvester Belmonté" appeared in 1913, as did the "'Maurice' Mattchiche (Brazilian Maxixe) by L. Dugue [*sic?*] and E. Costa," and the Chicago publishing house of McKinley Music had issued "La Sorella: Also Known as La Mattchiche" a few years earlier, probably in 1908. SDVC, Box 419 ("Maxixes"). On "La Mattchiche," see also Severiano and Mello, *A canção no tempo*, 31. In the popular music magazine *Metronome* in 1915, publishers advertised these and others, including "Amazon," "Amazonia (Parisian Tango)," "El Delirio, Maxixe do Brazil," "La Flor del Amazona," "Flor do Brazil," "Gypsy Maxixe," and the "Sans Souci Maxixe." *Metronome* 31, nos. 1–4 (January–April 1915), throughout. Retail-marketed sheet music shows that fans played this style themselves, but maxixe probably attracted more attention as a dance. Sheet music also appears to have attracted consumers as a fetishized commodity interesting in itself, purchased by people who did not necessarily intend to play it.

49. Antônio Amaral, *História dos velhos teatros de São Paulo*, 252–253.

50. Andrade, "Musica de coração" (1924), in *Música, doce música*, 115. He seems to have been referring to written scores.

51. "Joan Sawyer Maxixe," Columbia A 5561 (78A), LCDRS; "The 'Maurice' Mattchiche (Brazilian Maxixe) by L. Dugue and E. Costa" [sheet music] (New York: Jos. W. Stern, 1913); and "Bregeiro, Rio Brazilian Maxixe" by E. Nazareth [sheet music] (New York: Jos. W. Stern, 1914); both in SDVC, Box 419 ("Maxixes").

52. Castle and Castle, *Modern Dancing*, 107.

53. "Creole Girl, Maxixe, Vem Ca, Mulata, Frances Salabert, Castle House Orchestra; Frank W. McKee, director." Victor 35374 (78A), LCDRS.

54. James Reese Europe, "Amapa—Maxixe Bresilien" Victor recording, matrix #35360, dated to 1914 by Stephen C. Barr, *The Almost Complete 78 RPM Record Dating Guide (II)*; quote is Foreman, "Jazz and Race Records, 1920–1932," 18; see also J. Roberts, *The Latin Tinge*, 44–45.

55. Badger, *A Life in Ragtime*; Korman, roundtable talk on Brazil and jazz; and Welburn, "James Reese Europe and the Infancy of Jazz Criticism"; J. Roberts, *The Latin Tinge*.

56. "Brazilian Max-cheese," words by Muriel Window, music Ernesto Nazareth (New York: Jerome H. Remick, 1914), SDVC, Box 50, Series 8.62 (Geography: Brazil), Folder A ("Songs, 1914–1965; n.d.").

57. "Dance That Dengozo with Me, 'Oo-La-La,'" words by W. L. Beardsley, music [adapted by] George L. Cobb (Chicago: Will Rossiter, 1914), SDVC, Box 145B ("Dance"), no folder (loose in the bottom of the box). Cobb drops most of Nazareth's syncopation for a flatter, "pop" feel, but the reference is unmistakable.

58. Advertisement for Jerome H. Remick, *Metronome* 31, no. 2 (February 1915): 2.

59. "That Wonderful Dengoza Strain," words by William Jerome, music by Abner Greenberg (New York: Jerome H. Remick, 1914), SDVC, Box 50, Series 8.62 (Geography: Brazil), Folder A ("Songs, 1914–1965; n.d.").

60. On this dynamic, see Browning, *Infectious Rhythm*.

61. *Metronome* 31, nos. 1–4 (January–April 1915), throughout.

62. Advertisement for T. B. Harms, *Metronome* 32, no. 4 (April 1916): 7.

63. Advertisement for Jos. W. Stern, *Metronome* 32, no. 4 (April 1916): 4.

64. Antonio Ippolito, "O estudante brasileiro nos Estados Unidos: Suas primeiras impressões," *El Estudiante Latino-Americano* (1921): 7–10; Efegê, *Maxixe*, 154–55. Undated claims about the French dance-hall star Mistinguette's performance of a maxixe and of maxixe's presence at the Moulin Rouge are also suggestive, if inconclusive, in this regard. See Bret, *The Mistinguett Legend*, 135, and Pessis and Crépineau, *The Moulin Rouge*, 36. Essayist Brasílio Itiberê wrote in 1957 of hearing a Duque-Gaby maxixe in Paris, Italy, and Madrid; Itiberê, "Canções de Paris," in *Mangueira, Montmartre e outras favelas*, 75.

65. Walter Hirsch and May Hill, "On the Dreamy Amazon" (Chicago: Roger Graham Music, 1919); "Brazilian Chimes" (New York: Kendis-Brockman Music, 1920); Harold Dixon, "Braziliana" (St. Louis: Dixon-Lane, 1920); Raymond Klages and Paul Rebére, "Dreamy Amazon" (New York: Robbins-Engel, 1927); Don Drew and Cyril Crossing, "Rio" (Chicago: Forster Music, 1925); Elmer Vincent and Fisher Thompson, "Rio Nights" (New York: Fisher Thompson Music, 1920); "Rio Nights" (New York: A. J. Stasny Music, 1922); Ray Klages and Billy Fazioli, "Rose of Brazil" (New York: Leo Feist, 1923); Geo. Fairman and Frederick V. Bowers, "Sal-va-dor, Fox Trot Novelty and Song" (New York: Jos. W. Stern, 1920); see also Michael Gollatz, "My Old Guitar" (Chicago: Michael Gollatz, 1931); all Box 50, Series 8.62 (Geography: Brazil), Folder A ("Songs, 1914–1965; n.d."), SDVC, SI. See also Jack Levy, "Broken Heart (Corazon Roto)" (New York: Edward B. Marks, 1925), Box 96, Series 8.125 (Geography: Latin America/Spain—Miscellaneous), Folder A ("Songs, 1918–1956"), SDVC.

66. Thanks for help in musical analysis to musicologist Steven F. Pond (who heard *saudade* along with anacrusis) and flutist Jayn Rosenfeld.

67. Reflecting on this dynamic in other popular forms, Bianca Freire-Medeiros recalls Tzvetan Todorov's sharp analysis of the legacy of conquest in contemporary so-

cial relations across the Americas: "The woman and the country—the woman because she is a foreigner, the country because it is eroticized—both allow themselves to be desired, governed, and abandoned." Freire-Medeiros, "Hollywood Musicals," citing Tzvetan Todorov, *The Conquest of America: The Question of the Other*.

68. Watson, "Streetswing.com Dance History Archives."

69. Perry, "'The General Motherhood of the Commonwealth,'" 729.

70. Rivera, *Le tango et les danses nouvelles*, 73.

71. Advertisement for "Magic Love," pub. Oliver Ditson, *Metronome* 31, no. 2 (February 1915): 12; R. Penso's "The Grossmith Tango" (from *The Girl on the Film*) was described on its Columbia recording as a "tango-maxixe" (Columbia A 5543, LCDRS).

72. "Buenos Dias (Good Morning) American Maxixe by Kathryn L. Widmer" (New York: Jerome H. Remick, 1914); "Roguish Eyes: Brazilian Maxixe by Jose [*sic*] Santos" (New York: Will Wood, 1914), SDVC, Box 419 ("Maxixes"); "La Brasiliana—Tango by Sylvester Belmonté" (New York: Jerome H. Remick, 1913), SDVC, Box 50, Series 8.62 (Geography: Brazil), Folder C ("Instrumental, 1876–1941; n.d."); "La Flor del Amazona (The Flower of the Amazon)" [advertisement], *Metronome*, 31, no. 1 (January 1915): 2.

73. Will. H. Dixon, "Brazilian Dreams," described (on both cover and inside) as a "Tango-Intermezzo," (New York: Penn Music co., 1913); "Flor de Brazil (Flower of Brazil), Tango by Arturo de Castro" (Cleveland: Sam Fox, 1914); both SDVC, Box 50, Series 8.62 (Geography: Brazil), Folder C ("Instrumental, 1876–1941; n.d."); "Brazilian Love, Tango by Louis Ferrara" [sheet music] (New York: Jerome H. Remick, 1914), SDVC, Box 419 ("Maxixes").

74. "Every night, at Supper the celebrated Duque of Paris." Similarly, John Storm Roberts reports only that the Castles danced tango in *Watch Your Step*, but that was the revue Duque accompanied. Roberts, *The Latin Tinge*, 45.

75. "Maori-Tango or Maxixe (Tyers), Victor Military Band," Victor 35304; "La Rumba, Tango or Maxixe (Brymn)," Victor Military Band, Victor 17439 (78A); both LCDRS; advertisement for Jos. W. Stern, *Metronome* 31, no. 3 (March 1915): 2; same ad in *Metronome* 31, no. 4 (April 1915), inside front cover.

76. Advertisement for Oliver Ditson, publisher, in *Metronome*, 31, no. 2 (February 1915): 12; "Manana," advertised on the back cover of "The Uriel Maxixe (La Mattchiche Bresilienne) by Uriel Davis" (New York: Leo Feist, 1914), SDVC, Box 419 ("Maxixes"). These find an echo in a literary realm in the British aristocrat Osbert Sitwell's poem "Maxixe," about dancing Mexican dwarves. Sitwell, "Maxixe"; Sitwell, "Matchiche."

77. Even as early as the late 1930s, Tin Pan Alley simply listed maxixes *as* tangos in offerings of sheet music for sale: "Bregeiro (Rio Brazilian Maxixe)"; "Maurice (Tango Maxixe)"; and "Tango Dreams (Brazilian Tango)," listed under "The World's Foremost Tangos for Piano"; advertisement, back cover of sheet music for Juan de Dios Filiberto, "Clavel del Aire (Like Fragrant Carnations)" (New York: Edward B. Marks Music, 1938), SDVC, Box 48, Series 8.55 (Geography: Argentina), Folder A ("Songs, 1912–1976").

78. Sargeant, *Jazz*, 118. See also Natale, *Buenos Aires, negros y tango*; Prieto, *El dis-*

curso criollista en la formación de la Argentina moderna; Guy, *Sex and Danger in Buenos Aires*; Svampa, *El dilema argentino*; Andrews, *The Afro-Argentines of Buenos Aires*; Savigliano, *Tango and the Political Economy of Passion*.

79. See, for example, scholars' rankings of world civilizations compiled in Huntington, *Civilization and Climate*.

80. E. Nazareth, "Dengozo" (New York: Will Wood, 1914), and "The 'Maurice' Mattchiche (Brazilian Maxixe) by L. Dugue and E. Costa" (New York: Jos. W. Stern, 1913), both in sdvc, Box 419 ("Maxixes"); "La Mattchiche: Celebrated Parisien March on Spanish Melodies by C. Borel-Clerc" (Baltimore: P. J. Lammers, 1906), lc (Performing Arts Division). I am not sure why this song was called both "maxixe" and "march"—perhaps maxixe was not yet recognized as a genre in this moment?

81. "Sans Souci," Van Eps Banjo Orchestra, Columbia A 1594 (78A); and Europe, "Amapa—Maxixe Bresilien" and "Irresistible," tango argentine, Victor recording, matrix # 35360, both lcdrs; "Maxixe Briolette, Composée par H. Vincenzo Luzerno" [sheet music] (New York: Jerome H. Remick, 1914); "La Belle Sevilliene. International Maxixe, Antoinio Celfo [*sic*?]" [sheet music] (New York: Jerome H. Remick, 1914); "The 'Maurice' Mattchiche (Brazilian Maxixe) by L. Dugue and E. Costa" (New York: Jos. W. Stern, 1913); "A Brazilian Gem (Maxixe Brasilienne) by William T. Pierson" [inside prints "Maxixe Bresilienne"] (New York: W. T. Pierson, 1914); "Bregeiro: Rio Brazilian Maxixe by E. Nazareth" (New York: Jos. W. Stern, 1914), claimed as a "Tango Bresilienne"; all sdvc, Box 419 ("Maxixes"). Finally, the Castles entitled the maxixe chapter in their (English-language) dance manual "The Tango Brésilienne, or Maxixe," in Castle and Castle, *Modern Dancing*.

82. "Dance That Dengozo with Me, 'Oo-La-La,'" words by W. L. Beardsley, music [adapted by] George L. Cobb (Chicago: Will Rossiter, 1914), sdvc, Box 145B ("Dance"), no folder (loose in the bottom of the box).

83. "The Club De Vingt" [advertisement], *nyt*, December 18, 1914, 20; "Café des Beaux-Arts" [advertisement], *nyt*, March 9, 1915, 18; "Parisian Café Chantant" [advertisement], *nyt*, February 7, 1915, X6. Only a club that did not invoke France in its title, the Hotel Knickerbocker Grille, called Duque and Gaby "famous Brazilian Dancers," and even its copy immediately added that they were "celebrated in the leading Capitals of Europe." "Hotel Knickerbocker Grille" [advertisement], *nyt*, December 18, 1914, 4.

84. "Back from Paris" [advertisement], *nyt*, October 4, 1914, 15; "Authorized teacher" [advertisement], *nyt*, December 13, 1914, rpa7.

85. "Theatrical Notes," *nyt*, April 23, 1915, 13.

86. Alvarenga, *Música popular brasileira*, 336; Fryer, *Rhythms of Resistance*, 157, 237n5. To complicate matters further, Gérard Béhague considers Nazareth's "Odeon" (1909) and "Apanhei-te cavaquinho" (1913) "classical models of an erudite expression of *choro*"; Béhague, *Musiques du Brésil*, 75. See also Esteves, "O baile do samba com el tango"; cf Andrade, "Ernesto Nazaré." In Brazil even today, "tango" still often serves as a synonym for maxixe in musicological terms, according to one historian of music: "In truth here in Brazil the word 'tango' means something very different than Argen-

tine tango, and in fact is very close to 'maxixe.'" Tiago Gomes, electronic personal communication, February 5, 2001.

87. "Bregeiro—Rio Brazilian Maxixe by E. Nazareth" (New York: Jos. W. Stern, 1914), SDVC Box 419 ("Maxixes").

88. "Maid of Argentine: Tango tranquillo," by J. Tim Brymn (New York: Jerome H. Remick, 1914); "Nori: Tango Argentine by Uriel Davis" (New York: M. Witmark and Sons, 1913); both in SDVC, Box 419 ("Maxixes"); "Polka Bresilienne (Amazonia), by P. J. de O. Pinto" (New York: Jos. W. Stern, 1914), SDVC, Box 50, Series 8.62 (Geography: Brazil), Folder C ("Instrumental, 1876–1941; n.d.").

89. "The 'Maurice' Mattchiche (Brazilian Maxixe) by L. Dugue and E. Costa" [sheet music] (New York: Jos. W. Stern, 1913), SDVC, Box 419 ("Maxixes").

90. See, for example, "El Choclo (The Clog Dance), Tango Argentine, M Sarrablo" (Paris: L. E. Dotesio; New York: Jos. W. Stern, 1919); or "El Irresistible: Tango Argentino by L. Logatti" (New York: Jerome H. Remick, 1914), SDVC, Box 419 ("Maxixes"). Nor did "Argentine" groups fail to record maxixes, reveals the Argentine Marimba Band's 1924 recording of "Dengozo (Brazilian Maxixe-Tango)," Cameo 462 (78A), LCDRS. Recording date from Barr, *Dating Guide*.

91. Sachs, *World History of the Dance*, 444–45.

92. On syncretisms in jazz, see J. Roberts, *The Latin Tinge*; Ogren, *The Jazz Revolution*; Foreman, "Jazz and Race Records, 1920–1932," 40; on the travels of North American musics and musicians both high and low, see Sullivan, *New World Symphonies*, esp. 194; Oja, *Making Music Modern*; Blake, *Le tumulte noir*, esp. 27, 40, 49, 59; J. Jackson, *Making Jazz French*; Edwards, "Rendez-vous in Rhythm"; Unruh, *Latin American Vanguards*; Quintero-Rivera, *A cor e o som da nação*, esp. 111–13; Moody, *The Jazz Exiles*, 12; Rye and Green, "Black Musical Internationalism in England in the 1920s"; Riis, "The Experience and Impact of Black Entertainers in England, 1895–1920"; Jeffrey Green, "The Negro Renaissance and England"; Lotz, "The 'Louisiana Troupes' in Europe"; Lotz, "Will Garland and His Negro Operetta Company"; Rye, "The Southern Syncopated Orchestra"; Stovall, *Paris noir*, 3, 20–22, 38; Driggs, Frank, and Harris Lewine, *Black Beauty, White Heat*, esp. ch. 6, "Crow Jim Europe: Hangin' around Montmartre and Shanghai Gestures, 1919–1950"; and J. Leite and Cuti,—*E disse o velho militante José Correia Leite*, 39–40; on primitivist modernisms, see Blake, *Le tumulte noir*; Torgovnick, *Gone Primitive*; Aracy Amaral, *Blaise Cendrars no Brasil e os modernistas*; Alcala, *Vanguardia argentina y modernismo brasileño*.

93. Bushell and Montgomery, "Interview with Garvin Bushell," 142.

94. Wooding and Albertson, "Interview with Sam Wooding," 198–99.

95. Stovall, *Paris noir*, 42; Rye, "The Southern Syncopated Orchestra," 222; Goddard, *Jazz away from Home*, 219. Nightclubs in Paris highlight the presence of other South Americans, suggesting fruitful ground for further research. See, for example, nightclub owner Ada "Bricktop" Smith's memories of Argentine millionaires in Paris and their Montmartre hangout, El Garon, in Bricktop and Haskins, *Bricktop*, 148.

96. I use this term in the spirit of and inspired by Blake, *Le tumulte noir*. As Dalton

and Gates compile, "tumulte" can mean "uproar, commotion, tumult, turmoil, hubbub, storm, hullabaloo, turbulence, frenzy, sensation, rage, brouhaha, and craze. Thus, the title *Le Tumulte noir* conveys the energizing excitement African art and African American music and dance injected into the French capital after World War I." Dalton and Gates, "Josephine Baker and Paul Colin," 903n1.

97. Cooper, "What Is the Concept of Globalization Good For?"

98. Blake, *Le tumulte noir*, 113.

99. Szwed and Marks, "The Afro-American Transformations of European Set Dances and Dance Suites," 34.

100. Seigel, "The Disappearing Dance."

101. Briggs and Collier, "Interview with Arthur Briggs," 132; 147.

102. Cited in Goddard, *Jazz away from Home*, 273.

103. Efegê, *Maxixe*, 148, citing "O Brasil em Montmartre: O sucesso do *Vem cá, mulata*," *Gazeta de Notícias*, April 28, 1913.

104. N.a., n.t., *Revista da Semana*, March 7, 1913; cited in Efegê, *Maxixe*, 152.

105. Sucena, *A dança teatral no Brasil*.

106. On the related, contemporaneous rise of Afro-Brazilian characters and musics in theater revue and carnival song, which carved out niches for individual black people as stage performers there, see Seigel and Gomes, "Sabina's Oranges."

107. Cited in Foreman, "Jazz and Race Records, 1920–1932," 213.

108. The Harlem Renaissance's "guiding assumption was that 'excellence in art would alter the nation's perception of blacks, [leading] eventually to freedom and justice,'" notes Floyd, *The Power of Black Music*, 106, citing Arnold Rampersad, *The Life of Langston Hughes*; Floyd's ellipsis; see also Douglas, *Terrible Honesty*, 18, 106, and ch. 8 (303–45), esp. 323; Evans, *Writing Jazz*.

109. Foreman, "Jazz and Race Records, 1920–1932" 18, citing the *Chicago Defender*, March 7, 1914, 7, and 20–21, citing "Jazzing away Prejudice," *Chicago Defender*, May 10, 1919, 20.

110. Foreman, "Jazz and Race Records, 1920–1932," 27.

111. Cabral, *No tempo de Ari Barroso*, 416. The spelling of "Barroco" is the French program and record's error.

112. Tinhorão, *Música popular: Um tema em debate*, 13, 34–35; Vidossich, *Sincretismos na música afro-americana*, 59; cited in Lis, *Creating a New Tradition*, 70.

113. Lis, *Creating a New Tradition*, iv (my emphasis).

114. Wooding and Albertson, "Interview with Sam Wooding," 198–199.

115. Efegê, *Maxixe*, 101. See also Joshua Hochstein, "Announcements," *Hispania* 17, no. 2 (May 1934): 207–212, for details of the Pan-American day celebrations in high schools in Miami, San Francisco, and New York City in 1934, which suggest another route for the installation of the Carioca as "genuine" Brazilian dance. In New York, the superintendent of schools let twelve hundred students out of classes early to enjoy a program including "Carioca" as a musical number, along with pageants of good neighborliness, an Argentine "Café del Gaucho," "regional dances," "native music," and a Mexican history play. Hochstein, editor of *Hispania*, and clearly an adept of

Herbert Bolton's concept of "Greater America," hoped the celebrations would "make our young generation Greater-America-conscious" (212).

116. Veloso, *A Foreign Sound.*

117. Silva and Oliveira, *Pixinguinha*, 49–50.

Playing Politics

1. "Tumultuosa assembléa de negros," *O Clarim d'Alvorada*, October 21, 1928, 3. The São Paulo black press is introduced fully in chapter 5. *O Clarim da Alvorada* (1924–27) changed its name to *O Clarim d'Alvorada* (1928–1930), ceased publication until 1935, and then returned as *O Clarim*. For continuity I cite it as *Clarim* throughout.

2. Cabral, *Pixinguinha*, 25; see also R. Moura, *Tia Ciata e a pequena África no Rio de Janeiro*; Velloso, "As tias baianas tomam conta do pedaço"; and Sandroni, *Feitiço decente*. A useful caution regarding the state of research on Tia Ciata is T. Gomes, "Para além da casa da Tia Ciata."

3. Carvalho, "Brazil 1870–1914," 146; Lesser, *Welcoming the Undesirables*; Lesser, *Negotiating National Identities*; "outnumbering" is from Cowell, who estimates the disproportion at 56 to 44 percent in "Cityward Migration in the Nineteenth Century," 49.

4. Needell, "The Revolta Contra Vacina of 1904"; J. Love, "Political Participation in Brazil, 1881–1969." Nationally, literacy ranged from 14.8 percent literate in 1890 to 24.5 percent in 1920, Love claims on 8. See also Chalhoub, *Trabalho, lar e botequim*; Needell, *A Tropical Belle Epoque*; Adamo, "The Broken Promise."

5. Pixinguinha, deposition [oral history], *As vozes desassombradas do museu*; cited in Cabral, *Pixinguinha*, 22, 25, 27–28; Velloso, *A cultura das ruas no Rio de Janeiro (1900–1930)*; H. Vianna, *The Mystery of Samba*, 24–25, 29.

6. Cabral, *Pixinguinha*, 25–29. In addition to a conductor's baton, *batuta* also means "intelligent, sagacious; remarkable; agile, lively; brave." *Langenscheidt Pocket Portuguese Dictionary*, 412. Chasteen renders "Oito Batutas" as "eight 'batons,' 'pros,' or 'aces'" in his translation of H. Vianna, *The Mystery of Samba*, 82.

7. P. Gomes, *Humberto Mauro, Cataguases, cinearte*, notes on 298–299 that the percentage of all films shown in Brazil in 1922–24 that were Brazilian was negligible — around 4 percent. See also R. Moura, "O cinema carioca (1913–1930)"; Stam, *Tropical Multiculturalism*; and Stam and Johnson, *Brazilian Cinema*.

8. Aracy Amaral, *Blaise Cendrars no Brasil e os modernistas*; Martins, *O Modernismo*; Torgovnick, *Gone Primitive*.

9. Cabral, *Pixinguinha*, 32. Even this early, the exchange was two-way, with the research subjects picking up notes of interest as well, as Almirante's comments below on the "Turunas Pernambucanos" and his "Bando de Tangarás" confirm.

10. Ikeda, "Apontamentos historicos sobre o jazz no Brasil." H. Vianna asserts that the Batutas "became lovers of jazz" in Paris in 1922 (*The Mystery of Samba*, 83); if he means they began to love jazz *only* then, the comment requires some evidence to substantiate.

11. I am not weighing in on whether the music called "jazz" in Rio in this period was "really" jazz or not; I prefer to use the term "jazz" as a category of practice, as in Gabbard's definition—"the music that large groups of people have called jazz at particular moments in history"—to preserve the meanings "jazz" has held for musicians and audiences. Gabbard, *Jammin' at the Margins*, 8. J. Jackson offers a similar definition in *Making Jazz French*, 10. In the context at hand, one sophisticated application of this perspective is that of T. Gomes, who finds a wonderful detour around the overemphasis on genre definition in otherwise excellent social histories of music (in particular Eric Hobsbawm's *Uncommon People*, widely read in Brazil). Gomes argues that jazz was a way of playing, not a genre, and analyzes the jazz band as a discursive field in which people negotiated the meanings of "modernity." T. Gomes, "'Como eles se divertem' (e se entendem)," 60–63.

12. "Como se define o jazz-band," *Ariel: Revista de Cultura Musical*, September 1924, 440. See also Cabral, *Pixinguinha*, 50–51.

13. Tinhorão, *Música popular: teatro e cinema*, 101.

14. T. Gomes, *Um espelho no palco*, ch. 1; Santos et al., *Discografia brasileira 78 rpms, 1902–1964*.

15. Béhague, "Reflections on the Ideological History of Latin American Ethnomusicology," 57.

16. A perfect example is Tinhorão's defense of Pixinguinha from musicologist Cruz Cordeiro, who had accused the flutist of "transplanting North America musical resources to Brazilian music." Tinhorão explains that in 1929, popular music in Rio had not yet fixed its various genres, reflecting the lack of structure among the social classes (which were of equally recent formation) that those genres were to address. Happily, he continues, in the 1930s, *samba de morro* liberated itself from North American influence "in the bosom of the truly popular classes, segregated in certain neighborhoods and *morros*." That is, thanks to segregation, "pure" Brazilian music could emerge. Tinhorão, *Música popular: um tema em debate*, 36–37. This is precisely Béhague's complaint about Argentine musicologist Carlos Vega in "Reflections." While this approach is fading, it still exists; a contemporary scholar who insists on linking specific class formations to musical genres is Vicente, "Música popular e produção intelectual nos anos 40."

17. "Suffering" is in Almirante, *No tempo de Noel Rosa*, 33; Tinhorão, *Música popular: Um tema em debate*, 34–35; Cabral, *No tempo de Ari Barroso*, 54; Naves, *Da bossa nova à tropicália*, 13; "victim" comes from an appropriately penitent Ari Barroso, cited in Cabral, *No tempo de Ari Barroso*, 94, and Jota Efegê, "Ary Barroso, vitima da 'jazzificação' da música brasileira," *O Jornal*, December 12, 1965, n.p.; reprinted in Efegê, *Figuras e coisas da música popular brasileira*, vol. 1, 160–62; return to prelapsarian Brazilianness is in Almirante, *No tempo de Noel Rosa*, 33–34, 43; Tinhorão, *Música popular: um tema em debate*, 36–37. H. Vianna also discusses this in *The Mystery of Samba*, 84 and passim, for a primary interest of his is the question of samba's "authenticity."

18. "Donga" is the nickname of Ernesto Joaquim Maria dos Santos.

19. Cabral, *No tempo de Ari Barroso*, 35, 44, 47; see also Efegê, "Ary Barroso," re-

printed in Efegê, *Figuras e coisas da música popular brasileira*, vol. 1, 160–62. Also, composer Freire Júnior wrote at least one fox-trot, according to "Leopoldo Froes," n.d., in Santos et al., *Discografia brasileira 78 rpms, 1902–1964*, vol. 1, 256. The question of the foreign influence on the Batutas was a point of great consternation to nationalist music critics from an early moment; see, for example, Cruz Cordeiro, writing in *Phono Arte* in 1928; cited in Cabral, *Pixinguinha*, 57; and Tinhorão, *O samba agora vai*, 33n28.

20. Almirante suggests that the Bando de Tangarás, a group he and Noel Rosa formed in 1929, was in debt to the Turunas and therefore to Pixinguinha, música sertaneja, and Rio de Janeiro samba. Almirante, *No tempo de Noel Rosa*, 33, 38.

21. J. Moraes, *Metrópole em sinfonia*.

22. Gardel, *O encontro entre Bandeira e Sinhô*; T. Gomes, *Um espelho no palco*; T. Gomes, "Negros contando (e fazendo) sua história"; McCann, *Hello, Hello Brazil*; H. Vianna, *The Mystery of Samba*; for a slightly later moment, Lenharo, *Cantores do rádio*; and in the realm of erudite music, Contier, *Música e ideologia no Brasil*. See also Naves, who tries to take an interesting middle-ground position in allowing herself to be guided by her subjects when they claim to be "traditional" or "pure"; Naves, *Da bossa nova à tropicália*, 8.

23. Miller, "Segregating Sound"; Ikeda, "Apontamentos historicos sobre o jazz no Brasil"; Wallis and Malm, *Big Sounds from Small Peoples*.

24. Cabral, *No tempo de Ari Barroso*, 38; Guinle, *Jazz Panorama*, 90; Tinhorão, *O samba agora vai*, 36–39.

25. "New Liner Sets Record," *NYT*, September 7, 1921, 11.

26. Ari Barroso in *O Jornal*, November 21, 1955, n.p.; cited in Cabral, *No tempo de Ari Barroso*, 37.

27. This is suggested by news reports and program notes archived in Carpenter's personal papers: "Teatro Porteño" [advertisement], unattributed Argentine newspaper, January 25, 1935, n.p.; Elliot Carpenter papers, Helen Armstead-Johnson Theatre Collection, NYPL, Schomburg Branch, Box 16 ("Printed Material"), Folder 1 ("Programs").

28. Olliver and Mooney, Liner notes to *Argentine Swing 1936–1948*.

29. Guinle, *Jazz Panorama*, 90.

30. Ibid., claims that on this tour were "Eugene Sedric, Albert Wyn [*sic*], Willie Lewis and Ralph James, altos, Freddie Johnson, piano, and June Cole, bass, among others"; this contradicts *The New Grove Dictionary of Jazz*, 226–27, 1306, which implies that Cole and Wynn joined Wooding only after his South American tour, in 1928, and that the band instead included Tommy Ladnier, Herb Flemming, Garvin Bushell, and Gene Sedric. See also Wooding and Albertson, *Interview with Sam Wooding*. Bushell was certainly there, according to Goddard, *Jazz away from home*, 54; Bushell and Montgomery, *Interview with Garvin Bushell*, 34. Moody (*The Jazz Exiles*, 34) writes, "After a lengthy tour of South America, Bushell returned to New York in 1927," as if he had stayed two years, but Bushell's oral history suggests only a six-month tour. Kinkle, *The Complete Encyclopedia of Popular Music and Jazz, 1900–1950* (hereafter *EPM*), 3227, notes Willie Lewis's tour of Europe with Wooding but doesn't mention his South American travels; nor do the entries in that source for Johnny

Dunn (1655), Garvin Bushell (852), or Eugene Sedric (4809). Wooding notes that his band "toured throughout central and eastern Europe, Russia, Scandinavia, and the UK" but doesn't qualify his American travels as a tour: "On the way back to the USA the band visited South America" (*EPM*, 5913). See also Monk Mongomery's disinterest in South America in Bushell and Montgomery, "Interview with Garvin Bushell," 71, 74–75.

31. Cabral, *No tempo de Ari Barroso*, 35; Guinle, *Jazz Panorama*, 89; "Harry Kosarin and His Famous [Jazz Band]," *Brazilian American*, special edition for the Fourth of July, 1921; Ikeda, "Apontamentos historicos sobre o jazz no Brasil," 117, 122n28.

32. Thanks to Harold Flakser for this Pingatore brother's first name, which Guinle does not provide; personal communication, June 4, 2001. Flakser also claims Eugene Pingatore later lived several years in Australia.

33. Guinle, *Jazz Panorama*, 89; on 90, Guinle reports that Lipoff's band included "Chamek, piano, Kolman, saxophone and oboe, Abdon Lyra, trombone, and, finally, Simon Boutman, violin, who later organized numerous orchestras and who for many years played at the Copacabana Palace." Other than Boutman, whose activities surface occasionally (for example, in Cabral, *No tempo de Ari Barroso*, 87, 90), I have so far not been successful in finding more information on these musicians.

34. Matory, "The English Professors of Brazil"; Mann and Bay, *Rethinking the African Diaspora*; for a discussion of the "denial of coevalness" in another context, see Chakrabarty, "Postcoloniality and the Artifice of History."

35. Cabral, *Pixinguinha*, 31–32.

36. M. Silva and Oliveira, *Pixinguinha*, 53; Almirante, *No tempo de Noel Rosa*, 30; Cabral, *Pixinguinha*, 45–46. On Dempsey's time in Paris, see R. Roberts, *Jack Dempsey*, 133–34.

37. Donga, MIS deposition; quoted in Cabral, *Pixinguinha*, 44; M. Silva and Oliveira are overcredulous of Donga's count in *Pixinguinha*, 56.

38. Telegram from Paris reprinted in the *Jornal do Brasil*, February 17, 1922, n.p.; quoted (without comment) in Cabral, *Pixinguinha*, 44. On this erasure see Edwards, "Rendez-vous in Rhythm"; Rye and Green, "Black Musical Internationalism in England in the 1920s."

39. Cabral, *Pixinguinha*, gives a source for the Nélson Alves quote in M. Silva and Oliveira: an interview with the Rio newspaper *A Notícia* on August 16, 1922. Interestingly, Pixinguinha in his deposition remembered having heard Louis Armstrong in Paris in 1922, although Armstrong's first trip to Paris was in 1932; Cabral (*Pixinguinha*, 45) and M. Silva and Oliveira (*Pixinguinha*, 71–72) both point out this error. The latter use it to "prove" that the Batutas encountered only poor-quality jazz in this period, which, being inferior to the wonderful music they themselves played, could not possibly have "influenced" them. None comment on how revealing the Armstrong error is of Pixinguinha's perceptions. His experience of that trip prompted him later to add to his memories of Paris this jazz "great," a player now fully canonized—quite a convincing refutation of Silva and Oliveira's claims for the transcendence of their judgement.

40. Bushell and Montgomery, "Interview with Garvin Bushell," 142.

41. Ogren, *The Jazz Revolution*, 20, 40; see also McClary and Walser, "Theorizing the Body in African-American Music," and Small, *Music of the Common Tongue*. Brenda Dixon Gottschild extends this dynamic to all dance forms, suggesting, "whether it was a European-inspired adagio or African American forms like the Lindy or rhythm tap dance, the dancers reinvigorated the musicians" and vice-versa. Gottschild, *Waltzing in the Dark*, 48.

42. Cited in Almirante, *No tempo de Noel Rosa*, 30–31.

43. For Rio, see "Como se define o jazz-band"; Cabral, *Pixinguinha*, 50–51; on Paris, Goddard, *Jazz away from home*, 284, citing Arthur Briggs: "For the French people the jazz band was the drums. They called that the jazz band"; on the United States, Radano, "Hot Fantasies"; or see such erudite condescension as Dan Knowlton, "The Anatomy of Jazz," *Harper's Monthly Magazine* 152 (April 1926): 578–85.

44. M. Silva and Oliveira, *Pixinguinha*, 70; Cabral, *Pixinguinha*, 50; quoting Pixinguinha on 46.

45. Cabral, *Pixinguinha*, 51–52. "Hundreds" may have been the promoters' exaggeration.

46. M. Silva and Oliveira, *Pixinguinha*, 70; H. Vianna, *The Mystery of Samba*, 82.

47. Commission of the United States of America to the Brazilian Centennial Exposition, 1922–1923, *Final Report of the Commissioner General*, entry 1306, RG 43, NA A2; Pan American Union, *Trip to the Brazilian Centennial Exposition*; M. Silva and Oliveira, *Pixinguinha*, 70. Villa-Lobos spent 1923–25 and 1927–30 in Paris's richly transnational avant-garde high-art scene, entertaining widely and hosting a prestigious and popular salon; his Thursday and Sunday *assemblées*, writes one observer, became "one of the most typical images of Paris in the 'twenties." Pistone, "Les musiciens étrangers à Paris au XXᵉ siècle," 250; Timothy Brennan, electronic personal communication, April 24, 2000. Brennan also notes that Villa-Lobos befriended the Cuban writer Alejo Carpentier, who thought Villa-Lobos the greatest composer of the twentieth century.

48. M. Silva and Oliveira, *Pixinguinha*, 67.

49. Bret, *The Mistinguett Legend*; Dubeux, "Mistinguette"; Mistinguett, *Mistinguett by Mistinguett*; Pénet, *Mistinguett*; Pessis and Crépineau, *Les années Mistinguett*.

50. Guinle, *Jazz Panorama*, 90.

51. Cabral, *Pixinguinha*, 47.

52. On Forester's participation in the Southern Syncopated Orchestra, Harold Flakser, personal communication, June 4, 2001.

53. Guinle, *Jazz Panorama*, 90–91. Andreosi and Andreozzy were likely the same person.

54. "O jazz . . . O que nos disse o sr. Stretton" [author's ellipses], *A Patria*, September 22, 1923, 5.

55. Tinhorão, *O samba agora vai*, 42–43.

56. Vasconcelos, *Panorama da música popular brasileira na Belle Époque*, 91; see also D. Thompson, "Stalking Stokowski."

57. "O theatro em Paris: 'A Revista Negra' e suas extravagancias; Um espectaculo do seculo XX ultracivilisado," *A Notícia* January 8, 1926, 1. This is a rather dubious

suggestion; still, I wonder whether Pixinguinha and the Batutas played with Ba-ta-clan again in 1924, and therefore with Cook and Douglas. In any case, however, Cook and Douglas, along with any other members of the Southern Syncopated Orchestra or other U.S. performers who traveled with them, African American or not, would certainly have had the opportunity on this tour to perform with and listen to Brazilian musicians.

58. Sampson, *Blacks in Blackface*, 358; Spradling, *In Black and White*, 93; *Biographical Encyclopedia of Jazz*, 148–49; Kernfeld, *New Grove Dictionary of Jazz*, 244.

59. Jeffrey Green, "The Negro Renaissance and England," 160; Lotz, "Will Garland and His Negro Operetta Company," 134; Spradling, *In Black and White*, 121; Kernfeld, *New Grove Dictionary of Jazz*, 304.

60. U.S.-produced biographical sources on Cook and Douglas omit any mention of their Brazilian appearances: Sampson, *Blacks in Blackface*, 356–58; Spradling, *In Black and White*, 93; *Biographical Encyclopedia of Jazz*, 148–49; Kernfeld, *New Grove Dictionary of Jazz*, 244, 304 (mentions Douglas's travels to the United Kingdom, Paris, Egypt, and Berlin); Rye, "The Southern Syncopated Orchestra."

61. De Chocolat, *Tudo preto*.

62. T. Gomes, "Negros contando (e fazendo) sua história"; T. Gomes, *Um espelho no palco*.

63. M. Silva and Oliveira, *Pixinguinha*, 119, 117.

64. *Jornal do Brasil*, August 1, 1926; cited in T. Gomes, "'Como eles se divertem' (e se entendem)," 288.

65. H. Vianna, *The Mystery of Samba*, 7; M. Silva and Oliveira, *Pixinguinha*, 118 (the authors also note here that Cirino and Blassifera traveled to "the Orient"); Cabral, *Pixinguinha*, 54; Guinle, *Jazz Panorama*, 90; Tinhorão, *O samba agora vai*, 34–35. Tinhorão claims Carlitos was in Paris by 1924, while Cabral dates his departure to 1926, after *Tudo preto*'s debut.

66. Tinhorão, *O samba agora vai*, 38. Biagioni and Flemming, *Herb Flemming*, 47. A banjo and ukelele player whom Tinhorão calls only "Fernando," either French or North American, also joined Silva's band in Paris in 1925; Tinhorão, *O samba agora vai*, 38. Interestingly, Booker Pittman was the grandson of the president of Tuskegee who shared his first name, according to Southern, *Biographical Dictionary of Afro-American and African Musicians*, 309.

67. Bouillon, *Josephine*, 115–116. Brazilian commentators also note Josephine's visit to a place of worship (*terreiro*) of the then still heavily-policed Afro-Brazilian religion candomblé on her 1939 trip; see Jota Efegê, "Josephine foi à 'Macumba' no terreiro de Mãe Adedê," *O Globo* April 21, 1975, n.p.; reprinted in Efegê, *Figuras e coisas da música popular brasileira*, vol. 2, 191–92; and Cabral, *No tempo de Ari Barroso*, 179.

68. Cabral, *Pixinguinha*, 56–57.

69. Wooding's Symphonic Jazz Orchestra had traveled with the stage musical *Chocolate Kiddies*, which featured Greenlee and Drayton, among others. Biagioni and Flemming, *Herb Flemming*, 15; Wooding and Albertson, "Interview with Sam Wooding," 156.

70. Sampson, *Blacks in Blackface*, 371; Bushell, *Jazz from the Beginning*, 56.

71. Hennessey, *From Jazz to Swing*, 97. My suggestion about the timing is based on the Savoy's opening in Harlem in March 1926 and Hennessey's citation of *Chicago Defender* articles from March and April 1927 discussing King Oliver's (failed) appearance there. New work on the travels of jazz is beginning to remedy this shortfall, for example, Atkins, *Blue Nippon*; Jones, *Yellow Music*.

72. Cited in Stearns and Stearns, *Jazz Dance*, 296.

73. Cendrars, *Histoires vraies*, 97–98 (my translation). I cannot tell whether the St. Louis/Louisiana juxtaposition is Cendrars's confusion or not. Cendrars does not date this event, but he recounts it just after a story he claims took place in 1926, beginning with "The other year." He went to Rio for carnival many times in the 1920s; on these trips, in addition to *Histoires vraies*, see Cendrars, *Etc., etc.*; and Aracy Amaral, *Blaise Cendrars*.

74. R. Thompson, *Flash of the Spirit*; Kelley, "The Riddle of the Zoot."

75. Amado, *Mocidade no Rio e primeira viagem à Europa*; Velloso, *A cultura das ruas no Rio de Janeiro (1900–1930)*; Unruh, *Latin American Vanguards*. A fascinating figure among Brazilians in Paris was singer Elsie Houston, by some accounts the great-grandniece of Texas president Sam Houston, considered in the following chapter.

76. "On the Valorization of Things Black" is the title of a 1926 article written by Freyre; on this, see H. Vianna, *The Mystery of Samba*, 8, and on Cendrars, 67–73; Martins, "Cendrars e o Brasil," 985; Aracy Amaral, *Blaise Cendrars no Brasil e os modernistas*; Aracy Amaral, *Tarsila*, 84; see also H. Vianna's discussion of Cendrars's introduction of Donga to Prudente de Moraes Neto, in 1924, enabling the "encounter" Vianna describes, which he characterizes as another "interesting foreign intervention in the elite 'discovery' of Carioca popular culture" (*The Mystery of Samba*, 7); R. Moura, "A indústria cultural e o espetáculo-negócio no Rio de Janeiro," esp. 125–26.

77. Blake, *Le tumulte noir*; Naves, *O violão azul*; Wisnik, *O coro dos contrários*; H. Vianna, *The Mystery of Samba*; Gardel, *O encontro entre Bandeira e Sinhô*.

78. For example, Vasconcelos, *Panorama da música popular brasileira na Belle Époque*, vol. 1, 169, notes that "between 1904 and 1905 Villa-Lobos associated with the era's main figures of Brazilian popular music: Irineu de Almeida, Juca Kalut, Catulo da Paixão Cearense, Sátiro Bilhar, etc." Bryan McCann notes that Villa-Lobos "was famous—notorious in some circles—for using popular musical melodies as the themes for his erudite extrapolations." McCann, *Hello, Hello Brazil*, 73; in 257–258n70 McCann cites accusations of plagiarism brought by Catulo da Paixão Cearense and directs readers to Garcia, "The Choro, the Guitar, and Villa-Lobos." H. Vianna, in *The Mystery of Samba*, 24, also observes that Villa-Lobos had been listening to popular musicians in Rio since he was a little boy. Vianna takes this sort of social mixing as the occasion for his analysis, especially one evening of entertainment shared by Pixinguinha, Donga, and another sambista, Patrício, with Villa-Lobos and fellow classical composer Luciano Gallet and the elite writers Gilberto Freyre, Sérgio Buarque de Hollanda, and Pedro Dantas Prudente de Moraes Neto. Martha Abreu presents a similar picture of the always-already class and racially mixed nature of Brazilian

popular culture in *O império do divino*. M. Silva and Oliveira, *Pixinguinha*, 121, make a similar claim about Mário de Andrade—that is, that in 1926, for his Modernist novel, *Macunaíma, o herói sem nenhum caráter*, he sought out Pixinguinha to talk about Tia Ciata, the Bahian migrant whose Rio de Janeiro house was a trove of Afro-Brazilian culture.

79. Amado, speaking to the Brazilian Congress; cited in Cabral, *Pixinguinha*, 43–44.

80. D. Williams, *Culture Wars in Brazil*; Needell, "The Domestic Civilizing Mission."

81. Milhaud, *Notes without Music*; Collaer, *Darius Milhaud*.

82. Milhaud, *Notes without Music*, 118; M. Silva and Oliveira, *Pixinguinha*.

83. Cited in H. Vianna, *The Mystery of Samba*, 73.

84. Gendron, *Between Montmartre and the Mudd Club*, 9–10. I do not mean to suggest that Brazilian popular musicians were *more* active than others; surely popular music anywhere was created by people as alert as Donga, alongside others who were less so.

85. Jota Efegê, "Soprano Zaíra de Oliveira, a Marian Anderson do Brasil," *O Globo*, August 29, 1977, n.p.; reprinted in Efegê, *Figuras e coisas da música popular brasileira*, vol. 2, 260–62.

86. Andrade, "A música no Brasil," in Andrade, *Música, doce música*, 19. It is interesting to note how black-and-white Andrade's conceptualization is in this article, considering that in general the Modernists articulated a nationalism of mixture that emphasized indigenous rather than Afro-descended traits. The placement of this argument in a venue explicitly for English speakers (though sure to be conspicuous to Cariocas who cared), an issue of the *Anglo-Brazilian Chronicle* commemorating the visit of the Prince of Wales, suggests that Andrade tailored his remarks according to his (perception of his) readers' assumptions, offering them a comparison to a familiar situation to help them understand an unfamiliar place and embracing a dynamic he well knew they devalued (racial mixture, African cultural contributions to national cultural forms) to magnify his national pride. Andrade's own racial position is interestingly ambiguous. He was sometimes described as *mulato* but appears not to have been interested in identifying as such, or at least not in organizing his work around such an identification. See Martins, *O Modernismo*.

87. On scholarly critiques of racial democracy, see the preface, note 4. On music as a site for the working out of racial democracy nationalism, see McCann, *Hello, Hello Brazil*; H. Vianna, *The Mystery of Samba*; T. Gomes, *Um espelho no palco*; T. Gomes, *Lenço no pescoço*. A fascinatingly suggestive performance of elision between racial and musical categories is Carlos Sandroni's statement, "No Brasil, a separação entre diferentes categorias musicais parece ser menos marcada que em outros países" (In Brazil, the separation between different musical categories seems to be less fixed than in other countries); in Sandroni, *Feitiço decente*, 17. On related nationalisms placing music as a basis for racial democracy in Cuba, see Quintero-Rivera, *A cor e o som da nação*; Moore, *Nationalizing Blackness*; Fuente, "Myths of Racial Democracy."

88. For example, discussions of Herivelto Martins's 1932 song, "Não importa a nossa cor" (Our color makes no difference) in Efegê, "Tirei o Edredon da Cabeça e Fiz um Samba com Ele," *O Jornal* 1964, n.p., reprinted in *Figuras e Coisas*, vol. 1, 120–22; or De Chocolat and Ari Barroso's 1934 carnival piece, "Negro também é gente" (The Negro is one of us/is a person too), in Cabral, *No tempo de Ari Barroso*, 129; another rhetorical affirmation is Almeida, *Compêndio de história da música brasileira*, 11. This shift toward denials of racism in carnival songs corresponds to the disciplining of carnival itself; see M. Queiroz, *Carnaval brasileiro.*

89. On the popular production of the idea of racial democracy in the black press, see Andrews, *Blacks and Whites in São Paulo, Brazil, 1888–1988*, ch. 5; in popular music, see T. Gomes, *Lenço no pescoço*; T. Gomes, *Um espelho no palco*; and H. Vianna, *The Mystery of Samba*; on popular racial democracy discourse revealed in court records, see Caulfield, "Raça, sexo e casamento," and Caulfield, *In Defense of Honor*; on the importance of working-class *futbol* players in this process, see J. Lopes, "Class, Ethnicity, and Color in the Making of Brazilian Football." There is also a growing body of recent work outside the Brazilian context that wonderfully exposes the popular (cultural) production of race and nation, including Quintero-Rivera, *A cor e o som da nação*; Wade, *Music, Race, and Nation*; Moore, *Nationalizing Blackness*; and Lane, *Blackface Cuba, 1840–1895*. A related line of work, compatible with but not focused on the claim that the idea of racial democracy is popularly produced, is recent scholarship that insists on complicating the idea of racial democracy itself. I am referring neither to "neo-racial democracy" nor revisionist rejection, but to work that treats racial democracy as highly complex, certainly greater than illusion or false consciousness. See Burdick, *Blessed Anastácia*; D. Silva, *Toward a Global Idea of Race*; Caulfield, "Interracial Courtship in the Rio de Janeiro Courts, 1918–1940"; Weinstein, "Racializing Regional Difference"; J. Dávila, *Diploma of Whiteness*; and McCann, *Hello, Hello Brazil*, 43. I hope to hone all these insights further by highlighting the transnational connections sustaining the productive labor of race- and nation-building in general, and in Brazil specifically, the transnational aspects of the construction of the myth of racial democracy.

90. Jayme de Aguiar, "Nossos parabens!" *Clarim*, August 22, 1926, 1; Efegê, "Pixinguinha levou à Pretoria a estrela da Companhia Negra," *O Globo*, 26 October 26, 1972, n.p.; reprinted in Efegê, *Figuras e coisas da música popular brasileira*, vol. 2, 114–16. The *Enciclopédia da música brasileira* mentions De Chocolat's European stay, without citing sources, on 237 (thanks to Tiago Gomes for bringing this to my attention); J. Leite and Cuti, —*E disse o velho militante José Correia Leite*, 25.

91. Andrade, "Ernesto Nazaré," 32.

92. De Chocolat, *Tudo preto.*

93. T. Gomes, "Lenço no pescoço"; McCann, *Hello, Hello Brazil*, 53–56; and Roberto da Matta's classic *Carnavais, malandros e heróis.*

94. "Variedades," *Clarim*, May 13, 1929, 5.

95. "Chegou a Companhia Mulata Brasileira que vai trabalhar no República," *O Globo*, December 17, 1930, n.p. Tiago Gomes urges skepticism in reading such re-

ports, as journalists often glossed unremarkable material or simply put words in their subjects' mouths for the sake of good copy. Gomes, electronic personal communication, February 16, 2001.

96. J. Simões Coelho, *O Rio agacha-se*, theater revue (1928); cited in T. Gomes, "'Como eles se divertem' (e se entendem)," 215 (the original is "Quando eu caí no remelexo aquele pessoalzinho até virou borboleta!"). The phrasing ("Europe bows before Brazil") refers to the aviator Alberto Santos-Dumont's piloting triumphs.

97. An exemplary, long-accepted treatment of TEN as a break is Pinto, *O negro no Rio de Janeiro*, 36, 246–51.

98. Abdias do Nascimento, unpublished comments, meeting of the Brazilian Studies Association, Rio de Janeiro, June 2004; my translation and paraphrase. Somewhat confusingly, at the same time Abdias embraced the legacy of the Afro-Brazilian clown Benjamin de Oliveira, De Chocolat's equally popular contemporary.

99. "Companhia Negra de Revistas: A homenagem do 'Centro dos Homens de Côr'; Missa em acção de graças na igreja de N.S. do Rosario," *A Notícia*, August 19, 1926, 4.

100. "Tudo Preto," *Clarim*, October 24, 1926, 1; "Homenagem do 'Clarim' á Cia. Negra de Revistas," *Clarim*, November 14, 1926, 1; "Variedades," *Clarim*, May 13, 1929, 5.

101. Ferraz, "Ba-ta-clan," *O Kosmos*, May 18, 1924, 2; Julio Dantas, "Salomes negras," *Progresso*, January 13, 1929, 6; Laly, "Klaxonadas," *Clarim*, March 21, 1926, 1.

102. "Os pretos e o teatro moderno," *Progresso*, August 19, 1928, 2; see also "Passaros pretos em Paris," *Progresso*, August 31, 1929, 3, discussing Lew Leslie's "100 Negro Artists and the '*Plantation Orchestra*' to Put on the Famous Revue '*Blackbird*'" at the Moulin Rouge ("Plantation Orchestra" and "Blackbird" in English in the original).

103. "A musa negra e os seus triumphos na Europa," *Progresso*, January 13, 1929, 2.

104. "Na civilisáda Europa os rythmos da musica negra, provocam enthusiasmo e reclamam applausos," *Progresso*, March 24, 1929, 1. Readers will meet Houston again in chapter 4.

105. "A França, melhor amiga da raça negra!" *Clarim*, January 25, 1930, 4; Hellwig, *African-American Reflections on Brazil's Racial Paradise*.

106. Laly, "Klaxonadas." On Guedes's use of the nickname "Laly," see "O progresso," *Clarim*, July 1, 1928, 4; "Lino Guedes," *Clarim*, October 21, 1928, 1. In this review, Laly also praised the "rare star" Ascendina dos Santos, an actress. Laly was commenting on a *Correio da Manhã* review of dos Santos, full of distinctly backhanded compliments. Reprinting the critic's resigned acknowledgment of the force of public will, Laly changed a condescending dismissal of the masses' poor taste into a critique of the critic.

107. "Tudo Preto," *Clarim*, October 24, 1926, 1.

108. "Patacoadas," *Clarim*, August 22, 1926, 1.

109. "O negro, apesar de ser uma fonte inêsgotavel de motivos para toda manifestação de *Arte* não é, ainda, no Brasil, sufficientemente explorado," *Progresso*, July 28, 1929, 1.

110. Jayme de Aguiar, "Nossos parabens!" *Clarim*, August 22, 1926, 1–2.

111. *Correio da Manhã*, January 17, 1926; in Laly, "Klaxonadas."

112. "O jazz ... O que nos disse o sr. Stretton" [author's ellipses], *A Patria*, September 22, 1923, 5; Ferro, *A idade do jazz-band*.

113. "Como se define o jazz-band," *Ariel: Revista de Cultura Musical*, September 1924, 440.

114. "O *Brasil Musical*," *Brasil Musical* 1, no. 1 (March 1923): 2.

115. Abílio Rodrigues, "Chronica Social," *O Kosmos*, March 15, 1923.

116. "O avatar do 'jazz': Das selvas da Rhodesia aos salões da Europa; Os extremos se tocam ..." (author's ellipses), *A Notícia*, June 3, 1926, 1.

117. Bederman, *Manliness and Civilization*; Torgovnick, *Gone Primitive*; Mitchell, "Miguel Reale and the Impact of Conservative Modernization on Brazilian Race Relations."

118. *A Mascara*, April 22, 1927, 3 (a "Patria-Mãe do 'jazz'").

119. Magdalena Tagliaferro, cited in *Careta*, September 4, 1926, 13. On Brazilian Francophilia, see Carelli, "Les Brésiliens à Paris de la naissance du romantisme aux avant-gardes"; Carelli, "Deuxième partie," 134–35; Amado, *Mocidade no Rio e primeira viagem Europa*; Guerra calls Paris the "métropole intellectuel" in "La lumière et ses reflects," 175; Massa, "Paris lu, vu et rêvé par des écrivains portugais, brésiliens et de l'Afrique de langue portugaise"; P. Martin, *Latin America and the War*, 31–32; Miceli, *Imagens negociadas*; Sevcenko, *Orfeu extático na metrópole*, 277–302; "A lingua portugueza," *Clarim*, August 22, 1926; Martins, *O Modernismo*; Skidmore, *Black into White*; Graham, *The Idea of Race in Latin America*; Helg, "Los intelectuales frente a la cuestion racial en el decenio de 1920"; period examples include a Lycée Franco-Anglais ad, *Brazilian American*, July 9, 1921: "Teach your boys to speak French. ... In Brazil every educated person speaks French"; and Oscar Guanabarinho, "Pelo mundo das artes," *Jornal do Commercio*, March 2, 1920.

120. "Negro Venus" in "Atualidades," *Careta*, September 4, 1926, 22; see also "Actualidades," *Careta*, September 18, 1926.

121. Blake, *Le tumulte noir*, 148.

122. "O theatro em Paris: 'A Revista Negra' e suas extravagancias: Um espectaculo do seculo xx ultracivilisado," *A Notícia*, January 8, 1926. Author's ellipses in quote.

123. "O theatro Nacional," *A Mascara*, May 27, 1927, 14.

124. "Um 'jazz-band' de bebês," *Pró-Patria*, December 20, 1924, 29.

125. "Como se define o jazz-band," 440. This is an earlier version of Silva and Oliveira's confidence that the jazz the Batutas heard in Paris was inferior to their music and therefore not a possible "influence." M. Silva and Oliveira, *Pixinguinha*.

126. Silva, interviewed in "A música barulhenta," *A Notícia*, October 26, 1923, n.p.; cited in Cabral, *Pixinguinha*, 51.

127. Ukers, *A Trip to Brazil*, 30.

128. Cabral, *No tempo de Ari Barroso*, 38. In the *A Notícia* interview Silva also reveled in the high cost of his band's clothes.

129. Tinhorão, *O samba agora vai*, 36; Vasconcelos, *Panorama da música popular brasileira na Belle Époque*, vol. 1, 163–64; "Announcing/The World's Fair's Unique Night

Club/The Restaurant of the Brazilian Pavilion/Cocktails from 3 P.M./Dine and Dance to Romeo Silva's Brazilian Orchestra," *NYT*, June 9, 1939, 28; "Museum to Present Music of Brazilians: Rubenstein and Elsie Houston to Be Heard at Modern Art Here," *NYT*, September 29, 1940, 42; "Festival of Brazilian Music," *NYT*, October 6, 1940, 138; "Romeu Silva," *EPM*, 737.

130. Silva cited in Cabral, *Pixinguinha*, 51; *Correio da Manhã*, January 17, 1926, n.p.; reprinted and commented upon in Laly, "Klaxonadas," *Clarim*, March 21, 1926, 1; this rhetoric was also voiced by U.S. critics who opposed jazz but nonetheless recognized that such music "is the order of this barbarian day, and the minority can do little but endure." *Living Age*, July 31, 1920, 280; cited in Collier, *The Reception of Jazz in America*, 9.

131. Mario Noni, "Theatro," *O Malho*, July 27, 1929, n.p.

132. "A proposito de Josephina Baker no Rio," *A Patria*, July 21, 1929, 4.

133. J. A. Baptista Jr., "Josephina Baker, uma estrella que só brilha em Paris," *O Malho*, August 3, 1929, 9.

134. Author and title unknown, *Revista da Semana*, March 7, 1913; cited in Efegê, *Maxixe*, 152.

135. "Feeling King [*sic*] of Blue" and "Brown Eyes" [advertisements for Baker], *A Mascara*, April 29, 1927, 15; "Josephina Backer [*sic*] e a pata de coelho," *A Mascara*, July 29, 1927, 2, and August 26, 1927, back cover.

136. *O Paiz*, July 21, 1929, 14.

137. "A semana cinematographica," *O Paiz*, August 2, 1929, 8 ("Pickaninny" in English in the original); "'Follies' completa hoje 14 dias de exhibição," *O Paiz*, August 4, 1929, 11.

138. "'Follies' completa hoje 14 dias de exhibição"; "Josephina Baker" (photo and caption), *Clarim*, January 25, 1930, 4.

139. Costallat cited in the *Gazeta de Notícias*, January 22, 1922, 2; reproduced in M. Silva and Oliveira, *Pixinguinha*, 309–12. On the negotiation of concepts of honor in Brazil in this period, see Caulfield, *In Defense of Honor*.

140. José Fortunato, "Os 'Batutas' em Paris," *A Maça*, 1922; cited in Cabral, *Pixinguinha*, 17; *A Noite*, January 29, 1922; cited in Cabral, *Pixinguinha*, 42; Costallat in the *Gazeta de Notícias*; reproduced in M. Silva and Oliveira, *Pixinguinha*, 309–12.

141. Cabral, *Pixinguinha*, 37–38. H. Vianna agrees in *The Mystery of Samba*, 82: "The journalist [Costallat] may have exaggerated about the extent of the resistance to the Oito Batutas. Discontent cannot have been that widespread in view of what happened next" (that is, their wide acclaim, performance for the king and queen of Belgium, etc.).

142. Prudente de Moraes Neto, *Revista do Brazil*, September 15, 1926, n.p.; cited in Cabral, *Pixinguinha*, 54; Júlio Reis, in *A Rua*, n.d., and Xavier Pinheiro, "Teatro e sport," *Revista da Semana*, n.d.; both cited in Cabral, *Pixinguinha*, 30; Isaac Frankel cited in Cabral, *Pixinguinha*, 30–31.

143. Costallat in the *Gazeta de Notícias*; reproduced in M. Silva and Oliveira, *Pixinguinha*, 310–11. Such arguments found another erudite exponent in Mário de

Andrade, though in the context of his overall quite subtle view of nationality. Still, his 1928 polemic is fairly widely cited: "Every Brazilian artist who currently makes Brazilian art is an efficient being with human valor. Every one that makes international or foreign art, if he's not a genius, is useless, zero. And is a most highly revered beast." Andrade, *Ensaio sobre a música brasileira*; cited in Cabral, *No tempo de Ari Barroso*, 95. Forty years later Jota Efegê would echo this denunciation, adding a characterization of a contemporary trend, the rebellion against MPB (the Portuguese-language acronym for the genre "Brazilian popular music"), the "basest miscegenation." Efegê, "Ary Barroso, vitima da 'jazzificação' da música brasileira," *O Jornal*, December 12, 1965, n.p.; reprinted in Efegê, *Figuras e coisas da música popular brasileira*, vol. 1, 160–62.

144. Floresta de Miranda, letter published in *A Noite*, March 22, 1922, n.p.; quoted in Cabral, *Pixinguinha*, 43; also mentioned in Efegê, "Um Francês racista desaprovou a viagem dos '8 Batutas' a Paris," *O Globo*, June 18, 1973, n.p.; reprinted in Efegê, *Figuras e coisas da música popular brasileira*, vol. 2, 141–43, quote on 143.

145. *O Paiz*, n.d., n.p.; quoted in Cabral, *Pixinguinha*, 42–43.

146. Miranda in *A Noite*, March 22, 1922, n.p.

147. Rye, "The Southern Syncopated Orchestra," 220.

148. Ferro, *A idade do jazz-band*, 69–70. Ferro would later write an elegiac biography of fascist (or at least Franco-aligned) Portuguese dictator António de Oliveira Salazar.

149. Cited in Alencar, *O fabuloso e harmonioso Pixinguinha*, 45.

150. "Our own voice" is in Almeida, "Musica brasileira," 99–101; "a music 'genuinely ours'" is in "O folk-lore na musica actual," *Illustração Musical*, November 1930, 118.

151. Efegê, *Maxixe*, 152, citing *O Imparcial*, February 6, 1914.

152. "A approximação dos povos pela arte," *Diario Nacional* (São Paulo), November 4, 1928, 7.

153. Ferro, *A idade do jazz-band*, 69–70.

154. Guilherme de Almeida in ibid., 19.

155. The reference is to imperial advertisement for soap marketed as able to wash black bodies white or convince foolish black children that it might; see Burke, *Lifebuoy Men, Lux Women*; McClintock, "Soft-Soaping Empire: Commodity Racism and Imperial Advertising," ch. 5 in *Imperial Leather*.

156. "Atualidades," *Careta*, September 4, 1926, 22.

157. Fortunato, "Os 'Batutas' em Paris"; cited in Cabral, *Pixinguinha*, 17. Sérgio Cabral reproduces this satire without comment, although his view of the Batutas' fecund paternity is somewhat different: Pixinguinha, Cabral claims, "is without a doubt one of the fathers of Brazilian popular music. As such, he is also one of the fathers of our nationalism" (Cabral, *Pixinguinha*, 19). Cabral's claim is strikingly close to the nationalism articulated by the Batutas' champions in the 1920s, up to and including the inability to challenge even barely camouflaged racism. Overall, a striking feature of the contemporary scholarly work on Pixinguinha and the Batutas is how little distance it seems to have traveled in over seventy years. M. Silva and Oliveira call Costallat's nationalist riposte ("So what! They're Brazilian!") the "most beautiful and

convincing phrase of his missive," uninterested in changing the terms in any way. The three primary biographies of Pixinguinha, published in 1998, 1997, and 1979 (Silva and Oliveira's *Pixinguinha*, Cabral's *Pixinguinha*, and Alencar's *O fabuloso e harmonioso Pixinguinha*, respectively) tell a touching tale of progress. Remember, charges Cabral, "racism at that time was still not prohibited by law" (Cabral, *Pixinguinha*, 30). Happily, however, exult Silva and Oliveira, "The young men triumphed. . . . They were good—really good! . . . The evil tongues, suffocated by the truth of the valor of the Batutas, were quiet" (M. Silva and Oliveira, *Pixinguinha*, 39). Alencar goes furthest toward hagiography and nearest the edge of meaninglessness: "He was good throughout his whole existence. Phenomenal. . . . The goodness of the great Carioca musician was the only virtue that surpassed the virtues of his music" (Alencar, *O fabuloso e harmonioso Pixinguinha*, 75). All three biographers, like many other commentators, use the tale of the 1922 uproar as an opportunity to rejoice at the triumph of good over evil. The subtleties of racism and power have no place in these treatments.

158. See the wonderful discussion of ideas of cultural contagion in Browning, *Infectious Rhythm*.

159. Bushell, *Jazz from the Beginning*, 69.

Nation Drag

1. Rogers, *As Nature Leads*, 54–55.

2. Ibid., 57.

3. Historians have tried to pin down the moment at which the United States moved to a dichotomous racial system or the moment it left such a system behind: the 1924 immigration restriction, Third Reich, decolonization, civil rights, Black Power, and so on. Immigration historian Oscar Handlin, for example, cited restriction and postwar prosperity as axes of racial consolidation in *The Uprooted*, 299–300. More recently, Thomas A. Guglielmo, in *White on Arrival*, has suggested that Italian immigrants were always perceived as white, even as recent arrivals. Sociologist Howard Winant sees a shift in the other direction very recently, as if dichotomy were constant before that: "race is becoming more complicated and nuanced, largely as a result of the struggles of the recent past, so that the color line and the traditionally bipolar, black-white foundation of racial politics and identity is eroding." Winant credits the U.S. civil rights movement with forcing North Americans to see non-black and non-white people (Latinos and Asians, signally), making the United States multipolar. Winant, *Racial Conditions*, 159, 165. Such periodizations are fruitless ultimately; while emphases change, no single system ever consolidates its hegemony nationwide. On the shuttling back and forth possible in ethnic identification, helpful work includes Sollors, *Beyond Ethnicity*, and Sollors, *The Invention of Ethnicity*. On the existence of multiple, ranked racial categories in the early twentieth century, see Gossett, *Race*; Saxton, *The Rise and Fall of the White Republic*; Roediger, *The Wages of Whiteness*; Brodkin, *How Jews Became White Folks and What That Says about Race in America*; Ignatiev,

How the Irish Became White; Foley, *The White Scourge*; Jacobson, *Special Sorrows*; Jacobson, *Barbarian Virtues*; Jacobson, *Whiteness of a Different Color*; Haney Lopez, *White By Law*; Hunt, *Ideology and U.S. Foreign Policy*, 78–79.

4. Said, *Orientalism*; Stam and Shohat, *Unthinking Eurocentrism*. This is not to suggest that all non-black performers had easy access to whiteness or to the entitlement necessary to perform Orientalism as condescension; clearly there are complications for various sorts of people.

5. On the connections and tensions between colonialism and racism, see Renda, *Taking Haiti*; Rafael, *White Love and Other Events in Filipino History*; Hoganson, *Fighting for American Manhood*; A. Kaplan, "Black and Blue on San Juan Hill"; Michaels, "Anti-Imperial Americanism"; Bederman, *Manliness and Civilization*; Jacobson, *Barbarian Virtues*; Wexler, *Tender Violence*; Kramer, "Jim Crow Science and the 'Negro Problem' in the Occupied Philippines, 1898–1914."

6. A note on boundaries: while Brazil was a favorite object of exoticist attentions from all corners, it was only one of many such places in the imaginative lexicon of early-twentieth-century U.S. popular culture, alongside Cuba, Spain, Hawaii, France, "the South Seas," ancient Egypt, Greece, Rome, and so on. Evocations of Brazil are good starting points for *this* book's exploration of national masquerades during the exoticist culture of empire, given its expositions of Brazil-U.S. cultural exchange, the most concrete bases of ideas about Brazil circulating in U.S. intellectual, commercial, and political spheres. A discussion of this phenomenon that limited itself to a single manifestation, however, would not convey its multidirectional reach. As the discourse under discussion did not preserve Brazil's integrity, this chapter cannot hope to salvage it; it will instead contextualize Brazil's subsumption in the sea of exotic possibilities that rendered such tactics productive. In addition, this chapter ventures across the chronological borders of most of the others, accompanying several of the figures whose lives continued to engage questions of exoticist performance beyond the 1920s.

7. Krasner, *A Beautiful Pageant*, 4; and explaining the dynamic in a broader frame, Hammonds, "Black (W)holes and the Geometry of Black Female Sexuality."

8. See A. Davis, *Blues Legacies and Black Feminism*; Harrison, *Black Pearls*; Carby, "'It Jus Be's Dat Way Sometime'"; Kainer, "Sophie Tucker and Elsie Janis."

9. Lorde, *Uses of the Erotic*.

10. "Badge of color" is from Du Bois, *Dusk of Dawn*, 117. By 1923, the *Chicago Defender* could argue that black stage performance was quintessentially American. "Our peculiar gifts for the theater are a heritage of America," wrote a stage reviewer; a movie critic exulted, "There is nothing American unless the black man is in it." "American National Theater," *Chicago Defender*, May 12, 1923, 12; "The Silent Drama," *Chicago Defender*, June 23, 1923, 12. Excellent secondary sources on African American engagement with empire include Von Eschen, *Race against Empire*; Plummer, *Rising Wind*; Gatewood, *"Smoked Yankees" and the Struggle for Empire*; Gatewood, *Black Americans and the White Man's Burden, 1898–1903*; Marks, *The Black Press Views American Imperialism (1898–1900)*; Gaines, "Black Americans' Racial Uplift Ideology as 'Civilizing Mission'"; C. Robinson, "W. E. B. Du Bois and Black Sovereignty."

11. Lott, *Love and Theft*; Toll, *Blacking Up*; Spencer, *The New Negroes and Their Music*; Sampson, *Blacks in Blackface*; Spackman, "Passing for Colored."

12. L. Levine, *Highbrow/Lowbrow*; Kibler, *Rank Ladies*, "debate" on 7, citing Oberdeck, "Contested Cultures of American Refinement."

13. Gottschild, "Between Two Eras," 267.

14. Hoganson, *Fighting for American Manhood*; Jacobson, *Barbarian Virtues*; E. Love, *Race over Empire*.

15. Henriksen, "Black Patti"; citation from ch. 4, "Achievement Summary," 10, citing an article in the *Empire* (Toronto), author, title, date, and page not given; my emphasis. In folder "Black Patti (1868–1933)," Helen Armstead Johnson Miscellaneous Theater Collections, 1831–1993, NYPL, Schomburg Library (hereafter HAJ MTC). Although printed in a newspaper in Canada, not the United States, this piece evinces a shared North American imperial standpoint in title and content.

16. The others were at Buffalo, Pittsburgh, and Chicago. Tanner, *Dusky Maidens*. Jones did not appear in Chicago, apparently for contractual failure to make timely payment, reports Reed, *All the World Is Here!* It is interesting that Jones seems to have been particularly attractive or attracted to fairs in the border zone connecting the United States and Canada, whose imperial representations are likely to have affirmed an even more pointed view of the common destiny of Anglo-Americans in North America.

17. Rydell, *All the World's a Fair*; Rydell, Findling, and Pelle, *Fair America*; Burris, *Exhibiting Religion*; Harvey, *Hybrids of Modernity*; P. Bender, Brown, and Vasquez, *Savage Acts*.

18. Sampson, *Blacks in Blackface*, 386.

19. Ibid.

20. *Pittsburgh Post*, March 11, 1896, n.p.; cited in Henrikson, "Black Patti," ch. 2, p. 8.

21. Sampson, *Blacks in Blackface*, 9.

22. Stearns and Stearns, *Jazz Dance*; Sampson, *Blacks in Blackface*, 388; Tanner, *Dusky Maidens*; Henriksen, "Black Patti."

23. For example, the Oriental Troubadours, active 1889–1905, and a white burlesque show of the same name; see Peterson, *The African American Theatre Directory, 1816–1960*.

24. Southern, *The Music of Black Americans*.

25. Sampson, *Blacks in Blackface*, 386; Tanner, *Dusky Maidens*, citing newspaper reviews of the show.

26. Lott, *Love and Theft*.

27. Tanner, *Dusky Maidens*, 46.

28. Jeffrey Green, "The Negro Renaissance and England"; Bricktop and Haskins, *Bricktop*; Krasner, *A Beautiful Pageant*, 281; Bushell, *Jazz from the Beginning*, 55. Sampson, *Blacks in Blackface*, 194, offers the program from *Dixie to Broadway* (1924), in which Mills headlined a number called "Jungle Nights in Dixieland."

29. Walkowitz, "The 'Vision of Salome'"; "Salomania" on 344.

30. Krasner, *A Beautiful Pageant*, 62, 69.

31. Egan, *Florence Mills*; Sampson, *Blacks in Blackface*, 402.

32. Krasner, *A Beautiful Pageant*, 283; "They Say Florence Helped Irene Rebuke the Nobility," *New York Amsterdam News*, August 15, 1923, 5; cited in Regester, *Black Entertainers in African American Newspaper Articles*, 17.

33. Foreman, "Jazz and Race Records 1920–1932," 98; Peiss, *Hope in a Jar*, 220; advertisement in *Chicago Defender*, April 14, 1923, 19.

34. Leach, *Land of Desire*, 325.

35. Tanner, *Dusky Maidens*, 89, 93.

36. Ibid., 99, 101. Note that Sampson, *Blacks in Blackface*, 340–341, has a different version of events in Bowman's life, though the difference does not affect the argument made here.

37. Heard and Mussa, "African Dance in New York City," 143–153 on Efrom Odok, Asadata Dafora, and Momudu Johnson.

38. D. Baldwin, "Out from the Shadow of E. Franklin Frazier?"; Yelvington, "The Invention of Africa in Latin America and the Caribbean."

39. Tanner, *Dusky Maidens*, 71–73, 98, 100, 101; Foulkes, *Modern Bodies*, ch. 3.

40. Act I, Scene 2, p. 1, of Hall Johnson, *Run, Little Chillun!*, n.d., Box 3, Folder 9, HAJ MTC; see also Foulkes, *Modern Bodies*, 51.

41. This is the strategy African Americans would adopt using Brazil, as noted throughout this book; see also Hellwig, *African-American Reflections on Brazil's Racial Paradise*.

42. "Rise of Josephine Baker Not Possible in America," *Chicago Defender*, February 4, 1928, 10.

43. "Mme. Patti Brown Royally Received at Bahai [*sic*], Brazil," *Chicago Defender*, January 15, 1916, 1.

44. "Brazil Wants Educated Black Men," "Brazil's Black President," and "Brazil Ideal Country for Black Man," all in *Chicago Defender*, January 22, 1916, 1.

45. "Race Artists to Sing for Victrolas," *Chicago Defender*, January 8, 1916, page illegible [3 or 4].

46. Foreman, "Jazz and Race Records, 1920–1932," citing the *Chicago Defender*, January 8, 1916, 1, 4, and 5.

47. Cited in Stearns and Stearns, *Jazz Dance*, 296–297.

48. Ibid., 291–92.

49. Gottschild, *Waltzing in the Dark*, 42.

50. Ibid., 43.

51. Stearns and Stearns, *Jazz Dance*, 293.

52. "Those Two Colored Fashion Plates" (advertisement for Grenlee [*sic*] and Drayton), *Variety*, December 15, 1914, 54.

53. Bushell, *Jazz from the Beginning*, 56; Stearns and Stearns, *Jazz Dance*, 294.

54. Stearns and Stearns, *Jazz Dance*, 294.

55. Gottschild, *Waltzing in the Dark*, 41–43, 49.

56. Gottschild, "Between Two Eras"; quotation from 267.

57. Gottschild, "Between Two Eras."

58. Ibid.; Gottschild, *Waltzing in the Dark*.

59. Nella Larsen includes in her novel *Passing* a character who sometimes declines to correct people who read her as "an Italian, a Spaniard, a Mexican or a gipsy," understanding that these readings confer social privileges unlikely to be bestowed upon an African American woman. See Larsen, *Passing*, 150, and Ginsberg, introduction to *Passing and the Fictions of Identity*, 1–18, esp. 11. Larsen offers a wonderfully subtle portrait of the uses African Americans made of global racial variation through a character (the protagonist's husband) who yearns to move his family to Brazil, indexing the many journalists and activists at the time who juxtaposed supposedly better racial arrangements abroad to protest those in the United States. Such a move also appears in *Uncle Tom's Cabin* twice, as we will consider below. Also relevant is the protagonist of James Weldon Johnson's *Autobiography of an Ex-Colored Man*, who realizes that in Europe he would "have greater chances of attracting attention as a colored composer than as a white one" and alters his racial performance accordingly. Quoted in Pfeiffer, "Individualism, Success, and American Identity in *The Autobiography of an Ex-Colored Man*," 404. One historian who has documented the utility of foreign nationality in evading U.S. racial categories is Martha Hodes, who points out that in the antebellum U.S. South "a claim of Spanish or Portuguese nationality could erase counter-claims of blackness." For a Caribbean man in New England, "British nationality may have accomplished the same end." Hodes, "The Mercurial Nature and Abiding Power of Race," 103; see also Hodes, *White Women, Black Men*, 97, 100, 105, 119.

60. Foulkes, *Modern Bodies*, 55.

61. Ibid. Foulkes suggests Florence Warwick and Katherine Dunham may have leaned on their lightness in this way as well.

62. Gottschild, *Waltzing in the Dark*, 118–120, and "lightest, whitest" on 7.

63. Cited in Tanner, *Dusky Maidens*, 89, citing LeRoi Antoine, *Achievement: The Life of Laura Bowman*.

64. Cited in Foreman, "Jazz and Race Records, 1920–1932," 213.

65. George-Graves, *The Royalty of Negro Vaudeville*, 20.

66. "Got Your Habits On," words and music by John Queen; cited in Dennison, *Scandalize My Name*, 346 (attribution, 537n2).

67. Biagioni and Flemming, *Herb Flemming*, 55–57.

68. Gottschild agrees with this periodization, noting the difficulties Norton and Margot faced given the elite forms they preferred and the timing of their career, which was rising most steeply just after the twenties. Gottschild, "Between Two Eras," 267. This despite the Popular Front era of the 1930s, which gave some cultural *forms* (concert dance, for example), more room in the '30s than in the '40s. Foulkes, *Modern Bodies*, chs. 6–7.

69. Folder "Jarboro, Caterina (1903–1986)," HAJ MTC. On the National Negro Opera Company, founded in 1941 in Pittsburgh, see Cheatham, "African-American Women Singers at the Metropolitan Opera before Leontyne Price."

70. Everett, *Returning the Gaze*, 61. Everett finds in this *Bystander* report evidence of "the absurdities of early-twentieth-century race relations." Are they more logical today?

71. Clearly this was a person of no little mobility, in transit again at the fateful moment, and on a train, the vehicle most loaded with white racial anxieties in the period of the Great Migration. Elizabeth Marie Smith suggests that the "proliferation of discussions of passing" in the 1920s was a reflection in part of white Americans' fears of the Great Migration as a "racial threat" justifying great attention to "purity" in that period. E. Smith, "'Passing' and the Anxious Decade," 12, 13, citing Kevin Mumford. Smith also finds an abundance of fictional accounts of passing at the turn to the twenty-first century, a phenomenon she wryly leaves to future historians to decipher.

72. Cited in Gottschild, *Waltzing in the Dark*, 122, author's brackets.

73. Ibid., 121–22, author's ellipses.

74. Ibid., 46.

75. Ginsberg, *Passing and the Fictions of Identity*, 12.

76. Stern, "Spanish Masquerade and the Drama of Racial Identity in *Uncle Tom's Cabin*," 107. Kathleen Pfeiffer also discusses the runaways in *Uncle Tom's Cabin* who escape by dressing as Spanish aristocrats, disguising "their race, nationality, class, and gender"; Pfeiffer, "Individualism, Success, and American Identity in *The Autobiography of an Ex-Colored Man*," 417. Another use of George Harris's "Spanish Masquerade" as the axis of an argument about passing is Kosnik, "The Alien in Our Nation."

77. Stern, "Spanish Masquerade," 110.

78. Ibid., 110 and 126n16, citing Elizabeth Boone.

79. Cited in Gottschild, *Waltzing in the Dark*, 125.

80. Kosnik, "The Alien in Our Nation," 3, 8. Elizabeth Marie Smith offers another definition: "the process by which a person who is believed to be a member of one race identifies themselves or is identified by others with another race." Smith also offers Joel Williamson's definition, "crossing the color line and winning acceptance as white in the white world," preferring hers, she explains, to make clear "that ideas about race are grounded in beliefs not biology, and that race is not a stable, coherent identity." E. Smith, "'Passing' and the Anxious Decade," 2n3, citing Williamson, *New People*.

81. A. Robinson, "It Takes One to Know One," 716; Ginsberg, *Passing and the Fictions of Identity*, 4. See also A. Robinson, "To Pass/In Drag," on the "relation between passing and those visual models of identity that sustain its plausibility," p. vii; Kawash, "*The Autobiography of an Ex-Coloured Man*," on passing novels' "assumption that passing for white conceals or obscures a true black identity" (62); and Valerie Smith's critical widening of the lens, which seeks to situate passing within what she calls the "discourse of intersectionality," noting the critical roles of class and gender in motivating and structuring passing, which still restricts itself to black and white; V. Smith, "Reading the Intersection of Race and Gender in Narratives of Passing." Even Kristin Kosnik's wonderfully productive reading of passing narratives as refusals of "American" identity and of passing as a negotiation of national identity as much as of race is hampered by her unwillingness to articulate national identities available in the United States beyond "American." "In a nation defined by what Eric Sundquist aptly terms its 'dual citizenship' of white and black," writes Kosnik, "persons of mixed

race—those who resist classification as being neither white nor black—are ultimately relegated to the category *not American*, in some sense, entrapped in the role of being neither citizen nor alien." Kosnik, "The Alien in Our Nation," 5.

82. A. Robinson, "It Takes One to Know One," 727, citing Bertolt Brecht.

83. Halberstam, *Female Masculinity*, 236. Halberstam here is explicitly glossing Esther Newton's groundbreaking consideration of drag, *Mother Camp: Female Impersonators in America*.

84. J. Butler, *Gender Trouble*, 137.

85. A. Robinson, "It Takes One to Know One," 727.

86. "Cabarets," *Variety*, March 26, 1915, 13; "New Acts This Week," *Variety*, April 9, 1915, 14; *Chicago Defender*, March 23, 1918; Sampson, *Blacks in Blackface*, 470; "Lovejoy in K.C.," *Afro-American* (Baltimore), July 30, 1927, 9; *Charley's Aunt* [advertisement], *NYT*, April 5, 1925, X4; see also "Old Farce in Film Form Is as Cheery as of Yore," *NYT*, February 15, 1925, X5.

87. Henry Sampson's version, heavily cited by subsequent researchers, reports Burgoyne's birth "in 1885. She began her stage career in 1901 when she was six"—an error surely more typographical than mathematic; Sampson, *Blacks in Blackface*, 347. This math is reproduced in Perpener, *African-American Concert Dance*, 73. In her sixties, Burgoyne told a reporter that she first performed locally at age twelve, joined Isham's company at six*teen*, and went to Europe with a traveling troupe (not Isham's, she claimed in this account) at eighteen; Emmons, "Olga Burgoyne and Where She Danced."

88. Emmons, "Olga Burgoyne and Where She Danced," 4; "Negro Dancer Once Entertained Czar," no periodical title, n.d., n.p.; biographical clippings file for Ollie Burgoyne, Channing Pollock Theatre Collection, Howard University.

89. Sampson, *Blacks in Blackface*, 377; Helen Johnson, "Some International Implications of an Afro-American Theater Collection."

90. Hunter, "New Museum Traces Black Stage History," 22, citing Helen Armstead Johnson's essay in *Encore American and World Wide News*: "Cakewalkers such as the Due [*sic*] Eclatants, Olga Burgoyne, and Usher were in Russia in 1902." Jennifer Dunning, "'Dixie to Broadway,' Black Stage Tribute," *NYT*, February 11, 1977, n.p., reveals the actress admitting to birth in 1880: "Among the 'Dahomey' memorabilia on view is a photograph of a minx-eyed actress, inscribed in aged, shaky handwriting, 'From Olga, when I was 23.' Olga Burgoyne left for Russia after 'In Dahomey' closed, performed for Tolstoy and opened a lingerie shop there."

91. "Ollie Burgoyne," article attributed (in handwriting) to *Morning Telegraph* (New York), September 18, 1932, n.p.; folder "Burgoyne, Ollie (Olga) (1878? 1885?–1973)," HAJ MTC.

92. Emmons, "Olga Burgoyne and Where She Danced," credits the 1905 revolution; Perpener, *African-American Concert Dance*, 74, gives the First World War, citing an unattributed article in the Howard University collection. There are two such articles: "Negro Dancer Once Entertained Czar," which doesn't mention the reason for Burgoyne's departure from Russia, and "She Danced before the Tsar," unattrib-

uted article, biographical clipping file for Burgoyne, Channing Pollock Theatre Collection, Howard University, which writes simply, "While there, the war broke out."

93. Emmons, "Olga Burgoyne and Where She Danced."

94. Tanner, *Dusky Maidens*, 66, 86; Stearns and Stearns, *Jazz Dance*, 248, 293; Sampson, *Blacks in Blackface*, 483.

95. Cited in Emmons, "Olga Burgoyne and Where She Danced," 4.

96. Sampson, *Blacks in Blackface*, 347.

97. Ibid.

98. A. B., *Der Artist* 1182 (October 6, 1907); cited in Lotz, "The 'Louisiana Troupes' in Europe," 137.

99. Sampson, *Blacks in Blackface*, 318; could this song have cited "Creole Girl," the maxixe the Castles' house band had recorded a half-dozen years earlier?

100. Cited in "Negro Dancer Once Entertained Czar."

101. Cited in Emmons, "Olga Burgoyne and Where She Danced," 4.

102. Tanner, *Dusky Maidens*, 43.

103. Emmons, "Olga Burgoyne and Where She Danced," 4.

104. Had Burgoyne admitted to being twenty-three or more in 1903, as seems likely, she would have revealed herself to have been in her mid-fifties in *Run, Little Chillun!*, the occasion for this report. A photograph from this production in the HAJ MTC reveals a graceful, smooth-skinned woman who could easily have maintained the fiction of youth required for continued work as an actress. No wonder she fudged her birthdate in this discussion.

105. Cited in "She Danced before the Tsar."

106. Helen Johnson, "Some International Implications of an Afro-American Theater Collection."

107. "She Danced before the Tsar."

108. Sampson, *Blacks in Blackface*, 316; Peterson, *The African American Theatre Directory 1816–1960*, 112–13.

109. Sampson, *Blacks in Blackface*, 347.

110. "Thirteen Matinees for Election Day," *NYT*, November 3, 1942, 19.

111. For biographical information, see biographical clippings file for Burgoyne, Channing Pollock Theatre Collection, Howard University; folder "Burgoyne, Ollie (Olga) (1878? 1885?–1973)," HAJ MTC; Sampson, *Blacks in Blackface*, 347; Peterson, *The African American Theatre Directory 1816–1960*, 113, 151, 159, 203; Helen Johnson, "Some International Implications of an Afro-American Theater Collection"; Tanner, *Dusky Maidens*, 37, 43–44. Sampson's account, written in a format and moment in which formal citational practice was not necessary, is impossible to trace. Sampson based his work on playbills and newspaper accounts and may have been insufficiently source-critical of the latter. Researchers should take pains to cross-check his information lest they follow his mistakes as well as his generous leads.

112. Kawash, "*The Autobiography of an Ex-Coloured Man*," 70; J. Butler, *Gender Trouble*, 137; J. Butler, *Bodies That Matter*; J. Butler, "Imitation and Gender Insubordination." Another scholar who treats passing in this way, Harryette Mullen, suggests that pass-

ing be read as a technology for the production of whiteness. The theme of passing literature, she offers, is "the American mechanism for the cultural and genetic reproduction of whiteness." Mullen, "Optic White," 73.

113. Ginway, "Notes from My Talk with Captain Geyser Péret," 3. Many thanks to M. Elizabeth Ginway for invaluable assistance throughout this section. Dr. Ginway generously shared her notes from interviews with Houston's sister and son conducted in the course of work on Benjamin Péret. She also suggested further avenues of research and reflected helpfully on her sources.

114. Needell, *A Tropical Belle Epoque*. Perhaps the family's lack of sons allowed resources for study and travel abroad to be allocated to their daughters. Elsie's younger sister, Mary, also traveled to Paris (to some places before Elsie, she claimed); Ginway, "Conversa com Mary Houston Pedrosa," 1. About the older sister, I have no information. On Elsie's place among Brazilian artistic elites, see evidence of her friendships with Tarsila do Amaral in Aracy Amaral, *Tarsila*, 327n25; and with Patrícia Galvão (Pagu) in K. Jackson, "Alienation and Ideology in *A Famosa Revista* (1945)."

115. Aracy Amaral, *Tarsila*; Aracy Amaral, *Blaise Cendrars no Brasil e os modernistas*; Cendrars, *Etc., etc . . .* ; Cendrars, *Histoires vraies*; Milhaud, *Notes without Music*; Brito, *História do Modernismo brasileiro*; Martins, *O Modernismo*; Moraes Belluzzo, *Modernidade*.

116. It is important not to read a simple feminism into this decision, since "Houston" was a far more "noble" name than Péret in her circles, and if Elsie shared the standards of her elite family and class, she would have valued this prestige.

117. Houston, "La musique, la danse et les cérémonies populaires du Brésil," 162–164; Houston, *Chants populaires du Brésil*.

118. Photo in Courtot, *Introduction à la lecture de B. Péret*, 23; thanks again to M. Elizabeth Ginway for providing this source.

119. "Brazilian Diva Says Music'll Unite Americas," *Washington Post*, July 24, 1941, 17.

120. Blake, *Le tumulte noir*; Kelley, "A Poetics of Anticolonialism"; Edwards, *The Practice of Diaspora*; Stich, *Anxious Visions*; Chénieux-Gendron, "Surrealists in Exile"; cf. Caws, "Péret's 'Amour sublime,'" which argues that Péret, a Trotskyist, was "a firm believer in non-political poetry" (204); and Shelton, "Le monde noir dans la littérature dadaiste et surréaliste," who argues that surrealists' (including Péret's) exotic idealization of black people rarely led to reflections about black oppression or to questioning colonialism.

121. Ginway, "Conversa com Mary Houston Pedrosa," 2.

122. Ginway, "Surrealist Benjamin Péret and Brazilian Modernism." Apparently the study disappeared, Ginway laments on 548. Ginway points out that while Péret's vehement anticlericalism made him ambivalent about these religious traditions, still he was attracted to macumba because "it gave him the chance to comment on political oppression" and "allowed him to view a culture with access to the poetic 'marvelous'" (548, 547).

123. Ibid., 549; 545, citing the *Correio da Manhã*, February 21, 1929, 3.

124. Earl Warner, "Cavalcade of Songs Tells Story of America's Past," *Daily Worker*, June 7, 1941; "Programs of the Week," NYT, April 28, 1940, 122, on a benefit featuring Houston for the Little Red Schoolhouse (part of the New School); and "Benefit Takes Form of a Bassinet Dance," NYT, November 20, 1938, 46, another benefit, this one for a nursery. In 1941, a *Washington Post* reporter complained that Houston would not share her political opinions; "Brazilian Diva Says Music'll Unite Americas."

125. Ginway, "Notes from My Talk with Captain Geyser Péret," 2.

126. "On a pu constater dernièrement encore que l'élite intellectuelle brésilienne porte un intérêt toujours croissant à tout ce qui touche l'art populaire et nous espérons qu'une campagne sera entreprise pour divulguer des spectacles . . . que nous avons nommés, non seulement aux populations de notre capitale, mais aussi dans les autres pays." Houston, "La musique, la danse et les cérémonies populaires du Brésil," 164. Houston expressed a similar elitism in a 1929 conversation with a Brazilian press representative in São Paulo; "Na civilisáda Europa os rythmos da musica Negra, provocam enthusiasmo e reclamam applausos," *Progresso*, March 24, 1929, 1.

127. "Na civilisáda Europa os rythmos da musica Negra provocam enthusiasmo e reclamam applausos."

128. Tarsila mentions a concert by Elsie Houston that seems to have been in Brazil in 1933; see Aracy Amaral, *Tarsila*, 341n6.

129. Houston's U.S. performances bridge two long gaps: for all of 1939 and then the second half of 1942, the U.S. press was silent about her. She was apparently in Brazil in 1939. The writer Patrícia Galvão (Pagu) included in her novel *A Famosa Revista* (written with Geraldo Ferraz) a lightly fictionalized account of a visit Houston paid Pagu in jail in 1939. See K. Jackson, "Alienation and Ideology in *A Famosa Revista* (1945)," 301, 303n17.

130. NBC Symphony Orchestra in "Music Notes," NYT, November 19, 1937, 26; Kansas City and Rochester Philharmonics mentioned in "Latins Take Broadway by Storm," *Washington Post*, April 27, 1941, L9; solo recital at the Guild Theatre reviewed in "Elsie Houston of Brazil Heard," in "Music in Review: Segovia, Guitarist, Heard–Enesco Offers 'Emperor' Concerto–Modern Works Given–Other Programs," NYT, February 7, 1938, 10; "Composers' Group in Concert Here," NYT, March 11, 1940, 17; "Spanish Program Heard at Stadium; South American Works Also Presented at First Concert Conducted by Weissman; Elsie Houston Soloist," NYT, July 15, 1940, 20; Arthur Cohn, "Philadelphia Story," *Modern Music* 19, no. 3 (March–April, 1942): 187[?]–89; Donald Fuller, "Forecast and Review: Americans to the Fore—New York, 1941–42," *Modern Music* 19, no. 2 (January–February 1942): 113[?]–15; "Elsie Houston Soloist; Offers Latin-American Songs at Young People's Concert," NYT, January 17, 1943, 41.

131. "Benefit Takes Form of a Bassinet Dance"; "Programs of the Week" (April 28, 1940).

132. "Radio Programs Scheduled for Broadcast This Week," NYT, January 2, 1938, 11; "Today on the Radio," NYT, January 6, 1938, 42; also "Pan-American Talks Open," NYT, March 4, 1938, 6.

133. Jack Gould, "News of the Night Clubs," NYT, January 2, 1938, 2; "News and Gos-

sip of the Night Clubs," *NYT*, March 6, 1938, 150; "At the Night Clubs; Hotels," *NYT*, October 26, 1940, 18; "The Night Clubs during November," *NYT*, November 2, 1940, 18; "News of the Night Clubs," *NYT*, February 14, 1943, X2.

134. "Pan-American Talks Open"; "Festival of Brazilian Music" [at the Museum of Modern Art (MOMA)], *NYT*, October 6, 1940, 138; "Villa-Lobos Music Heard at Festival; Works of a Brazilian Composer on Second Program of Fete at Museum of Modern Art; Elsie Houston a Soloist," *NYT*, October 19, 1940, 24; "Night of Americas Voices Unity Theme; Diplomacy and Arts Join in Hemisphere Program Here," *NYT*, February 15, 1943, 12; "Music of the Week," *NYT*, February 14, 1943, X6; "Americas Night Tomorrow," *NYT*, February 13, 1943, 8.

135. Davidson Taylor, "The Enduring Elsie Houston."

136. "Latins Take Broadway by Storm."

137. "Elsie Houston of Brazil Heard," in "Music in Review: Segovia, Guitarist, Heard–Enesco Offers 'Emperor' Concerto–Modern Works Given–Other Programs," *NYT*, February 7, 1938, 10.

138. "News and Gossip of the Night Clubs," *NYT*, March 6, 1938, 150.

139. Colin McPhee, "Jungles of Brazil," *Modern Music* 18, no. 1 (November–December 1940): 42.

140. Minna Lederman, "Museum Pieces," *Modern Music* 18, no. 4 (May–June 1941): 265.

141. "News of the Night Clubs," NYT, February 14, 1943.

142. "Brazilian Soprano Is Found Dead Here," *NYT*, February 21, 1943, 20; "Elsie Houston, Noted Singer Dead; Listed as Suicide," *Washington Post*, February 21, 1943, 14.

143. Researchers of Afro–New World traditions had begun to call attention to the proximity of Haitian vodun and Brazilian candomblé by 1940; see Herskovits, "African Gods and Catholic Saints in New World Negro Belief"; and later, Bastide, *Les Amériques noires*, and Verger, book review of *Voodoo in Haiti*.

144. "Brazilian Girl to Sing with National Symphony," *Christian Science Monitor*, July 16, 1941, 16; "Hearing Ahead," *Washington Post*, July 19, 1942, L4.

145. "Composers' Group in Concert Here"; Colin McPhee, "Scores and Records," *Modern Music* 22, no. 1 (November–December 1944): 59.

146. Cited in Davidson Taylor, "The Enduring Elsie Houston."

147. Ibid.

148. "Elsie Houston, singer ambassadress," photo (Marcus Blechman, photo credit), *Theatre Arts*, April 1942, 279. In Houston's *NYT* obituary, Marcel Courbon (no "de") was identified as a "friend."

149. "Brazilian Girl to Sing with National Symphony"; "Elsie Houston, Noted Singer Dead."

150. Taylor, "The Enduring Elsie Houston."

151. Ibid.

152. McPhee, "Scores and Records," 42.

153. "Composers' Group in Concert Here."

154. Gould, "News of the Night Clubs," *NYT*, January 2, 1938.

155. After her death, Houston would be claimed by African Americans such as the radio personality Etta Moten Barnett, who used her recordings to demonstrate the proximity of black U.S. and Afro-Brazilian culture. See *Etta Moten Barnett's Return to the United States* (sound recording) (Chicago: WMAQ Radio, 1955), NYPL, Schomburg Branch, Recorded Sound Division. Moten's appearance in the 1933 movie *Flying Down to Rio*, singing the "Carioca" with a basket of fruit on her head, raises fascinating questions about Moten's own relationship to Brazil, to Houston, and to the U.S. circulation of the image Carmen Miranda would animate a half-dozen years later.

156. Tinhorão, *O samba agora vai*, 40: "a mulata americana Elsie Houston, nascida no Brasil por acaso, mas que dava entrevistas falando em nome da música brasileira e cantando canções folclóricas e populares."

157. Houston's death certificate listed her as a U.S. citizen. Borough of Manhattan Death Certificate no. 4387, Municipal Archives, New York.

158. "Brazilian Diva Says Music'll Unite Americas."

159. Ibid. As French composer Darius Milhaud wrote in his autobiography, "When I arrived in New York, I had told the newspapermen interviewing me that European music was considerably influenced by American music. 'But whose music?' they asked me; 'Macdowell's or Carpenter's?' 'Neither . . . ,' I answered; 'I mean jazz.' They were filled with consternation, for at that time most American musicians had not realized the importance of jazz as an art form and relegated it to the dance hall." Milhaud, *Notes without Music*, 135. Houston could easily have met Milhaud in Paris in the twenties; she certainly knew his music.

160. Davidson Taylor, "The Enduring Elsie Houston."

161. Ibid.

Another "Global Vision"

1. "Dr. Robert S. Abbott," *Jornal do Commercio*, May 11, 1923, n.p.; Maço [packet] 9691/92 (629), Arquivo Histórico do Itamarati (Ministry of Foreign Affairs; hereafter AHI). Italicized words in English in the original. The milreis was the currency in use in Brazil at that time; the extra zeroes reflect its notation. Deep thanks to Jeff Lesser for sharing this material from his research with me.

2. "Lack" in Hanchard, *Orpheus and Power*, 41; "absence" in Hanchard, *Orpheus and Power*, 74, and Winant, *Racial Conditions*, 130–131; see also Winant, *Racial Conditions*, 163; "inability" in Niani, "Black Consciousness vs. Racism in Brazil," 237 (see also the articles in Hellwig, *African-American Reflections on Brazil's Racial Paradise*, part 3, passim); "inability" in a slightly different context also in Hanchard, *Orpheus and Power*, 6; see also Frederickson, "Race and Racism in Historical Perspective." "Lack" is sometimes discussed via periodization, such that politicized racial identity in Brazil is seen as a recent phenomenon, as in Hanchard, "Black Cinderella?"; or Bastide and Fernandes, *Brancos e negros em São Paulo*, ch. 5.

3. This tradition is very old (e.g., José Correia Leite, "O grande problema nacional," *Evolução*, May 13, 1933, 9); its academic version dates at least to Oracy Nogueira's work in the 1950s. Nogueira characterized African Americans as collective in their racial consciousness and in their response to discrimination but Afro-Brazilians as having only an intermittent sense of racial identity and tending to respond to racism in individualistic ways, rarely in solidarity or cooperation with each other. Nogueira, "Preconceito racial de marca e preconceito racial de origem," 87–89, esp. 88n33. Other important scholarship of this camp includes Bastide and Fernandes, *Brancos e negros em São Paulo*; Bastide, "A imprensa negra do Estado de São Paulo"; Degler, *Neither Black nor White*; Ferrara, *A imprensa negra paulista (1915–1963)*; Hasenbalg and Silva, "Notes on Racial and Political Inequality in Brazil." Luiz de Aguiar Costa Pinto extended this logic to the whole country in "Associações tradicionais," ch. 1 in *O negro no Rio de Janeiro*; so did Carvalho in "Dreams Come Untrue." Carvalho contrasts the roles of myths in the United States and Brazil; in the former, they are a powerful organizing force; in the latter, "an instrument of self-delusion" (78).

4. Warren, *Racial Revolutions*, 269. Warren also reports a Brazilian activist's characterization of deniers of racism as "lobotomized." These characterizations outdozen the dozens, as Robin D. G. Kelley points out in *Yo' Mama's Disfunktional!* regarding the tradition of U.S. social science condemning African Americans. Perhaps the transnational version is more difficult to see?

5. The longer discussion is Seigel, "Beyond Compare." For readers of this book, this footnote highlights the errors courted by those who succumb to the seductions of comparing race in Brazil and the United States or African Americans and Afro-Brazilians. Most important, as briefly explained in the text preceding this note, comparison imagines its objects to have a hermetic integrity, historical and contemporary. It prohibits understanding of a conjoined process of construction, insinuating a clunky, essentialist conceptualization of race even into the analysis of scholars who embrace the tenets of social construction. If identity is formed in relation, comparison can't tell us much about it.

Next, it is almost impossible to prevent comparisons from resolving into value judgments of better or worse. The comparison of race in the United States and Brazil therefore recycles a familiar set of national characteristics. In only slightly modified terms it lauds pro-active, practical, progressive North Americans and chides South American laggards, providing yet another opportunity to reprise U.S. national superiority. Under its breath this comparison whispers a twisted congratulation to North American whites for the brutally explicit form of their racism. Much black nationalism is less nationalist than this national comparison, not in a strict definitional sense, but in that black nationalists often express a transnational sensibility and advance an anti-imperialist politics; see Singh, *Black Is a Country*; Stephens, "Black Transnationalism and the Politics of National Identity"; Stephens, *Black Empire*; Von Eschen, *Race against Empire*. This comparison runs counter in spirit to diasporic frameworks, which insist on connection. It indulges in the "denial of coevalness," the notion that some people are behind in evolutionary status, standing still in the time stream that has swept others along, in quintessential refusal of transnational connection, as set out in Fabian, *Time and the Other*.

Although many observers have taken issue with these implications when they emerge from comparative study, rarely do they object to the comparison as form. Most seem to think one should simply do the comparison better. One oft-voiced critique of comparisons of race in Brazil and the United States points out that their core harbors a U.S. black-white model as unacknowledged norm. This is undeniable. Unfortunately, the solution chosen is generally no more imaginative than to meet nationalism with nationalism: critics of U.S. supremacy defend "their" Brazil, articulating a "neo" version of the myth of racial democracy, denying the structuring force racism continues to wield in Brazilian (as in North American) society: Fry, "O que a Cinderela negra tem a dizer sobre a 'política racial' no Brasil"; see also Fry, "Politics, Nationality, and the Meanings of 'Race' in Brazil"; Fry, "Why Brazil Is Different"; see also Sansone, *From Africa to Afro*; Sansone, *Blackness without Ethnicity*; Segato, "The Color-Blind Subject of Myth." This is also the line of reasoning in Bourdieu and Wacquant, "Sur les ruses de la raison impérialiste," a wonderful refutation of which is French, "The Missteps of Anti-Imperialist Reason." Other highly useful responses include Bairros, "*Orfeu e poder*"; and while not responding directly to these provocations, Silva, "Facts of Blackness"; Silva, "Revisiting Racial Democracy"; Butler, *Freedoms Given, Freedoms Won*; and Burdick, *Blessed Anastácia*.

One way out of this dilemma is to refuse to compare the United States to Brazil or African Americans to Afro-Brazilians. Comparison distracts researchers from the pursuit of formative connections between the objects in question. It conceals the heterogeneity within the units compared, the salience of large-scale phenomena in small-scale environments, and the ways people grasp and mobilize global currents, including those currents that take form and walk down the streets of São Paulo.

6. In *Imagined Communities*, Benedict Anderson argues that newspapers offer the reflection and direction that forge an imagined community by refracting the boundaries and concerns of their writers and readers. The newspapers in question here trace the discursive formation of several national imagined communities, including black, North American, and Brazilian, sometimes in tension, sometimes juxtaposed.

7. Vogel, *The Black Press*; Detweiler, *The Negro Press in the United States*; Penn, *The Afro-American Press and Its Editors*; Wolseley, *The Black Press, U.S.A.*; Pride and Wilson, *A History of the Black Press*; Jordan, *Black Newspapers and America's War for Democracy, 1914–1920*. Kornweibel, "'The Most Dangerous of All Negro Journals,'" 157, estimates that the readership of the African American newspaper of greatest circulation, the *Chicago Defender*, approximated one million per week by the end of the First World War.

8. I disagree with historians who characterize the press as elite and who therefore dismiss its sense of community and political commitment as atypical—for example, Ferrara, "Imprensa negra paulista"; Ferrara, "A imprensa negra paulista (1915–1963): Estudo monográfico"; Bastide, "A imprensa negra do Estado de São Paulo"; J. Silva, "Negros em São Paulo," 87; Brookshaw, "Quatro poetas negros brasileiros"; Rolnik,

"São Paulo, início da industrialização"; or Rolnik, "Territórios negros nas cidades brasileiras." In the case of the United States, recent scholarship has allowed historians to "dispense with narrow readings that claim the [African American] press focused only on slavery or elite African Americans' concerns" (Vogel, *The Black Press*, 1). Similar attention is needed in Brazil. Certainly class distinctions were critical to writers' and readers' self-presentations, but they stood in complex relations to purchasing power and economic stability. Class divisions among Afro-Brazilians in São Paulo were important but porous, with crossings possible within an individual's lifetime and complicated by other factors, such as gender and geography. Other social categories could confuse themselves with class, such as skin color shade, a factor in Brazilian social positioning much noted by observers of race in Brazil, the journalists included. Less-noted categories were just as malleable; the journalists, overwhelmingly young men, expressed a sense of privilege and potential tied as much to age and gender as to wealth, in my view. Gender in particular was a critical facet of their self-representations, as we will shortly see. The question of whether there was anything that could be called a black Brazilian "middle class" is itself a subject of debate, for Afro-Brazilians have been unable to pass financial stability gained in one lifetime on to the next generation. Hasenbalg, "Anotações sobre a classe média negra no Rio de Janeiro"; see also Hasenbalg, *Discriminação e desigualdades raciais no Brasil*; Andrews, *Blacks and Whites in São Paulo, Brazil, 1888–1988*, ch. 5; see also Figueiredo, *Novas elites de cor*. These newspapers made nobody's fortune, as is clear from those few journalists whose paid occupations emerge in the papers' pages: *Getulino* poet Cumba Junior was a postal worker (Cumba Junior, "Holocaustos," *Getulino*, May 13, 1926, 1); orator Vicente Ferreira was homeless, often sleeping under a bridge; and José Correia Leite "hadn't even completed grade school" when Jayme de Aguiar asked him to collaborate in founding *Clarim*. He learned to write in part through his work on the paper, a situation his status as "co-editor" might not betray (J. Leite, "Um capítulo de nossas lutas sociais"; reproduced in J. Leite and Cuti, — *E disse o velho militante José Correia Leite*, 254–358; quote on 256). The mischaracterizations of the São Paulo black press as elite has to do, I think, with insufficient source-criticism leveled at the claims the journalists made about themselves. "Elite" was a term the journalists fought to include in their self-representations, to bolster claims of authority and give more weight to the frequent exhortations they addressed to their readers, and to insist to whiter readers that Afro-Brazilians were capable of achievement and discernment. Moreover, the press included voices other than those of editors and named contributors, for it reprinted funeral and graveside orations, public lectures, and other instances of popular public speech. Federação dos Homens de Côr president Jayme Batista de Camargo spoke at Rui Barbosa's funeral, for example; *O Paiz*, March 4, 1923; see also "Raymunda," *Progresso*, June 23, 1929, 1. Vicente Ferreira spoke frequently in cemeteries, mostly at the tombstones of beloved abolitionists; see Frederico Baptista de Souza, "A Jacintha," *Clarim*, July 14, 1929, 1. See also the report of a participant at the São Paulo School of Law conference in "Dr. Baptista Pereira," *Clarim*, July 1, 1928, 1. Finally, historians can read between the lines to find opinions the journalists refused to endorse. The editors' tireless exhortations betray the imprint of dissenters whose views didn't make it onto these printed pages. Their positions, registered in *capoeiragem* (i.e., engaging in the game-fight-dance form *capoeira*) vagrancy, or popular violence, for example, read in tandem with the press's emphases and silences, can help suggest the depth and diversity of the newspapers' producers, their contexts, and their targets. See Carvalho, *Os bestializados*; Cunha, *Intenção e gesto*; Soares, *A negregada instituição*; Pires, "Capoeira no jogo das cores"; Pires, *Movimentos da cultura afro-brasileira*; Pires, *Bimba, Pastinha e Besouro de Mangangá*; F. Gomes, *Histórias de quilombolas*.

9. For the paper's name changes, see note 1 of chapter 3.

10. *A Voz da Raça, Tribuna Negra, O Estimulo, A Raça, A Alvorada*, and *A Redentora* are some of these; they mostly fall outside the chronological parameters of this book's discussion.

11. Bastide, "A imprensa negra do Estado de São Paulo"; Ferrara, "Imprensa negra paulista"; Ferrara, "A imprensa negra paulista (1915–1963)" (doctoral dissertation); Ferrara, "A imprensa negra paulista (1915–1963): Estudo monográfico"; Andrews, *Blacks and Whites in São Paulo, Brazil, 1888–1988*; J. Silva, "Negros em São Paulo"; Pires, "As 'Associações dos Homens de Cor'"; J. Leite, "Um capítulo de nossas lutas sociais." Two collections of these newspapers are preserved on microfilm, one compiled by Michael Mitchell and archived at Princeton University, among other places, and the other by the University of São Paulo (USP) and available at USP, the Biblioteca Nacional in Rio de Janeiro, and other locations. There were a few other papers before and after these dates and outside São Paulo. Several are discussed in Bastide, "A imprensa negra do Estado de São Paulo," 131–132, such as *A Voz da Raça*, the organ of the Frente Negra Brasileira; its years of publication fall outside the time period considered here. Scholars who make excellent use of the São Paulo black press include J. Silva, "Negros em São Paulo"; Andrews, *Blacks and Whites in São Paulo, Brazil, 1888–1988*; K. Butler, *Freedoms Given, Freedoms Won*.

12. Ferrara, "A imprensa negra paulista (1915–1963): Estudo monográfico," 55. For the U.S. black press, researchers have calculated a readership of 17.1 people to each copy printed—four times as many as read each published exemplar of a mainstream newspaper. Young, "Reader Attitudes toward the Negro Press." Another clue to numbers is reader response: *Getulino*'s 1923 beauty contests received 400–800 weekly votes, contest organizers reported on August 12, 1923; August 26, 1923; and September 9, 1923, 3.

13. "Representantes," *Clarim*, July 1, 1928, 1.

14. "Outr'ora," *Clarim*, May 13, 1926, 7, introducing Dr. Cyro Costa's poem, "Pae João," recited by its author in Rio at an event organized by the Federation of Colored Men; "Rectificação," *A Liberdade*, May 9, 1920, 2; "Os pretos em São Paulo," *O Kosmos*, October 19, 1924, 1 (a far from exhaustive list). As to the Federação's publication, I have found no sign of a surviving copy.

15. "A nossa revista," *Clarim*, May 3, 1928, 1, notes congratulations on its May 13, 1928, issue received from *O Globo* and *A Notícia* in Rio and *O Combate, Diario Nacional, Jornal do Commercio*, and *A Gazeta* from São Paulo.

16. Quotes from Bastide, "A imprensa negra do Estado de São Paulo," 130; Hasenbalg and Silva, "Notes on Racial and Political Inequality in Brazil," 163; and Ferrara, "Imprensa negra paulista"; see also Ferrara, "A imprensa negra paulista (1915–1963): Estudo monográfico"; Ferrara, "A imprensa negra paulista (1915–1963)" (doctoral dissertation); and J. Leite and Cuti, *—E disse o velho militante José Correia Leite*.

17. J. Leite and Cuti, *—E disse o velho militante José Correia Leite*, 78–80. Remembering this exchange in the 1980s, when the Movimento Negro (Black Movement) was anxious to prove its "authentic" national character, *Clarim* editor José Correia Leite insisted that Afro-Brazilians repudiated Garvey, judging his ideas inappropriate for their context. *Clarim*'s record of publication in this regard suggests otherwise: "Os negros não precisam de protectores brancos: Do 'Negro World' de Nova York," *Clarim*, November 24, 1929, 2; items from the *Negro World and Defender* in *Clarim*, January 25, 1930, 4; on Garvey in *Clarim*, May 13, 1930; letter from Garvey and transcript from the Washington *Tribune* on imperialism and lynchings in *Clarim*, September 28, 1930, 4; and Frank St. Claire, "Sidelights on Brazil Racial Conditions," *Negro World*, January 13, 1923; cited in Hellwig, *African-American Reflections on Brazil's Racial Paradise*, 51–54. Kim Butler also reports that *Negro World* circulated in Porto Velho, a town in the Amazon basin now the capital of the state of Rondônia. K. Butler, personal communication, May 27, 2003. How this global current reached so deeply into Brazil's interior is instructive: Porto Velho grew up in the first years of the twentieth century around the construction of the doomed Madeira–Marmoré railroad by a workforce that was significantly Caribbean. These laborers may have been the source of the "foreign blacks" Leite notes in São Paulo, discussed below.

18. Detweiler, *The Negro Press in the United States*; Kornweibel, "'The Most Dangerous of All Negro Journals.'" Early *Defender* articles on Brazil include "Mme. Patti Brown Royally Received at Bahai [*sic*], Brazil," *Chicago Defender*, January 15, 1916, 1; "Brazil Wants Educated Black Men," "Brazil's Black President," and "Brazil Ideal Country for Black Man," all in *Chicago Defender*, January 22, 1916, 1. Robert Abbott's 1923 visit and subsequent reporting are detailed below.

19. "The *Chicago Defender*: World's Greatest Weekly," *Clarim*, November 24, 1929, 1; see also the favorable review of James Weldon Johnson's novel in "A questão das raças nos Estados Unidos," *Clarim*, February 3, 1929, 4. See also "Pr." [= proprietario, Argentino Wanderley?], "A formula igualitaria para resolver a questão racial americana," *Progresso*, Febuary 24, 1929 (mentions the *Defender*); Lino Guedes, "Illusão democratica norte-americana," *Progresso*, July 28, 1929 (a report on the invitation of a Chicago senator's wife to tea at the White House; it bears the mark of the *Defender*'s interpretations). On the exchange with *A Notícia*, see chapter 6.

20. Edwards, *The Practice of Diaspora*, 5.

21. Hellwig, *African-American Reflections on Brazil's Racial Paradise*; Guimarães, "Brasil–Estados Unidos"; Kelley, "'But a Local Phase of a World Problem'"; Singh, *Black Is a Country*; Stephens, "Black Transnationalism and the Politics of National Identity"; Stephens, *Black Empire*.

22. Sevcenko, *Orfeu extático na metrópole*; Padilha, *A cidade como espetáculo*; Morse, *From Community to Metropolis*; Dean, *The Industrialization of São Paulo*; Weinstein, *For*

Social Peace in Brazil; Rolnik, "São Paulo, início da industrialização"; J. Silva, "Negros em São Paulo"; Font, "City and Countryside in the Onset of Brazilian Industrialization," 32. See also the bibliography in Passos, *Evolução urbana da cidade de São Paulo*.

23. There seem to have been some ten or twenty of these organizations in existence at any given point in the twenties, sponsoring events, meetings, lectures, outings, picnics, and dances and launching variously fated serial publications. *Clarim*, January 15, 1927, 1, complimented the societies Auri-Verde; Brinco de Princezas; Campos Elyseos; Elite da Liberdade; 15 de Novembro; 28 de Setembro; 6 de Maio; 13 de Maio; Barão do Rio Branco; Eden Juvenil; Paulistano; Kosmos; Cravos Vermelhos; Princeza do Norte; União Miliar; União da Mocidade; Barra Funda; and two associations, the Centro Civico dos Palmares and C. H. José do Patrocinio. Francisco Lucrécio discusses the links between the press and the societies in Ferrara, "Imprensa negra paulista," 199.

24. José Correia Leite acknowledged the European immigrant groups as models in several places, including the pages of *Clarim* on December 7, 1924, and June 20, 1926. For a discussion of contemporaneous expressions of African associational traditions in urban Brazil, see F. Gomes, "No meio das aguas turvas"; Trochim, "The Brazilian Black Guard"; and Cruz, "Virando o jogo."

25. Historians have underemphasized the papers' ongoing connections to the recreational societies and their resulting political valence, seeing their projects as genuinely "political" only after 1930. Bastide and Fernandes, *Brancos e negros em São Paulo*, ch. 5, 277–284; Ferrara, "Imprensa negra paulista"; Pinto, *O negro no Rio de Janeiro*, esp. part 2, "Movimentos sociais." I think this conclusion requires revision. As the textual expression of the societies, the press shared their popular qualities, and as the structural bases of the press, the societies shared the papers' political functions. The societies held press fund-raisers and lent their premises for other press activities, while the press lavished many column inches on the societies' activities. Journalists sometimes regretted that members danced too much and played politics too little, but they also revealed that they considered the societies sites of organizing nonetheless. Even a meeting in a dancing club, claimed one, "becomes instructive for the *negro* himself" (Dionisio Barbosa, "A sociedade boa e a corrompida, do negro em S. Paulo," *Evolução*, May 13, 1933, 6). Perhaps, another hoped, the societies would provide the structural basis for a political party "composed exclusively of colored men [*homens de cor*]" ("A esmola," *Clarim*, November 15, 1925, 1. This call is noteworthy in that it dates from 1925; the bulk of calls for such a body were sounded at the decade's end). Consider the radical denunciation of racism against black job seekers in "Os pretos em São Paulo," *O Kosmos*, October 19, 1924, 1, at a moment when the masthead still credited the editorship of the paper to the directors of the "dramatic and recreational association 'Kosmos.'"

26. *Clarim*, January 6, 1924, 1 (this article also called São Paulo "the Brazilian New York"); Frederico B. de Souza, "Observando," *O Kosmos*, May 18, 1924; with bewilderment, the anonymous author of "Preconceito de côr," *Progresso*, January 13, 1929, wondered at the Paulista identity of some Brazilians exhibiting a very uncharacteristic sentiment (racism). See also the many reminders that Afro-Brazilians belonged

in São Paulo (and Brazil) far more than the immigrant newcomers who were taking their jobs, and the Paulista praise and pride in "A Guardia Civil e os pretos," *Progresso*, August 19, 1928, 2.

27. On São Paulo, see Sevcenko, *Orféu extático na metrópole*; on citizenship and cities, Carvalho reminds us: "Cities have traditionally been the classic site of the development of citizenship. The citizen was, even etymologically, the urban resident"; *Os bestializados*, 12. Statements of Paulista identity were often explicitly offered as entry points into national identity—for example, "Observando," *O Kosmos*, May 18, 1924, 1, celebrated the bravery of Paulista soldiers and urged *homens de côr* born in "this State [to] take an active part in this civilization." "A Guardia Civil e os pretos," 2, proclaims Paulista and Brazilian identity in the same breath, but Paulista first ("We who have the pride of being Paulistas and Brazilians will never forget this deed"). Even papers from smaller São Paulo cities (e.g., *O Patrocinio* and *Getulino*) used their urban identities to proclaim their national patriotism. See, for example, Gervasio de Moraes, "Á mocidade!" *Getulino*, August 5, 1923: "Campinas, sacred berth of the immortal Carlos Gomes, I and all your sons are proud to be Brazilians."

28. That is, *Progresso* and *Evolução*; see also "Patacoadas," and Aguiar, "Nossos parabens!" both in *Clarim*, August 22, 1926, 1; J. Leite, "Quem somos," *Clarim*, November 14, 1926, 3; "O grito chã," *Progresso*, September 7, 1928, 1–2; "Apresentando . . . ," *Evolução*, May 13, 1933, 3 (author's ellipses).

29. Mitchell, "Miguel Reale and the Impact of Conservative Modernization on Brazilian Race Relations"; Skidmore, *Black into White*; Borges, "'Puffy, Ugly, Slothful and Inert'"; Woodard, "Marketing Modernity."

30. See, for example, *Clarim*'s regular illustrations of its May 13 issues: "Salve 13 de maio" [illustration], *Clarim*, May 13, 1926, back cover; *Clarim*, May 13, 1927, back cover; *Clarim*, May 13, 1928, back cover; see also *O Patrocinio*, September 28, 1929.

31. Alberto Orlando, "Trecho de um capitulo do opusculo de proxima publicação, 'O negro na evolução brasileira,'" *Clarim*, January 15, 1927, 3–4; J. Leite, "O negro para o negro," *Clarim*, July 1, 1928, 1.

32. *Progresso*, August 19, 1928.

33. *Clarim* featured photographs in this style throughout; see October 12, 1924; January 25, 1925; January 24, 1926; March 21, 1926; July 24, 1926; January 15, 1927; January 6, 1929; also "Frente Negra Brasileira," *Evolução*, May 13, 1933, 5, and other head shots in this issue of *Evolução*, passim.

34. On portraiture, a highly relevant analysis is Painter, "Sojourner Truth's Knowing and Becoming Known."

35. Gervasio de Moraes, "A mocidade!" *Getulino*, August 5, 1923; "13 de maio," *Clarim*, May 13, 1930, 2; João Eugenio da Costa, "O despertar do gigante," *Clarim*, April 25, 1926.

36. "The *negro* built agricultural Brazil with his hands"; T. Camargo, "Echos do Projecto F. Reis," *Elite*, January 20, 1924, 1; "to [slaves] and all their descendants, Brazil owes its foundations"; "A redempção de nossa raça," *Clarim*, May 13, 1924, 1; "The *negro* here is the hero of work, element of great plasticity and adaptability which

society neither ignores nor disdains"; Dr. Theodoro Sampaio, quoted in (epigraph to) J. Leite, "Capacidade dos incapazes," *Clarim*, August 22, 1926, 2; "We owe to the manual labor of slaves from Africa a notable part of the economic wealth we enjoy"; *A Noite*, April 13, 1926, in "Monumento á Mãe Preta," *A Notícia*, April 24, 1926, 3; see also untitled article, *Clarim*, May 13, 1928, 1; "O Dia da Mãe Preta," *Clarim*, September 28, 1928, 1; Jayme de Aguiar, "O negro no Brasil," *Clarim*, June 3, 1928, 1; Mario Beni, "A contribução do preto na formação do poderio economio paulista," *Evolução*, May 13, 1933, 4; "O negro como factor do nosso progresso," *Evolução*, May 13, 1933, 17; *A Patria*, April 8, 1926, in "Publicações de ultima hora: Glorificando a raça negra; A idéa de um monumento á Mãe Preta suggerido pelos nossos collegas de '*A Notícia*,'" *A Notícia*, April 9, 1926, 4; *A Folha*, April 6, 1926, in "Tribuna publica," *A Notícia*, April 7, 1926, 3. Writing to convince white observers as much as to exhort Afro-Brazilians, the journalists emphasized the continued presence of hard-working, productive black Brazilians. Even musicians "in orchestras and jazz bands" in Paris, *Clarim* ventured, were performing "a veritable Herculean musical labor" ("Tumultuosa assembléa de negros," *Clarim*, October 21, 1928, 3).

37. *Progresso*'s issue of January 31, 1929, treated Africa with unusual depth; Pan-Americanist sentiment included Horacio de Cunha, "Sentimentalismo dos pretos," *O Clarim*, March 21, 1926, 4: "We Black South Americans" (Nós, os pretos da America do Sul); and a *Getulino* writer articulated a first-person plural as "we, colored Latins" [*latinos de côr*] in "O monumento á Mãe Preta e o presidente eleito da Republica," *Getulino*, May 13, 1926, 1.

38. "Morreu a popular organisadora de praticas africanas," *Progresso*, December 16, 1928, 2; "Em pleno seculo xx quatro milhões de *Escravos*, victimas de deshumanas crueldades," *Progresso*, March 24, 1929; Pe. Dubois, "Todos filhos do mesmo Deus," also in *Progresso* March 24, 1929; "Bushmen," *Progresso*, April 28, 1929; "A Africa berço da humanidade, affirme um illustre geologo," *Progresso*, August 31, 1929, 2; Boocker, "Negro!" *Clarim*, September 27, 1925, 3; "Voyage au Brésil," *Progresso*, January 13, 1929, 3. This edition of *Progresso* also reported some quite straightforward pieces on Africa—for example, "Na Africa: As linguas que ahi se falam" (p. 3).

39. Cruz, "Virando o jogo"; R. Moura, *Tia Ciata e a Pequena África no Rio de Janeiro*; Sevcenko, *Orféu extático na metrópole*; Chalhoub, *Trabalho, lar e botequim*; Chalhoub, *Cidade febril*; Chalhoub, "Medo branco de almas negras"; K. Butler, *Freedoms Given, Freedoms Won*.

40. To give a single example of a frequent phenomenon, "Os pretos em São Paulo," *O Kosmos*, October 19, 1924, 1, reports racism against *homens pretos*, urges the formation of an association of *homens de côr*; defends *nossa heroica raça* and identifies as *gente negra* all on a single page. Revealing that *negro* and *preto* could at times be interchangeable, rather than one a skin color designation and the other an umbrella term, a report on two boxers called one "the *negro* Tompson" and the other "the *preto* Brown." *Progresso*, November 15, 1928. Showing that color was not necessarily what distinguished *negro* and *preto*, an *Evolução* article in 1933 called African Americans "*negros* far darker black than *negros* from São Paulo!" *Evolução*, May 13, 1933.

41. "É NEGRO toda gente de côr, preto, mulato, moreno, etc., descendente do Africano e do Indigena"; in "Palavras aos paes negros," *Clarim*, May 13, 1927, 3. A similar intent lies behind the editors' naming the Black Mother the "Mãe Negra" instead of the more widely used "Mãe Preta," as chapter 6 will detail. For wonderfully subtle and sophisticated analysis of the shifting nature of words for race in the nineteenth century, including in the 1830s Afro-Brazilian press, see Castro, *Das cores do silêncio*; I. Lima, *Cores, marcas e falas*; Pires, "Movimentos da cultura afro-brasileira."

42. Luiz Barbosa, "O trabalho," *Clarim*, June 20, 1926, 3; *Clarim*, November 14, 1926; also see celebrations of U.S. "civilization" and "ingenuity" in articles such as "O meio centenario da lampada electrica: Edison, o seu inventor, terá uma participação interessantissima," *O Patrocinio*, September 28, 1929, 3. When these angry compliments were ironic, the irony lay in the contrast with the brutality of North American racism and did not cast doubt on the accuracy of the descriptions of the United States as modern. See also M. Lima, *The Evolution of Brazil Compared with That of Spanish and Anglo-Saxon America*, 39–40. I. Lima, *Cores, marcas e falas*, also notes much discussion of the United States in the pages of the 1830s Afro-Brazilian press.

43. Paulo Barreto, "O problema das raças nos Estados Unidos," *Patria*, October 2, 1921; *A Notícia*, passim throughout the 1920s; E. Moraes, *Brancos e negros nos Estados Unidos e no Brasil*; Lobo, *Brasilianos e Yankees*; Lobo, *Cousas americanas e brasileiras*; Lobato, *America*; Freyre, *Tempo de aprendiz*; A. Lima, *A realidade americana*; Athayde, "Eles e nós"; "Vida social," *O Paiz*, March 13, 1926, 6; "A resistencia dos negros," *Correio da Manhã*, July 18, 1925, 2; "Duas Biblias," *Correio da Manhã*, July 22, 1925, 2; "Hoover," *Crítica*, December 21, 1928, 3; "O chá presidencial," *Correio da Manhã*, July 28, 1929, 2; *Vida Policial* (December 1926), cover; cited in Cunha, *Intenção e gesto*, 199. See also T. Gomes, "Problemas no paraíso," 313. The theater, too, distributed this information: a 1930 revue by an author who had just returned from the United States, titled to refer to a recent U.S. movie, had an actor sing a song about the United States—in blackface. Cabral, *No tempo de Ari Barroso*, 104. Black press articles, which also covered U.S. racism extensively, are cited below.

44. "Negros retintos: No parlamento francês; Um advogado da raça exalta a liberalidade na grande Republica," *Getulino*, June 8, 1924, 1; E. Petrus, "O negro e o esporte," *Evolução*, May 13, 1933, 8.

45. Response to Paul Morand's *Rien que la terre* (untitled article), *Progresso*, June 23, 1929, 3.

46. Julio Dantas, "Salomes negras," *Progresso*, January 13, 1929, 6.

47. Oliveira, "A verdade," *O Alfinete*, October 12, 1918. This appears not to have been a suggestion of greater *mixture* in the United States; characterizing African Americans as *mestiço* and *preto* in the same breath, Oliveira suggested a relationship of synonyms varied mainly for poetic effect.

48. Petrus, "O negro e o esporte"; see also "A côr morena é cor de ouro," *Progresso*, January 13, 1929, 3.

49. "Associação Nacional para o Adiantamento da Raça Negra," *Progresso*, August 31, 1929, 4 ("não se coadunam com o espirito dos tempos modernos"); "Lynchamento:

É uma aberração da civilisação americana," *Progresso*, September 26, 1929, 6. An excellent argument regarding the "modernity" of racism is Cell, *The Highest State of White Supremacy*.

50. Fonseca Junior, "Um depoimento agradavel," *O Alfinete*, January 4, 1919, 2; Moysés Cintra, "Á mocidade paulistana," *Clarim*, December 7, 1924.

51. In other parts of the Americas, Afro-descended citizens made similar hortatory use of discourses of racial democracy (including the rhetoric of fraternal citizenship); see Fuente, "Myths of Racial Democracy," and Bronfman, *Measures of Equality*.

52. A. Oliveira, "Para os nossos leitores," *O Alfinete*, September 22, 1918.

53. A. Oliveira, "Aos nossos leitores," *O Alfinete*, September 3, 1918.

54. "Grave erro!" *O Bandeirante*, September 1918; author's ellipses. The ties some of these authors would develop to right-wing nationalisms in the 1930s (between Arlindo Veiga dos Santos, for example, and Integralism) are here eerily presaged in the resonance between "Brasil acima de tudo" (which I have translated as "Brazil first and foremost, above all") and "Deutschland Uber Alles." Dos Santos's corporativist support of Vargas led Leite to call him fascist, an association J. Silva, "Negros em São Paulo," 91, calls "logical."

55. Joaquim Cambará, "Deputado de cor," *O Bandeirante*, August 1918, 2 (this piece also cited in J. Leite, "Um capítulo de nossas lutas sociais," 255); Gastão Rodriguez de Silva, "Os agentes de policia em acção," *O Bandeirante*, April 1919, 2.

56. Matuto, "Vagando," *A Liberdade*, May 9, 1920; Benedicto Florencio, "Carta sem cor," *Alfinete*, November 1921, 2; "Os pretos e o jardim publico," *Clarim*, January 15, 1927, 3; "Os barqueiros do Volga," *Clarim*, July 17, 1927, 3; "A cor e a Guarda Civil," *Clarim*, July 14, 1929, 1, citing *Diario Nacional*, June 12, 1929; G. Moraes, "Carta aberta," *Patrocinio*, April 22, 1928, 1; J. Leite, "Mais um grito de dôr da raça desgraçada: Um orphanato que nào acceita orphãos negros," *Clarim*, October 21, 1928, 2; "Edificante!" *Progresso*, January 31, 1929, 5; Pe. Dubois, "Todos filhos do mesmo Deus," *Progresso*, March 24, 1929, 1 (on this nursing school controversy, see also *Getulino*, May 31, 1926, 3; and Antonio, "Black," *A Notícia*, March 1, 1925, 1); *Progresso*, April 28, 1929, 4; "Prefere-se branca," *Progresso*, September 26, 1929, 5; Jaime de Aguiar, "Ascenção do negro," *O Patrocinio*, September 28, 1929, 1.

57. Here is a count, incomplete and unsystematic, of São Paulo black press articles dealing with racism in Brazil, either denouncing or denying it, out of the newspapers I read: 1918: 4; 1919: 1; 1920: 1; 1921: 1; 1922: 0; 1923: 2; 1924: 4; 1925: 5; 1926: 9; 1927: 2; 1928: 13; 1929: 17; 1930: 4; the press then subsides until the May 13, 1933, issue of *Evolução*. Recall that the newspapers themselves rise and fall in similar peaks and valleys (thus the dip in 1927, for example).

58. Abbott met, among others, Rio's chief of police (unnamed); José do Patrocinio Filho; Juliana Moreira, a Bahian doctor; Eloy de Souza, a senator; Tito Carlos, a writer/journalist about to take a degree in medicine from the National University of Rio de Janeiro; the jurist Evaristo de Moraes; and Olympio de Castro, priest and scholar. "Sweet Liberty Wields Scepter Down in Brazil: Mr. Abbott Find Brazilians 'Sublime'; Sees the Spirit of Equality; Signally Honored," *Chicago Defender*, April 14, 1923, 2; "South America Gets Prejudice from the South: Mr. Abbott Tells Appomattox

Club Members Interesting Stories of His Travels," *Chicago Defender*, June 2, 1923, 5; Abbott, "My Trip through South America: Article 2—Personal Motives," *Chicago Defender*, August 11, 1923, 13–14; Abbott, "My Trip through South America: Article 3—São Paulo," *Chicago Defender*, August 18, 1923, 13–14; Abbott, "My Trip through South America: Article 4—Back in Rio de Janeiro," *Chicago Defender*, August 25, 1923, 13–14; Abbott, "My Trip through South America: Article 4 (Continued)—Rio de Janeiro," *Chicago Defender*, September 8, 1923, 13–14.

59. Abbott, "My Trip through South America: Article 3—São Paulo." On regional differences for Afro-Brazilians in São Paulo and Rio de Janeiro, see Fernandes, *A integração do negro na sociedade de classes* (translated as *The Negro in Brazilian Society*); C. Moura, *Sociologia do negro brasileiro*; Bastide, "The Development of Race Relations in Brazil"; Andrews, *Blacks and Whites in São Paulo, Brazil, 1888–1988*; Hanchard, *Orpheus and Power*, 29.

60. Abbott's *Defender* series, passim; quote from Ottley, *The Lonely Warrior*, 230–231. On African Americans' inability or unwillingness to see prejudice in Brazil, and Abbott's in particular, see Guimarães, "Brasil–Estados Unidos," 143.

61. Ottley, *The Lonely Warrior*, 240; see also 288.

62. "Brazilians Are Told Meaning of Liberty Statue: Symbol of Liberty in Books Only; Millions Fight for Freedom and Get Oppression," *Chicago Defender*, April 28, 1923, 3; "Uma carta do director de 'The Chicago Defender,'" *A Notícia*, April 23, 1926, 1; "Monumento á M P: A grande repercussão, na America do Norte, da iniciativa de 'A Notícia,'" *A Notícia*, June 18, 1926.

63. José do Patrocinio Filho, "Preto e branco," *A Patria*, March 14, 1923, 1; also reprinted in Abilio Rodrigues, "Preto e branco," *O Kosmos*, April 18, 1923.

64. "Cartas d'um negro," *Getulino*, October 21, 1923.

65. Luz, *A Amazônia para os negros americanos*; Hellwig, *African-American Reflections on Brazil's Racial Paradise*; unknown author to Booker T. Washington, November 28, 1906; enclosed in Booker T. Washington to S. L. Williams, December 3, 1906; Booker T. Washington Papers, Vol. 9: 1906–8, 148–49, available at http://www .historycooperative.org/btw/Vo1.9/html/149.html (accessed June 21, 2008). The suggestion in this letter is more of a threat than a collaboration. See also L. Hill, "Confederate Exiles to Brazil"; L. Hill, *The Confederate Exodus to Latin America*; C. Dawsey and Dawsey, *The Confederados*; Gussi, *Os norte-americanos (confederados) do Brasil*.

66. D. Leite, *O caráter nacional brasileiro*, 219, citing Rodrigues, *Os africanos no Brasil*.

67. Rodrigues, *Os africanos no Brasil*, 9. There is a possibility that it was up to ten years earlier than this as well.

68. Rodrigues's other work bears these stresses similarly. See Rodrigues, *L'animisme fétichiste des nègres de Bahia*; and with Afranio Peixoto, *As Raças humanas e a responsabilidade penal no Brasil*.

69. Skidmore, *Black into White*; Stepan, *"The Hour of Eugenics."*

70. Congresso Nacional do Brasil, *Annaes da Camera dos Deputados*, 1921, vol. 6 (July 20–30) (Rio de Janeiro: Imprensa Nacional, 1923), 623–35; Reis, *Paiz a organizar*.

71. Adriano de Souza Quartin, "Emigração de negros para o Brasil," instructions to consulates, n.d., ca. 1929, Maço 9691/92, AHI.

72. Senator Andrade Bezerra read the president of the state of Matto Grosso's telegram into the Congressional Record of July 29, 1921. He had read it in the newspapers, he explained, though he did not specify in which one. He also read similar material from a *Correio da Manhã* article from that same day. Bezerra in Congresso Nacional do Brasil, *Annaes da Camera dos Deputados*, 1921, vol. 6, 623 (July 29, 1921).

73. Quartin, "Emigração de negros para o Brasil"; NAACP to Helio Lobo, in Lobo to José Manoel de Azevedo Marques, minister of foreign affairs, April 19, 1922, Maço 9691/92, AHI; Lesser, "Are African-Americans African or American?"; Meade and Pirio, "In Search of the Afro-American 'Eldorado'"; T. Gomes, "Problemas no paraíso"; Hellwig, "A New Frontier in a Racial Paradise"; Hellwig, "Racial Paradise or Run-Around?," 52 and 60n35; Skidmore, *Black into White*. On the restriction of Jewish immigration in the 1930s, see Lesser, *Welcoming the Undesirables*.

74. Others who have made this same point include Mitchell, "Racial Consciousness and the Political Attitudes and Behavior of Blacks in São Paulo, Brazil," 122–123; Graham, "Economics or Culture?"; Graham, "Free African Brazilians and the State in Slavery Times"; J. Dávila, "Expanding Perspectives on Race in Brazil"; A. Marx, "Race-Making and the Nation-State"; and A. Marx, *Making Race and Nation*.

75. Quartin, "Emigração de negros para o Brasil," 2.

76. A. Alves de Fonseca, "Informão," June 11, 1921, Maço 9691/92, 3, AHI. The background to this reaction involves African Americans' opposition to anti-black restrictions at home; on this see Hellwig, "Black Leaders and United States Immigration Policy, 1917–1929."

77. NAACP to Helio Lobo, in Lobo to minister of foreign affairs, April 19, 1922, Maço 9691/92, AHI.

78. Quoted in Representative Henry R. Rathbone (Illinois) to Frank B. Kellogg (secretary of state), May 11, 1928; M519, roll 15: 832.111, NA; see also Quartin, "Emigração de negros para o Brasil."

79. "Effeitos da visita do sr. Abott ao Brasil: Os negros americanos pretendem provocar uma intervenção diplomatica para forçar o governo brasileiro a permitir a sua entrada e fixação em territorios nacionaes," *A Patria*, July 21, 1923, n.p.; Maço 9691/92 (629), AHI.

80. "A immigração dos negros," *O Paiz*, May 11, 1923, n.p.; Maço 9691/92 (629), AHI. See also "Effeitos da visita do sr. Abott ao Brasil" and "Dr. Robert S. Abott," *Jornal do Commercio*, May 11, 1923, n.p.; both Maço 9691/92 (629), AHI.

81. Fonseca, "Informão."

82. "A mais santa e significativa fraternidade" and "importações sociaes da America Irmã" in Gervasio Moraes, "A inquisição moderna," *Clarim*, November 14, 1926, 2. Moraes wrote this article three years after Abbott's departure, interestingly, after *Clarim* had begun the exchange with the *Defender* in which Leite found such reason for pride. It prompts me to wonder what specific reminder of Abbott might have sparked this rant. Perhaps another missive fired off to the ambassador?

83. *Getulino*, August 19, 1923; *"leader"* in English in the original. Nor were African Americans above invoking a similarly comparative nationalism, using supposedly radical European immigrants to demonstrate the superiority of native black labor. A pro-restriction *Defender* contributor, probably during the Depression, argued that U.S. employers should hire "acclimated, sympathetic labor," "neither bolshevistic, socialistic, anarchistic or any other kind of 'istic.'" Cited in Hellwig, "Black Leaders and United States Immigration Policy, 1917–1929," 115.

84. Another count: 1920–23: 0; 1924: 1; 1925: 1; 1926: 7; 1927: 2; 1928: 6; 1929: 5; and then, as before, nothing until *Evolução* in 1933. Also as noted above, the low numbers in 1927 reflect the demise of several papers; others start up in 1928.

85. "Os negros," *Clarim*, July 26, 1925, 4.

86. Ibid.

87. J. Leite, "Quem somos," *Clarim*, November 14, 1926, 3. I have translated "preto" as "Negro" rather than "black" or "negro" to preserve the sense of race pride and radicalism that using "preto" at this moment would have conveyed. It is a good example of a necessarily imperfect translation (readers may also note that in this piece Leite used "negro" and "classe" as synonyms).

88. Gervasio Moraes, "A inquisição moderna," *Clarim*, November 14, 1926, 2.

89. "Hatred" is ascribed to U.S. race relations in D'Alencastro, "Grave erro!," *O Bandeirante*, September 1918, 2; "Cartas d'um negro," *Getulino*, October 21, 1923; "O Ku Klux Klan," *Getulino*, November 23, 1924; Gervasio Moraes, "A inquisição moderna," *Clarim*, November 14, 1926, 2; "A questão de raça," *Auriverde*, April 29, 1928, 3; "Os pretos são sympathicos á Candidatura Smith," *Progresso*, November 15, 1928, 3; "O odio de raça: Problema de funda raizes nos Estados Unidos; Será soluccionado por Hoover?" *Progresso*, January 13, 1929, 5; "Pr. [= proprietario, Argentino Wanderley?]," "A formula igualitaria para resolver a questão racial americana," *Progresso*, February 24, 1929; "Lynchamento: É uma aberração da civilisação americana," *Progresso*, September 26, 1929; "Separando o joio do trigo," *Progresso*, November 24, 1929, 5.

Lynching and/or the KKK are mentioned in the first five of these articles and in the *Progresso* article of September 26, 1929; they are mentioned as well in two articles, both entitled "Ku-Klux-Klan," both *Clarim*, December 2, 1928, 2; Benedicto Florencio, "Os pretos em São Paulo," *O Kosmos*, October 19, 1924; "A raça branca posta em cheque pela raça negra," *Progresso*, September 7, 1928, 3; untitled review of *Rien que la terre*, *Progresso*, June 23, 1929, 3; "Associação Nacional para o Adiantamento da Raça Negra," *Progresso*, August 31, 1929, 4; J. Leite, "O grande problema nacional," *Evolução*, May 13, 1933, 9. See also A. J. Veiga dos Santos, "A acção dos negros brasileiros," *Clarim*, January 15, 1927, 5, which calls the Brazilian situation a question of "social distinctions" (*differentes sociaes*), not racism; and Horacio da Cunha, "Os pretos da America do Norte e os pretos da America do Sul," *Clarim*, February 5, 1928, 1. This list is surely not exhaustive.

90. On the performative, terroristic qualities of lynching, see T. Harris, *Exorcising Blackness*; Klotman, "'Tearing a Hole in History'"; Wiegman, *American Anatomies*; and O. Cox, *Caste, Class, and Race*.

91. For moralistic sermons and cautionary tales for wayward women or admonitions against adopting short hair or overly revealing fashions, see "Então, Alcides, é verdade que você não pretende se casar?" *O Patrocinio*, April 22, 1928, 2 (*O Patrocinio*, for some reason, was particularly sensitive to gender disruption); M. Teixeira de Carvalho, "Destino," *Elite*, February 17, 1924, 2; Mixto, "Falta de senso e de união," *Clarim*, September 27, 1925; see also Moysés Cintra's regular moralistic exhortations on marriage and family, as in "O dever," *Clarim*, February 3, 1924, 2, or "Ideal dos ideaes," *Clarim*, April 6, 1924 (Ferrara claims "Moysés Cintra" was one of Jayme de Aguiar's pseudonyms in *A imprensa negra paulista*, 55); "Observando," *O Kosmos*, November 1922; Gervasio de Moraes, "A mocidade!" *Getulino*, August 5, 1923; Horacio da Cunha, "La garçonne," *Clarim*, November 15, 1925; *O Alfinete*, March 9, 1919; "É por aqui," *Elite*, April 2, 1924, 1; Caio Telha, "Filha," *Getulino*, November 18, 1923, 1; *O Kosmos*, August 1922, 3; J. Leite, "Decadencia," *Clarim*, October 12, 1924; "F. R. J.," "Ruinas," *Clarim*, June 3, 1928, 2; "Apresentando," *Evolução*, May 13, 1933, 3; Abílio Rodrigues, "Chronica social," *O Kosmos*, March 15, 1923; "De ausculta e binoculo," *Getulino*, August 12, 1923, 2; and F. Baptista de Souza, "Charleston," *Clarim*, January 15, 1927, 5.

92. Gender changes were associated with the United States, "fast" morals, and co-education, notes Caulfield, *In Defense of Honor*, 73. Besse, *Restructuring Patriarchy*, 36, agrees that the changes were seen as foreign. The United States seemed the source of feminist electoral politics in part because throughout the 1920s Brazilian suffragists struggled for the gains their North American counterparts had achieved at the beginning of the decade. In April 1928, the first Brazilian women voted in Rio Grande do Norte; *O Patrocinio* reported it in "Os direitos civicos de Eva," *O Patrocinio*, April 22, 1928, reprinted from *Revista da Semana*, n.d. Those who wanted to blame Brazilian feminism on North American imports could look to the connections between the Federação Brasileira pelo Progresso Feminino (Brazilian Federation for Women's Progress) and the U.S. League of Women Voters, discussed in the mainstream press during president-elect Herbert Hoover's visit, just a few months after Rio Grande do Norte's early exercise of female suffrage: "O eleitorado feminino norte-americano," *Diario Nacional*, November 10, 1928, 8. See also "A infinita bondade da mulher brasileira," *A Notícia*, June 6, 1923, 1, on Carrie Chapman Catt and the Brazilian feminists she visited. Besse, *Restructuring Patiarchy*, also discusses Catt.

93. "A immoralidade nos cinemas," *A Notícia*, April 2, 1923, 1.

94. Horacio da Cunha, "O Charleston," *Clarim*, September 26, 1926, 2.

95. "Nacionalista até debaixo d'agua" (I have translated idiomatically); Tuca, "Amor e jazz," *Clarim*, March 21, 1926, 4. Ferrara claims "Tuca" was one of José Correia Leite's pseudonyms (Ferrara, *A imprensa negra paulista*, 55). See also the general preference many Afro-Brazilian journalists expressed for Brazilian forms with evident European roots (the waltz, contradances, the choro, the *violão*, the polka, the mazurka, the quadrilha). F. Baptista de Souza, in "Charleston," *Clarim*, January 15, 1927, 5, expressed his taste for the quadrilha, "the pride of our ancestors," and demanded, "Who talks about *pas de patiné*, Elihu Ruth [Root], Nacionalina etc.? Can we compare these dances to the Charleston? It can only be said that they had their moment; nevertheless we can-

not deny their elegance and delicacy, compared with those of today." See also Julio Dantas, "Salomes negras," *Progresso*, January 13, 1929, 6.

96. Ogren, *The Jazz Revolution*; Dennison, *Scandalize My Name*; Stearns and Stearns, *Jazz Dance*; Foreman, "Jazz and Race Records, 1920–1932."

97. "Ao 'jazz', aos 'a la garçonne', aos arranhacéus, chama-se com effusão e orgulho: Progresso!" "E a moral, senhores?" in Luiz Barbosa, "Alcoolismo," *Auriverde*, April 15, 1928. Barbosa here echoed widely audible criticisms of modernity, such as one in the conservative police journal *Vida Policial* by J. Ferrão, "O namoro nas ruas," *Vida Policial*, November 14, 1925, 2; cited in Caulfield, "Getting into Trouble," 157.

98. Abílio Rodrigues, "Chronica social," *O Kosmos*, March 15, 1923; see also "De ausculta e binoculo," *Getulino*, August 12, 1923, 2; F. Baptista de Souza, "Charleston," *Clarim*, January 15, 1927, 5; and "Romaria Civica," *Clarim*, April 1, 1928, 1.

99. Caulfield notes these expressions of dismissive contempt in *Vida Policial*. In addition to J. Ferrão, "O namoro nas ruas," cited above, she reprints "Elles e ellas," *Vida Policial*, May 3, 1925, 34: "for these days in the [lower class] clubs [*sociedades recreativas*] . . . there are masses of 'little negro girls' [*negrinhas*] covered in silk and jewels." Caulfield, "Getting into Trouble," 156; Caulfield's translation and brackets; and *Vida Policial*, July 24, 1926: "The 'clubs' of the kinky-heads should be proud, for they have imitators . . . in Rio de Janeiro's most elegant society." Caulfield, *In Defense of Honor*, 74; Caulfield's translation and ellipses. Tiago de Melo Gomes notes many similar expressions; see his *Um espelho no palco*. Caulfield explains that post–First World War changes in "fashion, leisure, the labor market, and the communications media" made many observers "perceive their era as one of unprecedented changes in gender norms" in Brazil, Europe, and North America; *In Defense of Honor*, 81; this concern over women in public space is also well explored in T. Gomes, "Massais, mulatas, meretrizes." Nor is this evidence of Afro-Brazilians' greater propensity to cede to conservative public mores; in the United States, African Americans often embraced bourgeois propriety to counter stereotypes of black promiscuity and licentiousness, walking the same class tightropes; see Gaines, *Uplifting the Race*; Giddings, "The Last Taboo"; Carby, "It Just Be's Dat Way Sometime"; and Floyd, *The Power of Black Music*.

100. See José Correia Leite, "Decadencia," *Clarim*, October 12, 1924, 1; Mixto, "Falta de senso e de união," *Clarim*, September 27, 1925, 1, criticizing women who travel "the path of ruin, without contemplating . . . the enormous moral and social prejudice they leave in the breast of the humble name of the black family" [o caminho de devassidão, sem contemplar . . . os enormes prejuizos moraes e sociaes que vão deixando no seio do humilde nome da familia preta]. See also Carby, "It Jus Be's Dat Way Sometime"; Carby, "Policing the Black Woman's Body in an Urban Context"; and Gaines, *Uplifting the Race*.

101. Alongside several love poems by Maria de Lourdes Sousa, *Clarim*, Febuary 3, 1924, printed a generous plea for other women to participate: "Temos o immenso prazer" (We take the greatest pleasure) in presenting her work, it wrote, and "Esperamos que outras procurem emital-a" (We hope that other women will try to imi-

tate her). This alongside news of Leite's daughter's baptism. Female contributors who took up the challenge include Dirce, Dutra Mendes, Maria Rosa, Anna Maria, Maria A. Silva, Evangelina Xavier de Carvalho, and Adalgisa Correa Lobo, though apparently some of these were male editors' pseudonyms; in *Clarim*, January 15, 1927. See also Maria das Dores de Sousa, "Sangue derramado pela crueldade!" *Evolução*, May 13, 1933, 23. Much of the female-bylined work is sentimental and ornamental (an exception is Xavier de Carvalho). On women's participation: *Clarim*, Febuary 3, 1924, thanked five women "que se encarregaram de vender no xv de Novembro" (who took responsibility for selling [*Clarim*] in the xv of November [plaza]); *Evolução*, May 13, 1933, 15, printed a photo of Gabriela de Almeida of Botucatú, "incansavel em pról de todas as iniciativas da raça. Devemos a ella, tambem, varias propagandas" (tireless in support of all the race's initiatives. We owe to her, as well, various ads [printed in the paper]); clearly Gabriela de Almeida was a respected, active businesswoman; "Honra ao merito," *Progresso*, Febuary 24, 1929, 2, honors Stellita Arruda, a.k.a. sra. Manoel Seraphim, three-time president of Campos Elyseos. Roberto Moura discusses women's economic importance in Rio in *Tia Ciata e a Pequena Africa no Rio de Janeiro*; J. Silva in "Negros em São Paulo" portrays Dona Eunice, who led the bloco Lavapés (a carnival group), as a sort of São Paulo equivalent to Tia Ciata.

102. R. Moura, *Tia Ciata e a Pequena Africa no Rio de Janeiro*; Velloso, "As tias baianas tomam conta do pedaço"; Dias, *Power and Everyday Life*; Landes, *The City of Women*; Carneiro, "Mulher negra"; and the issue on Afro-Brazilian women of *Estudos Feministas* 3, no. 2 (1995). Thanks to Denise Ferreira da Silva for guidance on this subject. The downside of portrayals of Afro-Brazilian "matriarchy," a rhetoric of black women's necessary leadership in the family given black men's absence or incompetence, recognizable to readers familiar with the Moynihan Report in the United States, dates to Fernandes, *A integração do negro na sociedade de classes*.

103. Souza, "Não querem trabalhar," *O Kosmos*, November 16, 1924, 2; "Prefere-se branca," *Progresso*, September 26, 1929, 5; *Progresso*, January 13, 1929; and "É por aqui," *Elite*, April 2, 1924, 1.

104. See F. Gomes, "No meio das aguas turvas"; Trochim, "The Brazilian Black Guard"; Q. Taylor, "Frente Negra Brasileira"; K. Butler, *Freedoms Given, Freedoms Won*; Linger, "Preconceito branco, consciencia negra e resistência a discriminação em São Paulo nos anos 30"; J. Silva, "Negros em São Paulo," 91. See also Flávio dos Santos Gomes's biography of Abdias do Nascimento.

105. C. Silva, *Discriminações raciais*; Andrews, *Blacks and Whites in São Paulo, Brazil, 1888–1988*; Adamo, "The Broken Promise."

106. Jayme de Aguiar, "Congregemo-nos (Á mocidade negra de Piracicaba)," *O Patrocinio*, July 7, 1929; "o negro (quer seja negro-preto ou o negro-mulato)" and "Nós, os pretos e os mulatos somos irmãos chegadinhos . . . quer queiramos ou não. Se não nos disser em plena face, será dita logo apoz o nosso primeiro passo, na retirada" in Mathias, "Preto-mulato," *Evolução*, May 13, 1933, 20; see also Arlindo Veiga dos Santos, "O 'divorcio nacional de raça'" ("poesia frentenegrina"), *Evolução*, May 13, 1933, 7.

107. "13 maio," *Clarim*, May 13, 1930. Interestingly, this comparison is to both North and *Central* American "negro" activists.

108. J. Leite, "O grande problema nacional," *Evolução*, May 13, 1933, 9.

109. Horacio da Cunha, "Os pretos da America do Norte e os pretos da America do Sul," *Clarim*, February 5, 1928, 1.

110. Quoting Dr. Saens Pennas, "Uma raça, nossa irmã de cor" in ibid.

111. Ottley, *The Lonely Warrior*, 234.

112. Horacio da Cunha, "Os homens pretos e a instrucção," *Clarim*, December 27, 1925, 3. Agreeing, José Correia Leite claimed the achievements of "our racial brothers [*nossos irmãos de raça*] fill us with enthusiasm" in "E, apoz *A Liberdade*," *Clarim*, August 30, 1925. Further Afro-Brazilian admiration for African American achievement (especially schools) is expressed in "Os pretos em São Paulo," *O Kosmos*, November 16, 1924, 2 (reprints Benedicto Florencio's piece in *Getulino* of September 28, 1924); "Os homens pretos e a instrucção," *Progresso*, June 23, 1928; "Associação Nacional para o Adiantamento da Raça Negra," *Progresso*, August 31, 1929, 4; *Progresso*, March 24, 1929. Booker Washington Theophilo, whose name itself bespeaks his parents' (and perhaps his own) identification and admiration for the North American educator, described the African American milieu in 1925 as "the most advanced sphere of our race [*nossa raça*]" over a series of articles (which, interestingly, suggest that he studied at Williams College): "Negro!" *Clarim*, September 27, 1925, 3; continued in issues for November 15, 1925, and March 21, 1926. In 1923, Abbott recounted his meeting with an Afro-Brazilian minister's son, Booker T. Washington de Castro. Was this the same person, and was he Olympio de Castro's son? If so, it is another point of entry for Abbott into the world of the São Paulo black press and another point of contact between Afro-Brazilian groups in Rio de Janeiro and São Paulo. Abbott, "My Trip through South America: Article 3 São Paulo," *Chicago Defender*, August 18, 1923, 13–14.

113. "Josephina Backer [*sic*], a condessa bailarinha, depois de reclamar no Velho Mundo a attenção para os *Pretos*, veio á America," *Progresso*, April 28, 1929; "Occaso de um astro," *Progresso*, June 23, 1929, 4; "Astro negro," *Progresso*, October 31, 1929; "Uma trinca de . . . *Negros*," *Progresso*, November 24, 1929, 6; "Separando o joio do trigo," *Progresso*, November 24, 1929, 5.

114. Cf. Hellwig, "Racial Paradise or Run-Around?"

115. "Associação Nacional para o Adiantamento da Raça Negra," *Progresso*, August 31, 1929, 4.

Black Mothers, Citizen Sons

1. See McElya, "Monumental Citizenship," and McElya, "Commemorating the Color Line." Many thanks to McElya for pointing me to the U.S. controversy and its significance and for collaboration on McElya and Seigel, "Confusing Relations."

2. For example, there is also a Black Mother monument in Guaratinguetá, Vale do Paraíba, São Paulo. Tiago de Melo Gomes, electronic personal communication, June

30, 2005. It is likely there are others elsewhere as well, given the movement's echoes in other parts of Brazil in the 1920s: "Grandes homenagens serão prestadas, hoje, á Mãe Preta, na Bahia." *Clarim*, September 28, 1929, 4; Yolanda de Camargo, "O dia da Mãe Preta em Botucatú," *Clarim*, October 27, 1929, 3; "Em Piracicaba," *Clarim*, October 27, 1929, 3; and "A Bahia, assistiu no dia 28 de setembro, uma manifestação inedita no Brasil," *Clarim*, November 24, 1929, 2.

3. Though students of "racial democracy" tend to date its emergence to the early 1930s, many 1920s phenomena, including the Mãe Preta movement, already contained the core of the claim. Michael Mitchell called the 1930s the apex of whitening's popularity in his "Miguel Reale and the Impact of Conservative Modernization on Brazilian Race Relations," while George Reid Andrews characterized it as defeated by the 1920s or '30s in "Brazilian Racial Democracy, 1900–1990." Though for the arc of this periodization scholars often cite or draw from Thomas Skidmore's influential *Black into White*, Skidmore actually ends the book by noting that whitening's basic tenets persist in later years.

4. Unsigned (Candido Campos), "O Brasil deve glorificar a raça negra erguendo um monumento á Mãe Preta; A significação desta figura luminosa; Appello de 'A Notícia' á imprensa brasileira," *A Notícia*, April 5, 1926. The statue of the Redeemer was finally inaugurated in October 1931. Another indication of Brazilians' care with their image abroad is Antonio Torres (Brazilian consul in London), article in *A Gazeta de Noticias* (Rio de Janeiro), read into the congressional record by Ephigenio de Salles, August 20, 1921, in Congresso Nacional do Brasil, *Annaes da Camera dos Deputados*, vol. 8 (August 16–31, 1921): 338–43.

5. "O Dia da Mãe Preta," *S. Paulo Jornal*, September 29, 1928; reprinted in "A nossa victoria de 28 de setembro," *Clarim*, January 6, 1929, 2.

6. José Amalio, "Galeria das ladras," *O Malho*, July 6, 1929, 10; "Sempre as domesticas: Um furto numa casa de familia," *A Notícia*, April 23, 1926, 4; Ernesto Silva, letter to the editor, *Diario Nacional*, October 5, 1928; reprinted in "Pede-se um pouco mais de respeito para com os pretos," *Clarim*, October 21, 1928, 6, responding to [not named], "No dia da mãe preta a Josephina foi para o xadrez" (On the Day of the Black Mother, Josephina went to the pen), *A Gazeta*, September 29, 1928. See also Pederneiras, *Scenas da vida Carioca*; and on urban Afro-Brazilian women, R. Moura, *Tia Ciata e a Pequena África no Rio de Janeiro*, and Dias, *Power and Everyday Life*. Disparaging images rose to the fore in, for example, the response by politician Antonio Torres, who connected the Mãe Preta to "the old black pastry vendor" [*a preta dos pasteis*], a figure of urban legend rumored to have murdered angelic white children and baked their flesh into pies. Antonio Torres, reprinted in [unsigned], "O Brasil deve glorificar a raça negra; Erguendo um monumento á Mãe Preta; O applauso de cinco illustres escriptores; Algumas considerações em torno da interpretação dado por Antonio Torres ao nosso pensamento," *A Notícia*, April 13, 1926, 1. Sr. Faria Neves Sobrinho agreed with Torres in *A Manhã*, April 29, 1926; reported in "Monumento á Mãe Preta," *A Notícia*, April 30, 1926, 1.

7. Gilberto Amado, reprinted in "Monumento á Mãe Preta; Luminoso parecer

do deputado Gilberto Amado na Commissão de Finanças; Opinando pela concessão do auxilio áquelle monumento, o illustre parlamentar escreve uma pagina brilhante de historia e sociologia do Brasil," *A Notícia*, November 8, 1926, 1. A photograph of Dr. Candido de Campos's long, pale jowls appears in *Clarim*, February 3, 1929, 4. Amado supported the monument to the tune of 200:000$000 milreis (this was the notational format for the milreis at the time), the amount he maneuvred into the monument drive's coffers as a member of the Congressional Finance Committee. "A nossa victoria de 28 de setembro," *Clarim*, January 6, 1929, 1, citing *A Notícia*, n.d., between September 29, 1928, and January 5, 1929.

8. "Mãe Preta: O Brasil deve glorificar a raça negra erguendo um monumento á Mãe Preta," *A Notícia*, April 13, 1926, 1. "Encerra, pois, a figura da Mãe Preta, dois sentidos diversos e igualmente profundos: o que resume e symbolisa a Raça Negra e os seus 'trabalhos', e o que indica a ligação intima e indestructivel de sua alma com a do branco." The possessive *sua* could be read as referring to the soul of the black race *or* the Black Mother.

9. Conrado Carneiro, "Monumento á Mãe Preta—Uma carta de applauso e um donativo enviados á '*A Notícia*,'" in *A Notícia*, April 8, 1926, 4; source of internal quote unclear.

10. *Diario da Noite*, September 27, 1928; reprinted in "A nossa victoria de 28 de setembro," *Clarim*, January 6, 1929, 1–2.

11. Excerpt from a Costallat "Chronica" in *Jornal do Brasil*, April 12, 1926; reprinted in "Tribuna pública: Monumento á Mãe Preta," *A Notícia*, April 24, 1926, 3 (Costallat's ellipses except for those following "all white"). See also *Redacção*, April 14, 1926; reprinted in "Publicações de ultima hora: Monumento á Mãe Preta," *A Notícia*, April 15, 1926, 4.

12. See Adamo, "The Broken Promise"; C. Silva, *Discriminações raciais*; Graham, "Free African Brazilians and the State in Slavery Times"; Andrews, *Blacks and Whites in São Paulo, Brazil, 1888–1988*.

13. Caulfield, *In Defense of Honor*; Besse, *Restructuring Patriarchy*; Besse, "Crimes of Passion"; Caulfield "Raça, sexo e casamento"; Caulfield, "Getting into Trouble"; T. Gomes, "Massais, mulatas, meretrizes."

14. Caulfield, *In Defense of Honor*, 81.

15. J. Ferrão, "O namoro nas ruas," *Vida Policial*, November 14, 1925, 2; cited in Caulfield, "Getting into Trouble," 157; Caulfield's translation.

16. Besse, *Restructuring Patriarchy*.

17. The Mãe Preta provided an excellent contrast to popular culture, having previously been a subject of elite European and Euro-American high-culture production; readers were reminded of this by such supporters as Costallat in his "Chronica" ("It is not enough that we mean well toward black men, nor simply make black women into stars of the theater. Blacks deserve our raising of this monument of Brazilian gratitude to them") or *A Notícia* in "A Engracia das fructas," *A Notícia*, April 16, 1923, 1 (recalling "'Mother,' playwright José de Alencar's famous drama"); the campaign also occasionally featured the painterly tradition of Mãe Preta portraits (e.g., Lucilio [or

Lucillo] de Albuquerque, Jean-Baptiste Debret). On changing views of the mulatta, see Sant'Anna, "A mulher de cor e o canibalismo erótico na sociedade escravocrata"; T. Gomes, "Lenço no pescoço"; R. Queiroz and Queiroz, *Preconceito de cor e a mulata na literatura brasileira*; Caulfield, *In Defense of Honor*, 146; and Besse, *Restructuring Patriarchy*, 18.

18. While other Brazilians of African descent surely also supported the movement, members of these three groups left traces in the historical record that allow observers outside their moment to identify them as such. See also the note on language following the preface.

19. Antunes da Cunha, "A mulher Negra e o Brasil," *Clarim*, September 28, 1930, 1. Lest his explicit differentiation of the modern world and the Mãe Preta's world seemed to overreach, Cunha reassured his readers of the continuity between the two. The Mãe Preta's sentiments were precisely those that ought to motivate contemporary Afro-Brazilan women and men to the different efforts required in their modern era: "Portanto damas!," he concluded: "Dentro de vossos corações, deve palpitar os mesmos sentimentos que nos leva á profissão de hoje que é a continuidade que ja vinha fazendo pelo Brasil, os nossos antepassados" (However, ladies! Within your hearts ought to beat the same sentiments that dedicate us to our tasks today, continuing what our ancestors had long done for Brazil).

20. Woodcut caption surrounded by "O Dia da Mãe Preta," *Clarim*, September 28, 1928, 1. Similarly, celebrating the "Day of the Mãe Preta" on the anniversary of the Lei do Ventre Livre (Law of the Free Womb) cast the Black Mother as agent of Afro-Brazilian emancipation rather than the otherwise much touted Princess Isabel. On the decision to commemorate this day, see Jayme D'Aguiar, "Mãe Preta," *Clarim*, September 28, 1930, 1.

21. Raul, "Ha negros no Brasil, sim," *Clarim*, January 6, 1929, 2.

22. Dr. Couto Esher, "Monumento á Mãe Preta," *Diario Nacional*, November 1, 1928, 8.

23. Raul, "Ha negros no Brasil, sim." Similar insistence appeared in the *Clarim* that printed Veiga dos Santos's call for the Congresso da Mocidade Negra Brasileira (Congress of Black Brazilian Youth), June 9, 1929, 1. This issue had quite a different tone, less tactful than earlier issues. A long sidebar quoted a number of non-Afro-Brazilians, such as Assis Chateaubriand: "Whether we will it or not, black blood does flow in the veins of all of us Brazilians," from *O Correio da Manhã*, n. 7780, 1920. Consider the same strategic distinction between good and bad whites made by Raul's North American contemporaries in the *Norfolk Journal and Guide*, February 1923; see also McElya, "Monumental Citizenship."

24. See also A. J. Veiga dos Santos, "A acção dos negros brasileiros," *Clarim*, January 15, 1927, 5. He turned the tables on North Atlantic racial "science" by denouncing "suspect anthropological and ethnologic sciences . . . with their foolish, apish [*macaqueadoras*] theories."

25. "Ivan," "Monumento symbolico á Mãe Preta," *Getulino*, May 13, 1926, 3.

26. José Correia Leite, "O Dia da Mãe Preta," *Clarim*, September 28, 1930.

27. "Dia da Mãe Preta," *Clarim*, September 28, 1929, 1; "Hoje é o Dia da Mãe-Preta: Symbolo de redempção e de penitencia! Ao embalo de seu cantico de saudade se construiu a nossa nacionalidade!" *Clarim*, September 28, 1929, 1; reprints of Mario Rodrigues (director of *Crítica*) in "A 'Mãe Negra,'" *Clarim*, September 28, 1929, 1; and Saul de Navarro, untitled; reprinted in "Mãe Preta," *Clarim*, May 13, 1927, 1 (on Navarro, see J. Leite, "O negro para o negro," *Clarim*, July 1, 1928, 1).

28. Mitchell, "Miguel Reale and the Impact of Conservative Modernization on Brazilian Race Relations."

29. Felski, *The Gender of Modernity*, 38; see also 9–10.

30. Cooper, "Modernity." See also Yack, *The Fetishism of Modernities*; Dussel, *The Underside of Modernity*; Mignolo, *Local Histories/Global Designs*; and Chakrabarty, *Habitations of Modernity*.

31. "Manifesto," *Elite*, February 17, 1924, 1; "Lima Barreto," *Clarim*, December 7, 1924, 2; Raul, "Ha negros no Brasil, sim"; "A memoria da viuva José Do Patrocinio," *Progresso*, September 26, 1929, 3; *Progresso*, October 31, 1929, 1, and November 24, 1929, 1; Amilcar Salgado dos Santos, "A herma de Luiz Gama," *Evolução*, May 13, 1933, 29; "Divida esquecida: Um justo appello em prol de um busto a Luiz Gama ou Patrocinio," *Clarim*, September 28, 1929, 4, claiming to reproduce an article with the same name by João Eugenio da Costa, from *O Progresso*, August 1929 (exact date unspecified); "Cruz e Souza," *Clarim*, November 24, 1929, 1; "Trigesimo nono," *Clarim*, May 13, 1927, 2–3; and Moyses Cintra, "Justiça e gratidão," *Clarim*, April 17, 1927, 3; on anonymous but noteworthy figures, see "Ainda ha juizes em Berlim," *Clarim*, October 15, 1927, 1; and Affonso Celso, "Joanna Angelica e Nicolau," *Getulino*, August 19, 1923, 1. The white politician Antonio Torres also proposed a statue to "a Herculean black [man], endowed with a musculature à la Miguel Angelo, Bernini, or Rodin," but no black press writer embraced it, perhaps because it came alongside the brutally disparaging mention of the witch-like *preta dos pasteis*. Antonio Torres, reprinted in [unsigned], "O Brasil deve glorificar a raça negra," *A Notícia*, April 13, 1926, 1.

32. See Ernesto Silva, letter to the editor, *Diario Nacional*, October 5, 1928; reprinted in "Pede-se um pouco mais de respeito para com os pretos," *Clarim*, October 21, 1928, 6, responding to [not named], "No dia da mãe preta a Josephina foi para o xadrez," *A Gazeta*, September 29, 1928.

33. Sueann Caulfield notes that Brazil's constitution in this period limited "active" citizenship "to literate males twenty-one or older." Caulfield, *In Defense of Honor*, 26; see also Carvalho, *Os bestializados*. The portrait tradition includes Lucillo [Lucilio] de Albuquerque's 1912 "Black Mother," which references French painter Jean-Baptiste Debret's "retrato de Dom Pedro II no colo da sua ama" (portrait of Don Pedro II in his nanny's lap). Rhetorically as well, the language used to refer to the Mãe Preta's children virtually always figured them as male; see especially Mario Rodriguez in *A Manhã*, April 9, 1926; reprinted as "Tribuna publica: Mãe Preta," *A Notícia*, April 10, 1926, 3; "Mãe Preta," *A Notícia*, April 13, 1926, 1; *Rio-Jornal*, April 6, 1926, in "Tribuna publica," *A Notícia*, April 7, 1926, 3; *Vanguarda*, April 13, 1926; reprinted in "Tribuna pública: Mãe Preta," *A Notícia*, April 17, 1926, 3. For children white or black, most

writers used the term *filhos*, meaning either the masculine "sons" or expressing the accepted wisdom of the time that the masculine generic could be neutral or inclusive—either way, the Mãe Preta never seemed to raise any girls.

34. "Jinarajadasa," *Progresso*, December 16, 1928, 2; Gervasio Moraes, "A inquisição moderna," *Clarim*, November 14, 1926, 2.

35. "Aonde pois, fraternidade nos Estados Unidos?" in *Progresso*, June 23, 1929, 3. See also D'Alencasiro [*sic*], "Grave erro!" *O Bandeirante*, September 1918, 2; Menotti Del Picchia (a.k.a. José Correia Leite, claims Ferrara, *A imprensa negra paulista*, 55), "Treze de maio," *Evolução*, May 13, 1933, 6.

36. Simão de Laboreiro, "Mãe Preta," *A Notícia*, June 3, 1926, 3. This name is suggestive: "Simão," a popular, even stereotypical, Afro-Brazilian name, the equivalent perhaps of "Mose" then in the United States; "Laboreiro," laborer or labor-ist; the two names together a pen name designating, I suspect, a writer who was neither, attempting to articulate the perspective he imagined such a subject would hold.

37. Washington Luis, "Monumento á Mãe Preta: Carta do Dr. Washington Luis presidente eleito da República a Vicente Ferreira," *A Notícia*, April 23, 1926, 1 (quoting his own presidential platform). Another elite celebration of fraternity is anthropologist Roquette-Pinto, "Archeologia e ethnographia," 57.

38. "O Dia da Mãe Preta," *Clarim*, September 28, 1928, 1, emphasis added.

39. "A 'União da Alliança' abre uma subscripção entre os seu socios: Expressiva mensagem do popular aggremiação," *A Notícia*, May 1, 1926, 4.

40. "O monumento á Mãe Preta e o presidente eleito da Republica," *Getulino*, May 13, 1926, 1. See also Evaristo de Moraes, *Rio-Jornal*, April 6, 1926; reprinted in "Tribuna publica," *A Notícia*, April 7, 1926, 3; and Moraes in *Jornal do Brasil*, April 14, 1926; reprinted in "A proposito da raça negra: Explicação de uma injustiça," *A Notícia*, May 27, 1926, 4. A journalist writing as far away as Portugal praised the monument for its Luso-Brazilian nationalism, using this same comparison. Mario Monteiro, untitled, *Primeiro de Janeiro* (Porto, Portugal), n.d., n.p.; reprinted in *A Notícia*, December 8, 1926, n.p.; reprinted in "Monumento á Mãe Preta," *Clarim*, September 28, 1928, 5.

41. *Pace* Paul Gilroy's cautions about the fascism supposedly inherent to masculinist, militaristic nationalism in *Against Race*. It is true that in the 1930s some members of the black press community would embrace fascism openly and organize or join right-wing political and military groups. But this decision would cause a serious schism in the larger group, alienating many who had enthusiastically embraced the idea of national fraternity, a reminder that no particular political position necessarily follows from any other.

42. Arauo and Costa, "O monumento á Mãe Preta: Uma captivante e significativa resolução da Irmandade de N.S. do Rosario e S. Benedicto dos Homens Pretos," *A Notícia*, April 21, 1926, 2, emphasis added.

43. *A Notícia* discussed the Mass on April 17, 1926; April 20, 1926; April 21, 1926; May 1, 1926; May 3, 1926 (featuring two large photographs and a long list of attendees); May 14, 1926; and August 19, 1926 (another long list with a photo).

44. De Chocolat, *Tudo preto*. See T. Gomes, "Negros contando (e fazendo) sua história"; T. Gomes, *Um espelho no palco*.

45. I know of no sources focusing on this organization, and that is unfortunate as it is unusual both in character and in its Rio location.

46. Camargo in "Monumento á 'Mãe Preta': Um officio da Federação dos Homens de Côr a '*A Notícia*,'" *A Notícia*, April 14, 1926, 2.

47. For distinctly critical implications in black support for the Mãe Preta, see Arlinda Veiga Dos Santos, "Congresso da Mocidade Negra Brasileira," *Clarim*, June 9, 1929, 1; Veiga dos Santos, "A acção dos negros brasileiros," *Clarim*, January 15, 1927, 5; Manoel Ignacio de Arauo, judge of N.S. do Rosario, and Sebastião de Arruda Costa, secretary, to *A Notícia*, printed in "O monumento á Mãe Preta: Uma captivante e significativa resolução da Irmandade de N.S. do Rosario e S. Benedicto dos Homens Pretos," *A Notícia*, April 21, 1926, 2; David R. de Castro, "Mãe Negra," *Progresso*, August 19, 1928, 1–2; Gervasio Moraes, "Dominicaes . . . ," *Clarim*, April 25, 1926, 1 (Moraes's ellipses); Lino Guedes, "Moda exotica," *Clarim*, April 25, 1926, 2–3; Evaristo de Moraes, "O Brasil deve . . . : O applauso ardente do Dr. Evaristo de Moraes á suggestão de '*A Notícia*,'" *A Notícia*, April 7, 1926, 1.

48. Lino Guedes, untitled, *Clarim*, January 15, 1927, 3.

49. Vagalume (director of Brasil-Politico), "E o monumento?" *Clarim*, September 28, 1929, 1; "Mãe Preta," *Clarim*, May 13, 1929, 1.

50. *Clarim* reprinted some of the responses its efforts earned on January 6, 1929, in "A nossa victoria de 28 setembro," 1–2, claiming notice in *O Correio de Botucatu, Diario da Noite, Correio Paulistano, S. Paulo Jornal, Jornal do Commercio, Nota do Dia, Folha da Manhã, Folha da Noite, Diario Nacional, O Estado de São Paulo, O Correio Popular de Campinas, Tribuna de Santos, A Folha de Santos, O Jornal do Rio, O Globo,* and others. The financial strain of this effort is evident in an untitled piece in *Clarim*, January 6, 1929, 3.

51. "*Clarim*," *A Notícia*, n.d., n.p.; untitled article in *O Correio de Botucatu*, n.d., n.p; "Amanhã é o Dia da Mãe Preta," *O Diario da Noite*, September 27, 1928, n.p.; D. X., "Cultuando a Mãe Preta," *Correio Paulistano*, September 28, 1928, n.p.; all reprinted in "A nossa victoria de 28 de setembro," *Clarim*, January 6, 1929, 1–2. *Clarim*'s distributory efforts did not begin or end with this issue, as "A nossa revista," on the front page of its issue of June 3, 1928, revealed: The priest Dr. Henrique de Magalhões, *Clarim* reported, spoke from the "sacred tribune of the Church of Saint Cecilia," on May 13, 1928, as follows: "In one of the streets of this capital [São Paulo], I met up with a man of color who gave me a magazine, '*Clarim d'Alvorada*,' and asked me to take it with me as a warm remembrance, and I am gratefully obliged for this homage lent to me by the descendants of the race that was the trunk of our nationality and to whom we owe the greatness of our dear fatherland." "A nossa revista" also reported that the writer Coelho Netto wrote "a kind note of thanks for the simple but deserved homage we paid him in our special May 13 issue" and that the issue also inspired *O Momento*, a newspaper from Macahé, Rio de Janeiro State, to print a "brilliant note." *Clarim*'s staff was obviously dedicated and effective in promoting the fruit of their labors.

52. C. Costa, *Julio Guerra*. The statue was sculpted in 1954 and commemorated São Paulo's IV Centennial. I do not know the process of its selection.

53. Kelley, "'But a Local Phase of a World Problem'"; Stephens, "Black Transnationalism and the Politics of National Identity."

54. This according to José Correia Leite's memoirs: J. Leite and Cuti, —*E disse o velho militante José Correia Leite*, 78–79.

55. "Brazil Pays High Honor to Dark Citizens: Brazil to Honor Her Women," *Chicago Defender*, May 22, 1926, part 1, 1; continued as "Brazil Plans to Honor Its Dark Citizens: Will Erect Statue to Women of Race," part 2, 1.

56. In a 1923 book comparing the United States and Brazil, Brazilian consul Hélio Lobo had lamented the fate of the Mãe Preta's U.S. counterpart: "In the South, the white man cannot ride the same railroad car as his beloved 'mammy,' who warms his childhood, weaves his dreams in summer, and whose image, passed down from parents to kids, invokes affection." Lobo, *Cousas americanas e brasileiras*, 72; "mammy" in English in the original. Oracy Nogueira also mentioned "mammy" in "Preconceito racial de marca e preconceito racial de origem," 87–89, 88n33.

57. "Rotten Service!" cartoon, *Chicago Defender*, March 17, 1923, 12; "Mockery," cartoon, *Chicago Defender*, April 7, 1923, 12; "'Mammy Statue' Opposed with Vet Memorial: National Memorial Association Would Have Monument to Dead Soldier Heroes," *Chicago Defender*, April 21, 1923, 13; see also J. Rogers, "Since Statues Seem to Be All the Rage, Suppose We Erect One," *Chicago Defender*, April 21, 1923, 12; A. L. Jackson, "The Black Mammy Statue," in "The Onlooker," column, *Chicago Defender*, April 21, 1923, 12; McElya, "Monumental Citizenship"; and McElya, "Commemorating the Color Line."

58. Liu, *Tokens of Exchange*; Derrida, "Des Tours de Babel"; Benjamin, "The Task of the Translator."

59. "Brazil Pays High Honor to Dark Citizens."

60. Ibid.

61. Ottley, *The Lonely Warrior*; Stuckey, *Slave Culture*, 394n135 and the chapter "Identity and Ideology: The Names Controversy," 193–244.

62. The Brazilian preference for visual terms here and in the emphasis on the Mãe Preta's white milk and red blood are intriguing in light of Oracy Nogueira's discussion of Brazilian racial prejudice of "mark" rather than "origin." Nogueira, "Preconceito racial de marca e preconceito racial de origem."

63. "Sweet Liberty Wields Scepter Down in Brazil: Mr. Abbott Finds Brazilians 'Sublime'; Sees the Spirit of Equality; Signally Honored," *Chicago Defender*, April 14, 1923, 2.

64. Abbott, "My Trip Through South America: Article 2—Personal Motives," *Chicago Defender*, August 11, 1923, 13–14.

65. Abbott, "My Trip Through South America: Article 4 (Continued)—Rio de Janeiro," *Chicago Defender*, September 1, 1923, 13–14.

66. Lynching's performative mobility is somewhat fleshed out in chapter 5; on lynchings in Brazil, see C. Silva, *Discriminações raciais*; Twine, *Racism in a Racial Democracy*.

67. "Monumento á MP: A grande repercussão, na America do Norte, da iniciativa de 'A Notícia'; Como o 'Jornal do Brasil' commenta o facto," *A Notícia*, June 21, 1926, 2, reprinting *Jornal do Brasil*, suelto, n.d.; and "Monumento á MP: A grande repercussão, na America do Norte, da iniciativa de 'A Notícia'; 'O Brasil' rende alta homenagem aos cidadões pretos', diz o 'The Chicago Defender,'" *A Notícia*, June 18, 1926, 1.

68. "Return Home to Keep Up Fight," *Chicago Defender*, May 26, 1923, 8; "Negro Martyr of Argentina," *Chicago Defender*, September 22, 1923, 13; Abbott, "My Trip through South America: Article 9—Panama and the Canal," *Chicago Defender*, October 13, 1923, 13–14. This is consistent with interest in monument building in the United States among whites, precisely the sentiment that fueled the UDC's proposal in 1923. On this phenomenon, see Mills and Simpson, *Monuments to the Lost Cause*, esp. McElya, "Commemorating the Color Line," and Hale, "Granite Stopped Time"; see also K. Savage, *Standing Soldiers, Kneeling Slaves*.

69. For example, "Os pretos são sympathicos á Candidatura Smith," *Progresso*, November 15, 1928, 3.

70. Gervasio Moraes, "A inquisição moderna," *Clarim*, November 14, 1926, 2; "Pr.," "A formula igualitaria para resolver a questão racial americana," *Progresso*, February 24, 1929.

71. *A Noite*, n.d.; reprinted in "Defender Head Made Welcome by Brazilians: Mr. Abbott Finds South American Metropolis Wonderful City; Ability Counts," *Chicago Defender*, March 31, 1923, 3.

72. "Sweet Liberty Wields Scepter."

73. Ibid.

74. "Friends Greet Mr. Abbott at Englewood Station," *Chicago Defender* photo, May 26, 1923, 1; "Brazil Pays High Honor to Dark Citizens."

75. Roscoe Simmons, "The Week," *Chicago Defender*, May 19, 1923, 13.

76. "Sweet Liberty Wields Scepter"; cited in ibid.

77. R. W. Merguson, "Glimpses of Brazil," *Crisis* 2, no. 1 (November 1915): 38–43; quote on 43; Merguson's capitals and emphasis.

78. Brown, "'What Has Happened Here'"; Crenshaw, "Mapping the Margins"; Higginbotham, "African-American Women's History and the Metalanguage of Race"; W. Johnson, *Soul by Soul*; Wiegman, *American Anatomies*; Bederman, *Manliness and Civilization*. Indeed, Bederman's analysis of the shift in models of masculinity in turn-of-the-century United States from genteel Victorian to Theodore Roosevelt–style "strenuous" masculinity suggests a need for interpretation of the exploding popularity among young people of sports and other aspects of the "strenuous life" in 1920s São Paulo, as recounted in Sevcenko, *Orféu extático na metrópole*.

79. J. Leite, "O negro para o negro," *Clarim*, July 1, 1928, 1; "O Hercules de ebano: A raça soffredora e forte na glorificação mais alta; A do trabalho," *Clarim*, October 15, 1927, 1, claiming to reprint *O Diario Nacional*, numero especial do Centenario do Café, n.d., n.p.; *Clarim*, May 13, 1927, 12; "D"*A Notícia*' dorio: Um jornal pelo interesse dos homens pretos; *Clarim* a exemplo do 'The Chicago Defender,'" *Clarim*, June 3, 1928, 2; "Dr. Baptista Pereira," *Clarim*, July 1, 1928, 1; "O Dia da Mãe Preta," *Clarim*, September 28, 1928, 1. This despite disproportionate forced recruitment of men of

color, a phenomenon many must have encountered in their lives. As Richard Graham has written, the Brazilian state "acted discriminatorily towards free African Brazilians in carrying out the military draft," using it "as a means of disciplining the poor." Graham, "Free African Brazilians and the State in Slavery Times," 35. This dates to at least the Paraguayan War; see Kraay, "Slavery, Citizenship, and Military Service in Brazil's Mobilization for the Paraguayan War." As a result, military service is a classic device with which to claim Afro-Brazilian belonging and citizenship; Kim Butler, personal communication, May 2003.

80. See, for example, a poem in *Clarim*, May 13, 1926, 7. Thanks to Tiago de Melo Gomes for pointing out the significance of the black press's avoidance of this figure during the monument campaign.

81. *Clarim*, May 13, 1928, 1. See also Alberto Orlando, "Trecho de um capitulo do opusculo de proxima publicação: 'O negro na evolução brasileira,'" *Clarim*, January 15, 1927, 3–4.

82. See Sterling Stuckey's nuanced discussions of black nationalism in *Slave Culture*; see also Summers, *Manliness and Its Discontents*; Wiegman, *American Anatomies*. On the "New Negro," see Locke, *The New Negro*; an excellent gloss is Childs, "Afro-American Intellectuals and the People's Culture."

83. In Uruguay, for example, Abbott observed, "Negro girls are conspicuous here and there as clerks in the department stores." Abbott, "My Trip through South America: Article 5—Montevideo," *Chicago Defender*, September 15, 1923, 13–14.

Conclusion

1. K. Marx, *Capital*; N. Smith, *Uneven Development*; Harvey, *Spaces of Global Capitalism* (the subtitle is *Towards a Theory of Uneven Geographical Development*).

2. Mignolo, *Local Histories/Global Designs*; Mignolo, *The Darker Side of the Renaissance*; Dussel, "The Invention of the Americas" (the subtitle is "Eclipse of 'the Other' and the Myth of Modernity"; Dussel, "Eurocentrism and Modernity"; Yack, *The Fetishism of Modernity*; Cooper, "Modernity."

3. "Global Empires: Local Encounters," Section 2 of Ballantyne and Burton, *Bodies in Contact* (the subtitle is *Rethinking Colonial Encounters in World History*); McAlister, *Epic Encounters*; Jacobson, *Barbarian Virtues* (the subtitle is *The United States Encounters Foreign Peoples at Home and Abroad, 1876–1917*); Linger, *Dangerous Encounters*.

4. Escobar, *Encountering Development*; Quijano, "Colonialidad del poder, cultura y conocimiento en América Latina."

Discography

Brymn, Tim. *La rumba, tango or maxixe*. Victor Military Band, Victor 17439, 78A rpm (1913).

Gallop, Sammy, Gil Rodin, and Bob Crosby. *Boogie-Woogie Maxixe*. Jack Richards and the Night Winds, Dick Jacobs, director. Coral 9–61063, 45 rpm (n.d.).

———. *Boogie-Woogie Maxixe*. Gil Rodin and Bob Crosby and His Orchestra. Decca 9–25114 (n.d.).

———. *Boogie-Woogie Maxixe*. The Ames Brothers with the Hugo Winterhalter Orchestra and Chorus. Victor 20–5530 and Victor 47–5530 (n.d.).

———. *Boogie-Woogie Maxixe*. Armed Forces Radio and TV Series P-3407, 16 (n.d.).

Green, Arthur N. *Sans Souci*. Van Eps Banjo Orchestra. Columbia A 1594 (78A).

Logatti, Lorenzo. *Irresistible, Tango Argentine*. Europe's Society Orchestra. Victor 35360, 78A rpm (1914).

Nazareth, Ernesto. "Apanhei-te, Cavaquinho," and "Odeon." *Carinhoso*. Paradoxx, CD (1996).

Olliver, Gillermo "Willy," and Tomás Mooney. *Argentine Swing 1936–1948*. Arquivo de Musica, Antiga/Portugal, LP (1989 [1984]).

Penso, R. *The Grossmith Tango*. Prince's Band. Columbia A 5543, 78A rpm (1911).

Salabert, Frances. "Creole Girl, Maxixe, Vem Cá, Mulata." Castle House Orchestra, Frank W. McKee, director. Victor 35374, 78A rpm (June 1914–January 1915).

Stagliano, James. *Joan Sawyer Maxixe*. Prince's Band. Columbia A 5561, 78A rpm (1914).

Storoni, J. *Amapa—maxixe bresilien*. Europe's Society Orchestra. Victor 35360, 78A rpm (1914).

Tyers, William H. *Maori-Tango or Maxixe*. Victor Military Band. Victor 35304, 78A rpm (1913).

Veloso, Caetano. *A Foreign Sound*. Caetano Veloso, Nonesuch, CD (2004).

Bibliography

Abreu, Marcelo de Paiva. "Argentina and Brazil during the 1930s: The Impact of British and United States International Economic Policies." In Thorp, *Latin America in the 1930s*, 127–42.

Abreu, Martha. *O império do Divino: festas religiosas e cultura popular no Rio de Janeiro, 1830–1900*. Rio de Janeiro: Editora Nova Fronteira; São Paulo: FAPESP, 1999.

Adamo, Sam. "The Broken Promise: Race, Health, and Justice in Rio de Janeiro, 1890–1940." Ph.D. diss., University of New Mexico, 1983.

Aita, Carmen Silva. "Discurso político e relações internacionais: o Estado Novo e o governo Roosevelt, 1936–1945." *Estudos Ibero-Americanos* 21, no. 2 (December 1995): 145–53.

Alcala, May Lorenzo. *Vanguardia argentina y Modernismo brasileño: años 20*. Buenos Aires: Grupo Editor Latinoamericano, 1994.

Alencar, Edigar de. *O fabuloso e harmonioso Pixinguinha*. Rio de Janeiro: Cátedra; Brasília: INL, 1979.

Almeida, Renato. *Compêndio de história da música brasileira*. Rio de Janeiro: F. Briguiet, 1948.

———. *História da música brasileira*, 2d ed. Rio de Janeiro: F. Briguiet, 1942.

———. "Musica brasileira." *Ariel: Revista de Cultura Musical*, December 1923, 99–101.

Almirante (a.k.a. Henrique Foreis). *No tempo de Noel Rosa*, 2d ed. Rio de Janeiro: Livraria Francisco Alves Editora, 1977.

Alvarenga, Oneyda. *Música popular brasileira*, 2d ed. São Paulo: Livraria Duas Cidades, 1982.

Amado, Gilberto. *Mocidade no Rio e primeira viagem à Europa*. Rio de Janeiro: J. Olympio, 1956.

Amaral, Antônio Barreto do. *História dos velhos teatros de São Paulo*. São Paulo: Governo do Estado de São Paulo, 1979.

Amaral, Aracy A. *Blaise Cendrars no Brasil e os modernistas*. São Paulo: Livraria Martins, 1970.

———. *Tarsila: Sua vida, sua obra*, 2 vols. São Paulo: Perspectiva, 1975.

Anderson, Benedict, *Imagined Communities: Reflections on the Origin and Spread of Nationalism*, 2d ed. London; New York: Verso, 1991 [1983].

Andrade, Mário de. *Ensaio sobre a música brasileira*. São Paulo: I. Chiarato, 1928.

——. "Ernesto Nazaré (Conferencia realizada na Sociedade de Cultura Artistica de São Paulo, 1926)." *Revista da Música Popular*, no. 3 (December 1954): 2–4, 32–33.

——. *Música, doce música*. São Paulo: Livraria Martins, 1964 [1933].

Andrews, George Reid. "Brazilian Racial Democracy, 1900–1990: An American Counterpoint." *Journal of Contemporary History* 31, no. 3 (1996): 483–507.

——. *Blacks and Whites in São Paulo, Brazil, 1888–1988*. Madison: University of Wisconsin Press, 1991.

——. *The Afro-Argentines of Buenos Aires, 1800–1900*. Madison: University of Wisconsin Press, 1980.

Anzaldua, Gloria. *Borderlands/La Frontera: The New Mestiza*. San Francisco: Spinsters/Aunt Lute, 1987.

Anzovin, Steven, and Janet Podell. *Famous First Facts, International Edition: A Record of First Happenings, Discoveries, and Inventions in World History*. New York: H. W. Wilson, 2000.

Appadurai, Arjun. *Modernity at Large: Cultural Dimensions of Globalization*. Minneapolis: University of Minnesota Press, 1996.

——, ed. *The Social Life of Things: Commodities in Cultural Perspective*. Cambridge: Cambridge University Press, 1986.

Appiah, Anthony. "The Uncompleted Argument: Du Bois and the Illusion of Race." *Critical Inquiry* 12 (autumn 1985): 21–37.

Applebaum, Nancy P., Anne S. Macpherson, and Karin Alejandra Rosemblatt, eds. *Race and Nation in Modern Latin America*. Chapel Hill: University of North Carolina Press, 2003.

Araújo, Ricardo Benzaquen de. *Guerra & paz: casa-grande & senzala e a obra de Gilberto Freyre nos anos 30*. Rio de Janeiro: Editora 34, 1994.

Ardizzone, Heidi. "Red-Blooded Americans: Mulattoes and the Melting Pot in U.S. Racialist and Nationalist Discourse, 1890–1930." Ph.D. diss., University of Michigan, 1997.

Associated Coffee Industries (ACI). *Convention Report*, September 12, 1932, 19–20. New York: NYPL.

Athayde, Tristão de (a.k.a. Alceu Amoroso Lima). "Eles e nós." *Estudos*, 2d series. Rio de Janeiro: Edição de Terra de Sol, 1928, 233–38.

Atkeson, Andrew, and Patrick J. Kehoe. "The Transition to a New Economy after the Second Industrial Revolution." NBER Working Paper no. 8676, December 2001; www.nber.org/papers/w8676 (accessed December 14, 2006).

Atkins, E. Taylor. *Blue Nippon: Authenticating Jazz in Japan*. Durham, N.C.: Duke University Press, 2001.

Aughinbaugh, William Edmund. *Selling Latin America: A Problem in International Salesmanship; What to Sell and How to Sell It*. Boston, Mass.: Small Maynard, 1915.

Azevedo, Celia Maria Marinho de. *Abolitionism in the United States and Brazil: A Comparative Perspective*. Studies in African American History and Culture New York: Garland, 1995.

Bacha, Edmar, and Robert Greenhill. *150 anos de café*. São Paulo: Lis Gráfica e Exportadores, 1992.

Badger, Reid. *A Life in Ragtime: A Biography of James Reese Europe*. Oxford: Oxford University Press, 1994.

Baer, Werner. *The Brazilian Economy: Growth and Development*, 4th ed. Westport, Conn.: Praeger, 2001 [1995].

Bairros, Luiza. "Orfeu e poder: uma perspectiva afro-americana sobre a política racial no Brasil." *Afro-Ásia* (Centro de Estudos Afro-Orientais, Universidade Federal da Bahia) 17 (1996): 173–86.

Baldwin, Davarian. "Out from the Shadow of E. Franklin Frazier? Middle-Class Identity and Consumer Citizenship in the Black Metropolis." *Journal of Urban History* 29, no. 6 (September 2004): 778–93.

Baldwin, James. "Color and American Civilization." In Westin, *Freedom Now!*, 3–9.

———. "The White Problem." In *100 Years of Emancipation*, ed. Robert A. Goldwin and Harry V. Jaffa. Chicago: Rand McNally, 1964, 80–88.

Balibar, Étienne, and Immanuel Wallerstein. *Race, Nation, Class: Ambiguous Identities*. Trans. Chris Turner. London: Routledge, Chapman and Hall, 1991.

Ballantyne, Tony, and Antoinette Burton, eds. *Bodies in Contact: Rethinking Colonial Encounters in World History*. Durham, N.C.: Duke University Press, 2005.

Bandeira, Moniz. *Presença dos Estados Unidos no Brasil*. Rio de Janeiro: Civilização Brasileira, 1973.

Barr, Steven C. *The Almost Complete 78 RPM Record Dating Guide (II)*. Huntington Beach, Calif.: Yesterday Once Again, 1992.

Barton, Bruce. *The Man Nobody Knows: A Discovery of Jesus*. Indianapolis: Bobbs-Merrill, 1925.

Basch, Linda, Nina Glick Schiller, and Cristina Szanton Blanc. *Nations Unbound: Transnational Projects, Postcolonial Predicaments, and Deterritorialized Nation-States*. Basel: Gordon and Breach, 1994.

Bastide, Roger. *Les Amériques noires: Les civilisations africaines dans le nouveau monde*. Paris: Payot, 1967.

———. "The Development of Race Relations in Brazil." In *Industrialisation and Race Relations: A Symposium*, ed. Guy Hunter. London: Oxford University Press, 1965, 9–29.

———. "A imprensa negra do Estado de São Paulo." In *Estudos afro-brasileiros*, 2ª série. São Paulo: Editora Perspectiva, 1973, 129–56.

Bastide, Roger, and Florestan Fernandes. *Brancos e negros em São Paulo: Ensaio sociológico sôbre aspectos da formação, manifestações atuais e efeitos do preconceito de côr na sociedade paulistana*, 2d ed. São Paulo: Companhia Editora Nacional, 1959.

Bates, Robert. *Open-Economy Politics: The Political Economy of the World Coffee Trade*. Princeton, N.J.: Princeton University Press, 1997.

Baudrillard, Jean. *The Consumer Society: Myths and Structures*. London: Sage, 1998 [1970].

———. *The System of Objects*. Trans. James Benedict. London: Verso, 1996 [1968].

Becker, William H. *The Dynamics of Business-Government Relations: Industry and Exports, 1893–1921*. Chicago: University of Chicago Press, 1982.

Bederman, Gail. *Manliness & Civilization: A Cultural History of Gender and Race in the United States, 1880–1917*. Chicago: University of Chicago Press, 1995.

Béhague, Gérard. *Musiques du Brésil: de la cantoria a la samba-reggae*. Arles: Cité de la Musique/Actes Sud, 1999.

———. "Reflections on the Ideological History of Latin American Ethnomusicology." In *Comparative Musicology and Anthropology of Music: Essays on the History of Ethnomusicology*, ed. Bruno Nettl and Philip V. Bohlman. Chicago: University of Chicago Press, 1991, 56–68.

Belluzzo, Ana Maria de Moraes, org. *Modernidade: vanguardas artísticas na América Latina*. São Paulo: Memorial: UNESP, 1990.

Bender, Pennee, Joshua Brown, and Andrea Ades Vasquez. *Savage Acts: Wars, Fairs, and Empire* (video recording). New York: American Social History Productions, 1995.

Bender, Thomas, ed. *Rethinking American History in a Global Age*. Berkeley: University of California Press, 2002.

Benjamin, Walter. "The Task of the Translator: An Introduction to the Translation of Baudelaire's *Tableaux parisiens*." In *Illuminations*, ed. Hannah Arendt, trans. Harry Zohn. New York: Schocken, 1973 [1955], 69–82.

Bento, Ma. Aparecida Silva. "Branqueamento e branquitude no Brasil." In *Psicologia social do racismo*, 25–57.

Beserra, Bernadete. *Brazilian Immigrants in the United States: Cultural Imperialism and Social Class*. New York: LFB Scholarly Publications, 2003.

Besse, Susan, "Crimes of Passion: The Campaign against Wife Killing in Brazil, 1910–1940." *Journal of Social History* 22, no. 4 (1989): 653–66.

———. *Restructuring Patriarchy: The Modernization of Gender in Brazil, 1914–1940*. Chapel Hill: University of North Carolina Press, 1996.

Bhabha, Homi. *The Location of Culture*. London: Routledge, 1994.

Biagioni, Egino, and Herb Flemming. *Herb Flemming: A Jazz Pioneer around the World*. Alphen Aan de Rijn: Micrography, 1977.

Biographical Encyclopedia of Jazz, The. New York: Oxford University Press, 1999.

Black, Jan Knippers. *United States Penetration of Brazil*. Philadelphia, Pa.: University of Pennsylvania Press, 1977.

Blake, Jody. *Le tumulte noir: Modernist Art and Popular Entertainment in Jazz-Age Paris, 1900–1930*. University Park: Pennsylvania State University Press, 1999.

Bloch, Marc. "Pour une histoire comparée des sociétés européennes." Paper presented at the Sixth International Congress of Historical Sciences, Oslo, August 1928. Printed in *Revue de synthèse historique* 46 (1928): 15–50.

Bolster, W. Jeffrey. *Black Jacks: African American Seamen in the Age of Sail*. Cambridge, Mass.: Harvard University Press, 1997.

Bolton, Herbert. "The Epic of Greater America." *AHR* 38 (April 1933): 448–74.

———. *History of the Americas: A Syllabus with Maps*. Boston, Mass.: Ginn, 1928.

Bonnard, Abel. *Océan et Brésil*. Paris: Flammarion, 1929.

Boorstin, Daniel J. *The Americans: The Democratic Experience*. New York: Random House, 1973.

Bordin, Ruth Birgitta Anderson. *Woman and Temperance: The Quest for Power and Liberty, 1873–1900*. Philadelphia, Pa.: Temple University Press, 1981.

Borges, Dain. "'Puffy, Ugly, Slothful and Inert': Degeneration in Brazilian Social Thought, 1880–1940." *Journal of Latin American Studies* 25 (1993): 235–56.

Bouillon, Jo. *Josephine*. Trans. Marian Fitzpatrick. New York: Harper and Row, 1977 [1976].

Bourdieu, Pierre, and Lois Wacquant. "Sur les ruses de la raison impérialiste." *Actes de la recherche en sciences sociales* 121/122 (March 1998): 109–18.

Brandes, Joseph. *Herbert Hoover and Economic Diplomacy: Department of Commerce Policy 1921–1928*. Pittsburgh: University of Pittsburgh Press, 1962.

Bret, David. *The Mistinguett Legend*. New York: St. Martin's Press, 1991.

Bricktop [Ada "Bricktop" Smith] and James Haskins. *Bricktop*. New York: Atheneum, 1983.

Briggs, Arthur, and James Collier. "Interview with Arthur Briggs." Washington, D.C.: Smithsonian Institution Oral History 1982; Institute of Jazz Studies, Rutgers University.

Briggs, Laura. *Reproducing Empire: Race, Sex, Science, and U.S. Imperialism in Puerto Rico*. Berkeley: University of California Press, 2002.

Brito, Mário da Silva. *História do Modernismo brasileiro: antecendentes da semana de arte moderna*, vol. 1, 6th. ed. Rio de Janeiro: Civilização Brasileira, 1997 [1978].

Brock, Lisa, and Digna Castañada, eds. *Between Race and Empire: African-Americans and Cubans before the Cuban Revolution*. Philadelphia, Pa.: Temple University Press, 1998.

Brodkin [Sachs], Karen. *How the Jews Became White Folks and What That Says about Race in America*. New Brunswick, N.J.: Rutgers University Press, 1999.

Bronfman, Alejandra. *Measures of Equality: Social Science, Citizenship, and Race in Cuba, 1902–1940*. Chapel Hill: University of North Carolina Press, 2004.

Brookshaw, David. "Quatro poetas negros brasileiros." *Estudos Afro-Asiáticos* 1, no. 2 (1978): 30–45.

Brown, Elsa Barkeley. "'What Has Happened Here': The Politics of Difference in Women's History and Feminist Politics." *Feminist Studies* 18 (summer 1992): 295–312.

Browning, Barbara. *Infectious Rhythm: Metaphors of Contagion and the Spread of African Culture*. New York: Routledge, 1998.

———. *Samba: Resistance in Motion*. Bloomington: Indiana University Press, 1995.

Bulmer-Thomas, Victor. *The Economic History of Latin America since Independence*. Cambridge: Cambridge University Press, 2003.

Burdick, John. *Blessed Anastácia: Women, Race, and Popular Christianity in Brazil*. New York: Routledge, 1998.

Burke, Timothy. *Lifebuoy Men, Lux Women: Commodification, Consumption and Cleanliness in Modern Zimbabwe*. Durham, N.C.: Duke University Press, 1996.

Burnett, Christina Duffy, and Burke Marshall, eds. *Foreign in a Domestic Sense: Puerto Rico, American Expansion, and the Constitution*. Durham, N.C.: Duke University Press, 2001.

Burns, E. Bradford. "Tradition and Variation in Brazilian Foreign Policy." *Journal of Inter-American Studies* 9, no. 2 (April 1967): 198–99.

———. *The Unwritten Alliance: Rio Branco and Brazilian-American Relations*. New York: Columbia University Press, 1966.

Burris, John P. *Exhibiting Religion: Colonialism and Spectacle at International Expositions, 1851–1893*. Charlottesville: University Press of Virginia, 2001.

Bushell, Garvin, as told to Mark Tucker. *Jazz from the Beginning*. New York: Da Capo Press, 1988.

Bushell, Garvin, and Monk Montgomery. "Interview with Garvin Bushell." Washington, D.C.: Smithsonian Institution Oral History, August 1977; Institute of Jazz Studies, Rutgers University.

Butler, Judith. *Bodies That Matter: On the Discursive Limits of "Sex."* New York: Routledge, 1993.

———. *Gender Trouble: Feminism and the Subversion of Identity*. New York: Routledge, 1990.

———. "Imitation and Gender Insubordination." In *The Lesbian and Gay Studies Reader*, Henry Abelove, Michèle Aina Barale, and David M. Halperin, eds. New York: Routledge, 1993, 307–320.

Butler, Kim D. *Freedoms Given, Freedoms Won: Afro-Brazilians in Post-Abolition São Paulo and Salvador*. New Brunswick, N.J.: Rutgers University Press, 1998.

Cabral, Sérgio. *No tempo de Ari Barroso*. Rio de Janeiro: Lumiar Editora, n.d.

———. *Pixinguinha: Vida e obra*. Rio de Janeiro: FUNARTE, 1978.

Caldeira, Teresa Pires do Rio. *City of Walls: Crime, Segregation, and Citizenship in São Paulo*. Berkeley: University of California Press, 2000.

Carby, Hazel V. "'It Jus Be's Dat Way Sometime': The Sexual Politics of Women's Blues." *Radical America* 20, no. 4 (1986): 9–24.

———. "Policing the Black Woman's Body in an Urban Context." *Critical Inquiry* 18, no. 4 (1992): 738–55.

Cárdenas, Enrique, José Antonio Ocampo, and Rosemary Thorp. "Introduction: The Export Age: The Latin American Economies in the Late Nineteenth and Early Twentieth Centuries." In Thorp, *Latin America in the 1930s*, 1–31.

Carelli, Mario, "Les Brésiliens à Paris de la naissance du romantisme aux avant-gardes." in Kaspi and Marès, *Le Paris des étrangers: depuis un siècle*, 287–98.

———. "Deuxième partie: Interactions culturelles franco-brésiliennes." In Carelli, Théry, and Zantman, *France-Brésil*, 107–71.

———. "Sottisier raisonné des stéréotypes franco-brésiliens." Introduction to Carelli, Théry, and Zantman, *France-Brésil*.

Carelli, Mario, Hervé Théry, and Alain Zantman. *France-Brésil: Bilan pour une relance*. Paris: Ed. Entente, 1987.

Carneiro, Sueli. "Mulher negra." In *Mulher negra: política governamental e a mulher.* São Paulo: Nobel, 1985, 1–54.

Carone, Iray, and Ma. Aparecida Silva Bento, orgs. *Psicologia social do racismo: estudos sobre branquitude e branqueamento no Brasil.* Rio de Janeiro: Vozes, 2002.

Carvalho, José Murilo de. *Os bestializados: o Rio de Janeiro e a República que não foi.* São Paulo: Cia. das Letras, 1987.

———. "Brazil 1870–1914. The Force of Tradition." *Journal of Latin American Studies* 24, Quincentenary Supplement (1992): 145–62.

———. "Dreams Come Untrue." *Daedalus* 129, no. 2 (spring 2000): 57–82.

Castle, Mr. and Mrs. [Irene and Vernon]. *Modern Dancing.* New York: Da Capo, 1980 [Harper and Row, 1914].

Castro, Hebe. *Das cores do silêncio: os significados da liberdade no sudeste escravista Brasil século XIX,* 2d ed. Rio de Janeiro: Editora Nova Fronteiroa, 1998 [1995].

Caulfield, Sueann. "Getting into Trouble: Dishonest Women, Modern Girls, and Women-Men in the Conceptual Language of *Vida Policial."* *Signs* 19, no. 1 (1993): 146–76.

———. *In Defense of Honor: Sexual Morality, Modernity and Nation in Early-Twentieth-Century Brazil.* Durham, N.C.: Duke University Press, 2000.

———. "Interracial Courtship in the Rio de Janeiro Courts, 1918–1940." In Applebaum, Macpherson, and Rosemblatt, *Race and Nation in Modern Latin America,* 163–86.

———. "Raça, sexo e casamento: crimes sexuais no Rio de Janeiro, 1918–1940." *Afro-Ásia* 18 (1996): 125–64.

Caws, Mary Ann. "Péret's 'Amour sublime': Just Another 'Amour fou'?" *French Review* 40, no. 2 (November 1966): 204–12.

Cell, John. *The Highest State of White Supremacy: The Origins of Segregation in South Africa and the U.S. South.* New York: Cambridge University Press, 1982.

Cendrars, Blaise, *Etc., etc. . . . : um livro 100% brasileiro.* São Paulo: Editora Perspectiva, 1976.

———. *Histoires vraies.* Paris: Bernard Grasset, 1927.

Cesaire, Aimé. *Discourse on Colonialism.* Trans. Joan Pinkham. New York: Monthly Review Press, 2000.

Chakrabarty, Dipesh. *Habitations of Modernity: Essays in the Wake of Subaltern Studies.* Chicago: University of Chicago Press, 2002.

———. "Postcoloniality and the Artifice of History: Who Speaks for Indian Pasts." *Representations* 37 (1992): 1–26.

———. *Provincializing Europe: Postcolonial Thought and Historical Difference.* Princeton, N.J.: Princeton University Press, 2000.

Chalhoub, Sidney. *Cidade febril: cortiços e epidemias na corte imperial.* São Paulo: Companhia das Letras, Editora Schwarcz, 1996.

———. "Medo branco de almas negras: escravos, libertos e republicanos na cidade do Rio." *Revista Brasileira de História* 8, no. 16 (1988): 83–105.

———. *Trabalho, lar e botequim: o cotidiano dos trabalhadores no Rio do Janeiro da belle époque.* São Paulo: Brasiliense, 1986.

Chasteen, John Charles. "The Prehistory of Samba: Carnival Dancing in Rio de Janeiro, 1840–1917." *Journal of Latin American Studies* 28 (1996): 29–47.

Cheatham, Wallace McClain. "African-American Women Singers at the Metropolitan Opera before Leontyne Price." *Journal of Negro History* 84, no. 2 (spring 1999): 167–81.

Chénieux-Gendron, Jacqueline. "Surrealists in Exile: Another Kind of Resistance." *Poetics Today* 17, no. 3 (fall 1996): 437–51.

Childs, John Brown. "Afro-American Intellectuals and the People's Culture." *Journal of Theory and Society* 13 (1984): 69–90.

Chin, Elizabeth. *Purchasing Power: Black Kids and Consumer Culture*. Minneapolis: University of Minnesota Press, 2001.

Chow, Rey. *Writing Diaspora: Tactics of Intervention in Contemporary Cultural Studies*. Bloomington: Indiana University Press, 1993.

Cobbs Hoffman, Elizabeth A. *The Rich Neighbor Policy: Rockefeller and Kaiser in Brazil*. New Haven, Conn.: Yale University Press, 1992.

Cohen, Lizabeth. *A Consumers' Republic: The Politics of Mass Consumption in Postwar America*. New York: Vintage Books, 2004.

Cohn, Arthur. "Philadelphia Story." *Modern Music* 19, no. 3 (March–April, 1942): 187[?]–89.

Collaer, Paul. *Darius Milhaud*. Trans. Jane Hohfeld Galante. San Francisco: San Francisco Press, 1988.

Collier, James Lincoln. *The Reception of Jazz in America: A New View*. Brooklyn: Institute for Studies in American Music, Brooklyn College, 1988.

Commission of the United States of America to the Brazilian Centennial Exposition, 1922–1923. *Final Report of the Commissioner General*. Entry 1306, RG 43, NA A2.

Congresso Nacional do Brasil. *Annaes da Camera dos Deputados*. Rio de Janeiro: Imprensa Nacional, all years.

———. *Annaes do Congresso*. Rio de Janeiro: Imprensa Nacional, all years.

Connell-Smith, Gordon. *The Inter-American System*. London: Royal Institute of International Affairs, Oxford University Press, 1966.

Contier, Arnaldo. *Música e ideologia no Brasil*. São Paulo: Novas Metas, 1985.

Cooper, Frederick. *Colonialism in Question: Theory, Knowledge, History*. Chapel Hill: University of North Carolina Press, 2005.

———. "Modernity." In Cooper, *Colonialism in Question*.

———. "What Is the Concept of Globalization Good For? An African Historian's Perspective." *African Affairs* 100, no. 399 (2001): 189–213.

Cooper, Frederick, and Ann Laura Stoler, eds. *Tensions of Empire: Colonial Cultures in a Bourgeois World*. Berkeley: University of California Press, 1997.

"Copy Writer Speaks, A." Oral history of George Cecil. Unpublished manuscript. New York: N. W. Ayer and Son Archives.

Costa, Cristina, cur. *Julio Guerra: um modernista marginal*. Text by Cristina Costa and Anna Maria Rahme. São Paulo: Pinacoteca do Estado, 1994.

Costa, Emilia Viotti da. "The Myth of Racial Democracy." Chapter 9 in *The Brazilian Empire: Myths and Histories*. Chicago: University of Chicago Press, 1985.

Coste, Felix (secretary-manager, Joint Coffee Trade Publicity Committee). "A Guide-Post for Co-operative Advertising Campaigns: Here, for the First Time, Is Told the Complete and Full Story of the Coffee Industry's Co-operative Advertising Campaign." *Printers' Ink*, June 19, 1924.

Courtot, Claude. *Introduction à la lecture de B. Péret*. Paris: Terrain Vague, 1965.

Cowell, Bainbridge, Jr. "Cityward Migration in the Nineteenth Century: The Case of Recife, Brazil." *Journal of Interamerican Studies and World Affairs* 17, no. 1 (February 1975): 43–63.

Cox, Ernest Sevier. *The South's Part in Mongrelizing the Nation*. Richmond, Va.: Society of a White America, 1926.

———. *White America*. Richmond, Va.: Society of a White America, 1923.

Cox, Oliver Cromwell. *Caste, Class, and Race: A Study in Social Dynamics*. New York: Doubleday, 1948.

Crenshaw, Kimberle. "Mapping the Margins: Intersectionality, Identity Politics, and Violence against Women of Color." *Stanford Law Review* 43, no. 6. (July 1991): 1241–99.

Cripps, Thomas. "The *Birth of a Race Company*: An Early Stride toward a Black Cinema." *Journal of Negro History* 59, no. 1 (1974): 28–37.

Cross, Gary. *An All-Consuming Century: Why Commercialism Won in Modern America*. New York: Columbia University Press, 2000.

Crowe, Charles. "Racial Violence and Social Reform: Origins of the Atlanta Riot of 1906." *Journal of Negro History* 53, no. 3 (1968): 234–56.

Cruz, Maria Cecilia Velasco e. "Virando o jogo: estivadores e carregadoreno Rio de Janeiro da Primeira República." Ph.D. diss., USP, 1988.

Cunha, Olívia Maria Gomes da. *Intenção e gesto: pessoa, cor e a produção cotidiana da (in)diferença no Rio de Janeiro, 1927–1942*. Rio de Janeiro: Arquivo Nacional, 2002.

———. "1933: Um ano em que fizemos contato." *Revista USP* 28 (1995–96): 142–63.

Dalton, Karen C. C., and Henry Louis Gates, Jr. "Josephine Baker and Paul Colin: African American Dance Seen through Parisian Eyes." *Critical Inquiry* 24, no. 4 (summer 1998): 903–34.

Daly, Ann. *Done into Dance: Isadora Duncan in America*. Bloomington: Indiana University Press, 1995.

Dávila, Arlene. *Latinos, Inc.: The Making and Marketing of a People*. Berkeley: University of California Press, 2001.

Dávila, Jerry. *Diploma of Whiteness: Race and Social Policy in Brazil, 1917–1945*. Durham, N.C.: Duke University Press, 2003.

———. "Expanding Perspectives on Race in Brazil." *Latin American Research Review* 35, no. 3 (2000): 188–98.

Davis, Angela. *Blues Legacies and Black Feminism: Gertrude "Ma" Rainey, Bessie Smith, and Billie Holiday*. New York: Vintage Books, 1998.

Davis, Simone Weil. *Living up to the Ads: Gender Fictions of the 1920s*. Durham, N.C.: Duke University Press, 2000.

Dawsey, Cyrus B., and James M. Dawsey. *The Confederados: Old South Immigrants in Brazil*. Tuscaloosa: University of Alabama Press, 1995.

Dawsey, John Cowart. "O espelho americano: Americanos para Brasileiros ver e 'Brazilians for Americans to See.'" *Revista de Antropologia* (Brazil) 37 (1994): 203–56.

Dean, Warren. *The Industrialization of São Paulo, 1880–1945*. Austin: University of Texas Press, 1969; translated as *A industrialização de São Paulo (1880—1945)*. São Paulo: Dif. Européia do Livro/Editora da USP, 1971.

DeBiaggi, Sylvia Duarte Dantas. *Changing Gender Roles: Brazilian Immigrant Families in the U.S.* New York: LFB Scholarly Publications, 2002.

Debret, Jean Baptiste. *Voyage pittoresque et historique au Brésil*. Paris: Firmin Didot, 1834.

De Chocolat. *Tudo preto*. "Revuette-charge," 2, Arquivo da 2a Delegacia Auxiliar de Polícia, Caixa 40, n.º 891, Arquivo Nacional, Rio de Janeiro.

Defrantz, Thomas F., ed. *Dancing Many Drums: Excavations in African American Dance*. Madison: University of Wisconsin Press, 2001.

Degler, Carl N. *Neither Black nor White: Slavery and Race Relations in Brazil and the United States*. New York: Macmillan, 1971.

Delfim Netto, Antônio. *O problema do café no Brasil*. Rio de Janeiro: Editora da Fundação Getulio Vargas, Ministério da Agricultura/SUPLAN, 1979 [1959].

Denis, Ferdinand. *Brésil*. Paris: Firmin Didot, 1837.

Dennison, Sam. *Scandalize My Name: Black Imagery in American Popular Music*. New York: Garland, 1982.

Derrida, Jacques. "'Des Tours de Babel' + Poststructuralism as Exegesis: The Insufficiency and Impossibility of the Translation of Languages." Trans. Joseph F. Graham. *Semeia* (1991): 3–34.

Detweiler, Frederick German. *The Negro Press in the United States*. Chicago: University of Chicago Press, 1922.

Dewitte, Philippe. *Les mouvements nègres en France pendant les entre-deux-guerres*. Paris: Harmattan, 1985.

———. "Le Paris noir de l'entre-deux-guerres." In Kaspi and Marès, *Le Paris des étrangers: depuis un siècle*, 156–69.

di Leonardo, Micaela. *Exotics at Home: Anthropologies, Others, American Modernity*. Chicago: University of Chicago Press, 1998.

Dias, Maria Odila Leite da Silva. *Power and Everyday Life: The Lives of Working Women in Nineteenth-Century Brazil*. Trans. Ann Frost. New Brunswick, N.J.: Rutgers University Press, 1995.

Donohue, Kathleen G. *Freedom from Want: American Liberalism and the Idea of the Consumer*. Baltimore: Johns Hopkins University Press, 2004.

Douglas, Ann. *Terrible Honesty: Mongrel Manhattan in the 1920s*. New York: Farrar, Straus, and Giroux, 1996 [1995].

Driggs, Frank, and Harris Lewine. *Black Beauty, White Heat: A Pictorial History of Classic Jazz, 1920–1950*. New York: William Morrow, 1982.

Dubeux, Albert. "Mistinguette." In *Acteurs . . . Neuf portraits hors-texte*. Paris: Librairie Théatrale, 1929, 173–90.

Dubois, Laurent. *A Colony of Citizens: Revolution and Slave Emancipation in the*

French Caribbean, 1787–1804. Chapel Hill: Omohundro Institute of Early American History and Culture, Williamsburg, by the University of North Carolina Press, 2004.

Du Bois, W. E. B. *Black Reconstruction*. New York: Harcourt, Brace, 1935.

———. *Dusk of Dawn: An Essay toward an Autobiography of a Race Concept*. New Brunswick, N.J.: Transaction Publishers, 1992 [1940].

———. *The Emerging Thought of W. E. B. Du Bois: Essays and Editorials from the Crisis*, ed. Henry Lee Moon. New York: Simon and Schuster, 1972.

———. "The Negro Race in the United States of America." *Papers on Inter-Racial Problems* (Communicated to the First Universal Races Congress, held at the University of London, 1911), ed. G. Spiller. London: P. S. King and Son, 1911, 348–64.

Duggan, Lisa. *Sapphic Slashers: Sex, Violence, and American Modernity*. Durham, N.C.: Duke University Press, 2000.

Dunn, Christopher. *Brutality Garden: Tropicalia and the Emergence of a Brazilian Counterculture*. Chapel Hill: University of North Carolina Press, 2001.

Duran, Gustavo. *Recordings of Latin American Songs and Dances: An Annotated Select List of Popular and Folk Music*. Washington, D.C.: Music Division, Pan American Union, 1942.

Dussel, Enrique, "Eurocentrism and Modernity (Introduction to the Frankfurt Lectures)." In *The Postmodernism Debate in Latin America*, special issue of *Boundary 2*, ed. John Beverley and José Oviedo (fall 1993): 65–76.

———. "The Invention of the Americas: Eclipse of 'the Other' and the Myth of Modernity." New York: Continuum, 1995 [1992].

———. *The Underside of Modernity: Apel, Ricoeur, Rorty, Taylor, and the Philosophy of Liberation*. Trans. and ed. Eduardo Mendieta. Atlantic Highlands: Humanities Press, 1996.

Duster, Troy. "Buried Alive: The Concept of Race in Science." In *Genetic Nature/Culture: Anthropology and Science beyond the Two-Culture Divide*, Alan H. Goodman, Deborah Heath, and M. Susan Lindee, eds. Berkeley: University of California Press, 2003, 258–77.

Eckes, Alfred E., Jr. *Opening America's Market: U.S. Foreign Trade Policy since 1776*. Chapel Hill: University of North Carolina Press, 1995.

Edelman, Lee. *No Future: Queer Theory and the Death Drive*. Durham, N.C.: Duke University Press, 2004.

Edwards, Brent Hayes. "On Critical Globality." *Ariel* 31, nos. 1–2 (January–April 2000): 255–74.

———. *The Practice of Diaspora: Literature, Translation, and the Rise of Black Internationalism*. Cambridge, Mass.: Harvard University Press, 2003.

———. "Rendez-vous in Rhythm." *Connect* 1 (fall 2000): 182–90.

Efegê, Jota [João Ferreira Gomes]. *Figuras e coisas da música popular brasileira*, 2 vols. Rio de Janeiro: FUNARTE, 1978 and 1980.

———. *Maxixe: a dança excomungada*. Rio de Janiero: Conquista, 1974.

Egan, Bill. *Florence Mills: Harlem Jazz Queen*. Lanham, Md.: Scarecrow Press, 2004.

Ellison, Ralph, and John F. Callahan. *The Collected Essays of Ralph Ellison*. New York: Modern Library, 1995.

Emmons, Steve. "Olga Burgoyne and Where She Danced." *Star Free Press* (Ventura, Calif.), April 9, 1967, 3–4.

Enciclopédia da música brasileira. São Paulo: Art Editora/Publifolha, 2000.

Epstein, Barbara Leslie. *The Politics of Domesticity: Women, Evangelism, and Temperance in Nineteenth-Century America*. Middletown, Conn.: Wesleyan University Press and Columbia University Press, 1981.

Epstein, Edward Jay. *The Diamond Invention: The Rise and Fall of Diamonds*. New York: Simon and Schuster, 1982.

Escobar, Arturo. *Encountering Development: The Making and Unmaking of the Third World*. Princeton, N.J.: Princeton University Press, 1995.

Esteves, Antônio. "*O baile do samba* con el tango." *Hispania (Revista Cultural Latinoamericana)*, no. 6 (1997).

Estudos Feministas 3, no. 2, special issue on Afro-Brazilian women (1995).

Etta Moten Barnett's Return to the United States (sound recording). Chicago: WMAQ Radio, 1955; NYPL, Schomburg Branch, Recorded Sound Division.

Evans, Nicholas M. *Writing Jazz: Race, Nationalism, and Modern Culture in the 1920s* New York: Garland, 2000.

Everett, Anna. *Returning the Gaze: A Genealogy of Black Film Criticism, 1909–1949*. Durham, N.C.: Duke University Press, 2001.

Ewen, Stuart. *Captains of Consciousness: Advertising and the Social Roots of the Consumer Culture*. New York: McGraw-Hill, 1976.

Ewen, Stuart, and Elizabeth Ewen. *Channels of Desire: Mass Images and the Shaping of American Consciousness*. New York: McGraw-Hill, 1982.

Fabian, Johannes. *Time and the Other: How Anthropology Makes Its Object*. New York: Columbia University Press, 1983.

Fabre, Michel. *From Harlem to Paris: Black American Writers in France, 1840–1980*. Urbana: University of Illinois Press, 1991.

Falk, Pasi. *The Consuming Body*. London: Sage, 1994.

Fanon, Franz. *Black Skin, White Masks: The Experiences of a Black Man in a White World*. New York: Grove, 1967 [1952].

Fein, Seth. "Culture across Borders in the Americas." *Blackwell History Compass*; http://www.history-compass.com/Pilot/northam/NthAm_CulturesArticle.htm (accessed October 16, 2004).

———. "New Empire into Old: Making Mexican Newsreels the Cold War Way." *Diplomatic History* 28, no. 5 (November 2004): 703–48.

———. *Transnational Projections: The United States in the Golden Age of Mexican Cinema*. Durham, N.C.: Duke University Press, forthcoming.

Fejes, Fred. *Imperialism, Media, and the Good Neighbor: New Deal Foreign Policy and United States Shortwave Broadcasting to Latin America*. Norwood: Ablex, 1986.

Felski, Rita. *The Gender of Modernity*. Cambridge, Mass.: Harvard University Press, 1995.

Ferguson, Niall. *Colossus: The Price of America's Empire*. New York: Penguin Press, 2004.

Fernandes, Florestan. *A integração do negro na sociedade de classes*. Trans. as *The Negro in Brazilian Society*, trans. Jacqueline D. Skiles, A. Brunel, and Arthur Rothwell. New York: Columbia University Press, 1969.

Ferrara, Miriam Nicolau. "Imprensa negra paulista." *Revista Brasileira de Historia* (São Paulo) 5, no. 10 (1985): 197–207.

———. "A imprensa negra paulista (1915–1963)." Master's thesis, University of São Paulo, 1981.

Ferro, António. *A idade do jazz-band*. São Paulo: Monteiro Lobato, 1923.

Fields, Barbara Jeanne. "Slavery, Race and Ideology in the United States of America." *New Left Review* 1, no. 181 (May–June 1990): 95–118.

Figueiredo, Angela. *Novas elites de cor: estudos sobre os profissionais liberais negros de Salvador*. São Paulo: Editora Annablume, 2002.

Findlay, Eileen. *Imposing Decency: The Politics of Sexuality and Race in Puerto Rico, 1870–1920*. Durham, N.C.: Duke University Press, 1999.

Fiol-Matta, Licia. *A Queer Mother for the Nation: The State and Gabriela Mistral*. Minneapolis: University of Minnesota Press, 2002.

Flexner, Stuart Berg. *I Hear America Talking*. Simon and Schuster, 1976.

Floyd, Samuel A., Jr. *The Power of Black Music: Interpreting Its History from Africa to the United States*. New York: Oxford University Press, 1995.

Foley, Neil. *The White Scourge: Mexicans, Blacks, and Poor Whites in Texas Cotton Culture*. Berkeley: University of California Press, 1997.

Fones-Wolf, Elizabeth. Review of James Hoopes, *False Prophets: The Gurus Who Created Modern Management and Why Their Ideas Are Bad for Business Today*. Cambridge: Perseus, 2003. *AHR* 109, no. 5 (December 2004): 1606.

Font, Mauricio A. "City and Countryside in the Onset of Brazilian Industrialization." *Studies in Comparative International Development* 27, no. 3 (fall 1992): 26–56.

———. *Coffee, Contention, and Change in the Making of Modern Brazil*. Cambridge: Basil Blackwell, 1990.

Foreman, Ronald Clifton, Jr. "Jazz and Race Records, 1920–1932: Their Origin and Significance for the Recording Industry." Ph.D. diss., University of Illinois, 1968.

Foulkes, Julia. *Modern Bodies: Dance and American Modernism from Martha Graham to Alvin Ailey*. Chapel Hill: University of North Carolina Press, 2002.

Fox, Richard Wightman, and T. J. Jackson Lears, eds. *The Culture of Consumption in America: Critical Essays in American History, 1880–1980*. New York: Pantheon Books, 1983.

Franco, Afonso Arinos de Melo. *O indio brasileiro e a revolução francesa: as origens brasileiras da teoria de bondade natural*, 2d ed. Rio de Janeiro: José Olympio, 1976.

Frank, Dana. *Buy American: The Untold Story of Economic Nationalism*. Boston, Mass.: Beacon Press, 1999.

Frank, Zephyr, and Aldo Musacchio. "Brazil in the International Rubber Trade, 1870–1930." In Topik, Marichal, and Frank, *From Silver to Cocaine*, 271–99.

Frazier, E. Franklin. *Black Bourgeoisie: The Rise of a New Middle Class in the United States.* Glencoe, Ill.: Free Press, 1957.

———. "Brazil Has No Race Problem." *Common Sense* 11, no. 11 (1942): 363–65.

———. "A Comparison of Negro-White Relations in Brazil and in the United States." In *Transactions of the New York Academy of Sciences*, Series 2, 6, no. 7 (1944): 251–69.

———. "Rejoinder to Melville J. Herskovits, 'The Negro in Bahia, Brazil': A Problem in Method." *ASR* 8, no. 4 (1943): 402–4.

Frederick, Christine McGaffey. *Selling Mrs. Consumer.* New York: Business Bourse, 1929.

Frederickson, George M. "Race and Racism in Historical Perspective." In *Beyond Racism: Race and Inequality in Brazil, South Africa, and the United States*, ed. Charles V. Hamilton. Boulder, Colo.: Lynne Rienner, 2001.

Freeland, Thornton, dir. *Flying Down to Rio.* RKO Radio Pictures, 1933.

Freire-Medeiros, Bianca. "Hollywood Musicals and the Invention of Rio de Janeiro, 1933–1953." *Cinema Journal* 41, no. 4 (2002): 52–67.

French, John D. "The Missteps of Anti-Imperialist Reason: Bourdieu, Wacquant, and Hanchard's *Orpheus and Power*." *Theory, Culture and Society* 17, no. 1 (2000): 107–28.

Freyre, Gilberto. *Casa-grande senzala: formação da família brasileira sob o regime de economia patriarchal.* Rio de Janeiro: Maia and Schmidt, 1933.

———. *Tempo de aprendiz*, org. José Antônio Gonsalves de Mello, 2 vols. São Paulo: IBRASA, and Brasília: INL, 1979.

Freyre, Gilberto, Arthur Ramos, and the Congresso Afro-Brasileiro, eds. *Novos estudos afro-brasileiros*, vol. 2: *Trabalhos apresentados ao 1. Congreso Afro-Brasileiro do Recife.* Rio de Janeiro: Civilizacao Brasileira, 1937.

Fried, Richard M. *The Man Everybody Knew: Bruce Barton and the Making of Modern America.* Chicago: Ivan R. Dee, 2005.

Fritsch, Winston. *External Constraints on Economic Policy in Brazil, 1889–1930.* Basingstoke: Macmillan, 1988.

Fry, Peter. "Politics, Nationality, and the Meanings of 'Race' in Brazil." *Daedalus* 129, no. 2 (spring 2000): 83–118.

———. "O que a Cinderela negra tem a dizer sobre a 'política racial' no Brasil." *Revista USP* 28 (1995–96): 122–36.

———. "Why Brazil Is Different." *Times Literary Supplement*, no. 8 (December, 1995): 6–7.

Fryer, Peter. *Rhythms of Resistance: African Musical Heritage in Brazil.* London: Pluto Press, 2000.

Fuente, Alejandro de la. "Myths of Racial Democracy: Cuba, 1900–1912." *Latin American Research Review* 34, no. 3 (1999): 39–73.

Fuller, Donald. "Forecast and Review: Americans to the Fore—New York, 1941–42." *Modern Music* 19, no. 2 (January–February 1942): 113[?]–15.

Gabaccia, Donna R. "Is Everywhere Nowhere? Nomads, Nations, and the Immigrant Paradigm of United States History." In *The Nation and Beyond: Transnational Perspectives on United States History*, special issue of *Journal of American History* 86, no. 3 (December 1999): 1115–34.

Gabbard, Krin. *Jammin' at the Margins: Jazz and American Cinema*. Chicago: University of Chicago Press, 1996.

Gaines, Kevin K. "Black Americans' Racial Uplift Ideology as 'Civilizing Mission': Pauline E. Hopkins on Race and Imperialism." In A. Kaplan and Pease, *Cultures of United States Imperialism*, 433–55.

———. *Uplifting the Race: Black Leadership, Politics, and Culture in the Twentieth Century*. Chapel Hill: University of North Carolina Press, 1996.

Gallicchio, Marc. *The African American Encounter with Japan and China: Black Internationalism in Asia, 1895–1945*. Chapel Hill: University of North Carolina Press, 2000.

Garcia, Thomas. "The Choro, the Guitar, and Villa-Lobos." *Luso-Brazilian Review* 34, no. 1 (1997): 57–66.

García Canclini, Néstor. *Consumers and Citizens: Globalization and Multicultural Conflicts*. Trans. George Yúdice. Minneapolis: University of Minnesota Press, 2001.

Gardel, André. *O encontro entre Bandeira e Sinhô*. Rio de Janeiro: Secretaria Municipal de Cultura, 1996.

Garfield, Seth. *Indigenous Struggle at the Heart of Brazil: State Policy, Frontier Expansion, and the Xavante Indians, 1937–1988*. Durham, N.C.: Duke University Press, 2001.

Garrod, Charles, and Bill Korst. *Bob Crosby and His Orchestra*. Zephyrhills, Fla.: Joyce Record Club, 1987.

Gatewood, Willard B. *Black Americans and the White Man's Burden, 1898–1903*. Urbana: University of Illinois Press, 1975.

———. *"Smoked Yankees" and the Struggle for Empire: Letters from Negro Soldiers, 1898–1902*. Urbana: University of Illinois Press, 1971.

Gendron, Bernard. *Between Montmartre and the Mudd Club: Popular Music and the Avant-Garde*. Chicago: University of Chicago Press, 2002.

George-Graves, Nadine. *The Royalty of Negro Vaudeville: The Whitman Sisters and the Negotiation of Race, Gender and Class in African American Theater, 1900–1940*. New York: St. Martin's Press, 2000.

Gereffi, Gary, and Miguel Korzeniewicz, eds. *Commodity Chains and Global Capitalism*. New York: Praeger, 1994.

Giddings, Paula. "The Last Taboo." In *Race-ing Justice, Engendering Power: Essays on Anita Hill, Clarence Thomas and the Construction of Social Reality*, ed. Toni Morrison. New York: Pantheon Books, 1992, 440–65.

Giele, Janet Zollinger. *Two Paths to Women's Equality: Temperance, Suffrage, and the Origins of Modern Feminism*. New York: Twayne, 1995.

Gill, Lesley. *The School of the Americas: Military Training and Political Violence in the Americas*. Durham, N.C.: Duke University Press, 2004.

Gilmore, Glenda. *Gender and Jim Crow*. Chapel Hill: University of North Carolina Press, 1996.

Gilroy, Paul, *Against Race: Imagining Political Culture beyond the Color Line*. Cambridge, Mass.: Belknap Press of Harvard University Press, 2000.

———. *The Black Atlantic: Modernity and Double Consciousness*. Cambridge, Mass.: Harvard University Press, 1993.

Ginsberg, Elaine K., ed. *Passing and the Fictions of Identity*. Durham, N.C.: Duke University Press, 1996.

Ginway, M. Elizabeth. "Conversa com Mary Houston Pedrosa." Unpublished interview conducted in Rio de Janeiro, March 17, 1983.

———. "Notes from My Talk with Captain Geyser Péret." Unpublished interview conducted in São Paulo, June 9, 1983.

———. "Surrealist Benjamin Péret and Brazilian Modernism." *Hispania* 75, no. 3 (September 1992): 543–53.

Ginzberg, Lori D. *Women and the Work of Benevolence: Morality, Politics, and Class in the Nineteenth-Century United States*. New Haven, Conn.: Yale University Press, 1990.

Giovannini, Francesco. *Balli d'oggi*. Milano: U. Hoepli, 1914.

Gladwell, Malcolm. "Java Man: How Caffeine Created the Modern World." *New Yorker*, July 30, 2001, 76–80.

Goddard, Chris. *Jazz away from Home*. New York: Paddington Press, 1979.

Gomes, Flávio dos Santos. Biography of Abdias do Nascimento, forthcoming.

———. *Histórias de quilombolas: mocambos e comunidades de senzalas no Rio de Janeiro—século XIX*. Rio de Janeiro: Arquivo Nacional, 1995.

———. "No meio das aguas turvas (Racismo e cidadania no alvorecer da República: a Guarda Negra na Corte—1888–1889)." *Estudos Afro-Asiáticos* 21 (1991): 75–96.

Gomes, P. E. Salles. *Humberto Mauro, cataguases, cinearte*. São Paulo: Editora Perspectiva, Editora da USP, 1974.

Gomes, Tiago de Melo. "'Como eles se divertem' (e se entendem): teatro de revista, cultura de massas e identidades sociais no Rio de Janeiro dos anos 1920." Doct. thesis, UNICAMP, 2003.

———. *Um espelho no palco: identidades sociais e massificação da cultura no teatro de revista dos 1920*. Campinas: Ed. Unicamp, 2004.

———. "Lenço no pescoço: o malandro no teatro de revista e na música popular— 'nacional,' 'popular' e cultura de massas nos anos 1920." Master's thesis, UNICAMP, 1998.

———. "Massais, mulatas, meretrizes: imagens da sexualidade feminina no Rio de Janeiro dos anos 1920." *Cadernos Pagu* 23 (July–December 2004): 121–47.

———. "Negros contando (e fazendo) sua história: alguns significados da trajetória da Companhia Negra de Revistas (1926)." *Estudos Afro-Asiáticos* 23, no. 1 (2001): 53–83.

———. "Para além da casa da Tia Ciata: outras experiências no universo cultural carioca, 1830–1930." *Afro-Ásia* 29/30 (2003): 175–98.

———. "Problemas no paraíso: a democracia racial brasileira frente à imigração afro-americana (1921)." *Estudos Afro-Asiáticos* 25, no. 2 (2003): 307–31.

Gomes, Tiago de Melo, and Micol Seigel. "Sabina das laranjas: gênero, raça e nação na trajetória de um símbolo popular, 1889–1930." *Revista Brasileira de História* 43 (July 2002): 171–93.

Gossett, Thomas F. *Race: The History of an Idea in America*. Dallas: Southern Methodist University Press, 1963.

Gottschild, Brenda Dixon. "Between Two Eras: 'Norton and Margot' in the Afro-American Entertainment World." In Defrantz, *Dancing Many Drums*, 267–87.

———. *Waltzing in the Dark: African American Vaudeville and Race Politics in the Swing Era*. New York: St. Martin's Press, 2000.

Goza, Franklin. "Brazilian Immigration to North America." *International Migration Review* 28, no. 1 (1994): 136–52.

Graden, Dale T. "An Act 'Even of Public Security': Slave Resistance, Social Tensions, and the End of the International Slave Trade to Brazil, 1835–1856." *HAHR* 76, no. 2 (1996): 249–82.

Graham, Richard. "Economics or Culture? The Development of the U.S. South and Brazil in the Days of Slavery." In *What Made the South Different? Essays and Comments*, ed. Kees Gispen. Jackson: University Press of Mississippi, 1990, 97–124.

———. "Free African Brazilians and the State in Slavery Times." In Hanchard, *Racial Politics in Contemporary Brazil*, 30–58.

———, ed. *The Idea of Race in Latin America*. Austin: University of Texas Press, 1990.

Green, James N. *Beyond Carnival: Male Homosexuality in Twentieth-Century Brazil*. Chicago: University of Chicago Press, 1999.

Green, Jeffrey P. "The Negro Renaissance and England." In *Black Music of the Harlem Renaissance*, ed. Samuel A. Floyd, Jr. Westport, Conn.: Greenwood Press, 1993, 150–71.

Gregg, Robert. *Inside Out, Outside In: Essays in Comparative History*. New York: St. Martin's Press, 2000.

Guerra, François-Xavier. "La lumière et ses reflects: Paris et la politique latino-américaine." In Kaspi and Marès, *Le Paris des étrangers: depuis un siècle*, 171–81.

Guglielmo, Thomas A. *White on Arrival: Italians, Race, Color, and Power in Chicago, 1890–1945*. New York: Oxford University Press, 2003.

Guimarães, Antônio Sérgio Alfredo. "Brasil–Estados Unidos: um diálogo que forja nossa identidade racial." *Estudos Afro-Ásiáticos* 26 (September 1994): 141–47.

———. *Classes, raças e democracia*. São Paulo: Ed. 34; Fundação de Apoio à Universidade de São Paulo(FUSP), 2002.

Guinle, Jorge. *Jazz Panorama*. Rio de Janeiro: Livraria Agir Ed., 1953.

Gussi, Alcides Fernando. *Os norte-americanos (confederados) do Brasil: Identidades no contexto transnacional*. Campinas: Área de Publicações CMU/UNICAMP, 1997.

Guterl, Matthew Pratt. *The Color of Race in America, 1900–1940*. Cambridge, Mass.: Harvard University Press, 2001.

Guy, Donna J. *Sex and Danger in Buenos Aires: Prostitution, Family, and Nation in Argentina*. Lincoln: University of Nebraska Press, 1991.

Halberstam, Judith. *Female Masculinity*. Durham, N.C.: Duke University Press, 1998.

Hale, Grace Elizabeth. "Granite Stopped Time: Stone Mountain Memorial and the Representation of White Southern Identity." In Mills and Simpson, *Monuments to the Lost Cause*, 219–33.

———. *Making Whiteness: The Culture of Segregation in the South, 1890–1940*. New York: Pantheon Books, 1998.

Halperín-Donghi, Tulio. *The Contemporary History of Latin America*. Trans. and ed. John Charles Chasteen. Durham, N.C.: Duke University Press, 1993.

Hammonds, Evelynn. "Black (W)holes and the Geometry of Black Female Sexuality." *differences* 6, nos. 2–3 (1994): 126–45.

Hanchard, Michael George. "Black Cinderella? Race and the Public Sphere in Brazil." In Hanchard, *Racial Politics in Contemporary Brazil*, 59–81.

———. *Orpheus and Power: The Movimento Negro of Rio de Janeiro and São Paulo, Brazil, 1945–1988*. Princeton, N.J.: Princeton University Press, 1994.

———, ed. *Racial Politics in Contemporary Brazil*. Durham, N.C.: Duke University Press, 1999.

Handlin, Oscar. *The Uprooted: The Epic Story of the Great Migrations That Made the American People*. Boston, Mass.: Little, Brown, 1951.

Haney López, Ian F. *White by Law: The Legal Construction of Race*. New York: New York University Press, 1996.

Haraway, Donna. *Primate Visions: Gender, Race, and Nature in the World of Modern Science*. New York: Routledge, 1989.

Harding, Rachel E. *A Refuge in Thunder: Candomblé and Alternative Spaces of Blackness*. Bloomington: Indiana University Press, 2000.

Hardt, Michael, and Antonio Negri. *Empire*. Cambridge, Mass.: Harvard University Press, 2000.

———. *Multitude: War and Democracy in the Age of Empire*. New York: Penguin Press, 2004.

Harlan, Louis R., Raymond W. Smock, and Nan E. Woodruff, eds. *The Booker T. Washington Papers*. Urbana: University of Illinois Press, 1980. Open Book Edition, http://stills.nap.edu/btw/.

Harris, Cheryl. "Whiteness as Property." *Harvard Law Review* 106 (1993): 1709–95.

Harris, Joseph E. *African-American Reactions to War in Ethiopia, 1936–1941*. Baton Rouge: Louisiana State University Press, 1973.

Harris, Trudier. *Exorcising Blackness: Historical and Literary Lynching and Burning Rituals*. Bloomington: Indiana University Press, 1984.

Harrison, Daphne Duval. *Black Pearls: Blues Queens of the 1920s*. New Brunswick, N.J.: Rutgers University Press, 1998.

Hart, Matthew. *Diamond: The History of a Cold-Blooded Love Affair*. London: Fourth Estate, 2002.

Harvey, Penelope. *Hybrids of Modernity: Anthropology, the Nation State and the Universal Exhibition*. London: Routledge, 1996.

Hasenbalg, Carlos Alfredo. "Anotações sobre a classe média negra no Rio de Janeiro." *Revista de Antropologia* (Brazil) 26 (1983): 53–63.

————. *Discriminação e desigualdades raciais no Brasil*. Rio de Janeiro: Graal, 1979.

Hasenbalg, Carlos Alfredo, and Nelson do Valle Silva. "Notes on Racial and Political Inequality in Brazil." In Hanchard, *Racial Politics in Contemporary Brazil*, 154–78.

Heard, Marcia E., and Mansa K. Mussa. "African Dance in New York City." In Defrantz, *Dancing Many Drums*, 143–53.

Helg, Aline. "Los intelectuales frente a la cuestion racial en el decenio de 1920: Colombia entre Mexico y Argentina." *Estudios Sociales* (FAES) 4 (March 1989): 37–53.

Hellwig, David J., ed. *African-American Reflections on Brazil's Racial Paradise*. Philadelphia, Pa.: Temple University Press, 1992.

————. "The Afro-American Press and Woodrow Wilson's Mexican Policy, 1913–1917." *Phylon* 48, no. 4 (winter 1987): 261–70.

————. "Afro-American Reactions to the Japanese and the Anti-Japanese Movement, 1906–1924." *Phylon* 38, no. 1 (winter 1977): 93–104.

————. "Black Leaders and United States Immigration Policy, 1917–1929." *Journal of Negro History* 66, no. 2 (summer 1981): 110–27.

————. "A New Frontier in a Racial Paradise: Robert S. Abbott's Brazilian Dream." *Luso-Brazilian Review* 25, no. 1 (1988): 59–67.

————. "Racial Paradise or Run-Around? Afro-North American Views of Race in Brazil." *American Studies* 31, no. 2 (1990): 43–60.

Hennessey, Thomas. J. *From Jazz to Swing: African American Jazz Musicians and Their Music, 1890–1935*. Detroit: Wayne State University Press, 1994.

Henriksen, Henry. "Black Patti." RR [acronym not explained], 1979. HAJ MTC.

Herskovits, Melville J. "African Gods and Catholic Saints in New World Negro Belief." *American Anthropologist* 39 (1937): 635–43.

Higginbotham, Evelyn Brooks. "African-American Women's History and the Metalanguage of Race." *Signs* 17 (winter 1992): 251–74.

Hill, Arlette Olin, and Boyd H. Hill Jr. "Marc Block and Comparative History." AHR 85, no. 4 (October 1980): 828–46.

Hill, Lawrence Francis. "Confederate Exiles to Brazil." HAHR 7 (1927): 192–210.

————. *The Confederate Exodus to Latin America*. Austin [?], 1936. Also in *Southwestern Historical Quarterly* (Austin), October 1935 and January and April 1936.

Hilton, Stanley. *Brazil and the Great Powers, 1930–1939: The Politics of Trade Rivalry*. Austin: University of Texas Press, 1975.

Hobsbawm, Eric J. *Uncommon People: Resistance, Rebellion and Jazz*. New York: New Press, 1998.

Hodes, Martha. "The Mercurial Nature and Abiding Power of Race: A Transnational Family Story." AHR 108, no. 1 (February 2003): 84–118.

————. *White Women, Black Men: Illicit Sex in the Nineteenth-Century South*. New Haven, Conn.: Yale University Press, 1997.

Hoganson, Kristin L. *Fighting for American Manhood: How Gender Politics Provoked the Spanish-American and Philippine-American Wars*. New Haven, Conn.: Yale University Press, 1998.

Holloway, Thomas H. *The Brazilian Coffee Valorization of 1906: Regional Politics and Economic Dependence*. Madison: State Historical Society of Wisconsin, 1975.

Holt, Thomas C. "Marking: Race, Race-Making, and the Writing of History." *AHR* 100 (February 1995): 1–20.

Hoover, Herbert. *The Memoirs of Herbert Hoover*, 3 vols. New York: Macmillan, 1952.

Horowitz, Daniel. *The Morality of Spending: Attitudes toward the Consumer Society in America, 1875–1940*. Baltimore: Johns Hopkins University Press, 1985.

Houston, Elsie. *Chants populaires du Brésil*, 1st series. Paris: Librairie Orientaliste Paul Geuthner, 1930.

———. "La musique, la danse et les cérémonies populaires du Brésil." In *Art populaire: travaux artistiques et scientifiques du 1er Congres international des arts populaires, Prague, 1928*. Paris: Ed. Duchartre, 1931, 162–64.

Hunt, Michael H. *Ideology and U.S. Foreign Policy*. New Haven, Conn.: Yale University Press, 1987.

Hunter, Charlayne. "New Museum Traces Black Stage History." *New York Times*, July 9, 1975, 22.

Huntington, Ellsworth. *Civilization and Climate*. New Haven, Conn.: Yale University Press, 1924.

Hurt, Douglas. *Problems of Plenty: The American Farmer in the Twentieth Century*. Chicago: Ivan R. Dee, 2002.

Ignatiev, Noel. *How the Irish Became White*. New York: Routledge, 1995.

Ikeda, Alberto Tsyuoshi. "Apontamentos historicos sobre o jazz no Brasil: primeiros momentos." *Comunicações e Artes* (ECA-USP) 13 (1984): 111–24.

Imada, Adria L. "Binding Hawai'i and New York in the American Empire: Hula and Hawaiian Music Circuits before Pearl Harbor." Paper presented at the 1999 annual meeting of the American Studies Association, Montreal, October 28–31, 1999.

Innis, H. A. "Technology and Public Opinion in the United States." *Canadian Journal of Economics and Political Science* 17, no. 1 (February 1951): 1–24.

Itiberê, Brasílio. *Mangueira, Montmartre e outras favelas: viagens e várias histórias*. Rio de Janeiro: Livraria São José, n.d. [December 1957].

Jackson, Jeffrey H. *Making Jazz French: Music and Modern Life in Interwar Paris*. Durham, N.C.: Duke University Press, 2003.

Jackson, K. David. "Alienation and Ideology in *A Famosa Revista* (1945)." *Hispania* 74, no. 2 (May 1991): 298–304.

Jacob, Heinrich Eduard. *The Saga of Coffee: The Biography of an Economic Product*. Trans. Eden and Cedar Paul. London: Allen and Unwin, 1935.

Jacobson, Matthew Frye. *Barbarian Virtues: The United States Encounters Foreign Peoples at Home and Abroad, 1876–1917*. New York: Hill and Wang, 2000.

———. *Special Sorrows: The Diasporic Imagination of Irish, Polish, and Jewish Immigrants in the United States*. Cambridge, Mass.: Harvard University Press, 1995.

———. *Whiteness of a Different Color: European Immigrants and the Alchemy of Race.* Cambridge, Mass.: Harvard University Press, 1998.

James, C. L. R. *The Black Jacobins: Toussaint L'Ouverture and the San Domingo Revolution.* New York: Vintage Books, 1963.

Jiménez, Michael. "'From Plantation to Cup': Coffee and Capitalism in the United States, 1830–1930." In Roseberry, Gudmundson, and Samper, *Coffee, Society, and Power in Latin America*, 38–64.

Johnson, Hall. *Run, Little Chillun!* Box 2, Folder 9, Helen Armstead-Johnson Play Script Collection, NYPL, Schomburg Branch, n.d.

Johnson, Helen A. "Some International Implications of an Afro-American Theater Collection." Article published online by the International Association of Libraries and Museums of the Performing Arts; http://www.theatrelibrary.org/sibmas/congresses/sibmas85/london85_05.html (accessed December 15, 2004).

Johnson, Walter. *Soul by Soul: Life inside the Antebellum Slave Market.* Cambridge, Mass.: Harvard University Press, 1999.

Jones, Andrew F. *Yellow Music: Media Culture and Colonial Modernity in the Chinese Jazz Age.* Durham, N.C.: Duke University Press, 2001.

Jordan, William G. *Black Newspapers and America's War for Democracy, 1914–1920.* Chapel Hill: University of North Carolina Press, 2001.

Joseph, Gilbert M., Catherine C. LeGrand, and Ricardo D. Salvatore, eds. *Close Encounters of Empire: Writing the Cultural History of U.S.-Latin American Relations.* Durham, N.C.: Duke University Press, 1995.

Kainer, Eden. "Sophie Tucker and Elsie Janis: Masked and Unmasked Performances of Blackness on the Early Vaudeville Stages." Unpublished paper presented to the International Association for the Study of Popular Music, Los Angeles, September 2003.

Kaplan, Amy. *The Anarchy of Empire in the Making of U.S. Culture.* Cambridge, Mass.: Harvard University Press, 2002.

———. "Black and Blue on San Juan Hill." In A. Kaplan and Pease, *Cultures of United States Imperialism*, 219–36.

———. "'Left Alone with America': The Absence of Empire in the Study of American Culture." In A. Kaplan and Pease, *Cultures of United States Imperialism*, 3–21.

Kaplan, Amy, and Donald E. Pease, eds. *Cultures of United States Imperialism.* Durham, N.C.: Duke University Press, 1993.

Kaplan, Edward S. *American Trade Policy, 1923–1995.* Westport, Conn.: Greenwood Press, 1996.

Karasch, Mary C. *Slave Life in Rio de Janeiro, 1808–1850.* Princeton, N.J.: Princeton University Press, 1987.

Karnes, David. "The Glamorous Crowd: Hollywood Movie Premieres between the Wars." *American Quarterly* 38, no. 4 (autumn 1986): 553–72.

Kaspi, André, and Antoine Marès, dirs. *Le Paris des étrangers: depuis un siècle.* Paris: Imprimerie Nationale, 1989.

Kawash, Samira. "*The Autobiography of an Ex-Colored Man*: (Passing for) Black Passing for White." In Ginsberg, *Passing and the Fictions of Identity*, 59–74.

Kelley, Robin D. G. "'But a Local Phase of a World Problem': Black History's Global Vision, 1883–1950." *Journal of American History* 86, no. 3 (December 1999): 1045–77.

———. *Hammer and Hoe: Alabama Communists during the Great Depression*. Chapel Hill: University of North Carolina Press, 1990.

———. "How the West Was One: The African Diaspora and the Re-Mapping of U.S. History." In T. Bender, *Rethinking American History in a Global Age*, 123–47.

———. "A Poetics of Anticolonialism." *Monthly Review*, November 1999; http://www.monthlyreview.org/1199kell.htm (accessed November 10, 2005).

———. "The Riddle of the Zoot: Malcolm Little and Black Cultural Politics during World War II." In *Race Rebels: Culture, Politics, and the Black Working Class*. New York: Macmillan, 1994, 161–81.

———. *Yo' Mama's Disfunktional!: Fighting the Culture Wars in Urban America*. Boston, Mass.: Beacon Press, 1997.

Kelley, Robin D. G., and Sidney J. Lemelle, eds. *Imagining Home: Class, Culture and Nationalism in the African Diaspora*. London: Verso, 1994.

Kernfeld, Barry, ed. *New Grove Dictionary of Jazz*, 2 vols. London: Macmillan Press, 1988.

Kibler, M. Alison. *Rank Ladies: Gender and Cultural Hierarchy in American Vaudeville*. Chapel Hill: University of North Carolina Press, 1999.

Kinkle, Roger D. *The Complete Encyclopedia of Popular Music and Jazz, 1900–1950*, vol. 2: *Biographies*. Westport, Conn.: Arlington House Publishers, 1974.

Kinney, Troy, and Margaret West. *Social Dancing of Today*. New York: Frederick A. Stokes, 1914.

Kirby, Jack Temple. "D. W. Griffith's Racial Portraiture." *Phylon* 39, no. 2 (1978): 118–27.

Klein, Christina. *Cold War Orientalism: Asia in the Middlebrow Imagination, 1945–1961*. Berkeley: University of California Press, 2003.

———. "*Crouching Tiger, Hidden Dragon*: A Diasporic Reading." *Cinema Journal* 43, no. 4 (summer 2004): 18–42.

Klotman, Phyllis. "'Tearing a Hole in History': Lynching as Theme and Motif." *Black American Literature Forum* 19 (summer 1985): 55–63.

Korman, Clifford. Roundtable talk on Brazil and jazz, December 14, 2000. Unpublished transcript, Institute of Jazz Studies, Rutgers University.

Kornweibel, Theodore, Jr. "'The Most Dangerous of All Negro Journals': Federal Efforts to Suppress the *Chicago Defender* during World War I." *American Journalism* 11, no. 2 (1994): 154–68.

Kosnik, Kristin Costello. "The Alien in Our Nation: Complicating Issues of 'Passing' and Miscegenation in the American Narrative." Ph.D. diss., Columbia University, 2001.

Kraay, Hendrik. "Slavery, Citizenship, and Military Service in Brazil's Mobilization for the Paraguayan War." *Slavery and Abolition* 18, no. 3 (December 1997): 228–56.

Kramer, Paul. "Jim Crow Science and the 'Negro Problem' in the Occupied Philippines, 1898–1914." In *Race Consciousness: African-American Studies for the New Century*, ed. Judith Jackson Fossett and Jeffrey A. Tucker. New York: New York University Press, 1997, 227–46.

Krasner, David. *A Beautiful Pageant: African American Theatre, Drama, and Performance in the Harlem Renaissance, 1910–1927*. New York: Palgrave Macmillan, 2002.

LaFeber, Walter. "United States Depression Diplomacy and the Brazilian Revolution, 1893–1894." *HAHR* 40, no. 1 (February 1960): 107–18.

———. "The World and the United States." *AHR* 100, no. 4 (October 1995): 1015–33.

Landes, Ruth. *The City of Women*. New York: Macmillan, 1947.

Lane, Jill. *Blackface Cuba, 1840–1895*. Philadelphia, Pa.: University of Pennsylvania Press, 2005.

Langenscheidt Pocket Porgtuguese Dictionary. New York: Langenscheidt Publishers, 1989.

Larsen, Nella. *Passing*. In *Quicksand and Passing*, ed. Deborah McDowell. New Brunswick, N.J.: Rutgers University Press, 1986.

Leach, William. *Land of Desire: Merchants, Power, and the Rise of a New American Culture*. New York: Pantheon Books, 1993.

Lears, T. J. Jackson. *Fables of Abundance: A Cultural History of Advertising in America*. New York: Basic Books, 1994.

———. "From Salvation to Self-Realization: Advertising and the Therapeutic Roots of the Consumer Culture, 1880–1930." In Fox and Lears, *The Culture of Consumption in America*, 1–38.

———. *No Place of Grace: Antimodernism and the Transformation of American Culture, 1880–1920*. New York: Pantheon Books, 1981.

Lederman, Minna. "Museum Pieces." *Modern Music* 18, no. 4 (May–June 1941): 265.

Lee, C. H. "The Effects of the Depression on Primary Producing Countries." *Journal of Contemporary History* 4, no. 4 (October 1969): 139–55.

Leff, Nathaniel. *Economic Structure and Change, 1822–1947*. Vol. 1, *Underdevelopment and Development in Brazil*. London: George Allen and Unwin, 1982.

———. *Reassessing the Obstacles to Economic Development*. Vol. 2, *Underdevelopment and Development in Brazil*. London: George Allen and Unwin, 1982.

Leite, Dante Moreira. *O caráter nacional brasileiro: história de uma ideologia*, 5th ed. São Paulo: Ed. Ática, 1992 [1954].

Leite, José Correia. "Um capítulo de nossas lutas sociais: história dos nossos periódicos (de 1916 a 1926)." *Alvorada*, May 1947, 5–6.

Leite, José Correia, and [Luiz Silva] Cuti.—*E disse o velho militante José Correia Leite*. São Paulo: Secretaria Municipal de Cultura, 1992.

Lenharo, Alcir. *Cantores do rádio: A trajetória de Nora Ney e Jorge Goulart e o meio artístico de seu tempo*. Campinas: Ed. Unicamp, 1995.

Léon-Martin, Louis. *Le music-hall et ses figures*. Paris: Les Éditions de France, 1928.

Lesser, Jeffrey H. "Are African-Americans African or American? Brazilian Immagination Policy in the 1920s." *Review of Latin America Studies* 4, no. 1-2 (1991): 115–37.

———. *Negotiating National Identities: Immigrants, Minorities, and the Struggle for Ethnicity in Brazil*. Durham, N.C.: Duke University Press, 1999.

———, ed. *Searching for Home Abroad: Japanese-Brazilians and Transnationalism.* Durham, N.C.: Duke University Press, 2003.

———. *Welcoming the Undesirables: Brazil and the Jewish Question.* Berkeley: University of California Press, 1995.

Levine, Bruce, et al., eds. *Who Built America? Working People and the Nation's Economy, Politics, Culture, and Society.* New York: Pantheon Books, 1989–92.

Levine, Lawrence W. *Highbrow/Lowbrow: The Emergence of Cultural Hierarchy in America.* Cambridge, Mass.: Harvard University Press, 1988.

Lewis, Earl. "To Turn as on a Pivot: Writing African Americans into a History of Overlapping Diasporas." *AHR* 100, no. 3 (June 1995): 765–87.

Lima, Alceu Amoroso (a.k.a. Tristão de Athayde). *A realidade americana: ensaio de interpretação dos Estados Unidos,* 2d ed. Rio de Janeiro: Livraria AGIR Editora, 1955.

Lima, Ivana Stolze. *Cores, marcas e falas: sentidos da mestiçagem no Império do Brasil.* Rio de Janeiro: Arquivo Nacional, 2003.

Lima, Manuel de Oliveira. *The Evolution of Brazil Compared with That of Spanish and Anglo-Saxon America,* ed. Percy Alvin Martin. New York: Russell and Russell, 1966 [1914].

Linebaugh, Peter. "All the Atlantic Mountains Shook." *Labour/Le Travailleur* 10 (1982): 87–121.

Linebaugh, Peter, and Marcus Buford Rediker. *The Many-Headed Hydra: Sailors, Slaves, Commoners, and the Hidden History of the Revolutionary Atlantic.* Boston, Mass.: Beacon Press, 2000.

Linger, Daniel Touro. *Dangerous Encounters: Meanings of Violence in a Brazilian City.* Stanford, Calif.: Stanford University Press, 1992.

———. *No One Home: Brazilian Selves Remade in Japan.* Stanford, Calif.: Stanford University Press, 2001.

———. "Preconceito branco, consciencia negra e resistência a discriminação em São Paulo nos anos 30." *Cadernos de Pesquisa* (São Luis) 4, no. 1 (1988): 120–34.

Lipsitz, George. *Class and Culture in Cold War America: A Rainbow at Midnight.* New York: Praeger, 1981.

———. *A Life in the Struggle: Ivory Perry and the Culture of Opposition.* Philadelphia, Pa.: Temple University Press, 1988.

———. *Time Passages: Collective Memory and American Popular Culture.* Minneapolis: University of Minnesota Press, 1990.

Lis, Eduardo. "Creating a New Tradition: The Brazilian Jazz Experience in North America." Master's thesis, York University, Ontario, 1996.

Liu, Lydia, ed. *Tokens of Exchange: The Problem of Translation in Global Circulations.* Durham, N.C.: Duke University Press, 1999.

Lobato, José Bento Monteiro. *America: Os Estados Unidos em 1929.* São Paulo: Ed. Brasiliense, 1946.

———. *How Henry Ford Is Regarded in Brazil.* Trans. Aubrey Stuart. Rio de Janeiro: *O Jornal*/n.p., 1926.

Lobo, Hélio. *Brasilianos e Yankees*. Rio de Janeiro: Pimenta de Mello, 1926.

———. *Cousas americanas e brasileiras*. Rio de Janeiro: Imprensa Nacional, 1923.

Locke, Alain, ed. *The New Negro*. New York: Atheneum, 1968 [1925].

Lopes, José Sergio Leite. "Class, Ethnicity, and Color in the Making of Brazilian Football." *Daedalus* 129, no. 2 (spring 2000): 239–70.

Lopes, Nei. *O Negro no Rio de Janeiro e sua tradição musical: partido-alto, calango, chula e outras cantorias*. Rio de Janeiro: Pallas, 1992.

Lorde, Audre. *Uses of the Erotic: The Erotic as Power*. Brooklyn: Out and Out Books, 1978.

Lott, Eric. *Love and Theft: Blackface Minstrelsy and the American Working Class*. New York: Oxford University Press, 1993.

Lotz, Rainer E. "The 'Louisiana Troupes' in Europe." *Black Perspective in Music* 11 (fall 1983): 133–42.

———. "Will Garland and His Negro Operetta Company." In Lotz and Pegg, *Under the Imperial Carpet*, 130–44.

Lotz, Rainer E., and Ian Pegg, eds. *Under the Imperial Carpet*. Crawley, England: Rabbitt Press, 1986.

Love, Eric T. L. *Race over Empire: Racism and U.S. Imperialism, 1865–1900*. Chapel Hill: University of North Carolina Press, 2004.

Love, Joseph L. "Political Participation in Brazil, 1881–1969." *Luso-Brazilian Review* 7, no. 2 (December 1970): 3–24.

———. *São Paulo in the Brazilian Federation, 1889–1937*. Stanford, Calif.: Stanford University Press, 1980.

Lowe, Lisa. *Immigrant Acts: On Asian American Cultural Politics*. Durham, N.C.: Duke University Press, 1996.

Luz, Nicia Vilela. *A Amazônia para os negros americanos (As origens de uma controvérsia internacional)*. Rio de Janeiro: Editora Saga, 1968.

Mahony, Mary Ann. "The Local and the Global: Internal and External Factors in the Development of Bahia's Cacao Sector." In Topik, Marichal, and Frank, *From Silver to Cocaine*, 174–203.

Mann, Kristin, and Edna G. Bay, eds. *Rethinking the African Diaspora: The Making of a Black Atlantic World in the Bight of Benin and Brazil*. London: F. Cass, 2001.

Marable, Manning. *How Capitalism Underdeveloped Black America: Problems in Race, Political Economy, and Society*. Boston, Mass.: South End Press, 1983.

Marchand, Roland. *Advertising the American Dream: Making Way for Modernity, 1920–1940*. Berkeley: University of California Press, 1985.

Margolis, Maxine L. *An Invisible Minority: Brazilians in New York City*. Boston, Mass.: Allyn and Bacon, 1998.

———. *Little Brazil: An Ethnography of Brazilian Immigrants in New York City*. Princeton, N.J.: Princeton University Press, 1994.

Marks, George P. *The Black Press Views American Imperialism (1898–1900)*. New York: Arno Press, 1971.

Martin, Emily. *Flexible Bodies: Tracking Immunity in American Culture from the Days of Polio to the Age of AIDS*. Boston, Mass.: Beacon Press, 1994.

Martin, Percy Alvin. *Latin America and the War*. Baltimore: Johns Hopkins University Press, 1925.

Martins, Wilson. "Cendrars e o Brasil." *Hispania* 75, no. 4 (October 1992): 979–87.

———. *O Modernismo*, vol. 6: *O Modernismo (1916–1945)*, 4th. ed. São Paulo: Editora Cultrix, 1973.

Marx, Anthony W. *Making Race and Nation: A Comparison of the United States, South Africa, and Brazil*. Cambridge: Cambridge University Press, 1998.

———. "Race-Making and the Nation-State." *World Politics* 48, no. 2 (1996): 180–208.

Marx, Karl. *Capital: A Critique of Political Economy*. Trans. Ben Fowkes. London: Penguin Books in association with New Left Review, 1990–92.

Massa, Jean-Michel. "Paris lu, vu et rêvé par des écrivains portugais, brésiliens et de l'Afrique de langue portugaise." In *Paris et le phénomenène des capitales littéraires*, vol. 1. Paris: Université de Paris–Sorbonne, 1984, 103–14.

Matory, James Lorand. *Black Atlantic Religion: Tradition, Transnationalism, and Matriarchy in the Afro-Brazilian Candomblé*. Princeton, N.J.: Princeton University Press, 2005.

———. "The English Professors of Brazil: On the Diasporic Roots of the Yoruba Nation." *Comparative Studies in Society and History* 41, no. 1 (1999): 72–103.

Matta, Roberto da. *Carnavais, malandros e heróis: para uma sociologia do dilema brasileiro*. Rio de Janeiro: Zahar Editores, 1983 [1978].

Mazzarella, William. *Shoveling Smoke: Advertising and Globalization in Contemporary India*. Durham, N.C.: Duke University Press, 2003.

McAlister, Melani. "'The Common Heritage of Mankind': Race, Nation, and Masculinity in the King Tut Exhibit." *Representations* 54 (spring 1996): 80–103.

———. *Epic Encounters: Culture, Media, and U.S. Interests in the Middle East, 1945–2000*. Berkeley: University of California Press, 2001.

McCann, Bryan. *Hello, Hello Brazil: Popular Music in the Making of Modern Brazil*. Durham, N.C.: Duke University Press, 2004.

McClary, Susan, and Robert Walser. "Theorizing the Body in African-American Music." *Black Music Research Journal* 14, no. 1 (1994): 75–84.

McClintock, Anne. *Imperial Leather: Race, Gender, and Sexuality in the Colonial Conquest*. New York: Routledge, 1995.

McElya, Michele Paige. "Commemorating the Color Line: The National Mammy Monument Controversy of the 1920s." In Mills and Simpson, *Monuments to the Lost Cause*, 203–218.

———. "Monumental Citizenship: Reading the National Mammy Memorial Controversy of the Early Twentieth Century." Ph.D. diss., New York University, 2003.

McElya, Michele Paige, and Micol Seigel. "Confusing Relations: Mammy, Mãe Preta and the Shape of Black Citizenship in 1920s U.S. and Brazil." Paper presented at the annual conference of the American Studies Association, Montreal, October 27–31, 1999.

McGovern, Charles. "Consumption and Citizenship in the United States, 1900–1940." In Strasser, McGovern, and Judt, *Getting and Spending*, 37–58.

McGuire, Phillip, ed. *Taps for a Jim Crow Army: Letters from Black Soldiers in World War II*. Santa Barbara, Calif.: ABC-Clio, 1983.

McPhee, Colin. "Jungles of Brazil." *Modern Music* 18, no. 1 (November–December 1940): 42.

———. "Scores and Records." *Modern Music* 22, no. 1 (November–December 1944): 59.

Meade, Teresa, and Gregory Alonso Pirio. "In Search of the Afro-American 'Eldorado': Attempts by North American Blacks to Enter Brazil in the 1920s." *Luso-Brazilian Review* 25, no. 1 (1988): 85–110.

Mencke, John G. *Mulattoes and Race Mixture: American Attitudes and Images, 1865–1918*. Ann Arbor: UMI Research Press, 1979 [1976].

Merguson, R. W. "Glimpses of Brazil." *Crisis* 2, no. 1 (November 1915): 38–43.

Metcalf, Alida C. "Millenarian Slaves? The Santidade de Jaguaripe and Slave Resistance in the Americas." *AHR* 104, no. 5 (December 1999): 1531–59.

Miceli, Sergio. *Imagens negociadas: retratos da elite brasileira (1920–40)*. São Paulo: Editora Schwarcz, 1996.

Michaels, Walter Benn. "Anti-Imperial Americanism." In A. Kaplan and Pease, *Cultures of United States Imperialism*, 365–91.

———. "Race into Culture: A Critical Genealogy of Cultural Identity." *Critical Inquiry* 18 (summer 1992): 655–85.

———. *The Trouble with Diversity: How We Learned to Love Identity and Ignore Inequality*. New York: Metropolitan Books, 2006.

Mignolo, Walter D. *The Darker Side of the Renaissance: Literacy, Territoriality, and Colonization*. Ann Arbor: University of Michigan Press, 2003 [1995].

———. *Local Histories/Global Designs: Coloniality, Subaltern Knowledges, and Border Thinking*. Princeton, N.J.: Princeton University Press, 2000.

Milhaud, Darius. *Notes without Music*. New York: Alfred A. Knopf, 1953 [1952].

Miller, Karl. "Segregating Sound: Folklore, Phonographs, and the Transformation of Southern Music, 1888–1935." Ph.D. diss., New York University, 2002.

Mills, Cynthia, and Pamela H. Simpson, eds. *Monuments to the Lost Cause: Women, Art, and the Landscapes of Southern Memory*. Knoxville: University of Tennessee, 2003.

Mintz, Sidney. "The Localization of Anthropological Practice: From Area Studies to Transnationalism." *Critique of Anthropology* 18 (June 1998): 117–33.

———. *Sweetness and Power: The Place of Sugar in Modern History*. New York: Viking, 1985.

Mistinguett. *Mistinguett by Mistinguett—Queen of the Paris Night*. Trans. Lucienne Hill. London: Elak Books, 1954.

Mitchell, Michael. "Miguel Reale and the Impact of Conservative Modernization on Brazilian Race Relations." In Hanchard, *Racial Politics in Contemporary Brazil*, 116–37.

————. "Racial Consciousness and the Political Attitudes and Behavior of Blacks in São Paulo, Brazil." Ph.D. diss., Indiana University, 1977.

Mokyr, Joel. "The Second Industrial Revolution, 1870–1914." In *Storia dell'economia mondiale*, ed. Valerio Castronovo. Rome: Laterza Publishing, 1999, 219–45.

Moody, Bill. *The Jazz Exiles: American Musicians Abroad*. Reno: University of Nevada Press, 1993.

Moore, Robin. *Nationalizing Blackness: Afrocubanismo and Artistic Revolution in Havana, 1920–1940*. Pittsburgh: University of Pittsburgh Press, 1997.

Moraes, Evaristo de. *Brancos e negros nos Estados Unidos e no Brasil*. Rio de Janeiro: Typ. Miccolis, 1922.

Moraes, José Geraldo Vinci de. *Metrópole em sinfonia: história, cultura e música popular na São Paulo dos anos 30*. São Paulo: Estação Liberdade, 2000.

Moraga, Cherríe, and Gloria Anzaldúa, eds. *This Bridge Called My Back: Writings by Radical Women of Color*. Watertown: Persephone Press, 1981.

Moreno, Julio. *Yankee Don't Go Home! Mexican Nationalism, American Business Culture, and the Shaping of Modern Mexico, 1920–1950*. Chapel Hill: University of North Carolina Press, 2003.

Morris, William W. "Rolling Down to Rio with Hughes." *Outlook*, October 18, 1922, 286–88.

Morrison, Toni. *Playing in the Dark: Whiteness and the Literary Imagination*. New York: Vintage Books, 1992.

Morse, Richard. *From Community to Metropolis: A Biography of São Paulo, Brazil*. Gainesville: University of Florida Press, 1958.

Mosse, George L. *Nationalism and Sexuality: Respectability and Abnormal Sexuality in Modern Europe*. New York: H. Fertig, 1985.

————. *Toward the Final Solution: A History of European Racism*. New York: H. Fertig, 1978.

Moura, Clóvis. *Sociologia do negro brasileiro*. São Paulo: Editora Ática, 1988.

Moura, Roberto. "O cinema carioca (1913–1930)." In *Historia do cinema brasileira*, org. Fernão Ramos. São Paulo: Art Editora, 1987, 49–62.

————. "A indústria cultural e o espetáculo-negócio no Rio de Janeiro." In *Entre Europa e África: A invenção do carioca*, org. Antônio Herculano Lopes. Rio de Janeiro: Edições Casa de Rui Barbosa, 2000, 113–54.

————. *Tia Ciata e a Pequena África no Rio de Janeiro*. Rio de Janeiro: FUNARTE/ Instituto Nacional de Música, 1995 [1983].

Mullen, Harryette. "Optic White: Blackness and the Production of Whiteness." *diacritics* 24, nos. 2–3 (1994): 74–89.

Natale, Oscar. *Buenos Aires, negros y tango*. Buenos Aires: Peña Lillo Editor, 1984.

Naves, Santuza Cambraia. *Da bossa nova à tropicália*. Rio de Janeiro: Jorge Zahar Editor, 2001.

————. *O violão azul: modernismo e música popular*. Rio de Janeiro: Fundação Getulio Vargas, 1998.

Needell, Jeffrey D. "The Domestic Civilizing Mission: The Cultural Role of the State in Brazil, 1808–1930." *Luso-Brazilian Review* 36, no. 1 (summer 1999): 1–18.

————. "The Revolta Contra Vacina of 1904: The Revolt against 'Modernization' in Belle-Epoque Rio de Janeiro." *HAHR* 67, no. 2 (May 1987): 233–69.

————. *A Tropical Belle Epoque: The Elite Culture of Turn-of-the-Century Rio de Janeiro*. New York: Cambridge University Press, 1987.

Niani [Dee Brown]. "Black Consciousness vs. Racism in Brazil." In Hellwig, *African-American Reflections on Brazil's Racial Paradise*, 225–48. Also in *Black Scholar*, January–February 1980, 59–70.

Nobles, Melissa. *Shades of Citizenship: Race and the Census in Modern Politics*. Stanford, Calif.: Stanford University Press, 2000.

Nogueira, Oracy. "Preconceito racial de marca e preconceito racial de origem." In *Tanto preto quanto branco: Estudos de relações raciais*. São Paulo: T. A. Queirós, 1985 [1957 (1954)].

Oberdeck, Kathryn. "Contested Cultures of American Refinement: Theatrical Manager Sylvester Poli, His Audiences, and the Vaudeville Industry, 1890–1920." *Radical History Review* 66 (1996): 40–91.

Ogren, Kathy J. *The Jazz Revolution: Twenties America and the Meaning of Jazz*. Oxford: Oxford University Press, 1989.

Oja, Carol. *Making Music Modern: New York in the 1920s*. New York: Oxford University Press, 2000.

Olliver, Gillermo "Willy," and Tomás Mooney. Liner notes to *Argentine Swing 1936–1948*. Antiga, Portugal: Arquivo de Musica, 1989 [1984].

Olney, Martha L. *Buy Now, Pay Later: Advertising, Credit, and Consumer Durables in the 1920s*. Chapel Hill: University of North Carolina Press, 1991.

Olson, Joel. "W. E. B. Du Bois and the Race Concept." *Souls* 7, nos. 3–4 (summer–fall 2005): 118–28.

Ong, Aiwah. *Flexible Citizenship: The Cultural Logics of Transnationality*. Durham, N.C.: Duke University Press, 1999.

Ottley, Roi. *The Lonely Warrior: The Life and Times of Robert S. Abbott*. Chicago: Henry Regnery, 1955.

Ownby, Ted. *American Dreams in Mississippi: Consumers, Poverty, and Culture*. Chapel Hill: University of North Carolina Press, 1999.

Padilha, Marcia. *A cidade como espetáculo: Publicidade e vida urbana na São Paulo nos anos 20*. São Paulo: Annablume, 2001.

Painter, Nell Irvin. "Sojourner Truth's Knowing and Becoming Known." *Journal of American History* 81, no. 2 (September 1994): 461–92.

————. *Standing at Armageddon: The United States, 1877–1919*. New York: W. W. Norton, 1987.

Pan American Union. *Trip to the Brazilian Centennial Exposition*. Washington., D.C.: GPO, 1922. Reprinted from *Bulletin of the Pan American Union*, May 1922.

Parker, Andrew, ed. *Nationalisms and Sexualities*. New York: Routledge, 1992.

Passos, Maria Lúcia P. F., coord. *Evolução urbana da cidade de São Paulo: estruturação de uma cidade industrial, 1872–1945*. São Paulo: ELETROPAULO, 1989.

Peard, Julyan G. *Race, Place, and Medicine: The Idea of the Tropics in Nineteenth-Century Brazilian Medicine*. Durham, N.C.: Duke University Press, 1999.

Pederneiras, Raul. *Scenas da vida Carioca: caricaturas de Raul*, vol. 1. Rio de Janeiro: Officinas Graphicas do "Jornal do Brasil,"1924. Rio de Janeiro: Jornal do Brasil, 1935.

Peiss, Kathy. *Hope in a Jar: The Making of America's Beauty Culture*. New York: Metropolitan Books, 1998.

Peláez, Carlos Manuel, and Instituto Brasileiro do Café. *Essays on Coffee and Economic Development*. Rio de Janeiro: Fundação Getulio Vargas 1973. Published for Instituto Brasileiro do Café.

Pendergrast, Mark. *Uncommon Grounds: The History of Coffee and How It Transformed Our World*. New York: Basic Books, 1999.

Pénet, Martin. *Mistinguett: La reine du music-hall*. N.p.: Éditions du Rocher, 1995.

Penn, Irvine Garland. *The Afro-American Press and Its Editors*, reprint ed. New York: Arno Press, 1969 [Springfield, Mass.: Willey, 1891].

Perpener, John O., III. *African-American Concert Dance*. Urbana: University of Illinois Press, 2001.

Perrone, Charles A., and Christopher Dunn, eds. *Brazilian Popular Music and Globalization*. Gainesville: University Press of Florida, 2001.

Perry, Elisabeth I. "'The General Motherhood of the Commonwealth': Dance Hall Reform in the Progressive Era." *American Quarterly* 37, no. 5 (winter 1985): 719–33.

Pessis, Jacques, and Jacques Crépineau. *Les années Mistinguett*. Paris: Vade Retro, 2001.

———. *The Moulin Rouge*. New York: St. Martin's Press, 1990 [1989].

Peterson, Bernard L., Jr. *African American Theatre Directory, 1816–1960: A Comprehensive Guide to Early Black Theatre Organizations, Companies, Theatres, and Performing Groups*. Westport, Conn.: Greenwood Press, 1997.

Pfeiffer, Kathleen. "Individualism, Success, and American Identity in *The Autobiography of an Ex-Colored Man*." *African American Review* 30, no. 3 (1996): 403–19.

Pierre. "Maxixe—1910, samba—1920, caterête—1930." *Amateur Dancer* (London), no. 5 (February 1931): 17–19.

Pierson, Donald. *Negroes in Brazil: A Study of Race Contact at Bahia*. Carbondale: Southern Illinois University Press, 1967.

Pinto, L. A. [Luiz de Aguiar] Costa. *O negro no Rio de Janeiro: relações raciais numa sociedade em mudança*, 2d ed. Rio de Janeiro: Editora UFRJ, 1998 [São Paulo: Editora Nacional, 1953].

Pires, Antônio Liberac Cardoso Simões. "As 'Associações dos Homens de Cor': política e 'cultura negra' no Brasil, na primeira metade do século XX." Unpublished paper, UNICAMP, 1999.

———. *Bimba, Pastinha e Besouro de Mangangá: tres personagens da capoeira baiana*. Tocantins/Goiânia: NEAB/Grafset, 2002.

———. "Capoeira no jogo das cores: criminalidade, cultura e racismo na cidade do Rio de Janeiro (1890–1937)." Master's thesis, UNICAMP, 1996.

———. "Movimentos da cultura afro-brasileira: A formação histórica da capoeira contemporânea, 1890–1950." Doct. thesis, IFCH-UNICAMP, 2001.

Pistone, Danièle. "Les musiciens étrangers à Paris au XXᵉ siècle." In Kaspi and Marès, *Le Paris des étrangers depuis un siècle*, 245–255.

Pixinguinha. Deposition [oral history]. *As vozes desassombradas do museu*. Rio de Janeiro: Museu de Imagem e Som, 1970.

Plummer, Brenda Gayle. *Rising Wind: Black Americans and U.S. Foreign Affairs, 1935–1960*. Chapel Hill: University of North Carolina Press, 1996.

Pollan, Michael. *The Botany of Desire: A Plant's Eye View of the World*. New York: Random House, 2001.

Pomeranz, Kenneth, and Steven C. Topik. *The World That Trade Created: Society, Culture, and the World Economy, 1400–the Present*. Armonk, N.Y.: M. E. Sharpe, 1999.

Prado Jùnior, Caio. *História econômica do Brasil*, 15th ed. São Paulo: Brasiliense, 1972 [1945].

Prakash, Gyan, ed. *After Colonialism: Imperial Histories and Postcolonial Displacements*. Princeton, N.J.: Princeton University Press, 1995.

Pride, Armistead Scott, and Clint C. Wilson II. *A History of the Black Press*. Washington, D.C.: Howard University Press, 1997.

Prieto, Adolfo. *El discurso criollista en la formación de la Argentina moderna*. Buenos Aires: Editorial Sudamericana, 1988.

Queiroz, Maria Isaura Pereira de. *Carnaval brasileiro: o vivido e o mito*. São Paulo: Brasiliense, 1992.

Queiroz, Romano de, and Teofilo de Queiroz, Júnior. *Preconceito de cor e a mulata na literatura brasileira*. São Paulo: Editora Ática, 1975.

Quijano, Aníbal. "Colonialidad del poder, cultura y conocimiento en América Latina." *Anuario Mariateguiano* (Lima) 9, no. 9 (1997).

Quintero-Rivera, Mareia. *A cor e o som da nação: a idéia de mestiçagem na crítica musical do Caribe hispânico e do Brasil (1928–1948)*. São Paulo: Annablume Editora, 2000.

Race, Ethnicity, and Genetics Working Group, National Human Genome Research Institute (Bethesda). "The Use of Racial, Ethnic, and Ancestral Categories in Human Genetics Research." *American Journal of Human Genetics* 77 (2005): 519–32.

Radano, Ronald. "Hot Fantasies: American Modernism and the Idea of Black Rhythm," *Music and the Racial Imagination*, Ron Radano and Philip V. Bohlman, eds. Chicago: University of Chicago Press, 2000, 459–80.

Rafael, Vicente L. *White Love and Other Events in Filipino History*. Durham, N.C.: Duke University Press, 2000.

———. "White Love: Surveillance and Nationalist Resistance in the U.S. Colonization of the Philippines," in *Cultures of United States Imperialism*, 185–218.

Reed, Christopher Robert. *All the World Is Here!: The Black Presence at White City*. Bloomington: Indiana University Press, 1999.

Regester, Charlene B. *Black Entertainers in African American Newspaper Articles*, vol. 1. Jefferson, N.C.: McFarland and Co., 2002.

Reichmann, Rebecca, ed. *Race in Contemporary Brazil: From Indifference to Inequality.* University Park: Pennsylvania State University Press, 1999.

Reis, Fábio Wanderley. "Mito e valor da democracia racial." In *Multiculturalismo e racismo: uma comparação Brasil-Estados Unidos*, ed. Jesse Souza. Brasilia: Paralelo 15, 1997, 221–32.

Reis, Fidelis. *Paiz a organizar.* Rio de Janeiro: Typ. A Gloria, 1924.

Reis, João José. *Slave Rebellion in Brazil.* Trans. Arthur Brakel. Baltimore: Johns Hopkins University Press, 1993.

Reis, João José, and Flávio dos Santos Gomes, orgs. *Liberdade por um fio: história dos quilombos no Brasil.* São Paulo: Companhia das Letras, 1996.

Renan, Ernest. *Qu'est-ce qu'une nation?* Trans. Wanda Romer Taylor. Toronto: Tapir Press, 1996.

Renda, Mary A. *Taking Haiti: Military Occupation and the Culture of U.S. Imperialism, 1915–1940.* Chapel Hill: University of North Carolina Press, 2001.

"Report of the 1925 Conferences between the Sao Paulo Institute for the Permanent Defense of Coffee and the Representatives of the National Coffee Roasters Association of the United States." N.p., n.d. [New York: NCRA, 1925?]. In *Coffee Pamphlets, 1925–1960.* Baker Library, Harvard School of Business.

Reuter, Edward Byron. *The Mulatto in the United States: Including a Study of the Rôle of Mixed-Blood Races throughout the World.* New York: Haskell House, 1969 [1918].

Richards, Thomas. *The Commodity Culture of Victorian England: Advertising and Spectacle, 1851–1914.* Stanford, Calif.: Stanford University Press, 1990.

Riis, Thomas L. "The Experience and Impact of Black Entertainers in England, 1895–1920." *American Music* 4 (spring 1986): 50–58.

Rivera, Max. *Le tango et les danses nouvelles.* Paris: Pierre Lafitte, 1913.

Robbins, Bruce. "Commodity Histories." *PMLA* 120, no. 2 (March 2005): 454–63.

Roberts, John Storm. *The Latin Tinge: The Impact of Latin American Music on the United States*, 2d ed. New York: Oxford University Press, 1999 [1979].

Roberts, Randy. *Jack Dempsey: The Manassa Mauler.* Baton Rouge: Louisiana State University Press, 1979.

Robinson, Amy. "It Takes One to Know One: Passing and Communities of Common Interest." *Critial Inquiry* 20 (summer 1994): 715–36.

———. "To Pass/In Drag: Strategies of Entrance into the Visible (Passing, Sexual Preference, Racial Preference, Identity)." Ph.D. diss., University of Pennsylvania, 1993.

Robinson, Cedric J. *Black Marxism: The Making of the Black Radical Tradition*, 2d ed. Chapel Hill: University of North Carolina Press, 2000.

———. "W. E. B. Du Bois and Black Sovereignty." In Kelley and Lemelle, *Imagining Home*, 145–57.

Rocha, Edmar, and Robert Greenhill for Marcellino Martins and E. Johnson (corp. author). *150 anos de café.* Rio de Janeiro: Salamandra Consultoria Editorial, 1993.

Rodrigues, Raymundo Nina. *Os africanos no Brasil*, 6th ed. Brasília: Editora Universidade de Brasília, 1982 [1905].

————. *L'animisme fétichiste des nègres de Bahia.* Bahia: Brésil Reis, 1900.

————. *As Raças humanas e a responsabilidade penal no Brasil,* 3d ed. São Paulo: Companhia Editora Nacional, 1938.

Roediger, David R., ed. *Black on White: Black Writers on What It Means to Be White.* New York: Schocken Books, 1998.

————. *The Wages of Whiteness: Race and the Making of the American Working Class.* London: Verso, 1991.

Rogers, J. A. [Joel Augustus]. *As Nature Leads: An Informal Discussion of the Reason Why Negro and Caucasian Are Mixing in Spite of Opposition.* Baltimore: Black Classic Press, 1987 [1919].

————. *Nature Knows No Color-Line: Research into the Negro Ancestry in the White Race,* 3d. ed. St. Petersburg, Fla.: Helga M. Rogers, 1980.

Rogin, Michael. "'The Sword Became a Flashing Vision': D. W. Griffith's *The Birth of a Nation.*" *Representations* 9 (1985): 150–95.

Rolnik, Raquel. "São Paulo, início da industrialização, o espaço e a política." In *As lutas sociais e a cidade,* ed. Lúcio Kowarik. Rio de Janeiro: Paz e Terra, 1988.

————. "Territórios negros nas cidades brasileiras (Etnicidade e cidade em São Paulo e no Rio de Janeiro)." *Estudos Afro-Asiáticos* 17 (1989): 29–40.

Roquette-Pinto, Edgar. "Archeologia e ethnographia." In *Impressões do Brasil no século vinte: sua historia, seo povo, commercio, industrias e recursos,* ed. W. Feldwick, L. T. Delaney, and Joaquim Eulalio. London: Lloyd's Greater Britain Publishing, 1913, 52–58.

Rose, Phyllis. *Jazz Cleopatra: Josephine Baker in Her Time.* New York: Doubleday, 1989.

Roseberry, William. "Americanization in the Americas." In *Anthropologies and Histories: Essays in Culture, History, and the Political Economy.* New Brunswick, N.J.: Rutgers University Press, 1989, 80–121.

Roseberry, William, Lowell Gudmundson, and Mario Samper Kutzchbach, eds. *Coffee, Society, and Power in Latin America.* Baltimore: Johns Hopkins University Press, 1995.

Rosenberg, Emily. *Spreading the American Dream: American Economic and Cultural Expansion, 1890–1945.* New York: Hill and Wang, 1982.

————. *World War I and the Growth of United States Predominance in Latin America.* New York: Garland, 1987.

Rotundo, E. Anthony. *American Manhood: Transformations in Masculinity from the Revolution to the Modern Era.* New York: Basic Books, 1993.

Rubin, Gayle. "Thinking Sex: Notes for a Radical Theory of the Politics of Sexuality." In *Pleasure and Danger: Exploring Female Sexuality,* ed. Carole Vance. Boston, Mass.: Routledge and Kegan Paul, 1984, 267–319.

Rutherford, Janice Williams. *Selling Mrs. Consumer: Christine Frederick and the Rise of Household Efficiency.* Athens: University of Georgia Press, 2003.

Rydell, Robert W. *All the World's a Fair: Visions of Empire at American International Expositions, 1876–1916.* Chicago: University of Chicago Press, 1984.

————. "The Culture of Imperial Abundance: World's Fairs in the Making of American Culture." In *Consuming Visions: Accumulation and Display of Goods in America, 1880–1920*, ed. Simon Bronner. New York: Norton, 1989, 191–216.

Rydell, Robert W., John E. Findling, and Kimberly D. Pelle, eds. *Fair America: World's Fairs in the United States.* Washington, D.C.: Smithsonian Institution Press, 2000.

Rye, Howard. "The Southern Syncopated Orchestra." In Lotz and Pegg, *Under the Imperial Carpet*, 217–32.

Rye, Howard, and Jeffrey Green. "Black Musical Internationalism in England in the 1920s." *Black Music Research Journal* 15, no. 1 (spring 1995): 93–107.

Sachs, Curt. *World History of the Dance*. Trans. Bessie Schönberg. New York: W. W. Norton, 1937.

Said, Edward. *Orientalism*. New York: Vintage Books, 1978.

Saldaña-Portillo, Maria Josefina. *The Revolutionary Imagination in the Americas and the Age of Development*. Durham, N.C.: Duke University Press, 2003.

Saldívar, José David. *Border Matters: Remapping American Cultural Studies*. Berkeley: University of California Press, 1997.

————. *The Dialectics of Our America: Genealogy, Cultural Critique, and Literary History*. Durham, N.C.: Duke University Press, 1991.

Salisbury, Richard V. *Anti-Imperialism and International Competition in Central America, 1920–1929*. Wilmington: SR Books, 1989.

Sampson, Henry T. *Blacks in Blackface: A Source Book on Early Black Musical Shows*. Metuchen, N.J.: Scarecrow Press, 1980.

Sandoval, Chela. *Methodology of the Oppressed*. Minneapolis: University of Minnesota Press, 2000.

Sandroni, Carlos. *Feitiço decente: transformações do samba no Rio de Janeiro (1917–1933)*. Rio de Janeiro: Jorge Zahar/Editora UFRJ, 2001.

Sansone, Livio. *Blackness without Ethnicity: Constructing Race in Brazil*. New York: Palgrave Macmillan, 2003.

————. *From Africa to Afro: Use and Abuse of Africa in Brazil*. Amsterdam: SEPHIS, 1999.

Sant'Anna, Affonso Romano de. "A mulher de cor e o canibalismo erótico na sociedade escravocrata." In *O canibalismo amoroso: o desejo e a interdicão em nossa cultura através da poesia*. São Paulo: Ed. Brasiliense, 1984, 17–60.

Santos, Alcino, Gracio Barbalho, Jairo Severiano, and M. A. de Azevedo (Nirez). *Discografia brasileira 78 rpms, 1902–1964*, vol. 2. Rio de Janeiro: Funarte, 1982.

Sargeant, Winthrop. *Jazz: Hot and Hybrid*, 3d ed. New York: Da Capo Press, 1975 [1938].

Sassen, Saskia. *The Global City: New York, London, Tokyo*. Princeton, N.J.: Princeton University Press, 1991.

————. *Globalization and Its Discontents*. New York: New Press, 1998.

Savage, Barbara Dianne. *Broadcasting Freedom: Radio, War, and the Politics of Race, 1938–1948*. Chapel Hill: University of North Carolina Press, 1999.

Savage, Kirk. *Standing Soldiers, Kneeling Slaves: Race, War, and Monument in Nineteenth-Century America*. Princeton, N.J.: Princeton University Press, 1997.

Savigliano, Marta. *Tango and the Political Economy of Passion*. Boulder, Colo.: Westview Press, 1995.

Saxton, Alexander. *The Rise and Fall of the White Republic: Class Politics and Mass Culture in Nineteenth-Century America*. London: Verso, 1990.

Scanlon, Jennifer. *Inarticulate Longings: The Ladies' Home Journal, Gender, and the Promises of Consumer Culture*. New York: Routledge, 1995.

Schulten, Susan. *The Geographical Imagination in America, 1880–1950*. Chicago: University of Chicago Press, 2001.

Schultz, Kirsten. *Tropical Versailles: Empire, Monarchy, and the Portuguese Royal Court in Rio de Janeiro, 1808–1821*. New York: Routledge, 2001.

Schurz, William L. *Valorization of Brazilian Coffee*. Washington, D.C.: GPO, 1922.

Schwarcz, Lilia Moritz. *Retrato em branco e negro: Jornais, escravos e cidadãos em São Paulo no final do século XIX*. São Paulo: Editora Schwarcz, 1987.

Scott, Julius. "The Common Wind: Currents of Afro-American Communication in the Era of the Haitian Revolution." Ph.D. diss., Duke University, 1986.

Scott, William R. *The Sons of Sheba's Race: African-Americans and the Italo-Ethiopian War, 1935–1941*. Bloomington: Indiana University Press, 1993.

Sedgwick, Eve Kosofsky. *Between Men: English Literature and Male Homosocial Desire*. New York: Columbia University Press, 1985.

Segato, Rita Laura. "The Color-Blind Subject of Myth; or, Where to Find Africa in the Nation." *Annual Review of Anthropology* 27 (1998): 129–51.

Seigel, Micol. "Beyond Compare: Historical Method after the Transnational Turn." *Radical History Review* 91 (winter 2005): 62–90.

———. "The Disappearing Dance: Maxixe's Imperial Erasure." *Black Music Research Journal* 25, no. 1 (spring/fall 2005): 93–118.

———. "The Point of Comparison: Transnational Racial Construction, Brazil and the United States, 1918–1933." Ph.D. diss., New York University, 2001.

———. "World History's Narrative Problem." *HAHR* 84, no. 3 (August 2004): 431–46.

Seigel, Micol, and Tiago de Melo Gomes. "Sabina's Oranges: The Colors of Cultural Politics in Rio de Janeiro, 1889–1930." *Journal of Latin American Cultural Studies* 11, no. 1 (March 2002): 5–28.

Sensabaugh, Leon F. "The Coffee-Trust Question in United States–Brazilian Relations, 1912–1913." *HAHR* 26 (November 1946): 480–96.

Sevcenko, Nikolau. *Orféu extático na metrópole: São Paulo sociedade e cultura nos frementes anos 20*. São Paulo: Editora Schwarcz, 1992.

Severiano, Jairo, and Zuza Homem de Mello. *A canção no tempo*, vol. 1: *1901–1957*. São Paulo: Editora 34, 1997.

Sewell, William H., Jr. "Marc Bloch and Comparative History." *History and Theory* 6 (1967): 208–18.

Shannon, A. H. *The Racial Integrity of the American Negro*. N.p.: Smith and Lamar, 1907.

Shapiro, Nat, and Bruce Pollock, eds. *Popular Music, 1920–1979: A Revised Cumulation*. Detroit: Gale Research, 1985.

Shelton, Marie-Denise. "Le monde noir dans la littérature dadaiste et surréaliste." *French Review* 57, no. 3 (February 1984): 320–28.

Silva, Cleber Maciel da. *Discriminações raciais: negros em Campinas (1888–1926)*. Campinas: Área de Publicações CMU/UNICAMP, 1997 [1987].

Silva, Denise Ferreira da. "Facts of Blackness: Brazil Is Not (Quite) the United States . . . and Racial Politics in Brazil?" *Social Identities* 4, no. 2 (1998): 201–34.

———. "Revisiting Racial Democracy: Race and National Identity in Brazilian Thought." *Estudos Afro-Asiáticos* 16 (1989): 157–70.

———. *Toward a Global Idea of Race*. Minneapolis: University of Minnesota Press, 2007.

Silva, José Carlos Gomes Da. "Negros em São Paulo: espaço público, imagem e cidadania (1900–1930)." In *Além dos territórios: Para um diálogo entre a etnologia indígena, os estudos rurais e os estudos urbanos*, ed. Ana Maria de Niemeyer and Emília Pietrafesa de Godoi. Campinas: Mercado de Letras, 1998, 65–96.

Silva, Marília T. Barboza da, and Arthur L. de Oliveira Filho. *Pixinguinha: filho de Ogum Bexiguento*. Rio de Janeiro: Gryphers, 1998.

Simpson, Amelia. *Xuxa: The Mega-Marketing of Gender, Race, and Modernity*. Philadelphia, Pa.: Temple University Press, 1993.

Singh, Nikhil Pal. *Black Is a Country: Race and the Unfinished Struggle for Democracy*. Cambridge, Mass.: Harvard University Press, 2004.

Sitwell, Osbert. "Matchiche." *Living Age* 8, no. 312 (July/September 1922): 55.

———. "Maxixe." *Poetry* 20 (April/September 1922): 126.

Skidmore, Thomas E. "Bi-Racial U.S.A. vs. Multi-Racial Brazil: Is the Contrast Still Valid?" *Journal of Latin American Studies* 25 (1993): 373–86.

———. *Black into White: Race and Nationality in Brazilian Thought*. Durham, N.C.: Duke University Press, 1993 [1974].

———. "Toward a Comparative Analysis of Race Relations since Abolition in Brazil and the United States." *Latin American Studies* 4, no. 1 (1972): 1–28.

Skinner, David. "Racialized Futures: Biologism and the Changing Politics of Identity." *Social Studies of Science* 36, no. 3 (June 2006): 459–88.

Slenes, Robert. *Na senzala, uma flor: esperanças e recordações na formação da família escrava: Brasil Sudeste, século XIX*. Rio de Janeiro: Editora Nova Fronteira, 1999.

Small, Christopher. *Music of the Common Tongue: Survival and Celebration in Afro-American Music*. New York: Riverrun Press, 1987.

Smith, Elizabeth Marie. "'Passing' and the Anxious Decade: The *Rhinelander* Case and the 1920s." Ph.D. diss., Rutgers University, 2002.

Smith, Joseph. *Unequal Giants: Diplomatic Relations between the United States and Brazil, 1889–1930*. Pittsburgh: University of Pittsburgh Press, 1991.

Smith, Neil. *American Empire: Roosevelt's Geographer and the Prelude to Globalization*. Berkeley: University of California Press, 2003.

————. "The Satanic Geographies of Globalization: Uneven Development in the 1990s." *Public Culture* 10, no. 1 (1997): 169–89.

————. *Uneven Development: Nature, Capital, and the Production of Space*. New York: Blackwell, 1984.

Smith, Peter H. *Talons of the Eagle: Dynamics of U.S.–Latin-American Relations*. New York: Oxford University Press, 1996.

Smith, Valerie. "Reading the Intersection of Race and Gender in Narratives of Passing." *diacritics* 24 (summer–fall 1994): 43–57.

Soares, Carlos Eugênio. *A negregada instituição: os capoeiras no Rio de Janeiro*. Rio de Janeiro: Prefeitura da Cidade do Rio de Janeiro, 1994.

Sollors, Werner. *Beyond Ethnicity: Consent and Descent in American Culture*. New York: Oxford University Press, 1986.

————. *The Invention of Ethnicity*. New York: Oxford University Press, 1988.

Southern, Eileen. *Biographical Dictionary of Afro-American and African Musicians*. Westport, Conn.: Greenwood Press, 1982.

————. *The Music of Black Americans: A History*. New York: W. W. Norton, 1971.

Spackman, S. G. F. "Passing for Colored: Meanings for Minstrelsy and Ragtime." *Reviews in American History* 23, no. 2 (1995): 237–42.

Spalding, John W. "1928: Radio Becomes a Mass Advertising Medium." *Journal of Broadcasting* 8 (1963–64): 31–44.

Spencer, Jon Michael. *The New Negroes and Their Music: The Success of the Harlem Renaissance*. Knoxville: University of Tennessee Press, 1997.

Spradling, Mary Mace, ed. *In Black and White*, 3d ed., suppl. Detroit: Gale, 1985.

Stam, Robert. *Tropical Multiculturalism: A Comparative History of Race in Brazilian Cinema and Culture*. Durham, N.C.: Duke University Press, 1997.

Stam, Robert, and Randal Johnson, eds. *Brazilian Cinema*. East Brunswick, N.J.: Associated University Presses, 1982.

Stam, Robert, and Ella Shohat. *Unthinking Eurocentrism: Multiculturalism and the Media*. London: Routledge, 1994.

Stearns, Marshall Winslow, and Jean Stearns. *Jazz Dance: The Story of American Vernacular Dance*. New York: Macmillan, 1968.

Stein, Stanley J. *Vassouras, a Brazilian Coffee County, 1850–1900*. Cambridge, Mass.: Harvard University Press, 1957.

Stepan, Nancy Leys. *"The Hour of Eugenics": Race, Gender, and Nation in Latin America*. Ithaca: Cornell University Press, 1991.

Stephens, Michelle Ann. *Black Empire: The Masculine Global Imaginary of Caribbean Intellectuals in the United States, 1914–1962*. Durham, N.C.: Duke University Press, 2005.

————. "Black Transnationalism and the Politics of National Identity: West Indian Intellectuals in Harlem in the Age of War and Revolution." *American Quarterly* 50, no. 3 (September 1998): 592–608.

Stern, Julia. "Spanish Masquerade and the Drama of Racial Identity in *Uncle Tom's Cabin*." In Ginsberg, *Passing and the Fictions of Identity*, 103–30.

Stich, Sidra. *Anxious Visions: Surrealist Art*. New York: University Art Museum; Abbeville Press, 1990.

Stoddard, Lothrop. *The Rising Tide of Color against White World-Supremacy*. New York: Scribner's Sons, 1920.

Stolcke, Verena. "Brasil: uma nação vista através de raça." *Revista de Cultura Brasileña* 1 (March 1998): 207–20.

———. *Coffee Planters, Workers, and Wives: Class Conflict and Gender Relations on São Paulo Plantations, 1850–1980*. New York: St. Martin's Press, 1988.

———. "The Labors of Coffee in Latin America: The Hidden Charm of Family Labor and Self-Provisioning." In Roseberry, Gudmundson, and Samper, *Coffee, Society, and Power*, 65–93.

Stoler, Ann Laura. *Carnal Knowledge and Imperial Power: Race and the Intimate in Colonial Rule*. Berkeley: University of California Press, 2002.

———. *Race and the Education of Desire: Foucault's* History of Sexuality *and the Colonial Order of Things*. Durham, N.C.: Duke University Press, 1995.

———. "Tense and Tender Ties: The Politics of Comparison in North American History and (Post) Colonial Studies." *Journal of American History* 88, no. 3 (2001): 829–65.

Stone, Alfred Holt. *Studies in the American Race Problem*. New York: Negro Universities Press, 1969 [1908].

Story of Coffee and How to Make It, The. Nashville: Cheek-Neal Coffee, 1925. Advertising Ephemera Collection, Database #A0160, Emergence of Advertising On-Line Project, John W. Hartman Center for Sales, Advertising and Marketing History, Duke University Rare Book, Manuscript, and Special Collections Library; http://scriptorium.lib.duke.edu/eaa/.

Stovall, Tyler. "Music and Modernity, Tourism and Transgression: Harlem and Montmartre in the Jazz Age." *Intellectual History Newsletter*, 2000, 36–48.

———. *Paris noir: African Americans in the City of Light*. Boston, Mass.: Houghton Mifflin, 1996.

Strasser, Susan, Charles McGovern, and Matthias Judt, eds. *Getting and Spending: European and American Consumer Societies in the Twentieth Century*. Cambridge: Cambridge University Press, 1998.

Streeby, Shelley. *American Sensations: Class, Empire, and the Production of Popular Culture*. Berkeley: University of California Press, 2002.

Striffler, Steve. *In the Shadows of State and Capital: The United Fruit Company, Popular Struggle, and Agrarian Restructuring in Ecuador, 1900–1995*. Durham, N.C.: Duke University Press, 2002.

Stuckey, Sterling. *Slave Culture: Nationalist Theory and the Foundations of Black America*. New York: Oxford University Press, 1987.

Stychin, Carl. *A Nation by Rights: National Cultures, Sexual Identity Politics, and the Discourse of Rights*. Philadelphia, Pa.: Temple University Press, 1998.

Sucena, Eduardo. *A dança teatral no Brasil*. Rio de Janeiro: Fundação Nacional de Artes Cênicas, Ministério da Cultura, 1988.

Sullivan, Jack. *New World Symphonies: How American Culture Changed European Music*. New Haven, Conn.: Yale University Press, 1999.

Summers, Martin. *Manliness and Its Discontents: The Black Middle Class and the Transformation of Masculinity, 1900–1930*. Chapel Hill: University of North Carolina Press, 2004.

Susman, Warren. *Culture as History: The Transformation of American Society in the Twentieth Century*. New York: Pantheon Books, 1984.

Svampa, Maristella. *El dilema argentino: Civilización o barbarie: De Sarmiento al revisionismo peronista*. Buenos Aires: El Cielo por Asalto, Imago Mundi, 1994.

Szwed, John, and Morton Marks. "The Afro-American Transformations of European Set Dances and Dance Suites." *Dance Research Journal* 21, no. 1 (summer 1988): 29–36.

Tannenbaum, Frank. *Slave and Citizen: The Negro in the Americas*. New York: Alfred A. Knopf, 1946.

Tanner, Jo A. *Dusky Maidens: The Odyssey of the Early Black Dramatic Actress*. Westport, Conn.: Greenwood Press, 1992.

Taylor, Davidson. "The Enduring Elsie Houston." *Saturday Review*, July 31, 1954, 55.

Taylor, Diana. *Disappearing Acts: Spectacles of Gender and Nationalism in Argentina's "Dirty War."* Durham, N.C.: Duke University Press, 1997.

Taylor, Frederick Winslow. *The Principles of Scientific Management*. New York: Harper and Brothers, 1911.

Taylor, Quintard. "Frente Negra Brasileira: The Afro-Brazilian Civil Rights Movement, 1924–1937." *Umoja: A Scholarly Journal of Black Studies* 2, no. 1 (spring 1978): 25–40.

Thelen, David. "Rethinking History and the Nation-State: Mexico and the United States." *Journal of American History* 86, no. 3 (1999): 438–52.

Théry, Hervé. "Première partie: Territoire et institutions: Une originalité des stéréotypes franco-brésiliens." In Carelli, Théry, and Zantman, *France-Brésil*, 29–106.

Thomas, William Isaac, and Florian Znaniecki. *The Polish Peasant in Europe and America: Monograph of an Immigrant Group*. Boston, Mass.: Richard G. Badger, Gorham Press, 1918–20.

Thompson, Daniella. "Stalking Stokowski." *Brazzil*, February 2000; http://www.brazzillog.com/pages/musfeb00.htm (accessed May 7, 2007).

Thompson, Robert Farris. *Flash of the Spirit: African and Afro-American Art and Philosophy*. New York: Vintage Books, 1983.

Thorp, Rosemary, ed. *Latin America in the 1930s: The Role of the Periphery in World Crisis*. Vol. 2 of *An Economic History of Twentieth-Century Latin America*. Oxford: Palgrave/St Antony's College, 2000 [1984].

———, ed. *Progress, Poverty and Exclusion: An Economic History of Latin America in the Twentieth Century*. Washington, D.C.: Inter-American Development Bank and the European Union, Johns Hopkins University Press, 1998.

Tinhorão, José Ramos. *Música popular: teatro e cinema*. Petrópolis: Editora Vozes, 1972.

————. *Música popular: um tema em debate*. Rio de Janeiro: Editôra Saga, 1966.

————. *O samba agora vai: a farsa da música popular no exterior*. Rio de Janeiro: JCM Editôres, 1969.

Toll, Robert C. *Blacking Up: The Minstrel Show in Nineteenth-Century America*. New York: Oxford University Press, 1974.

Tomlinson, John. *Cultural Imperialism*. Baltimore: Johns Hopkins University Press, 1991.

Topik, Steven C. "Coffee." In Topik and Wells, *The Second Conquest of Latin America*.

————. "Historicizing Commodity Chains: Thinking about Things, Structures, Systems, and Especially Coffee." Unpublished paper, London School of Economics, fall 2002.

————. *The Political Economy of the Brazilian State, 1889–1930*. Austin: University of Texas Press, 1987.

————. "Representaçoes nacionais do cafecultor: Zé Prado e Juan Valdez." *Revista Brasileira de História* 15, no. 29 (1995): 157–72.

————. *Trade and Gunboats: The United States and Brazil in the Age of Empire*. Stanford, Calif.: Stanford University Press, 1996.

Topik, Steven C., and Mario Samper Kutschbach. "The Latin American Coffee Commodity Chain: Brazil and Costa Rica." In Topik, Marichal, and Frank, *From Silver to Cocaine*, 118–46.

Topik, Steven C., Carlos Marichal, and Zephyr Frank, eds. *From Silver to Cocaine: Latin American Commodity Chains and the Building of the World Economy, 1500–2000*. Durham, N.C.: Duke University Press, 2006.

Topik, Steven C., and Allen Wells. "Epilogue." In Topik and Wells, *The Second Conquest of Latin America*.

————, eds. *The Second Conquest of Latin America*. Austin: University of Texas Press, 1998.

Toplin, Robert Brent. "Reinterpreting Comparative Race Relations: The United States and Brazil." *Journal of Black Studies* 2, no. 2 (December 1971): 135–55.

Torgovnick, Mariana. *Gone Primitive: Savage Intellects, Modern Lives*. Chicago: University of Chicago Press, 1990.

Triner, Gail D. "Race, with or without Color? Reconciling Brazilian Historiography." *Estudios Interdisciplinarios de América Latina y el Caribe* (EIAL) 10, 1 (January–June 1999); online at http://www.tau.ac.il/eial/X_1/triner.html (accessed May 13, 2000).

Trochim, Michael. "The Brazilian Black Guard: Racial Conflict in Post-Abolition Brazil." *The Americas* 44, no. 3 (1988): 286–90.

Trouillot, Michel-Rolph. *Silencing the Past: Power and the Production of History*. Boston, Mass.: Beacon Press, 1995.

Tuttle, William M. *Race Riot: Chicago in the Red Summer of 1919*. New York: Atheneum, 1970.

Twine, Frances Winddance. *Racism in a Racial Democracy: The Maintenance of White Supremacy in Brazil*. New Brunswick, N.J.: Rutgers University Press, 1997.

Tyler, Bruce M. "Racist Art and Politics at the Turn of the Century." *Journal of Ethnic Studies* 15, no. 4 (1988): 85–103.

Ukers, William H. *All about Coffee*, 2d ed. New York: Tea and Coffee Trade Journal, 1935.

———. *A Trip to Brazil*. New York: Tea and Coffee Trade Journal, 1924. NMAH Warsaw Business Administration Collection, Coffee Series, Box 4.

Unruh, Vickey. *Latin American Vanguards: The Art of Contentious Encounters*. Berkeley: University of California Press, 1994.

Uribe-Compuzano, Andrés. *Brown Gold: The Amazing Story of Coffee*. New York: Random House, 1954.

U.S. Congress, House, Committee on Interstate and Foreign Commerce. *Crude Rubber, Coffee, Etc.: Hearings before the Committee on Interstate and Foreign Commerce* (on H. Res. 59). 69th Cong., 1st sess., January 6–22, 1926.

———. *Hearings on Crude Rubber, Coffee, Etc.* (on H. Res. 59). 69th Cong., 1st sess., 1926.

———. *Preliminary Report on Crude Rubber, Coffee, Etc.*, 69th Cong., 1st sess., 1926.

Valla, Victor Vincent. "Os Estados Unidos e a influência estran[j]eira na economia brasileira . . . , 1904–1928." *Revista de História* (Brazil) 42 (1960): 147–74; 43 (1960): 169–85; 44 (1960): 173–95; 45 (1961): 143–67.

———. *A penetração norte-americana na economia brasileira, 1898–1928*. Rio de Janeiro: Ao Livro Técnico; Brasília: INL, 1978.

Vallotton, Henry. *Brésil: Terre d'amour et de beauté*. Lausanne: Payot, 1945.

Vasconcelos, Ary. *Panorama da música popular brasileira na Belle Époque*. 2 vols. Rio de Janeiro: Livraria Sant'anna, 1977.

Velloso, Mônica Pimenta. *A cultura das ruas no Rio de Janeiro (1900–1930): Mediações, linguagens e espaço*. Rio de Janeiro: Edições Casa de Rui Barbosa, 2004.

———. "As tias baianas tomam conta do pedaço: Espaço e identidade cultural no Rio de Janeiro." *Estudos Históricos* 3, no. 6 (1990): 207–28.

Verger, Pierre. Book review of *Voodoo in Haiti* by Alfred Metraux. *Man* 60 (July 1960): 111–12.

Vianna, Hermano. *The Mystery of Samba: Popular Music and National Identity in Brazil*. Trans. John Chasteen. Chapel Hill: University of North Carolina Press, 1999 [1995].

Vianna, Larissa Moreira. "As dimensões da cor: um estudo do olhar norte-americano sobre as relações inter-étnicas, Rio de Janeiro, primeira metade do século XIX." Master's thesis, UFF — Fluminense Federal University, Nitteroi, Rio de Janeiro, 1998.

Vicente, Eduardo. "Música popular e produção intelectual nos anos 40." *Cadernos de Sociologia* (UNICAMP) 2 (July/December 1996): 157–72.

Vidal, Armando, ed. *Defesa do café no Brasil: coletanea de documentos oficiais*. Rio de Janeiro: Departamento Nacional do Café, 1935.

Vidossich, Edoardo. *Sincretismos na música afro-americana*. São Paulo: Edições Quiron, 1975.

Vinhosa, Francisco Luis Teixeira. "As relações Brasil–Estados Unidos durante a primeira república." *Revista do Instituto Histórico e Geográfico Brasileiro* 378–79 (April–June 1993): 280–94.

Vogel, Todd, ed. *The Black Press: New Literary and Historical Essays*. New Brunswick, N.J.: Rutgers University Press, 2001.

Von Eschen, Penny M. *Race against Empire: Black Americans and Anticolonialism, 1937–1957*. Ithaca: Cornell University Press, 1997.

————. *Satchmo Blows up the World: Jazz Ambassadors Play the Cold War*. Cambridge, Mass.: Harvard University Press, 2004.

Wade, Peter. *Music, Race, and Nation: Música Tropical in Colombia*. Chicago: University of Chicago Press, 2000.

Wagnleitner, Reinhold, and Elaine Tyler May, eds. *Here, There and Everywhere: The Foreign Politics of American Popular Culture*. Hanover, N.H.: University Press of New England, 2000.

Walkowitz, Judith R. "The 'Vision of Salome': Cosmopolitanism and Erotic Dancing in Central London, 1908–1918." AHR 108, no. 2 (April 2003): 336–77.

Wallis, Roger, and Krister Malm. *Big Sounds from Small Peoples: The Music Industry in Small Countries*. New York: Perdagon Press, 1984.

Warren, Jonathan W. *Racial Revolutions: Antiracism and Indian Resurgence in Brazil*. Durham, N.C.: Duke University Press, 2001.

Watkins-Owens, Irma. *Blood Relations: Caribbean Immigrants and the Harlem Community, 1900–1930*. Bloomington: Indiana University Press, 1996.

Watson, Sonny. "Streetswing.com Dance History Archives"; www.streetswing.com/histmai2/d2movet1.htm (accessed August 22, 2004).

Weinstein, Barbara. *The Amazon Rubber Boom, 1850–1920*. Stanford, Calif.: Stanford University Press, 1983.

————. *For Social Peace in Brazil: Industrialists and the Remaking of the Working Class in São Paulo*. Chapel Hill: University of North Carolina Press, 1996.

————. "Racializing Regional Difference: São Paulo versus Brazil, 1932." In Applebaum, Macpherson, and Rosemblatt, *Race and Nation in Modern Latin America*, 237–62.

Welburn, Ron. "James Reese Europe and the Infancy of Jazz Criticism." *Black Music Research Journal* 7 (1987): 35–44.

Wesson, Robert. *The United States and Brazil: Limits of Influence*. New York: Praeger, 1981.

Westin, Alan F., ed. *Freedom Now! The Civil-Rights Struggle in America*. New York: Basic Books, 1964.

Wexler, Laura. *Tender Violence: Domestic Visions in an Age of U.S. Imperialism*. Chapel Hill: University of North Carolina Press, 2000.

White, Richard. "The Nationalization of Nature." *Journal of American History* 86, no. 3 (December 1999): 976–86.

Wickizer, Vernon Dale. *The World Coffee Economy, with Special Reference to Control Schemes*. Stanford, Calif.: Food Research Institute, Stanford University, 1943.

Wiegman, Robyn. *American Anatomies: Theorizing Race and Gender.* Durham, N.C.: Duke University Press, 1995.

Williams, Daryle. *Culture Wars in Brazil: The First Vargas Regime, 1930–1945.* Durham, N.C.: Duke University Press, 2001.

Williams, Eric. *Capitalism & Slavery.* Chapel Hill: University of North Carolina Press, 1994.

Williamson, Joel. *New People: Miscegenation and Mulattoes in the United States.* Baton Rouge: Louisiana State University Press, 1995 [New York: Free Press, 1980].

Williamson, Judith. *Decoding Advertisements: Ideology and Meaning in Advertising.* London: Boyars, 1978.

Williamson, William F., and National Coffee Association of USA. *The Retail Market for Coffee: A Study Based on the Retail Census of Distribution.* New York: Associated Coffee Industries of America, 1932.

Winant, Howard. *Racial Conditions: Politics, Theory, Comparisons.* Minneapolis: University of Minnesota Press, 1994.

Wisnik, José Miguel. *O coro dos contrários: a música em torno da semana de 22.* São Paulo: Duas Cidades, 1977.

Witt, Doris. *Black Hunger: Food and the Politics of U.S. Identity.* New York: Oxford University Press, 1999.

Wolseley, Roland E. *The Black Press, U.S.A.*, 2d ed. Ames: Iowa State University, 1990 [1971].

Woodard, James P. "Marketing Modernity: The J. Walter Thompson Company and North American Advertising in Brazil, 1929–1939." *HAHR* 82, no. 2 (May 2002): 257–90.

Wooding, Sam, and Chris Albertson. "Interview with Sam Wooding." Unpublished Smithsonian Institution oral history. Washington, D.C., April–May, 1975; Institute of Jazz Studies, Rutgers University.

Woodward, C. Vann. *American Counterpoint: Slavery and Racism in the North-South Dialogue.* Boston, Mass.: Little Brown, 1971.

Yack, Bernard. *The Fetishism of Modernities: Epochal Self-Consciousness in Contemporary Social and Political Thought.* Notre Dame: University of Notre Dame Press, 1997.

Yelvington, Kevin A., ed. *Afro-Atlantic Dialogues: Anthropology in the Diaspora.* Santa Fe: School of American Research Press, 2006.

———. "The Invention of Africa in Latin America and the Caribbean: Political Discourse and Anthropological Praxis, 1920–1940." In Yelvington, *Afro-Atlantic Dialogues.*

Young, Consuelo C. "Reader Attitudes toward the Negro Press." *Journalism Quarterly* 21 (June 1944): 148–52.

Index

Abbaye de Thélème (Paris), 75, 88–89

Abbey, Don, 103

Abbott, Helen, 193–94, 204

Abbott, Robert S., 179–80, 182, 192–95, 197–98, 203–5, 230, 231, 237; on Mãe Preta monument, 222–29, 233. *See also* *Chicago Defender*

Abolitionists, 6–7, 9, 76, 221, 232, 297 n. 8. *See also* Slavery (African)

Abreu, Martha, 276 n. 78

"Absent presence," 53, 72, 90

Acioly (musician), 107

Advertising (of coffee), 4, 8, 9, 13–66, 235, 236; consumer citizenship in, 15–18, 20–27, 33, 43, 49–50, 61–63; erasure of Brazil in later, 44, 51–53, 57, 59, 61, 66, 178; financial aspects of joint campaign by Brazil and United States, 26, 57–58, 236, 258 n. 122; gender in, 13–15, 26, 29–31, 35–37, 42, 48, 50, 61–63; magazines for, 22; Orientalism in, 144–45; on radio, 23, 61–63; as source material for scholars, 23–24; tours as part of, 126. *See also* Coffee; Coffee trade

African Americans: attempts by, to compare blackness across national contexts, 6, 120, 139, 144, 183; Brazilians' views of, 188–205, 311 n. 112; in coffee ads, 29–33; foreign language fluency of, 111, 149–50, 153–55, 160, 164; global vision of, 3, 183; interest of, in Brazil as place of racial harmony, 8–10, 120, 135, 147, 158, 179–80, 192–93, 195–98, 204–5, 222–25; segregation for, in Rio de Janeiro, 111, 131–32, 135, 192; as term, xvii; use of exoticism

by, 136–78; violence against, 10, 30, 57, 71, 91, 155, 166, 188, 198–200, 202–3, 217, 218, 224, 227–28, 234; work open to female, 160. *See also* Africans and Afro-descendents; Afro-diasporic forms and traditions; Citizenship; Jazz; "Negro vogue"; Pan-Africanism; Racism; Segregation; Slavery; *Names of specific African Americans*

African diaspora studies, xiii, xiv, xvii

Os africanos no Brasil (Nina Rodrigues), 195

Africans and Afro-descendents: as backward and primitive, 122–23, 187, 216; Brazilian immigration policy on, 195–98; common history of, 190–91; as cultural producers claiming authorship and public space, 90–91, 95, 116–24; erasure of influence of, in cultural performances, 71, 72, 83–84, 113–15; as exotic, 144; in France in First World War, 1, 9–10, 79, 87, 105, 192, 232, 319 n. 79; influence of, on Brazil, 72, 83–85, 104, 113–16, 122–23, 127, 170, 187, 209–11, 213–17, 231; in Latin America, 37. *See also* African Americans; African diaspora studies; Afro-Brazilians; Afro-diasporic forms and traditions; Exoticism; Pan-Africanism; Race; Slavery; *Specific African countries*

Afro-American (term), xvii–xviii. *See also* African Americans; Afro-Brazilians

Afro-Brazilians: attempts by, to compare blackness across national contexts, 6, 120, 183; expressions of national loyalty and denial of racism by, 179–80, 185, 187,

Afro-Brazilians (*continued*)
190–92, 197–205; on Mãe Preta monument issue, 206, 213–19; married to white ex-Confederates, 167; as a term, xvii; traditions of, 168, 169–70. *See also* Afro-diasporic forms and traditions; "Negro vogue"; Non-elites; Whitening; *Specific Afro-Brazilians*
Afro-Cariocas (term), 10
Afro-Cubans, 153
Afro-descendents (term), xvii. *See also* Africans and Afro-descendents
Afro-diasporic forms and traditions: as adored in centers of civilization, 76, 107, 116, 117, 119–21, 123, 124, 138, 176; characteristics of, 105, 112; jazz as, 92, 94, 102–6, 112–13, 116–23, 176, 236; maxixe as, 72–79, 88–90, 92, 93, 106, 112, 127, 138; mobility and, 5, 95–96, 100–104, 106, 108, 110, 111, 114–15, 120–21, 126–30, 135, 138, 142, 148–50, 160–61, 167–68; modernity and, 5, 117–21, 123–25, 132, 200–201, 236, 271 n. 11; Paris as mediating cultural exchanges of, 102–7, 109–10, 112–21, 123–25, 127–29, 135, 138, 170, 175, 189, 235, 236; sambas as, 92, 94, 112, 113
Afro-Paulistas (term), 3
Aguiar, Jayme de, 121, 202, 297 n. 8
Aida Walker and Her Abyssinia Girls (vaudeville group), 144
Aimoré, Jacy, 118
Alaska, 65
Alcazar d'Èté (Paris), 75
Alcohol, 36, 254 n. 66
Alencar, Edigar de, 283 n. 157
Alencar, José de, 313 n. 17
O Alfinete (São Paulo newspaper), 181, 189, 190
Algeria, 161, 163–64
All-America Cables, 37, 39
Almeida, Gabriela de, 310 n. 101
Almeida, Guilherme de, 132
Almeida, Irineu de, 276 n. 78
Alves, José, 105
Alves, Nélson, 105
Amado, Gilberto, 113, 210
Amaral, Tarsila do, 113, 291 n. 114

Ambassadeur (Paris), 75
Americana (Brazil), 167
American Jazz (musical group), 100
American Jazz-Band (Bernard Kay's), 105
American Legion (ship), 102
Americano, Luís, 108–9
American studies, xiv–xv
Amorim Diniz, Antônio Lopes de. *See* "Duque"
Anderson, Benedict, xii, xv, 296 n. 6
Andrade, Mário de, 77, 115–16, 118, 167–68, 277 n. 78, 281 n. 143
Andrade, Oswald de, 113
Andreosi (musician), 108
Andreozzy, José, 108
Andrews, George Reid, 312 n. 3
Anglo-Brazilian Chronicle, 277 n. 86
Antoine, LeRoi, 145
AP (Associated Press), 224
Apache (dance), 150
Apollo Theater (Paris), 88
"Aquarela do Brasil" (samba), 100
"Arab on the Can" (ad), 55, 235
Argentina: Afro-descended performers in, 168; as influence on jazz, 88, 89; maxixe in, 75, 77, 86; tango in, 73, 79, 85, 87, 88, 105, 131; as whiter and more European than its neighbors, 85. *See also* Buenos Aires
Arias, José, 108
Arinos, Alfonso, 98
Armstrong, Louis, 273 n. 39
Arruda (musician), 108
Arruda, Stellita, 310 n. 101
Art: high vs. low, 113–15, 122, 123–26, 128–30, 140, 142, 154, 170–73; prevention of war through, 130–31, 168; "primitivism" and, 138. *See also* Dance; Music
Asians, xii, 52, 98, 184, 195, 283 n. 3
As Nature Leads (Rogers), 136
Assírio (Rio de Janeiro), 94, 97, 103, 104, 107–8
Associated Press, 9
Astaire, Fred, 112
"Aunt Jemima," 30, 235
Auriverde (São Paulo newspaper), 181, 201
Australia, 142
Austria-Hungary, 149

Autobiography of an Ex-Colored Man (Johnson), 287 n. 59
Ayer and Son, 22, 23, 27–29, 37

BACPC (Brazilian-American Coffee Promotion Committee), 22, 51, 59–63
BACS (Brazilian American Colonization Syndicate), 196
Baker, Josephine, 92, 110–11, 119, 120, 123, 127, 147, 204
Balle Noir, 89
Ballet, 151–52, 163
Ballroom dance duos, 150–52
Baltimore *Afro-American* (newspaper), 224
O Bandeirante (São Paulo newspaper), 181, 190–91
Bando de Tangarás, 272 n. 20
Baptista, J. A., Jr., 127
Barbarity and savagery, 13, 27, 29, 37, 42, 143, 145, 146, 184; Africa and Africans associated with, 122–23, 187, 216; maxixe associated with, 73; of slavery in United States, 198. *See also* Civilization; Exoticism; Primitivism
Barbosa, Luiz, 201
Barbosa, Rui, 98, 296 n. 8
Barnett, Claude, 144
Barnett, Etta Moten, 93, 112, 294 n. 155
Barroso, Ari, 92, 100, 102, 126, 278 n. 88
Ba-ta-clan (revue troupe), 107–10, 114, 117, 275 n. 57
Batuque, cateretê e maxixe (play), 118
Batutas, 100, 101, 104–15, 128–33. *See also* Oito Batutas
Bechet, Sidney, 109
Bederman, Gail, 319 n. 78
Beeson, Emmet, 47, 50
"Begin the Beguine" (Porter), 89
Béhague, Gérard, 100, 267 n. 86, 271 n. 16
Belgium, 128, 132
Berensdorff, Edith de, 112
Bernard Kay's American Jazz-Band, 105
Besse, Susan, 308 n. 92
Bilhar, Sátiro, 276 n. 78
Billy King Stock Company (Atlanta), 163
Bi-Orquestra Os Batutas, 106
Biracial. *See* Racial mixing (miscegenation)
Birth of a Nation (film), 30, 229–30

Black (as term), xviii, 226–27. *See also* Blackness
"Black Ba-ta-clan," 117, 118. *See also* Companhia Negra de Revistas
"Blackbird." *See* Mills, Florence
Black bottom (dance), 73, 100, 112
Black Mother (of slavery times). *See* Mãe Preta
Black nationalism (U.S.), 183
Blackness: Brazilian discourse of nation as superseding, 128–31, 171–76, 197–205, 208–22; differences in definitions of, and terms for, xvii–xviii, 6, 120, 139, 144, 187–88, 198, 200, 203–4, 226–30, 307 n. 87; elites' attempts to come to terms with, 115–17, 121–34, 206–34; as fluid concept, 136–41, 175–76; modernity and, 188–89; "Negro vogue" as emphasizing value of, 5, 97, 113, 116–17, 119–21, 166. *See also* Nationalism; Race; Racism
"Black Patti." *See* Jones, Matilda Sissieretta Joyner
"Black Patti's Troubadours" (vaudeville group), 142
Black press. *See Chicago Defender*; São Paulo (Brazil): black press in
Blake, Jody, 88, 268 n. 96
Blassifera, Carlos ("Carlitos"), 110
Blues music, 68, 88, 89, 112, 122
"Le boeuf sur le toit" (Milhaud), 114
"O boi no telhado" (Brazilian maxixe), 114, 115
Bolero (dance), 150
Bolshevik Revolution, 42–43
Bolton, Herbert, 270 n. 115
Bonita Company (vaudeville group), 144
"Boogie-Woogie Maxixe" (song), 67–69, 81
Boogie-woogie music, 68–69, 93
Borbee's Tango Orchestra, 91
Bossa nova, 68, 69, 93
Bowman, Laura, 145–46, 152, 153
Brasil Musical (magazine), 122
Brazil: African Americans performing as natives of, 158–66; African influence on, 72, 83–85, 104, 113–16, 122–23, 127, 170, 187, 209–11, 213–17, 231; coffee advertising by, 4, 8, 19–29, 44, 51–53, 57–63, 66, 178, 236, 258 n. 122; coffee production in,

Brazil (*continued*)
    19–20, 25, 26, 44, 51–53, 59, 65; coffee's
    price protection by, 18, 24, 44–61, 65,
    254 n. 78; constitutions of, 98, 193, 196,
    216, 315 n. 33; in First World War, 20; in-
    digenous groups in, 118; Josephine Baker
    and, 110–11; Mãe Preta monuments in,
    206–34; as a monarchy, 7, 98; "national"
    music genres from, 99–101, 104, 106;
    opposition to racism in, xvii, 6, 10, 116–
    21, 178, 182, 185–92, 200–208, 213–18, 228,
    236–37, 295 n. 3; "racial democracy" in,
    as a trait of nationalism in, xii, 4, 6–10,
    96–97, 115–17, 120, 128–35, 147, 158, 179–
    80, 185, 187, 189–92, 197–205, 208–22,
    224, 228–31, 234, 237–39; racial mixing
    in, xii, 7, 8, 118–19, 133, 208, 210, 213–15,
    226–27, 277 n. 86; racism in, xii, 169, 184,
    190–99, 205, 218, 237; as a republic, 7,
    98, 190; 1930 revolution in, 11, 45, 221;
    slavery abolished in, 7, 97; songs refer-
    ring to, 82–83, 93; trade between United
    States and, 9, 11, 18, 20–21, 44–59, 101–
    2, 157–58, 188; unequal power relations
    between United States and, 183, 198,
    203–4, 236, 237, 247 n. 2; U.S. migrants
    to, 7, 179–80, 192, 195–98, 204–5; United
    States' influence on, 8, 21. *See also* Folk
    culture; Maxixe; Rio de Janeiro; São
    Paulo; Slavery; Whitening
"Brazil" (dance), 163
"Braziliana" (song), 82
Brazilian-American Coffee Promotion
    Committee (BACPC), 22, 51, 59–63
Brazilian American Colonization Syndi-
    cate (BACS), 196
"Brazilian Chimes" (song), 82
"The Brazilian dance." *See* Maxixe (Brazil-
    ian dance)
Brazilian Jazz (musical group), 100
Brazilian Music Festival (Museum of Mod-
    ern Art), 171, 175
"Brazilian Nut" (vaudeville singer), 157
Brazilian Press Association, 195
"Bregeiro, Rio Brazilian Maxixe" (Naza-
    reth), 77, 86
Brennan, Timothy, 274 n. 47
Breton, André, 169

Briggs, Arthur, 89, 109
Britain: African American performers in,
    130, 138, 142, 159; alleged lack of racism
    in, 142, 147; Brazilian performers in, 75,
    76; Brazil's trade with, 20; after First
    World War, 21; as imperial power, 50, 115
Brown, Anita Patti, 147–48
Buenos Aires (Argentina): as influence on
    jazz, 88, 89; inter-American encounters
    in, 103–5, 108, 110; maxixe in, 75
Burgoyne, Olive (Olga), 141, 143, 158–67,
    174, 178
Burns, Billy, 110
Bushell, Garvin, 88, 105, 111, 135, 149, 272
    n. 30
Butler, Judith, 157
Butler, Kim, 299 n. 17
Butter-Nut coffee ads, 13–16, 23, 27, 43
Byrd, Charlie, 68

Cabral, Sérgio, 101, 111, 126, 282 n. 157
Café des Beaux-Arts (New York), 77, 84, 86
Cakewalk (dance), 73, 74, 77, 94, 100, 112
Camargo, Jayme Baptista de, 220, 297 n. 8
Campinas (São Paulo), 181, 206
Campos, Candido, 206, 209, 210, 213, 219–
    21, 223, 228–29
Candomblé (Brazilian religious tradition),
    169, 275 n. 67, 293 n. 143
Canero (band), 88
Capitalism: consumer, 15, 16, 23; link be-
    tween violence and, 35, 42–43, 47, 48,
    65; transnationalism and, xiii, 2, 239
Careta (Rio de Janeiro magazine), 123, 132
Caribbean, 19, 87, 88
Caribou Coffee (company), 64, 65
"Carioca" (dance), 74, 75, 93, 111–12, 150,
    294 n. 155
"Cariocas." *See* Rio de Janeiro
Carlitos Jazz-Band, 110
Carlos, Tito, 231
Carneiro, Conrado, 211
Carnival in Rhythm (film), 155
Carnival music, 99, 100
Carpenter, Elliott, 103
Carpentier, Alejo, 274 n. 47
Carter, Macy, & Co., 37, 38
Carvalho, Evangelina Xavier de, 310 n. 101

Carvalho, José Murilo de, 295 n. 3, 301 n. 27
Casa-grande & senzala (Freyre), 194
Castle, Vernon and Irene, 76, 77, 79, 81, 82, 266 n. 74, 290 n. 99
Castro, Booker T. Washington de, 311 n. 112
Castro, Olympio de, 222
Catumbi (Rio de Janeiro neighborhood), 97–99
Caulfield, Sueann, 308 n. 92, 309 n. 99, 315 n. 33
CBS Radio, 172, 173
Cearense, Catulo da Paixão, 276 n. 78
Cendrars, Blaise, 112–14, 276 n. 76
Centennial Exposition (Rio de Janeiro), 107, 113
Central American coffee, 51, 52, 65
C'est Paris (musical revue), 110
Chamek (musician), 108
Charleston (dance), 73, 100, 107, 200, 201, 213
Charley's Aunt (play), 158
Chateaubriand, Assis, 314 n. 23
Chez Duque (Paris), 76, 105
Chicago (Illinois): Olive Burgoyne's origins in, 158–59, 161. *See also Chicago Defender*
Chicago Defender, 4, 91, 147–48, 192, 237, 276 n. 71, 296 n. 7; Afro-Brazilian press and, 6, 178–83, 222–25; on black stage performance, 284 n. 10; on Brazilian matters, 182, 230, 231; on Mãe Preta monument, 222–29, 231, 233; on UDC's "Mammy statue," 224–25. *See also* Abbott, Robert S.
Chicago *Evening Post*, 50
Chicago Opera Company, 154
Chin, Elizabeth, 244 n. 6
China (Pixinguinha's brother), 105
Choro (dance), 99, 106, 308 n. 95
Christianity, 146, 219–20, 232–33
Ciata, Tia, 276 n. 78
Cirino, Sebastião, 110, 118
Citizenship: consumer, 15–18, 20–21, 26–27, 33, 43, 49–50, 61–63; gendered notions of, 208, 216–22, 225, 229, 230–31, 234, 315 n. 33; "Negro vogue" as bringing attention to, 5, 116, 135, 138; in São Paulo, 184; women's suffrage and, 308 n. 92. *See also* Visas

Civilization: Afro-diasporic performance adored in centers of, 76, 107, 116, 117, 119–21, 123, 124, 138, 176; appeals to, in coffee ads, 17, 25–27, 29, 37, 42, 52; elites' emphasis on, 123, 132, 184; vs. exoticism, 141, 236; fears of over-, 14, 16, 31; as site of racial mixing, 214–15. *See also* Barbarity and savagery; Elites; Modernity; Paris; Primitivism; Whitening
Clarim (São Paulo newspaper), 95, 181, 184, 229, 297 n. 8; on African American matters, 182, 197–98, 200, 237, 299 n. 17; on Afro-Brazilian performers, 118–21; on Mãe Preta monument, 213–14, 217, 220–22, 224; on male slaves, 232; organizations supporting, 300 n. 23; racial terms used by, 187–88; on slavery in Brazil and the United States, 198
O Clarim d'Alvorada (newspaper). *See Clarim*
Class: among Afro-Brazilians in São Paulo, 297 n. 8; coffee and, 34, 35–37, 53–55; as form of "whiteness," 203–4; maxixe and, 79, 80; morality and, 309 n. 99; music as cutting across, 98–99, 105, 113, 271 n. 16; in post-slavery Brazil, 212; as a social construct, 17, 18, 30–33; vaudevillians as performing high, 148–50, 162–63, 166. *See also* Elites; Non-elites
Club De Vingt (New York), 77, 85
Cocteau, Jean, 113
Coelho, Olga, 172
Coelho Netto, Henrique, 317 n. 51
Coffee: advertising of, 4, 8, 13–66; as "American drink," 26, 33–36, 59, 62; as an import, 4, 15, 25, 29, 51, 57; Brazil's attempts to protect price of, 18, 24, 44–61, 65, 254 n. 78; health and, 19, 26, 34; producers vs. consumers of, 13–15, 18–25, 27, 29–33, 46, 57–58, 61–63, 256 n. 90. *See also* Advertising; Coffee trade
Coffee as an Aid to Factory Efficiency (pamphlet), 34
Coffee trade: as Brazilian monopoly, 47–50; 1929 "crack" in, 45, 63; elites in, 5, 6, 45, 126; history of, 19–20; as "industry," 250 n. 32; in São Paulo, 25, 27, 33, 44, 183, 185; transnational aspects of, 13–14, 16–18. *See also* Advertising; Coffee

Cold War, 43

Cole, June, 272 n. 30

Colombia, 11, 65

Colonial Exposition (Paris 1930), 110

Colonialism (internal), xiv, 138, 139, 153. *See also* Imperialism

Colonization ventures, 179–80, 192, 195–98, 204–5

The Comedy of Errors (Shakespeare), 145

"Commodity chains," 17

Communication: after First World War, 9, 87, 136–37; before First World War, 1–2, 7–8; during slavery, 2, 6

Communities. *See* Imagined transnational communities; *Specific places*

Companhia Mulata Brasileira, 117, 118

Companhia Negra de Revistas (revue troupe), 109–10, 117–21, 129, 132

Comparison: black press's use of, between Brazilian and U.S. racism, 189–92, 198–203, 224–25; defects of, as methodology, xi–xii, 103, 130, 179–80, 207–8, 225, 238, 295 n. 5; transnationalism as alternative method to, xii–xiii, 235–39, 295 n. 5. *See also* Translation

Confederates (U.S.), 7, 167. *See also* United Daughters of the Confederacy

Confederation of Black Youth conference, 120

Conjur (play), 146

Consumer citizenship, 15–66, 238

Consumerism (defined), 15–16

Continental (dance), 150

Cook, Jenny, 75

Cook, Will Marion, 108, 109, 123, 129

Cooper, Frederick, 8

Copacabana Palace (Buenos Aires), 110

Le Corbusier, 123

Cordeiro, Cruz, 271 n. 16

Correio da Manhã (newspaper), 121, 126

Costa, Cyro, 181

Costallat, Benjamin, 128, 129, 131, 211–12, 282 n. 157, 313 n. 17

Coste, Felix, 26

Courbon, Marcel de, 174

Creole (as term), 161, 163–64

"Creole Girl" (song), 79, 290 n. 99

"Cristo nasceu na Bahia" (Cirino), 110, 118

Crosby, Bob, 67

Cross, Gary, 23

Cuba, 11, 20, 50, 153

Cultural exchange (in the Americas), 10–11, 76, 102–15

Cunha, Antunes da, 213–14

Cunha, Horacio da, 200, 203, 204

Cuppy, Will, 61–62

D'Alencastro, J., 190–92

Dance, 4, 5; difficulty in studying, 74, 262 n. 27; European forms of, 308 n. 95; exoticism of foreign forms of, 69–94, 119–20, 130, 138, 144, 145, 148–50, 162–64, 236; influence of, on jazz musicians, 105–6; "Negro vogue" in, 119; transnational aspects of, 102, 110–12, 235. *See also Names of specific dances, especially maxixe*

"Dance That Dengozo with Me, 'Oo-La-La'" (song), 80, 81, 85

Dancing Palace (Coney Island), 70, 76

Daniels, Jimmy, 174

Davis, Belle, 143

Davis, Simone, 23

Day of the Mãe Negra, 220, 221

Dean, Dora, 143

De Chocolat, 117, 119, 121, 278 n. 88

Delfim Netto, Antônio, 50–51

Delirio and Luis (dancers), 77

Delsarte, 160

Delson and Nata (dancers), 111

Dempsey, Jack, 105

"Dengozo" (Nazareth), 80, 86–87

Denmark, 160

Diamond's Club (Rio de Janeiro), 112

Diario da Noite (newspaper), 211

Diario Nacional (São Paulo newspaper), 131, 214

Dias Braga Company, 77

Diasporas, xiii. *See also* African diaspora studies; Afro-diasporic forms and traditions

Dirce (journalist), 310 n. 101

Donga (musician), 100, 105, 110, 114–15, 131, 276 n. 76, 276 n. 78

Dos Santos, Arlindo Veiga, 304 n. 54

Douglas, Louis, 109, 118, 123
Drag, xiv, 6, 137–41, 150–55, 157, 166
Drayton, Thaddeus, 111–12, 135, 148–50
"Dreamy Amazon" (song), 82
Drums, 145, 146
Drums of Voodoo (play), 146
Du Bois, W. E. B., 10
Dunbar, Paul Lawrence, 109
Dunham, Katharine, 155
Dunn, Johnny, 110, 272 n. 30
Duo Eclatant, 159, 161
"Duque" (Antônio Lopes de Amorim
    Diniz), 76–79, 83–86, 93, 118, 266 n. 74;
    Pixinguinha and, 94, 95, 97, 104–6, 108
"Duque Walk" (dance), 77
Dvorák, Anton, 109

Earth (play), 146
Edna and Wood Mysteries and Novelties
    (vaudeville troupe), 77
Efegê, Jota, 75, 101, 282 n. 143
Egypt, 70–71, 82, 103, 144–45, 150, 160
Elite (São Paulo newspaper), 181
Elites: African American, 188–89, 203–4;
    African-American performers giving
    themselves names associated with, 76;
    Brazilian, 7, 98–99, 193; coffee ads and,
    13, 23–24, 27, 36, 43, 63; in coffee trade,
    5, 6, 45, 126; high vs. low art and, 113–15;
    Houston's background among, 167–76;
    masculinity as bridging gap between
    non-elites and, 230–34; maxixe fears of,
    90; non-elite cultural producers and,
    112–17, 121–34; racial harmony rheto-
    ric used by Brazilian, 10, 115–17, 128–35,
    208–10, 215–16, 221, 224, 237; as term,
    xviii; white dancers associated with, 112;
    on whitening, 71–72, 123, 184, 188–92,
    195, 199, 233. *See also* Civilization; Class;
    Non-elites; Whiter people
Ellington, Duke, 76, 109
Empire: exoticist culture of, 5, 27, 42, 69–
    72, 83, 86, 90, 119, 126, 130, 138–53, 166,
    236, 238. *See also* Imperialism
English language, 62, 194, 231. *See also*
    Translation
"Entertainer" (Joplin), 74
Esher, Couto, 214

Espirito Santo, Antonio Feliciano do,
    132–33
Estado Novo, 181
Ethiopian Art Players (vaudeville group),
    145
Eugenics, 55, 184. *See also* Racial purity
Europe, James Reese, 79, 91
Eve, Marie, 174
Everett, Anna, 287 n. 70
Evolução (São Paulo newspaper), 181, 185,
    186, 189
Ewen, Stuart and Elizabeth, 23
Exoticism: in advertising, 62–63; African
    Americans' use of, 136–78; imperialism
    and, 5, 27, 42, 69–72, 83, 86, 90, 119, 126,
    130, 138–53, 166, 236, 238; of maxixe, 68,
    73, 83–84, 236; "primitivism" as, 119–20,
    138, 146–47, 236; sensuality's association
    with, 137, 139, 142, 144, 150, 158, 161–64,
    166, 173, 236. *See also* "Negro vogue";
    Primitivism
Exploitation. *See* Slavery; Violence and
    resistance

Fabian, Johannes, 296 n. 5
A Famosa Revista (Galvão), 292 n. 129
Fascism, 316 n. 41
"Father John" (Pãe João), 232
Favelas, 98
Federação dos Homens de Côr (Afro-
    Brazilian mutual aid organization), 182,
    193, 220, 227, 230
Fein, Seth, xv, 224 n. 9, 224 nn. 13, 14
Felski, Rita, 216
Ferrara, Miriam Nicolau, 308 n. 95
Ferreira, Vicente, 181, 220, 297 n. 8
Ferro, António, 130, 131–32
First World War: advertising and, 21; anti-
    colonial efforts after, 145; black par-
    ticipation in, 1, 9–10, 79, 87, 192, 232,
    319 n. 79; Brazil's involvement in, 20;
    changes following, 71, 87, 191, 212–13;
    efforts to diminish hatred after, 130–31,
    168; jazz following, 96, 105; savagery
    yoked to civilization in, 42
Fischer-Witmark, Carl, 70–71
Flakser, Harold, 273 n. 32
Fleming, R. D., 256 n. 94

Flemming, Herb, 88, 110, 153–54, 272 n. 30

Florianópolis (Brazil), 111

Flying Down to Rio (film), 74, 75, 93, 111–12, 150, 294 n. 155

Folger's Coffee (company), 52

Folies Bergères (Paris), 75, 123, 132

Folk culture, 89, 99, 104, 113, 114, 167, 169, 171, 172, 175, 176

Follies (film), 127

Ford, Henry, 34–35, 53

Foreign languages: African Americans' fluency in, 111, 149–50, 153–55, 160, 164. *See also Specific languages*

A Foreign Sound (album), 92

Foreman, Ronald Clifton, Jr., 91–92

Forester, John, 107–9

Forgetting, 53–56, 66, 68, 69, 178. *See also* Ignorance

Forsyne, Ida, 160, 161

Fortunato, José, 128, 132–33

Foulkes, Julia, 152

Fox trot (dance), 70, 73, 106, 107, 122

France: alleged lack of racism in, 1, 3, 120, 236; imperialism of, 105, 236; prestige associated with, 161. *See also* Paris

Frankel, Isaac, 129

Frazier, E. Franklin, 146

Freire-Medeiros, Bianca, 265 n. 67

Freitinhas (José Francisco de Freitas), 100

Frente Negra Brasileira (political group), 202

Freyre, Gilberto, 8, 194, 221–22, 276 n. 78

Futurism, 9, 113, 167, 200

Gabbard, Krin, 271 n. 11

Gabriel (musician), 108

Gaby des Fleurs, 76, 94

Galdo, Arindo, 167, 174

Gallet, Luciano, 167, 276 n. 78

Gallop, Sammy, 67

Galvão, Patrícia, 291 n. 114, 292 n. 129

Garvey, Marcus, 182, 235, 299 n. 17

Gender: in advertising, 13–15, 26, 29–31, 35–37, 42, 48, 50, 61–63; among Afro-Brazilian journalists, 297 n. 8; changes in conventions relating to, 200–202, 212–13; citizenship and, 208, 216–22, 225, 229, 230–31, 234, 315 n. 33; constancy of, as

category, 6; of consumerism ("Mrs. Consumer"), 61–63; drag as mocking of, 157, 166; exoticism and, 150, 154–55; in national identity, xiv, 29–33, 205, 208–34. *See also* Masculinity; Men; Women

Gendron, Bernard, 115

Geraldos. *See* Magalhães, Geraldo; Teixeira, Nina

Germany: African American performers in, 159–61, 167; after First World War, 21; language of, 154; maxixe in, 76, 77; Third Reich in, 171; vaudeville in, 149

Getulino (São Paulo newspaper), 181, 194, 198, 215, 218, 297 n. 8

Getz, Stan, 68

Gilberto, João, 68

Gilroy, Paul, 316 n. 41

Ginway, M. Elizabeth, 169, 291 n. 113

Globalization, 2–3, 65, 96; as "lumpy," 8, 88, 92

Gold, 20

Gomes, Tiago, 268 n. 86, 271 n. 11, 278 n. 90, 279 n. 95, 309 n. 99, 320 n. 80

Good Neighbor Policy (U.S.), 11, 108–9, 168, 171, 173, 176

Gottschild, Brenda Dixon, 150–52, 155–56, 271 n. 41, 287 n. 59

Graham, Richard, 320 n. 79

Grand Negro Jubilee (1892), 142

Great Depression, 10, 11, 61, 63, 143, 154–55, 164, 166, 171

Great Migration (U.S.), 288 n. 71

Grecian dances, 150

Greenlee, Rufus, 111–12, 135, 148–50, 154, 158

Griffith, D. W., 30, 229–30

Guedes, Lino, 120–21, 221

Guerra, Júlio, 221

Guglielmo, Thomas A., 283 n. 3

Guibout (Paris), 75, 90

Guinle, Arnaldo, 104, 106, 130

Guinle, Jorge, 107, 108, 273 n. 32

Gusikoff, Michel, 62

Guy, Edna, 151

Gypsy routines, 150

Habanera (dance), 73, 74, 122

Haiti, 11, 145, 146

Handlin, Oscar, 283 n. 3

Harlem (New York City), 88–89, 145, 269 n. 108

Harlem Renaissance, 269 n. 108

Harms, T. B., 81

Harrison, Benjamin, 142

Hawaii, 20, 50, 152; music from, 70, 71, 82, 144; vaudeville based on, 144, 145, 152

Hayman, Joe, 110

Herskovits, Melville, 146

Hesitation (dance), 80, 83

Hills Bros. coffee ad, 30, 52–55, 65, 166

His Honor the Barber (vaudeville performance), 144

Hispania (publication), 269 n. 115

Historical method, 238. *See also* Comparison; Forgetting; Transnational method

Hobsbawn, Eric, 271 n. 11

Hochstein, Joshua, 269 n. 115

Hodes, Martha, 287 n. 59

Hollanda, Sérgio Buarque de, 276 n. 78

Hollywood, 8, 81, 99, 200, 213. *See also* Motion pictures

Honduras, 11

Hoover, Herbert, 45–51, 53, 59, 61, 256 n. 94, 257 n. 96

Hornez, André, 92

Hotel Flamengo (Rio de Janeiro), 111, 135

Hotel Gloria (Rio de Janeiro), 193

Hotel Knickerbocker Grille (New York), 77

Hotel Odeste (São Paulo), 193

Houston, Elsie, 119, 141, 166–78, 276 n. 75

Houston, James Franklin, 167, 174

Houston, Sam, 174

Hula (dance), 70, 138

Hungary, 149, 160

Identity, xiv, 137, 209–10, 217–18, 231, 234. *See also* Class; Gender; National identity; Race

Ignorance: of maxixe dance steps and movements, 74; as privilege of power, 8, 55–58, 84, 236; as refusal to know, 237. *See also* Forgetting

Imagined Communities (Anderson), 296 n. 6

Imagined transnational communities, xii–xiii, 14–15, 29, 33, 56, 183, 232, 236,

296 n. 6. *See also* Pan-Africanism; Pan-Americanism

Immigrants: African Americans as, to Brazil, 147, 179–80, 192, 195–98, 204–5; to Brazil, 7, 10, 98, 115, 173, 212, 262 n. 32, 299 n. 17, 300 n. 26; in Rio de Janeiro, 97–98; in São Paulo, 184; in the United States, 7, 53. *See also* Migrants (rural Brazilian)

Imperialism (empire): African Americans as extending, to Brazil, 192–205; construction of racial and national identity and, 8, 239; exoticism and, 5, 27, 42, 69–72, 83, 86, 90, 119, 126, 130, 138–53, 166, 236, 238; internal colonialism and, xiv, 138, 139, 153; racism and, 69–70, 72; resistance to, 42–43, 238; transnationalism and, xiii, 2, 101, 139, 239; of United States, xiv–xv, 11, 20–21, 37, 42–58, 69–70, 93, 138–40, 188. *See also* Colonialism

In Dahomey (operetta), 159

India, 142, 151

Indianapolis (Indiana), 145, 152, 153

Indians (Native Americans), 37, 52, 118, 153, 156

Industrial Digest, 48

Industrialization, 183–85

Instituto do Café do Estado de São Paulo, 45, 46, 58, 59

Instituto Paulista de Defesa Permanente do Café, 44–46

Integralism, 304 n. 54

International Congress of Popular Arts, 168

Interracial relationships. *See* Racial mixing (miscegenation)

Irmandade de Nossa Senhora do Rosario e São Benedicto dos Homens Pretos (black church in Rio), 119, 213, 218–19, 222

Isabel, Princess, 185, 229, 314 n. 20

Isham, John, 142, 158

Italy, 76, 98, 111

Itapira (Brazil), 117, 118

"Ivan" (writer), 215

J. Walter Thompson advertising company (JWT), 30, 252 n. 52

Jackson, Hardtack, 157–58
Jackson, J., 271 n. 11
James, Ralph, 272 n. 30
Jarboro, Caterina, 154
Jazz: as Afro-diasporic form, 92, 94, 102–6, 112–13, 116–23, 176, 236; as "American" musical form, 79, 84, 87, 91–92, 94, 101, 123, 132, 176, 200, 201; defined, 271 n. 11; Latin roots of, 79, 84, 87, 92–93; post–First World War interest in, 9; in Rio de Janeiro, 4–6, 99–101
Jazz-Band Sul-Americana, 102, 125, 126
JC. *See* Joint Coffee Trade Publicity Committee
Jercolis, Jardel, 75, 90
Jim Crow. *See* Segregation
Jiménez, Michael, 252 n. 54
Jobim, Antonio Carlos, 68
Johnson, Freddie, 272 n. 30
Johnson, Helen Armstead, 159
Johnson, Helen Louise, 252 n. 52
Johnson, Jack, 204
Johnson, James Weldon, 287 n. 59
Joint Coffee Trade Publicity Committee (JC), 18, 21–30, 34–37, 43, 44, 49, 57, 62, 65, 252 n. 51; Brazil's representation on, 258 n. 112; collapse of, 46, 53; successor to, 51, 59–61
Jolson, Al, 149
"Jones" (Joel Augustus Rogers' fictional character), 136–41, 151
Jones, Matilda Sissieretta Joyner ("Black Patti"), 141–43, 147, 154, 166
Joplin, Scott, 74
Jornal do Brasil (newspaper), 110
Jornal do Commercio (publication), 195
Junior, Cumba, 297 n. 8
JWT (J. Walter Thompson advertising company), 30, 252 n. 52

Kalut, Juca, 276 n. 78
Kansas City Philharmonic, 171
Kaplan, Amy, xiv–xv
Kay, Bernard, 105
Kelley, Robin, xiii, 295 n. 4
Kirkpatrick, Sidney, 145, 152, 153
KKK (Ku Klux Klan), 188, 199, 217, 235
Klein, Christina, xv
Korman, Clifford, 74

Kornweibel, Theodore, Jr., 296 n. 7
Kosarin, Harry, 103
O Kosmos (Afro-Paulista newspaper), 122, 181, 201
Kosnik, Kristin, 288 n. 81
Krasner, David, 144
Ku Klux Klan (KKK), 188, 199, 217, 235

Labor: available to female African Americans, 160; coffee as increasing efficiency of, 30–44, 252 n. 54; in coffee production, 26–27, 37, 42–43, 49, 254 n. 78; in elite nightclubs, 131–32; household, in ads, 29–33, 252 n. 51; musical, 95–135; after slavery, 212, 213; in urbanizing Rio de Janeiro, 98. *See also* Slavery
Ladnier, Tommy, 272 n. 30
Lafayette Theatre, 145
Lambada (dance), 73
Lansbury, George, 130
La Reserve de Saint Cloud (Paris), 76, 105
Larsen, Nella, 287 n. 59
Latin America: coffee production in, 19; Good Neighbor Policy and, 171; stereotypes of, 13–14, 27, 37, 49; United States as chief moneylender to, 49, 56. *See also* Central American coffee
Latinos, xii, 283 n. 3
Legião Negra, 202
Lehmann, Lilli, 167
Lei do Ventre Livre, 220
Leite, Dante Moreira, 195
Leite, José Correia ("Tuca"): on African Americans, 299 n. 17, 311 n. 112; as agent of transnational exchange, 1–3, 6; background of, 297 n. 8; on De Chocolat, 117–18; on European dance forms, 308 n. 95; on First World War, 1, 9, 10; on immigrants, 300 n. 24; on jazz, 200; on Mãe Preta monument, 215; on racism, 199, 202–3
Le Ruban Bleu (New York), 171, 174
Lewis, Willie, 272 n. 30
A Liberdade (São Paulo newspaper), 181
Liberty Bond campaigns, 21
Librairie Orientaliste Paul Geuthner, 168, 170
Liga Comunista, 169
Lima, Firmina Rosa de, 120

Lina, Maria, 76
Lincoln, Abraham, 229
Lipoff, Raul, 103
Lis, Eduardo, 92
Lobo, Hélio, 318 n. 56
London *Daily Herald*, 130
Lorde, Audre, 139
Lott, Eric, 143
Louisiana (play), 146
Lucrécio, Francisco, 300 n. 23
Lugné-Poe, Aurélien, 168
Luis, Washington, 217, 231
Lundu (dance), 73, 112
Lynchings: in Brazil, xii, 227–28; as not modern, 189; in United States, 10, 57, 155, 188, 199–200, 202–3, 217, 218, 227–28

A Maça (publication), 128, 132
Macon (Georgia), 153–54
Macumba (Brazilian religious tradition), 169, 172
Macumbas (musical form), 111, 112
Madison Avenue. *See* Advertising
Mãe Preta (Black Mother of slavery times), 6, 206–34, 252 n. 49, 312 n. 6
Magalhães, Geraldo ("the Geraldos"), 75, 79, 88, 90
Magalhões, Henrique de, 317 n. 51
"Maison Creole" (lingerie boutique in Russia), 161, 162
Malandragem (revue), 118
O Malho (publication), 127
"Mammy": in ads, 30–31, 235, 252 n. 49; proposed statue to, in the United States, 206, 224–25, 229, 233–34; segregation and, 318 n. 56. *See also* Mãe Preta; Slavery
Maori people, 84–85
Marchand, Roland, 23, 249 n. 18
Marcosson, I. F., 256 n. 94
Marginalized people. *See* Non-elites
Maria, Anna, 310 n. 101
Marigny (Paris), 75
Marshall Rogers' "Brazilian Nuts" (comedy troupe), 158
"Martha" (African-American character in ad), 30–33
Martins, Alfredo, 75, 79, 90
Martins, Herivelto, 278 n. 88

Martins, João, 75, 79, 90
Marx, Karl, xiv
A Mascara (journal), 127
Masculinity: alcohol and, 254 n. 66; as bridging gap between Brazilian elites and non-elites, 230–34; citizenship and, 208, 216–22, 225, 229, 230–31, 234, 315 n. 33; in coffee advertising, 13–14, 26, 35–37, 42, 63; in depictions of male slaves, 185, 231–32; fascism and, 316 n. 41; as feature of anti-black racism and its rebuttal in Brazil, 184–85; of the Martins brothers, 90. *See also* Gender; Men
Mass culture, 9, 87, 212, 213, 235. *See also* Advertising; Motion pictures; Radio; *Specific newspapers*
"Mathias" (journalist), 202
Matto Grosso (Brazilian state), 196
Maurice and Florence (dancers), 77
Maxixe (Brazilian dance), 5, 66–94; African American performers of, 141, 158–66; as Afro-diasporic form, 72–79, 88–90, 92, 93, 106, 112, 127, 138; conflation of tango and other dances with, 84–87, 91–92, 266 n. 77, 267 n. 86; dates of popularity of, 69, 70, 73, 79–83; erasure of, 66, 68, 69, 72, 83–86, 93, 94, 96; as "low" art, 122; as a set dance, 74, 86; sheet music for, 70, 74, 77, 84–85, 264 n. 48, 266 n. 77; as a transnational phenomenon, 67–94, 111–12, 114–15, 131, 235; whitening of, 71–72
"Maxixe" (Sitwell), 266 n. 76
Maxwell House coffee, 30, 51–52
Mayes, Jack, 110
McCann, Bryan, 276 n. 78
McCarthy and Fisher (sheet music publishers), 70
McElya, Michele Paige, 311 n. 1
Men: figure of young, in Mãe Preta monument, 216–17; images of slaves as, 185, 231–32; proposals for statues celebrating Afro-Brazilian, 216, 232. *See also* Gender; Masculinity
Mendes, Dutra, 310 n. 101
O Menelick (São Paulo newspaper), 181
Meredith Sisters (performers), 153, 156
Merguson, R. W., 231
Metronome (magazine), 81

Migrants (rural Brazilian), 97, 98, 184
Milhaud, Darius, 113, 114–15, 176
Mills, Florence ("Blackbird"), 144, 145
Ministry of Foreign Relations (Brazil), 126, 196
Minstrelsy, 102, 140, 143, 149, 150, 153
Miranda, Carmen, 70, 93, 155, 173, 294 n. 155
Miranda, Floresta de, 130
Miscegenation. *See* Racial mixing
Mistinguette (French actress), 107, 118, 265 n. 64
Mitchell, Michael, 312 n. 3
Mobility (travel): of coffee, xiv, 17, 19, 43, 62, 126; contamination metaphors associated with, 81, 133; of jazz and Afro-diasporic performance, 5, 95–96, 100–104, 106, 108, 110, 111, 114–15, 120–21, 126–30, 135, 138, 142, 148–50, 160–61, 167–68; of journalists and journalism, 179–83, 192–93; of lynching, 227–28; of maxixe, 5, 68, 72–79, 81, 86, 87, 94; by train, 288 n. 71; transnationalism and, xvi, 2, 7, 9, 12, 18, 142, 147, 155. *See also* Translation
Modern Dancing (Castle and Castle), 79
Modernism: in Brazil, 99, 113, 167, 185, 277 n. 86; literary, 183; Péret's, 169; debt to the popular, 99, 113, 167; primitivist, 87
Modernity: Afro-diasporic performance and, 5, 117–21, 123–25, 132, 200–201, 236, 271 n. 11; blackness and, 125, 188–89, 215–16; in coffee ads, 25, 26, 31, 49–50; as (hyper)valorized concept, 25, 49–50, 108, 117, 237; critiques of, 200–01, 216, 239, 315 n. 30; as gendered concept, 216, 315 n. 29; in São Paulo, 184, 185; United States as symbol of, 188–89, 200–202, 237
Modern Music (publication), 172
Monte Carlo (New York), 172
Monteiro, José ("Zé Boiadeiro"), 105, 114
Montreal (Canada), 151, 152
Monuments (public), 4, 6, 205, 206–34
Moraes, Gervasio (de), 197, 199, 217, 229
Moraes, José Geraldo Vinci de, 101
Moralism, 73, 200–201, 210, 308 n. 91, 309 n. 99
Morand, Paul, 113

Morly, Derminy and Paule, 75
Morrison, Toni, 53
Morton, Jelly Roll, 89
Moten, Etta. *See* Barnett, Etta Moten
Motion pictures, 81, 99, 127, 140, 164, 200. *See also* Hollywood
Mouvet, Maurice, 77, 83
Movimento Negro (Brazil), 299 n. 17
"Mrs. Consumer," 61–63
"Mrs. Stevens" (in coffee ad), 29–31
"Mrs. Thomas Was Housecleaning" (ad), 30–33, 35, 53, 55, 252 n. 51
Mulatto, 137. *See also* Racial mixing (miscegenation)
Mullen, Harryette, 290 n. 112
Munson Steamship Line, 102
Murray, Moons, 110
Museum of Modern Art (New York), 171, 172, 175
Music, 4; Afro-diasporic, 92, 94, 95–135; blues, 68, 88, 89, 112, 122; boogie-woogie, 68–69, 93; Brazilian, as hybrid mixture, 96, 99–104; Brazilian, in radio ads for coffee, 62; Brazilian "national" genres of, 99–101, 104, 106; as cutting across class, 98–99, 105, 113, 271 n. 16; popular Brazilian, 167–69, 171, 172, 175; ragtime, 73, 89, 100; regional Brazilian, 99, 106, 107, 113; relations that bring about transnational, 69, 119–21. *See also* Dance; Folk culture; Jazz; Tin Pan Alley
Musical Record, 71
Música sertaneja, 99, 106, 107

NAACP, 196, 204
Nascimento, Abdias do, 119
National Art School (Harlem), 145
National Coffee Roasters Association (NCRA), 22, 34, 45–46, 57–58
National Coffee Trade Council, 255 n. 82
"National explosions," xv
National identity: Brazilian, and Afro-diasporic performance, 5–6, 67–135, 200–201; coffee as drink associated with United States', 26, 33–36, 59, 62; as constructed in relation to other categories, xiv, 15, 137, 209–10, 217–18, 234; consumer citizenship as replacing produc-

tion in United States, 15–18, 20–21, 26–27, 33, 43, 49–50; jazz as musical form associated with United States', 79, 84, 87, 91–92, 94, 101, 123, 132, 176, 200, 201; music identified with Brazilian, 99–101, 104, 106; public monuments and, xiv, 29–33, 205, 208–34; race as intertwined with, in Brazil, xi–xii, 4, 6–10, 96–97, 115–17, 120, 128–35, 147, 158, 179–80, 185, 187, 189–92, 197–205, 208–22, 224, 228–31, 234, 237–39; as social construct, 3–4, 8, 11, 15, 18; substitution of, for racial categories, 150–53, 172–76; transnational method's critique of, xv, xvi, 3; as woman, 61, 63. *See also* Nationalism

Nationalism: black, 183, 299 n. 17; as fraternity, 208, 216–22, 225, 229, 230–31, 234, 315 n. 33; right-wing, 304 n. 54; transnational alternatives to, xiii, 16–17; transnational method's critique of, xiii, xv, 4; violence associated with, xiii, xiv. *See also* National identity

National Negro Opera Company, 154

National Press Association (Rio de Janeiro), 193

National Symphony (Washington, D. C.), 172

Native Americans. *See* Indians

Nazareth, Ernesto, 74, 77, 80, 86, 267 n. 86

NBC Symphony Orchestra, 171

NCRA. *See* National Coffee Roasters Association

"Negro" (as term), 187–88

"Negro vogue," 5, 95, 101, 102–3, 109, 116–21, 142, 159, 166, 170, 201. *See also* Afro-diasporic forms and traditions; Exoticism; Primitivism

Negro World, 299 n. 17

Nelson, D. C., 159, 161

The New Grove Dictionary of Jazz, 272 n. 30

"New Negro," 233

New Negro Art Theatre Dance Company, 162

New Orleans (Louisiana), 89, 104

New York *Amsterdam News* (newspaper), 224

New York Dramatic Mirror, 90–91

New York International Fair, 126

New York Public Library, 159

New York Times: on Brazil's price protectionism, 47–51; on "Duque," 86; on Elsie Houston, 171, 172, 175; on Jarboro, 154; on radio show, 61; on steamship between Rio and New York, 102

New York World's Fair, 171

Nigeria, 145

Nogueira, Oracy, 295 n. 3, 318 n. 62

A Noite (publication), 128, 227, 230

Non-elites: activism of, 2–3, 6, 116–21, 213–21; Afro-Brazilian journalists as, 296 n. 8; Brazilian, on racial democracy, 183–92, 213–21, 228–31; power of, xv, xvi, 95–121, 135; as primary subject of this book, xiv, 235; slurs of, 52, 244 n. 6. *See also* African Americans; Afro-Brazilians; Class

"Norton and Margot" (ballroom dance duo), 150–53, 155, 287 n. 68

"Nossa raça," 230

Nostalgia, 212, 213, 215, 216. *See also Saudade*

A Notícia (Rio de Janeiro newspaper): on Afro-diasporic performances, 122, 123–25; *Chicago Defender* and, 182, 223, 224, 230; Mãe Preta monument and, 206, 211, 221, 223–25, 228, 233; on nationalism as fraternity, 217–21. *See also* Campos, Candido

N.W. Ayer and Son. *See* Ayer and Son

"Odeon" (Nazareth), 74, 267 n. 86

Odeon cinema (Rio de Janeiro), 111, 127, 135

Ogren, Kathy, 106

Oito Batutas, 99, 106, 112–14, 128–34. *See also* Batutas

Okeh (record label), 144

Oliveira, A., 189, 190, 192

Oliveira, Benjamin de, 279 n. 98

Oliveira, Luis de, 105

Oliveira, Zaíra de, 115

Oliveira Filho, Arthur L. de, 273 n. 39, 277 n. 78, 282 n. 157

Oliver, King, 76, 276 n. 71

Olympic Games (Los Angeles, 1932), 126

One-step (dance), 73, 77, 81, 100, 107, 112, 123

"On the Dreamy Amazon" (song), 82

Opera, 89, 140–43, 154

"Oriental America" (vaudeville group), 142–43, 158, 160

Orientalism, 27, 70, 85, 138, 140, 141–45, 150, 163

Orquestra Sul-Americana-Brasileira, 102

Ottley, Roi, 193–94

Oxnard (California), 166

Pãe João (Father John), 232

O Paiz (newspaper), 127, 130

Palace Hotel (São Paulo), 193

Palais Cinema (Rio de Janeiro), 99, 104, 128, 129

Pan-Africanism, 6, 10, 120, 139, 144, 145, 183, 202, 203, 222, 225, 229

Panama, 20

Panama Trio (vaudeville group), 144

Pan-Americanism, 9–11, 20, 21, 168, 171, 172, 187, 269 n. 115

Pan-American Union (Washington, D. C.), 171, 172

Paris (France): Afro-descended musicians and performers in, 95–97, 104–11, 113–21, 123–25, 127–29, 132, 135, 138, 147, 167–68, 170, 174–76, 189, 236; Colonial Exposition in, 110; elites' exposure to, 167; as influence on jazz, 88, 89, 95–97, 104–7; maxixe in, 75–77, 85–86, 90, 94; as mediating Afro-American cultural exchanges, 102–7, 109–10, 112–21, 123–25, 127–29, 135, 138, 170, 175, 189, 235, 236. *See also* Civilization; "Negro vogue"

Paris Casino (Paris), 110

Parisian Café Chantant (New York), 77

Passing, xiv, 5–6, 137, 140, 150–52, 154–57, 166, 193, 287 n. 59, 288 n. 80

A Patria (Rio de Janeiro newspaper), 108, 127, 194

Patrício (musician), 276 n. 78

O Patrocinio (São Paulo newspaper), 181

Patrocinio Filho, José do, 76, 194

"Paulista" (defined), 184

"Paulistano" (defined), 184

Pauvre Noir (song), 92

Pederneiras, Raul, 195

"Pensão Viana," 98–99

Péret, Benjamin, 168–70, 175, 291 n. 113

Perpener, John O., III, 290 n. 111

Petrópolis (Brazil), 167

Pfeiffer, Kathleen, 288 n. 76

Philippines, 20, 51

Phonograph recordings, 144, 148

Photography, 185

"Pick" (defined), 148, 150

"Pickaninny" (defined), 148

Pingatore, Eugene and Mike, 103

Pinheiro, Xavier, 129

Piracicaba (Brazil), 181

Pittman, Booker, 110

Pittsburgh Post (newspaper), 142

Pixinguinha (Alfredo da Rocha Viana Filho), 94–100, 104–6, 108–10, 276 n. 78, 277 n. 78, 282 n. 157; Brazilian racial democracy myth and, 128–35; on Companhia Negra de Revistas, 117

Platt Amendment, 11

Poland, 159, 161

Polka (dance), 73, 74, 87, 106, 308 n. 95

Pomeranz, Kenneth, 19, 252 n. 53

Pond, Stephen F., 265 n. 66

Porter, Cole, 89

Porto Rico Girls (vaudeville group), 144

Porto Velho (Brazil), 299 n. 17

Portuguese immigrants (to Brazil), 98, 115, 173

Portuguese language, 62, 111, 135, 150. *See also* Translation

Postcolonial theory, xiv, xv, 238

Power: ignorance as privilege of, 8, 55–58, 84, 236; of non-elites, xv, xvi, 95–121, 135; unequal, between Brazil and United States, 183, 198, 203–4, 236, 237, 247 n. 2. *See also* Imperialism

Prague, 168, 169

Pratt, Alfred, 110

Preciado, A. A., 258 n. 116

Press. *See* São Paulo (Brazil): black press in; *Specific newspapers*

Prestes de Albuquerque, Julio, 214

Primitivism, 9, 31, 87, 104, 119, 120, 138, 139, 142, 144, 145, 148, 159, 161, 164, 167, 168, 236

Printer's Ink (trade journal), 55–57

Production: images of Afro-Brazilian slaves

engaged in, 185, 231–32; as part of U.S. national identity, 15–18, 20–21, 26–27, 33–35, 252 n. 54

Progress, 25, 26, 195. *See also* Modernity

Progresso (São Paulo newspaper), 181, 182, 185; on black performances, 119–21, 189; on blacks in United States, 189, 204; Houston's remarks in, 170; on Mãe Preta monument, 221; on nationalism as fraternity, 217, 229

Prohibition, 36

Pró Patria (magazine), 125

Providence (Rhode Island), 142–43

Prudente de Moraes Neto, Pedro Dantas, 129, 276n. 76, 276 n. 78

Puerto Rico, 20, 50, 144

Quaker Oats, 30, 31

Queer theory, xiv, xv. *See also* Drag; Passing

Race: as constructed in relation to other categories, 31, 137, 180, 203–4, 231, 234; dichotomous construction of, in United States, xii, 136–37, 151, 155, 157, 164, 283 n. 3, 296 n. 5; global imaginaries based on, 10, 145, 183, 202, 203, 222, 225, 229; as intertwined with nationalism in Brazil, xii, 4, 6–10, 96–97, 115–17, 120, 128–35, 147, 158, 179–80, 185, 187, 189–92, 197–205, 208–22, 224, 228–31, 234, 237–39; as multi-category system, 136–37, 151, 155–57, 164; power and, 91; as social construct, xviii, 3–4, 8, 11, 15, 18, 53, 166, 180; terms for, xvii–xviii, 6, 120, 139, 144, 187–88, 198, 200, 203–4, 226–30, 307 n. 87; transnational construction of, xii, xv, xvi, 3, 7, 15. *See also* Blackness; Passing; Racial mixing; Racial purity; Racism; Social hierarchy; "Whiteness"

Racial democracy (racial harmony): as Brazilian nationalism, xii, 4, 6–10, 96–97, 115–17, 120, 128–35, 147, 158, 179–80, 185, 187, 189–92, 197–205, 208–22, 224, 228–31, 234, 237–39; historiography, 243 n. 4; discourse of, in music, 116, 277 n. 87; periodization of, 208–09, 215, 221–22, 296 n. 5, 312 n. 3; as popular production, 96–97, 116–17, 128–32, 180, 189–94, 278

n. 89; as transnational product, 6, 116–17, 194, 210–21, 278 n. 89

Racial mixing (miscegenation), 136–41, 282 n. 143; Abbott's lack of references to, 233–34; in Brazil, xii, 7, 8, 118–19, 133, 208, 213, 226–27, 277 n. 86; in Brazil as source of national strength, 208, 210, 214–15; in the United States, xii, 9, 123, 189, 224, 234, 238

Racial purity, xi, xii, 53–55. *See also* Eugenics

Racism: alleged lack of, in Brazil, xii, 6–10, 96–97, 115–17, 120, 128–35, 147, 158, 179–80, 185, 189–94, 196–99, 204–5, 208–25, 228, 234, 237, 238; alleged lack of, in Britain, 142, 147; alleged lack of, in Europe, 153; alleged lack of, in France, 1, 3, 120, 236; in Brazil, xii, 169, 184, 190–99, 205, 218, 237; Brazil seen as haven from United States, 7, 237; imperialism and, 69–70, 72, 94; as neither natural nor inevitable, 9, 147, 178; opposition to, 72, 87, 130, 135, 198; opposition to, in Brazil, xvii, 6, 10, 116–21, 178, 182, 185–92, 200–208, 213–18, 228, 236–37, 295 n. 3; opposition to, in United States, 10, 90–91, 93, 136–37, 139, 142, 144, 145, 147, 196, 198, 222–25, 295 n. 3; in United States, 1, 7, 9–10, 30, 57, 71, 116, 129, 147, 154–55, 188, 190–91, 198–200, 202–3, 217–18, 224–25, 227–29, 237, 318 n. 56. *See also* Citizenship; White supremacy

Radio, 23, 61–63, 171, 172, 235

Ragtime music, 73, 89, 100

Rainbow Room (New York), 171, 172

Rasimi, Madame, 107–8

"Raul," 214–15

Recife (Brazil), 101

Redeemer statue (Rio de Janeiro), 209

"Red Scares," 166

"Red Summer" (1919), 10, 30

Reis, Júlio, 129

Remick, Jerome H., 70

Retinto (defined), 189

La revue nègre (revue), 109, 118, 123–25

Rieuse and Nichette (performers), 75

"Rio" (song), 82

O Rio Agache-se (revue), 118

Rio Branco, Jose Maria da Silva Paranhos, Jr., Baron of, 20, 304 n. 54

Rio de Janeiro, 181–82, 187; Abbott's lectures in, 193, 194; black church in, 119, 213, 218–19, 222; Centennial Exposition in, 107, 113; Elsie Houston's birth in, 166–67, 175; jazz as transnational cultural production in, 4–6, 95–96, 104–18, 127–28, 236; links between New York and, 102, 107–9; Mãe Preta monument issue in, 206, 211, 221, 223–25, 228, 233; maxixe in, 77, 86; racial segregation in, 111, 131–32, 135, 192; Redeemer statue in, 209; rural migrants in, 97, 98. *See also* Afro-Cariocas

"Rio Nights" (song), 82

Rivera, Max, 84

Roberts, John Storm, 266 n. 74

Rochester Philharmonic, 171

Rodin, Gil, 67

Rodrigues, José, 100

Rodrigues, Raimundo Nina, 195

Rogers, Ginger, 112

Rogers, Joel Augustus, 136–37, 139, 151

Rogers, Marshall, 158

Roosevelt, Franklin D., 11

Roosevelt, Theodore, 50, 191

Roriz, Nelson, 108

Rosa, Maria, 310 n. 101

Rosa, Noel, 272 n. 20

Rosenfeld, Jayn, 265 n. 66

"Rose of Brazil" (song), 82

A Rua (São Paulo newspaper), 181

Rubber, 51

Rubinstein, Artur, 168

Rumba (dance), 73, 84, 150

Run, Little Chillun! (play), 146, 161, 164

Rural areas: Mãe Preta associated with, 213; migrants from, 97, 98, 184. *See also* Folk culture

Russia, 76, 111, 159–63, 166. *See also* Soviet Union

Sachs, Curt, 73, 87

Said, Edward, 138

Sailors, 7–8

"St. Louis Blues" (song), 88

Salnave, Bertin Depestre, 88

"Salomania," 144

Salome (dance), 70, 144, 145, 163

Salomé, 144, 145

Saloons, 36

Salvador (Brazil), 181

"Salvador" (song), 82

Sambas, 72, 77, 106, 111, 114, 155, 271 n. 16; as Afro-diasporic form, 92, 94, 112, 113; jazz blends with, 68, 100; maxixe and, 74, 93

Sampaio, Sebastião, 62

Sampson, Henry, 111, 142, 159, 163, 289 n. 87, 290 n. 111

Sandroni, Carlos, 277 n. 87

Santos (Brazil), 181

Santos, Ascendina dos, 121

Santos, Plácida dos, 75, 90

Santos, Sizenando, 105

Santos-Dumont, Alberto, 279 n. 96

São Paulo (Brazil): Afro-Brazilian musical performances in, 117–19, 126; black press in, 1–4, 6, 95, 119–21, 131, 170, 178, 179–205, 213–21, 228–31, 236–37, 296 n. 8, 300 n. 23, 300 n. 25; coffee production in, 25, 27, 33, 44, 183, 185; Elsic Houston in, 168; immigrants in, 7, 98, 183–84, 300 n. 24, 301n. 26; Mãe Preta statue in, 206, 207, 221; Sociedade Promotora da Defesa do Café established in, 22; terms for "blackness" in, 187–88; United States' ignorance about, 56. *See also* Clarim

Saudade, 82–83. *See also* Nostalgia

Savage Rhythm (play), 146

Savoy Bearcats (musical group), 111

Sawyer, Joan, 77

Saxophones, 102, 106, 108, 126

Scanlon, Jennifer, 23

Scheherazade (Paris), 105

Schulten, Susan, 257 n. 96

Schurz, William, 47–48

"Second Industrial Revolution," 19

Second World War, 135, 146, 181

Sedric, Eugene (Gene), 272 n. 30

Segregation: of black vaudeville performances, 90–91, 139–40, 144, 152; in Brazil, 111, 131–32, 135, 192, 193, 271 n. 16; in Jim Crow United States, 10, 154, 171, 188, 198, 318 n. 56; in U.S. Army, 1, 9–10

Senegalese troops, 1

A Sentinella (São Paulo newspaper), 181

Shapiro and Bernstein (vaudeville agents), 149

Sheet music industry. *See* Tin Pan Alley

Shelton, Marie-Denise, 291 n. 120

Shimmy (dance), 73, 100, 122

Ships: in coffee ads, 37, 42, 43; as promoting transnationalism, 102, 147, 193. *See also* Mobility

Sierra Leone, 145

Silva, Denise Ferreira da, 310 n. 102

Silva, Maria A., 310 n. 101

Silva, Marília T. Barboza da, 273 n. 39, 277 n. 78, 282 n. 157

Silva, Romeu, 102, 110, 125–26

Silva Azevedo, Antônio da, Júnior, 56

Silvera, Frank, 156

Simão de Laboreiro, 217

Simmons, Roscoe, 231

Sitwell, Osbert, 266 n. 76

Skidmore, Thomas, 312 n. 3

Slavery (African): Brazil's abolition of, 7, 97; coffee trade and, 19; communication during, 2, 6; comparisons between Brazilian and United States', 198–99; contributions of, to Brazil, 185–87, 198, 206–34; dance forms associated with North American, 74; males as minority in Brazilian, 232; opposing views of, 7; sexual violence in, 224, 234; steps toward abolition of, 220; transnationalism and, xiii, 3. *See also* Abolitionists; Mãe Preta; "Mammy"

Smith, Ada "Bricktop," 144, 268 n. 95

Smith, Elizabeth Marie, 288 n. 71, 288 n. 80

Smith, Frederick, J., 90–91

Smith, Valerie, 288 n. 81

Smoot-Hawley Act (1930), 45

Snake dances, 70, 163–64

Social hierarchy: Brazil's maintenance of, through racial democracy rhetoric, 128–35, 209–10, 221–22, 228; in coffee ads, 27, 30–33, 65; jazz and, 87, 117–34; "race" use to structure, xii, 10. *See also* Class; Gender; National identity; Race

Sociedade Promotora da Defesa do Café, 22, 259 n. 122

Society Orchestra (James Reese Europe's), 79, 91

Soldiers (black), 1, 9–10, 192, 232, 319 n. 79. *See also* Sailors; War

Sousa, Maria de Lourdes, 309 n. 101

South Africa, 142, 153, 156

Southern, Eileen, 143

Southern Syncopated Orchestra, 89, 108, 129, 130

Soviet Union (USSR), xv, 43, 110, 111. *See also* Russia

Spain, 75, 76, 151, 153, 163–64

Spanish-American War, 153

Spanish dance, 163–64

Spanish language, 84

Spice Mill (trade magazine), 22

Steamships, 102, 147, 193

Stearns, Marshall and Jean, 149

"Stepin Fetchit," 204

Stern, Joseph W., 77, 81

Stock market crash (1929), 45, 63. *See also* Great Depression

Stoddard, Lathrop, 10

Stokowski, Leopold, 109

Stolcke, Verena, 253 n. 54

The Story of Coffee and How to Make It (pamphlet), 51–52

Stowe, Harriet Beecher, 156

Straight, Gordon, 107–9

Stretton, Sr. *See* Straight, Gordon

Sucena, Eduardo, 263 n. 36

Sugar, 20

Sundquist, Eric, 288 n. 81

Surrealism, 10, 167, 169, 291 n. 120

Sweden, 160

Switzerland, 160

Tango, 73, 79–83, 106, 150, 266 n. 74; Argentine, 73, 79, 85, 87, 88, 105, 131; blacks' associations with, 90–91, 122, 138, 152; Brazilian, 76, 77, 79, 84; jazz and, 88, 91–93; maxixe and other dances conflated with, 84–87, 91–92, 266 n. 77, 267 n. 86

Taylor, Frederick Winslow, 35, 47

Teatro Experimental do Negro (TEN), 119

Teatro Lírico (Rio de Janeiro), 106–7, 131

Teixeira, Nina ("the Geraldos"), 75, 79, 88, 90

Terra seca (song), 92

"That American Boy of Mine" (song), 126

"That Wonderful Dengosa Strain" (song), 80–81

Theatre Arts (publication), 174

Théâtre des Champs Elysées (Paris), 129

Theophilo, Booker Washington, 311 n. 112

They're Off (play), 163

"Thoroughbreds" (ad), 53–55

Time and the Other (Fabian), 296 n. 5

Tinhorão, José Ramos, 101, 108–10, 271 n. 16

Tin Pan Alley: defined, 70; impact of, on Brazil, 8, 101–2; publications of, 70, 74, 77, 81–82, 84–85, 100, 264 n. 48, 266 n. 77

Todorov, Tzvetan, 265 n. 67

Tomás, J., 100

Topik, Steven, 19, 251 n. 42, 252 n. 53, 256 n. 90, 260 n. 151

Toronto *Empire* (newspaper), 141–42

Toronto World's Fair (1892), 141

Torres, Antonio, 312 n. 6, 315 n. 31

Town Top-Piks (show), 161

Translation, 205, 235–36, 250 n. 32; as mode of transnational exchange, 225–31; racial terms used in, xviii, 307 n. 87

Transnational method: African American performers and, 136–78, 235; as alternative method to comparison, xii–xiii, 235–39, 295 n. 5; author's "bottom-up" approach to, xiv, 235; black press in Brazil and the United States and, 179–205, 235, 237; coffee advertising and, 13–66, 235; defined, xii–xiv, 16–17; jazz and, 95–135, 235; local and global bound together in, xv, 1–3, 96, 148, 183–92; maxixe and, 67–94, 235; monuments to Black Mother and, 206–34; nationalism and, xiii, xv, 4

Travel. *See* Mobility

Trot (dance), 79–80, 83. *See also* Fox trot; Turkey-trot

Trotskyism, 169

Troupe Negra de Revistas e Variedades, 117, 118

"Tuca." *See* Leite, José Correia

Tudo preto (play), 109–10, 213, 219

Tumulte noir, 88–90, 92, 95, 97, 105, 110, 170, 236

Tupinambá, Marcelo, 77

Turkey, 110, 160

Turkey-trot (dance), 73

Turunas Pernambucanos (musical group), 100–101

Tutankhamen, 71, 144–45

"Two Nuts from Brazil" (play), 157–58

Two-step (dance), 107, 112

UDC (United Daughters of the Confederacy), 206, 224, 319 n. 68

Ukers, William, 125–26

Uncle Eph's Christmas (play), 159, 160

Uncle Tom's Cabin (Stowe), 156, 287 n. 59, 288 n. 76

União da Alliança, 218

United Daughters of the Confederacy (UDC), 206, 224, 319 n. 68

United States: on Brazilian coffee price protectionism, 45–61, 65; Brazilians in, 7; coffee advertising by, 4, 8, 13–66; coffee as drink associated with, 26, 33–36, 59, 62; consumer citizenship as replacing production in national identity in, 15–18, 20–21, 26–27, 33, 43, 49–50; democratic rhetoric of, 9; dichotomous construction of race in, xii, 136–37, 151, 155, 157, 164, 283 n. 3, 296 n. 5; Elsie Houston in, 170–78; hybridity of culture in, 5, 88, 89, 92, 176, 238 (*see also Specific cultural forms*); imperialism of, xiv–xv, 11, 20–21, 37, 42–58, 69–70, 93, 138–40, 188; influence of, on Brazil, 8, 21; jazz as musical form associated with, 79, 84, 87, 91–92, 94, 101, 123, 132, 176, 200, 201; as Latin America's chief moneylender, 49, 56; maxixe in, 76–77, 79–86, 93; migration to Brazil from, 7, 179–80, 192, 195–98, 204–5; myths of racial purity in, xi–xii, 53–55; opposition to racism in, 10, 90–91, 93, 136–37, 139, 142, 144, 145, 147, 196, 198, 222–25, 295 n. 3; in post–First World War Paris, 105; racial mixing in, xii, 9, 123, 189, 224, 234, 238; racism in, 1, 7, 9–10, 30, 57, 71, 116, 129, 147, 154–55, 188, 190–91, 198–200, 202–3, 217–18, 224–25, 227–29, 237, 318 n. 56; São Paulo black press's interest in, 188; slavery in, 198, 233; as symbol of modernity, 188–89,

200–202, 237; trade between Brazil and, 9, 11, 18, 20–21, 44–59, 101–2, 157–58, 188; unequal power relations between Brazil and, 183, 198, 203–4, 236, 237, 247 n. 2. *See also* African Americans; Confederates; Good Neighbor Policy; Imperialism; Slavery; West; White supremacy

U.S. Congress, 47, 48

UPI (United Press International), 224

Urbanization, 9, 21, 87, 97–98, 183–85, 212

Uruguay (ship), 108–9

USSR. *See* Soviet Union

"Valdez, Juan," 65, 251 n. 42

Vallin, Ninon, 168

Valorization (price protection of coffee), 18, 24, 44–61, 65, 254 n. 78

"Valyda and Brazilian Nuts" (vaudeville group), 157, 158

Vargas, Getúlio, 11, 181, 304 n. 54

Variety (magazine), 149

Vasconcelos, Ary, 101

Vasconcelos, Mário de, 182

Vauchant, Leo, 89

Vaudeville, 4, 136–78; maxixe and, 76, 77; "nation drag" as a strategy for African-American performers in, 138, 142–43, 150–54; rise of, 140; transnational aspects of, 102. *See also Specific performers and acts*

Vega, Carlos, 271 n. 16

Velloso, Reis, 131

Veloso, Caetano, 93

"Vem cá, mulata" (song), 75, 79

Ventura (California) *Star Free Press*, 160

Viana Filho, Alfredo da Rocha. *See* Pixinguinha

Vianna, Hermano, 270 n. 10, 276 n. 76, 276 n. 78, 281 n. 141

Vicente, Eduardo, 271 n. 16

Victory Bond campaigns, 21

Vienna (Austria), 34

Villa-Lobos, Heitor, 98, 107, 113, 168, 170, 276 n. 78

Violence and resistance: against African Americans, 10, 30, 57, 71, 91, 155, 166, 188, 198–200, 202–3, 217, 218, 224, 227–28, 234; associated with nationalism, xiii, xiv; capitalism's link to, 35, 42–43, 47, 48, 65; global links forged in, 3; in Rio de Janeiro, 98. *See also* First World War; Lynchings; Slavery

Virility. *See* Masculinity

Visas (Brazilian, for Afro-descendents), 193, 196–97, 204–5, 237

Voodoo (vodun), 146, 164, 171–74, 293 n. 143

W. R. Grace & Co., 37, 40–42

Walker, Aida Overton, 144, 145, 166

Walton, Florence, 77

Waltzes, 106, 150, 151–52, 308 n. 95

War: in coffee ads, 35, 36–37; multiculturalism as solution to, 130–31, 168. *See also Specific wars*

Warren, Jonathan W., 295 n. 4

Washington Post (newspaper), 172, 176

Watch Your Step (vaudeville performance), 76, 79, 266 n. 74

Waterson, Berlin and Snyder (sheet music publishers), 70

Watson, John B., 252 n. 52

Watts, Usher, 159–61

Webb, Margot, 150–52, 155, 156

The West (U.S.), 17, 35, 52, 56, 65

Whiteman, Paul, 103, 125, 126

"Whiteness": class as form of, 203–4; as a fraternity, 229–30; as hybrid in the United States, 238; as modern condition in Brazil, 210–11; performing, 152; of "Spanish" people, 151, 155–56; U.S. immigration and, 53. *See also* Drag; Passing; Racial mixing; Whitening; Whiter people

Whitening: of Afro-diasporic influences, 71–72, 123; of the *Chicago Defender* in Brazil, 228; discourse of, in Brazil, 184, 188–92, 195, 199, 233; racial democracy as replacing discourse of, 209, 215, 221–22

Whiter people: in advertising, 15; Argentina as dominated by, 85; Mãe Preta monument and, 206–34; sent to Paris to offset Afro-Brazilians' influence, 113–14; as a term, xviii. *See also* Elites

White supremacy, xii, 56, 243 n. 3; advertising's evocation of, 30, 33; black colonization schemes and, 195–97, 205; challenges to, 130, 183. *See also* Racism

Wilde, Oscar, 145

Wilkes, Mattie, 143

Williams, Lavinia, 155

Williams and Walker's vaudeville productions, 144

Williamson, Joel, 288 n. 80

Williamson, Judith, 23

The Willow and I (play), 166

Winant, Howard, 283 n. 3

Women: changes in conventions for, 200–202, 212–13; as consumers, 61–63; as household workers in ads, 252 n. 51; images of black sexual, 139, 144, 150, 173, 201, 210, 213, 216, 224, 234; nation conceived as, 61, 63; suffrage for, 308 n. 92; uses of maternal image of slave, 30–31, 206–22, 224–25, 229, 233–35, 252 n. 49, 310 n. 102, 318 n. 56. *See also* Gender

Wooding, Sam, 88, 89, 93, 103, 105, 111, 13, 272 n. 30

Woodward, James P., 245 n. 14

World's fairs and expositions, 107, 110, 113, 141–42, 171

World War I. *See* First World War

World War II. *See* Second World War

Wynn, Albert, 272 n. 30

O Xauter (São Paulo newspaper), 181

Young, James Webb, 30

Zé Boiadeiro. *See* Monteiro, José

Zelli, Joe, 88

MICOL SEIGEL is an assistant professor in the department of African American and African Diaspora Studies and the program in American Studies at Indiana University, Bloomington.